Chapter 4

Find around 8 secondary sources

Stay the Hand of Vengeance

*

PRINCETON STUDIES IN

INTERNATIONAL HISTORY AND POLITICS

Series Editors
Jack L. Snyder
Marc Trachtenberg
Fareed Zakaria

———————————

Stay the Hand of Vengeance

THE POLITICS OF WAR CRIMES TRIBUNALS

*

With a new afterword by the author

GARY JONATHAN BASS

PRINCETON UNIVERSITY PRESS

PRINCETON AND OXFORD

Copyright © 2000 by Princeton University Press
Published by Princeton University Press, 41 William Street,
Princeton, New Jersey 08540
In the United Kingdom: Princeton University Press,
3 Market Place, Woodstock, Oxfordshire OX20 1SY
All Rights Reserved

Third printing, and first paperback printing,
with a new afterword, 2002
Paperback ISBN 0-691-09278-8

The Library of Congress has cataloged the cloth edition of this book as follows

Bass, Gary Jonathan, 1969–
Stay the hand of vengeance : the politics of war crimes
tribunals / Gary Jonathan Bass.
p.   cm. — (Princeton studies in international history and politics)
Includes bibliographical references and index.
ISBN 0-691-04922-X
1. International criminal courts. 2. War crimes trials.
3. Law and politics. I. Title. II. Series.
KZ6310 .B37 2000
341.6′9—dc21   00-036692

British Library Cataloging-in-Publication Data is available

This book has been composed in New Baskerville

Printed on acid-free paper. ∞

www.pup.princeton.edu

Printed in the United States of America

5   7   9   10   8

ISBN-13: 978-0-691-09278-2

ISBN-10: 0-691-09278-8

FOR THE

PEOPLE OF BOSNIA,

TOO LATE,

AND IN MEMORY OF MY GRANDFATHERS,

NATE BASSERABIE

AND

CHONA (JOE) BOBROW

*

Contents

❋ *Abbreviations* ❋

CUP	Committee of Union and Progress, a Young Turk nationalist party
EU	European Union
FRY	Federal Republic of Yugoslavia (the republics of Serbia and Montenegro)
HVO	the Bosnian Croat militia
ICC	International Criminal Court, a proposed permanent war crimes court
ICTY	International Criminal Tribunal for the former Yugoslavia
ICTR	International Criminal Tribunal for Rwanda
IFOR	NATO's initial Implementation Force, in Bosnia
IMT	International Military Tribunal, at Nuremberg
IMTFE	International Military Tribunal for the Far East, at Tokyo
JAG	Judge Advocate General
JNA	Yugoslav National Army; since April 1992, known as VJ
KFOR	Kosovo Force, the NATO–led mission in Kosovo
KLA	Kosovo Liberation Army, also known as UCK
NATO	North Atlantic Treaty Organization
NDH	the World War II–era fascist Independent State of Croatia
OHR	Office of the High Representative, the civilian agency implementing the Dayton accords in Bosnia
RPF	Rwanda Patriotic Front
SFOR	Stabilization Force, the successor force to IFOR
UN	United Nations
UNWCC	United Nations War Crimes Commission— in World War II
UNPROFOR	United Nations Protection Force
VRS	Bosnian Serb Army; also known as BSA

Stay the Hand of Vengeance

*

[W]hen these matters are discussed by practical people, the standard of justice depends on the equality of power to compel and that in fact the strong do what they have the power to do and the weak accept what they have to accept.
—Thucydides, *History of the Peloponnesian War*

That four great nations, flushed with victory and stung with injury, stay the hand of vengeance and voluntarily submit their captive enemies to the judgment of the law is one of the most significant tributes that Power has ever paid to Reason.
—Justice Robert Jackson, U.S. opening statement at Nuremberg

✻ CHAPTER ONE ✻

Introduction

Tihomir Blaskic was brought into court in The Hague on June 24, 1997, flanked by two policemen wearing the baby-blue of the UN. An unexceptional dark man with wispy thinning black hair and gold glasses, dressed for the occasion in a gray civilian suit, Blaskic looked constantly grim. He did not change his expression as the morning wore on. He gave no hint of emotion, even when the prosecutor, a square-jawed American draped in a black robe, described the 1993 sack of Ahmici, a small, innocuous village in central Bosnia's Lasva Valley.

Blaskic had then been a colonel and the commander of the Bosnian Croat army's operations in central Bosnia. In April 1993, Dario Kordic, the young local Bosnian Croat leader, decided to take the Lasva Valley, a rugged area populated both by Muslims and Croats. Forces under Blaskic's command launched an assault on the Bosnian government's forces and the Muslim towns of the Lasva Valley. The rain of shells took a heavy toll on Muslim civilians. Men allegedly under Blaskic's command rounded up hundreds of Muslims who remained in the valley, and held them in makeshift facilities in Vitez and Busovaca. They forced the prisoners, hungry and thirsty, to dig trenches on confrontation lines or used them as human shields to deter the Bosnian government forces from striking back at the Croat forces. The atrocities in Ahmici, a mostly Muslim village, were the most notorious: its mosques and the homes of its Muslim inhabitants had been razed, and ninety-six civilians were killed.[1]

But that was all a world away. Now Blaskic could only see Ahmici—with its Muslim houses gutted, and Croatian nationalist graffiti spray-painted on a toppled Muslim minaret—in stark black-and-white video images, filmed by a swooping camera that had been carried by a NATO helicopter. Blaskic's old headquarters at the Hotel Vitez, only about five kilometers from Ahmici and mere blocks away from what became a mass grave site, were also just pictures on the screens in a hushed and darkened courtroom on the other side of Europe. Instead, Blaskic was surrounded by the self-important trappings of a new effort at international justice.

The courtroom is in fact a rebuilt conference room, which until 1994 housed Dutch businesspeople working for Aegon, the insurance firm with which the tribunal was sharing its sprawling, shabby building on Churchillplein in the northern part of The Hague. The courtroom, which cost the UN about three million Dutch guilders, boasts ultramodern computer and video monitors, immediate computerized stenography, and simultaneous translation broadcast in three languages: English, French, and what used to be called Serbo-Croatian and is now prudently listed by the UN as "Bosnian, Croatian, Serbian."[2] Visitors and the press are separated from Blaskic only by a pane of bulletproof glass. The courtroom is sleek and gleaming white, with baby-blue drapes and two big UN flags flanking the judges. They are robed in black and red, with faintly ridiculous white bibs in the Continental style; the attorneys wear simpler black robes, with the same bibs. The air is a riot of international accents: the presiding judge is French, his two colleagues are from Egypt and Guyana, the defense team are from Croatia and Los Angeles, and the prosecutors have American accents (one of them distinctly from New York). It is all built to impress. There was no sign that day that it had made any impact on Blaskic.

Nor were his superiors in Croatia any more impressed. Croatia was resisting the tribunal's attempts to subpoena its records on the Lasva Valley attacks, presumably fearing that such papers might implicate men of greater rank than Blaskic. Dario Kordic was still at large, widely assumed to be living comfortably in Zagreb. The mere fact that Blaskic was in court at all was an anomaly. On the day Blaskic walked into the dock, only eight out of seventy-five men publicly indicted by the tribunal were in custody.[3] Blaskic was the only high-ranking one. Over three years after the UN set up the first international war crimes tribunal since World War II, all it had to show for it were these eight men: whiling away their days by playing chess, reading a spy novel by John Le Carré, and, in the case of a man who had brutalized prisoners at the Omarska concentration camp, doing a series of paintings for an exhibition in a London restaurant.

Most of what really mattered for the tribunal was going on far from the former insurance office in The Hague. The machinery of justice was here, still a bit creaky with its new duties, but, it was hoped, up to the task. What was missing, as the tribunal's staff constantly says, was the world's political will. The crucial decisions that had brought Blaskic to the dock had mostly been made elsewhere: by the member states of the UN Security Council when they created the Hague tribunal in 1993 but then kept it underfunded and understaffed; by ex-Yugoslav authorities as they flouted the tribunal's authority; by Britain and France as they limited the duties of their peacekeeping troops; by Russia as it interfered with the tribunal to shelter the Serbs; and above all by America, an inattentive superpower.

Those decisions had left the tribunal's staff grumbling that the West was not remotely serious about the work being done here. "We are not offering anywhere enough justice," said a tribunal staffer, recently back from Bosnia. "All the old grievances are still there." There was no triumphalism in The Hague, only a gnawing fear that the entire effort would prove pointless, or would discredit the Nuremberg legacy by failing.

This book is about idealism in international relations, and its sharp limits. It asks why some countries will sometimes be strikingly idealistic in the face of foreign wickedness, and at other times will cynically abandon the pursuit of justice. For those who were glad to see the likes of Blaskic on trial, the crucial question is: What makes governments support international war crimes tribunals? And, conversely: What makes governments abandon them? Those are the basic questions that this book will try to answer.

The answers, such as they are, are in patterns of politics from historical events that have largely been forgotten. The dominant—and incorrect—view of war crimes tribunals centers on Nuremberg as an almost unique moment.[4] In fact, war crimes trials are a fairly regular part of international politics, with Nuremberg as only the most successful example. International war crimes tribunals are a recurring modern phenomenon, with discernible patterns. Today's debates about war criminals in Rwanda, Bosnia, and Kosovo are partial echoes of political disputes from 1815, 1918, and 1944.

There are at least seven major comparable times when states confronted issues of international justice: abortive treason trials of Bonapartists in 1815 after the Hundred Days; botched trials of German war criminals after World War I; an abortive prosecution of some of the Young Turk perpetrators of the Armenian genocide; the great trials of top German war criminals at Nuremberg after World War II; a parallel but less successful process for major Japanese war criminals at the Tokyo international military tribunal; the current ex-Yugoslavia tribunal; and a twin tribunal for Rwanda.[5] There are even less well-known cases too. The United States set up war crimes trials after the Spanish-American War, as did Britain after the Boer War.[6] After World War I, Yugoslavia pushed Bulgaria into trying some of its own.[7] Indira Gandhi, India's premier, called for trials of Pakistanis accused of atrocities in Bangladesh in 1972.[8] There was also some discussion in America of trials for North Koreans after the Korean War.[9] The Bush administration threatened trials for Iraqi cruelty in Kuwait,[10] and the Clinton administration is considering a tribunal for Iraq's so-called Anfal atrocities against the Kurds.[11] The sudden capture of Pol Pot in the summer of 1997 prompted a chorus of calls for his trial; after his death, the UN is planning a tribunal for other Khmer Rouge leaders, with Cambodian and foreign judges. And in July 1998, a UN conference in Rome approved a plan for a permanent international criminal court (ICC) to judge war crimes and crimes against humanity.

This book is a systematic and comparative account of the politics of international war crimes tribunals.[12] It is meant to be part of a growing debate about reconciliation and reconstruction after political violence, whether after democratization at home or war abroad. But unlike cases like South Africa and Chile, where heated arguments about justice and forgiveness and truth take place within one country, the war crimes tribunals in this book are all international. They rely on foreign political will and on military force. They carry special dangers of nationalist backlash caused by Western arrogance—and, perhaps, special opportunities to impose justice.

Why support a war crimes tribunal?[13] The treatment of humbled or defeated enemy leaders and war criminals can make the difference between war and peace.[14] If the job is done well, as after World War II, it may lay the foundation for a durable peacetime order; if botched, as when Napoleon was exiled to Elba, it may spark a new outbreak of war.

Still, if one wants to get rid of undesirables, using the trappings of a domestic courtroom is a distinctly awkward way to do it. Sustaining a tribunal means surrendering control of the outcome to a set of unwieldy rules designed for other occasions, and to a group of rule-obsessed lawyers. These lawyers have a way of washing their hands of responsibility for the political consequences of their own legal proceedings. "It's a political decision as to whether you should execute these people without trial, release them without trial, or try them and decide at the end of the trial what to do," said Robert Jackson, the U.S. Supreme Court justice who served as America's chief prosecutor at Nuremberg. "That decision was made by the President, and I was asked to run the legal end of the prosecution. So I'm not really in a position to say whether it's the wisest thing to do or not."[15] Did Richard Goldstone, the first chief prosecutor of the ex-Yugoslavia tribunal, worry about the consequences to the Bosnian peace process of indicting Radovan Karadzic and Ratko Mladic, the wartime political and military leaders of the Bosnian Serbs? "But it was really done as, if you like, as an academic exercise," Goldstone says. "Because our duty was clear." That kind of professional detachment may make sense to lawyers; it is bizarre to diplomats.

There are easier ways to punish vanquished enemies. Victorious leaders have come up with an impressive array of nonlegalist fates for their defeated foes. One could shoot them on sight.[16] One could round them up and shoot them en masse later. One could have a perfunctory show trial and then shoot them. One could put them in concentration camps. One could (as both Winston Churchill and Franklin Roosevelt suggested) castrate them.[17] One could deport them to a neutral country, or perhaps a quiet island somewhere. Or one could simply ignore their sordid past and do business with them. Of all things, why bother to go to the trouble of a bona fide trial, with the possibility of acquittals, of cases being thrown out on technicalities, of embarrassing evidence and irritating delays, of uncooperative judges, of a vigorous defense? After World War I, one of the reasons why efforts to punish German and Ottoman war criminals failed was that the Allies found they could not get convictions in the respective courts. Why give up direct state control to independent lawyers?

There is a flip side to these questions, too, which is just as puzzling. American diplomats had no great enthusiasm for the prosecution of Balkan war criminals. Some of these men, like Mladic, have powerful domestic followings. Arrests could spark violence, or turn Bosnian Serb sentiment even more bitterly against NATO. And the Hague tribunal has a way of reminding the world of the savage habits of men like Slobodan Milosevic (indicted in 1999 by Louise Arbour, Goldstone's successor) and Franjo Tudjman, who have often been deemed essential to America's plans for a stable region. Despite that, America has offered grudging support to the tribunal since its creation. Why take the risk?

The core argument of this book—fleshed out in this chapter and running throughout the historical chapters—is that some leaders do so because they, and their countries, are in the grip of a principled *idea*. There is nothing structural that necessitates the adoption of this idea. A tribunal is not necessarily part of a punitive peace, nor of a generous one.[18] Nevertheless, some decision makers believe that it is right for war criminals to be put on trial—a belief that I will call, for brevity's sake, legalism.

There are strict limits to the influence of legalism. Above all, legalism is a concept that seems only to spring from a particular kind of liberal domestic polity. After all, a war crimes tribunal is an extension of the rule of law from the domestic sphere to the international sphere. Although illiberal or totalitarian states accustomed to running domestic show trials might try to do the same at the international level, the serious pursuit of international justice rests on principled legalist beliefs held by only a few liberal governments. Liberal governments sometimes pursue war crimes trials; illiberal ones never have.

Still, the power of legalist ideas alone is not wholly sufficient as an explanation, because nonrhetorical calls for international justice are fitful. Why is it right at some times for some states, and not at other times for other states? If principled ideas are so important to foreign policy, why do states so often fail to live up to those ideas? These questions lead to the two other major arguments of this book. First, even liberal states almost never put their own soldiers at risk in order to bring war criminals to book. Second, even liberal states are more likely to seek justice for war crimes committed against their own citizens, not against innocent foreigners. These two arguments are flip sides of a common coin: the selfishness of states, even of liberal ones. We put our own citizens first— by an amazing degree. The war crimes policy of liberal states is a push-and-pull of idealism and selfishness.

IDEALISM IN INTERNATIONAL RELATIONS

Victors' Justice

Tojo Hideki had few doubts about the true character of the Allies' international military tribunal at Tokyo. In December 1948, he said, "In the last analysis, this trial was a political trial. It was only victors' justice."[19] When Nuremberg's prison psychiatrist asked Hermann Göring to sign a copy of Göring's own indictment as a unique souvenir, the former Reichsmarschall could not resist editorializing: "The victor will always be the judge, and the vanquished the accused."[20] Wilhelm II, hiding in Holland after World War I, scorned Allied efforts to bring him to book: "[A] tribunal where the enemy would be judge and party would not be an organ of the law but an instrument of political tyranny aiming only at justifying my condemnation."[21] Zeljko Raznatovic, the indicted Serb paramilitary leader better known as Arkan, once said, "I will go to a war-crimes tribunal when Americans are tried for Hiroshima, Nagasaki, Vietnam, Cambodia, Panama!"[22] Even the victors sometimes make this argument. "I suppose if I had lost the war, I would have been tried as a war criminal," said Curtis LeMay, who targeted some sixty-three Japanese cities for annihilation by American bombing in World War II. "Fortunately, we were on the winning side."[23]

It is perhaps not surprising that these men felt this way. What is striking is the extent to which their skepticism is reflected in typical good-faith beliefs about war crimes tribunals today.[24] Even Immanuel Kant unhappily admitted that, in the state of war, "where no tribunal empowered to make judgments supported by the power of law exists," judgment would rest on power: "neither party can be declared an unjust enemy (since this already presupposes a judgment of right) and the outcome of the conflict (as if it were a so-called 'judgment of God') determines the side on which justice lies."[25] The frequently expressed argument that war crimes tribunals are simply victors' justice has deep roots. As Thrasymachus says in Plato's *Republic*, "[E]verywhere justice is the same thing, the advantage of the stronger."[26]

The Thrasymachus tradition in the study of international relations is usually called realism. Realists—the dominant thinkers in America and Britain since at least 1945—argue that international relations differ from domestic politics in the lack of a common ruler among self-interested states.[27] To survive in such conditions of anarchy, states must rely on self-help for their own security; they become, in the great sociologist Raymond Aron's vivid phrase, "cold-blooded monsters."[28] In the dangerous brawl of international anarchy, realists argue, idealistic and legalistic policies are a luxury that states can ill afford. In his classic history of the Peloponnesian War, Thucydides has Cleon, a cruel Athenian, say:

> Our business, therefore, is not to injure ourselves by acting like a judge who strictly examines a criminal; instead we should be looking for a method by which, employing moderation in our punishments, we can in future secure for ourselves the full use of those cities which bring us important contributions. And we should recognize that the proper basis of our security is in good administration rather than in the fear of legal penalties.[29]

Thus to realists, international moralizing in general—and punishing war criminals in particular—is mystifying.[30] Writing on the eve of World War II, E. H. Carr insisted that "politics are not (as utopians pretend) a function of ethics, but ethics of politics." Contemptuous of "utopianism," Carr scorned efforts to blame Wilhelm II for World War I.[31]

In a sweeping book that lavishes attention on the Krüger telegram and the Fashoda crisis, Henry Kissinger does not even mention Nuremberg.[32]

In 1954, the British historian A.J.P. Taylor asked, "Who cares now whether William II and Berchtold were 'war-criminals'?"[33] Later, under fire for praising Munich, Taylor dug himself in further: "In international affairs there was nothing wrong with Hitler except that he was a German."[34] Underlying this apology for Nazi Germany was Taylor's incomprehension of the application of moral standards to diplomacy: "I have never seen any sense in the question of war guilt or war innocence. In a world of sovereign states, each does the best it can for its own interest; and can be criticised at most for mistakes, not for crimes."[35] Taylor even suggested that moralizing only made wars more vicious: "Bismarck's planned wars killed thousands; the just wars of the twentieth century have killed millions."[36]

Other realists quibble less with the notion of punishment than with the use of legal methods. George Kennan, the American diplomat who created the cold war doctrine of containment, warned, "I see the most serious fault of our past policy formulation to lie in something I might call the legalistic-moralistic approach to international problems."[37] And some realists simply cannot be bothered with legal niceties. Kennan preferred summary execution for Nazi leaders. And at the end of World War II, Hans Morgenthau, the father of American realism,[38] said, "I am doubtful of the whole setup under which these [Nuremberg] trials will be conducted. What, in my opinion, they should have done is to set up summary courts-martial. Then they should have placed these criminals on trial before them within 24 hours after they were caught, sentenced them to death, and shot them in the morning."[39]

Realists often fear that war crimes tribunals will interfere with the establishment of international order. Carrying the hatreds and moral passions of war over into a peace settlement is dangerous. Kissinger admired the Congress of Vienna's generous treatment of France after the Napoleonic Wars: "A war without an enemy is inconceivable; a peace built on the myth of an enemy is an armistice. It is the temptation of war to punish; it is the task of policy to construct. Power can sit in judgment, but statesmanship must look to the future."[40] Overheated moral judgments and particularly "personal retribution," Kissinger implied, risk undermining a peace.[41]

The most recent updating of realism, in the twilight of the cold war, maintains these themes. Such neorealism argues that in an anarchic international system, unitary states facing potential threats from *tous azimuts* will attempt to maximize either power or security. The result will be a balance of power. As Kenneth Waltz put it in the founding book of neorealism, "Self-help is necessarily the principle of action in an anarchic order."[42] The states in Waltz's system are all essentially alike, behaving the same abroad regardless of how they run their domestic politics: "[S]o long as anarchy endures, states remain like units."[43]

Like Taylor and Kissinger, Waltz hopes that removing overheated moral debates from the international arena will have a pacifying effect: "If might decides, then bloody struggles over right can more easily be avoided." And he is skeptical about injecting justice into international politics: "Nationally, the force of a government is exercised in the name of right and justice. Internationally, the force of a state is employed for the sake of its own protection and advantage." He is equally wary of international law: "National politics is the realm of authority, of administration, and of law. International politics is the realm of power, of struggle, and of accommodation. The international realm is preeminently a political one."[44] Law, to Waltz, is the antithesis of the anarchic international system.

These neorealists take a dim view of international legalism. International norms and institutions are epiphenomenal, mere veils over state power. As John Mearsheimer, a realist political scientist, puts it, "Realists maintain that institutions are basically a reflection of the distribution of power in the world. They are based on the self-interested calculations of the great powers, and they have no independent effect on state behavior."[45] To realists, a war crimes tribunal is simply something that the countries that decisively win a war inflict on the helpless country that loses it. It is punishment, revenge, spectacle—anything but justice.

It is hard not to be impressed with the force of much of the realist line of argument. Kennan, sensibly, recoiled at the notion of a Soviet judge sitting at Nuremberg despite the Soviet Union's own complicity, aggressions, and atrocities.[46] When the Ottoman Empire was defeated, it faced war crimes trials; when Atatürk drove Britain and Greece back, the new peace treaty dropped those demands. Criminals such as Stalin, Mao, and Pol Pot never faced justice from Western states appalled at their atrocities because they had not been militarily defeated first.

Realism also deflates much of the high-flown rhetoric of victorious states as self-serving. Throughout this book, states abandon lofty projects of international justice when that endangers their soldiers. Finally, realism provides a welcome corrective against the occasionally otherworldly musings of some international lawyers. To make rabbit stew, first catch a rabbit.

So why not adopt a realist approach? I will argue that war crimes tribunals are more than just vehicles for the crude application of power. There is no way of determining what will be done to accused war criminals without reference to ideas drawn from domestic politics.[47] In particular, there are five main anomalies that confound realism.

First, critically, there is a distinctive legalism to the notion of war crimes tribunals. These efforts are not simply disguised purges, although they often do have the result of getting rid of undesirable enemy leaders. The victors were not just trying to dispose of enemies; they were aiming at men they saw as *criminals*.[48] The documentary record clearly shows that the motivations for the trials at Leipzig, Constantinople, Nuremberg, Tokyo, The Hague, and Arusha were not merely to purge. Victorious liberals saw their foes as war criminals deserving of just punishment. Realists would either be baffled by this or deplore it.

After all, one hardly needs trials to dispose of accused war criminals. Why not just shoot them? If one considers such a brutal solution to be out of the question, that only a barbarian state would do such a thing, that only testifies to the extent to which legalism has permeated our political culture. Even liberal countries have been tempted to skip trials. Lloyd George swept to victory in the 1918 elections with his supporters chanting, "Hang the kaiser!" At the Québec Conference, Churchill and Roosevelt agreed to the Morgenthau Plan, which envisioned the summary execution of the Nazi leadership (they later reconsidered). Muhamed Sacirbey, Bosnia's UN ambassador and a former foreign minister, pointedly remembers this: "[A]fter World War II, before Nuremberg, the British and Russian view of Nuremberg was that we don't need a trial: let's just take them out in the back and shoot them." More recently, Gérard Prunier, a respected scholar of the Rwandan genocide, singled out "maybe 100 men who have committed not only a crime against humanity but a sin against the Spirit by locking up a whole nation into the airless sadomasochistic inferno. They have to die."[49]

Even some people who are otherwise dedicated to the rule of law believe that some atrocities go beyond the realm of law. The application of municipal law to war crimes is in many ways the legal equivalent of a bad analogy. The worst crimes in Western law are utterly pallid next to crimes against humanity.[50] A war crimes trial applies an old precedent to deeds that are a universe away from the conditions that created that precedent. As Robert Penn Warren's fictional demagogue Willie Stark put it,

I know a lot of law. . . . But I'm not a lawyer. That's why I can see what the law is like. It's like a single-bed blanket on a double bed and three folks in the bed and a cold night. There ain't ever enough blanket to cover the case, no matter how much pulling and hauling, and someone is always going to nigh catch pneumonia. Hell, the law is like the pants you bought last year and the seams are popped and the shankbone's to the breeze. The law is always too short and too tight for growing humankind.[51]

There is no such thing as *appropriate* punishment for the massacres at Srebrenica or Djakovica; only the depth of our legalist ideology makes it seem so. Watching the unfolding spectacle at Nuremberg, political theorist Hannah Arendt wrote, "For these crimes, no punishment is severe enough. It may well be essential to hang Göring, but it is totally inadequate. That is, this guilt, in contrast to all criminal guilt, oversteps and shatters any and all legal systems. That is the reason why the Nazis in Nuremberg are so smug."[52] This is no theoretical abstraction. Anthony Eden, the British foreign secretary, made the same point in 1942: "The guilt of such individuals is so black that they fall outside and go beyond the scope of any judicial process."[53] Today, who could really say it would be totally unjust to shoot thugs like Théoneste Bagosora or Ratko Mladic?

War crimes tribunals risk the acquittals of history's bloodiest killers in order to apply legal norms that were, after all, designed for lesser crimes. The Allied efforts to punish German and Turkish war criminals after World War I ended in fiasco, in large part because of the law. The British high commissioner in Constantinople complained, for instance, that a top Ottoman official was surely morally and criminally guilty, but that without "definite proof against him," he might escape justice.[54] Eden worried, "[T]he precedent of public trials of prominent statesmen shows that the procedure is rarely advantageous to the prosecution."[55] Nuremberg had its acquittals, and the court red-facedly dismissed a case against Krupp because the British thought they were trying Gustav Krupp (*père*) while the Americans were aiming for Alfried Krupp (*fils*).[56] Of 1,409 Japanese defendants tried in American courts after World War II, only 163 were sentenced to death.[57] Dusan Tadic, the first person to stand trial in The Hague, was initially acquitted on seven murder charges, and the judges dismissed 11 of 31 charges against him on the grounds that he could not have violated the Geneva Conventions because the war in Bosnia was not an international one—a vindication for Serbia.[58] And when

Augusto Pinochet's cruelty was brought before Britain's Law Lords, they at one point ruled that he could be extradited only for crimes committed after December 1988, when Britain implemented the Torture Convention at home—letting Pinochet off the hook for all but the last fifteen months of his seventeen years of dictatorship. British authorities later ruled Pinochet too ill to stand trial. Why risk this kind of thing? The only sturdy answer to these questions is the power of the legalistic norm.

Second, it seems that some norms of domestic politics occasionally spill over into the international realm.[59] After all, states do not only try defeated enemies; sometimes they try their own soldiers and leaders. Edmund Burke, while a member of Parliament in Britain, impeached Warren Hastings, the corrupt former governor general of Bengal, on twenty-two charges of high crimes and misdemeanors; Hastings was dramatically tried in the House of Lords in 1788–95.[60] In October 1956, an Israeli patrol massacred forty-three Israeli Arab villagers of Kfar Qassem, who had unwittingly violated a curfew imposed for the Suez War; after public outcry, the Israeli soldiers were tried by a military court and jailed, although the sentences were later shortened.[61] The United States half-heartedly put a handful of its own soldiers on trial after the My Lai massacre, although only one was ever convicted (and Richard Nixon helped get his sentence reduced to a mere three years).[62] In 1982, Menachem Begin's government was hounded from power after an Israeli judicial committee concluded that Begin and Ariel Sharon, his defense minister, bore indirect responsibility for the Sabra and Shatila massacres.[63] These cases can hardly be said to be victors' justice. Rather, they suggest that a country's norms can be so sincerely held that it will put its *own* soldiers and leaders on trial even in times of national upheaval.

Third, sometimes states pursue justice for victims who are not citizens of the victor states. British sympathy for the Armenians in 1915 and after was quite sincere. Even if Henry Stimson, the American secretary of war who was the architect of Nuremberg, took no great interest in the Holocaust, the administration was pressured to take account of the extermination of the Jews by Henry Morgenthau Jr., the treasury secretary, and by American Jews. Lackadaisical as the Clinton administration's response to the slaughters in Bosnia and Rwanda was, America did ultimately push for the establishment of international tribunals for these horrors. It is hard to find a NATO interest in Kosovo except humanitarianism. This is hardly a triumph of idealism, but it is not the complete absence of it either.

Fourth, war crimes tribunals seem to make an impact even in the absence of a military victory—suggesting that norms may have a certain independent power even when not fully backed up by states. To be sure, the Hague tribunal, forced to rely on the whims of NATO countries for its enforcement, lacks the scope and comprehensiveness of Nuremberg. But the tribunal has had an impact on Balkan diplomacy. During the NATO war over Kosovo, The Hague indicted Milosevic and other top Yugoslav leaders. Goldstone's indictment of Karadzic and Mladic, at a minimum, made it embarrassing to do business with them. Since then, American diplomats have been progressively more insistent on the need to punish indicted war criminals. For an underfunded international institution that until recently shared its office space with a Dutch insurance firm, the Hague tribunal has made a clear difference.

Similarly, the UN criminal tribunal for Rwanda is not easily explained as victors' justice. In Rwanda there was both a victory and an attempt at international justice, with the latter set up mostly to mitigate the excesses of the former. In 1994, over half a million people, mostly Tutsi, were killed by Hutu extremists. After that genocide, the Tutsi-dominated Rwandan Patriotic Front's guerrillas took back the capital city of Kigali and put tens of thousands of suspected Hutu *génocidaires* in appalling jails. The UN court is distinct from the Rwandan regime's own prosecutions, which aim at low-level perpetrators while leaving more important figures to the UN's jurisdiction. The UN tribunal was established partly because of dissatisfaction with the quality of justice likely to be dispensed by the overburdened, penniless, and understandably vengeful Rwandan regime.

Fifth, critically, not all victors' justice is the same. Göring's argument was not just that he was in the dock because he lost the war. He also implicitly argued that Allied leaders would too be in the dock if they had lost instead, and that therefore there was nothing to recommend the Allied brand of justice over the Nazi one. This argument has somehow found a certain amount of public currency. Oddly, although there are precious few people who would be indifferent if asked to choose between standing trial in a Soviet domestic court or an American one, there are plenty who think that there is not much difference between an *international* Soviet or American tribunal. Aron, hardly an unclear thinker, wrote: "It is easy to imagine the use that the victorious Reich would have made of its right to punish the 'criminal' states (Poland, France, Great Britain)."[64] Had the Nazis won, there is no reason to believe they would have set up a bona fide war crimes tribunal—even for acts like the fire-

15

bombing of Dresden, which could easily be considered a war crime. The Nazis might have set up a show trial, but it is wildly unlikely that they would have created anything more impartial. Nazi domestic courts were heavily rigged toward political persecution.[65] It seems safe to assume that the Nazis would have been equally as cynical in their use of the courts after a victory in World War II as they were after their victory in German domestic politics. There is in fact an empirical example of what a totalitarian state might have done as a victor in World War II: the Soviet Union's heavy-handed attitude toward Nuremberg and Tokyo.[66]

Nor is it difficult to tell a show trial from a truly legalistic one. A bona fide trial includes an independent judiciary, the possibility of acquittal, some kind of civil procedure, and some kind of proportionality in sentencing. As D. B. Somervell, the British attorney general, put it in 1944, "A trial involves a charge or charges for offences against some law, a decision on evidence, arguments on each side, and, if the accused is found guilty, the imposition by the Court of a penalty."[67] "The modern view of criminal justice, broadly," wrote Max Weber, "is that public concern with morality or expediency decrees expiation for the violation of a norm; this concern finds expression in the infliction of punishment on the evil doer by agents of the state, the evil doer, however, *enjoying the protection of a regular procedure*."[68] In contrast, a show trial has no chance of returning an acquittal, keeps the judges in thrall to the prosecution and behind that the state, cares little for procedure or standards of evidence, and has a propensity toward the quick execution. In 1946, Vyacheslav Molotov, the Soviet foreign minister, explained to shocked Western officials what awaited sixteen Polish underground leaders in Soviet custody: "The guilty ones will be tried."[69]

For all these reasons, the phrase "victors' justice" is in the end a largely uninformative one. The kind of justice one gets depends on the nature of the conquering state. The question is not whether we are looking at victors' justice. Probably. But *which* victor? And what justice?

The Liberal Approach

Realists argue that the exigencies of anarchy force states to similar behavior—an amoral struggle for security—regardless of their domestic ideals. So democracies and dictatorships alike do what they need to do to survive.[70] This runs contrary to a long tradition of seeing domestic politics as crucially important for foreign policy. Plato accused tyrants of stirring up wars to distract their subjects from their misery at home.[71] Rousseau

16

blamed states for causing wars.[72] Lenin, Hobson, and Schumpeter saw domestic roots for imperialism.[73] And in a more optimistic vein, Kant relied on republican constitutions to bring perpetual peace.[74]

So the foreign policy of liberal states might reflect liberal principles, at least up to a point. This opens the door to idealism in foreign policy. The reintroduction of domestic norms even in the extremities of wartime shows that states have options, and that their choices can therefore be morally judged.

An enduring dilemma of American foreign policy is the difficulty of maintaining American domestic ideals abroad: of being as pure in conducting foreign policy as in conducting domestic policy. "It was assumed that the foreign-policy institutions, like other [American] political institutions, would reflect the basic values of the preexisting and overwhelmingly preponderant ideology," wrote Samuel Huntington, an eminent political scientist. "Yet precisely these institutions—foreign and intelligence services, military and police forces—have functional imperatives that conflict most sharply and dramatically with the liberal-democratic values of the American Creed."[75] Elsewhere, Huntington worried that, in American civil-military relations, "[t]he real problem was the ideological one, the American attitude of mind which sought to impose liberal solutions in military affairs as well as in civil life."[76] Political scientist Aaron Friedberg argues that America's cold war technology-based nuclear deterrence strategy was largely determined by American domestic liberalism, which was ideologically opposed to the kind of intrusive, militarized garrison state that would be necessary to support a war-fighting strategy against the Soviet Union.[77]

There is an increasing body of evidence by political scientists suggesting that domestic preferences are reflected in a state's approach to international affairs. Making an argument similar to mine, David Lumsdaine writes, "The values and practices of domestic political life are apt to be preferred in international politics."[78] In a sweeping study of foreign aid, he shows that the most generous foreign aid donors were those countries that had generous social welfare programs at home.[79] Andrew Moravcsik argues that states act purposefully abroad to represent the interests of some part of the domestic polity.[80] And Huntington argues that American liberalism tends to "transpose its domestic successes to foreign relations," especially lawyerly measures like a World Court and outlawing war.[81]

Liberals argue that democracies almost never fight each other.[82] Democratic peace theorists believe that some combination of liberal institutions and norms combines to make democratic states behave radically

17

differently from other states on the fundamental question of international relations—whether to go to war. My argument is related to the democratic peace school: I argue that liberal ideals make liberal states take up the cause of international justice, treating their humbled foes in a way utterly divorced from the methods practiced by illiberal states.[83]

What does this mean for war crimes tribunals? If a war crimes tribunal is victors' justice, it makes a difference who the victors are. Victorious legalist liberal states tend to operate abroad by some of the same rules they observe at home.[84] "A trial, the supreme legalistic act," wrote liberal political theorist Judith Shklar, "like all political acts, does not take place in a vacuum. It is part of a whole complex of other institutions, habits, and beliefs. A trial within a constitutional government is not like a trial in a state of near-anarchy, or in a totalitarian order."[85]

As Kennan, Huntington, and others have (often disapprovingly) noted, liberal America has a propensity toward a lawyerly foreign policy. From the *Paquete Habana* (a 1900 case with the Supreme Court sitting as an international court of prize)[86] to the recent use of the 1789 Alien Tort Statute[87] to try to bring Karadzic before a New York court, American courts have not shied away from stepping outside of American borders. The Alien Tort Statute, strengthened by the *Filartiga* decision in 1980, and joined with the Torture Victim Protection Act of 1991, has been used against such figures as a former Guatemalan defense minister, a former president of Haiti, and the estate of the late Ferdinand Marcos, the ex-dictator of the Philippines.[88] Yamashita Tomoyuki, a Japanese general charged with not preventing his troops from committing war crimes in the Philippines, appealed his case all the way up to the Supreme Court.[89] Warren Christopher, Clinton's first secretary of state—and a prominent Los Angeles lawyer—says of the Hague tribunal: "I had a sort of a lawyer's sense of not wanting to interfere with the proceedings of the tribunal."

Liberal diplomats can be startlingly explicit about their exportation of domestic norms. In 1918, as the Imperial War Cabinet decided to seek Wilhelm II's trial, Frederick Smith, the British attorney general, said, "Grave judges should be appointed, but we should . . . take the risk of saying that in this quarrel we, the Allies, taking our stand upon the universally admitted principles of the moral law, *take our own standards of right and commit the trial of them to our own tribunals.*"[90] As Woodrow Wilson put it in his address to Congress on declaring war in 1917, "We are at the beginning of an age in which it will be insisted that the same standards of conduct and of responsibility for wrong shall be observed among nations and their governments that are observed among the individual citizens of civilized states."[91] And Robert Jackson wrote to Truman that

> *our test of what is legally crime gives recognition to those things which fundamentally outraged the conscience of the American people* and brought them finally to the conviction that their own liberty and civilization could not persist in the same world with the Nazi power. . . . The feeling of outrage grew in this country, and it became more and more felt that these were crimes committed against us and against the whole society of civilized nations by a band of brigands who had seized the instrumentality of a state. *I believe that those instincts of our people were right and that they should guide us as the fundamental tests of criminality.*[92]

Even those who do not welcome such statements agree on the underlying dynamic. Kennan wrote that such international legalism "undoubtedly represents in part an attempt to transpose the Anglo-Saxon concept of individual law into the international field and to make it applicable to governments as it is applicable here at home to individuals."[93] Idealism begins at home.

There are two strong pieces of evidence to support the liberal view of international relations. First, *every* international war crimes tribunal that I am aware of—Leipzig, Constantinople, Nuremberg, Tokyo, The Hague, and Arusha—has rested on the support of liberal states. Second, conversely, when illiberal states have fought each other, they have *never* established a bona fide war crimes tribunal. They may trade accusations of atrocities as propaganda, but nothing more legalistic. Think of the Chaco War between Bolivia and Paraguay, the 1970 Syrian invasion of Jordan, the 1985–87 Sino-Vietnamese War, or the Iran-Iraq War.[94]

After the Franco-Prussian War, Bismarck scorned any talk of putting Napoleon III on trial.[95] While the liberal Allies were having a series of war crimes trials in the Pacific, the Soviet Union did not bother with any sort of judicial proceedings for the hundreds of thousands of Japanese prisoners of war captured in Stalin's brief foray into Manchuria.[96] The seriousness of the Soviet Union's commitment to legality can perhaps be judged by the fact that the Soviets tried to include the Katyn forest massacre at the Nuremberg trials—despite the fact that the massacre had actually been committed by the *Soviets.* The Soviet judge was the only one to dissent from the Nuremberg judgment, objecting to three acquittals and the sentencing of Rudolf Hess to life in prison instead of hanging.[97] The Soviets wanted a show trial, and were piqued when the other three Allies would not let them have it.[98] The exportation of domestic habits is not always a welcome development.

War Crimes Legalism

Due Process across Borders

Much of this book chronicles the principled belief that war criminals must be put on trial—a legalistic solution to a complex moral and political problem. Legalism, as defined by Shklar, is "the ethical attitude that holds moral conduct to be a matter of rule following, and moral relationships to consist of duties and rights determined by rules."[99] In this book, legalism mostly manifests itself as a fixation on process, a sense that international trials must be conducted roughly according to well-established domestic practice—not just rule-following, but rule-following when it comes to war criminals. (I properly ought to say "war crimes legalism," but that seems cumbersome.) Liberal states are legalist: they put war criminals on trial in rough accordance with their domestic norms.

There is a growing academic interest in the power of ideas in international relations.[100] But it is difficult to trace precisely the influence of ideas. One problem is that it can be difficult to anticipate which ideas will prove influential.[101] Another is that it is hard to specify *ex ante* what exactly the content of these ideas is, which can lead to circular explanations that infer ideas backward from the actions of states. And another is that one will confuse ideas with self-interest.[102] But one can sidestep these hazards by locating the sources of ideas in clear, well-established domestic politics, and then tracing their functioning in the international arena. Neither the source nor the presence of the idea of legalism is hard to discern. The common (and correct) statement that international law lags behind domestic law shows that causality runs from domestic norms to international ones.

Liberal states believe, with varying degrees of intensity and seriousness, in universal rights. Such states also have well-established judicial systems and domestic norms of nonviolent contestation in politics. From such peaceful ways of politics and tribunals, liberal leaders learn a respect for due process. And because of their belief in the universal applicability of their liberal principles, liberal leaders are tempted to use those methods of fair trial even outside their own borders.[103]

The Universal Application of Domestic Norms

Liberal states—that is, states that respect civil and political rights—almost never commit atrocities at home.[104] Liberal politicians do not profess radical violence or revolution, do not rise to power by killing, and do not stay there by repression.[105] The quietude of liberal polities is enhanced by a strong, well-respected judicial system. Whatever the domestic imperfections and ethnic hatreds in liberal states, in their domestic nonviolence and well-established judicial systems they are still qualitatively different from illiberal states.[106] Accustomed to such norms, liberal leaders can be genuinely shocked by overseas atrocities. As Ernest Pollock, the British solicitor general, said while preparing lists of German war crimes suspects in 1919: "The test that had been applied by himself and his French colleagues was: 'Do these charges shock any plain man's conscience?' "[107] Liberal elites think: we do not do such things here.[108] Even in the darkest days of World War II, when he wanted to execute the top Nazis, Churchill did not trust his country to tolerate such killings, "for I am certain that the British nation at any rate would be incapable of carrying out mass executions for any length of time, especially as we have not suffered like the subjugated countries."[109]

There is more underlying liberal states' legalism than just the rule of law. After all, some authoritarian states also respect the rule of law, albeit often harsh laws. But the liberal acceptance of the rule of law comes in the context of rights, often protected by the courts. Political trials cut deeply against the liberal grain.

These rights, whether resting on natural law (as in Vattel), a Rawlsian thought-experiment, divinity, or a process of discourse, are often seen as universal, or at least not strictly domestic rights.[110] In 1788, in Parliament, Burke dismissed the venal Hastings's notion of

a plan of Geographical morality, by which the duties of men in public and in private situations are not to be governed by their relations to the Great Governor of the Universe, or by their relations to men, but by climates, degrees of longitude and latitude, parallels not of life but of latitudes. As if, when you have crossed the equinoctial line all the virtues die. . . . [T]he laws of morality are the same every where, and. . . there is no action which would pass for an action of extortion, of peculation, of bribery and of oppression in England, that is not an act of extortion, of peculation, of bribery and of oppression in Europe, Asia, Africa, and all the world over.[111]

The most important practical liberal document, the American Declaration of Independence, says that all men are created equal, with inalienable rights. It does not specify that those men must be Americans, not Bosnians. Approvingly citing Justice Hugo Black, Louis Henkin, a distinguished scholar of the Constitution, argues that the Constitution was "not only a social contract by citizens for citizens. It was not only for home consumption. It established a community of conscience and righteousness and the people directed their representatives to respect individual human rights wherever they exercised the people's authority, in or outside the United States."[112] For Henkin, there is little difference between foreign and domestic rights-based constraints: "In principle, then, the Bill of Rights limits foreign policy and the conduct of foreign relations as it does other federal activities."[113] Political scientists echo the theme. "Within a transnational domestic culture," wrote Bruce Russett, "as within a democratic nation, others are seen as possessing rights and exercising those rights in a spirit of enlightened self-interest."[114]

Because these rights can be seen as universal, they can be spread. Strictly speaking, a British-imposed war crimes tribunal on behalf of British prisoners of war need not rely on universal rights, but on a sense of British responsibility for Britons. But liberal states often go beyond that. The notion of human rights is axiomatic to today's liberal citizens. When seeking justice for the Armenians, the Jews, the Kurds, the Bosnian Muslims, the Rwandan Tutsi, or the Kosovars, liberal states rest their efforts on universal rights—hence the famous category of crimes against *humanity*. This category is not just an invention of Nuremberg; it dates back at least to the 1915 Armenian massacres. Universal human rights do not respect "geographical morality" or sovereignty.

Theoretically, any ideology that transcends sovereignty—like pan-Arabism, pan-Slavism, or Marxism—can extend its jurisdiction beyond national borders. But Marxist and pan-Arabist states are not necessarily legalist, so this might result in political support for a group of victims but not in trials: outrage, but not legalism. Many Muslim countries sympathized with the plight of Muslims in Bosnia, which built pressure for the creation of the Hague tribunal; but American proposals for trying Iraqi war criminals for atrocities against Kuwaitis and Kurds have generated scant enthusiasm among the Persian Gulf monarchies, even though all of the parties in question are Muslim. Israel abducted and tried Adolf Eichmann according to the constraints of Israeli legalism, but it would not do the same for war criminals who were not perpetrators of the Holocaust.[115]

The roots of Western universalism may partially lie, ironically enough, in a pan-Christian concern for the laws of war. Hugo Grotius was moved to write by cruelty among warring Christians, and Thomas Aquinas claimed the Greek tradition of natural law for Christianity.[116] In practice, European Christian sympathy for fellow Christians under Ottoman rule resulted in numerous semi-humanitarian interventions. In 1774, Russia was granted a right to intervene in the Ottoman Empire to help Russian Orthodox Christians; Britain and Russia sided with the Greeks in their war of independence in 1821–30; in 1860, France sent six thousand troops to Syria and Lebanon to help Maronites being massacred by Druse; and in 1876 Gladstone raged against the "Bulgarian horrors."[117] In the 1915 Armenian massacres, British solicitude rested on both a kind of pan-Christian solidarity as well as a more universal humanitarianism.

Whatever its precise lineage, in practice, it is only liberalism that has looked so far beyond its own borders. Lloyd George's legalism did not respect sovereignty, monarchy, empire, or even divinity: he once told the Imperial War Cabinet that Alexander the Great and Moses should have been tried as war criminals.[118]

This universalistic legalism can be baffling to the war criminals who face it. During the Armenian massacres, Henry Morgenthau Sr., America's ambassador to the Sublime Porte, tried to appeal to the conscience of Talaat Pasha, the Ottoman minister of the interior and one of the masterminds of the atrocities. Talaat once told Morgenthau, "You are a Jew; these people are Christians." Morgenthau snapped, "[A]t least in my ambassadorial capacity I am 97 per cent. Christian. . . . I do not appeal to you in the name of any race or any religion, but merely as a human being."[119]

There is of course the danger that liberal states will overreach. Shklar warned: "When, for example, the American prosecution at the Tokyo Trials appealed to the law of nature as the basis for condemning the accused, he was only applying a foreign ideology, serving his nation's interests, to a group of people who neither knew nor cared about this doctrine. The assumption of universal agreement served here merely to impose dogmatically an ethnocentric vision of international order."[120] My point is not whether it is wise for liberal states to impose their norms on Turks, Iraqis, Serbs, and so on. The point is that it happens.

The Importance of Due Process

What exactly does it mean to be legalist? From World War I to Kosovo, liberal states have consistently seen attacks on civilians and cruelty to prisoners of war as criminal acts. Even with foggier and less easily justifiable charges, like aggression, legalists remain devoted to the idea that a *trial* is the proper way of dispensing justice. This is only one rule among many that could guide the legalistic mind, but it is a crucial one. As Henkin notes, "The constitutional provisions that afford fair criminal procedures apply also to persons charged with violating foreign affairs statutes, even to foreign nationals accused of espionage."[121] Legalism is above all about due process. Thus, Jackson, in his report on the London Conference, wrote of the importance of

> provisions which assured to the defendants the fundamentals of procedural "due process of law." Although this famous phrase of the American Constitution bears an occasionally unfamiliar implication abroad, the Continental countries joined us in enacting its essence— guaranties securing the defendants every reasonable opportunity to make a full and free defense. Thus the charter gives the defendant the right to counsel, to present evidence, and to cross-examine prosecution witnesses.[122]

America might have been willing to fudge a bit by creating new categories of crimes, but it was conservative about the essential modalities for a trial: jurists steeped in Western domestic legal traditions, the possibility of acquittal, standards of evidence, proportionate punishment, and so on. A court-martial or an international military tribunal is not the same thing as, say, the U.S. Court of Appeals for the Second Circuit, and American and Continental law are hardly identical; but an amalgam of basically fair liberal legal arrangements is still easily discernible from a Soviet-style show trial. The American lawyers trying Japanese war criminals conducted themselves "just like 'the boys back home.' "[123] "It was as if Sullivan & Cromwell or Milbank, Tweed, Hadley & McCloy decided to conduct a trial," writes one commentator on Nuremberg. "The aura of the prevailing New York corporate law firm culture drifted across the Atlantic and landed in Nuremberg."[124]

The accusation may be murder, rape, or theft—or genocide, or aggression—but the case will wind up in a court. Cruelty to prisoners of war, or mass killing of civilians, have been criminal throughout this century— and well before.[125] (True, some legalists have not shown a particular horror of setting new precedents, such as when arguing about whether sovereignty entitles a government to slaughter its own subjects. The novelty of some charges, like genocide or rape, was not the result of a desire to convict the accused on trumped-up charges; it was generally a product of the accused's innovations in cruelty.[126]) To be sure, there is a distinct danger that politicized charges, of which Wilhelm's "supreme offence against international morality and the sanctity of treaties" is the most glaring example ever put up by liberal states, may make a mockery of the method of a trial. There are charges so unfair that they undo any notions of due process. But such excesses are usually checked by the judges who will eventually hear such cases. Liberal states have not been willing to seriously compromise their domestic standards of a fair trial when putting foreign leaders on trial.[127] Nuremberg was a stripped-down version of domestic British or American trials, but not so much that it could fairly be called a naked exercise of state power. State power was exercised before Nuremberg, to put the Nazis in the dock; but once they were there, they faced full-blown Western legalism as it had developed in its domestic context.

This is not always to the liking of some lawyers, who worry that extending the law abroad will only corrupt the law. This is a kind of lawyerly isolationism: our laws are too good for just anybody. Lawyers, after all, take precedent seriously, which can be paralyzing in the face of innovations in atrocity.[128] Robert Lansing, Wilson's secretary of state, frowned at the idea of trying Wilhelm II for starting World War I, and at the idea of crimes against humanity—anything, that is, that expanded the scope of international law. Stimson hesitated to prosecute German crimes against German Jews. Nuremberg and Tokyo's charges of aggressive war raised many eyebrows. In *Profiles in Courage,* John Kennedy lauded Robert Taft for opposing plans for Nuremberg.[129] And at the Supreme Court, Chief Justice Harlan Fiske Stone noted,

> It would not disturb me greatly . . . if that power were openly and frankly used to punish the German leaders for being a bad lot, but it disturbs me some to have it dressed up in the habiliments of the common law and the Constitutional safeguards to those charged with crime. . . .
>
> Jackson is away conducting his high-grade lynching party in Nuremberg. . . . I don't mind what he does to the Nazis, but I hate to see the pretense that he is running a court and proceeding according to common law. This is a little too sanctimonious a fraud to meet my old-fashioned ideas.[130]

25

Stone does not dwell on the alternative to a high-grade lynching: the usual type of lynching.[131]

Once a president or prime minister has turned the judgment of defeated enemies over to the judges, the outcome is in the hands of laws that developed from domestic traditions. Arendt, suspicious of the motives of David Ben-Gurion, Israel's prime minister, in trying Eichmann, was nevertheless impressed by the fairness of the Israeli judges: "[T]he trial is presided over by someone who serves Justice as faithfully as Mr. Hausner [the prosecutor] serves the State of Israel."[132] America sent some of its finest jurists to Nuremberg; Jackson, a Supreme Court justice, was in the habit of ignoring executive wishes. (Stalin sent Vishinsky.) Richard Goldstone had headed the Goldstone commission investigating atrocities in democratizing South Africa—another good way of learning to defy your own government.[133] The leaders of the executive branch understand perfectly well what risks—acquittals, technicalities, tedium— they are taking. But a liberal executive still sometimes leaves the fate of war criminals up to the courts.

Legalism's Antithesis: Totalitarian Show Trials

Political trials have earned a bad reputation since those of Socrates and Jesus. In France before the Revolution, the poor who defied the state faced special rigged trials.[134] But such illiberal trials reached their apotheosis in modern totalitarian states. These regimes show the opposite of liberal legalism: the complete subversion of legal norms. The judiciary has no independence. Predictable bureaucratic authority is replaced with arbitrary terror. Nazi and Soviet show trials, Shklar wrote, have "nothing to do with justice. Their end is elimination, terror, propaganda, and re-education. . . . They are part of regimes that have already abandoned justice as a policy, and our judgment of these courts must depend on our view of the ends they serve, not of their 'betrayal' of justice, since the ideologies which inspire them are profoundly unlegalistic and indeed hostile to the whole policy of justice."[135] These trials took a terrible toll. From 1933 to 1945, Nazi civilian courts executed an estimated 16,560 people, plus 40,000 to 50,000 German soldiers killed after courts-martial. Even setting aside the use of courts in collectivization, the Soviet Union sentenced a million people to death in the 1937–39 purges, and perhaps twelve million people died from 1936 to 1953 in camps after being purged.[136]

In *Mein Kampf*, Hitler had written that "one day a German national tribunal must condemn and execute several tens of thousands of the criminals who organized and are responsible for the November treason and everything connected with it."[137] Nazi domestic trials, instruments of the Nazi state rather than checks upon it, aimed at discovering if the accused had become an enemy of the race. As legal scholar Ingo Müller has noted: "As a result, the purpose of a trial now became not so much to determine whether the accused had broken a law, but rather 'whether the wrongdoer still belongs to the community'; the criminal trial was supposed to be 'an evaluation and segregation of types.' A decisive characteristic of National Socialistic theory was that emphasis was placed less on the act committed than on the 'criminal personality.'"[138] Nazi "jurisprudence" ordered purges, established concentration camps, wrote the Nuremberg Laws, and took away the civil rights of Jews.[139] In 1934, the Nazi regime created its special *Volksgerichtshof* (People's Court) to realize Hitler's ambition in *Mein Kampf.* In 1944, after the failure of the Stauffenberg plot to kill Hitler, Hitler gave a glimpse of his idea of justice: "This time the criminals will be given short shrift. No military tribunals. We'll haul them before the People's Court. No long speeches from them. The court will act with lightning speed. And two hours after the sentence it will be carried out. By hanging—without mercy."[140]

The story was much the same in the Soviet Union. Hitler even once referred to Roland Freisler, the president of the *Volksgerichtshof,* as "our Vishinsky."[141] Russia had an unhappy history of rigged tsarist political trials, but the Communist version of the practice, under Andrei Vishinsky's prosecution, reached unprecedented depths. Robert Tucker described the 1938 show trial as "a gigantic texture of fantasy into which bits and pieces of falsified real history have been woven along with outright fiction."[142] As historian Adam Ulam put it,

> The Bolshevik mind—and not only Stalin's, though his was the extreme case in point—was unable to distinguish between theoretical and factual reality, between the world of ideologically inspired dreams or suspicions and the world of hard facts. . . . They [Bukharin and Rykov] must have realized, as Stalin did during the purge trials, that the indictment was manufactured and the confessions exacted through pressure. But these were "details"; the essential fact was that the accused were of hostile class origin and hence *capable* of the crimes of which they were charged. The principle "innocent until proven guilty" is not so much alien as incomprehensible to someone nurtured on Communist dogmas and categories.

Does one have to *prove* that the *kulak* is an enemy of the Soviet power?
... Freedom, wrote an English jurist, was secreted in the interstices of
procedure. Stalinist terror bred upon Communist semantics: terms like
class war, class justice, enemy of the people, encouraged a frame of mind
in which individual guilt or innocence was the consequence not of facts
but of political and social imperatives of the moment.[143]

Reporting on the 1976 trial of four Czech rock musicians, Václav Havel
wrote that the court system had become "a judiciary fully aware of how
it is manipulated by power, but incapable of defying that power and so,
ultimately, accepting the pitiful role of a subordinated employee of the
'masters.' "[144] The contrast with real legalism is stark.

The Politics of War Crimes Tribunals

Five Propositions

Liberals need to ask why liberal states so often fail to pursue war crimes
tribunals, and realists need to ask why war crimes trials happen at all.[145]
Moving from theory to practicalities, there are at least five important
recurring themes in the politics of war crimes tribunals.[146] First, it is only
liberal states, with legalist beliefs, that support bona fide war crimes tribunals. That much, at least, is a minor triumph for idealists. Illiberal states,
in contrast, are more cynical: they may support a show trial only as a way
of pursuing a Carthaginian peace.

There are sharp limits to liberal idealism. As the second proposition,
even liberal states tend not to push for a war crimes tribunal if so doing
would put their own soldiers at risk. From the Napoleonic Wars to Bosnia, this is perhaps the single biggest impediment to the creation of robust institutions of international justice.

Third, there is a distinctly self-serving undertone to liberal campaigns
for international justice. Even liberal states are more likely to be outraged
by war crimes against their own citizens than war crimes against foreigners. The more a state has suffered, the more likely it is to be outraged.

Fourth, even liberal states are most likely to support a war crimes tribunal if public opinion is outraged by the war crimes in question. And they
are less likely to support a war crimes tribunal if only elites are outraged.

Finally, nonstate pressure groups can be effective in pushing for a tribunal, by shaming liberal states into action and providing expertise. This

theme does not come up as much as the other four, for these nonstate groups only came of age after World War II. Taken together, these five propositions constitute a sketch of the politics behind the support, or abandonment, of war crimes tribunals.

FIRST PROPOSITION: THE LEGALISM OF LIBERAL STATES

Only liberal states have legalist domestic norms that have a clear impact on foreign policy. Illiberal states can do things the easy way: summary executions, show trials, or ignoring the issue of war crimes altogether. Liberal states find it much tougher to do so.[147] No doubt, there will be decision makers in liberal governments who scoff at the idea of war crimes trials. But liberal governments, even if they might otherwise prefer to either ignore war criminals or summarily execute them, tend to be bound by their own liberalism.

Ironically, this legalism can interfere with war crimes prosecutions. The recourse to law brings in a series of standards that can make it difficult to prosecute. Robert Lansing had legal objections to putting Wilhelm II on trial; some American officials were reluctant to include Nazi atrocities against German Jews in the Nuremberg charges; and it has been difficult to find adequate evidence to convict Arkan or Milosevic. Liberal diplomats often find themselves squirming at the challenge of exporting their domestic standards.

SECOND PROPOSITION: PROTECTING SOLDIERS

For want of a better term, call this the Scott O'Grady phenomenon. In June 1995, O'Grady, an American F-16 pilot, was shot down by the Bosnian Serb Army. While the White House still refused to send American troops to save Bosnian civilians, America went to extraordinary lengths to bring O'Grady home safe, sending Marine commandos into hostile Serb territory. O'Grady got a hero's welcome back in America, and his name is still fairly well known. What is striking is not just that even liberal states value the lives of their own more than those of foreigners, but how *radically* the lives of foreigners are discounted. There is no doubt that O'Grady's life is precious; the puzzle is why Bosnian lives were seen as so cheap.

To realists, this makes a kind of sense. Security is paramount, and if there is a trade-off between protecting soldiers and protecting the innocent, the innocent are liable to get the worst of it. Hans Morgenthau wrote, "[T]he principle of the defense of human rights cannot be consistently applied in foreign policy because it can and it must come in conflict with other interests that may be more important than the defense of human rights in a particular instance."[148] Here, the protection of soldiers stands as a kind of rough proxy for some of these other interests.[149] Liberal universalism only goes so far. "Americans are basically isolationist," Clinton said in 1993, as American soldiers were dying in Somalia. "They understand at a basic gut level Henry Kissinger's vital-interest argument. Right now the average American doesn't see our interest threatened to the point where we should sacrifice one American life."[150]

This proposition is also perhaps a way of explaining the absence of a call for a war crimes tribunal in the aftermath of the horrors committed by Mao, Stalin, or (until very recently) Pol Pot. Western complicity aside, what country was going to risk its soldiers to bring them to trial? This also explains why war crimes tribunals are almost invariably linked to a peace settlement. In war, the soldiers are already at risk. If a proposed tribunal puts them at greater risk, the tribunal idea is in serious trouble; if the proposal calls for putting them in harm's way in the first place, it has even slimmer chances.

This is not only the military's fault. True, militaries are often the center of opposition to war crimes prosecutions; as Samuel Huntington noted, "The military man normally opposes reckless aggressive, belligerent action."[151] It is unexceptionable that officers and military commanders want to protect their troops; but civilian leaders also shrink from casualties in the pursuit of international justice, as shown repeatedly in Bosnia. Conversely, one of the reasons Nuremberg went off so well was that the Allies had already decided to occupy Germany even before settling on a war crimes policy. It was assumed that catching war criminals would not increase the danger to troops, and in the event even Göring and Frank surrendered quietly. Whenever the safety of one's own is at stake, considerations of justice for others melt away.

THIRD PROPOSITION: PUTTING CITIZENS BEFORE FOREIGNERS

When will states be outraged at war crimes? Countries are first and foremost outraged by wars waged against them. The playwright Eugène Ionesco has a character say, "If only it had happened somewhere else, in some other country, and we'd just read about it in the papers, one could discuss it quietly, examine the question from all points of view and come to an objective conclusion. . . . But when you're involved yourself, when you suddenly find yourself up against the brutal facts you can't help feeling directly concerned—the shock is too violent for you to stay cool and detached."[152] There is no doubting the sincerity of British outrage during the Blitz, or the depth of Russian feeling during Hitler's invasion—or, for that matter, German outrage during the fire-bombing of Dresden, or Japanese outrage at the atomic bombings of Hiroshima and Nagasaki. The fact that the names of O'Grady and Nurse Edith Cavell (a Briton executed by Germans in World War I) are widely known shows a great concern for even a handful of one's own citizens. Any state, liberal or otherwise, may be solicitous of its own citizens.

Even liberal states are primarily concerned with war crimes against their own. During World War I, eagerness for war crimes trials increased in proportion to the severity of suffering: Wilson was less interested in hanging the kaiser than Lloyd George was, and Belgium and France were, in turn, more enthusiastic about it than Britain. British officials came to worry more about prosecuting Turks who had mistreated British prisoners of war than Turks who had killed Armenians. Britain has shown more interest in prosecuting Libyans for the Lockerbie terrorist incident than in punishing Serbs for atrocities against Bosnian Muslims. A liberal state that has suffered in a war will be more likely to seek international justice than one that has not. And a liberal state will probably be more concerned with prosecuting war crimes against its own citizens than those against foreigners, even when the suffering of the foreigners far outweighs that of the citizens of that liberal state.

Liberal states do make universalistic arguments for the protection of those who are *not* their citizens. Liberal states are more apt to pursue prosecution for war crimes committed against their own citizens; but because they are universalists, liberal states may also be outraged by crimes against humanity committed against noncitizens.[153] Selfishness predominates, but not totally.

FOURTH PROPOSITION: OUTRAGE, MASS AND ELITE

Legalism alone is not enough; one also needs outrage. Any country, liberal or not, can be outraged by an enemy's war crimes. Such fury is a necessary but not sufficient condition for supporting a war crimes tribunal. Outrage alone could result in summary executions, as proposed by Prussia in 1815 and, on a vast scale, by the Soviet Union in 1943. Conversely, legalism without outrage could result in a dreary series of futile legal briefs.

Liberal domestic institutions can be conducive to voicing mass outrage for two reasons. First, they do not offer elites the option of using certain methods to silence public opinion. If Stalin had decided for some reason not to punish the Nazis, he would have had ways of stifling the outrage of average Russians that were not available to Churchill or Roosevelt. Nor can liberal states muzzle an inconvenient press. Second, by definition, democracies are responsive to public opinion.

Polls from World War II show that the British and American publics were bitterly punitive toward the Axis, and policymakers responded to that. As Kennan disapprovingly wrote, "[A] good deal of our trouble seems to have stemmed from the extent to which the executive has felt itself beholden to short-term trends of public opinion in the country and from what we might call the erratic and subjective nature of public reaction to foreign-policy questions."[154] The dynamic can work in reverse, too: elite outrage can stoke mass outrage, through speeches and propaganda. The British election of 1918, in which Lloyd George's government rode and stoked public anger at Wilhelm II, is a fine example of both. One could equally well explain British enthusiasm for war crimes trials for Wilhelm II and other Germans by pointing to the British public's anger, or to that of Lloyd George and Curzon.

This is not to say that liberal diplomats will not sometimes try to stand against their public's wishes. In France in 1815, Castlereagh, Britain's foreign secretary, did not mind doing business with Bonapartists whom the English public could not stomach. In such situations, one would expect the elites to win out in the short term. Elites are simply closer to policy decisions; mass opinion may not influence them fast enough. A determined leader can act now and worry about public opinion later. This is less likely in liberal states, where elites know that the price of flouting public opinion may yet be paid on election day, but still not impossible.

In the long term, such elites are taking a real risk. Wilson preferred the League of Nations to punitive war crimes trials, although many Americans disagreed. Today, Madeleine Albright's push for a tougher war crimes policy may manage to win out, but it always risks being swamped in bureaucratic infighting or overruled—by the Pentagon, Bill Clinton, or an American electorate with no stomach for casualties. The best guarantee of an idealistic policy is consistent idealistic pressure from the electorate.

FIFTH PROPOSITION: NONSTATE ACTORS

Some idealists have long hoped to tame a world of Realpolitik by relying on international public opinion. In 1870, Gladstone wrote:

> Certain it is that a new law of nations is gradually taking hold of the mind, and coming to sway the practice, of the world; a law which recognises independence, which frowns upon aggression, which favours the pacific, not the bloody settlement of disputes, which aims at permanent and not temporary adjustments; above all, which recognises, as a tribunal of paramount authority, the general judgment of civilised mankind.[155]

It was on that kind of foundation that the League of Nations briefly rested, and it is that hope that inspires human rights groups to push for war crimes tribunals.

Since the 1960s, international human rights groups have grown stronger. In the debates over ex-Yugoslavia and Rwanda, nongovernmental organizations (NGOs) have been a noticeable voice—although states are still by far the most powerful international actors. The Hague tribunal has taken advantage of NGO resources: forensic experts from Physicians for Human Rights, documentation from Human Rights Watch, funding for the commission of experts by the Soros Foundation, and so on.[156] But in the end, these NGOs can claim credit, or bear responsibility, for the establishment of the tribunal mostly insofar as they were able to persuade the liberal members of the Security Council. The pleas of Human Rights Watch presumably had little impact in Beijing, but they were a source of embarrassment in Washington.[157]

Pressure from NGOs is not a necessary condition for the establishment of a war crimes tribunal. The courts at Leipzig, Constantinople, Nuremberg, and Tokyo were set up without the benefit of today's human rights NGOs. But now that they do exist, these NGOs can provide expertise and raise the domestic costs in a liberal country for ignoring foreign atrocities.

This book is primarily about the politics of international justice. For the sake of truth in advertising, it is *not* about three closely related topics—not for any lack of interest, but in the hopes of focusing an already large book.

33

First, this book is not about domestic transitions to democracy. That is why Bosnia features here and South Africa does not. In democratizations, there is some consensus on what the national community is; not so in wars. More important, democratizations usually involve an amnesty for the ancien régime as a negotiated price of a peaceful transition.[158] In contrast, all of my cases here involve defeat in war: an opportunity for the sheer imposition of justice that is exceedingly rare in democratization. Students of democratization tend to view Latin America and Eastern Europe as having distinct dynamics in confronting authoritarian human rights violations; international justice has its own dynamics, too.

Second, this book is not primarily about international institutions. It is true that institutions, domestic or international, are often the repositories of ideas.[159] Realists and institutionalists both agree that these institutions are the creation of a powerful state—a hegemon, in political scientist Robert Keohane's formulation.[160] Realists tend to believe that these institutions remain tools of states; neoliberal institutionalists argue that "sticky" institutions can linger long after the hegemon has faded from the scene, playing a powerful role even without backing from a state.[161] This book does not address this debate because my case studies tend to come at the very moments when international institutions—the Holy Alliance, the League of Nations, the International Court of Justice, the UN—are being created. Nuremberg was part and parcel of a post–World War II network of institutions that included the UN and the Bretton Woods organizations,[162] and Leipzig was linked to the creation of the League of Nations.

The major exceptions are the twin UN tribunals for ex-Yugoslavia and Rwanda, and the nascent permanent ICC. The Hague tribunal has stigmatized Karadzic and Milosevic as indicted war criminals, showing the power of international institutions. The Hague has shown surprising independence and durability, despite fitful political support. Although they have almost certainly never read Keohane, the tribunal's staff sound like neoliberal institutionalists. "It's a sort of Frankenstein," said an official in the prosecutor's office, neatly summing up much of the neoliberal institutionalist argument. "You create the monster and then you can't control it." Did Goldstone, the first chief prosecutor, think that the Security Council had realized in 1993, when it first set up the tribunal, that the court would indict Karadzic and Mladic? "Probably not," says Goldstone. "But that's what happens when you create an institution. They really take on a life of their own."

Finally, this book is not about international law. There has been a great deal written about international criminal justice, but this book is mostly interested in the politics that underpin (and undermine) international law.

To reiterate, my argument is that the pursuit of war criminals can only be explained with reference to domestic political norms in liberal states. Authoritarian and totalitarian powers may seek to punish defeated foes, or they may choose to do business with them. When they have chosen punishment, they did not use legal methods; rather, they took arbitrary steps like shooting their enemies, or at best putting on an obviously rigged show trial. And in one respect, liberal and illiberal states are similar: they have tended not to put their own soldiers at risk for international justice.

But unlike illiberal states, liberal states are often constrained by their domestic norms. Liberal states commonly see their enemies not as mere foes, but as war criminals deserving legal punishment. Liberal states are unlikely to shoot war criminals, although they can be tempted by that prospect. Rather, even when liberal decision makers are painfully aware of the risks of acquittal, delay, and embarrassment posed by a war crimes tribunal, domestic norms push them to apply due process beyond their own borders. Liberal states are most likely to seek such legalistic punishment when it is their own citizens who have suffered war crimes, but they also sometimes pursue war criminals for atrocities against foreigners. So in the crucial question of how to treat a defeated foe, liberal states are profoundly different from illiberal ones.

The bulk of this book will be spent developing these themes across five historical chapters: the aftermath of the Napoleonic Wars; World War I; the Armenian genocide; World War II and the Holocaust; and the wars of Yugoslavia's disintegration. This book also considers three other cases throughout the course of the narrative: the Tokyo trials for Japanese war criminals after World War II; the abortive American pursuit of Iraqi Ba'thists during the Persian Gulf crisis; and the UN war crimes tribunal, in Arusha, Tanzania, for the 1994 Rwandan genocide. In an epilogue, I will consider, more speculatively, whether war crimes tribunals seem to be effective tools for reconciliation in shattered societies.

In their closing arguments in Tihomir Blaskic's trial, over two years later, the prosecutors blamed Croatia's president, Franjo Tudjman, for the "ethnic cleansing" of the Lasva Valley. For its part, Croatia, fearing an indictment of Tudjman, was refusing to turn over subpoenaed documents that might be incriminating, and dragging its heels on the extradition of two other war crimes suspects. The Hague formally complained to the Security Council, while Tudjman himself publicly denounced the prosecutors as "dilettantes." Justice was still grinding slow.

Tudjman died of cancer before the trial ended. Blaskic finally heard the verdict against him on March 3, 2000. Convicted on nineteen charges of command responsibility and individual responsibility for the ravaging of the Lasva Valley and Ahmici, Blaskic was sentenced to forty-five years imprisonment—the stiffest sentence handed down by the tribunal to date, for the highest-ranked military officer to be convicted. In his summary of the court's findings, Judge Claude Jorda of France made a point of blaming Tudjman's Croatia for "pitting the Muslims and Croats of central Bosnia against each other." The verdict was received angrily by Bosnian Croat leader Ante Jelavic, the Croat member of Bosnia's three-person presidency, who denounced it as a sentence "against Croatian people in Bosnia as a whole." Ivica Racan, the prime minister of the more moderate government that had emerged in Croatia after Tudjman's death, called for an appeal of "a really severe sentence." But Bosnian officials applauded the verdict, calling it a step towards reconciliation.

For Blaskic, justice will now be measured in the creeping minutes of those forty-five years. For the liberal states that brought Blaskic to the dock, justice is measured in the ability of such trials to bring a sense of fairness and dignity to Bosnians, and maybe even a sense of order to a violent world.

St. Helena

O NE HUNDRED AND FOUR YEARS after the end of the Napoleonic Wars, in 1919, the British government found itself thinking through the fate of Wilhelm II by reconsidering what it had done to Napoleon Bonaparte. The attorney general, Gordon Hewart, commissioned a lengthy scholarly report on the British decision to detain Napoleon at St. Helena.[1] In meetings of the Imperial War Cabinet and in inter-Allied conferences, the fate of Napoleon came up repeatedly.[2]

What had changed since 1815? In most regards, the way the Allies had dealt with the Bonapartists was in line with realism. Enemies were treated as enemies, no more and no less. Wellington did not see his opponents as war criminals. Nor was he much concerned with legal niceties like trials. British leaders did not even discuss putting Napoleon before an international tribunal before whisking him off to Elba and to St. Helena.

This is a far cry from Nuremberg. The great powers knew they wanted to dispose of Napoleon, and they were willing to use extralegal methods to do so. Napoleon did not have the benefit of anything like the stern insistence of Georges Clemenceau or Henry Stimson or (maybe) Madeleine Albright that enemy leaders were also war criminals who had to be put on *trial*, not merely gotten rid of as undesirables. In short, 1815 largely saw the exercise of naked state power. In that sense, the aftermath of the Hundred Days makes the aftermaths of the Armenian genocide, World War I, and World War II all the more striking. They did not bother with a trial for Napoleon in 1815; and yet they were obsessed with trials a century later.

The aftermath of the Napoleonic Wars is a favorite case for realists. In an implicit rebuke to harsher and more moralistic peaces, Henry Kissinger writes approvingly of the magnanimous (if not particularly effective) decision to send Napoleon to Elba: "The early nineteenth century was not yet a period which measured the extent of its triumph by the degree of personal retribution exacted."[3] For Kissinger, the great virtue of the era of the Congress of Vienna is that it avoided self-righteous punishment for France: "It is to the credit of the statesmen who negotiated the settlement of the post-Napoleonic period that they resisted the temptation of a punitive peace. This may have been due to the very quality which is usually considered their greatest failing: their indifference to popular pressures. But whatever the cause, they were seeking equilibrium and not retribution, legitimacy and not punishment."[4]

This is simply too strong, and not only because of Kissinger's emphasis on Elba rather than on St. Helena. Elba was Russia's over-generous choice—a decision made without reference either to domestic politics or even to the Allies. As such, there was little chance for domestic politics or other factors to influence Tsar Alexander's decision. By the time Castlereagh got to Paris in the spring of 1814, Alexander had already given Elba to Napoleon; Britain's dissatisfaction was expressed only in refusing to recognize Napoleon as emperor.[5] But, in contrast, the St. Helena decision involved both Britain and Prussia—a somewhat liberal and illiberal power respectively—and is thus more tangled.

On closer examination, it turns out that the aftermath of the Hundred Days was *largely* in keeping with the expectations of Kissinger and other realists, but not exclusively. Both British and Prussian policy was profoundly influenced by popular pressures. After all, Realpolitik might dictate that the victors would not attempt to punish the Bonapartists at all. But domestic politics, in this case mostly meaning public opinion, closed that option for both Britain and Prussia.

It turns out that banishment was the third option that the Allies came up with for Napoleon. Initially, Prussia wanted the simplest solution: shoot Napoleon. But Britain would have none of this, because of an idiosyncratic intrusion of its domestic traditions into its foreign policy—in this case, the gallant or priggish refusal of Wellington to have anything to do with so sordid a deed. Britain then turned to the cleanest solution: having Napoleon tried by the twice-restored Bourbon monarchy. But the Bourbons did not think they were strong enough to survive such a trial. Stymied, Britain turned to banishment.

In several important respects, Britain was constrained by its own domestic politics and legal traditions—even in 1815. Most importantly, Liverpool, the prime minister, pushed for the punishment of Bonapartists in order to satisfy British public outrage, despite Castlereagh's desire to avoid a punitive peace. British public outrage in 1815 may not have been as overwhelming as it would be in 1918 or 1945 (nor were anywhere near as many Britons capable of making their voices heard by their government), but it still had a noticeable impact on policy. As for Prussia, it was even more outraged and therefore more punitive.

What was largely missing was legalism. To this day, "the Napoleonic precedent" means the use of extralegal means to get rid of an enemy. But there were weak stirrings of some kind of British legalism, an embryonic preference for postwar trials rather than arbitrary methods. A kind of proper-minded restraint is not the same thing as legalism, but it is at least a step in that direction. There are four examples. First, Britain would have preferred to see Napoleon on trial, albeit in a French court. Second, two prominent Bonapartists, Michel Ney and Charles de la Bédoyère, did in fact get French trials (even so their conviction and execution scandalized British Whigs). At one point, when a French court-martial ruled it had no competence to try Ney, it actually seemed as if Ney might escape thanks to French law. Third, Wellington himself would not hear of the summary execution of his bitter enemy—just as Henry Stimson and George Marshall in 1944 would be reluctant to use the American military for the summary executions of German war criminals. Fourth, Savary and L'Allemand, two of Napoleon's top deputies, who had surrendered along with Napoleon without realizing France considered them criminals, were briefly detained by Britain at Malta but freed at the end of the war. The British did not want to release them, but Lord Bathurst explained himself to Castlereagh in a sentence that neatly sums up much of the argument of this book: "As our laws are strict as to questions of this nature, and the disposition of the people alive on the subject, we are obliged to act with a delicacy which does not appear to be necessary in other countries."[6]

On these occasions, popular outrage and even a weak legalism forced even the unsentimental architects of the Vienna system to act in ways that contradicted their own understanding of the national interest. Of course, these pressures mostly came to bear on Britain, which was partially liberal.[7] Despotic Prussia, its soldiers amok in Paris, was perfectly comfortable calling for vengeance and summary execution. But these twin pressures of popular outrage and legalism, still weak in 1815, would slowly grow stronger. A century later, Britain would loudly call for justice for German and Turkish war criminals—not just enemies, but war criminals—and a century and a half later, America would bring the idea to its apotheosis at Nuremberg.

BRITAIN

War without War Crimes

The Napoleonic Wars were an unprecedented catastrophe for Europe, all the more shocking coming after a period of seeming enlightenment and progress. "Even the rules of war, last resort of the will to violence, had been humanized," Alexis de Tocqueville remembered wistfully after the disaster.[8] The casualty tolls were numbingly high. Rory Muir, a historian, estimates the 1793–1815 wars left perhaps 200,000 British soldiers dead—roughly proportionate to the toll World War I took on a larger British population.[9]

Thus, as one would expect, much of the British public—or at least that segment of the public whose opinions could influence the cabinet—was outraged at the Bonapartists. In 1814, British public opinion had blocked peace with Napoleon. "The disposition of the country for *any* peace with Napoleon becomes more unfavourable every day," Liverpool, the prime minister, noted in February 1814. "I hear it from all quarters and from all classes of the people."[10] Liverpool was undoubtedly influenced by this public rage a year later, pushing for harsher steps against France than Castlereagh, his foreign secretary, wanted.[11] In 1815, the anger focused on Napoleon himself, not on all of France—unlike Prussian public opinion, which drew no such distinction. In his classic history of the events of 1815, Henry Houssaye wrote that English journals were capable of reserving their worst insults for Napoleon, not France. *The Times*, for instance, wrote of the disasters caused by the "bloody Corsican" in his pillage of Europe.[12] This is hardly flattering, but it is significantly milder than what appeared in the Prussian press. In addition, Sir Francis Burdett championed a significant Whig minority (derisively known the Napoleonist Whigs) who saw the choice between emperor and king as a French one, and did not think that the return of Napoleon necessitated any British reaction.[13] Altogether, this slightly muted public mood gave Liverpool and Castlereagh a little room for maneuver in the summer of 1815.

In 1815, British diplomats could still often afford to flout public opinion. Wellington, unimpressed with brayings from below, griped that Liverpool's cabinet was "taking up a little too much the tone of their rascally newspapers."[14] Castlereagh worried that public opinion might not be the best arbiter of British policy: "Fouché, I understand, is horribly unpopular in England: I don't wonder at it, as far as the mass are concerned; but those who know how impossible it is to find men of character in France who can be employed ought to be very cautious about encouraging this clamour."[15]

That kind of moralistic clamor was not a luxury that Castlereagh would let himself indulge in, even if he had wanted to. His responsibility was to prevent another outbreak of the carnage that had ravaged the Continent. If that meant dealing with the despised Joseph Fouché, or showing lenience toward the Bonapartists, so be it.[16] But Castlereagh, for all his skill, sometimes lost out to more moralistic Britons.

Les Coupables

"The Decision of the Duke of Wellington's March, and the commanding Character of his Victory, have reduced the Question to one of Political Management," cheered Castlereagh on his arrival in Paris.[17] Waterloo had brought the Hundred Days to a crashing halt, and Paris had fallen to British and Prussian armies on July 3, 1815.[18] The Allies now faced two interwoven dilemmas: what to do with the Bonapartists, and with Napoleon himself.

Liverpool had a clear and consistently tough view on these issues. He wanted to trim France's borders to make it less threatening should revolutionaries ever take power again. But he also wanted to interfere with French domestic politics to ensure the permanent exclusion of the dangerous elements. Even before Paris fell, he had written to Castlereagh:

> It appears to be quite indispensable that in the event of the restoration of Louis XVIII. a severe example should be made of those commanding officers of garrison or corps who deserted the King and went over to Buonaparte. Such a proceeding is not only become necessary with a view to the continuance of the power of the House of Bourbon, but likewise for the security of the object for which the Allies have been contending, a safe and lasting peace.[19]

Much as Liverpool dreaded the French armies, he did not see the Bonapartist officers as anything like war criminals as the term is used today.[20] The British did occasionally refer to them as criminals (in French, *les coupables*), but this seemed more an insult than a formal indictment. If there was a crime, it was for the most part treason, not a war crime as we would understand it today—nor as they understood the general concept of *jus in bello* in 1815. Throughout the summer of 1815, as Liverpool was deciding the Bonapartists' fate, he never raised any objection to their conduct during the wars. (As that British report on war crimes would note in 1919, "Napoleon was not charged with having during the Hundred Days carried on war contrary to the usages of civilised nations.")[21] In this respect, Britain differed from Prussia, which was furious at French executions of Prussian prisoners—a violation of the laws of war, then and now. To the British, the Bonapartists were Britain's enemies, and the enemies of the Bourbon monarchy; but their crime was mostly treason

41

against the French crown.[22] Punishment, for Liverpool, was mostly a matter of pleasing British opinion and deterring future treason:

> Considering the elements for conspiracies and rebellion which must exist in France for some years, there can be no chance of stopping them but by an exemplary punishment on the present occasion of those who were forward to join the standard of Buonaparte.
>
> With respect to the conspirators who were not military, it might be proper, likewise, to make an example of those who are the most dangerous, subjecting the most criminal to the pains of high treason, and those who were less so to that of banishment.[23]

Castlereagh, in Paris and therefore insulated from public pressure, took a softer line than Liverpool. Like Liverpool, he did not see the Bonapartists primarily as war criminals. Castlereagh also worried that territorial concessions—a crowd-pleasing notion in Britain—would spark French rage, potentially plunging Europe back into war. He hoped that Britain would show "some Attention to the feelings and Interests" of France to help Louis XVIII consolidate his grip on power, which would prove "valuable beyond all other Securities we can acquire." The key was generosity to the French:

> If, on the contrary, we push things now to an Extremity, we leave the King no Resource in the Eyes of his own people but to disavow us, and when once committed against us in Sentiment, He will soon either be obliged to lead the Nation into War himself, or possibly be set aside to make way for some more bold and enterprising Competition. . . . [T]he European Alliance can be made powerfully instrumental to his [Louis XVIII's] support, if our Securities are framed in such a manner as not to be ultimately hostile to France, after she shall have given *protracted Proofs* of having ceased to be a revolutionary state.[24]

Castlereagh was backed up by the ultimate military authority. Wellington, with the fresh glory of Waterloo on his shoulders, shared Castlereagh's belief in the primacy of French domestic politics: "Revolutionary France is more likely to distress the world than France, however strong in her frontier, under a regular Government; and that is the situation in which we ought to endeavor to place her."[25]

From the first, Liverpool tried to impress upon Castlereagh the importance of British popular rage. The military convention by which Paris had capitulated to Wellington included a broad amnesty for Frenchmen regardless of "their conduct and their political opinions."[26] Liverpool nervously hoped this applied "only to the foreign military authorities, and is not considered as granting an indemnity to all persons in Paris, whatever their offences may have been against the legal national tribunals, either civil or military."[27]

Liverpool was greatly worried about how to reinstall Louis XVIII on his throne, and especially about what would happen once the Allies withdrew.[28] In particular, "there are three questions which occur to every person one meets—What is to become of Buonaparte? What course is to be adopted with respect to those who assisted him in resuming his authority? What is to be done with the French armies?"[29] Liverpool repeatedly warned Castlereagh that British public opinion tied the prime minister's hands. If the Bonapartists were not dealt with, Liverpool wrote, "the country will expect, and justly, I think, expect further securities for the continuance of peace on an improved frontier," especially considering that the British had "wasted so much of the best blood of the country" in the wars.[30] This was not just a threat against France, but also against Castlereagh. Castlereagh had a horror of what Liverpool had in mind: a more punitive peace, involving some dismemberment and humiliation of France. If Castlereagh was to avoid that, Liverpool told his independent-minded foreign secretary, Castlereagh would have to deal with the Bonapartists firmly.

Already, Castlereagh had demonstrated his lack of enthusiasm for cracking down on the Bonapartists. Instead, he hoped to co-opt the Bonapartists by including some of their top men in the Bourbon regime: "The Nomination of Fouché, Gouvion St. Cyr [the new minister of war], and of others ought to assure the Revolutionists as to the King's Intentions," wrote Castlereagh.[31] This was the exact opposite of Liverpool's idea of securing the Bourbons through harsh measures against the Bonapartists. The inclusion of Fouché in Louis XVIII's government brought British public opinion to what historian C. K. Webster called a "high fever."[32] Castlereagh insisted Fouché's inclusion was "essential to His Majesty's restoration,"[33] but added a sheepish apology to Liverpool: "You will perceive Fouché has played us a shabby trick at starting; but we must forgive him, as I believe he has been of essential use to the King. I was amused with Talleyrand's apology for him."[34]

Liverpool, presumably, was not. Castlereagh was not above reminding Liverpool that doing business in France would occasionally require offending British opinion. Castlereagh knew that Fouché was "horribly unpopular in England . . . but those who know how impossible it is to find men of character in France who can be employed ought to be very cautious about encouraging this clamour."[35]

The Bourbons dragged their heels at first. Castlereagh informed his prime minister: "With respect to arrests, none have yet taken place; perhaps the Government has hardly existed long enough to admit of any act of Vigour, and the absence of all Military Force except the National Guards, enfeebles sadly as yet the Kings Authority."[36] Louis XVIII was aware of how precarious his grip on power was, and feared that stiff measures against prominent Bonapartists would spark rage, especially in the untamed army. "I would not be in his place for anything in the world," Metternich, Austria's foreign minister, wrote of the king.[37] The British knew the monarchy had little public support, and scorned the king's "extreme inefficiency" and "inimical disposition to liberal ideas and forms of government."[38] Louis XVIII knew that much of France saw him as a foreign imposition. Royal proclamations still started with the declaration, "Louis, by the Grace of God, King of France & Navarre"; but if so, He was acting on this earth through the instruments of the British and Prussian armies. The net result was royal timidity.

So the impetus for arrests came mostly from Britain. As far as Liverpool was concerned, Louis XVIII's soft line could only encourage the Jacobins and the restless army:

> The forbearance manifested at the present moment can be considered in no other light than as weakness, and not mercy. . . . A severe example made of the conspirators who brought back Bonaparte could alone have any effect in counteracting these dangers: but this is not now to be expected, and perhaps would have been very difficult, considering the share in the Government which the King has been obliged to assign to some members of the Jacobin party.[39]

Some of those Jacobins, of course, had been pushed on Louis XVIII by none other than Castlereagh, a point surely not lost on either Liverpool or Castlereagh. Liverpool, without any confidence that the Bourbons could keep France friendly toward the Allies, once again invoked British public opinion to suggest adjusting France's borders. He wrote, "[W]e owe it to ourselves now to provide, in the best manner we can, for our own security. These, I can assure you, are the generally received opinions in this country at present."[40]

Even before he received this letter, Castlereagh seemed to be taking a harsher line on the Bonapartists. Although he could tolerate Fouché and was amused by Talleyrand, Castlereagh fully grasped the dangers posed by the army and the more committed Bonapartists. The Allies, Castlereagh wrote, "owe no forbearance" to the army and to anti-Bourbon conspirators. Napoleon's army, "faithless and perjured as it is, collectively and regimentally," should be dissolved, lest it threaten the Bourbons and then Europe. Castlereagh was coming around to Liverpool's harder line on Bonapartists. The three "Principal Dangers" Castlereagh saw were, "1st. The Person of Buonaparte still being at large"; second, the unpurged army and national guards, still organized so as to "[consecrate] their Treason, Perjury and hostile Relations towards their own Sovereign and Europe"; and, "3dly. The Presence of those notorious Traitors and Agitators in France who will inevitably organize a New Revolution and whose Impunity is in itself a recorded Proof of the Weakness of the Sovereign or the Insecurity of his Advisors."[41]

With Liverpool and Castlereagh in some kind of uneasy accord, Britain took the lead. Castlereagh beseeched the Allies to get Louis XVIII "to adopt Measure of Vigour against the most criminal of the Traitors." The Allies agreed that Louis XVIII's authority risked "utter Contempt if some Step of this Nature was not taken without loss of Time." This message was sent to Talleyrand, while Castlereagh went to the king himself. In order to impress "the necessity of exertion" upon a reluctant Louis XVIII, Castlereagh warned, "in proportion as Measures of just Severity against the Agitators were neglected, that the Allies must be the more severe in their precautions both against the Government and Nation." Talleyrand did not fight this, and "promised me that the Measures to be taken against the most Criminal of Buonaparte's adherents should be forthwith decided, and that his own View of the policy to be adopted entirely coincided with that which the Allies recommended."[42] Evidently not yet satisfied, Castlereagh took the issue to the French again. He met with Talleyrand and Fouché later, lecturing them on "the necessity of acting with more Vigour against the Traitors."[43]

There was, of course, a catch. Britain was pushing for the arrest of the Bonapartists; but Britain had also appointed a Bonapartist to do the arresting. Thanks to Castlereagh, Fouché ran the police. After Waterloo, Fouché had asked Wellington for amnesties for his fellow Bonapartists, and had objected (unsuccessfully) to the idea of punishing some of the top French army officers.[44] Had Castlereagh planned to have such an unenthusiastic enforcer? Or was he embarrassed? Either way, he had caught a whiff of the impending disaster, and tactfully braced Liverpool for what was to come:

It is perhaps unlucky that Fouché's office should be at this moment that of the Police, altho' the most competent of any to discharge it's functions in an ordinary case, it is difficult for him to be otherwise than indulgent to those who have been supporting the same cause as himself.

... It is not that he is not now hearty in The King's Cause: I believe he really is and must be so from Interest, but having always played a Game of Personal Popularity, by covering his Friends when they got into a Scrape, he has now additional Motives for endeavouring to screen them, that he may retain some Character, or perhaps what he more values, influence with his party. Talleyrand assured me he had spoken to him very strongly this morning upon this subject.[45]

On July 24, Louis XVIII, under no small pressure from his foreign saviors, duly issued "Measures of Publick Police or Publick Safety."[46] According to Talleyrand, Fouché had originally suggested blacklisting one hundred men, but Louis XVIII cautiously trimmed the list of this (Talleyrand's phrase) "odious measure."[47] The ordinance was signed by Fouché, but not without reservations:

It will be asked, how I could countersign such an act, which affected individuals who had pursued the same line of politics as myself. . . . [T]housands of names, obscure as well as notorious, were pointed out to the police department for the purpose of being involved in a general measure of proscription. Heads were demanded of the minister of police, as pledges of his sincere devotion to the royal cause. There only remained two paths for me to follow; that of making myself an accomplice in acts of vengeance, or that of giving up my office. To the first I could not subscribe; the second, I was too deeply compromised to adopt. I discovered a third expedient, and that was to reduce the list to a small number of names, selected from persons who had acted the most conspicuous part during the late events: and here I must confess that I met in the council, and more especially in the eminently French feelings of the monarch, with everything that was calculated to mitigate those measures of excessive rigour, and to diminish the number of victims.[48]

Louis XVIII even couched his arrest warrant in a general amnesty, with fifty-seven specific exceptions—nineteen military men to be arrested immediately, plus thirty-eight to be exiled under surveillance to the interior before their fate was decided. He insisted on "the punishment of an unprecedented assassination attempt" and on safeguarding "our people, the dignity of our crown and the tranquility of Europe." The accused traitors against the first Bourbon restoration would face court-martial. But Louis XVIII focused only on those who had gone over to the Bonapartists in March 1815, not on any prior offenses against the monarchy.[49]

There were few surprises on the lists. Heading the first one was Michel Ney, with the "N" written with a giant flourish. Ney had earned this dubious honor. Hailed by Napoleon as "the bravest of the brave," the marshal had been the pride of the French forces throughout the emperor's campaigns, including the rout in Russia in 1812. Having somehow won the Bourbons' confidence again after that not inconsiderable indiscretion, they had—in a staggering act of bad delegation—sent Ney to capture Napoleon immediately after the defeated emperor escaped from Elba. Ney reached Napoleon in late March 1815, had a moment of inspiration, and went Bonapartist again. "I was in the storm," Ney would say later. "I lost my head."[50] For that, the monarchy put Ney at the top of its list.

To the best of its ability, at least. Fouché saw his chance. He warned the fifty-seven accused traitors that his police were coming after them. As even Talleyrand later admitted, the Bonapartists were "all warned in time to be able to escape if they wanted."[51] Despite the surreptitious efforts of a nervous Louis XVIII to let Ney get away, the marshal was arrested in August 1815.[52] In the end only three men were caught: Ney, General Charles de la Bédoyère, and Count Lavalette.[53]

Liverpool, in a passage that could have been copied straight out of Machiavelli, stubbornly insisted on seeing heads roll:

[O]ne can never feel that the King is secure upon his throne till he has dared to spill traitors' blood. It is not that many examples would be necessary; but the *daring* to make a few will alone manifest any strength in the government. It is a curious circumstance that, after the sanguinary scenes which we recollect at the beginning of the French Revolution, all parties now appear to have an insuperable repugnance to executions. This arises not from mercy, but from fear. Every government that has been recently established in France has felt its situation so weak and uncertain, that the persons composing it have not ventured to make examples of their enemies for fear of retaliation.[54]

Liverpool soon got first blood. In August, La Bédoyère was tried before a military council, and then shot.[55]

Ney's trial was a massive sensation, and remains a source of considerable fascination in France to this day.[56] The spectacle of France's great military hero before a French court was agonizing for the Bourbons, and that agony was only prolonged by the messy business of lawyering. To Bourbon chagrin, the court-martial at the Palais de Justice ruled itself incompetent to try Ney ("Those fellows would have killed me like a rabbit!" Ney said with relief). Instead, the Chamber of Peers voted to hear the case itself, "in the name of Europe." The trial started in the Palais du Luxembourg in November, with a curious Metternich attending. Ney, calm and slightly pale as the prosecution denounced him as a traitor, at one point exploded, pointing to heaven to appeal to "a higher tribunal."[57] Down here, Ney was condemned and, on December 7, shot by a Bourbon firing squad.[58] One of the twelve French soldiers, incapable of shooting a national hero, intentionally fired high and missed.[59] Liverpool had got two "sanguinary scenes" all his own after all.

Despite Fouché's best efforts, Britain had also picked up two other catches. Aboard H.M.S. *Bellerophon*, the British ship carrying Napoleon after his surrender, were, as Castlereagh put it, "two very flagrant criminals, Savary and L'Allemand."[60] At first, Castlereagh and the admiralty were ready to hold onto them.[61]

But British domestic norms were quick to interfere—albeit norms of a different nature from the public calls for revenge against the Bonapartists. This time, a kind of British military honor interfered, urging clemency. Savary and L'Allemand feared that they were likely to wind up facing a Bourbon court, and after that probably Bourbon bullets, and thus asked the British for the mercy due a prisoner under the laws of war.[62] This appeal worked. Just as Wellington would not simply shoot Napoleon (see below), so too Captain Frederick Maitland, commanding the *Bellerophon*, asked Lord Melville to

> make allowance for the feelings of an officer, who has nothing so dear to him as his honour, and who could not bear that a stain should be affixed to a name he has ever endeavoured to bear unblemished.
>
> These two men, Savary and Lallemand (what their character or conduct towards their own country may be I know not,) threw themselves under the protection of the British flag; that protection was granted them with the sanction of my name; 'tis true no conditions were stipulated for; but I acted in the full confidence that their lives would be held sacred.[63]

Maitland got his way. Sir Samuel Romilly, a prominent member of Parliament, brought the case to the lord chancellor, who reassured Romilly that "there was no intention in Government to deliver up Savary or Lallemand to the French Government." Savary and L'Allemand wound up at Malta, and were later freed.[64]

Maitland's honor is not a direct precursor of the legalism that would dominate British policy after World War I, but it does show restraint from pursuing vengeance *à outrance*. To be sure, Britain in 1815 was far more high-handed than in 1918. But there is a glimmer of potential for a more serious legalism here.

"He Thinks and Acts as a Briton": How Wellington Saved Napoleon's Neck

It was the considered opinion of Tsar Alexander I that Napoleon Bonaparte was the Antichrist.[65] This may have put the tsar a little ahead of general sentiment in the victorious Allied countries, but not that much. (Tolstoy opens *War and Peace* with a Russian aristocrat ranting about "the infamies and horrors perpetrated by that Antichrist—I really believe that he is Antichrist."[66]) When Napoleon surrendered to Britain, his presence off Plymouth fairly drove the British public wild. "The newswriters are in the daily habit of loading him with the lowest and meanest abuse," Romilly noted.[67] Liverpool explained:

> [W]hy so much importance is attached to one man, it is because I am thoroughly convinced that no other man can play the same part as he has done, and is likely to play again if he should be allowed the opportunity. Independent of his personal qualities, he has the advantage of fourteen years' enjoyment of supreme power. This has given him a title which belongs to no other man, and which it would be difficult for any one to acquire.[68]

Metternich, too, focused on Napoleon: "If we seize Bonaparte, the aspect changes in many respects, for from that moment, the seditious will have lost their rallying points."[69] Otherwise sober British diplomatic letters had a way of refusing to even mention Napoleon's name, as if it were an unholy tetragrammaton, and instead blazing at "the USURPER."[70]

It is not so easy to know what to do with the Antichrist should one catch him, but Prussia had a simple suggestion. Marching on Paris, Prussia's Field Marshal Gebhard von Blücher told Wellington that "as the Congress of Vienna had declared Napoleon outlawed, it was his intention to have him shot whenever he caught him."[71] (Not quite: Blücher actually meant "to execute Bonaparte on the spot where the Duc D'Enghien was shot," avenging the Bourbon nobleman's 1804 killing.[72]) Prussia knew that British domestic politics might rebel at the prospect, and Count Neithardt von Gneisenau, at the head of the Prussian forces, therefore generously offered to do the deed without British participation:

Bonaparte has been declared under outlawry by the Allied Powers. The Duke of Wellington may possibly (from parliamentary considerations) hesitate to fulfil the declaration of the Powers. Your Excellency will therefore direct the negociations to the effect, that Bonaparte may be delivered over to us, with a view to his execution.

This is what eternal justice demands, and what the declaration of March the 13th decides; and thus the blood of our soldiers killed and mutilated on the 18th and 19th will be avenged.[73]

Wellington was, as predicted, appalled. In March 1815, he had argued against a proposal by Talleyrand that might have let any peasant shoot Napoleon on sight.[74] Now, when his Prussian liaison, General von Müffling, passed on Blücher's proposal, Wellington "stared at me in astonishment."[75] Appealing to the conscience of Europe, Wellington

disputed the correctness of this interpretation of the Viennese declaration of outlawry, which was never meant to incite to the assassination of Napoleon. He therefore did not think that they could acquire from this act any right to order Napoleon to be shot, should they succeed in making him a prisoner of war. But be this as it may, as far as his own position and that of the Field-Marshal with respect to Napoleon were concerned, it appeared to him that, since the battle they had won [Waterloo], they were become much too conspicuous personages to justify such a transaction in the eyes of Europe.

I [Müffling] had already felt the force of the Duke's arguments before I most reluctantly undertook my mission, and was therefore little disposed to dispute them. "I therefore," continued the Duke, "wish my friend and colleague to see this matter in the light I do; such an act would hand down our names to history stained by a crime, and posterity would say of us, that we did not deserve to be the conquerors of Napoleon; the more so as such a deed is now quite useless, and can have no object."[76]

Wellington had known that Prussia might make such an appeal:

The Prussians think the Jacobins wish to give him over to me, believing that I will save his life. [Blücher] wishes to kill him; but I have told him that I shall remonstrate, and shall insist upon his being disposed of by common accord. I have likewise said that, as a private friend, I advised him to have nothing to do with so foul a transaction; that he and I had acted too distinguished parts in these transactions to become executioners; and that I was determined that if the Sovereigns wished to put him to death they should appoint an executioner, which should not be me.[77]

This silenced Blücher. It comes as a bit of a shock to the modern reader, weaned on a century of total war. At the end of World War II, Churchill and Eden, while insisting on trials for lower-level German war criminals, still pushed hard for the summary execution of the top echelon of the Nazi leadership. It is all the more striking how unthinkable such acts were in 1815. Napoleon, after all, was the most aggressive conqueror Europe had ever seen, and posed a mortal danger to the political order in every court in Europe. Would posterity really have been so shocked if someone had decided simply to shoot the man? And yet Wellington would not hear of "so foul a transaction."

The Prussians were angered and confused. Gneisenau saw Wellington's act not as noble, but self-serving:

> *When the Duke of Wellington declares himself against the execution of Bonaparte, he thinks and acts in the matter as a Briton.* Great Britain is under weightier obligation to no mortal man than to this very villain; for by the occurrences whereof he is the author, her greatness, prosperity, and wealth, have attained their present elevation. The English are the masters of the seas, and have no longer to fear any rivalry, either in this dominion or the commerce of the world.
>
> It is quite otherwise with us Prussians. We have been impoverished by him. Our Nobility will never be able to right itself again.
>
> Ought we not, then, to consider ourselves the tools of that Providence which has given us such a victory for the ends of eternal justice? Does not the death of the Duc d'Enghien call for such a vengeance? Shall we not draw upon ourselves the reproaches of the people of Prussia, Russia, Spain, and Portugal, if we leave unperformed the duty that devolves upon us?
>
> But be it so!—If others will assume a theatrical magnanimity, I shall not set myself against it. We act thus from esteem for the Duke and— weakness.[78]

Gneisenau did not talk of war crimes in so many words, but that is clearly what he was thinking of. He was furious at French violations of accepted standards of military conduct: shooting prisoners and mutilating soldiers. But his outrage was not tempered by any kind of legalism (even the weak hints in Britain); it found its expression in a call for summary vengeance.

After Napoleon threw himself on Britain's mercies, his actual seizure was a delicate matter. The British squadron flew a white Bourbon flag as it advanced on Napoleon at Rochefort, hoping that this would prevent the ex-emperor's guard from opening fire for perhaps ten minutes while the arrest was made. It is not just the NATO mission in Bosnia that has a horror of casualties in the course of arrests; the British of 1815 sounded uncannily like the British of 1996. The squadron was instructed "that it was very desirable to take Buonaparte alive, and with as little violence, and even inconvenience to him personally, as possible, *but that he was to be taken*; and that the life of any British sailor was as dear to the King of England as that of Buonaparte."[79] Even after the Hundred Days, the British equated the life of a single British sailor with the man who had ravaged Europe. John Major, who as British prime minister went to great lengths to protect British peacekeeping troops in Bosnia, was only taking a long British tradition to new levels.

Liverpool and Castlereagh would have preferred to see the French courts deal with Napoleon. Even Metternich admitted that the Allied declaration outlawing Napoleon could be seen as calling for a trial.[80] Liverpool only grudgingly accepted the idea of a trial:

> The most easy course would be to deliver him up to the King of France, but then we must be quite sure that he would be tried and have no chance of escape. I have had some conversations with the civilians, and they are of opinion that this would be, in all respects, the least objectionable course. We should have a right to consider him as a French prisoner, and as such to give him up to the French Government.[81]

Even Castlereagh had no hesitation about hounding Bonaparte.[82] He wanted to ensure that any Bonapartist power grabs would be met with "European Invasion": "[I]f we can once lead the Publick Mind of France completely to dismiss Buonaparte and his Race, as pregnant with calamity to the Nation, we give the stability to the King's Title which it wants."[83]

The king begged to differ. Whatever they thought of Napoleon, the Bourbons were leery of arresting him, still in British custody aboard the *Bellerophon*. Castlereagh thought that "the King of France's Government will not, and perhaps have not sufficient authority to, charge themselves with the judging and executing Buonaparte, as a Traitor." He did not consider summary execution: "If so, and he should fall into our hands, there is no other Course than to confine him as a Prisoner."[84] When Napoleon finally gave himself up, Castlereagh congratulated Liverpool "heartily," and immediately added: "You must make up your mind to be his Gaolers. The French Government will not try him as a Traitor."[85] If France could not hold Napoleon, then Castlereagh wanted Britain to do it. There was even a poetic justice to it: "[A]fter fighting him for twenty years, as a Trophy, he seems to belong to us."[86]

The trophy would have to be kept far from Britain and Europe. Liverpool worried about British law and British public opinion:

> We are all decidedly of the opinion that it would not answer to confine him in this country. Very nice legal questions might arise upon the subject, which would be particularly embarrassing. . . . [Y]ou know enough of the feelings of people in this country not to doubt he would become an object of curiousity immediately, and possibly of compassion, in the course of a few months: and the circumstances of his being here, or indeed anywhere in Europe, would contribute to keep up a certain degree of ferment in France.[87]

After all, when Napoleon was brought to Britain's shores on the *Bellerophon*, his presence had caused a sensation. "Bonaparte is giving us great trouble at Plymouth," Liverpool had complained.[88] There had been an explosion of public anger, curiosity, and even in some cases sympathy from Whigs who either sympathized with the Bonapartist cause or, like Wellington, did not want to see Napoleon suffer arbitrary punishment.[89] In an extension of domestic civil law reminiscent of the recent use of America's Alien Tort Claims Act against Radovan Karadzic, Napoleon was subpoenaed to testify in a libel case in London, forcing the *Bellerophon* to take evasive active to avoid being served.[90]

In the end, Britain settled on exile to St. Helena for Napoleon. Technically, he was a prisoner of the Allies.[91] Liverpool and Castlereagh allowed weak commissioners from the other European powers to oversee the ex-emperor's captivity as a way "to tranquillize the publick Sentiment in the respective States with respect to this man."[92] Napoleon, wasting away on St. Helena, was not just the prisoner of Europe; he was the prisoner of European public passions.

PRUSSIA

"We Must Exterminate Them, Kill Them Like Mad Dogs"

The only people who made Castlereagh more nervous than his former enemies were his current allies. Castlereagh might chuckle at Fouché and Talleyrand, but the Prussians scared him stiff. In Prussia he saw a wild and untamed public opinion, to which British diplomacy was now linked:

Their [the Allies'] Politicks at this Moment receive an Extraordinary Impulse from the publick Sentiment of Germany. . . . No doubt the prevailing Sentiment throughout Germany is in favour of territorially reducing France. After all the people have suffered, and with ordinary Inducements of some fresh acquisitions, it is not wonderful that it should be so, but it is one thing to wish the thing done and another to maintain it when done.[93]

Indeed, Prussia reminded Castlereagh of Napoleonic France: "[T]here is a temper in the Prussian Army little less alarming to the Peace of Europe, and little less menacing to the Authority of their own Sovereign, than what prevails in the Army of France, and when they get their new Parliament, the spirit of Military Democracy will be found not less loud at Berlin, than at Paris."[94] In the summer of 1815, there was nothing nastier Castlereagh could have written.

British and Prussian policy toward France shows the difference between a partially liberal and an illiberal victor. There is no reason to doubt the basic gist—if not the tone—of Castlereagh's analysis. Prussia had suffered at French hands, and now Prussian public opinion demanded a punitive peace. This outrage, both elite and mass-based, was not fettered by any kind of legalism, even the vestigial stuff at work in Britain in 1815. As discussed above, Blücher saw no reason not to shoot Napoleon, and fumed at Wellington's priggishness. This kind of lack of restraint is of a piece with Prussia's broader drive for a Carthaginian peace.[95]

In 1815, Prussia was anything but liberal. The considerable imperfections of the liberalism of Liverpool's Britain paled next to those of the Hohenzollern monarchy. The Prussian state was still despotic, with a monarchy largely immune from liberal impulses, buttressed by the power of the reactionary Junkers. The Rhineland had been under arbitrary rule even before its occupation by absolutist France.[96]

The stirrings of liberal dissatisfaction were weak, even with the catalyst of the need to resist France. The reform movement in Prussia resented Frederick the Great's treatment of individuals as, in the words of one historian, "mere means to an end." The government did not require the free consent of the governed, resting instead only on coercion and obedience. But these bureaucratic reformers lacked support from either the conservative Junkers or popular sentiment. Instead, even Baron Stein's reformers had to trust the absolutism of the monarchy in the very process of amending it. And the reform movement had mostly fallen apart by the time Prussia, in 1812, offered Napoleon help should he fight Russia. Shocked, many reformers quit public life; Stein and Clausewitz went to St. Petersburg.[97]

On top of this, there was the chaos of wartime and defeat. The Holy Roman Empire had finally vanished in 1806. Prussia was crushed in 1793–94 and 1806–7, and under French control from 1807 to 1813. Even the victory at Leipzig (and later at Waterloo) could not erase the taint of collaboration: of the 600,000 troops in the Grande Armée when it disastrously invaded Russia in 1812, no less than 180,000 were Germans. France kept 150,000 troops in Prussia and wrecked Prussia's economy by imposing crushing indemnities and halting grain exports.[98] Without any serious liberal institutions or intentions, or a tradition of restraint on despotic power, one would not expect Prussia to create legalistic barriers to its executive.

So in 1815 the furious Prussians behaved without any legalistic restraints. "Only the Prussians spoke of an inherently wicked France," wrote Kissinger.[99] Prussia seemed bent on flattening France. Even before reaching Paris, Prussia issued a list of Carthaginian demands for a truce, including forts, indemnification, and the "delivering up of Bonaparte alive or dead."[100] Ney, knowing all was lost, had tried so hard to get himself killed at Waterloo that five horses had died beneath him; but even Ney did not want to be taken prisoner by the Prussians.[101]

Houssaye, perhaps the definitive historian of the Napoleonic Wars, basically agreed with Castlereagh's evaluation of Prussian rage. He wrote:

> From the Rhine to the Oder, the whole country resounded with the press's barking: "We were wrong to be merciful with the French. We should have exterminated them all. Yes, we must exterminate this bunch of 500,000 robbers. We must do more than that: we must outlaw the French people." . . . "No treaties with the French. The proscription pronounced by the Congress [of Vienna] against their chief must be extended to the whole nation. We must exterminate them, kill them like mad dogs."[102]

In a minor masterpiece of understatement, Liverpool noted that "those who are near to France, and consequently in the post of danger, have the deepest interest in the issue of the contest."[103]

Prussia expressed this deep interest mostly by sacking Paris. Müffling, who had been appointed governor of Paris, did not show much fondness for his charges: "The great mass of the French people are very intelligent, but there are many vain, egotistical, and quarrelsome individuals amongst them, who must be summarily dealt with."[104] "The immediate Difficulty is now to keep Blucher and the Prussians within any bounds towards this Town," wrote Castlereagh from Paris. Prussia was charging the Parisians for costs of the occupation army, and "they are at this Moment mining the Bridge of Jena with a View of blowing it up."[105]

Small surprise that Prussia also pushed vigorously for the punishment of Bonapartists. Müffling, as the Prussian commander, wrote to Wellington: "With respect to the Arrest and Punishment of the Principal Traitors, Civil and Military, I think there is a great Repugnance to shed Blood, the Result in a great Measure of fear and party compromise, and that they look rather to an extensive Deportation and outlawry." When Müffling had urged "the importance of adequately vindicating the King's Authority and the Authority of the Laws," Talleyrand had said that the Bourbons would be "severe" when they could do so safely. "It was," Müffling wrote, "impossible for one to do more than represent, how much the King's Authority must be brought into Contempt, so long as the most notorious criminals were not only at large, but seen abroad defying the Laws."[106] This hard line was of a piece with Prussia's other harsh demands.

This kind of Prussian behavior sparked French backlash, and drove the British to distraction. Usually unflappable, Wellington warned Castlereagh that "the useless, and if was not likely to be attended with serious consequences, I should call it ridiculous, oppression" would "excite a national war" if not stopped.[107] Castlereagh warned Liverpool that "If Discipline and Order are not upheld [in the Allied ranks], King Army and People will forget their Differences in one common feeling of Resentment against the Foreign Troops."[108]

In short, Prussia in 1815 behaved as a vengeful, stung power. It was only restrained by moderation from Britain. Unlike the British, the furious Prussians saw the Bonapartists as something close to war criminals. But Prussia's solution was simple: summary execution, in the broader context of an uncompromisingly punitive peace. There was no constraining legalism.

A WORLD REMOVED

A realist account can explain much of the 1815 decisions about punishing Bonapartists. Only Prussia leveled accusations of war crimes against France, and even then those grievances were not the heart of Prussia's case against the Bonapartists. For the most part, the Bonapartists were seen as traitors, usurpers, and enemies—but not as war criminals. And the decision to exile Napoleon to St. Helena was made with scant discussion of judicial mechanisms. The weaknesses in the realist account emerge mostly in the case of Britain. Britain, at least, was substantially constrained by its own domestic norms, both by public anger and even some embryonic stirrings of legalism. It was only the Prussians who were totally comfortable doing things the easy way.

But even so, the realist account makes sense only in what was, after all, the golden moment of realism. Diplomats could continue to act this way only so long as they represented illiberal countries. Thus, in the wars of German unification, which would utterly put an end to the Vienna system, Otto von Bismarck could defy the rabble's calls for vengeance. After the 1866 war, Bismarck resisted Wilhelm I's calls for punishing Austria (with the loss of territory, not with trials). Then, after France capitulated to Prussia at Sedan, it was still possible for Bismarck—no great democrat—to resist the calls from Prussian public opinion to flatten France and punish Napoleon III. The great practitioner of Realpolitik had no interest in legalism: "The politician has to leave the punishment of princes and peoples for their offences against the moral law to Divine providence."[109]

But this illiberal—or preliberal—moment passed. By the time the British government, in 1919, had that report drawn up on the punishment of Napoleon, the deliberations of Castlereagh and Liverpool must have seemed quaint.[110] Lloyd George could not possibly have ignored British public opinion as Castlereagh did. The British government insisted on legalistic methods. "[Wilhelm II] should be put on his trial; he and his son, as the two persons primarily responsible for this great war and for all the suffering which it has entailed," Lloyd George said.[111] What would Castlereagh have said to that? Here was a British prime minister who was utterly uninterested in turning a blind eye to an enemy's misdeeds for the sake of a conciliatory peace, and who insisted on using judicial mechanisms to mete out punishment. This was, in short, a different Britain from that of 1815. With the pressures of public and elite outrage and of an ingrained legalism playing a huge role in foreign policymaking, Lloyd George's Britain was a world removed from that of Castlereagh.

Leipzig

FURIOUS at the end of a long and unprecedentedly cruel world war, the victorious Allies decided to put Germans on trial for aggression and other war crimes. It was a crashing failure. This was not the aftermath of World War II, but World War I.[1]

When planning Nuremberg, Allied leaders sometimes remembered with chagrin this earlier catastrophic effort. On the British side, Anthony Eden cringed at "that ill-starred enterprise at the end of the last war."[2] For the Americans, John Pehle of the War Refugee Board thought it "abominable,"[3] and Henry Morgenthau Jr. a "fiasco."[4] Much of the skepticism about Nuremberg on the Allied side came from those who, like Winston Churchill, had been stung by the Allies' failure to prosecute war criminals after World War I.

From the start of the Great War, the Allies were enraged at German atrocities. For the most part, this outrage was self-serving: Britain railed at German submarine warfare, France at the German occupation of northern France, and both at Germany for—as they saw it—starting the war in the first place. Even while maintaining lofty neutrality, America was furious when German U-boats sank neutral ships and thus killed Americans. There were moments of anger at war crimes against foreigners—mostly Belgians, and Armenians in the Ottoman Empire—but Britain, France, and America were overwhelmingly concerned with their own citizens.

The countries that suffered more pushed harder for prosecutions. The most enthusiastic supporters were Belgium and France, which had taken the brunt of the German attack; then Britain, uninvaded on the other side of the Channel, and thus ultimately more willing than France to drop the war crimes issue; and finally America, almost diffident on the other side of the Atlantic—except, of course, regarding U-boat warfare against Americans. Their passion for war crimes trials matched their relative death tolls: about 1.4 million or perhaps as many as two million for France, 950,000 for Britain, and 100,000 for America.[5] In Britain and France, leaders were acutely aware that their publics were enraged at German war crimes. Elites usually shared that sentiment, but even when they did not, they knew the risks of appearing in public to seem indifferent to German villainy. Woodrow Wilson's administration was only moved to talk of war crimes trials when German U-boats killed Americans on the high seas. In 1918, Britons spoke of Edith Cavell, a British nurse executed by the Germans; French citizens spoke of Lille, a French town sacked by German forces; and Americans spoke of the *Lusitania.*

For all their rage, British and French leaders still called for due process in judging even Wilhelm II. As written, the war crimes provisions of the Treaty of Versailles envisioned a revolution in international law. Although the idea of charging Wilhelm II for a novel and retroactive offense—aggression—was troublesome to some Allied jurists, even David Lloyd George and Georges Clemenceau were prepared to give the defeated kaiser the advantages of a roughly British- or French-style court. Three liberal states—Britain, France, and America—took a broadly legalist attitude toward the punishment of Germans for war crimes. British diplomats often drew analogies between British domestic norms and the punishment of German war criminals.

America clung to international law, but not primarily through war crimes trials. To be sure, during the Great War, the Wilson administration had rumbled about trials for U-boat attacks on neutral ships carrying Americans. After the war, America kept the door open for U-boat trials, but not for other war crimes efforts. The Wilson administration preferred the League of Nations—a purer and more impartial way of expanding the rule of law than even a trial of Wilhelm II—to Lloyd George and Clemenceau's vengeful calls for war crimes trials.[6] To more conservative lawyers, among them Robert Lansing, America's secretary of state, trying Wilhelm II stretched international law beyond the breaking point. American objections were not based on a lack of faith in law, but on an excess of it.[7]

"The difficulty, of course, arose in 1919 from the fact that the defeated countries were not occupied," remembered Britain's law officers in 1942.[8] Unlike after World War II, Germany in 1919 could still resist the Allies. Wilhelm II fled to Holland, and Allied thundering was not enough to extricate him. Germany, stung by the vengefulness of the Treaty of Versailles, resisted the humiliation of turning over its leaders and soldiers to face international tribunals. The Allies grudgingly agreed to let a German court, in Leipzig, hear a few test cases. But the court either acquitted the suspects or let them off with light sentences; they had, the German court ruled, merely been following superior orders. Short of military action, there was little the Allies could do other than voice protests.

The only obvious effect of Allied efforts was to undermine the fledgling Weimar Republic by galvanizing the nationalist right to resist British and French calls for the trials of German citizens. Of course, it was not only the Allied pursuit of German war criminals that ushered in fascism, and one can envision future cases where, for instance, a robust economy would offset nationalist backlash. But the war crimes issue was not a trivial one. In the chaos of Weimar Republic politics, Göring first encountered Hitler at a rightist rally against French demands for the trial of German war criminals.

Forewarned by this cautionary tale, Nuremberg managed to avoid most of the pitfalls of Leipzig; but for the ex-Yugoslavia and Rwanda tribunals currently sitting, Leipzig is all but forgotten. The selfishness of liberal states—in focusing on the suffering of their own citizens and in an extreme reluctance to risk their soldiers to pursue war criminals—is as relevant to Western policy on ex-Yugoslavia and Rwanda as it was to Leipzig. Thinking about war crimes tribunals only in terms of Nuremberg analogies is as reckless as thinking of crises and wars only in terms of Vietnam or Munich analogies.

BRITAIN

The Great Crusade

There is a stereotype, not least among the British, that British diplomacy is cynical and cold-hearted. Nothing could worse describe Britain's reaction to German war crimes.

The war, to Lloyd George, was nothing less than "a great crusade."[9] As early as 1915, Britain formally made war crimes trials—including almost certainly that of Wilhelm II himself—a part of its war aims. Lloyd George and other leaders pressed passionately for such trials, which were broadly popular with the British public. In November 1918, the British cabinet had a sweeping debate on the issue; after a remarkable peroration from the attorney general, the cabinet threw caution to the winds and approved war crimes trials.

Public opinion crusaded, too. Even before Allied governments came to see the usefulness of anti-German propaganda, British and French citizens were up in arms at the German invasion of neutral Belgium.[10] But British suffering came first, and there was a stupefying amount of it. By the end of the war, Britain would lose almost a million men, with 37 percent of those men mobilized ending up as casualties.[11] King George V fumed at German treatment of British prisoners of war.[12] In January 1915, German Zeppelins began bombing British cities. And in February 1915, Germany started using U-boats against merchant shipping to Britain, including many neutral ships.[13]

For all the fury at German criminality, even Wilhelm II would be afforded British-style due process. The cabinet never considered simply shooting him. Lloyd George, in a campaign speech in 1918, remained legalistic: "There is no right you can establish, national or international, unless you establish the fact that the man who breaks the law will meet inevitable punishment."[14]

There were limits to this idealism. Paradoxically, British threats of prosecution could sometimes spark German reprisals that actually made conditions worse for the Britons at risk. To protect British prisoners of war in German hands, the British sometimes had to mute their calls for war crimes trials. After the war, Britain worried about undermining the Weimar Republic, and would not use military might to enforce the Treaty of Versailles—in particular, apprehending Wilhelm II or other accused German war criminals. What had started as a crusade ended with a whimper.

During the War

The first British leader to take concrete steps to press for a firm and legalistic policy on German war criminals was Winston Churchill. He would wrestle with the issue of war crimes through both World Wars, eventually despairing. After World War I, he would ask the cabinet to free Turkish accused war criminals in exchange for British prisoners, and late in World War II, he would press for the summary execution of a small number of top Axis leaders. But in 1915 Churchill's first instincts were distinctly legalistic.

When Lord Fisher wanted to shoot all the German prisoners of war in reprisal for the Zeppelin attacks, Churchill refused.[15] As first lord of the admiralty, Churchill was particularly troubled by U-boat attacks. When Britain captured two U-boats, Churchill's admiralty had their crews segregated in the barracks. The U-boat crews were accused of "offenses against the law of nations and . . . common humanity" and would thus be investigated and punished.[16]

Germany responded in kind. As Gottlieb von Jagow, the German foreign secretary, had threatened,[17] Germany put thirty-nine British officers—many of them well-connected aristocrats—into barrack arrest or criminal jails, to be returned to regular quarters as soon as Britain treated the U-boat men as normal prisoners of war.[18] Lord Curzon—who would later lock horns with Churchill over Turkish war criminals—accused Churchill of acting rashly and without the cabinet's support.[19]

Churchill, already seen as a loose cannon by the king and others, vehemently stuck to his view of U-boat crews as criminals.[20] Forming a new government, Herbert Henry Asquith quietly dumped Churchill as first lord of the admiralty.[21] Even after the deaths of 1,198 people in the sinking of the *Lusitania* by a German U-boat—perhaps the single most notorious war crime of the Great War[22]—the British government kept its emphasis on its thirty-nine captive officers, leaving Churchill isolated.[23] King George V himself pleaded for a quick capitulation.[24] Asquith obliged, putting the U-boat crews in normal prisoner-of-war jails.[25] Germany reciprocated.[26] The next time Britain captured a submarine crew, the government completed its repudiation of Churchill's legalistic venture by delicately postponing the issue of punishment until the war's end.[27]

Britain balked at other times when a stern line on war criminals seemed to put its soldiers at risk. In April 1915, Lord Kitchener, the war secretary, suggested holding responsible all Germans guilty of atrocities against British prisoners, from Wilhelm II on down,[28] and publicly declaring that the war would not stop until these war criminals were delivered to the British government. But the cabinet, including Lloyd George, demurred, fearing that Germany would fight on for three extra years.[29]

British opinion could be horrified at atrocities against non-Britons, such as the 1914 sack of the Belgian town of Louvain and the Armenian genocide. But the greatest outbursts came when Britons suffered in striking ways. The most famous was Edith Cavell, a British nurse executed by Germans for sheltering Allied soldiers in Brussels. Britain protested fiercely, to no avail.[30] (Cavell is immortalized to this day in a statute near Trafalgar Square. And Hitler, visiting Paris in triumph in June 1940, pointedly ordered the demolition of a French monument to Cavell.)[31]

In July 1916, Germany captured, tried, and executed Captain Charles Algernon Fryatt, a merchant marine officer who had rammed a German submarine.[32] Edward Grey, Britain's foreign secretary, formally protested this "judicial murder" of a prisoner of war.[33] British opinion was enraged. There was a slew of questions in Parliament about Fryatt's executioners,[34] and protests flooded in from steamship owners and private citizens furiously calling for trials for the Germans.[35] The press was scorching. Invoking Fryatt, Cavell, Louvain, the Zeppelins, and the Armenians, an editorial in *The Weekly Dispatch* demanded the kaiser's execution: "Kaiser rule is the rule of the Devil. The cannibal knows no better."[36]

The government, its sentiments largely in line with those of the public, moved decisively. Condemning the "atrocious crime" in the House of Commons in July, Asquith made a bold legalistic call for criminal punishment for Fryatt's killers and, without being too oblique about it, Wilhelm II: "[T]he man who authorises the system under which such crimes are committed may well be the most guilty of all."[37]

Grey followed this up by asking France and Russia to agree to a joint Allied threat against the Germans responsible for Fryatt's death.[38] France and Russia quickly agreed in principle,[39] but a secret Franco-German prisoner exchange agreement muzzled France.[40] Asquith had to content himself with warning that Britain would not restore diplomatic relations after the war until reparations had been made for Fryatt's death—a threat aimed directly at Wilhelm II, in light of Asquith's speech in the Commons.[41]

For the rest of the war, Britain did not issue new threats. There was not much that Lloyd George, who became prime minister in December 1916, could add to what Asquith had already said. And Britain often kept quiet for a cruder reason: Germany might win the war. When Germany in January 1917 said that its U-boats would start sinking hospital ships without warning, Britain decided that war crimes trials would be unlikely, and instead opened talks with Germany about better treatment of prisoners.[42]

The tide finally turned and Germany asked for an armistice on October 4, 1918, a month before the actual end of the war. The British were emboldened as victory drew closer. In September, Lloyd George had publicly thundered:

> The first indispensable condition, in my judgment, is that civilisation shall establish beyond doubt its power to enforce its decrees. . . . The German people must know that if their rulers outrage the laws of humanity, Prussian military strength cannot protect them from punishment. There is no right you can establish, national or international, unless you establish the fact that the man who breaks the law will meet inevitable punishment. Unless this is accomplished, the loss, the suffering, and the burdens of this war will have been in vain.[43]

Amid a public outcry over the treatment of British prisoners, George Cave, the home secretary and head of a special committee on prisoners of war, wanted to formally warn Germany that its "abominable" treatment of British prisoners would be punished.[44] Curzon wanted "the trial and punishment of the principal criminals, possibly including the Kaiser, unless he abdicated."[45]

But war crimes trials were intentionally left out of the armistice. Despite "a very strong feeling in the country" about British prisoners of war, as well as the scorched earth left by Germany's retreat,[46] the cabinet was not prepared to put war crimes trials before an armistice:

> It was suggested that we might make it a condition of the peace that those individuals who had been responsible for the ill-treatment of our prisoners should be tried by a court of law. It was pointed out, however, that it would be very difficult to fix responsibility. In addition, no nation, unless it was beaten to the dust, would accept such terms. If England had been beaten in this war, we should never agree to our officers being tried by German tribunals.[47]

Quietly, the cabinet agreed to warn Germany that the guilty must be punished.[48] The armistice itself said nothing about war criminals.[49]

Secretly, Britain started its planning. Frederick Smith, the attorney general, had people sift through the evidence in the Foreign Office and War Office files and consider an international tribunal.[50] Smith drew up a list of forty Germans, "guilty of the greatest atrocities in respect to our prisoners of war," to be brought to trial. Curzon suggested reminding Lloyd George of the promises made in the Commons.[51] Once again, public and elite fury at crimes against Britons mingled with British faith in the rule of law. And now, with the end of the fighting, war crimes trials would no longer put British lives at risk.

Putting Wilhelm II on Trial: The Cabinet's Great Debate

On November 11, 1918, an armistice ended World War I. Wilhelm II abdicated and—handing his sword to a baffled Dutch border guard—fled to the Netherlands, which gave him asylum.[52] Weighed down by his luggage, stuffed full of his military regalia, the toppled monarch was not an awe-inspiring figure. He was, a French diplomat noted with evident satisfaction, "visibly surprised and terrified" by a Dutch heckler yelling, "Down with the assassin!"[53]

That heckler was in good company. As Lloyd George wrote in his memoirs, toward the war's end, "British feeling was roused to a pitch of irrepressible wrath" by German sinking of merchant ships, with Wilhelm II widely held personally responsible. Lloyd George noted "a growing feeling that war itself was a crime against humanity, and that it would never be finally eliminated until it was brought into the same category as all other crimes by the infliction of condign punishment on the perpetrators and instigators."[54] After hearing Clemenceau push for a trial for Wilhelm II (see France section below), Curzon, lord president of the council, urged Lloyd George:

> I pray you to consider it seriously. Public opinion will not willingly consent to let this arch-criminal escape by a final act of cowardice. The supreme and colossal nature of his crime seems to call for some supreme and unprecedented condemnation. Execution, imprisonment, these are not, or may not be, necessary. But continued life, an inglorious and ignoble exile, under the weight of such a sentence as has never been given in the history of mankind, would be a penance worse than death.[55]

Lloyd George agreed to bring the issue to the Imperial War Cabinet at its next meeting. There, and in the next such meeting, the British and Commonwealth governments would have one of the most extraordinary debates over international justice on record, unmatched until Henry Morgenthau Jr. and Henry Stimson waged their great argument over the future of Nazi Germany.

On November 20, Curzon opened the debate by pushing hard for a trial for the German kaiser and crown prince for starting the war and for war crimes. His case rested on a legalistic belief that Wilhelm II had been a criminal, and therefore should be treated just as any other criminal would be treated under British domestic law:

> I do not think I need argue the case about the desirability, still less the fairness, or the equity of trying him and the Crown Prince. We know the war was started by the Kaiser, and have reason to believe that all the cruelty, the iniquities, and the horrors that have been perpetrated, if not directly inspired by him, have been countenanced and in no way discouraged by him. *In my view the Kaiser is the arch-criminal of the world, and just as in any other sphere of life when you get hold of a criminal you bring him to justice, so I do not see, because he is an Emperor and living in exile in another country, why he should be saved from the punishment that is his due.*[56]

On the need for a trial, Curzon simply said, "I have not thought it necessary to argue the case on its merits." He also waved off the possibility of execution: "I do not think he [Clemenceau] said much about execution; I do not think that entered into our minds."[57] For all the hatred toward Wilhelm II, legalism precluded shooting him.

Lloyd George now unleashed some of the ferocity that had made meeker Britons like Asquith shake their heads at Lloyd George's "Celtic capacity for impulsive and momentary fervour."[58] The prime minister stormed:

> *If he is guilty at all then he is guilty of a criminal offence.* He has put to death hundreds of thousands of prime young fellows from this country and did it very recklessly, and a still greater culprit is the Crown Prince, who had been advocating this war for many years, and who hailed it with joy when it started. These people have been very irresponsible. Kings have been tried and executed for offences which are not comparable with the offences which these two culprits have been guilty of, and I think rulers who plunge the world into all this misery ought to be warned for all time that they must pay the penalty sooner or later. I do not think it is sufficient punishment to this man that he should get away with twenty millions of money, as I see is stated, to Holland or Corfu, or wherever he goes. *I think he ought to stand his trial.* With regard to the question of international law, well, we are making international law, and all we can claim is that international law should be based on justice. I think if we demanded this man, if he is not responsible, he could then make his case. . . . There is a sense of justice in the world which will not be satisfied so long as this man is at large.[59]

Lloyd George even gave a nod to impartiality—far beyond what the Allies would do at Nuremberg—by suggesting the inclusion of German judges. Although Lloyd George was vague about the precise charges, he was clearly for a trial: "[T]he sooner they are tried, the better."[60]

But Curzon and Lloyd George would not be able to sway the cabinet in this first meeting. They were bombarded with political and legal objections. Jan Smuts, South Africa's defense minister and an opponent of a punitive peace, recognized that there had been standard war crimes at Lille and Ostend, but was not sure what Wilhelm II's crime was. Lloyd George replied: "The crime for which he is responsible is plunging this world into war." Robert Borden, Canada's prime minister, agreed: "It is a crime against humanity." W. M. Hughes, Australia's prime minister, was not convinced. "You cannot indict a man for making war. War has been the prerogative of the right of all nations from the beginning, and if you say, well, as a result of this war, millions have died, you can say that much of Alexander and of Moses and of almost anybody." Ringingly, Lloyd George fired back: "I am not sure that they also ought not to be brought to justice!"[61]

Hughes wanted to cut through the legalism and take a simple stance: "If you say that it is a good thing that he should die, let us say so, but you cannot say he should die because he plunged the world into war, because he had a perfect right to plunge the world into war, and now we have conquered, we have a perfect right to kill him, not because he plunged the world into war, but because we have won. You cannot indict him, Mr. Prime Minister, for breaking the law."[62] Churchill, now minister of munitions but destined to find himself both in Lloyd George's office and dilemma, had more complicated doubts. He did not want to stretch the concept of command responsibility too far.[63] Evidently sobered by his U-boat crew fiasco, and with a wariness of legalism that he would maintain in the planning for Nuremberg, Churchill said:

> [I]t is within our rights to kill him as an act of vengeance, but it does seem to me, if you are going to deal with him on the basis of what is called justice and law, it is difficult to say that the ex-Kaiser's guilt is greater than the guilt of a great many very important persons in Germany who supported him, including the Parliament of the nation, which supported him unanimously. It does seem to me that you might easily set out hopefully on the path of hanging the ex-Kaiser and have general public interest taken in it, but after a time you might find you were in a very great *impasse*, and the lawyers all over the world would begin to see that the indictment was not capable of being sustained. It might even be found that the ex-Kaiser was not altogether a free agent and that he was carried away by the tremendous influences around him. I think it should be looked at very carefully by the Government before committing itself to any decision.[64]

In 1918, Churchill had his doubts even *before* Allied war crimes policy began to crash and burn. He saw the ambiguities of meting out blame, and the risk that legal procedure would let Wilhelm II off the hook.

Austen Chamberlain had another objection. He feared that trying the kaiser might imply an exoneration of the German people, and—presciently—that a trial might generate German nationalist backlash: "Let us beware that we do not create a Hohenzollern legend like the Napoleonic legend. . . . The Napoleonic legend grew with St. Helena." On top of that, Chamberlain had no confidence in legalistic methods: "You must say about this what President Roosevelt said of the seizure of the Panama Canal: 'Let there be no taint of legality about it.' "[65]

By this point, it was clear that Lloyd George and Curzon were losing the argument. Lloyd George would only accept the cabinet's disagreement "under strong protest." He said: "I am entirely with Lord Curzon on this matter. I think this man ought to be tried for high treason against humanity. That is my view, and I regret to see there is hesitation upon that subject. I think it is a cardinal mistake. There is no legend you can create about a creature of this kind."[66] Trying to compromise, Hughes tried to shift the debate away from Wilhelm II's responsibility for the war. The kaiser, Hughes argued, was widely blamed for "treason against humanity, but unfortunately that is not a crime at all." Instead, Hughes suggested "a public declaration of policy that all those persons who have committed crimes against international law, persons of the type who were responsible for the death of Captain Fryatt, the sinking of the 'Lusitania,' and anything of that kind, whether they were Generals or Admirals or Kaiser or peasant, whoever they were, should be brought to justice."[67] Lloyd George would have none of this. "That is letting off the greatest criminal of the lot," he said.[68]

Against the objections of most of the cabinet, Lloyd George then began, in essence, to play out the trial of Wilhelm II right there in 10 Downing Street. In a bizarre scene, Lloyd George—with something of the temperament of a prosecutor anyway—made the case against the kaiser, while the Imperial War Cabinet found itself sounding like Hohenzollern defense counsel. "His defence might be our trial," warned Chamberlain. Churchill worried that proving that Germany started the war might involve indelicate questions about Russia's runaway role in the July 1914 crisis. "Russia has been given very many hundreds of millions by the French to complete strategic railways," Churchill said, "and if Russia was in the hands of a couple of women they might persuade her either this way or that." Balfour singled out the crown prince, pointing out that "you cannot drag him before a Court of Law because his father went to war." Hughes, uneasy with the prospect of a trial, warned, "It would be a very serious thing if this man was brought up for trial and not convicted." This was the last straw for Lloyd George, who made his final prosecutorial statement: "All those who have no confidence in our case are right in voting against it, but, as I say, I have complete confidence in the Allied case, and would like to see it put forward before the strongest body of jurists."[69]

Stymied, Curzon took the obvious legalist step: he suggested going to the lawyers. The Imperial War Cabinet deferred its decision until hearing the report of Smith's committee.[70] Lloyd George had faced a host of objections: that a trial might be inconclusive or impossible or provocative. But the most telling one seemed to be that the trial might be bad law.

So the triumph of the rule of law would come from the official repositories of the British legal tradition. Eight days later, the Imperial War Cabinet (minus Churchill and Chamberlain) reconvened to hear from Smith, the attorney general. An extraordinary orator, he launched into an extemporaneous forty-five-minute peroration that would lay to rest the cabinet's objections.[71]

Smith's argument was a more temperate version of Lloyd George's. And the attorney general, speaking for the crown's law officers and a blue-ribbon committee of lawyers who had mulled over a trial of Wilhelm II,[72] had a legal credibility that Lloyd George in full cry lacked.[73] Smith started by rejecting the option of letting Wilhelm II enjoy a luxurious exile. If Britain was to have war crimes trials for any Germans at all, Smith argued, then it would be a mockery not to indict their leader:

> The ex-Kaiser's personal responsibility and supreme authority in Germany have been constantly asserted by himself, and his assertions are fully warranted by the constitution of Germany. Accepting, as we must, this view, we are bound to take notice of the conclusion which follows: namely, that the ex-Kaiser is primarily and personally responsible for the death of millions of young men; for the destruction in four years of 200 times as much material wealth as Napoleon destroyed in twenty years; and he is responsible—and this is not the least grave part of the indictment—for the most daring and dangerous challenge to the fundamental principles of public law which that indispensable charter of international right has sustained since its foundations were laid centuries ago by Grotius. These things are very easy to understand, and ordinary people all over the world understand them very well. How then, I ask, are we to justify impunity? Under what pretext, and with what degree of consistence, are we to try smaller criminals? Is it still proposed—it has been repeatedly threatened by the responsible representatives of every Allied country—to try, in appropriate cases, submarine commanders and to bring to justice the governors of prisons? Is it proposed to indict the murderers of Captain Fryatt? In my view you must answer all these questions in the affirmative. I am at least sure that the democracies of

69

the world will take that view, and among them I have no doubt that the American people will be numbered. How can you do this if, to use the title claimed by himself, and in itself illustrative of my argument, "the All Highest" is given impunity? Must we not, at the moment of our triumph, avoid the sarcasm: *Dat veniam corvis, vexat censura columbas?* In order to illustrate the point which is in my mind I will read to the Imperial War Cabinet a very short extract, which represents our view with admirable eloquence, from Burke's speech in the trial of Warren Hastings:—

> "We have not brought before you an obscure offendor, who, when his insignificance and weakness are weighed against the power of the prosecution, gives even to public justice something of the appearance of oppression; no, my Lords, we have brought before you the first man of India in rank, authority, and station. We have brought before you the chief of the tribe, the head of the whole body of eastern offenders; a captain-general of iniquity, under whom all the fraud, all the peculation, all the tyranny in India are embodied, disciplined, arrayed, and paid. This is the person, my Lords, that we bring before you. We have brought before you such a person, that, if you strike at him with the firm and decided arm of justice, you will not have need of a great many more examples. You strike at the whole corps if you strike at the head."

Prime Minister, in my judgment, if this man escapes, common people will say everywhere that he has escaped because he is an Emperor. In my judgment they will be right. They will say that august influence has been exerted to save him. . . . It is necessary for all time to teach the lesson that failure is not the only risk which a man possessing at the moment in any country despotic powers, and taking the awful decision between peace and war, has to fear. If ever again that decision should be suspended in nicely balanced equipoise, at the disposition of an individual, let the ruler who decides upon war know that he is gambling, amongst other hazards, with his own personal safety.[74]

Some twenty-seven years before Nuremberg, Smith had delivered an eloquent call for command responsibility.[75]

What should be done with Wilhelm II? Smith did not reject out of hand the option of punishing the kaiser for "high crimes and misdemeanours" without trial, on the model of Napoleon. That way, "we should avoid the risks of infinite delays and of a long drawn-out impeachment," Smith said. "We should carry with us the sanction and support of the overwhelming mass of civilisation, and we are bold enough to feel that we have nothing to fear from the judgment of the future."

Alternatively, Wilhelm II could face an international court. If so, Smith argued, Britain's own domestic legal standards, joined with those of its liberal allies (in this, at least, Russia's absence was a mercy), should not be compromised:

> There are obvious advantages in this method upon the moral side, if this method of dealing with the situation be carried to a logical conclusion. It is, of course, very desirable that we should be able to say that this man received fair-play, and that he has had a fair trial, but grave difficulties beset this course in its complete application. In this connection, how is the Court to be constituted? Are neutrals to be members of the Court? Are Germans to be members of the Court?
>
> The only advantage of judicial procedure over the other alternative—a high exercise of executive and conquering force submitting itself to the judgment of history—lies in the fact that for all time it may claim the sanction of legal forms and the protection—in favour of the prisoner—of a tribunal whose impartiality can be established in the face of any challenge. This advantage, it must be observed, largely disappears if the fairness of the tribunal can be plausibly impeached. The Law Officers are not, indeed, of opinion that before a tribunal which consisted in part even of Germans, as Germany appears to be developing to-day, an indictment would necessarily fail. But it is unwise to ignore the difficulties. . . .
>
> On the whole, if a Court be constituted, I confess that I myself incline on the whole to the view that the members of the Court should consist only of citizens of the Allied countries. Grave judges should be appointed, but we should, as it seems to me at present, take the risk of saying that *in this quarrel we, the Allies, taking our stand upon the universally admitted principles of the moral law, take our own standards of right and commit the trial of them to our own tribunals.*[76]

Unlike Lloyd George, Smith did not overplay his hand. At the very end of the meeting, Smith would say that "I am not at present wholly convinced" that Wilhelm II should get a trial, although his committee preferred a formal trial. Whatever Smith's fears about a drawn-out trial, the cabinet seemed to take his speech as a legitimation of a legalist approach.

What would Wilhelm II be charged with? Smith did not offer any judgment as to whether or not aggression was a crime; he simply argued that he was not sure that Wilhelm II could be easily convicted for it.

An aggression charge would invite "infinite disputation," an unwelcome "meticulous examination of the history of European politics for the past twenty years" that would sprawl to questions like Russia's strategic railways. To avoid this, Smith preferred to emphasize the strongest parts of the Allied case. First, Smith suggested a "decisive" indictment "charging the Kaiser with responsibility for the invasion of Belgium in breach of international law, and for all the consequent criminal acts which took place. That is an absolutely clear issue," Smith said, "and upon it I do not think that any honest tribunal could hesitate." Invoking the *Lusitania*'s sinking, Smith also focused on "unrestricted submarine warfare":

[I]t will, in my judgment, be absolutely impossible for us to charge or punish any subordinate if the ex-Kaiser escapes with impunity all responsibility for the submarine warfare. . . . [T]housands of women and children, in our clear and frequently expressed view, have been brutally murdered. I am dealing with the case where a ship is torpedoed carrying no munitions of war, but which it is known must or may be carrying women and children, and where it is equally known that such passengers had no possible means of escape, and I do not in this connection deal with the vile cases of assassination when helpless boats, vainly attempting to escape, have been fired on and destroyed. Excluding the last class of cases, it is our view, and the view of the whole civilised world, that these acts amount to murder. It is surely vital that if ever there is another war, whether in ten or fifteen years, or however distant it may be, those responsible on both sides for the conduct of that war should be made to feel that unrestricted submarine warfare has been so branded with the punitive censure of the whole civilised world that it has definitely passed into the category of international crime. "If I do it and fail," the Tirpitz of the next war must say, "I, too, shall pay for it in my own person." How can we best secure that no one in future will dream of resorting to submarine warfare of this kind? You can best secure it by letting the whole world know that, by the unanimous consent of the whole of that part of the civilised world which has conquered in this war, the man responsible for those acts is responsible in his own person for that which he has done. To us of all people it is not possible to exaggerate the weight and force of these considerations. Nothing more vitally concerns these islands than that it should be recognised that these acts are crimes. The commission of such crimes, and their possible future development, menace us more directly than any other nation in the world.[77]

Here, Smith struck a self-serving note, pointing out Britain's unique interest in humane law at sea.

Smith's splendid speech had done the job. After sounding arguments that were more respectably legalist and less politicized than Lloyd George's, Smith concluded by invoking his legal authority once again: "As chief Law Officer of the Crown I say quite plainly that I should feel the greatest difficulty in being responsible in any way for the trial of subordinate criminals if the ex-Kaiser is allowed to escape."

Throughout, Smith had emphasized the importance of using British standards to judge German war criminals. Lloyd George, sensing victory, underlined that he had the lawyers on his side. "The case has been very ably stated by the Attorney-General, and his views are supported by the strongest legal body that you can possibly summon together in a matter of this kind in this country," Lloyd George said. "Does anybody dissent?"[78]

Nobody did. At the end of the greatest war in history to date, the decision about the fate of Britain's chief adversary had not been made on the basis of the arguments of the general staff, or foreign secretary, or war secretary. It had been made on the authority of the attorney general and a committee of lawyers.

The December 1918 Election

"Why do the English hate me so?" asked Wilhelm II, in exile.[79] In 1918, Lloyd George's anti-German feelings were widely held in Britain, so much so that Wilhelm II would become an electoral issue. Lloyd George wrote (with Belgium's integrity in mind) that "public opinion ultimately dominates the actions of Government here to a degree incomprehensible in lands subject to pre-War autocracies and post-War dictatorships."[80]

The government had called an election for December, and British members of Parliament were eager to translate Wilhelm II's massive unpopularity into votes. Immediately after swaying the Imperial War Cabinet, Smith turned to crass politicking. "As I shall be going to my constituency very soon," Smith asked Lloyd George, "is one at liberty to say anything in that strain?" "I propose to say something to-morrow," Lloyd George replied, hesitating just long enough to be assured by the general staff that so doing would not endanger British soldiers during the armistice.[81]

The next day, as promised, Lloyd George hit the hustings in Newcastle-on-Tyne. "The Kaiser must be prosecuted," Lloyd George told a cheering crowd:

The war was a hideous, abominable crime, a crime which has sent millions of the best young men of Europe to death and mutilation, and which has plunged myriads of homes into desolation. Is no one responsible? Is no one to be called to account? Is there to be no punishment? Surely that is neither God's justice nor man's. The men responsible for this outrage on the human race must not be let off because their heads were crowned when they perpetrated the deeds.[82]

Throughout Britain, the notion of punishing Wilhelm II was overwhelmingly popular. Candidates spoke openly of hanging the kaiser. As one historian writes, "[T]he aroused electorate probably would have compelled any leadership to adopt such a program."[83] Even Churchill, despite private doubts, found it easier on the stump simply to call for the kaiser's trial.[84] The government's electoral victory ringingly vindicated Lloyd George's call for war crimes trials.

Britain's allies were also enthusiastic. At an inter-Allied conference in Paris on December 2, Clemenceau led the charge for trying Wilhelm II, while the British distributed copies of the British war crimes commission's report and of Smith's cabinet speech. Vittorio Orlando, Italy's president, soaringly declared that "the question was exclusively one of sentiment; it had nothing to do with interests." For Orlando, this "was a matter of universal sentiment which touched the highest moral laws. We had just witnessed the reaction of the world from a veritable crime against humanity."[85]

The only note of discord came from Sidney Sonnino, Italy's skeptical foreign secretary. "Was not the nation responsible as a whole?" Sonnino asked. "[A] nation usually gets the Government it deserves. He questioned the desirability of making a scape-goat. Was not St. Helena useful to the Bonapartists? The answer was 'Yes'; and the *régime* of Napoleon III had been the result." Lloyd George replied sharply "that St. Helena was not so useful to the Bonapartists as the ex-Kaiser in Holland with £30,000,000 at his disposal would be to his party in Germany."[86]

Lloyd George, Clemenceau, and Orlando quickly agreed that Wilhelm II would be personally punished. Clemenceau was unwaveringly legalist, preferring a trial to an Allied declaration formally denouncing Wilhelm II. Lloyd George said that a trial "was much more striking." Only Balfour, the British foreign secretary, voiced some caution. Administrative action, he said, would be "a clear and simple course, but it would lose the advantages of a legal trial." But a trial would lay the Allies open to all the delays of the law which would weary the whole world. There had been a famous British political trial which had lasted seven years. It would be possible to drag into the trial all questions such as to whether Germany was justified in anticipating the completion of the Russian railway system. There would be all the arguments of lawyers, which would draw attention off the main fact that this man was the ringleader in the greatest crime against the human race on which the eyes of the whole world ought to be fixed.[87]

Lloyd George had no qualms about victors' justice: "[E]very judge tried an offence against the society of which he was a member."[88]

Having quickly reached a consensus, the Allies drew up a telegram notifying Wilson that they would demand Holland surrender "the arch-criminal" Wilhelm II to face an international tribunal for aggression and war crimes. The judges would be from those countries that had won the war. Trials for Germany's leaders were what "justice requires." Playing to Wilson's respect for international law, the Allies argued that "the certainty of inevitable personal punishment for crimes against humanity and international right will be a very important security against future attempts to make war wrongfully or to violate international law, and is a necessary stage in the development of the authority of a League of Nations."[89] With that, the Allies had made their decision: a historic demand not merely for the overthrow of a defeated enemy leader, but for a trial of a man who had been a monarch but was now seen in Britain as simply a criminal.

The Paris Peace Conference

The first item on the agenda of the Paris Peace Conference was the punishment of war criminals.[90] Balfour, heading Britain's delegation, pushed for making Germany hand over any accused officers "for breaches of laws of war and humanity."[91] In January 1919, the preliminary peace conference established an Allied and American commission to look into creating a war crimes tribunal.[92]

In this commission, the British delegation argued strongly for a trial of the kaiser, often basing its arguments on Britain's domestic rule of law. One British delegate noted that if the king of England had ordered an assassin to murder a lowly Briton, the king would be tried.[93] Driven by Britain and France, the commission blamed the war on "a dark conspiracy" between Germany and Austria, and secondarily on Turkey and

Bulgaria. Wilhelm II bore personal responsibility for attacking Belgium, France, and Serbia, and for "barbarous and illegitimate methods in violation of the established laws and customs of war and the elementary laws of humanity." Although the war crimes were mostly against Allied citizens, the report did include the 1915 Armenian genocide as "systematic terrorism" (see Constantinople chapter). For these crimes, there would be a special tribunal, with judges mostly from the big victorious powers.[94]

Lansing, America's secretary of state and the chair of the commission, dissented (see America section below). Germany protested bitterly, but to no avail.[95] On June 28, Germany was forced to sign the Treaty of Versailles.[96] Amid its other punitive clauses, there were four articles on German war crimes. Those who had committed crimes against Allied citizens would face military trials run by the victimized country. Article 227 was revolutionary: "The Allied and Associated Powers publicly arraign William II of Hohenzollern, formerly German Emperor, for a supreme offence against international morality and the sanctity of treaties." This dubious wording allowed a trial for aggression, but relied less on codified law and more on substantive justice as seen by the Allies—whose definition of justice was hardly universally shared.[97]

If this charge was not exactly impeccable law, the proposed process was at least more fair. Wilhelm II would face five judges, one each from America, Britain, France, Italy, and Japan. The court would assure him "of the guarantees essential to the right of defence" and would adjudicate on the basis of "the highest motives of international policy, with a view to vindicating the solemn obligations of international undertakings and the validity of international morality." And Article 228 focused on any other Germans who had "committed acts in violation of the laws and customs of war," who would be surrendered by Germany for an Allied trial.[98]

The war guilt and war criminals clauses were roundly condemned in Germany. Much of Matthias Erzberger's cabinet, with the support of Field Marshal Paul von Hindenburg, demanded the removal of the war guilt and war criminals clauses. The government fell. Erzberger scrabbled together a new government, promising not to acknowledge German war guilt or hand over war criminals. Lloyd George and Clemenceau issued an ultimatum: sign the treaty as written, or Allied troops would storm into Germany. Germany helplessly signed.[99] But Articles 227 and 228, wildly unpopular in Germany, would only inflame German politics, undermining the fledgling Weimar Republic.

Article 227: Wilhelm II

Hiding out in Holland, Wilhelm II said, "I do not want to be dragged like the basest criminal through the streets of Paris or London where I will be spit upon and so that those bastards can cut off my head."[100] Having granted asylum, the Dutch government was not to be easily budged, to Lloyd George's surprise. Holland, neutral in the shadow of its huge German neighbor, took a dim view of Allied victors' justice. Nor did the Dutch monarchy relish the precedent of turning another monarch over for trial.[101] Repeated harangues from Clemenceau and Curzon, now Britain's foreign secretary, cut no ice.[102]

With the trial blocked, a series of bizarre alternative suggestions floated around. France suggested a trial without Wilhelm II in custody, which, Curzon shrugged, would "be rather in the nature of a *brutum fulmen*—all the more so that the sentence, if passed, could apparently not be put into execution."[103] Theobald von Bethmann Hollweg, as ex-chancellor, offered to stand trial on behalf of his ex-king.[104] When rumors reached London that Wilhelm II was contemplating suicide, Parliament ("HON. MEMBERS: 'Let him!' ") urged the British government to "do its best to facilitate this expeditious and inexpensive solution."[105] Lloyd George— still incapable of getting the kaiser out of Holland—somehow contrived to announce, to cheers, that Wilhelm II would face trial in London.[106] The cabinet hastily recanted, with Lloyd George modestly admitting that "London was not a very suitable place, and it had been his intention, in his speech on the subject, to say that it would take place in *England*. The relative advantages of Hampton Court and Dover were discussed. The Acting Secretary of State for Foreign Affairs made the suggestion of the Channel Islands."[107] This was not noticeably more realistic.

Despite continued Dutch obstinacy, in January 1920, the Allies formally demanded Wilhelm II from the Netherlands under Article 227.[108] The note, wrote Britain's ambassador, "occasioned a great flutter in Dutch Dovecotes,"[109] but Holland stood firm.[110] Lloyd George, thwarted, had his ambassador lecture the Dutch foreign minister about "a very strong, powerful and easily roused public opinion in England."[111] (On the bright side, floodwaters were rising at Wilhelm II's castle; if they rose a bit higher, the British ambassador mused, they would be met with "unmitigated relief."[112]) In fact, Britain was softening its line a bit.[113] Lloyd George floated the idea of a German tribunal with Allied prosecutors: "In his mind the fundamental essential is that the criminals should be strictly and sternly tried, and that punishments suited to their proven crimes should be rigorously inflicted upon them."[114] Secretly, some British officials would accept some kind of banishment for Wilhelm II,[115] which in practice led only to diplomats wasting time weighing the relative merits of Chile and Java and Curaçao, while Wilhelm II sat tight in Holland.[116] The nadir came when a Dutch diplomat likened Wilhelm II to a dog that the neighbors consider dangerous but which Holland would look after. The British ambassador, not exactly flattering anyone, replied that "if the dog in question had already severely bitten the neighbours and their children in the tenderest portions of their anatomy, they were entitled to demand not only that it should be chained up, but that it should be removed altogether from the neighbourhood."[117]

Eventually, Holland agreed to confine Wilhelm II to a "narrow circle" around his residence, which the former emperor accepted "with a good grace, remarking that he was well aware how embarrassing his presence must be for Netherlands Government."[118] He finally wound up at Doorn. Appropriately enough, this was a location that the British had repeatedly deemed entirely unsuitable.[119]

Article 228: Germany's War Criminals

From the start, many Germans resented the Allied demands for war crimes trials. The German army warned it would not turn over Wilhelm II or other leaders for trial, even if the German government wanted to.[120] The Prussian war ministry set up a legal defense office for accused war criminals.[121] Even Erzberger wanted the Allies to waive their demands for arrests.[122]

Not without trepidation, the Allies drew up lists of suspects to be demanded under Article 228. These lists showed a kind of rough mathematical ratio of wartime suffering. Belgium alone had originally wanted 1,132 people,[123] and the first combined list had come out to 3,000 names.[124] After cutting some lower-level suspects, this was brought down to 1,580: 800 named by Belgium, 600 by France, 130 by Britain, and 50 by Italy. Even Lloyd George declared himself "startled at the numbers" and "rather taken aback at the idea of more than 1,500 separate trials."[125] After another round of cuts, France and Belgium accused 334 men each, Britain accused 97, and smaller countries rounded out the total to 854.[126]

About half of the ninety-seven on Britain's list were accused of mistreating British prisoners of war. Grand Admiral Alfred von Tirpitz and six admirals were accused of unrestricted submarine warfare. There were charges for Zeppelin attacks on London, Hull, and Essex. Two officers, one of them an admiral, were charged with Fryatt's murder. Nurse Cavell's killers—in a striking irony of legalism—could not be charged, because Britain's law officers decided she had been treated fairly.[127] The list ended with nine Ottoman leaders (see Constantinople chapter), accused not of crimes against Britons but against Armenians.[128]

With Britain's long-sought goal in sight, the risks of war crimes trials became more noticeable. Lloyd George understood that demanding too many Germans would increase the backlash in the Weimar Republic. Instead, he "only wanted to make an example. Trying very large numbers, would create great difficulties for the German Government, which he believed to be better than either a Bolshevist Government or a Militarist Government."[129] Chamberlain warned "that a prolonged series of trials might have the opposite effect and even arouse sympathy."[130] Smith wanted to pare the lists, reckoning that "the vindication of the moral law of the world" was best served by naming a number small enough that Germany would actually turn them over. This, Smith knew, meant "excluding some persons who undoubtedly had been guilty of criminal acts." Even Lloyd George managed to put himself in Erzberger's shoes: "[E]ven now we were asking more than any Government could be expected to comply with. . . . [I]f in different circumstances, a demand had been made by a German Government on a British or French Government for the handing over of 800 officers, he did not believe that they would ever comply with it. No British or French Government could do so."[131]

As expected, the Allied lists were met with shock in Germany. Erzberger warned (accurately, Balfour thought) that his government would fall if the Allies pressed their demands.[132] Clemenceau suggested targeting only the top war criminals for now,[133] and Lloyd George's "strong opinion" was that "we should confine our demands to surrender of the most important and notorious offenders and let the rest go."[134]

The British embassy in Berlin warned that the imminent Allied demand for accused war criminals "arouses passionate resentment amongst all classes" in Germany.[135] Germany protested that no magistrates would sign arrest orders, and no policemen would carry them out.[136] Baron von Lersner, chair of Germany's delegation at the peace conference, predicted "most serious disturbances."[137] When finally slapped with the formal Allied demand, he returned it, resigned, and took the first train out of Paris.[138] When the list reached Germany, the British embassy reported, "feeling is very strong a most serious situation . . . about to arise here."[139] The embassy warned this "great sensation"—exacerbated by the inclusion of the hugely popular Hindenburg—might topple the government, opening the way for either the right or a "Soviet regime."[140]

The Allies inched back. France suggested dropping Hindenburg, General Erich Ludendorff, and Bethmann Hollweg from its list if Britain would drop Tirpitz. Despite bitter objections from the admiralty, Tirpitz's name was deleted.[141] The process was falling apart.

Leipzig as Seen from London

Germany had floated a compromise proposal: trying the accused before Germany's highest court, the Supreme Court (*Reichsgericht*) at Leipzig.[142] In February 1920, the shaken Allies agreed to this.[143] For a start, they would cull forty-five test cases from the overall Allied list to see if, as Lloyd George wrote, Germany was "actually determined to judge them themselves before the Court of Leipsig."[144] The breakdown of cases was, once again, proportionate to Allied suffering: sixteen from the Belgian list, eleven from the French, seven British, five Italian, and four from smaller countries.[145]

This compromise was unpopular in Britain. "The difficulty no doubt is that something must be done here to satisfy *our* public opinion," the Foreign Office worried.[146] Britain's seven suspects were accused of crimes that would scandalize most Britons: one for sinking without warning the *Llandovery Castle*, a hospital ship, and then sinking the lifeboats, killing 234 people; one for torpedoing the *Dover Castle*, a British hospital ship, killing six people; one for sinking the S.S. *Torrington*, and then drowning the crew; and four for cruelty to British prisoners of war.[147]

The Leipzig war crimes trials were a disaster. German authorities claimed they could not find the commanders of the U-boats that sank the *Llandovery Castle* and the *Torrington*, as well as one of the officers accused of mistreating prisoners of war.[148] The trials finally got started in May 1921, after a year of dithering while the Allies fumed at a suspicious German tendency to try "certain obscure offenders" not accused of anything by the Allies.[149] The British list went first. The first suspect, accused of assaulting British prisoners, got a mere ten months' imprisonment.[150] Two others got six months each. (To confuse matters, two more Germans, not on the British lists, were tried for the sinking of the *Llandovery Castle* and sentenced to four years each. They were hailed as heroes by the German right,[151] and one of them would later escape.[152]) In the *Dover Castle* case, the accused was acquitted, largely because the Leipzig court accepted the defense that he had merely been following superior orders—a precedent that would make further U-boat warfare convictions almost impossible.[153]

Thus, of Britain's seven suspects, three had escaped, one had been acquitted, and the other three had gotten jail sentences of a few months.[154] An Allied commission on Leipzig would conclude that "in almost all the cases the court has given no satisfaction in that certain accused have been acquitted when they should have been condemned, and that even in those cases where the accused have been judged guilty the penalty applied has not been sufficient."[155] As Alexander Cadogan in the Foreign Office summed it up, the Leipzig "experiment has been pronounced a failure."[156] Perhaps the only person impressed was Ernest Pollock, the British solicitor general, who attended and pronounced himself "much impressed by the Supreme Court of Leipzig—the trials were conducted very impartially with every desire to get at the truth." Pollock knew that "the British Public may have desired and expected more startling sentences," but predicted "a wide-reaching and permanent effect" in Germany.[157] This did not endear Pollock to Parliament or the Foreign Office, where a diplomat sniffed that he "seems better pleased than the general public in this country."[158]

In June 1921, the court acquitted a German secret police chief accused of torturing Belgian children; Belgium, furious, withdrew its delegation.[159] By July, France ostentatiously gave up on Leipzig, pulling out its representatives and witnesses. But Britain, though disgusted with the Leipzig experiment, was no longer prepared to risk the stability of the Weimar Republic for the sake of a futile pursuit of war criminals. Britain feared "a most dangerous situation in Germany" and the fall of Josef Wirth's government, and thought France was using Leipzig as an excuse to maintain sanctions.[160]

By now the British government was heartily sick of the whole business. "[E]verybody concerned—most of all the Attorney General—is only too anxious to let the whole war criminals question sleep," wrote a Foreign Office official, when some suspects were discovered. "It only brings us trouble both the French & with the Germans."[161] "I hardly need tell you that we have not the slightest intention of making any representations to the Dutch Government," added another. "[P]ersonally, I think that the less that is said about, and the fewer enquiries that are made as to the whereabouts of escaped war criminals, the better."[162]

By 1922, British officials knew that Article 228 was a dead letter.[163] Any more demands, Curzon thought, were "quite certain" to be met with "a blank refusal."[164] The French ambassador in London reminded Curzon that British public opinion during the 1918 election "was no less passionate than French opinion on this issue." But now Curzon would not even sanction France's idea of holding trials *par contumace*—without the presence of the accused—for "English criminal procedure does not allow them."[165]

In the end, the only way to carry out Lloyd George's plans for war crimes trials would have been to occupy and control Germany completely, so that the Allies could hunt down the war criminals themselves, as after World War II. But after World War I, the Allies had not occupied Germany outright, and they were not about to do so simply in order to catch suspected war criminals. As a Foreign Office diplomat wrote, "The question was never one of practical politics unless we were prepared (which we were not) to march into Germany and arrest the criminals."[166] In principle, Britain had been strongly legalist; but not at the price of sending soldiers.

FRANCE

The Greatest of the Victims

No major power was more traumatized by the Great War than France. Most French citizens were either terrified of Germany or simply hated it, or both, seeing the country as an infernal and perpetual menace.[167] In addition to an unprecedented death toll from the war, France had endured the agony of partial German occupation, looting, and rape. The wartime fear of German reprisals could muzzle France, but with victory came the opportunity for French retribution.

It is hard to separate France's harshly punitive impulses toward German war criminals[168] from a variety of other anti-German policies: economic reparations, military sanctions, and occupation of the Rhineland. But that does not mean that France was cynically using war crimes as an excuse for hostility to Germany. To a considerable extent, the war crimes issue was the *reason* why France was hostile to Germany. After the horrors of the Great War, France did not see Germany simply as an enemy power, but as a criminal one.[169]

During the War

France was the first major country to start gathering evidence of German war crimes. Once German troops were in France, behaving not so differently from Germans in Belgium, France set up special military courts for German prisoners of war charged with war crimes in France. In October 1914, one of these courts issued the first war crimes judgment of the Great War, convicting three Germans of pillage. Other trials followed.[170]

These trials caught Germany's attention. Demanding the release of Germans convicted of committing war crimes, Germany threw six French officers—one of them the son of Théophile Delcassé, the foreign minister—into Berlin's Spandau prison, not as war crimes suspects but as simple hostages. France did much the same thing to the sons of German notables, who were not charged with war crimes. This seemed to silence French leaders throughout 1914 and 1915, who did not dare risk further German reprisals either against French citizens under occupation or held as prisoners.[171]

France felt particularly victimized by German forces. French leaders were shocked at a systematic assault on French prisoners, both in Germany and in the occupied parts of France, who were forced to do labor, malnourished, and terrorized.[172] But for all the sincerity of French public and elite outrage, France was prepared to overlook punishing war crimes against its own citizens in order to protect other French citizens. In the summer of 1916, France held secret talks with Germany about a prisoner exchange, which freed the young Delcassé and other Frenchmen. The price for their freedom was an agreement not to take any more legal measures against prisoners of war until the end of the war.[173] Thus, France proposed making only a rather vague public statement after the Fryatt killing—"No peace without the suppression of atrocities"[174]—while at the same time joining in secret with Britain in elaborate plans to draft a war crimes tribunal for after the end of hostilities.[175] To protect its own soldiers and residents of occupied French areas, France fell silent until 1918.

Indicting the Kaiser

At the war's end, German forces left behind scorched earth as they retreated.[176] Marshal Ferdinand Foch, the French commander, wanted a loud Allied declaration telling Germany to stop devastating French lands and villages.[177] "During the last few months of the War there had been a growing feeling in France—which was the greatest sufferer—also in Britain and America, that punishment should be meted out to those who had been guilty of barbarities," Lloyd George later wrote. "The French population in the occupied areas had suffered from these excesses."[178] Once again, France asked the Allies for punishment for German war criminals.[179]

The government was pushed along by pressure from below. Andrew Bonar Law, the British chancellor of the exchequer, knew that threats against the kaiser would in France "appeal to the public mind tremendously."[180] The press returned over and over to the theme: "they are *boches*, they will remain *boches*." In January 1919, *Le Matin* started a drumbeat: "Wilhelm II will be judged by the tribunal of Nations, or the S.D.N. [League of Nations] will be nothing but a word." The paper was joined by other publications, rural and urban, across the political spectrum, from *Le Temps* to *Le Radical*. The only note of debate was how broadly guilt should be spread. Many French citizens, usually on the right, felt it unfair to lay all the blame on the kaiser. *La Presse* wrote: "The *Boches* remain immutably *Boches*, all guilty, so all responsible."[181]

For all this fury, France's outrage was tempered at least at the elite level with a legalistic insistence that even Wilhelm II face an actual trial. If anything, Clemenceau, France's president, was more forthright in his calls for a trial than even Lloyd George. There is no evidence in these debates that summary execution was considered. In November 1918, meeting Curzon in Paris to discuss the issue, Clemenceau said he "thought that as an act of international justice, of world retribution, it would be one of the most imposing events in history and that the conception was well worthy of being pursued."[182] As Curzon later reported to the Imperial War Cabinet, Clemenceau "said that, as far as he knew, the French jurists had not looked at it from the point of view of international law and of the questions that will arise in respect of internment and extradition, but he said public opinion in France, as represented by the press, was strongly in favour of steps being taken for the trial of the Kaiser and that he himself shared that view." Clemenceau, Curzon said, evidently "had the idea of an international tribunal," made up of Allied and neutral delegates. Clemenceau would have preferred "a successful demand for the person of the Kaiser himself and putting him up for trial before a body to which he himself could answer for his misdeeds," but if Holland would not allow that, "[h]e did not think that would be a fatal bar." Instead, "the terms of indictment might be drawn up and that they might be sent to the Kaiser, if we could not get hold of him." Finally,

Curzon reported, summary execution was off the table: "As regards punishment, the idea which he mentioned—I do not think he said much about execution; I do not think that entered into our minds—was that of treating the Kaiser as a universal outlaw so that there should be no land in which he could set his foot."[183]

Whether or not the perpetually skeptical Clemenceau entirely believed all of his own high-flying rhetoric, or if he was just following public opinion, he clearly meant for his words to become French policy. At the December 1918 meeting of the Allies in London, Clemenceau took the lead in arguing for a trial for Wilhelm II, overshadowing even Lloyd George:

> M. *Clemenceau* said that he thought it would show an immense progress if we could punish the man who was guilty of a great historic crime like the declaration of war in August, 1914. All the Governments represented here to-day were proud of the principle of responsibility. As a rule, it only meant responsibility in newspaper articles and books, which the great criminals of the world could afford to laugh at. He was not one of those who was sure we could immediately set up a League of Nations. A great step, however, would have been taken towards internal understanding if the peoples of the world could feel that the greatest criminals, such as the ex-Kaiser, would be brought to trial. He therefore supported energetically the proposal of Mr. Lloyd George that the ex-Kaiser and his accomplices should be brought before an international tribunal.
>
> *Baron Sonnino* asked who were the accomplices?
>
> M. *Clemenceau* said that the Court must determine this. The ex-Crown Prince would certainly be the first of them. The same could not be said of the great soldiers, who had merely obeyed orders. If, however, we could get seven or eight persons, and make them responsible before an international tribunal, this would be an enormous progress for humanity. Hence, he regretted to have to separate himself from his friend Baron Sonnino and rally to Mr. Lloyd George. The ex-Kaiser was the person really responsible for the war, and this case must be entirely separated from that of camp commandants and others who had been guilty of ill-treating prisoners. These latter ought to be court-martialled.—(*Mr. Lloyd George* interjected that he agreed.)—Frankly, he himself had no other idea than to bring the ex-Kaiser to justice. The people everywhere would be satisfied if this could be done. They will feel that justice will in future be done in the case of Kaisers and Kings just as

much in the case of common men. If this could be achieved, it would be a magnificent advance and a moral revolution.[184]

Clemenceau was unabashedly revolutionary on this point. He was hoping for something like an international Magna Carta that would extend the rule of law to kings and to foreign policymakers—and he knew how popular this stance would be in France.[185]

Clemenceau betrayed no particular anxieties about the difficulty of holding a trial for Wilhelm II. Clemenceau told the Allies simply that he "stood for trial." He was unimpressed by Balfour's warning that a trial could drag on for years:

> *M. Clemenceau* said he knew nothing about the methods on which the political trials were conducted in England. In France, however, an important political trial was now being held. The case was before the Senate. The Senate made its own procedure and gave instructions. It was a sovereign body and made its own law. If this course were followed, all Mr. Balfour's objections in regard to procedure would disappear. There would be no neutrals on the Tribunal. They had no right to it, they had not intervened in the war, and had undergone no sacrifices. The Allies had secured this right by their immense losses in men and sacrifices of all kinds.
>
> *Mr. Balfour* asked if this course would not take away all appearance of impartiality? If the Allies set up the Court themselves, where would be the moral effect before the world?
>
> *M. Clemenceau* said that all justice was relative, and that the impartiality of all judges was liable to be questioned. It was a misfortune which could not be helped. But when a crime took place on a scale so unprecedented in history, he thought that France, Great Britain, Italy, and the United States must place themselves high enough to take the responsibility for dealing with it.[186]

For all Clemenceau's legalism, he had a way of only being moralistic when it concerned France. Thus, when Balfour suggested also putting Talaat Pasha on trial, Clemenceau was not interested. France kept its sights on Germany: "*M. Clemenceau* thought that Talaat and the others could be brought in later on. But he would deprecate mixing them up with the ex-Kaiser. He thought for the moment people were not particularly interested in Talaat. It would be sufficient to begin with the chief culprit."[187] Moments after Clemenceau sniffed at the idea of prosecuting the Young Turks, Lloyd George suggested putting the Hohenzollern crown prince on the Allies' blacklist. This time, Clemenceau quickly agreed.[188] He had his eye firmly fixed on his own country's suffering.

Article 227: Wilhelm II

If anything, France was even angrier at Wilhelm II than Britain was. In the peace conference's deliberations on war crimes issues, France repeatedly invoked its own wartime miseries.[189] French bitterness was so intense that Lloyd George would suggest to Clemenceau that the kaiser be tried "in some Allied country removed from those where resentment at the Kaiser was naturally the most acute"—in Britain or America, not France.[190]

Like Lloyd George, Clemenceau had at first thought that Holland would quickly surrender the kaiser,[191] and was startled to be thwarted. Clemenceau harshly told Holland that it would be an international crime to let the kaiser escape.[192] French diplomats accused Holland of being undisturbed by Germany's war crimes, and, like Lloyd George, made a point of citing Grotius.[193] The Allies hinted that they might sever diplomatic relations.[194]

Compromise solutions went nowhere. The Dutch government suggested an exile in the Falkland Islands,[195] and France reluctantly considered sending Wilhelm II to a quiet island somewhere.[196] France entertained one idea that Britain would not. Under French domestic law, absent suspects could be tried *par contumace*. This might allow for a symbolic trial of the kaiser, even if he could not be captured.[197] In 1920, Alexandre Millerand, then French president, also proposed trying Wilhelm II *par contumace*.[198] But British law had no equivalent procedure, and France could hardly take such a dramatic step alone. Wilhelm II would die of old age in Holland.

Article 228: Germany's War Criminals

France did not share Britain's predilection for negotiated agreements about how to enact the Treaty of Versailles, instead insisting on standing firm behind every article—including those on war criminals. To France, any sign of weakness would open the door to German revision of the treaty and even a potential resumption of hostilities.[199]

France drew up massive lists of accused German war criminals. During the war, the French Ministry of War gathered files on no fewer than 2,000 German suspects. From that, a French list was made of 800 names, which was slowly whittled down to 334 names for the joint Allied list of war criminals to be demanded under Article 228.[200] As Britain's Pollock said, "[I]t was impossible to ask France and Belgium to reduce their big numbers to something comparable with ours, as the difference was due . . . to the fact that British soil had not been occupied by the enemy."[201] Clemenceau, unfazed by the length of the list, said that "the effect would be admirable upon public opinion."[202] When Lloyd George suggested a shorter list, Clemenceau said pointedly that "some people felt very keenly on this question." After Lloyd George argued that no British or French government would ever give up 800 officers to face German courts, Clemenceau said that "the British or French officers would not have perpetrated such abominable crimes." Clemenceau bitterly continued: "[T]he difficulty was to give a reply when women came up from the provinces and told him that their daughters had been carried off by the Germans and that they had their names and yet they were not included in the list." After much cajoling, Clemenceau grudgingly agreed to try to trim his list.[203]

Even so, France's list was one of the most punitive, to British chagrin and German horror.[204] It included such major figures as the Hohenzollern crown prince, former chief of staff Helmuth von Moltke, Hindenburg, and Ludendorff, plus at least fifteen generals and those men accused of sacking Lille, Liège, Maubeurge, and other French towns.[205] On February 3, 1920, under Articles 228–230 of the Treaty of Versailles, France gave Germany its list.[206] Evidently frustrated at having had to trim the list, Millerand, Clemenceau's successor as president, accompanied it with a warning that the list did not imply amnesty for other "innumerable crimes."[207]

Leipzig as Seen from Paris

Only in Belgium, perhaps, was the Leipzig compromise more unpopular than in France. The enforcement of the Treaty of Versailles was going poorly: in April 1921, Aristide Briand, France's new president, had wanted to occupy the Ruhr because German reparations offers seemed inadequate.[208] Going into Leipzig, France was no more generous on the implementation of the treaty's other provisions. The fact that France had gone from keeping files on some two thousand German war crimes suspects to now asking for a mere eleven rankled with some in the French Ministry of War.[209] It gives a sense of French bitterness that some of the French witnesses, who had been prisoners of the German army, wanted to stop in Cassel en route to Leipzig and lay a wreath on the graves of their old brothers in arms.[210]

By the time France's cases came to trial, the Allies were already more than a little leery of the Leipzig proceedings. First, Britain had faced its run of acquittals, short sentences, and vanished suspects. Then, in Belgium's test case, the German court had acquitted a German secret police chief accused of the torture of Belgian children. Horrified, Belgium pulled out of Leipzig.[211]

France fared no better. Two of the German officers accused of killing French prisoners turned out to be dead, and a third, Germany claimed, could not be found.[212] Paul Matter, the attorney general at the Cour de Cassation and the head of the French team, was convinced this was all a judicial farce. The most high-profile suspect was General Karl Stenger, notorious in France for war crimes against French prisoners; in 1914 French courts-martial had tried four Germans under Stenger's command. But Stenger's trial, Matter reported, had turned into an occasion for claiming that German troops had been provoked beyond endurance by French soldiers.[213] Stenger, who claimed he had not given the order to shoot French prisoners, was acquitted. A German captain, who had nevertheless had them shot, was declared to have been depressed at the time and thus got two and a half years in jail.[214] There was an anti-French demonstration outside the court.[215]

The next trial—another acquittal—was the last straw.[216] Briand pronounced the trials "ridiculous" and ordered Matter and the French delegation to return to Paris.[217] The day after the French witnesses left, the Leipzig court acquitted two German generals, thereby ending its consideration of the French test cases.[218] When they returned, Matter and other distinguished jurists sent stinging reports about Leipzig's "disastrous results" to Briand.[219] Briand asked Belgium and Britain to join in a démarche complaining about Leipzig.[220] Britain balked, because of Pollock's favorable impression of Leipzig and British fears of German instability and French opportunism.[221]

Briand's outrage sparked a furious reaction in Germany. The German press continued "without party distinction, to throw fire and flames against France because of its attitude on the issue of the guilty," reported France's ambassador.[222] In Leipzig, reported the French envoy there, the local press demanded punishment for French army war crimes.[223] When Briand called Stenger's acquittal a "parody of justice,"[224] the German justice minister stormed against an effort to "maintain the hatred and passions of the war."[225] The Weimar Republic was lashing back.

War Criminals and Other Sanctions

Briand, worried that public opinion on all sides was "overexcited," had no stomach for more Leipzig cases. He preferred to set up an Allied commission on Leipzig, which would take time and thus allow tempers to cool.[226] Like Clemenceau and Millerand before him, Briand pushed a trial for Wilhelm II *par contumace*—a feature of the secret 1916 draft plans for a war crimes tribunal.[227]

The French dilemma was clear. Trials were politically impossible, the Foreign Ministry knew, but some solution was needed "to give public opinion the necessary appeasements."[228] One French group, called Remember, claimed to have gathered more than two million signatures on a petition calling for the punishment of those who started the war and committed atrocities during it.[229] France, stymied by Germany, had already been holding such trials for absent German soldiers over a year. The concept of trials *par contumace* was an accepted part of French domestic law.[230] But it was not part of British domestic law, and made the British distinctly uncomfortable.[231] (The wrangling continues to this day. Claude Jorda, a French judge in The Hague, wishes ex-Yugoslav war crimes suspects could be tried *par contumace*.) France once managed to seize three German soldiers and sentenced them at a court-martial in Nancy.[232] But most cases, at Lille and Nancy, went on without anyone in custody.[233]

In September 1921, in No. méyy, the French justice minister declared that "France from now on loses its interest in what is deliberated, but not judged, in Leipzig."[234] Briand declared that the whole Leipzig scheme had been unrealistic, and that instead, France had decided to "judge *par contumace*, by our tribunals, by our courts martial."[235] These trials continued throughout 1921 and 1922.[236] Even after an Allied commission heaped scorn on Leipzig,[237] France knew that it would risk provoking "unanimous protest" in Germany if it asked for the surrender of war criminals.[238] Raymond Poincaré, France's president, though more anti-German than his predecessor Briand, thought that trials *par contumace* were the bare minimum that French public opinion would accept.[239] Poincaré ordered André Maginot, the war minister, to have the Nancy court-martial go to work on the list of forty-five names that had been given to the Leipzig court.[240]

Having endured German occupation, French officials and ordinary citizens were loath to abandon entirely the issue of war crimes. This stood in contrast to Britain, which had noticeably backed off from Lloyd George's firebreathing speeches and had thus begun to spark French complaints about the fickleness of Anglo-Saxon Protestantism.[241] Poincaré wrote: "[T]he United Kingdom's population, which did not have to suffer an invasion, cannot take the same interest in the punishment of the guilty as the inhabitants of Belgium and the north of France, who, in the same degree, were the victims of German occupation and who would feel the injustice of an impunity for their oppressors."[242]

French bitterness over the impunity of Germany's war criminals only aggravated tensions between the two countries, which were on a perpetual war footing. In April 1920, when German soldiers were sent—without Allied authorization—to fight leftists in the Ruhr, French troops had marched into Frankfurt.[243] And on January 11, 1923, France would occupy the Ruhr.[244]

In 1922, France tried to use Germany's failure to punish war criminals to justify extending other sanctions under the Treaty of Versailles.[245] France's ambassador to Britain told the Foreign Office that France wanted to put on the record a formal note that Germany had breached the Treaty of Versailles. This was important, the ambassador said, "not only for the moral reasons which appealed to public opinion, but also because they strongly held to their view that the progressive evacuation of the occupied territories contemplated by the Treaty of Versailles would not be justified so long as the German Government did not carry out the terms of the treaty; and they regarded the refusal of the surrender of the criminals as one of the most flagrant instances of the German failure to do so."[246] France repeatedly brought the matter up, and Britain repeatedly shrugged it off.[247] After the occupation of the Ruhr, the Weimar government mollified German nationalists by allowing the return of Frederick Wilhelm, the former crown prince. Poincaré invoked Article 228 to demand his trial, or, failing that, suggested occupying Hamburg in retaliation.[248] Britain refused, fearing that such actions would only strengthen the German right.[249]

It is hard to disentangle the various strands motivating French sanctions policy: Poincaré's own anti-German stance, French public opinion, and the need to keep Germany down. But by not giving France satisfaction on the issue of war crimes, Germany had made it all too easy for a hostile French government to continue to hound Germany.

For France, Leipzig was a disaster on several levels. It stirred up French public opinion without offering any prospect of satisfaction; it made French leaders look both vengeful and feeble; it annoyed Britain; and, worst, it sparked nationalist backlash within Germany. There were many causes for the demise of the Weimar Republic, and it is possible that German democracy could have survived war crimes trials if only hyperinflation had not happened, or if the Weimar parties had been quicker to understand the Nazi threat, or any number of other hypotheticals. But protesting Allied demands on war criminals was a simple way for the German far right to undermine the Weimar Republic.

The most grotesquely ironic example of backlash came in 1922. After the Allied commission rendered its dismal verdict on Leipzig, Wirth declared that Germany would never turn over those Germans suspected by the Allies of war crimes. There were demonstrations throughout Germany to cheer on Wirth's defiance. It was at one of these flashpoints for the far right that Hermann Göring—who would end his life as the most prominent German war criminal in the dock at Nuremberg—for the first time saw Adolf Hitler whipping up German nationalism.[250]

AMERICA

Moral Isolationism

Woodrow Wilson drove British and French leaders to distraction over war crimes issues. The self-declared greatest of the democracies remained detached from the passions on the Continent. Entering the war only in April 1917, America lost 100,000 men—at most, one-fourteenth of the French tally.[251] During its long neutrality, America reserved its loudest moralizing for the one war crime that specifically threatened Americans: Germany's submarine attacks on neutral shipping around the British Isles. This aroused American indignation—complete with discussions of possible war crimes trials for the guilty—in a way that German depredations in Lille and over London did not.

More than any American administration before or since, the Wilson administration based its vision of world order on international law.[252] But Wilson's plans for the League of Nations were so forward-looking that they left little room for lesser issues like German war crimes. Although America shared the Allies' sense that domestic liberal legal principles should be brought to bear on world politics, Lloyd George and Clemenceau's plans struck the administration as more punitive than just, as legally dubious, and as a sop to febrile public opinion. At the Paris Peace Conference, the Americans left open the possibility of trials for U-boat warfare, while shrugging off the other offenses that had enraged the Allies. America had not suffered enough to make war crimes trials a political necessity, and the Wilson administration had a kind of legalism too pure for anything that smacked of victors' justice.

"None of Our Business"

Until April 1917, America was neutral in the Great War, with a simple war crimes policy: it was not America's place to condemn, unless Americans happened to be the victims. As late as November 1916, Lansing, as Wilson's secretary of state, wrote, "I have firmly supported the policy of avoiding all protests on account of inhuman methods of warfare by belligerents which are in violation of international law."[253] The great exception was U-boat warfare, which threatened American lives and shipping, and thus not only drew White House condemnations but dragged America into the war.

At first, America strove for neutrality. Protests over war crimes might have pulled America into a war that the White House did not condone. William Jennings Bryan, Wilson's first secretary of state, was almost a pacifist. Once, when an American died on a ship sunk by a German U-boat, Bryan asked that Wilson not protest the war crime itself but speak of "the tens of thousands who are dying daily in this 'causeless war.' "[254] When a German military balloon bombarded Antwerp in August 1914, Lansing, then State Department counselor, considered the attack "an outrage against humanity," but preferred not to make any protest unless Americans were the victims. He asked Bryan: "[I]f we begin to make protests general in nature as to violations of civilized and humane methods of slaughter where are we going to stop?"[255] Wilson mulled the situation: "[W]e ought to be very slow to make formal protests, chiefly because we shall no doubt be called upon by every one of the belligerents before the fighting is over to do something of this kind and would be in danger of becoming chronic critics of what was going forward. I think the time for clearing up all these matters will come when the war is over and the nations gather sober counsel again."[256] When the British ambassador agitatedly protested German Zeppelin attacks on London in 1915, Wilson remained aloof: "[I]t is none of our business to protest against these methods of 'warfare,' no matter what our opinion of them may be."[257]

The supposedly arch-moralist Wilson administration did not protest the German invasion of Belgium—a policy of silence that Lansing defended stoutly.[258] Even the 1916 German deportations of French and Belgian civilians for forced labor[259] earned nothing worse than a protest given "in a friendly spirit, but most solemnly."[260] Lansing, though privately appalled about the Belgians, continued to think America's refusal to condemn war crimes "wise" and worth continuing.[261]

Public opinion was more voluble. In general, the American public was neutralist, with some belligerently anti-German Republicans and pacifist Democrats at the respective fringes.[262] But German war crimes in Belgium and on the high seas shocked Americans. Wilson's efforts to maintain "a real neutrality of public opinion here" were, he feared, being "wholly nullified" by German aerial bombings.[263] When pressed by Congress to explain why the White House had not lodged protests under the Hague conventions, to which America was a signatory, Lansing and Wilson argued that, as a neutral, America had no obligations unless American citizens were affected.[264] When a group of prominent critics of Wilson—including Henry Stimson, who would be the architect of Nuremberg—asked for government information on German abuses in Belgium, Wilson worried that the request would "embarrass us."[265] Nationalists like Theodore Roosevelt, who wanted to plunge into war to stop German cruelty, saw Wilson as a coward.[266] German atrocities continued to give fodder to the Republican critics of American neutrality, like Elihu Root and Henry Cabot Lodge.[267] But despite several major bursts of public outrage over German use of poison gas and the execution of Edith Cavell, Wilson stayed the course.[268]

U-Boats

The U-boats were a different matter altogether. The administration that ignored Lille and Louvain railed against unrestricted submarine warfare, which posed a direct threat to American lives and ships.[269]

In February 1915, Germany, itself under embargo, declared British waters a war zone. German submarines aiming at British ships often sunk neutral vessels, although they were ostensibly protected—a policy Lansing described as if "a man who has a very dim vision should go out on the street with a revolver in search of an enemy and should see the outline of a figure and should immediately fire on him and injure him seriously and then go up and apologize and say he made a mistake."[270] In May, a German U-boat sank the *Lusitania*, killing 1,198 people—including 128 American citizens. Americans were transfixed and horrified.[271] Public outrage reached a new high.[272] Six months after, Lansing even worried that Congress might declare war on Germany.[273]

Lansing saw the sinking of the *Lusitania* as a violation of international law. "It seems to us a shame that Mr. Lansing should insist that we declare the *Lusitania* sinking illegal," said Jagow, Germany's foreign secretary. "He is acting like a technical lawyer."[274] Germany had gone too far, even for neutral America. Bryan, although personally so conciliatory that he would resign over Wilson's tough line on the *Lusitania*,[275] asked for reparation and a disavowal of the U-boat commander's actions, but said nothing specific about war crimes trials.[276] An agonized and deeply torn Wilson issued notes warning that America would insist on "strict accountability" for attacks on Americans.[277]

As historian Ernest May points out, "strict accountability" could mean anything from a threat of war to some kind of litigation after the war[278]— including, presumably, some kind of war crimes trial. This option was certainly on Lansing and Wilson's minds. Lansing talked of "the crime of submarine warfare,"[279] and suggested demanding a German admission of guilt and that "the officer of the German Navy responsible for the sinking of the *Lusitania*, will be punished for having committed a lawless and inhumane act in thus causing the death of citizens of the United States."[280] When an Austro-Hungarian submarine sank the *Ancona*, an Italian liner bearing twelve Americans,[281] Lansing demanded that Austria-Hungary denounce the sinking and that "the officer who perpetrated the deed be punished."[282] Lansing told Austria-Hungary, "Either the Commander is guilty, or your Government is guilty. If your Government desires to take the responsibility they should frankly say so, exonerating the Commander, but they should assume his guilt."[283]

In March 1916, there was another spectacular incident: the steamer *Sussex* was sunk in the English Channel, evidently by a U-boat, killing some Americans. America threatened to break diplomatic relations with Germany.[284] Lansing threatened tougher warnings. Had this been an isolated incident, America

> might consider that the officer responsible for the deed had wilfully violated his orders and that the ends of justice would be satisfied by imposing upon him an adequate punishment and by a formal disavowal of the act by the Imperial Government. But the *Sussex* is not an isolated

case, though the attack was so utterly indefensible and caused a loss of life so appalling that it stands forth today as one of the most terrible examples of the inhumanity of submarine warfare as it is now being waged by Germany.[285]

With American lives being lost because of German war crimes, the lawyerly Lansing suddenly sounded more like Lloyd George than like Bryan. Wilson's personal foreign policy advisor, E. M. House, more florid, thought Tirpitz deserved to be "hanged at the end of a yardarm like any pirate of old."[286]

Lansing wrote to Wilson that "we can no longer temporize in the matter of submarine warfare when Americans are being killed, wounded or endangered by the illegal and inhuman conduct of the Germans." Lansing wanted to sever ties with Germany immediately, and House urged action.[287] Wilson, according to House, was "set in his determination to make Germany recede from her position regarding submarines. He spoke with much feeling concerning German responsibility for this world-wide calamity, and thought those guilty should have personal punishment."[288]

In May, Wilson considered making a call for an international tribunal, which would appeal to the Allies: "The only inducement we can hold out to the Allies is one which will actually remove the menace of Militarism."[289] Although Wilson never went through with this legalistic suggestion, it was a war crime—submarine warfare against Americans—that made him for the first time threaten Germany with war, even though he personally was anxious to avoid war.[290]

Bethmann's limitations on the U-boats held until 1917, when Hindenburg, Wilhelm II and the Reichstag managed to reinstate unrestricted submarine warfare.[291] This risked war with America.[292] On several occasions, Lansing had suggested severing diplomatic relations with Germany if it did not acknowledge its guilt in killing Americans aboard the *Lusitania*.[293] As Lansing recognized, American public opinion worried mostly when American lives were lost: "[P]ublic opinion in this country would not support drastic action unless Americans were killed or imperiled by the submarine warfare."[294]

In February, when Wilson announced to Congress that he had severed relations with Germany, his speech to Congress was entirely about U-boat warfare against Americans.[295] And on April 2, declaring war against Germany, Wilson's speech to Congress again was almost entirely about U-boat warfare: passing "all restraints of law or of humanity," it was "warfare against mankind."[296] For Wilson, the time had come to impose liberal domestic standards universally: "We are at the beginning of an age in which it will be insisted that the same standards of conduct and of responsibility for wrong done shall be observed among nations and their governments that are observed among the individual citizens of civilized states."[297] In the end, it was to a huge extent a German war crime—unrestricted submarine warfare—that brought America out of neutrality and into the Great War.[298]

"America Must Paddle Her Own Canoe"

"He was the product, not, it is true, of a different world, but of another hemisphere," Lloyd George wrote of Wilson, grudgingly admitting that Wilson was actually from this planet.[299] America found itself in the unusual position of having helped win the war, but without the same kind of suffering as the Allies. (America was an Associated Power, not one of the Allies.) Britain had lost over nine times as many men in combat as America, and France at least fourteen times as many.[300] Australia's W. M. Hughes pointed out to the Imperial War Cabinet that his country had lost more men than had America.[301]

So one could hardly expect America to match the heights of outrage reached by Lloyd George and Clemenceau. To Europeans, Wilson himself seemed a cold fish. Lloyd George was furious that, on Wilson's triumphant arrival in Paris, the American president gave no mention of British contributions to the war. The French fared no better. "I never heard one sentence which would give an impression that President Wilson was even cognisant of the ravages wrought by the War in the homes of France," Lloyd George later wrote.[302] He bitterly noted:

> Whilst we were dealing every day with ghastly realities on land and sea, some of them visible to our own eyes and audible to our ears, he [Wilson] was soaring in clouds of serene rhetoric. When the Allied Armies were hard pressed and our troops were falling by the hundred thousand in vain endeavours to drive back our redoubtable foe, we could with difficulty even approach him to persuade him to view the grim struggle below, and to come down to earth to deal with its urgent demands before the accumulating slaughter should bury our cause in irreparable disaster. When he came to France, the French Government and people were anxious that he should visit the devastated areas so as to acquaint him with the demoniac actualities of war. He managed to elude their request and to ignore their hints right to the end.[303]

After persuading the Imperial War Cabinet in November 1918 to seek the punishment of Wilhelm II, Lloyd George was not much concerned about America's reaction. "America must paddle her own canoe," Lloyd George said. "We have responsibilities in this matter greater than hers. Our sufferings have been very much greater."[304]

As the war drew to a close, American policy on war criminals was a curious mixture of self-centered indifference and faith in international law. The Wilson administration wavered between its own anger at German war crimes and seeing British and French fury at German war crimes as an impediment to peace. In 1916, Lansing worried that Germany's brutality in Belgium would make it impossible to make peace.[305] Similarly, he warned in early 1917 that unrestricted U-boat warfare would make the Allies "so enraged" that they would not make peace.[306] In September 1918, Wilson publicly warned: "The nations associated against Germany cannot be expected to agree to a cessation of arms while acts of inhumanity, spoliation and desolation are being continued which they justly look upon with horror and with burning hearts."[307]

Lansing was aware that America had not suffered in the same way that France and Belgium had. He once tried to imagine America in their position:

> [A]s our own people and territory are . . . spared the horrors of a German invasion, it seems to me that we should view the situation very much as if our own land had been occupied and our own people subjected to the privations and brutal treatment which for four years have been the portion of the Belgians and French. . . .
>
> If these criminal acts were perpetrated against American citizens on American soil, I believe that we would be warranted in attempting to prevent it by threatening reprisals upon the territory and property of the Germans and by declaring that full reparation would be required for all property destroyed or carried away.[308]

At the very end of the war, Lansing made a legalistic suggestion, in a departure from America's wartime quiescence: "[I]t might stay these ruffians if we made a general statement that if those atrocities continued it would be necessary to hold those responsible liable therefor."[309]

Wilson frequently hinted that the Hohenzollern monarchy would need to be overthrown in order to build a stable peace, but he said almost nothing about war crimes trials.[310] Privately, the subject was evidently on his mind. According to a telegram brought to the British cabinet in October 1918, Wilson was "inclined to take Germany to task for recent atrocities, *e.g.*, the sinking of the *Leinster,*" an Irish mailboat.[311] In December 1918, arriving in France, Wilson warned of "the certainty of just punishment" for those who had carried out acts of terror.[312] But Wilson, whose country had suffered so much less, was far less committed to vengeance than were the Allies.

War Crimes Trials or the League of Nations?

This is not to say that Woodrow Wilson was not a legalist or a moralist.[313] He was both, with a singular kind of purity that irritated the more worldly Lloyd George and Clemenceau almost beyond endurance. Lloyd George witheringly described Wilson as thinking himself "a missionary whose function it was to rescue the poor European heathen from their age-long worship of false and fiery gods." And Clemenceau, a serious cynic even in less trying circumstances, opened his eyes wide when Wilson couched an appeal for the League of Nations in a less than modest explanation of why Jesus Christ had not succeeded in bringing the whole world to Christianity: "It is because He taught the idea without devising any practical means of attaining it. That is the reason why I am proposing a practical scheme to carry out His aims."[314]

Wilson did not want to associate himself with crude victors' justice. His vision of a world ruled by law did not make any allowance for Allied vengeance. In September 1918, Wilson said: "[T]he impartial justice meted out must involve no discrimination between those to whom we wish to be just and those to whom we do not wish to be just. It must be a justice that plays no favourites and knows no standards but the equal rights of the several peoples concerned."[315] This kind of purity stood in the way of the Allied project of trying German war criminals. Wilson's pure and narrow kind of American legalism clashed with a looser Allied brand of legalism. The top French delegate in the commission on war crimes at the peace conference said the Americans "to a certain extent, have a higher idea of legality than we have, and I . . . beseech them not to stand for the narrow point of view,—not to stand, as it were, as prosecuting magistrates, attorneys, and lawyers, but as great men of law,—as great jurists."[316] Wilson's sketches of a European peace emphasized the grand project of the League of Nations—the ultimate expression of the liberal quest for an international order resting on law—not Lloyd George and Clemenceau's plans to try Wilhelm II.[317]

The Allies billed the trial of the kaiser as part and parcel of the new law-governed world Wilson craved.[318] Lloyd George and Clemenceau, neither of them otherwise great League enthusiasts,[319] consistently linked the two grand legal projects. In November 1918, Clemenceau said, "if the nations set up this tribunal [for Wilhelm II] a League of Nations will be in existence, and this will be its first act."[320] At Clemenceau's suggestion, the Allies told Wilson that Wilhelm II's trial "is a necessary stage in the development of a League of Nations."[321]

This Allied sop to Wilson seemed, for one brief second, to succeed. House told the British that he agreed entirely with a trial for Wilhelm II, and, "though he cannot remember exactly what [Wilson] replied he is sure that he expressed no dissent."[322] Lloyd George wrote in his memoirs: "President Wilson subsequently intimated that he was in agreement with the decision arrived at by the Allies on this subject."[323] If Wilson agreed, he quickly changed his mind.

In the end, despite America's occasional rumbles about war crimes trials, the Wilson administration did not associate itself with the war crimes provisions of the Treaty of Versailles. Wilson told Lloyd George and Clemenceau that "he had always felt that this [the surrender of German war criminals] was the weak spot in the Treaty of Peace."[324] While in transit from America to France, Wilson had implicitly disapproved of any plans for a trial of Wilhelm II by telling reporters: "I am not wholly convinced that the Kaiser was personally responsible for the war or the prosecution of it. There are many evidences that he was coerced to an extent, that the war was the product of the Great General Staff by which he was surrounded. . . . The Kaiser was probably a victim of circumstance and environment. In a case of this sort you can't with certainty put your finger on the guilty party."[325] In Paris, Wilson did agree that Holland was "morally obliged to surrender the Kaiser, but he wished to make it as easy for her as possible," presumably by avoiding saber-rattling.[326] When Lloyd George panicked that Wilhelm II might be about to return to Germany, Wilson somewhat priggishly said that legally the kaiser "had the right to leave the country" if he wanted to, although allowing that this was undesirable.[327]

Nowhere were the differences between the American and European viewpoints more stark than in the peace conference's commission on war criminals, grandly named the Commission on the Responsibility of the Authors of the War and the Enforcement of Penalties. It was chaired by Lansing, who, like Wilson, seemed to have forgotten his earlier interest in war crimes trials.[328] His objections to Allied proposals for war crimes trials became so frequent that, at one meeting Lansing skipped, Pollock, the British solicitor general, sitting as chairman in Lansing's absence, joked, "I shall make a reservation on behalf of the United States."[329]

Lansing was driven by two motivations: a narrower kind of legalism that would not allow prosecutions for which there was no clear precedent, and a muted American sensitivity to British and French outrage. Recommending a formal condemnation of Wilhelm II rather than an unprecedented trial that broke the principle of sovereign immunity, Lansing suggested the commission conclude:

> Restrained by reverence for law which is inseparable from that high sense of justice which is essential to social order, the nations, which have suffered so grievously, may be unable to mete out through judicial channels retribution to the guilty. . . . [In] the name of those who sacrificed their lives that liberty might live, in the name of the helpless who endured unspeakable atrocities, in the name of those whose ruined and plundered lands bear witness to the wickedness of the accused, in the name of humanity, of righteousness and of civilization, an outraged world denounces as infamous and demands the judgment of the ages against Wilhelm of Hohenzollern, once German Emperor and King of Prussia, etc. etc. etc.
>
> . . . [I]n view of the immunity from suit and prosecution which a Monarch and Chief of State enjoys according to the municipal law of every civilised country and also according to the Common Law of Nations, and lest because of this immunity from judicial process, the ex-Kaiser escape the condemnation which his misdeeds require, the . . . sub-Commission recommends that, instead of attempting to hale the ex-Kaiser before a Court of Justice for which there is no precedent in the accepted Law of Nations, an International Commission of Inquiry be instituted to investigate and to report upon the extent of the responsibility of the ex-Kaiser from the political, legal, and moral point of view for the acts of the German authorities civil and military in violation of the laws and customs of war.[330]

This was met with predictable horror by the Allied delegations, who did not merely claim to speak for the war's victims, but had to account to them in their own domestic politics.[331] It is far less likely that a British or French or Belgian diplomat could, or would want to, say, as Lansing did: "The people of the world demand that in some form the judgment of the world should be registered, but at the same time we are all nations which have a very high reverence and veneration for the law, and for submission to the rules of law. If there is no instrument of justice by which we can operate, we may be helpless, but it does not prevent us from registering our abhorrence of these acts."[332] Lloyd George and Clemenceau were aware of the difficulties of trials but had nevertheless chosen them. Lansing, constrained by his narrower version of legalism, would not go so far.

Except, of course, when the victims were Americans. Then Lansing managed to widen his otherwise cramped version of legalism. Pollock said, "When the Lusitania was sunk, the Americans, in spirit that we should expect of them, called upon the world to decry and denounce such outrages." The top French delegate, a law professor, added that "when the Lusitania was sunk, when women and children were sent to the bottom ... [i]t was the United States then that cried loudly ... against such outrages." He bitterly continued: "I cannot ... believe that the United States will not be with us at the end, and that they will not come with us when we want to have right and justice prevail against those outrages. What is the good, men, of saying that right is the master of the world if you come out scot-free, as it were, after such crimes, because no technical law exists?"[333] Making a self-interested exception to his loftiness, Lansing said that the *Lusitania*

> approached, to my mind, very nearly an act of war on the part of Germany against the United States, and it is reasonable to suppose that it might be included in a judicial proceeding in which the United States would take part. I do not wish to commit myself directly upon that, but I feel that there is a possibility of such an interpretation of the position which the United States will take,—we have been, I will say, in a measure, unwillingly compelled to take into account not our feelings but our conception of what justice demands, and what the law imposes upon us.[334]

Lansing here came out with much the same kind of legalism as Britain and France: still insisting on trials, but prepared to take a broader view of what was a war crime.

Wilson and Lansing yielded no ground. At the end of these increasingly bitter deliberations, Wilson ordered Lansing to write "a minority report rejecting High Tribunal and opposing trial of Kaiser."[335] After filing a lengthy memorandum outlining their disagreements with the Allies, the American delegates concluded that America would not participate in the creation of the proposed war crimes tribunal, nor would it send cases before it.

In this memorandum, Lansing and James Brown Scott, the other American delegate, wrapped themselves in their version of legalism.[336] The Americans drew a distinction between offenses "of a legal nature" and those of "a moral nature," which were not necessarily the same thing (although, of course, Americans had loudly criticized German submarine warfare as both illegal and immoral). The lines between the two had been blurred, Lansing and Scott wrote, in a slap at the Allies, "due in large measure to a determination to punish certain persons, high in authority, particularly the heads of enemy States, even though heads of States were not hitherto legally responsible for the atrocious acts committed by subordinate authorities."[337] Lansing and Scott added that the Americans objected to the fact that "[i]t was frankly stated [by the Allies] that the purpose was to bring before this tribunal the ex-Kaiser of Germany, and that the jurisdiction of the tribunals must be broad enough to include him even if he had not directly ordered the violations."[338] To the contrary, Lansing and Scott cited an 1812 U.S. Supreme Court case that exempted sovereigns from "judicial process."[339]

For Lansing and Scott, what the Allies had in mind was simply bad law. The two Americans argued against punishments "created after the commission of the act," and insisted that a head of state could only be tried by his own country, not by others. "The laws and customs of war are a standard certain, to be found in books of authority and in the practice of nations," Lansing and Scott wrote. "The laws and principles of humanity vary with the individual, which, if for no other reason, should exclude them from consideration in a court of justice, especially one charged with the administration of criminal law." Aggression, the Americans thought, was not a crime against positive law, and the most they would accept was a formal reprimand. The American delegates wrote, "These are matters for statesmen, not for judges."[340]

Lansing and Scott did manage to leave some room for prosecuting war crimes against Americans. They wrote that America could set up "a military tribunal within its own jurisdiction to pass upon violations of the laws and customs of war" for crimes "committed upon American persons or American property."[341]

But perhaps the most important fact underlying Lansing and Scott's reservations was America's relatively limited wartime suffering. They revealingly concluded that they had "confined themselves to law in its legal sense, believing . . . that to have permitted sentiment or popular indignation to affect their judgment would have been violative of their duty as members of the Commission on Responsibilities."[342] In other words, Lansing thought that the British and French delegates had been swept away by public opinion, whereas Lansing had not. Of course, Lansing had been furious when Americans had been the victims of German war crimes, as in the sinking of the *Lusitania* and the *Sussex;* but he was above all that now. One cannot conceive of a French or British foreign secretary writing such words. In the 1945 negotiations leading to Nuremberg, Robert Jackson would specifically repudiate Lansing and Scott's views as immature.[343]

With this memorandum, the Wilson administration washed its hands of the issue of war crimes. Wilson would concentrate his efforts on the larger goal of establishing a League of Nations, leaving cruder projects like war crimes trials to lesser legalists like Lloyd George and Clemenceau. In the end, Wilson reluctantly agreed to include provisions for war crimes trials in the Treaty of Versailles, emphasizing Germany's offense in violating Belgian neutrality.[344]

In one of their final debates on the issue, Wilson and Clemenceau managed to sum up neatly the core difference between American and European positions. Wilson told Lloyd George and Clemenceau, "You think me unfeeling. But I constantly struggle against emotion, and I have to exert pressure on myself to maintain my reliability of judgment." Clemenceau replied, "Nothing is accomplished without emotion. Was Jesus Christ not carried away by passion the day he chased the money changers from the Temple?"[345] The passions that swept away Europeans left no lasting imprint on Woodrow Wilson.

AFTER LEIPZIG

The debacle of Leipzig drives home the difficulties of putting on war crimes trials. Allied demands had seemed unimpeachable when they were formed, and German resistance had been seen as yet another sign of the incorrigibly wrong-headed nature of Germany. But as the issue curdled, the Allied pursuit of German war criminals invited disaster: it made the Allies look vindictive and weak; it divided America and Britain and France from each other; it showed that Germany could get away with failing to comply to the Treaty of Versailles; it kept wartime passions from cooling; and worst of all, it galvanized the German right and thus helped to undermine democracy in the Weimar Republic. For many thoughtful leaders, most notably Churchill, Leipzig was proof of the folly of entrusting a political problem to legal methods.

During the Great War, Allied leaders knew the risks they were taking by pressing for trials of German war criminals, but in an abstract way. After Leipzig, the problems were depressingly concrete. No one could pretend that idealism alone would be enough to bring such a task to a successful conclusion.

Constantinople

THE CONSTANTINOPLE WAR CRIMES TRIALS, had they not fallen apart, would have been remembered as comparable only to Nuremberg and Tokyo. In April 1919, an Ottoman court—created under massive British pressure—had before it some of the most important leaders from the wartime Ottoman government: men who had once held the mighty titles of minister of foreign affairs, minister of justice (two of them), party secretary-general, and even grand vizier. They were there to stand trial for war crimes and for the 1915 genocide of about a million Armenians.[1] The Constantinople tribunal also held trials for the deportation and slaughter of Armenians from Yozgat and Trebizond. British and Ottoman jails were crammed with cabinet ministers, provincial governors, senior military officers, and other major war crimes suspects. Out of the eight Ottoman leaders who drew up the decree taking the empire into war against the Allies, fully five of them—the grand vizier, the *shaikh ul-Islam* (the top religious official), the president of the council of state, and the ministers of justice and public instruction—wound up in custody.[2]

And yet the tribunal has been completely forgotten in the West, except among some Armenian communities.[3] Constantinople is the Nuremberg that failed. What Constantinople shows, most of all, is that the enormous political difficulties of mounting prosecutions against foreign war criminals can be so great that a tribunal can *crumble*. With the collapse of the Ottoman Empire came the collapse of the tribunal. There is as much to learn from failure as from success.[4]

British efforts at international justice after the Great War focused on Germany (see Leipzig chapter). But there were also more universalistic strands in British war crimes policy. The Constantinople trials were driven at first by a striking display of British idealism and universalism. Even though the Armenian victims of the 1915 massacres were foreigners (albeit Christians), the British public and much of its elite were outraged. The British government was egged on by an influential pro-Armenian lobby. This all rested on a liberal concept of universal rights: Britons did not think that the fact that Armenians were not British citizens excluded them from the protection of law.

British liberalism manifested itself in another related way. Britain's universalistic indignation found its expression in legalism: a demand that the Young Turks be held individually criminally accountable. The domestic standards of British due process would be called into service in demands for trials, not summary punishment. As early as May 1915, the Allies formally accused the Ottoman Empire of crimes against humanity—a category that is usually thought of as being established only thirty years later, in the London Charter for the Nuremberg tribunal. Following up on this declaration in 1919, Britain pressured the defeated Sublime Porte into setting up a special court-martial in Constantinople. Ironically, Britain's own legalism worked against its hopes of punishing the Turks. As they tried to set up trials, the British realized that finding sufficient evidence, like testimony from scattered Armenian witnesses and documents secreted away in Ottoman archives, would be dauntingly difficult.

But Britain was also in many ways self-serving. During World War I British prisoners of war were often abused by Ottoman authorities. This spurred Britain on to demand justice for its own soldiers, in much the same way that German and Japanese cruelty to Allied prisoners of war would in World War II. This self-serving element in Britain's outrage at the Ottoman Empire was both a blessing and a curse. The British government proved more eager to prosecute Turks for war crimes against Britons than against Armenians. By 1920, the question of justice for the Armenians had been lumped in with efforts to try Turks who had mistreated British prisoners, and with a purge of Turkish political prisoners. British demands caused a nationalist backlash among Turks.

So the project degenerated, until all that was left was a group of Turkish prisoners in indefinite British custody. When the British cabinet realized this, it reasserted its commitment to due process, ordering the release of those Turks who could not be prosecuted; but by then the entire enterprise was clearly headed for failure anyway. The end was still stunningly embarrassing. As Turkey descended into civil war, in 1921, Mustafa Kemal Atatürk's Nationalists took hostage a handful of British soldiers, and proposed a prisoner swap: all the Britons in exchange for all the war crimes suspects in British custody. Even though the British Foreign Office suspected many of these men of atrocities against Armenians, Britain agreed to the deal. Torn between the demands of its legalism and the need to protect its own soldiers, Britain scrapped what might have been a Nuremberg.

Britain

Taking the Lead

The Constantinople affair was a British creation, almost as much as Nuremberg was American. Three-quarters of the Allied fleet in the Aegean were British, and Britain had fought the biggest campaigns against the Ottoman Empire: Gallipoli, Egypt, Palestine, and Mesopotamia.[5] (As Lloyd George said to Clemenceau, "The other Governments had only put in a few nigger policemen to see that we did not steal the Holy Sepulchre!")[6] And more than any of the other Allied and Associated Powers—France, Russia, and America—Britain took the plight of the Armenians seriously.

France, although it had a small number of troops on the ground in Turkey, let Britain take the lead. Like Britain, France's preoccupation was with German war criminals, not Turks. When, at an Allied conference in London in December 1918, Arthur Balfour, Britain's foreign secretary, asked that Talaat's name be added to a declaration calling for Wilhelm II's trial, he got a lukewarm response from Clemenceau: "Talaat and the others could be brought in later on. But he [Clemenceau] would deprecate mixing them up with the ex-Kaiser. He thought for the moment people were not particularly interested in Talaat. It would be sufficient to begin with the chief culprit, the ex-Kaiser, and his principal accomplices."[7] Clemenceau was quite explicit about a lack of public concern for the Armenians. So, while France did go along with some of Britain's less unrestrained demands, France kept the emphasis on Turkey's role in starting World War I.[8] France took some interest in this issue, but spent much of its time in 1919 pursuing rapprochement with Francophile Young Turks and haranguing the British about petty issues. While France shared Britain's legalism and its outrage at Germany, France seems to have been much less enthusiastic about pursuing the perpetrators of the Armenian massacres.[9]

America's position was more complicated. Despite the anguished pleadings of Henry Morgenthau Sr., America's ambassador in Constantinople,[10] the American government did not take serious measures to dissuade the Young Turks in 1915.[11] America did not threaten war, although some historians think that might have saved the Armenians.[12] Although many Americans sympathized with the Armenians, there was no pro-Armenian lobby or outcry comparable to that in Britain. There were some American protests in 1916, but Lansing admitted that his State Depart-

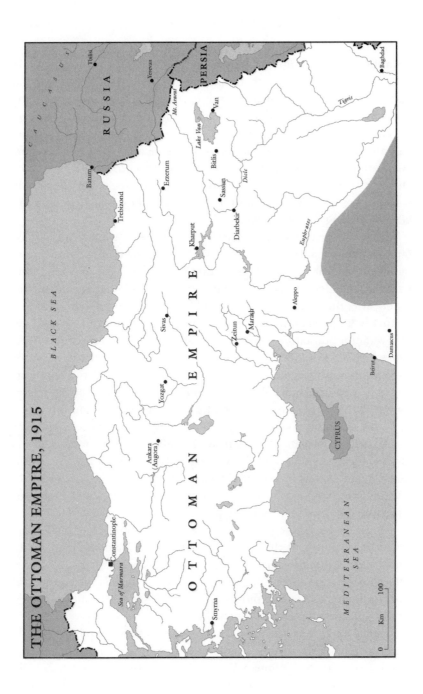

THE OTTOMAN EMPIRE, 1915

ment had actually been keeping some of the facts about the massacres from the American public.[13] For America to take steps against the Ottoman Empire would have meant embroiling the United States in a war that it had hitherto struggled mightily to avoid. The extermination of the Armenians did prompt an American tilt toward the Allies.[14] But Woodrow Wilson would keep America neutral for two more years, and even when he entered the war against Germany, he made a point of not breaking off relations with the Ottoman Empire.[15] In the end, in 1917 it was the Ottomans who broke ties with the Americans, not vice versa.[16] Britain, in contrast, was already at war with the Ottoman Empire in 1915, and lost little by making threats.

Wilson was of course the preeminent advocate of international law, but he came to fear that Allied efforts regarding war criminals were more punitive than just. Instead, Wilson supported the League of Nations and national self-determination—including an independent Armenia. When, after the war, Lloyd George and Balfour proposed sending troops to Turkey "to prevent the Armenians from being massacred," Wilson was evasive and opposed to sending American troops to enforce territorial issues.[17] "Not having declared war upon Turkey," wrote the chief of the Near Eastern division of the American delegation to the Paris Peace Conference, "we were always, during the period of discussion, outsiders, impotent to affect the actual course of the negotiations or put our stamp upon the decisions taken."[18] At the Paris Peace Conference, Lansing led the American delegation's split from the Allied plans for war crimes trials, specifically writing that "the United States could not institute a military tribunal within its own jurisdiction to pass upon violations of the laws and customs of war, unless such violations were committed upon American persons or American property, and that the United States could not properly take part in the trial and punishment of persons accused of violations of the laws and customs of war committed by the military or civil authorities of Bulgaria or Turkey."[19] American officials offered some assistance with gathering evidence against the Young Turk war criminals, but America mostly preferred to leave the remote problem of the Constantinople trials to Britain.[20]

Russia's position was simpler. There seems to have been little genuine legalism, just tsarist wartime politics. Russia had special Armenian units fighting against the Ottoman Empire, and in 1915 wanted to use the Armenian massacres as a way of rallying its Armenian troops. Perhaps Russia would have championed trials for the Young Turks after the Great War, but after 1917 the preferences of tsarist Russia were not of much import. There is no sign that the Soviet Union took an interest in British and French projects, and it is unlikely that Leninists would have wanted to taint themselves with Western colonialism. If there was to be justice for the Armenians, Britain was the only Allied power that would deliver it.

British and Ottoman Christians

British fury at Ottoman atrocities was no new phenomenon. In 1879, William Ewart Gladstone waged his epic electoral campaign in Midlothian against Benjamin Disraeli's Tories largely on the basis of Disraeli's support of the Ottoman Empire against Russia.[21] This, thundered Gladstone, was a deal with the devil. The Ottoman Empire's subjugation of Bulgaria had won it Gladstone's lasting enmity.[22] In his famous broadside, *Bulgarian Horrors and the Question of the East,* published in September 1876, Gladstone had written:

> [W]e now know in detail that there have been perpetrated, under the immediate authority of a Government [Turkey] to which all the time we have been giving the strongest moral, and for part of the time even material support, crimes and outrages, so vast in scale as to exceed all modern example, and so unutterably vile as well as fierce in character, that it passes the power of heart to conceive, and of tongue and pen adequately to describe them. These are the Bulgarian horrors; and the question is, What can and should be done, either to punish, or to brand, or to prevent?[23]

Gladstone's fury was enough to doom Disraeli's tilt toward the Ottoman Empire, which the Tories saw as a way of checking Russia. There was no equivalent popular moralism in any other European country.[24] At the very end of his career, Gladstone devoted his final foray in public life to denouncing the Ottomans again, this time rallying not to the side of the Bulgarians but that of the Armenians.[25]

That Gladstonian tradition was very much in evidence by 1915. More so than any other European power or America, Britain had largely humanitarian motives in its initial outrage at the 1915 Armenian massacres. British sensibilities, accustomed to a self-appointed role as protector of Christians under Ottoman rule, were genuinely shocked by the reports of slaughter in the Turkish interior.

More cynical interpretations do not hold up well. To be sure, Britain had no objection to fomenting unrest among Ottoman subjects, as spectacularly demonstrated in the Hashemite-led Arab revolt. But it is clear that Britain's motives were not just to weaken the Ottoman Empire: Britain thought the Armenians were militarily useless and repeatedly refused to have anything to do with Armenian uprisings.[26] As for propaganda, Britain's efforts focused mostly on (largely unsuccessful) efforts to implicate German consuls in the Armenian atrocities.[27]

In contrast, both Russia and France saw the Armenians as potentially useful in the war against Turkey. France saw the arrival of a wave of Armenian refugees in Egypt as a military opportunity, recruiting the able-bodied Armenian men to go fight at Gallipoli.[28] Russia had been fomenting Christian uprisings against the Ottomans since before the Crimean War.[29] When war broke out with the Ottoman Empire, Tsar Nicholas II, belatedly discovering a hitherto well-hidden regard for his Armenian subjects, had recruited Armenians. Russia fielded four much-decorated Armenian volunteer units in Russia's Caucasus Army, which saw bloody clashes against Enver's forces in the winter campaign of 1914, and organized three more volunteer units in 1915.[30] Sergei Sazonov, Russia's foreign minister, hoped to arm the Armenians.[31] Russia took advantage of the 1915 slaughter to recruit desperate and embittered Armenians into its army.[32] And, of course, Russia also had its eye on the Straits and on Armenia as a future protectorate.[33] Unlike Russia, with its Armenian soldiers, Britain had little to gain from publicizing the atrocities. Russia lost interest, and after the Bolshevik Revolution in 1917 was not about to do anything to bring the Young Turks to justice. But Britain stuck with the issue until years after the war had ended.

Armenian Horrors

The 1915 Armenian massacres were met with the same kind of fury as the "Bulgarian horrors." At all levels, Britons clamored for punishment of the Turks responsible for the slaughter.

Most important, some of the most powerful members of the cabinet were horrified. Lloyd George wrote, "From the moment war was declared, there was not a British statesman of any party who did not have it in mind that if we succeeded in defeating this inhuman Empire, one essential condition of the peace we should impose was the redemption of the Armenian valleys for ever from the bloody misrule with which they had been stained by the infamies of the Turk."[34] Balfour, who by 1918 was foreign secretary, was consistent in his calls for the trial of Talaat, Enver, and Djavid. Balfour's successor, Lord Curzon, who was, as these things go, far less anti-Turkish than Lloyd George,[35] was horrified at Ottoman war crimes against British prisoners and at the Armenian massacres. He told the cabinet "that he had no desire whatever to deal gently with the Turks. The Turks had voluntarily sided with Germany; they had treated our prisoners with unexampled barbarity; they had massacred hundreds of thousands of their own subjects. They therefore deserved any fate which was inflicted upon them."[36]

The pro-Armenian mood was also strong in British society generally. Whitehall was not enthusiastic about the idea of trying the Young Turks ("The weapon of personal responsibility, whether effective or not, is one which will get blunted by too frequent use," wrote a Foreign Office official),[37] but the government was under tremendous pressure from below.

Spurred by an effective pro-Armenian lobby, Parliament and press alike were in full cry.[38] For instance, in Parliament, the influential Viscount James Bryce[39]—one of the most prominent friends of the Armenians—asked what could be done "to save what remains of the Christian population of Armenia." Such protests were taken seriously within Whitehall.[40] In a widely distributed pamphlet based on another speech in Parliament, Bryce wrote, "the only chance of saving the unfortunate remains of this ancient Christian nation is to be found in an expression of the public opinion of the world."[41] Into the fall of 1915, the drumbeat in Parliament kept up, with members of the House of Lords accusing the Ottoman Empire of making "government by massacre part of their political system,"[42] and of proceeding "systematically to exterminate a whole race out of their domain."[43] The government replied that "when the day of reckoning arrives the individuals who have perpetrated or taken any part in these crimes will not be forgotten."[44]

These sentiments were amplified by several influential pro-Armenian organizations and Christian relief groups, most of them set up in the late 1890s in response to earlier Ottoman massacres: the Friends of Armenia, the Anglo-Armenian Association (founded by Bryce), and the British Armenia Committee.[45] These groups were well connected; in 1919, the chairman of the British Armenia Committee managed to meet with both Lloyd George and Curzon. Arnold Toynbee, perhaps the most respected foreign-policy expert of his day, was a prolific member of the British Armenia Committee's propaganda subcommittee.[46] In 1915, he published a widely read pamphlet accusing the Ottomans of planning "nothing less than the extermination of the whole Christian population within the Ottoman frontiers."[47]

The mass media played its role, too.[48] One of the London editors of the Boston-based *Christian Science Monitor* started sending his correspondent's cables directly to the Foreign Office. Blaming Talaat and Enver, the reporter wrote of "massacre on wholesale scale accompanied by brutalities hitherto unheard of."[49] Far from shunning such stinging reporting, the Foreign Office went so far as to ask the British embassy in Petrograd whether they could get photographs of the atrocities, or of refugees.[50]

British diplomats took careful note of international humanitarian sentiment. Atrocity reports flooded in,[51] as did pleas from Armenians and pro-Armenian groups.[52] The pope sent a letter to the sultan in September 1915, asking for end to the killings.[53] The picture, in short, is of a democracy in high dudgeon.

Of course, not all of Britain's rage at Turkey was because of the slaughter of the Armenians. In World War I, Turkish prisoner-of-war facilities acquired a special reputation for inhumane conditions, much like Japanese prisoner-of-war camps in World War II.[54] At the end of the war, the return of British prisoners set off another wave of anti-Turkish sentiment as stories of Turkish cruelty circulated in Britain. In January 1919, Admiral Somerset Calthorpe, the British high commissioner in Constantinople, angrily lectured Rechid Pasha, the Ottoman foreign minister:

> I said that the released prisoners were now arriving in England and were relating their experiences, and that the same indignation which I had felt myself was already showing itself as prevalent throughout public opinion in England, as evidenced by the news telegrams which were reaching this country. . . . [T]he treatment of these prisoners . . . cut at the very root of any such [pro-Turkish] feeling. With regard to the Armenians, knowledge of what had happened was only now becoming really known. In this case also, the signs of public indignation were perfectly clear.[55]

It was no exaggeration when, in March 1919, Richard Webb, a subsequent British high commissioner, explained to the Turkish grand vizier why Britain was so consistently angry at Turkey: "I told His Highness that if I had adopted a severe tone in my note to Turkish Government this was merely in order that I might be a true interpreter of sentiments of British Government and people."[56]

"Crimes against Humanity": The May 1915 Threat

Britain's outrage was from the first expressed in legalistic terms. As early as 1915, British officials sounded all of the themes that are usually thought of as having been born at Nuremberg: individual criminal responsibility of leaders, the importance of due process as it had evolved at home in Britain, and even the notion of crimes against humanity.

Although Britain's motives were mostly high-minded, it was not quick to act during the genocide.[57] Russia made the first diplomatic protests.[58] This, of course, was anything but untainted idealism. When, in late April 1915, Russia asked its French and British allies to join in a threat to the Sublime Porte,[59] the Russians made no secret of their domestic necessities. After meeting Russia's ambassador, Sir Edward Grey, Britain's foreign secretary, wrote, "in order to satisfy Armenian opinion in Russia, his Government are anxious to make a public declaration."[60]

Ironically enough, cynical Russia moved faster than idealistic Britain. Britain's initial official reaction to Russia's proposal was unenthusiastic. (Théophile Delcassé, France's foreign minister, agreed immediately.)[61] After Britain failed to reply until mid-May, Sergei Sazonov, Russia's foreign minister, had to ask again. Britain was still uncertain about the situation on the ground.[62] Unlike much of the British public, cautious Foreign Office diplomats had no stomach for formal threats. Grey worried, "A message to the Porte would have but little effect in restraining them from reprisals on Armenians—and we ourselves have no direct knowledge of what has been occurring at Van and elsewhere."[63] So Sazonov was told that while Britain would consider drafts, "[W]e do not possess sufficiently trustworthy data on which to base such a message, and that it is doubtful if the publication of such a message would have the desired effect, and might indeed lead the Porte to adopt serious measures against the Armenians."[64]

Sazonov quickly sent a draft text to Britain and France.[65] His proposed declaration did not mince words: "In face of these fresh crimes committed by Turkey against Christianity and civilisation, Allied Governments announce publicly to Sublime Porte that they will hold all the members of the Ottoman Government, as well as such of their agents as are implicated, personally responsible for Armenian massacres."[66]

Britain was familiar with the legalistic principle of individual punishment. Britain had recently threatened Turkish ministers with personal responsibility—but, self-servingly, "for action agst. British (and French) nationals sent to Gallipoli: and it is undesirable to use the threat too frequently." Another Foreign Office official wrote: "Official publications in London, Paris and Petrograd will not save the life of a single Armenian." Grey did not see much point in a public pronouncement, although he did want to bring Turkey to justice eventually: "With the Turks in their present mood I am afraid such public announcements will have no effect whatever beyond possibly inciting them to be still more oppressive on Christians of all nationalities. We can do no good & we might do harm. Moreover our hands will be quite free, with or without an announcement, to exact reparation when we are in a position to do so."[67]

There was a strong universalist current in Britain's condemnation of the Ottoman killings of Armenians. Sazonov's draft referred to "these fresh crimes committed by Turkey against Christianity and civilisation." Britain accepted the general idea of a war crime that transcended national borders without much debate, but, strikingly, balked at another point: Sazonov had couched the issue in overtly pan-Christian terms.

By 1915, Britain was moving fitfully from pan-Christian solidarity toward a truly universal conception of human rights. In 1876, Gladstone's fury at the "Bulgarian horrors" and at subsequent attacks on Armenians had had a strong element of High Church Anglicanism to it. By the 1910s and 1920s, British humanitarianism was still often—although not always—couched as a kind of pan-Christian solidarity in the face of Muslim cruelty.[68] Western diplomatic telegrams were thick with almost unconscious references to Muslim barbarism, and the victims were regularly referred to by the British not as Armenians but as "native Christians."[69] But while Russia was comfortable framing the issue as civilized Christendom under attack by barbaric Islam, Britain was not. "[W]ould it not be well," asked the British ambassador in Paris, "from a British point of view, to omit from the declaration respecting massacre of Armenians proposed by Russian Minister for Foreign Affairs . . . the word 'Christianity',"[70] so that Turkey would be accused simply of "crimes . . . against civilization." Britain preferred to see this as an issue of civilization versus barbarism, not Christians versus Muslims. (Delcassé wanted to strike the words "against Christianity and civilisation," leaving it simply as "crimes."[71])

To mollify the British, Sazonov came up with a compromise solution that rings familiar decades later. The British ambassador in Paris reported that "Monsieur Sazonov will insert in published declaration 'against humanity and civilisation.' "[72] So it was, of all people, Sazonov who coined the famous phrase "crimes against humanity"—fully thirty years before Nuremberg would make it a household term.[73]

Possibly by now convinced of the facts of the massacres, and quite likely nudged along by public pressure, Grey agreed to the declaration,[74] which was duly published on May 24. Morgenthau Sr., presumably to his considerable satisfaction, delivered the threat to the Sublime Porte:

For about a month the Kurd and Turkish population of Armenia has been massacring Armenians with the connivance and often assistance of Ottoman authorities. Such massacres took place in middle April . . . at Erzerum, Dertchun, Eguine, Van, Bitlis, Mush, Sassun, Zeitun, and through Cilicia. Inhabitants of about one hundred villages near Van were all murdered. In that city Armenian quarter is besieged by Kurds. At the same time in Constantinople Ottoman Government ill-treats inoffensive Armenian population. In view of these new crimes of Turkey against humanity and civilization, the Allied governments announce publicly to the Sublime Porte that they will hold personally responsible [for] these crimes all members of the Ottoman Government and those of their agents who are implicated in such massacres.[75]

Rather than simply shoot the Young Turkish leadership, the Allies wanted to see justice done. Talaat, Enver, and their subordinates risked not just war, but trial; their deeds were seen by the British not as acts of state but as crimes.

From Leipzig to Constantinople

Despite its slow start, Britain was as good as its word when the war was won. Once Britain began to fixate on bringing Wilhelm II to trial, the cabinet quickly added in the Young Turks. Britain's outrage at Germany for starting the Great War was more self-serving than its concern for the Armenians, and it was the former that drove British war criminals policy after World War I. In much the same way, the Holocaust would take second place in Allied planning for Nuremberg after the crime of aggression.

When Britain drew up its list of ninety-seven suspected war criminals, mostly Germans, it included nine Turkish leaders in a separate category for the Armenian massacres.[76] At the Paris Peace Conference, the commission looking into war crimes considered Turkey's guilt alongside Germany's. In the commission's report, the Ottoman Empire was accused of secondary responsibility for aggression (primary responsibility went to Germany and Austria), plus "systematic terrorism" for the death of over 200,000 Armenians.[77]

There was support at the highest levels for punishing Turks as well as Germans. On November 20, 1918, the Imperial War Cabinet debated Lloyd George and Curzon's proposal of trying Wilhelm II and the Hohenzollern crown prince. This was not enough for Balfour, the foreign secretary: "I must put in a plea for Talaat and Enver, who certainly ought to be hanged."[78] At the Allied conference in London in December 1918, Balfour once again called for Talaat's punishment alongside Wilhelm II, pointing specifically to the Armenian massacres. Balfour singled out "people under the ex-Kaiser, such as Talaat, who had deliberately committed murders; and those individuals should also be brought to trial."[79]Thus, with public pressure and elite sentiment largely in accord, in 1919, Britain began to make good on its promise of May 1915.

At the end of World War I, the Ottoman sultan's regime was led first by Ahmed Tevfik Pasha and then Damad Ferid Pasha, grand viziers most notable for accommodating the victorious Allies.[80] Talaat, Enver, and the other major Young Turk leaders had fled to Germany. But the sultanate still faced pressure from the main Young Turk organization, Ittihad ve Terraki (the Committee of Union and Progress, or CUP), still active in spirit and in various offshoot parties after being formally outlawed.[81] Later, the sultanate would be confronted by Atatürk's Ankara-based Nationalist uprising. But despite these domestic challenges, Ahmed Tevfik and then Damad Ferid, hoping to ingratiate themselves with the Allies and thus win a generous peace, were most threatened by Britain's easy willingness to hound the collapsing Ottoman Empire with British military strength.[82]

Thus, in his first appearance at the Paris Peace Conference, in June 1919, Damad Ferid preempted Allied anger at Ottoman war crimes:

> In the course of the war nearly the entire civilised world was shocked by the recital of the crimes alleged to have been committed by the Turks. It is far from my thought to cast a veil over these misdeeds, which are such as to make the conscience of mankind shudder with horror for ever; still less will I endeavour to minimise the degree of guilt of the actors in the great drama. The aim which I have set myself is that of showing to the world with proofs in my hand, who are the truly responsible authors of these terrible crimes.[83]

To rehabilitate Turkey, Damad Ferid tried to shift blame for the Armenian massacres away from Turkey generally—which was where, he thought, Europeans tended to put it—to the Ittihadists specifically. He asked the Allies to press a recalcitrant Germany to extradite Talaat, Enver, and Djemal ("the three very guilty persons") to face trial, and to seize their German bank accounts.[84]

The Ottoman sultanate had good reason to fear Britain. After the Ottoman Empire's capitulation in October 1918,[85] Britain had a massive occupation army: over a million men. Technically, Constantinople was not occupied (it would be formally occupied only in March 1920), but Turkey's coasts were under the British navy and the Ottoman capital was full of British and French troops.[86] Lloyd George and Edmund Allenby, at the peak of his power after taking Jerusalem, had no compunctions about browbeating the Ottomans.[87] In a typical display of British high-handedness, Allenby (as a British official recorded) told the Turkish foreign minister

> that if he thought he had come all the way to Constantinople to argue these points he was mistaken: he had brought certain demands which had to be carried out by the Turkish Government: that his time was short and that he had no more to say.
>
> The interview ended.
>
> The Minister had almost visibly shrunk into nothing. The Minister of War (a man in his sixties) had not even got in a word. The Staff Officers in the corridor had not even unpacked their maps and papers. It was a sad party that disappeared down the Embassy staircase. It began to dawn on them, I think, how Palestine and Syria had been conquered.[88]

It was on that kind of deliberate intimidation that the trials rested. Small wonder that Damad Ferid was, in Lloyd George's dismissive description, "pliable."[89]

Pressuring the Sublime Porte

Britain started mulling proposals for trials in 1919. Since November 1918, two Ottoman commissions—the Fifth Committee of the Ottoman Parliament and the special Mazhar Inquiry Commission—had been collecting evidence and holding hearings, a bit like similar commissions preceding Nuremberg and The Hague. But these Ottomans commissions investigated corruption and military ineptitude, too, as well as the Armenian massacres.[90]

In January 1919, Calthorpe, Britain's high commissioner in Constantinople, asked London for permission to start pressing Turkey to turn over suspects for mistreating British prisoners of war and for Armenian atrocities. Calthorpe, wanting "some fresh form of action" to protect the Armenians against oppression that reportedly stopped short only of massacres, wrote: "I can think of nothing more likely to be efficacious than to authorize me to demand immediate arrest and delivery to Allied Military Authorities of such persons against whom there appears to be a prima facie good case."[91] The sultan, Calthorpe thought, would be glad to move against the Ittihadists. Calthorpe knew that such efforts would be backed by "powerful assistance" from Allied troops, and would drive home to the Turks their defeat and protect the Armenians.[92] Calthorpe told Rechid Pasha, the Ottoman foreign minister: "I was certain, speaking as a private Englishman and without any instructions, that these [abuses of British prisoners, and the Armenian massacres] were matters on which His Majesty's Government had an inflexible resolve: the authors of both would have to be punished and with all rigour."[93]

Turkey quickly obliged, although not without trepidation. Sultan Mehmed VI was prepared to shuffle his cabinet to install more vigorous ministers on this issue, but nervously warned the British that the "guilty are members [of the] largest and strongest organization in country [Ittihad ve Terraki] and if they see themselves the subject of really serious action it is likely that they would grow desperate; he fears an outbreak against himself and those who share his views, which include ultimate friendship with and dependence on Great Britain."[94] The sultan, according to an earlier note from Calthorpe,

> knew that His Majesty's Government desired the punishment of those guilty of barbarous treatment of our prisoners of war as well as of those responsible for the massacres, and he was ready to cause the arrest and punishment of every single person we might desire, and in accordance with our desire. Only he feared that if he took action on a large scale, it would provoke a revolution, and he himself would be overthrown and probably killed, without any good coming of it. If he did take strong action, he wanted to know if he could count on the support of the Allies, or would they merely hold aloof saying it was a purely internal Turkish affair.[95]

Ahmed Tevfik's cabinet followed their sultan's line. As Calthorpe noted, Rechid told him that

> he would be prepared to adopt any recommendation that I might make to him. With regard to the Armenian massacres, it was not merely the intention but the firm decision of the Government to punish the guilty. A Court Martial was already engaged in trying them, and granted only a little time, justice would be done. Public opinion in Turkey was de-

manding this, and only the Committee of Union and Progress, which possessed a powerful organization, were opposing it: the Government were acting with the support of public opinion and he hoped he might count also on that of H.M. Government. He said that he himself was insisting on the infliction of proper punishment and that he would resign from the cabinet if this were not done.[96]

The Ottoman interior minister drew up a list of sixty people in Constantinople responsible for Armenian massacres, who would soon be seized.[97]

The prospects seemed bright. Calthorpe asked Curzon for "authority, without the consent of the Turkish Government, to arrest Enver, Talaat, and their leading confederates, if he could do so." Curzon and the cabinet agreed. Curzon thought that "Admiral Calthorpe would hardly have asked for it [arrest authority] unless there was information that Enver was somewhere near."[98] If he was, Calthorpe never found him.

With that clear mandate from London, on January 18, Calthorpe once again harangued Ahmed Tevfik, telling him and his foreign minister to "have proper punishment inflicted on those responsible for treatment of prisoners of war and for Armenian massacres and they professed their readiness to carry out our wishes."[99] When one important suspect in the Armenian massacres escaped Turkish jails, Calthorpe furiously reminded the grand vizier "that when massacres became known in England British statesmen had promised civilised world that persons concerned would be held personally responsible, and that it was firm intention of His Majesty's Government to fulfil promise."[100] Calthorpe demanded more arrests to compensate, and the grand vizier, evidently realizing the "extreme gravity of matter," agreed.[101] Two days later, the Porte started the first wave of arrests, both of suspected war criminals and of Turks opposing the armistice—a total between fifty and a few hundred.[102]

Calthorpe thought the arrests "very satisfactory," and planned more. The captives were "little known in Europe, but of great importance. . . . My colleagues are deeply impressed by this mark of energy and good intentions on the part of Turkish Government."[103] Calthorpe headily envisioned the capture of the notorious top seven or eight wartime Turkish leaders—including Talaat and Enver—hiding out in Germany:

It is only natural that at present moment when Turkish Government are arresting minor members of Committee here, they should be anxious to secure great criminals who have fled to Germany, but we must allow them credit for attempt, and effect of arrests of those here would be

121

enormously enhanced if almost simultaneously we could lay hands on Djemal, etc, and I would beg you to leave nothing undone in order to obtain this. It would be enormously valuable.[104]

Balfour carefully noted the names of the top seven, planning to insert them in the peace treaty with Germany.[105] "Effect of arrests has been in every way excellent and has, I think, somewhat daunted the Committee of Union and Progress at any rate in Constantinople," Calthorpe reported.[106]

It was easy for Britain to be high-handed. British soldiers were not making the arrests, so there were no great risks in a firm war crimes policy. The Foreign Office found the fragile Ottoman regime easier to push around than Germany.[107] No less than Balfour, who despised Talaat and the Young Turk leadership, kept a watchful eye on the process, demanding the arrest of a former finance minister for whom he bore a particular animus.[108]

In February, Turkey arrested about thirty prominent Ittihadist leaders, including a former interior minister and the leading Ittihadist intellectual.[109] The most important arrests came in March. In early March, Damad Ferid, soon after replacing Ahmed Tevfik as grand vizier, told his provincial authorities,

> All the higher and lower officials should know that from today onwards all tyranny, injustice, atrocities, deportation, and massacres are banished from this country. . . . The authors of these evils are not only considered by Ottomans as not belonging to the nation, but they are severely condemned by the entire civilized world. We regard these persons who have been so dangerous to their fellow mortals with a pity mingled with horror. However, every civilized Government has the duty of punishing all those who make themselves guilty of crimes against humanity and against liberty.[110]

So on March 10, Damad Ferid arrested twenty-two more prominent Young Turks to face trial before a special court-martial.[111]

It was an altogether remarkable catch, comparable only to Nuremberg and Tokyo. Topping the list was Said Halim Pasha, who had been the grand vizier from June 1913 to February 1917—including during the 1915 massacres.[112] Other captives had served as justice minister, finance minister, minister of public works and governor of the Lebanon, interior minister, minister of public instruction, yet another justice minister, and a foreign minister.[113] There were plenty of slightly lesser lights, too: a

former *shaikh ul-Islam,* a former head of the political section of the direc-
torate-general of police, and the owner of the nationalist newspaper *Is-
tiklal.*[114] The *shaikh ul-Islam* when the Ottoman Empire issued a declaration of *jihad* against the Allies was too ill to be arrested and instead was
under surveillance.[115] (The former finance minister wanted by Balfour
evaded arrest.[116]) Some seventeen of the top men were suspected by the
British of command responsibility for the Armenian atrocities.[117] "Altogether they are a good bag," noted the Foreign Office.[118]

These kinds of dramatic arrests continued, aiming at eminent Turkish
leaders: a former director of intelligence,[119] a former Senate president,
and the commander of the garrison at Yozgat, the site of some of the
most infamous Armenian massacres. The backbone of provincial administration was also now in jail, with an impressive list of former *valis* (provincial governors) from Smyrna, Bogazlian, Mosul, Broussa, and Diarbekir.[120] By April, Ottoman prisons held no less than 107 suspects.[121]

No matter how pliant the sultan and grand vizier,[122] these arrests would
foment nationalist unrest.[123] The Ottoman cabinet's choices of men to
arrest were often noticeably politicized, to the anger of Ittihadists. Calthorpe admitted to Balfour that the "list of persons selected for arrest
bears traces of having been partly inspired by motives of political vengeance." Such accusations would dog British efforts, but Calthorpe was
unruffled: "This matters little, as the majority of the persons arrested
deserve to be put on trial, but it is somewhat unfortunate in-as-much as
this High Commission is widely credited with responsibility for all the
arrests, and the Turkish Government are naturally not unwilling in present circumstances that this impression should prevail."[124] This highly
public wave of arrests of prominent diplomats was a risky thing in a country as wretched as Turkey. Even Calthorpe, no Turcophile, warned of
"something approaching despair regarding Turkish national future."[125]
Already, there were signs of nationalist backlash—even before Atatürk's
revolt gained steam.[126]

Britain preferred to fight backlash by pursuing war criminals. Enver,
for instance, was still widely seen as a great hero, complete with wild
rumors of his returning to expel the Allies. But British military intelligence thought that such rumors only "show the necessity of apprehending as many of the Leaders of the Committee of Union and Progress
and anti-Entente elements as possible, and of conducting an intelligent
and sober campaign of propaganda." Trials, in other words, would quell

nationalism. The War Office hoped to "spread the truth about the war and dispel the fog of illusions prevailing throughout the country."[127]

The pace of arrests had outrun whatever mechanisms the British might have had in mind for trying the suspects. Many of them would presumably come before an Allied tribunal to be set up by the Paris Peace Conference, but this was still up in the air as late as June 1919.[128] This haphazardness left Britain looking less like the instrument of impartial justice and more like a bully.[129]

After the March arrests, Webb, the deputy high commissioner, presciently began to warn that Britain might undermine Damad Ferid's legitimacy. Webb wrote that it had been "practically impossible" to find and arrest suspects without Ottoman support, and was "anxious lest we overdrive a willing horse." Britain had asked Damad Ferid for more arrests, but Webb wanted to "proceed gently and not in haste."[130]

Even Damad Ferid might not have been a totally willing horse. To be sure, he told Webb repeatedly that the "hopes of himself and his master the Sultan were centred after God in (. . . H.M.) Government," and promised that those Turks "guilty of cruelty to prisoners and of Armenian massacres" would be "arrested and punished." But, Damad Ferid admitted, the lists of these suspected war criminals had somehow disappeared from the Sublime Porte's archives—possibly incompetence, or Ittihadist sabotage, or a hedge by the new grand vizier. Webb had planned to demand that the Turks suspected of abusing Britons and Armenians be turned over to British custody, but he skittishly decided that he "did not think it polite at a first interview to point out that we had made so large a demand."[131] The risks of backlash were becoming alarmingly clear.

The Ottoman Extraordinary Courts-Martial

Soon after the March arrests, the Ottomans opened a special Turkish court-martial. There were four major trials: for Armenian massacres and deportations in Yozgat and in Trebizond, of Ittihadist leaders, and finally for wartime Turkish cabinet members. There were also lesser trials for atrocities against Armenians in Harput, Mosul, Baiburt, and Erzinjan. More trials—for atrocities against Armenians in Adana, Aleppo, Bitlis, Diarbekir, Erzerum, Marash, and Van—were planned but never held.[132]

The tribunal almost instantly proved itself politically explosive. In April, the court handed down its first judgment in a case against Kemal Bey, the lieutenant governor of the Yozgat district (*sandjak*), and Major

Tevfik Bey, commander of the Yozgat police, accused of carrying out the deportations of Armenians there. Decades before Nuremberg and the *Yamashita* case, this was a command-responsibility conviction on something very close to crimes against humanity. Echoing the 1915 Allied declaration, the court convicted the two men of acting "against humanity and civilization." The two men, the court ruled, had

> issued awesome orders to their subalterns at the time of the deportations of the Armenians. Acting under these orders, their underlings (first) (fell on the Armenians) and, without regard to ill-health, treating men, women and children alike, organized them into deportation caravans.
>
> ... [I]llegal orders were handed down for the murder of the males. . . . [T]hey were premeditatedly, with intent, murdered, after the men had had their hands tied behind their backs. . . . The officials then practiced all methods of murder. . . . Nor did they make any attempt to prevent further killings. . . .
>
> All these facts are against humanity and civilization. They are never compatible in any manner to human considerations.
>
> Moslem supreme justice consider these events as murder, pillage, robbery and crimes of enormous magnitude.[133]

Tevfik was sentenced to fifteen years of hard labor, and Kemal to death.[134]

This death sentence sparked a blast of nationalist unrest. The Ottomans hanged Kemal, trying to dodge nationalists by surreptitiously doing it in the afternoon rather than in the morning as would be usual. British officials were satisfied with this first move by the "special Courts-Martial now trying persons responsible for deportations and massacres of Christians during war. This is first instance of condign punishment for participation in massacres. It remains to be seen whether Government will have courage to take equally drastic action on any large scale especially in regard to highly placed criminals."[135] But this was hardly the time for more drastic moves against war criminals. Kemal's funeral was a disaster. Perhaps a thousand Ittihadists gathered to pay their respects, with wreaths reading, "To the innocent victim of the nation." British intelligence officers fumed that the "weakness of the present Government in allowing a funeral of this kind to take place is unpardonable, especially as the man is one of no importance and a criminal."[136] A British intelligence report described a wild scene:

The MOLLA, who directed the ceremony was a certain DERGHIAN SHEIKH MOUNIB EFFENDI. . . . Mounib Effendi ordered Dervishes to attend the ceremony. Many officers and soldiers were present, as well as the students of the medical college. One of the students, holding a bunch of flowers in his hand stood at the head of the grave and made a speech from which the following are some extracts, literally translated; "Hark oh people! Hark oh Musslmen! He whom we leave lying here is the hero KEMAL BEY. The English have been ejected from Odessa, let us drive them out of Constantinople. What are you waiting for? This is our duty. We must destroy the English who have brought our doom, and with the help of God we will soon be able to crush their heads."

After this student, another man made a speech in the same strain. It was evident that the tone of both speeches was one calculated to incite revolt. The Dervishes themselves admitted this, and gave details about the funeral.[137]

Calthorpe was enraged: "The perpetrator of crimes, the nature of which would send a shudder through any civilized Community, was treated as a hero and martyr amongst Moslems; but then, his victims were Christians."[138]

Worse, the trial had not convinced Turks that they had done wrong during the war. Even the Ottoman government's supporters "regard executions as necessary concession to Entente rather than as punishment justly meted out to criminals," Calthorpe wrote.[139] "Not one Turk in a thousand will think that any other Turk deserves to be hanged for massacring Christians," a Foreign Office diplomat complained. The Ittihadists "stand to make a good deal of capital out of these punishments if they continue, & more still if they cease." The official even considered using an Allied court instead: "If the Grand Vizier is too frightened to proceed with penalties he might be glad to hand the offendors over."[140]

On April 27, the court nevertheless opened its trial of the wartime Turkish leadership. Before it stood the most prominent men arrested in March, including Said Halim Pasha and others. There were also charges against top Young Turks who had fled to Germany and were thus being tried in absentia, including Talaat and Enver.[141] The five military judges of the Constantinople court heard the Ottoman attorney general's command-responsibility indictment of Talaat, Enver, and the other top Young Turks:

The principal subject matter of this investigation has been the event of the disaster befalling the deported Armenians. . . . The disaster visiting the Armenians was not a local or isolated event. It was the result of a premeditated decision taken by a central body composed of the above-mentioned persons; and the immolations and excesses which took place were based on oral and written orders issued by that central body.[142]

There would not be even a roughly equivalent moment until 1945, when Nazi leaders stood accused of crimes against humanity at Nuremberg.

But at the same time, the Constantinople tribunal was starting to be destroyed by politics. British military might was dissipating fast. From a peak of over a million soldiers, the British army presence in the Ottoman Empire had dwindled by the summer of 1919 to 320,000 soldiers—a cut of over two-thirds. Sticking to a timetable—reminiscent of the original one-year time limit for America's military participation in Bosnia after the Dayton accords—Britain inexorably shrunk its own authority.[143] Worse still, Britain had helped Greece occupy Smyrna, and reports of Greek atrocities undermined what limited public credibility Britain still had in Turkey.[144]

Despite its promising start, the British came to view the ongoing Ottoman court-martial with considerable jaundice. Damad Ferid, after Kemal's funeral, may have realized the dangers of nationalist backlash. "Political prisoners in Turkey rarely remain in prison long," wrote a Foreign Office official. "If they are not despatched early they manage to escape either by a private intrigue or at the next coup d'état."[145] Another time, the Foreign Office groused about "the beating around the bush which is common to all Turkish judicial proceedings"[146] and about "the dilatory procedure of the Turkish Court Martial and the constant risk of prisoners escaping."[147] A Reuters correspondent shook his head at "the constant resignations of officers and officials of the [Ottoman] Special Military Court, the interminable delays of procedure, the tendency of Crown counsel to allow all sorts of side issues to be dragged into the case, and above all, the fact that the authorities allowed the only person hitherto executed [Kemal] to be given the funeral of a patriotic martyr by their opponents."[148] Another diplomat complained that Ottoman "judicial procedure was so incompetent, and their methods of guarding the offenders so inadequate, that they themselves realised that there was a danger of the criminals escaping justice unless some other measures were taken."[149]

If Turkish justice could not be trusted, Britain would look to its own courts. On May 1, the Ottoman foreign minister asked to retain custody of some of the lower-level war crimes suspects on the British lists; Webb refused, promising that Britain's own trials "will be conducted with scrupulous regard to justice and that facilities will be provided for the attendance of all relevant witnesses."[150]

In May, Britain got a rude shock from the Ottoman courts-martial for the wartime Ottoman cabinet ministers and for the Trebizond massacres: "26 of the accused are to be released as there is no case against them."[151] Then Webb, the deputy high commissioner (Calthorpe was in Smyrna), got word that the Ottomans, under Ittihadist pressure, were about to free a total of forty-one prominent prisoners "guilty of the most heinous crimes" from Seraskerat prison[152] (evidently without Damad Ferid's authorization).[153] Webb acted fast. On May 28, the British military suddenly deported sixty-eight Turks from Ottoman custody to British detention at Mudros and Malta[154]—emptying out the jails of the Ottoman courts-martial.

All of the prominent Turks who had been in Ottoman hands, from Said Halim down, were now held by Britain.[155] "There are some very important members of the C.U.P. among them & the fact that we hold them safely in custody at Malta may be very valuable to us," cheered a Foreign Office diplomat. "Hussein Jadid, Ismail Djanbolat & Ahmed Agahif are particularly valuable catches & I notice the that the list includes Rahmi, the ex-Vali of Smyrna & Said Halim, ex-Grand Vizier." Also on the list were "12 ex-Ministers or politicians of the 1st rank," who wound up at Mudros; "41 ex-Ministers, politicians or ex-Valis of slightly lower rank," headed for Malta; and 14 soldiers accused of mistreating British prisoners of war.[156] Calthorpe, once so enthusiastic, had given up on Ottoman justice. He wrote: "Even if there were no reasons for fearing that these men would be set free either by the Authorities themselves in a panic or as the result of a popular upheaval, yet the proceedings in connection with their trials have been so dilatory and half hearted as to render them little less than a farce."[157]

With the most important indicted Turks now either hiding out in Germany or in British custody on Malta or Mudros, the Ottoman court-martial was left toothless.[158] British officials seemed incapable of referring to the tribunal without using the word "farce." More often than not, the court was pronouncing sentence on men who stood no chance of appearing before it. Of seven men being investigated by one of the courts-martial, five were fugitives and one had been hauled off to Malta by the British.[159] "This trial has long been a farce," wrote a British diplomat.[160]

The sultanate, hard-pressed by the nationalist opposition, was not above using the tribunal as a pretext for purging Ittihadists. A substantial proportion of those in Seraskerat prison were charged with crimes in the Armenian massacres, but many others were accused unsubtly of "disturbing internal security."[161] Other prisoners, with ties to the nationalists, had a way of escaping from jails in the most suspicious of circumstances. The trial of two former cabinet ministers was called off when one of them managed to flee.[162] One night in August, twenty armed men mysteriously appeared and freed from Seraskerat three prominent Ittihadists with close ties to Talaat and Enver.[163]

To appease the nationalists, the Ottomans began to free some of the prisoners. In June 1919, one hundred Turks were under arrest; but fifty were freed in one swoop, plus a few more on subsequent occasions.[164] "Owing to Nationalist Movement, Courts Martial more of a farce than ever," wrote a Foreign Office diplomat. A few British officials had belatedly come to realize the dangers of running roughshod over the Turks: "Safe custody difficult and further deportations politically undesirable."[165] By July, the War Office had given up on the Ottoman trials, which would "almost certainly result in the escape without punishment, except of a nominal character, of many of the worse offendors." Instead, the War Office preferred to write provisions for international trials into the peace treaty being hammered out in Paris.[166]

The court-martial did not do much better even when it handed down judgment in its most spectacular case. In July, the Ottoman court-martial sentenced Talaat, Enver, and two other Young Turk leaders to death, and sentenced three others to fifteen years' imprisonment. The tribunal also acquitted two men.[167] But only three of these people were actually in custody: the two acquitted men and Moussa Kiazim, the former *shaikh ul-Islam* sentenced to a jail term. "It is interesting to see how skilfully the Turkish penal code has been manipulated to cover the acts attributed to the accused," wrote Webb, now acting high commissioner in Constantinople, "and the manner in which the sentences have been apportioned among the absent and the present so as to effect a minimum of real bloodshed."[168] The Foreign Office was equally unimpressed: "The net result is that the only person to be punished is Mussa Kiazim Effendi, the free-thinking ex-Sheikh-ul-Islam, & his condemnation is on such flimsy grounds that if he does not escape some other means he will be able to do so by appeal."[169] Sure enough, his sentence was commuted to fifteen years in exile.[170] Soon after that, J. M. de Robeck, the new British high commissioner after Calthorpe and Webb, wrote that the "Court Martial has been such a dead failure that its findings cannot be held of any account at all, if it is intended to make responsibility for deportations and massacres a matter of inter-Allied concern."[171] A bit later, using the well-worn British insult of choice, he called it "more of a farce than ever."[172]

Legalism

One advantage of British trials over Ottoman ones was that they would conform to British standards. British officials simply assumed that they would put on fair British-style trials. The idea of summary executions was dismissed out of hand. In April 1919, Webb, then deputy high commissioner, had insisted on trials: "To punish all persons guilty of Armenian atrocities would necessitate wholesale execution of Turks and I therefore suggest punishment should rather take form nationally of dismemberment of late Turkish Empire and individually in trial of high officials, such as those on my lists, whose fate will serve as an example."[173] Even though he knew that trials would not punish all the guilty, Webb preferred legalism. Nor were these to be sham trials. In the only law review article on the Constantinople trials, historian Vahakn Dadrian was impressed by Britain's commitment to fair trials: "The British were quite sensitive to the need to separate executive from judicial acts and to bar, as much as possible, political considerations from intruding into legal proceedings."[174]

The British were prisoners of their own legalism, often to their considerable chagrin. Even the king yielded before British legalism. King George V was personally concerned with a German general in Turkey, Otto Liman von Sanders: "His Majesty trusts that no mercy or pity will be shown him, and that everything possible will be done to bring him to justice."[175] But Sanders's connection with the Armenian massacres could not be proved, and he went free.[176] When Balfour asked Calthorpe about Djavid Bey, the former finance minister against whom Balfour had a grudge, Calthorpe answered the foreign secretary with legal considerations: "Djavid Bey was undoubtedly deeply implicated in the crimes of which he is accused, and his moral responsibility is enormous. There is, however, a lack of definite proof against him, and it will probably be a matter of considerable difficulty to prove his individual responsibility."[177]

Legalists confronted an unusual problem: the atrocities had been carried out under Ottoman sovereignty. Worrying about potential defenses

that Talaat might offer, in December 1918 Balfour told an Allied conference that the perpetrators of the Armenian massacres "strictly speaking,
had committed no definite legal offences. . . . It was necessary to consider how they could be got at. Talaat had said that the Armenians were
a constant trouble. He had made up his mind to get rid of them, and, in
consequence, he had massacred them *en masse*. That was merely a policy,
and the offenders could not be tried by court-martial, as they had committed no definite legal offence."[178] Balfour said this in the hopes of
bringing the law into line with the demands of substantive justice, not to
exonerate Talaat. To him, a new kind of war crime demanded a new kind
of criminal law; his fear was that British courts might not agree with him.
Similarly, the Greek-Armenian section of the British high commission in
Constantinople wanted "to leave no doubt that Turks accused of having
ordered or executed a policy of extermination of their Armenian or
Greek subjects would become amenable to Allied Jurisdiction."[179] Balfour's problem would later bedevil the planners of Nuremberg, and the
solution was much the same in both cases: putting the atrocities in a new
category of war crime, a crime against all humanity. The term, minted
in 1915, stuck: in January 1919, Calthorpe talked of bringing "to trial
those guilty of crimes against humanity."[180]

The insistence on due process was echoed at lower levels. The Constantinople high commission shared Balfour's assumption that there
must be trials: "As however it will be impossible for any Court or Courts
to try all those implicated in deportations, massacres, etc. it is desirable
that some line of demarcation should be laid down between those we
propose should be tried by the Allies and those who could be proceeded
against in the time to come under the ordinary process of local municipal laws."[181] There is no evidence that the British considered summary
executions or show trials. At the outset, Calthorpe, the high commissioner in Constantinople, asked for permission to demand the arrest "of
such persons against whom there appears to be a prima facie good
case,"[182] rather than simply rounding up prominent nationalists. In January 1919, Calthorpe told the Foreign Office that he was "convinced of
necessity of arriving at perfectly clear decision as to procedure which is
to be adopted for trial of accused, nationality of judges and execution of
sentences before presenting our demand to Turkish Government for
their apprehension. It seems probable His Majesty's Government will
wish to use same procedure in case of Turks as of Germans."[183]

After the March arrests, Webb, the new high commissioner, warned
that it would not be easy to design a judicial process that would be to

Britain's credit, but wanted to try it anyway: "It must be borne in mind that degrees of guilt of accused vary very greatly and that in regard to Massacres question of evidence will be extremely difficult. No less so will be the composition of the tribunal which will judge them, which indeed would seem only capable of formation by such an institution as the League of Nations."[184] By July, British lawyers and diplomats were figuring out the legal status of their Malta prisoners. Curzon—who succeeded Balfour as foreign secretary in October 1919—asked the crown's law officers for a memorandum outlining his legal options, including questions like Britain's legal authority to try Turks, whether the suspects should be returned to Ottoman custody, and what legal provisions needed to be included in the peace treaty.[185]

But having set these legal standards for themselves, the British were forced to admit that they often could not meet them. "It is obvious that in these circumstances it might be very difficult to sustain definite charges against many of these persons before an Allied tribunal," de Robeck, then British high commissioner, wrote of Turks at Malta accused of Armenian massacres.[186] The high commission's Greek-Armenian section admitted, "In very few cases could the section produce a statement of evidence to be placed before a Court."[187] Even when faced with such problems, there was no discussion of steps like executions or show trials. Britain's desire to punish the Young Turks was stymied by Britain's own legalism.

In the chaos of Turkey's descent into civil war, Britain's legalistic intentions were sometimes overwhelmed by events in Turkey. As the Ittihadists and Atatürk's Nationalists grew bolder, Ottoman and British arrests began to spin out of control. Often the arrests were of those suspected of war crimes. The high commission's Greek-Armenian section—whose very existence was a testament to institutionalized British solicitude for Ottoman Christians—had a list of over six hundred Turks "against whom lies a strong suspicion of complicity in 'Atrocities'."[188] The Foreign Office overruled a request from the director of military intelligence to free a former senior Turkish commander, because he was accused of atrocities against Armenians.[189]

But the arrests were not always for war crimes. In April 1919, the British asked the Sublime Porte to turn over a group of Turks composed both of minor war criminals and simple thugs, only some of whom were accused of persecuting Armenians. Britain's charges were not always criminal: "Insolent and contumacious," or "A dangerous intriguer."[190] De Robeck admitted that "[i]n practice, this . . . was very freely construed. The deportees were selected from a list of persons whom the Turkish Government had themselves considered dangerous or criminal enough to place under arrest, and the real object was to avert, at a highly critical moment, the possibility of those politically most dangerous and most criminal, being let loose in Turkey."[191] British motives were not always pure. "The people on these lists are drawn from all classes of the community," wrote one diplomat, "& while we hold them we shall possess a pledge for the good behaviour of the C.U.P. elements remaining at large. In case of need we might make it known that they will be regarded as hostages."[192]

In the slide into civil war, British officials did not always resist the temptation to arrest subversives. By de Robeck's calculation, at least twenty-two of the men in Malta were, not to put too fine a point on it, innocent: those who "cannot be said to have been actually concerned in the policy that led to, or in the commission of, the atrocities."[193] British lists sometimes explicitly distinguished between political prisoners and suspected war criminals.[194] The charge against one prisoner was simply "Being one of the Ministers responsible for the fate of the Turkish Empire"; a former minister of public instruction was held for "His rank"; and Enver's father, a former war minister, was weakly charged with "Peculation."[195]

This situation was meant to be temporary. It was assumed that those who had been sent to Malta primarily for "public security in time of war and only secondly for their indirect complicity in massacres of Christians" would be freed after a peace treaty was ratified, if the Ottomans felt confident enough. But those accused of Armenian massacres would face an international tribunal.[196]

Then there was the role of incompetence. The British lists, rife with misspellings, were often baffling.[197] "Most of the names or descriptions are hopelessly vague or incorrect," a Foreign Office official complained.[198] Even the lists of those charged with Armenian massacres were far from reliable: "These are offendors against Ottoman Christians & we have always contemplated that there [sic] surrender to the Allies for trial would be provided for in the Turkish treaty," the Foreign Office noted. "We have however never had satisfactory lists . . . there seems to be a good deal of doubt between F.O., Consple."[199] "The selection was necessarily made very hurriedly," de Robeck admitted, "and where it was impossible to rely on known facts, general principles were applied."[200]

The British government planned to include its plans for the war criminals in a peace treaty. Until that treaty was signed, trial planning was frozen.[201] The result, de Robeck concluded, was "in many respects unsatisfactory and even chaotic."[202] Even after the signing of the Treaty of Sèvres in August 1920, its war crimes clauses would take time to be implemented, if indeed they ever could be. In October 1920, the British were still talking of trials for the Armenian massacres, as specified in the Treaty of Sèvres, but were slow to set up the tribunal.[203]

British officials knew that leaving these men languishing was improper. De Robeck noted that those accused of Armenian massacres "have now been in British custody sufficiently long to make it desirable that our attitude towards them should be defined as soon as possible." De Robeck was also irritated by the haphazard results of the arrests. He wanted to punish the most guilty, and worried that "the choice of persons . . . placed on their trial should not be determined by the more or less fortuitous circumstance of their being now in custody"[204]—words that would resonate at The Hague now too.

Shrewdly, the prisoners complained that indefinite detention violated Britain's own standards. Ali Munif, who had been Ottoman public works minister in 1917 and was suspected of indirect responsibility for Armenian atrocities, mustered impressive sarcasm:

> I am at a loss to understand the reason of my being detained in Malta indefinitely. There is, of course, the remote possibility that we are held here for the account of the present partisan government in Turkey. . . . It is, however, very hard to believe that Great Britain would act blindly as a gaoler for the good pleasure of the Turkish Government. Therefore, this possibility must be dismissed from the mind.[205]

Ahmed Bey Agayeff, a propagandist, wrote, "I demand neither mercy nor pity: I demand justice, English justice!!"[206]

All of this meant that Britain had no idea what to do with the men at Malta. So, in their confusion and high-handedness, the British simply let the Turks languish without being charged. This is no triumph of legalism; the gentlest thing one can say is that it seems more a matter of ad hoc confusion than of systematic policy. At no point in these documents did anyone argue for holding the Turks indefinitely; to the contrary, officials worried about keeping them in jail as long as they had. The men were taken on the assumption that there would be trials, and as it became increasingly obvious that there would not be, the British did not want to just free their prisoners and thus held on. When the cabinet finally noticed these long-term detentions (see below), it moved to free the Turks. The end was far less impressive and purposeful than the beginning, but the entire process, though far from perfect, was shot through with British legalism.

Backlash

Underlying the collapse of the Ottoman courts-martial was the threat of Atatürk's explosion of Turkish nationalism, which would destroy the sultanate.[207] Atatürk's Nationalists now controlled most of Anatolia and Thrace. The days of pliant Turkish cabinets were numbered. In October 1919, the beleaguered Damad Ferid resigned, to be replaced by a more pro-Kemalist grand vizier, who immediately sent a minister to open talks with Atatürk.[208]

Meanwhile the Paris Peace Conference was drawing up plans for a treaty, including war crimes trials. The British delegation had given up on writing provisions for the extradition of Talaat, Enver, and five other top Young Turks into the Treaty of Versailles with Germany, and Germany had rebuffed the Porte's requests for extradition. Still, Britain planned to insert war crimes clauses, modeled on those in the Treaty of Versailles, into other peace treaties, "with a special provision to cover those responsible for the Armenian and Greek massacres."[209] De Robeck wanted Talaat, Enver, and the other five to face the equivalent of Article 227 of the Treaty of Versailles—the article arraigning Wilhelm II. He also wanted to try other perpetrators of the Armenian massacres before an Allied or Turkish war crimes tribunal.[210]

In the end, the Treaty of Sèvres—signed in August 1920—included five articles on war crimes, much like the Treaty of Versailles.[211] One article stipulated that those Turks "guilty of criminal acts against the nationals of one of the Allied Powers shall be brought before the military tribunals of that Power"—covering abusers of Allied prisoners of war. Another article committed the Ottomans to surrender those accused of "the massacres committed during the continuance of the state of war on territory which formed part of the Turkish Empire" to face an international tribunal.[212] The treaty also carved up the Ottoman Empire, including a new independent state of Armenia.[213]

This treaty would not last long. Signing it, Atatürk's Nationalists declared, was an act of treason. When Britain demanded that the new grand vizier crack down on the Nationalists, he resigned instead. Damad Ferid was brought back as grand vizier, in a last-ditch attempt to stave off Atatürk before the outbreak of full-scale civil war.[214] It would not work.

In September 1919, de Robeck, nervous about "the unfavourable general conditions now prevailing" in Turkey, had decided not to ask for any more Turks suspected of atrocities against Armenians and to cease deportations to Malta and Mudros.[215] Two months later, he wrote that the Porte was "so dependent on the toleration of the organisers of the National Movement that I feel it would be futile to ask for the arrest of any Turk accused of offences against Christians, even though he may be living openly in Constantinople." Should Atatürk demand the release of the remaining prisoners, the Sublime Porte might "prefer to risk the displeasure of the Entente Powers rather than break definitely with the Mustafa Kemal party."[216]

British officials would continue to draw up lists of wanted Turks, and a few would even get arrested in all the chaos. But the Foreign Office knew the process was over: "We cannot expect that the Turks will surrender anybody."[217] "[T]here is a regrettably large number of offendors who will never be brought to justice," wrote a Foreign Office diplomat.[218]

By early 1920, Britain was cutting its losses. Six Turks were freed, some for lack of evidence.[219] The director of military intelligence was pressing for releases, forcing the Foreign Office to admit it often was not sure why some Turks were being held.[220] De Robeck, sensing that the Malta and Mudros jails might soon be emptied, was reluctant to free any of the fifty-two Turks at Malta charged with Armenian massacres.[221] (The number of such Turks ranged in British estimates from sixteen to sixty.)[222] The Nationalist revolt gained strength, defeating French forces in Cilicia. In March, Britain took the desperate move of formally occupying Constantinople and declaring martial law there, which did nothing to quell an uprising based in Ankara.[223] The question was no longer which Turks would be tried, but which would be freed.

Churchill Sways the Cabinet

The chaos in Constantinople had managed to avoid the attention of the cabinet. No longer. Winston Churchill, now war secretary, was sick of the whole affair.

Churchill had once been the most pro-Turkish member of the cabinet. Before the war, he had met and liked Talaat. He had been the only minister to push for a pro-Turkey policy before 1914.[224] But during World War I, he became capable of impressive paranoia about Turkish intentions (he once told the cabinet that he "foresaw danger in letting the Sultan be in Brusa, where would gradually collect round him Mustapha Kemal, Enver, Trotsky and others, who would help him build up a huge hostile force, and turn Asia Minor and Arabia into a seething cauldron of trouble"),[225] and suggested using poison gas against Turkey at Gallipoli.[226] By 1920, he wanted to be sure that Atatürk would not be pushed into the

arms of the Soviet Union.[227] Equally important, Churchill had been sting-
ingly criticized for trying to treat German U-boat crews as war criminals
(see Leipzig chapter), leaving him wary of legalistic projects.

The issue of British prisoners dominated Churchill's thinking. He expected a prisoner swap between Britain and Atatürk, and suggested releasing some Anglophile Turks to get the ball rolling.[228] Churchill, the
War Office noted, "remains of the opinion that the expediency of releasing several of our less guilty and less hostile Turkish prisoners should be
considered lest we are compelled to release in the first instance the most
guilty and the most hostile in exchange for British officers and men captured by Nationalist forces."[229] Churchill would have preferred to hold
onto the war criminals; but given a choice between prosecuting Turkish
war criminals and protecting British soldiers, Churchill did not hesitate.

After sounding out a reluctant Foreign Office, Churchill went to the
cabinet in July:

> I circulate to the Cabinet a long list of prominent Turkish politicians,
> ex-Ministers, Generals, Deputies and others whom we are still keeping
> as prisoners at Malta. It seems to me that this list should be carefully
> revised by the Attorney-General, and that those men against whom it is
> not proposed to take definite proceedings should at the first convenient
> opportunity be released. They are a burden and a cost to us while they
> are on our hands, and I am not at all clear how long we are expected to
> go on holding them.[230]

Curzon, now foreign secretary, as well as Churchill's old antagonist
over German war criminals in 1915, met Churchill's challenge.[231] The
Foreign Office argued, variously, that freeing the Turks would undermine Damad Ferid and hand Atatürk a victory; that some sixty-four important Turks should not be freed before a peace treaty was signed;
and—answering Churchill's intimation that there were scant legal
grounds for holding some of the Turks—that the law officers had ruled
that such detentions were "an act of State, the propriety of which cannot
be questioned in any Court of Law."[232]

But Churchill was backed up by the crown's law officers: Gordon Hewart, the attorney general, and Ernest Pollock, the solicitor general. Hewart and Pollock were critical of ineptitude and arbitrariness in the Malta
detentions, but their concern was only with Turks who were suspected of
abusing British prisoners of war, not persecuting Armenians. There were
only six Turks "whose detention on the ground of ill-treatment of Prisoners of War seems desirable."[233]

The cabinet reasserted its legalism against the more dubious arrests made by the high commission in Constantinople. Together, Churchill and the law officers swayed the cabinet:

> The Cabinet had before them . . . a list of prominent Turkish politicians, ex-Ministers, Generals, Deputies, and others, who are still being kept as prisoners at Malta. . . .
>
> The Cabinet agreed—
>
> That the list should be carefully revised by the Attorney-General with a view to selecting the names of those it was proposed to prosecute, so that those against whom no procedures were contemplated should be released at the first convenient opportunity.[234]

Only those suspected of war crimes would be kept in custody.

But it would not be so easy to convict those suspected war criminals. The law officers wanted to throw out any weak cases.[235] A Foreign Office diplomat explained: "Our difficulty is that while we have good reason to know that they are guilty, we have practically no *legal* evidence . . . & that we do not want to prepare for proceedings that will be abortive. Besides this, we shall sooner or later receive demands from the Angora Turks for their release, & we must know which internees we really mean to prosecute."[236] Another Foreign Office official wrote, "There is probably not one of these prisoners who does not deserve a long term of imprisonment if not capital punishment. But . . . it appears that the chances of obtaining convictions are almost nil."[237] Curzon had sent the law officers to look at the still-considerable list of Turks being held for Armenian massacres to see if "there is a reasonable prospect of obtaining a conviction,"[238] and Hewart was reviewing cases of abuse of British prisoners.[239] After it was clear that the chances of convictions in British-style trials were slim to nonexistent, British officials worried that trials that exonerated the Turks might make Britain look bad.[240] Now that the cabinet had reasserted British legalism, British officials feared that they could not meet their own standards.

Putting British People First

In the chaos, Britain remained more interested in punishing crimes against Britons than crimes against Armenians.[241] Britain put most of its energy into the prosecution of German war criminals. The most important British committee gathering evidence on the Central Powers was "concerned only with the ill treatment of British prisoners of war & Brit-

138

ish interned civilians."[242] Hewart, too, was "only concerned with the eight Turks whose prosecution he desires for cruelty to British P.W.," while the Foreign Office fixated on forty-three Turks to be "prosecuted for massacre" under the Treaty of Sèvres.[243]

There were still over one hundred Turks in Ottoman jails, likely to escape at any moment; but, as they were charged either with "general political offences and with massacres, but not with cruelty to British prisoners of War," Britain let them stay in Ottoman custody.[244] When de Robeck warned that he feared Turkish jailbreaks,[245] a Foreign Office diplomat did not disguise his priorities: "I trust that if any of these are offenders against British subjects they will not be allowed to escape."[246] With the signing of the Treaty of Sèvres, de Robeck wondered about the implementation of an article calling for trials of those accused of Armenian massacres.[247] It is perhaps a sign of how serious Britain was about the issue that both Pollock and the Foreign Office had no idea.[248] The universalism of 1915 was a faint memory; by 1920, justice for Britons came first.

"It Is in a Measure Yielding to Blackmail but Seems Justified"

If Britain would take such steps to punish those who had abused its soldiers, what might it do to save some of its soldiers? Atatürk's Nationalists, shrewdly, had taken a small group of Britons prisoner, including Colonel Alfred Rawlinson. This was an inspired choice; his elder brother was the influential Major General Lord Rawlinson, commander of British forces in India.[249] There were, in total, a mere twenty-nine Britons in Turkish custody—but they would come to drive British policy.[250]

It was clear to the Foreign Office what Atatürk had in mind: "to use those [Britons] still detained as the means of pressure on His Majesty's Government to release all Turkish prisoners in Malta including the worst war criminals."[251] Britain knew that Atatürk had found a soft spot: "[T]he Nationalists might like to use what they would call our 'squeamishness' over a couple of officers as a lever to revise the Treaty." Lord Rawlinson asked Curzon to save his younger brother by a prisoner exchange.[252] Curzon preferred not to free any Turks until Rawlinson and the others were freed too.[253]

At first, Britain tried only to free political prisoners, as specified by the cabinet. The Foreign Office insisted that Rawlinson "cannot well be exchanged" for Turks at Malta accused of abusing British prisoners of war or of atrocities against Armenians.[254] But Churchill's War Office was, as the Foreign Office noted, "pressing to release all the internees possible."[255] Of course, any sizable prisoner exchange would be at the expense of international justice. By one accounting (the numbers skipped around depending on which official was doing the counting), there were twenty-five political prisoners, twelve Turks accused of abusing British prisoners of war, and around sixty Turks accused of atrocities against Armenians.[256]

In the spring of 1921, in the midst of the civil war in Turkey, the British started to free the political prisoners.[257] After talks with Atatürk's foreign minister, Britain and Atatürk's Ankara-based government agreed to free sixty-four Turkish prisoners.[258] The law officers "expressly kept out of the agreement" eight Turks accused of cruelty to British prisoners.[259] But according to a list given to the cabinet, thirty-six of those accused of a role in the Armenian massacres were to be freed.[260] At least four of these charges seemed dubious,[261] but that still leaves over thirty men suspected of massive crimes being traded for Rawlinson and the other British hostages.

More would follow. The Foreign Office decided "H.M.G. must contemplate including in the general settlement of Turkey the release of the 43 Turks who remain at Malta on charges of cruelty to native Christians."[262] "We may be able to convict the 8 prisoners charged with cruelty to British prisoners of war," wrote a Foreign Office diplomat, "but all things considered it seems as if we must not count much on enforcing art 230"—the article of the Treaty of Sèvres calling for trial of persecutors of Armenians before an international tribunal.[263] Another official was even gloomier: "We are holding the internees as an international duty under a moribund Treaty of Sevres. It is bad enough that our British prisoners should suffer retaliation because of our discharge of this duty. But it is intolerable if half the internees can really hardly be prosecuted, much less convicted."[264] Britain, much as it might have liked to punish the Turks at Malta, had bound itself to its own domestic legal standards. A legal officer wrote about

> the inherent difficulties with which the prosecution will be faced, if the Military Tribunals, before which these persons are to be arraigned, *require the production of evidence of a character which alone would be admissible before an English Court of Justice.* Up to the present no statements have been taken from witnesses who can depose to the truth of the charges made against the prisoners. It is indeed uncertain whether any witnesses

can be found and it is hardly necessary to dwell upon the difficulty of finding witnesses in a country so remote and inaccessible as Armenia, especially after so long a lapse of time and so many political changes. If the charges made are substantially true, it seems more than probable that the great majority of those who could appear as witnesses against the accused are dead or have been irretrievably dispersed.[265]

Without better evidence from Turkish archives, Hewart could not offer "any opinion" about the chances of successful prosecutions.[266]

By now, Britain was mulling swapping all of those accused of Armenian massacres, except for four "gravely implicated," and the eight charged with abusing British prisoners.[267] Those exceptions aside, wrote Horace Rumbold, the latest high commissioner in Constantinople, the armed forces should be able to use "all the deportees . . . for the purpose of exchange." Five years after the crimes in question, it would be

> practically impossible to conduct a trial which would be fair either to the accusers or to the accused, and *that fact alone seems a good ground for dropping the prosecution. Failing the possibility of obtaining proper evidence against these Turks which would satisfy a British Court of Law, we would seem to be continuing an act of technical injustice in further detaining the Turks in question.* In order, therefore, to avoid as far as possible losing face in this matter, I consider that all the Turks except the 8 and the 4 . . . should be made available for exchange purposes and that we should in the last resort even contemplate the release of the four, should the Angora Government make their release a condition of the release of the British prisoners of war. We should however, insist in any event on the retention of the eight Turks accused of cruelty to British prisoners of war.[268]

The military hoped for a prisoner exchange.[269] The War Office, asking Curzon to drop Britain's claims against even those eight Turks accused of abusing British prisoners, wrote that they felt

> that the release of the British prisoners in Anatolia, whose health is already suffering from continued confinement in conditions of great hardship and privation, is a matter of urgent necessity. They feel that if these prisoners are compelled to remain in Anatolia during another winter, we must expect to learn that several have died in captivity. They consider that it is vastly more important to save the lives of these British subjects than to bind ourselves by the strict letter of the law as regards the Turkish prisoners at Malta.[270]

Not everyone could stomach the abandonment of Britain's war crimes program. A disgusted Foreign Office staffer wrote:

> As Sir H. Rumbold himself . . . seems to recommend the release of the sole remaining Turks in our custody against whom there is any real evidence of implication in the massacres, we can, perhaps, hardly refuse the War Office request that he be offered with all the rest. It is also difficult on humanitarian grounds to resist the W.O. plea that the eight be released as well. . . .
>
> The total release suggested by the War Office virtually tears up Part VII (Penalties) of the Treaty of Sèvres, as we can hardly ask the Turks to hand over these people whom we now release. . . . The whole transaction is tantamount to a complete capitulation to Turkish blackmail.[271]

But another Foreign Office official, Lancelot Oliphant, took it in stride: "[T]he W.O. doubt the feasibility of satisfactory trials being held forthwith; some military authorities have bungled matters outrageously by allowing the escape of the men at Malta; & with winter approaching, the need for securing the release of all our men becomes daily more urgent."[272] Oliphant summed up the collapse of the Constantinople war crimes trials with a bit of cynicism that stands out even by the distinguished standards of the British Foreign Office: "It is in a measure yielding to blackmail but seems justified by present conditions."[273]

Finally, Rumbold was given permission by Curzon and the law officers to negotiate that blackmail: an "all for all" swap, including all the war criminals and even the "bad eight."[274] The Foreign Office was perfectly explicit about putting the release of British prisoners above all else:

> Proposal put forward by War Office and concurred in by Attorney-General and myself is that in last resort eight should be released unconditionally, claim to bring them to trial, whether by Turkish or other courts, being entirely waived. Apart from the difficulty of collecting witnesses so long after offences and therefore of securing conviction which would ensure exemplary sentence, gravity of charges against them, possible deterrent effect of trial and probability that release may lead to withdrawal of part or all of Penalty clauses of Treaty of Sevres were fully realised but held to be outweighed by necessity of obtaining release of our prisoners before the winter.[275]

Atatürk did not disappoint. His negotiator insisted on the release of all the accused war criminals, including those eight. When the Nationalists said that the Turks would face a Turkish court, Rumbold gave up any claims to try them before any court.[276]

There was nothing left but recriminations. As preparations got under way to ship fifty-one Turks from Malta in October 1921, Rumbold resented the "confession of weakness on our part."[277] De Robeck, by now commander-in-chief in the Mediterranean, was undisguisedly bitter at freeing "8 now at Malta guilty of abominable crimes to our prisoners. I feel I have no option but to help Military in the course they have decided on and will therefore arrange transport by Man of war or otherwise as necessary but I consider any concession to Turks highly regrettable and to have any part in the liberation of the 8 Turks specially held as prisoners Malta a deplorable act which is forced on me."[278] The Foreign Office was unmoved: "Deplorable, no doubt, but necessary to obtain release of our prisoners. There will probably be P.Qs [Parliamentary questions] about this."[279] In a faint echo of the public uproar of 1915, *The Times* complained about freeing the eight without trial.[280]

When the deal was done in the early days of November 1921, Rawlinson turned up at Erzerum.[281] He had evidently "suffered abominable treatment," the Foreign Office noted.[282] Britain got back two officers, three other soldiers, and nineteen civilians.[283] Rawlinson got a hero's welcome (reminiscent of American pilot Scott O'Grady's return from being shot down in Bosnia in 1995): an audience with the king and no less than three meetings with Curzon, who "told me he had on many occasions done his best to obtain our release or exchange, without success."[284] It is not clear if Curzon told Rawlinson exactly what those efforts had involved. Rawlinson, like O'Grady, celebrated his freedom by quickly writing a memoir.[285]

Rawlinson's freedom was bought by selling out a substantial amount of international justice. All fifty-nine remaining Turks were freed, without distinctions among political and military prisoners, alleged abusers of British prisoners of war, and accused murderers of Armenian civilians.[286] It is not clear exactly how many Turks suspected of crimes against humanity were set free, because Britain's own estimates had a way of fluctuating from sixteen to sixty.[287] But the number was substantial, especially given that many of them—like Said Halim, grand vizier in 1915—were prominent leaders and thus likely bore some command responsibility. To take one middle-range British estimate, in August 1921 there had been forty-three Turks at Malta accused of Armenian massacres.[288] All of them went free.

The Treaty of Lausanne, signed in July 1923 with Atatürk's triumphant Nationalists, replacing the defunct Treaty of Sèvres, contained no clauses on war criminals.[289] Lloyd George called the treaty an "abject, cowardly and infamous surrender."[290]

FORGETTING CONSTANTINOPLE

The British, humiliated, did not look back. During the planning of Nuremberg, British (and a few American) officials often recalled the disastrous precedent of Leipzig and even the exile of Napoleon to St. Helena; but nobody mentioned Constantinople. Even when casting about for a precedent for the Nuremberg category of crimes against humanity, the Allies did not remember that they had used that precise term as early as 1915.

Today, Constantinople is once again forgotten. Seeing today's efforts in the light of Constantinople makes one more nervous at the prospect of outright failure. In particular, the aftermath of the fiasco in Turkey shows two cautionary examples of what could happen if Arusha and The Hague go the way of Constantinople.

First, the forgetting of the Constantinople trials has been closely linked to the forgetting of the Armenian genocide. Unlike Germany, which made a relatively clean break with its dark past, Atatürk's Republic has never confronted the deeds of 1915 or distanced itself adequately from them.[291] Tansu Ciller, a recent prime minister of Turkey, was typical when asked if Turkey had done enough to address the Armenian genocide. "In the history of every nation, there's war or strife, and controversial incidents like this," Ciller says. "Turkey is no better or no worse than any nation. It is a two-sided story that took place at a time of war. This is not to excuse massacre on both sides."

Of course it is. Or, rather, it is to excuse massacre on the Turkish side. Nor are these apologetics limited to Turkish leaders. A standard history of the Ottoman Empire, published by Cambridge University Press, denies that the Armenians were deliberately killed.[292] The evidence from high-level testimony and from a more complete search of the Ottoman archives, had Britain been able to get such documents as stipulated in the Treaty of Sèvres, would have made it harder for subsequent Turkish governments to deny or minimize Turkish culpability. Trials can help bring out truth.

Second, Britain walked away, but the Armenians did not. In 1919, de Robeck had warned that if the punishment of the Young Turks was ignored, "it may safely be predicted that the question of retribution for the deportations and massacres will be an element of venomous trouble in the life of each of the countries concerned."[293] He was right.

Some Young Turks proved themselves to be almost as disruptive under Atatürk's Republic as they had been before. Ali Ihsan Pasha—the highest-ranked Turkish soldier who had languished to the end at Malta, having been accused of Armenian atrocities—was immediately given command of a Turkish division in Anatolia, to fight Greece.[294] In 1926, Ahmed Shukri Bey and Nazim were hanged for trying to overthrow Atatürk.[295]

Talaat, Enver, and many of the other top Young Turks had fled to Germany in 1918. The Allies had never managed to get ahold of them for trial.[296] Having been failed by both Ottoman and British justice, some Armenians now took matters in their own hands. The guerrilla wing of the Armenian Dashnak party hunted down the Young Turks relentlessly across Europe and Central Asia, in their "Operation Nemesis." One group tracked down and killed Djemal, former navy minister, in Tiflis in July 1922.[297] Said Halim, the former grand vizier, had outlasted both Ottoman and British jailers, only to be killed by an Armenian assassination cell in Rome in December 1921.[298] Enver managed to escape these cells, but died in battle with Bolsheviks in Bukhara in August 1922.[299] Behaeddin Shakir was shot by an Armenian in Berlin in April 1922.[300] And on March 14, 1921, Talaat himself was killed on a street in Berlin, shot once through the neck and brain by Soghomon Tehlirian, an Armenian from Turkey who had lost his family to Talaat's deportations.[301]

These desires for vengeance and justice are just as present today in ravaged places like Bosnia, Kosovo, and Rwanda. They come not just from average citizens or survivors or thugs, but also from the highest levels of government. Muhamed Sacirbey, Bosnia's former foreign minister and one of three top Bosnian negotiators at Dayton, now serves as Bosnia's ambassador to the United Nations and is known among the press as a smooth-talking, Tulane-educated diplomat who puts the Bosnian case in the most American terms. Would Sacirbey expect to see Bosnians hunting down Karadzic and other Serb nationalist leaders, as the Armenians hunted down Talaat and Said Halim? "You know, if there is no justice delivered by the international community, not only would I see that happening, but I would condone it." One of Bosnia's top leaders would condone *assassination*? Sacirbey's explanation would presumably not have sounded so alien to the ears of Soghomon Tehlirian:

I would condone the assassination—delivery of justice—if there was no other alternative path to justice. But we do have alternative paths to justice. And that's why I think the war crimes tribunal is so important. But remember, the concept of even assassination here isn't revenge. The concept is that . . . there needs to be a sense of justice being accomplished. And the war crimes tribunal, frankly, is the biggest hope for that to be done. But if you take away that hope, then what else is left? The Israelis certainly have gone out and hunted down individuals—we know certainly they brought some of them back to stand trial, and that's what I would be in favor of, but I don't know if they've assassinated others. . . . So, I don't see any reason why we . . . would be held to a different standard.

When a war crimes tribunal fails, it is easy enough for a third party to walk away. Britain did not look back after the fiasco at Constantinople and Malta. But the victims did not forget then. Karadzic and Milosevic have a lesson to learn here too, one way or the other.

Nuremberg

T HAT FOUR GREAT NATIONS, flushed with victory and stung with injury, stay the hand of vengeance and voluntarily submit their captive enemies to the judgment of the law is one of the most significant tributes that Power has ever paid to Reason."[1] With that flourish, on November 21, 1945, Robert Jackson opened the American case against the captive leadership of Nazi Germany at Nuremberg. Jackson was a U.S. Supreme Court justice, a former attorney general and solicitor general, now serving as the American chief prosecutor at Nuremberg. There could not have been a more powerful symbol that America, victorious in the greatest war in history, had turned the fate of its despised enemies over to the highest legal authority.

Because of the spectacular success of Nuremberg, it is hard, over fifty years later, to reconstruct the decision to hold the trials without making the choice seem overdetermined.[2] It was anything but. To the three Allies who decided to hold Nuremberg (France, defeated by Germany, played almost no role in the decision), it was not at all obvious that trials were the best way to deal with the defeated Germans.

At the Tehran Conference in 1943, Stalin proposed shooting 50,000 or 100,000 Germans. When he realized that was unlikely, the Soviets tried instead to make Nuremberg a show trial, not too different from those instrumental in Stalin's purges. Stalin did not want to let the process out of his control, risking acquittals or embarrassment.

Not so America and Britain, two liberal states. Both found themselves constrained by their domestic standards. In the end, legalism triumphed; but it was a near thing. At first, Henry Morgenthau Jr., America's treasury secretary, persuaded Franklin Delano Roosevelt to support summary executions for the top Nazi leaders. The British and American publics would have preferred simply to shoot the Nazis, without bothering with a trial. Britain, while insisting on trials for lesser war crimes suspects, called for the execution of the top Axis leaders, until being overruled by America. (The case of Britain does cut against the general tendency of liberal states to adopt legalism—the only case in this book that does not fit the model.)

It was only after Morgenthau's plans for pastoralizing Germany leaked to the press and embarrassed the White House that Roosevelt turned to his secretary of war, Henry Stimson, who argued, against Morgenthau, that war criminals had to be put on trial because of America's own domestic respect for due process. Not only did Stimson argue for trials that conformed to the Bill of Rights, he even drew up the plans for a conspiracy indictment against Nazi organizations on the basis of his own American legal experience fighting a sugar trust—resting the punishment of the SS and Gestapo on American law's provisions for dealing with the American Sugar Refining Company. Harry Truman sent Jackson to represent America at the London negotiations over Nuremberg's charter, and then turned the prosecution at Nuremberg over to Jackson.

Nuremberg was created as the result of unswerving political will on the part of the Allies—in stark contrast to the tokenistic efforts undertaken on behalf of Bosnians, Rwandans, and Kurds. Toward the end of World War II, there was little to dissuade the Allies from punishing Nazis, for two reasons. First, the biggest sticking point in the Leipzig, Constantinople, and Hague processes—the desire to protect one's own soldiers— had been largely obviated by the Allied decision to get Germany's unconditional surrender. There would be few additional risks to Allied soldiers, who were going to be occupying Germany no matter what, in arresting Nazi war crimes suspects in the process.

Second, as in the case of Leipzig, and part of the time in the case of Constantinople, the Allies saw themselves as the victims of German criminality, and were thus resolute in their desire for some sort of justice. Over fifty years later, it is often forgotten that the Allied efforts to punish Germany were undertaken mostly out of anger at the Nazi instigation of World War II. One of the great ironies of Nuremberg's legacy is that the tribunal is remembered as a product of Allied horror at the Holocaust,[3] when in fact America and Britain, the two liberal countries that played major roles in deciding what Nuremberg would be, actually focused far more on the criminality of Nazi aggression than on the Holocaust. Nuremberg was self-serving in ways that are usually forgotten today.[4]

Whatever the flaws and temptations, America and Britain still crafted something spectacular. It is not that liberal states are automatically and unthinkingly legalistic. They can be tempted by nonlegalistic solutions, and are acutely aware of the disadvantages of choosing trials. They are self-centered. But America and Britain were at least partially constrained by a strong influence from liberal domestic norms, which in the end was enough to produce the great trials at Nuremberg.

Faltering First Steps

There was little serious planning of Allied war crimes policies until the eve of victory in Europe. In 1941 Roosevelt vaguely threatened "fearful retribution" for executed French hostages,[5] and in 1942 the Big Three said they would bring war criminals to justice, without being particularly specific.[6] As early as June 1942, the Polish and Czechoslovak exile governments, taking the brunt of Nazi occupation, were asking the Big Three to threaten war criminals with reprisals.[7] As a concession to these pressures, the first concrete step in Allied war crimes policy was the establishment in October 1943 of the United Nations War Crimes Commission (UNWCC), a weak evidence-collecting body that left investigations to its member states, many of whom were under German occupation.[8] ("United Nations" here, as throughout this period, means the Allies.) The UNWCC was criticized for its decision not to include the Holocaust in its purview.[9] By the time Nuremberg was in the works, the UNWCC was unceremoniously killed off.[10]

A more serious step toward Nuremberg came in November 1943, when Roosevelt, Stalin, and Churchill issued their Moscow Declaration. Churchill, its author, wrote to Stalin and Roosevelt that he was "not particular about the phraseology," but thought a tripartite statement "would make some of these villains reluctant to be mixed up in butcheries now they realize they are going to be defeated."[11] Fearing that specificity might provoke German retaliation against Allied prisoners of war, they kept the wording vague.[12] The Moscow Declaration warned that Germans "responsible for, or have taken a consenting part in the above atrocities, massacres and executions, will be sent back to the countries in which their abominable deeds were done in order that they may be judged and punished according to the laws of these liberated countries and of the free governments which will be created therein."[13] The Holocaust was mentioned only in passing as "the slaughters inflicted on the people of Poland," without reference to the Jews. Nor was there much concern for legal niceties: the Germans were to be "judged on the spot by the peoples whom they outraged." And the declaration was pointedly "without prejudice to the case of the major criminals, whose offences have no particular

149

geographical localisation and who will be punished by the joint decision of the Governments of the Allies."[14] There was no mention of a judicial process for that punishment.

The big decisions had not been taken. As the Allied armies drew ever closer to conquering Germany, there was still no Allied war crimes plan. That debate would not begin in earnest until after D-Day.

AMERICA

Nuremberg was largely an American creation.[15] ("Typical American humor," scoffed Karl Dönitz, in his Nuremberg cell.)[16] Britain and the Soviet Union were forced to follow America's lead. Roosevelt's free-wheeling and haphazard administration thus offers the single most important and vivid example of how governments argue about international justice.

This grand American debate over Nuremberg was waged mostly between two of Roosevelt's most powerful cabinet members: Henry Stimson, the secretary of war, and Henry Morgenthau Jr., the treasury secretary. Stimson insisted on trials for the top Nazis; Morgenthau wanted summary executions. In March 1945, Stimson, while emphasizing postwar economic and political issues over the question of war criminals, gave a good firsthand outline of the way the decision was made:

> Never has anything which I have witnessed in the four years shown such instance of the bad effect of our chaotic administration and its utter failure to treat matters in a well organized way. . . . Morgenthau advanced his project for destroying industrial Germany and turning it into a "pastoral" country. . . . Then the President pranced up to the meeting at Quebec in September taking Morgenthau and leaving Hull and me behind, and there he put his initials to the fantastic "pastoral Germany" program which was drawn by Churchill and Morgenthau. Morgenthau came back and told us about it, and the character of the paper leaked out evidently through somebody in the Treasury Department. It was at once torn to pieces by public opinion and the President hastily retreated from his position. At a luncheon with me in the White House he spoke of this paper as something that had been put over him in Quebec and which he had never fathered. I had a copy of it in my pocket, fished it out, and showed his initials at the bottom of it. Then he said he had

made a great mistake and has admitted that with great frankness since. Then for a while Morgenthau was in the doghouse.[17]

While more than a little self-congratulatory, this account is basically accurate.[18] The Morgenthau Plan, which Churchill and Roosevelt initialed at the Québec Conference in September 1944, called for the summary execution of the Nazi leadership as war criminals. But Stimson managed to triumph, insisting that even Nazi war criminals be given the benefit of due process as it had evolved in America.

Protecting Soldiers

Throughout these debates, the Allies were not much hamstrung by what is typically the biggest impediment to the prosecution of war crimes: a terrific reluctance to expose soldiers to unusual risks in order to apprehend suspected war criminals. In January 1943, long before anyone in the White House started thinking seriously about the punishment of war criminals, Roosevelt and Churchill had demanded unconditional surrender from the Axis. When the question of war criminals finally came to the administration's attention, it therefore seemed that capturing the suspects would not require additional risks for American forces.[19] Germany was going to be occupied regardless; no extra risks were required to pursue a firm policy of prosecuting German war criminals.

To be sure, in those rare cases where apprehending war criminals put American troops at unusual risk, America was as eager to protect its soldiers as any other country. Japan did in fact get to impose one term of its surrender—that Hirohito not be dethroned, and certainly not be charged with war crimes. As Stimson noted in his diary, Japan only accepted the Potsdam terms "with the understanding that the said declaration does not comprise any demand which prejudices the prerogatives of his majesty as a sovereign ruler."[20] America was not about to suffer through a devastating land campaign simply in order to try Hirohito. So MacArthur was told not to name Hirohito as a suspected war criminal.[21]

In October 1944, the Combined Chiefs of Staff wanted their field commanders to run speedy trials of captured war criminals who directly affected security or military operations; otherwise, "principally in order to avoid the danger of reprisals," the suspects were to be caught and tried later.[22] The War Department viewed the Soviet Union's Kharkov trials, in 1943, with "grave concern . . . since it fears that such action during the course of the war may lead to reprisals against American prisoners of

151

war."[23] And the White House was aware of the risks that American prisoners of war might face as Germany grew increasingly desperate.[24]

America was as jealous of its soldiers' lives as any state. But because of the preexisting policy of unconditional surrender, during the great White House argument over whether to have trials, the question of protecting American lives mostly did not come up.

"Let Somebody Else Water It Down": Morgenthau

Morgenthau was the most prominent American official who did not want war crimes trials. This was not because he did not want punishment. To the contrary, Morgenthau was more outraged than anyone in the cabinet at Nazi atrocities against Jews[25] (Morgenthau was himself Jewish, a point not lost on Stimson). Morgenthau spent much of 1944 bombarding the White House with proposals for harsh treatment of Germany after the war—part and parcel of which was the summary execution of many Nazi war criminals. He had no patience for plodding legalism. His justice was to be swift and terrible.

Half a century after Nuremberg, it is hard to remember that it was perfectly intellectually acceptable during and after World War II to express doubt—as Arendt did—that Nazi horrors could rightly be lumped under the rubric of municipal law. Morgenthau, in his blazing anger, said, "it's a question of attacking the German mind." He did not shirk from harsh measures:

> . . . [W]hen it gets down to it, it may be a question of taking this whole S.S. group, because you can't keep the concentration camps forever and deporting them somewhere—out of Germany to some other part of the world. Just taking them bodily. And I wouldn't be afraid to make the suggestion just as ruthlessly as it is necessary to accomplish the act. . . .
> Let somebody else water it down.[26]

In another outburst, in a Treasury Department meeting in September 1944, Morgenthau proposed mass deportations of millions of Germans—on the precedent, of all things, of Turkish expulsions of ethnic Greeks while Morgenthau's father, Henry Morgenthau Sr. (see Constantinople chapter), was ambassador to the Ottoman Empire:

> I will give you people an example which I lived through in the eyes of my father. One morning the Turks woke up and said, "We don't want a Greek in Turkey". They didn't worry about what the Greeks were going

152

to do with them. They moved one million people out. . . . They said, "We don't want any more Greeks in Turkey."

Now, whether it is one million, ten million, twenty million it still has to be done. A whole population was moved. The people lived. They got rehabilitated in no time. They moved them.

If you can move a million, you can move twenty million; and you move twenty million. It is just a question; no one has thought about it. It seems a terrific task; it seems inhuman; it seems cruel. We didn't ask for this war; we didn't put millions of people through gas chambers. We didn't do any of these things. They have asked for it.[27]

Morgenthau, an old friend of Roosevelt, was no minor crank. Eleanor Roosevelt called him "Franklin's conscience" and said that her husband treated Morgenthau "as a younger brother."[28] Morgenthau was one of the most powerful men in Washington, and he interpreted his portfolio broadly. On a host of issues, from the Ruhr to reparations, Morgenthau took a hard line against Germany. When Morgenthau's aides balked at smashing the industrial capacities of the Ruhr, Morgenthau snapped, "Why the hell should I care what happens to their people?" He continued: "[F]or the future of my children and my grandchildren, I don't want these beasts to wage war."[29] When the Morgenthau Plan was criticized as immoral, he snapped, "I suppose putting a million or two million people in gas chambers is a godlike action."[30]

At first, Morgenthau dominated the White House's postwar German policy. "Everybody is toying with the thing," he complained, "and here we are with one toe in Germany and just starting on it."[31] Even Stimson at first considered the most expedient policy: simply shooting the Nazi leaders. In notes for a meeting with Roosevelt in August 1944, Stimson jotted:

3. Policy vs. liquidation of Hitler and his gang.
Present instructions seem inadequate beyond imprisonment.
Our officers must have the protection of definite instructions if shooting is required.
If shooting is required it must be immediate; not postwar.
4. Treatment of Gestapo? To include what levels?[32]

Executions were clearly not unthinkable to Stimson and Roosevelt. (One irony: Stimson insisted that his soldiers must be able to claim afterward that they were merely following superior orders—the defense that would be famously discredited at Nuremberg.)

Morgenthau was hardly alone in his fury. In July 1944, General Dwight Eisenhower, the supreme Allied commander in Europe, wanted to "exterminate all of the General Staff," which he figured would be 3,500 people, as well as the entire Gestapo and all Nazi Party members above the rank of mayor. He also might have exiled the German general staff to an "appropriate St. Helena." Eisenhower was initially amenable to letting the Soviets do the extermination, but wanted to reserve special treatment for the 12th SS Panzer Division, which had in June 1944 killed 64 Allied prisoners of war: "I think that the American Army as a unit will handle the 12th SS, every man they can get a hold of. They are the men that killed our people in cold blood. . . . We hate everybody that ever wore a 12th SS uniform."[33] Morgenthau wrote that even Eleanor Roosevelt, "who was a great pacifist before this," approved of Morgenthau's plan for the Ruhr. "It doesn't bother her at all. She said, 'Put the thing under lock and key and shut it down completely.' "[34]

Roosevelt left few written records of his attitudes on postwar Germany, but his instinct evidently was to follow Morgenthau's hard line. After his meeting with the president, Stimson noted that Roosevelt "showed some interest in radical treatment of the Gestapo"[35]—a possible reference to summary executions. Roosevelt, irked by what he saw as a generous War Department proposal to restore Germany, vehemently wrote:

> It is of the utmost importance that every person in Germany should realize that this time Germany is a defeated nation. I do not want them to starve to death but, as an example, if they need food to keep body and soul together beyond what they have, they should be fed three times a day with soup from Army soup kitchens. That will keep them perfectly healthy and they will remember that experience all their lives. The fact that they are a defeated nation, collectively and individually, must be so impressed upon them that they will hesitate to start any new war. . . .
>
> Too many people here and in England hold to the view that the German people as a whole are not responsible for what has taken place— that only a few Nazi leaders are responsible. That unfortunately is not based on fact. The German people as a whole must have it driven home to them that the whole nation has been engaged in a lawless conspiracy against the decencies of modern civilization.[36]

Roosevelt refused to draw a veil over Germany's deeds. To the contrary, he placed the widest possible blame for those deeds. Presumably the element of the Nuremberg trials that would have most appealed to Roosevelt was their educational value: the Germans would be fed soup and truth. It is not at all clear that Roosevelt's first instinct was to give the Nazi leaders the benefit of trials.

"A Better Respect for the Law": Stimson

"Let somebody else water it down," Morgenthau had said. Stimson, Morgenthau's chief rival in making America's policy on war criminals, was just the man for that job. In many ways, Stimson was just the opposite of his voluble cabinet colleague.[37] Morgenthau was a New Deal Democrat; Stimson was a Republican who had served as Herbert Hoover's secretary of state. Unlike Morgenthau, Stimson was a lawyer, a product of the white-shoe American legal establishment. Morgenthau often spoke of the gas chambers. Stimson's diaries almost never mention the Holocaust. Morgenthau pressed for American action to help Europe's Jews; Stimson opposed immigration.[38] Stimson was mostly worried about winning the war; Morgenthau was also obsessed with Nazi atrocities. But Stimson had long been a believer in punishing war crimes; in 1916, he had signed a letter to Woodrow Wilson protesting Germany's deportation of Belgians, "in violation of law and humanity."[39] It was, in the final account, Stimson's cooler head that allowed America to constrain Morgenthau's calls for harsh punishments of German leaders within a legalistic framework.

But Morgenthau held the field at first. Stimson was not above thoughts of vengeance; he once suggested to Morgenthau that SS troops should be put in the concentration camps they had set up for the Jews.[40] But Stimson soon came to resist Morgenthau's sweeping plans for pastoralizing Germany, questioning whether Germany could really be somehow reduced to its 1860 size of forty million. "Well," Morgenthau replied, "that is not nearly as bad as sending them to gas chambers." "I find," Morgenthau concluded, "that Mr. Stimson tires very easily."[41]

Morgenthau was not the only hard-liner wearing Stimson out. Stalin's grisly toast at Tehran—to shooting at least 50,000 Germans—hung on Stimson's mind, and he feared that such mass killings would embarrass the entire war effort.[42] He had warned Roosevelt that

there would be methods used . . . in the liquidation of the military clique in Germany which the United States would not like to participate in directly. I reminded the President of the story he had told . . . of his conversation with Stalin concerning the liquidation of 50,000 German officers and indicated that this rather confirmed my view. Under all these circumstances I felt that the further we were away from North Germany and the less responsibility we had in the conduct of German affairs in that region the better. I felt that repercussions would be sure to arise which would mar the page of our history if we, whether rightly or wrongly, seemed to be responsible for it.[43]

Stimson was clearly repelled at the prospect of Soviet executions, as something beneath America's standards—even for Nazi war criminals.

These standards grew out of Stimson's respect for basic American legal rights, with explicit reference to the Bill of Rights. Stimson, who equated the OGPU with the Gestapo, was horrified at Soviet domestic terror. "Stalin recently promised his people a constitution with a bill of rights like our own," Stimson wrote. "It seems to me now that our success in getting him to carry out this promised reform, which will necessarily mean the abolition of the secret police, lies at the foundation of our success."[44] This was a very American remedy for Stalinism.

Stimson clung to the idea of individual responsibility for war crimes, which would focus Allied vengeance against the guilty rather than all Germans. "In particular I was working up and pressing for the point I had initiated," he wrote,

> namely that we should intern the entire Gestapo and perhaps the SS leaders and then vigorously investigate and try them as the main instruments of Hitler's system of terrorism in Europe. By so doing I thought we would begin at the right end, namely the Hitler machine and punish the people who were directly responsible for that, carrying the line of investigation and punishment as far as possible. I found around me, particularly Morgenthau, a very bitter atmosphere of personal resentment against the entire German people without regard to individual guilt and I am very much afraid that it will result in our taking mass vengeance on the part of our people in the shape of clumsy economic action. This in my opinion will be ineffective and will inevitably produce a very dangerous reaction in Germany and probably a new war.[45]

Stimson's disagreement with Morgenthau was not just about the wisdom of pastoralizing and partitioning Germany. Stimson, after his initial fumblings, became more and more appalled at Morgenthau's idea of summarily killing war criminals.

Stimson's legalism ran deep. Like the Treasury Department, the War Department agreed that the entire Gestapo should be detained. But while Morgenthau wanted to deal with such terror organizations in toto, Stimson and John McCloy, the assistant secretary of war, initially preferred to focus on individual criminal responsibility for specific Gestapo members. Stimson also worried, "How far can we go under the Geneva Convention in educating war prisoners against Nazism?" This respect for law also encompassed a fondness for trials. Stimson's reasoning revealed a blend of pragmatism and ingrained legalism:

> We should always have in mind the necessity of punishing effectively enough to bring home to the German people the wrongdoing done in their name, and thus prevent similar conduct in the future, without depriving them of the hope of a future respected German community. (Those are the two alternatives.) Remember this punishment is for the purpose of prevention and not for vengeance. An element in prevention is to secure in the person punished the conviction of guilt. The trial and punishment should be as prompt as possible and in all cases care should be taken against making martyrs of the individuals punished.[46]

Stimson's insistence on fair trials even led him to yield some of the military's prerogatives. When he won the approval of George Marshall, the chief of staff, for war crimes trials, the two agreed on using civilian judges where possible, rather than military men. Afterward, Stimson wrote in his diary: "It was very interesting to find that Army officers have a better respect for the law in those matters than civilians who talk about them and who are anxious to go ahead and chop everybody's head off without trial or hearing."[47]

The Morgenthau Plan

That desire to chop off heads without trial was quickly enshrined in a now-notorious Treasury Department plan. On September 5, 1944, Morgenthau sent Roosevelt what would become known as the Morgenthau Plan—synonymous with a devastatingly punitive peace. It proposed, among other things, a partition giving large tracts of land to Poland, France, and Denmark, the complete demilitarization of Germany, internationalization of the Ruhr, political decentralization, reparations, and reeducation of the German people.

For the Nazi leadership, the Morgenthau Plan was perfectly clear:

> A list of the arch criminals of this war whose obvious guilt has generally been recognized by the United Nations shall be drawn up as soon as possible and transmitted to the appropriate military authorities. The military authorities shall be instructed with respect to all persons who are on such list as follows:

A. They shall be apprehended as soon as possible and identified as soon as possible after apprehension, the identification to be approved by an officer of the General rank.

B. When such identification has been made *the person identified shall be put to death forthwith by firing squads* made up of soldiers of the United Nations.[48]

Lower-level perpetrators of "crimes . . . against civilization," including racist killings, would get a trial before Allied military commissions, and then swift execution upon conviction. All senior Nazi Party and government officials, as well as the entire SS, Gestapo, and SA, would be detained until a determination was made of their guilt. Nazi Party members and sympathizers, as well as military officers and Junkers, were to be barred from public life. And SS men were to form reconstruction battalions in countries devastated by the war.[49]

Compared to this, prior or subsequent American proposals for punishing war criminals look pallid. Morgenthau did make some concessions to legalism in the belief that the Nazis were criminals and in the willingness to afford some kind of trial for lesser offenders. But what stands out is the call for summary execution for German leaders.

On September 4, in a stunning meeting at the Treasury Department, Morgenthau and some of his top aides discussed how to go about these summary executions. This was not idle talk. Their concern, in fact, seems to have been with making sure that a queasy American military, not used to such things, would not balk at carrying out such orders. Harry Dexter White, a Treasury Department official close to Morgenthau (subsequently found to be a Soviet agent),[50] spoke approvingly of a suggestion made by Major General John Hilldring, a War Department official drafting American occupation plans. Hilldring, White told the meeting,

> said if you could draw up a list of people to present to the commanding officer and the commanding officer has to apprehend them and identify them by some responsible authority and those people are immediately shot that there is not a question of discretion by the military. He has his orders. They didn't know how long that this would be. Hilldring mentioned about 2,500, whether it was in connection with that or not, I don't know.[51]

Hilldring's suggestion of summarily executing 2,500 people went without comment from his colleagues. (In hindsight, once again, Hilldring's position has a sharp irony to it: if there were to be executions, the American army wanted to have the excuse of following superior orders.)

Compared to some rhetorical flourishes by Morgenthau, this may seem a relatively small figure. Morgenthau once suggested eliminating all Nazi Party members; when told by McCloy that there were perhaps thirteen million of them, Morgenthau said there were no more than five million.[52] To get a proper sense of the scale of 2,500 summary executions, consider what the total scale of the American effort against lower-level war criminals would ultimately be.[53] The judge advocate general (JAG) would be given responsibility for war crimes committed either against American troops or in concentration camps liberated by American forces, which led to trials for 1,600 Germans. Of those, over 250 were killed, plus 11 at Nuremberg. In total, Telford Taylor later calculated, by spring 1948, some 3,500 Germans and 2,800 Japanese had faced war crimes trials. That is, if the Morgenthau Plan had been followed as its planners at the Treasury Department had envisioned it in this meeting, then the Allies would have summarily shot about 70 percent of the Germans who were ultimately *charged* with war crimes. In fact, after these trials, the total number of Germans executed was under 300.[54]

Even compared to Britain, which preferred the execution of fifty to one hundred top Axis war criminals (see Britain section below), 2,500 was a remarkable number. Unfazed, the Treasury Department team moved briskly to the logistical details of mass executions. White worried that the UNWCC seemed to have no list of war criminals to be shot. "American soldiers wouldn't shoot them," he added—an implicit recognition that it would be hard to get American soldiers to do such a thing. "Somebody else would probably, but the commanding officer would not have to decide whether or not they are to be shot but rather merely to identify them." White's plan included identification by a senior Allied officer before the execution. "Churchill didn't go that far," Morgenthau replied, sticking with the most summary of summary executions. "He said that any soldier meeting any of these people, their orders were to shoot them on sight." "And identify them afterwards," said Morgenthau aide Dan Bell. Herbert Gaston, the assistant secretary of the treasury, joked: "None of these people should be shot more than three times, Dan." Morgenthau then launched into a disquisition on the difficulty of doing summary shootings properly:

> If they shoot them at the rate they shot them in Italy—all they do there is put them back in the house and set them up in fine style. Just to give you an example, we landed in Sardinia and this . . . English General . . . said, "I never thought I would live to remove a Lt. General but there are

250,000 troops here, and I removed the Italian Lt. General in charge because he was a Fascist." I said, "What did you do, shoot him?" The man said, "Oh, no." I said, "Where is he?" "He is over with the King at Bari." . . . So I mean the shooting was not very good over there.[55]

Morgenthau planned to do better.

John Pehle, the executive director of the War Refugee Board (which helped Jews from Europe), made the only legalistic argument in the meeting, worrying about shooting people on the basis of insufficient evidence, and proposing trials as a partial solution: "I think if there is a list prepared of people that everyone agrees ought to be shot, it has got to be within a limited number in character. You can't take one of those things of any little evidence of some name and put it on the list. It has to be a list of names about which there would be no question. The rest would be subject to trial."[56] "Stalin has a list with 50,000," replied Morgenthau, evidently unimpressed by Pehle's reticence.[57] This might have been the kind of joke Morgenthau liked to throw into meetings, a self-parodying poke at his own toughness. (The presence of White makes it particularly bizarre.) Or maybe Morgenthau really did want to use the Soviet list. At a minimum, it showed that Morgenthau was just as aware of Stalin's notorious Tehran suggestion as Stimson was—but that Morgenthau did not object as bitterly as Stimson did.

Public Opinion

The vast majority of Americans would have agreed with Morgenthau. Legalism seems to have been largely an elite phenomenon. While Stimson was insisting on the norms of the American domestic legal system, the American public was quick to disregard those same norms. There were overwhelming public calls for revenge, but of the swift and certain kind. Typically, as few as 10 percent or even 1 percent of Gallup poll respondents favored trials.

In July 1942, 39 percent of Americans thought Hitler should be hanged or shot, 23 percent thought he should be imprisoned or put in an asylum, and 3 percent preferred slow torture. Only 1 percent said he should be given a court-martial. The results were roughly the same for the Nazi leaders: 35 percent for shooting, 31 percent for jailing, 5 percent for treating them as the Nazis had treated others, 2 percent for torturing, and 2 percent for a court-martial.[58] In June 1945, only 4 percent said Göring should be given a trial, but 67 percent said he should be killed—many respondents emphasizing "that the manner of death should be made as unpleasant as possible."

There was a slightly greater interest in legalism for lower-level war criminals in 1945. Some 45 percent of Americans wanted to kill Gestapo agents and Storm Troopers: " 'Kill them . . . hang them . . . wipe them off the face of the earth' are typical replies." Only about 10 percent would try them: about as many as wanted to torture them.[59] As for Nazi Party members who claimed they had just been following orders, 42 percent of Americans wanted to imprison them, 19 percent wanted to kill them, and 19 percent wanted to try them and punish them only if found guilty.[60]

This lack of legalism was, if anything, more pronounced when it came to Japan. In December 1944, 33 percent of Americans wanted to destroy Japan as a country after the war, 28 percent wanted to supervise and control Japan—and fully 13 percent wanted to kill *all* Japanese people. In another poll, while 88 percent wanted to punish the Japanese military leaders, only 4 percent of Americans wanted to "Treat them justly, handle them under International Law, (or) demote them." Instead, typical suggestions included:

> "We should string them up and cut little pieces off them—one piece at
> a time."
> "Torture them to a slow and awful death."
> "Kill them, but be sure to torture them first, the way they have tortured
> our boys."
> "Take them to Pearl Harbor and sink them."
> "Put them in Siberia and let them freeze to death."
> "Turn them over to the Chinese."
> "Put them in foxholes and [throw] fire bombs and grenades at them."
> "Kill them like rats."[61]

In sum, these polls suggest that wartime public opinion is untamed and violent, and that a democratic government that takes its cues directly from that public mood is likely to want revenge, not trials. Democratic mass outrage may make it impossible for a government to ignore the question of war criminals, but it is no guarantee of legalism. To the contrary, it was the liberal norms of elites like Stimson and Jackson that foreclosed the idea of summary punishment. When, in May 1945, the Treasury Department confronted Jackson with a Gallup poll showing that the American public wanted to use Germans for forced labor in the Soviet Union, Jackson stuck to his legalism: "I don't give a damn what the Gallup Poll says."[62]

Morgenthau versus Stimson

The Treasury and War Departments were on a collision course. The night of September 4, 1944, after spending part of his day mulling 2,500 executions, Morgenthau had Stimson and McCloy over for dinner—and ran into the first overt opposition to those execution plans. "[W]e were all aware of the feeling that a sharp issue is sure to arise over the question of the treatment of Germany," Stimson wrote. "Morgenthau is, not unnaturally, very bitter and as he is not thoroughly trained in history or even economics it became very apparent that he would plunge out for a treatment of Germany which I feel sure would be unwise."[63] In particular, Stimson, according to a Treasury Department memorandum, was "most interested" in the war criminals issue, and emphasized the importance of "a fair trial though not necessarily a public trial."[64]

When a cabinet-level committee on postwar Germany met at the State Department the next day, there was a predictable explosion. Stimson met fierce opposition not just from Morgenthau, but also from Cordell Hull, the secretary of state, and Harry Hopkins. "[T]o my tremendous surprise," Stimson "found that Hull was as bitter as Morgenthau against the Germans."[65] Before this meeting, Hull had told Morgenthau, "The reason that I got along so well with the Russians was when I went to Moscow, the first thing I told them I would do was to bring up all these people before a drumhead court martial, and I would shoot them before sunset, and from that day I got along with the Russians beautifully."[66] Hull, according to Morgenthau, said, "This Nazism is down in the German people a thousand miles deep, and you have just got to uproot it, and you can't do it by just shooting a few people." Stimson, as Morgenthau noted, "didn't even seem to like that and he went into a long legal discussion of how you would have to have legal procedure before you shot the people, and had to do all this on a legal basis. Well, Hull doesn't want to wait; he just wants to shoot them all at dawn."[67]

Morgenthau was elated. "I wanted to get up and kiss Cordell for the first time," Morgenthau cheered to Hopkins after the meeting. "I nearly fell through the floor," Hopkins said. Hopkins was particularly irritated by Stimson: "My God, he was terrible." Morgenthau agreed, sarcastically echoing Stimson's views: "All you've got to do is let kindness and Christianity work on the Germans." Both Hopkins and Morgenthau were confident that Roosevelt would be on their side.[68]

Stimson despaired. "I found myself a minority of one and I labored vigorously but entirely ineffectively against my colleagues," Stimson wrote in his diary after the meeting. "In all the four years that I have been here I have not had such a difficult and unpleasant meeting."[69] McCloy found Stimson "more depressed after the conference than he had ever seen him."[70]

Stimson spent the rest of his day dictating a memorandum for posterity ("I feel that I had to leave a record for history that the entire government of this Administration had not run amuck at this vital period of history") detailing his objections to the Morgenthau Plan, which he sent to Roosevelt, Morgenthau, Hull, and Hopkins. Stimson's "basic objection" was to "the dangerous weapon of complete economic oppression. Such methods, in my opinion, do not prevent war; they breed war." Instead of partition, Stimson preferred war crimes trials:

> It is primarily by the thorough apprehension, investigation, and trial of all the Nazi leaders and instruments of the Nazi system of terrorism, such as the Gestapo, with punishment delivered as promptly, swiftly and severely as possible, that we can demonstrate the abhorrence which the world has for such a system and bring home to the German people our determination to extirpate it and all its fruits forever.[71]

Despite his drubbing, Stimson stuck by his legalism.

Stimson's trial plans rested largely on his own understanding of American domestic norms. Even while Morgenthau's view seemed triumphant, Stimson was thinking through the modalities of war crimes trials that would be a credit to the American legal tradition. In the middle of a heated cabinet-level fight at the end of the greatest war America had ever fought, the secretary of war was spending his time carefully reading an article from the *American Bar Association Review*. Stimson turned to the Pentagon's top lawyer, Myron Cramer, the judge advocate general, for legal advice. They discussed Allied military tribunals, for which Stimson wanted to supply "simply the skeleton of what we call the requisitional fair trial." The accused would get a chance to hear and answer the charges against them, perhaps have the benefit of counsel, and maybe get to call witnesses; but "it must be free from all the delays that would go with the technicalities of courts-martial or the United States jurisprudence procedure should go in, absolutely." Cramer insisted that the accused have the right to call witnesses, to prevent "any charges of railroading these people." "A great many people think that the question of guilt of some of these people is already decided," Stimson said. "I'm taking the position that they must have the substance of a trial. I just

wanted to know whether you agreed with me." "I agree with you absolutely," said Cramer.[72]

If anything, Stimson's legalism grew stronger. He showed Marshall one
of Morgenthau's memorandums

> demanding that the leaders of the Nazi party be shot without trial and
> on the basis of the general world appreciation of their guilt, and it met
> with the reception that I expected—absolute rejection of the notion
> that we should not give these men a fair trial. Marshall called attention
> to the fact that it was the same sort of thing that happens after every war
> and that the bitterness of this one was sure to be extreme. I told him that
> I was not a bit surprised at what I had found but that I was appalled—a
> different thing. The attitude of these typical soldiers towards this wave
> of hysteria which seems to be sweeping over some of the members of
> the government was symptomatic of what I have always found among
> good soldiers—they are in many respects the best educated men of the
> country in regard to the basic principles of our Constitution and tradi-
> tional respect for freedom and law.[73]

Strikingly, Stimson explicitly equated his trial proposal with nothing less
than the Constitution, the holy of holies in American domestic politics.
For Stimson and Marshall, Morgenthau's summary executions simply
stood against American domestic legal tradition.

Having invoked the Constitution, Stimson then went one better. He
summoned a trusted friend to a private dinner at his house, "so that I
might enlist him in this battle": no less than Felix Frankfurter, a prominent Supreme Court justice. The famed jurist, Stimson wrote,

> was very helpful as I knew he would be. Although a Jew like Morgenthau,
> he approached this subject with perfect detachment and great help-
> fulness. I went over the whole matter from the beginning with him,
> reading him Morgenthau's views on the subjects of the Ruhr and also
> on the subject of the trial of the Nazis, at both of which he snorted with
> astonishment and distain. He was very helpful in regard to the trials
> because he had sat in the Supreme Court on the opinion that they had
> rendered in the saboteurs' case and was very familiar with the subject
> of the "common law of war offenses". He fully backed up my views and
> those of my fellows in the Army that we must give these men the sub-
> stance of a fair trial and that they cannot be railroaded to their death
> without trial. Also we discussed a little the limitations of jurisdiction
> which are involved in the fact that most of these Nazi crimes have not

been directed at the American government or at the American Army but at the people and armies of our allies. . . . By the time the evening was over I felt refreshed and encouraged by the help he had given me.[74]

Stimson was not just invoking the Supreme Court to show that war crimes trials were in keeping with American domestic traditions; he was enlisting it.

Roosevelt met with his dueling cabinet officers on September 9. But Stimson's carefully crafted memorandum made no impact on the president. As Stimson wrote in his diary, Morgenthau launched into "a new diatribe on the subject of the Nazis," and Roosevelt limited himself to once again stating "his predilection for feeding the Germans from soup kitchens instead of anything heavier." Stimson wrote: "It was a very discouraging meeting and I came away rather low in my mind."[75]

Unbowed, Stimson gave a memorandum to Roosevelt that in essence proposed the scheme that would become Nuremberg. "Prompt and summary trials shall be held of those charged with such crimes and punishment should be swift and severe," Stimson suggested. The basic mechanism of trials was of tremendous importance:

> The other fundamental point upon which I feel we [Stimson and Morgenthau] differ is the matter of the trial and punishment of those Germans who are responsible for crimes and depredations. Under the plan proposed by Mr. Morgenthau, the so-called arch-criminals shall be put to death by the military without provision for any trial and upon mere identification after apprehension. The method of dealing with these and other criminals requires careful thought and a well-defined procedure. *Such procedure must embody, in my judgment, at least the rudimentary aspects of the Bill of Rights,* namely, notification to the accused of the charge, the right to be heard and, within reasonable limits, to call witnesses in his defense. I do not mean to favor the institution of state trials or to introduce any cumbersome machinery but the very punishment of these men in a dignified manner consistent with the advance of civilization, will have all the greater effect upon posterity. Furthermore, it will afford the most effective way of making a record of the Nazi system of terrorism and of the effort of the Allies to terminate the system and prevent its recurrence.
>
> I am disposed to believe that at least as to the chief Nazi officials, we should participate in an international tribunal constituted to try them. They should be charged with offenses against the laws of the rules of

war in that they have committed wanton and unnecessary cruelties in connection with the prosecution of the war. *This law of the Rules of War has been upheld by our own Supreme Court and will be the basis of judicial action against the Nazis.*[76]

Once again, Stimson's argument relied on the export of American norms into Germany. It was not just that he insisted on "well-defined procedure" and "a dignified manner consistent with the advance of civilization"—a distinctively legalistic way of thinking about the punishment of enemy leaders, particularly in contrast with the furious Treasury Department plans. More strikingly, Stimson relied explicitly on the Bill of Rights. Fortified by his dinner with Frankfurter, and with a clear reference to their discussion of the common law of war, Stimson argued that the virtue of an international tribunal was that it was in keeping with no lesser authority than the Supreme Court. Morgenthau had complained before that Stimson wanted to reform the Germans with kindness and Christianity; here, Stimson seemed to want to reform them with the Bill of Rights and the Supreme Court.

The Québec Conference

On September 14, Roosevelt was to meet Churchill in Québec City to discuss many of the same German issues that were tearing the White House apart. Frankfurter, cheering Stimson up over another dinner at Stimson's house, was confident that Morgenthau's punitive paper "would not go anywhere and that the President himself would catch the errors and would see that the spirit was all wrong."[77] Not so. Roosevelt invited only one cabinet member to Québec: Morgenthau. Morgenthau, Stimson wrote, "is so biased by his Semitic grievances that he is really a very dangerous adviser to the President at this time."[78] If Morgenthau won out, Stimson thought, "it will certainly be a disaster."[79]

The Québec Conference was a triumph for the Morgenthau Plan. Roosevelt and Churchill—after some strong initial reluctance—agreed to crush Germany's industrial capacities and to convert "Germany into a country primarily agricultural and pastoral in its character," as the Québec directive put it.[80] "The Treasury viewpoint was wholly accepted," Morgenthau reported to his staff. "[T]he President put it this way: He said he had been groping for something, and we came along and gave him just what he wanted."[81]

On the war criminals issue, the British government, which had been leaning toward summary executions for the top Nazis (see Britain section below), lined up with Morgenthau and Roosevelt: "The President and Prime Minister have agreed to put to Marshal Stalin Lord Simon's proposals for dealing with the major criminals and to concert with him a list of names."[82] There is scant doubt what this meant. Stimson complained of Roosevelt's "recklessness" in using the army for summary executions, after McCloy reported that "he had heard from the British representatives here that the President was very firm for shooting the Nazi leaders without trial."[83]

Morgenthau was elated. "The thing up at Quebec, all together, was unbelievably good," Morgenthau enthused on his return to Washington. "And as far as I went personally, it was the high spot of my whole career in the Government. I got more personal satisfaction out of those forty-eight hours than with anything I have ever been connected with."[84]

Stimson once again plunged into an equal and opposite gloom. He railed privately against Roosevelt's and Churchill's ignorance and naïveté, and resorted again under pressure to an antisemitic analysis of Morgenthau's influence:

[T]he cloud of it has hung over me pretty heavily over the weekend. It is a terrible thing to think that the total power of the United States and the United Kingdom in such a critical matter as this is in the hands of two men, both of whom are similar in their impulsiveness and their lack of systematic study. Since the matter has come up two weeks ago I have been studying it as carefully and hard as I can and I have discussed it with many men and I have yet to meet a man who is not horrified with the "Carthaginian" attitude of the Treasury. It is Semitism gone wild for vengeance and, if it is ultimately carried out (I cannot believe that it will be), it as sure as fate will lay the seeds for another war in the next generation.[85]

Stimson sent yet another memorandum to Roosevelt (without the antisemitic references). The Treasury Department plans, Stimson wrote, "will tend through bitterness and suffering to breed another war," and, in a burst of hyperbole, "would be just such a crime as the Germans themselves hoped to perpetrate upon their victims—it would be a crime against civilization itself." Once again, Stimson tried to appeal to Roosevelt in terms of American domestic ideals, this time invoking both the

Declaration of Independence and Roosevelt's own "Four Freedoms" speech:

> This country since its very beginning has maintained the fundamental belief that all men, in the long run, have the right to be free human beings and to live in the pursuit of happiness. Under the Atlantic Charter victors and vanquished alike are entitled to freedom from economic want. But the proposed treatment of Germany would, if successful, deliberately deprive many millions of people of the right to freedom from want and freedom from fear. Other peoples all over the world would suspect the validity of our spiritual tenets and question the long range effectiveness of our economic and political principles as applied to the vanquished.[86]

Riding high after Québec, Morgenthau had no patience for this. "I do not know what he means when he says he does not plead for a 'soft' treatment of Germany," Morgenthau wrote to Roosevelt in a rebuttal. "It was this same attitude of appeasement that was so fruitful in helping Germany plunge the world into the present war." Morgenthau's interest was in "preventing World War III," by depriving the Germans of any "spark of hope for world conquest."[87]

For reassurance, Stimson turned once again to his two favorite legalists, Marshall and Frankfurter. Marshall was "very much troubled, particularly about the report of Roosevelt's attitude towards shooting without trial and that to me is the problem before us which is fraught with the most danger." Over yet another dinner, Frankfurter agreed. "As to the shooting without trial," Stimson wrote, "he said that was preposterous and he agreed wholly with me that I should resist it with all means within my power."[88]

The Collapse of the Morgenthau Plan

Stimson, or some other enemy of the Morgenthau Plan, did have one final trick within his power: a perfect piece of Washingtonia. The Morgenthau Plan leaked. On September 24, *The New York Times* ran a front-page story under the headline, "Morgenthau Plan on Germany Splits Cabinet Committee," reporting that Stimson "violently opposed" the plan.[89] As far as the press knew, the issue at stake was Morgenthau's pastoralization proposals; this story did not mention executing war criminals.

The leak hit the Morgenthau Plan in its one weak spot. Most of Morgenthau's ideas were fairly popular,[90] but not pastoralization. In an April 1945 poll, only 13 percent of Americans approved of pastoralizing Germany, while 56 percent wanted only to keep close supervision over German industry.[91] Stimson's protestations of innocence notwithstanding, if someone had meant to use public opinion against Morgenthau, pastoralization was a clever issue. Roosevelt also worried that the Morgenthau Plan would stiffen German resolve on the Western front, putting American soldiers at risk.[92]

"Now the pack is in full cry," Stimson wrote in his diary.[93] Morgenthau immediately saw the danger. After follow-up stories and editorials in *The New York Times* and its rival, *The New York Herald Tribune*, Morgenthau asked Hull to plug the leaks: "I had understood that the War Department had been talking to Walter Lippmann,"[94] the most influential columnist in Washington. Public opinion quickly swung against pastoralization. "Give them another month," a Morgenthau aide said, "and it will be as dead as a doorknob as far as trying to get public acceptance."[95]

That was optimistic. A mere three days after the Morgenthau Plan hit the front pages, Roosevelt called Stimson to recant. Roosevelt said that he had not really planned to pastoralize Germany. Roosevelt, Stimson wrote, "was evidently under the influence of the impact of criticism which has followed his decision to follow Morgenthau's advice. The papers have taken it up violently and almost unanimously against Morgenthau and the President himself, and the impact has been such that he had already evidently reached the conclusion that he had made a false step and was trying to work out of it."[96] Roosevelt backed away from the Morgenthau Plan and the Québec Conference with an easy flexibility of conviction. Lunching with Stimson, Roosevelt "grinned and looked naughty and said 'Henry Morgenthau pulled a boner' or an equivalent expression, and said that we really were not apart on that."[97]

The whole Morgenthau Plan was destroyed by American public opinion, but not because of its summary execution plans. Had Americans evaluated the Morgenthau Plan on war criminals, they would probably have sided with Morgenthau. In practical terms, the Morgenthau Plan's demise signaled a sudden reversal in America's nascent war criminals policy. Trials became the order of the day. Stimson—the great advocate of exporting America's domestic legal norms—suddenly found himself in charge.

From the Morgenthau Plan to the Bernays Plan

"I am sorry for Morgenthau for never has an indiscretion been so quickly and vigorously punished as his incursion into German and Army politics at Quebec," wrote Stimson.[98] The center of gravity on war crimes policy shifted with breathtaking speed to the War Department. For all the twists and turns in the road, American war crimes policy was in its essence set: there would be trials for the German leadership and for lower-level perpetrators. To be sure, the exact nature of these trials would preoccupy officials well into 1945; fierce debates about international law would rage; White House officials would try to divine Roosevelt's position. But the basic legalistic policy was set.

The War Department proved adept at drafting trial plans. Stimson had already found support for war crimes trials among military men like Marshall, and the department had well-established mechanisms for dispensing military justice, like the judge advocate general. By the time the Morgenthau Plan met its leaky demise, Stimson's general preference for trials had already been more thoroughly elaborated by Murray Bernays, a young colonel in a special projects unit of the War Department's personnel branch.

The Bernays Plan echoed Stimson's objections to Morgenthau's hard line. Summary execution, Bernays argued, "would not solve the problem of punishing the thousands of less outstanding culprits." Anything less than American legalism "would do violence to the very principles for which the United Nations have taken up arms, and furnish apparent justification for what the Nazis themselves have taught and done. It would also help the Nazis elevate Hitler to martyrdom. The [Treasury Department's] suggested procedure would taint an essential act of justice with false color of vindictiveness."[99] If Nazi war criminals were not tried, "Germany will simply have lost another war. The German people will not know the barbarians they have supported, nor will they have any understanding of the criminal character of their conduct and the world's judgment upon it."[100] To Stimson's satisfaction, Cramer, Bernays, and other JAG officials had concluded that the Allies could set up local and international war crimes tribunals, the latter for war crimes that did not pertain to any one particular country. "[D]eeply interesting," Stimson noted.[101] He had found a way to export the basics of American law.

In another way, the Bernays Plan bore unique signs of its American parentage. The War Department worried about the virtual impossibility of trying every single member of the SS, SA, Gestapo, and other Nazi terror organizations. Bernays and Stimson's creative solution to this problem drew explicitly upon American domestic precedents: charging groups with a conspiracy to commit a crime. So Bernays proposed charging the German government, the Nazi Party, and the terror organizations with "conspiracy to commit murder, terrorism, and the destruction of peaceful populations in violation of the laws of war."[102] Once these organizations had been convicted, any member of them could be swiftly punished; instead of proving individual guilt, national or Allied courts would only have to prove that the defendant had been a member of a criminal group.

This odd idea sprang from American domestic law—in particular, American domestic law as practiced by Henry Stimson. As a federal prosecutor under Theodore Roosevelt, a young Stimson had successfully slapped the sugar trust with conspiracy charges, convicting the organization of putting holes (seventeen of them, a fact Stimson never tired of repeating)[103] in the scales at a port in order to underweigh the imported sugar and thereby dodge tariffs.[104] When Bernays mentioned convicting the Nazis of a conspiracy to wage World War II, Stimson "told them of my experience as United States Attorney in finding that only by conspiracy could we properly cope with the evils which arose under our complicated development of big business. In many respects the task which we have to cope with now in the development of the Nazi scheme of terrorism is much like the development of big business."[105] What exactly did the American Sugar Refining Company have in common with the Gestapo? And yet Stimson's inapposite analogy came to drive much of the formulation of American war crimes policy. Stimson had in mind "my picture of a big trial for conspiracy involving the leaders and actors all the way down who had taken part in the different atrocity camps and mass murder places."[106] McCloy told a skeptical Morgenthau, "After Justice Jackson puts the Gestapo on the stand and has indicted them like the American Sugar Company or whatever it was, then he says, 'By God, you're guilty.' "[107]

This is one of the more bizarre tributes ever paid to the rule of precedent, but it gives a telling impression of the extent to which America could be driven by a respect for its own law—even law that bore as little relation to the new situation at hand as seventeen holes in a sugar scale did to the German atrocities.[108] (The conspiracy charges worked particularly badly at the Tokyo trials.[109]) To Stimson's satisfaction, the War Department's plans gave "the great powers a chance to handle this difficult question in a way which is at the same time *consistent with our traditional judicial principles* and also will be effective in dispensing adequate punishment and also will leave a permanent record in the shape of the evidence collected of the evils against which we have fought this war."[110] What mattered was domestic legal norms.

On January 3, 1945, Roosevelt gave his imprimatur to the idea of war crimes trials. In a somewhat enigmatic memorandum to Edward Stettinius, now secretary of state, the president wrote: "The charges against the top Nazis should include an indictment for waging aggressive warfare, in violation of the Kellogg Pact. Perhaps these and other charges might be joined in a conspiracy indictment."[111] Oblique as the memorandum was, Roosevelt's position was a vindication for Bernays and Stimson's conspiracy plan.

Trounced, Morgenthau remained skeptical of legalism. When confronted with plans for Nuremberg, he was displeased enough to compose a long memorandum to Harry Truman, although he never sent it. Caving to Stimson, Morgenthau accepted the idea of "simple and expeditious" trials, using "regular legal methods" even against the Nazis. But he worried that Allied legalists had "failed to produce a simple and uncomplicated procedure for the prompt punishment of war criminals which will be understood by common men everywhere as a means of doing essential justice rather than a maze constructed by lawyers to baffle laymen and to delay punishment of the guilty."[112] Morgenthau feared that the German criminals might "go free again" (presumably a Leipzig reference), if the Allies stuck to "all the technicalities and complexities of Anglo-American jurisprudence in the prosecution of war criminals." He feared trying "to transplant our technical legal procedures to Germany." Morgenthau concluded:

> If we force these military tribunals to follow the technical procedures and customs of an American court, such as the Supreme Court of the United States, I greatly fear that notorious criminals will be permitted to delay or avoid punishment by reliance on technical legal rules. . . .
> . . . The respect which the people of the world have for international law is in direct proportion to its ability to meet their needs.[113]

This was a remarkable mirror image of Stimson's arguments, right down to the references to the Supreme Court. Morgenthau feared that American legal mechanisms would let the Nazis dodge true justice. Much as Morgenthau had disagreed with Stimson, the two men had understood each other perfectly: the issue at hand was the appropriateness of exporting America's domestic legal norms.

It was only after all of this cabinet-level dueling that Truman plucked Jackson from the Supreme Court to represent America at the negotiations in London over Nuremberg's charter, and then to lead the American prosecution at the tribunal. When Morgenthau doggedly raised some of his old objections to Jackson, Jackson could respond that he was simply doing his duty as a lawyer in the American tradition:

> You want to execute them for the right reasons, if you want to do anything for the future peace of the world. If we stand for all the things we've been saying we stand for, we can hardly refuse to make an inquiry. It's difficult for me to see why you can hesitate to record here the evidence and make it available—the record of its rise and that barbarism and all that—to have it available, and this is the only real official way to do it. Now, as far as I'm concerned, that decision is passed. It's a political decision as to whether you should execute these people without trial, release them without trial, or try them and decide at the end of the trial what to do. That decision was made by the President, and I was asked to run the legal end of the prosecution. So I'm not really in a position to say whether it's the wisest thing to do or not.[114]

It was only after Stimson had confronted Morgenthau broadly that such a narrow argument could suffice. At the end of America's most brutal war ever, the Germans would be accorded the benefit of legal procedure as it had evolved in America, because of an American belief in the rightness of its own domestic legalism.

What the Americans Were Putting on Trial: The War First, the Holocaust Second

America prosecuted war crimes much as it had prosecuted the war. That is, the charges that were of greatest interest to America were those that bore directly on America: the German instigation of World War II. The Allies had been largely passive as the Holocaust went on, although there was in the end a visceral Allied revulsion at the Nazi concentration camps when Dachau and Belsen were liberated by Western soldiers in April 1945—long after the basics of Stimson's plans for Nuremberg were Allied policy.[115] This lends support to the notion that war crimes prosecutions are usually self-serving, with even liberal states most commonly outraged by war crimes against their own citizens.

Nuremberg is often incorrectly remembered as if it had been mostly a trial for the Holocaust. This confuses Nuremberg with other trials in Israel and West Germany, like the 1961 Eichmann trial, the 1963–65 Auschwitz trials in Frankfurt, and the 1975–81 Majdanek trials in Düsseldorf. Indeed, much of the Israeli motivation for bringing Eichmann to stand his trial in an Israeli court was a sense that the Allies had not paid sufficient concern to the Holocaust at Nuremberg. As Arendt put it (quoting from the Israeli prosecutor's opening statement), the spectators in Jerusalem "were to watch a spectacle as sensational as the Nuremberg Trials, only this time 'the tragedy of Jewry as a whole was to be the central concern.' "[116]

America aimed mostly at prosecuting the Nazis for the crime of aggressive war. Jackson's very first words at Nuremberg were: "The privilege of opening the first trial in history for crimes against the peace of the world imposes a grave responsibility." He spoke of the Allied "practical effort . . . to utilize International Law to meet the greatest menace of our times—aggressive war."[117] Britain's prosecutor at Nuremberg, Hartley Shawcross, noted: "The Americans are primarily concerned with establishing that the prisoners conspired together to wage a war of aggression—a very vital part of the case."[118]

This American attitude was obvious at all levels. In a rare explicit statement on war criminals, Roosevelt had called for indicting the top Nazis for waging war.[119] He mentioned aggression, not the Holocaust, atrocities against civilians, or war crimes. At Nuremberg's conclusion, Truman echoed Roosevelt: "The principles established and the results achieved place International Law on the side of peace as against aggressive war."[120]

Stimson is a fine illustrative case. The prime mover behind Nuremberg was a rather mild and genteel antisemite, no worse but no better than the bulk of the American establishment in the 1930s and 1940s.[121] (It was only over Japanese-Americans that Stimson's ethnic prejudices overwhelmed even his respect for law. He admitted that the 1942 internment of Japanese-Americans in California would "make an awful hole in our constitutional system," but considered internment a necessity because "their racial characteristics are such that we cannot understand or trust even citizen Japanese."[122]) Stimson understood that private antisemitic remarks were inappropriate in some public settings, and saw himself as more tolerant than many other Americans. After the demise of the Morgenthau Plan, Stimson—in what might not have been his most self-aware moment—told Roosevelt that he "had shuddered when he [Morgenthau] took the leadership in such a campaign against Germany, knowing how a man of his race would be mis-represented for so doing."[123]

Stimson was not particularly concerned with the Holocaust.[124] Throughout the war criminals debate, Stimson's diaries make almost no mention of the Holocaust, except, for instance, when Marshall brought up "the Lublin mass murder"—that is, the Majdanek death camp, just liberated by the Soviets.[125] Stimson wrote vastly more about the summer humidity in Washington than about the extermination of European Jewry.[126] His War Department repeatedly refused to divert resources to enfeebling the German machinery of mass death.[127] In an important memorandum to Roosevelt spelling out trial plans, Stimson spent almost as much space arguing *against* trying Nazis for persecution within Germany as he did arguing for holding the trials at all. Without pressure from others more troubled by the Holocaust, Stimson might well have set up a Nuremberg that did not prosecute crimes against humanity:

> Even though these offenses have not been committed against our troops, I feel that our moral position is better if we take our share in their conviction. Other war criminals who have committed crimes in subjugated territories should be returned in accordance with the Moscow Declaration to those territories for trial by national military commissions having jurisdiction of the offense under the same Rules of War. *I have great difficulty in finding any means whereby military commissions may try and convict those responsible for excesses committed within Germany both before and during the war which have no relation to the conduct of the war.* I would be prepared to construe broadly what constituted a violation of the Rules of War but there is a certain field in which I feel that external courts cannot move. Such courts would be without jurisdiction in precisely the same way that any foreign court would be without jurisdiction to try those who were guilty of, or condoned, lynching in our own country.[128]

Stimson's approach is the kind of legal reasoning that would not have considered it a murder when Cain slew Abel, because such a crime had not been committed before. The argument, resting on the legal principle of *nullum crimen sine lege*,[129] is legally unexceptionable, although not even the Nuremberg judges remembered Allied threats against "these crimes of Turkey against humanity and civilization" during the 1915 Armenian genocide—thirty years *before* Nuremberg.

Instead, Stimson was primarily interested in prosecuting Nazi aggression. His conspiracy format could equally well have been applied to the Holocaust; the Nazis had colluded as much to exterminate the Jews as they had to launch World War II. And yet when he brought the issue up with Roosevelt, Stimson used his precious moments with the president to emphasize "the importance as a matter of record of having a state trial with records and one that would bring out and show the full nature of the Nazi conspiracy or evil plan to wage a war of terrorism on the European world involving totalitarian war and breaches of the laws of war."[130] Aggression came first.

The picture was much the same at the Justice Department. Herbert Wechsler, an assistant attorney general, emphasized aggression.[131] So did Telford Taylor, who would succeed Jackson as America's chief Nuremberg prosecutor.[132] Stimson noted that officials including McCloy, Francis Biddle, the attorney general, and Samuel Rosenman, an old Roosevelt confidant, were coming to back his proposal of "a big trial in which we can prove the whole Nazi conspiracy to wage a totalitarian war of aggression violating in its progress all of the regular rules which limit needless cruelty and destruction."[133]

Jackson's view of German criminality also centered on aggression. In 1941, as attorney general, he had publicly stated that Axis aggression violated the Kellogg-Briand Pact.[134] At the London Conference, André Gros, France's delegate, told Jackson, "[O]ur differences are more or less this: the Americans want to win the trial on the ground that the Nazi war was illegal, and the French people and other people of the occupied countries just want to show that the Nazis were bandits." Jackson agreed fully with that comment, precisely because America had not suffered from Nazi occupation:

> I think Professor Gros put his finger on it when he said the American Delegation wants to show that war is illegal, while they only want to show that the Nazis were bandits. Without boring you too much, I will tell you why we are interested in that and explain what our basic difference is here, as I see it.
>
> It is probably very difficult for those of you who lived under the immediate attack of the Nazis to appreciate the different public psychology that those of us who were in the American Government dealt with. Our American population is at least 3,000 miles from the scene. Germany did not attack or invade the United States in violation of any treaty with us. The thing that led us to take sides in this war was that we regarded Germany's resort to war as illegal from its outset, as an illegitimate attack on the international peace and order.[135]

It is not clear if Jackson understood how self-serving this sounded, nor how it might have stung the French delegates to shrug at the experience of Nazi occupation. Jackson subsumed all Nazi atrocities as part of the Nazi plan of aggression:

> [O]ur view is that this isn't merely a case of showing that these Nazi Hitlerite people failed to be gentlemen in war; it is a matter of their having designed an illegal attack on the international peace, which to our mind is a criminal offense by common-law tests, at least, and *the other atrocities were all preparatory to it or done in execution of it.*[136]

On returning from negotiating the London Charter, Jackson wrote that it "ushers international law into a new era where it is in accord with the common sense of mankind that a war of deliberate and unprovoked attack deserves universal condemnation and its authors condign penalties." Jackson triumphantly ended his report on the conference by writing that "all who have shared in this work have been united and inspired in the belief that at long last the law is now unequivocal in classifying armed aggression as an international crime instead of a national right."[137] Jackson even defined crimes against humanity as ancillary to aggression:

> The reason that this program of extermination of Jews and destruction of the rights of minorities becomes an international concern is this: it was a part of a plan for making an illegal war. Unless we have a war connection as a basis for reaching them, I would think we have no basis for dealing with atrocities. They were a part of the preparation for war or for making an illegal war in so far as they occurred inside of Germany and that makes them our concern.[138]

Amid all this effort on aggression, crimes against humanity got relatively short shrift.

In addition to giving pride of place to aggressive war, America was self-interested in its concern over war crimes committed against American soldiers. "Principal emphasis, doubtless," noted an American memorandum at the San Francisco Conference, "will be placed in the trial upon those patent violations of the customs of war which most shock the Allies (e.g., murder of prisoners of war, abuse of populations in occupied territories, deportation of Allied peoples for use as slave labor, etc.)."[139] Stimson—whose diaries pay such meager attention to the Holocaust—made a point of being briefed by a former American prisoner of war in Germany, and recorded the miserable conditions in his diary.[140] Stimson and McCloy were angered at Germany's failure to obey the Geneva Convention, and feared German executions of American prisoners as Allied forces approached.[141] Gordon Dean, a Jackson aide, was blunt: "Whatever the other countries of the world had suffered, and admittedly some had suffered much more than the United States, American blood had been spilled in the holocaust of war—a war that had been none of America's doing. American airmen taken as prisoners of war had been brutally killed. Such crimes could not pass unnoticed. Americans had an interest in this problem."[142] Japan came in for particular hatred, far more than Germany in some polls, because of Pearl Harbor and Japanese cruelty toward American prisoners.[143]

By far the worst shock to American public opinion—and to the planners of Nuremberg—came during the Battle of the Bulge. In an incident that became instantly notorious, the SS machine-gunned some seventy American prisoners of war near Malmédy, Belgium. This was not a particularly unusual event for the SS, which had carried out countless worse atrocities against Soviet prisoners of war.[144] But now the victims were Americans. The American government was outraged.[145] Stimson wrote that "it seems to be clear that their troops have been guilty of many violations of the laws of war against us."[146] The impact on Americans was comparable to that on Britons of the death of Fryatt or Cavell in World War I: galvanizing the planning of a war criminals policy.

In all of this, America was no worse than other liberal countries. Even liberal states tend to hound war criminals who have committed atrocities against citizens, rather than foreigners. Because of America's domestic liberal ideology, sympathizers with Europe's Jews could at least couch a universalistic appeal in terms that had some broad resonance in America. But that did not mean that America would put crimes against humanity before crimes against Americans.

This relative lack of interest in prosecuting the Holocaust was of a piece with the Roosevelt administration's inattentive reaction to the Holocaust while it was happening.[147] Most of the pressure from the American Jewish community, a powerful component of the New Deal coalition, went unheeded. Some administration officials did give powerful speeches about Germany's anti-Jewish enormities, as Hull did before Congress in November 1943.[148] But even this statement was almost an afterthought, spurred by the eyebrow-raising fact that the Moscow Declaration had made no mention of the Jews at all. Hull himself had paid scant attention to efforts to rescue the European Jews, and the State Department often opposed such moves.[149]

Early in the drafting of American war crimes policy, American Jews realized that the White House might leave Jewish victims out altogether.

Herbert Pell, the American delegate on the UNWCC—"no doubt," as Taylor indelicately put it later, "sensitive to ethnic factors in New York politics"—had to push for the inclusion of crimes against German Jews and Catholics. This did not go over well with some in the State Department, and Roosevelt warned Pell that persecution committed before the outbreak of war "may not fall within the category of war crimes" and thus should be left to the Allies.[150] But the Treasury Department—which under Morgenthau had pushed for action to help the European Jews—insisted that no atrocities be excused.[151] Taylor later wrote that the establishment of the UNWCC "made astonishingly—indeed shamefully—little impact on the public mind. I myself did not become aware of the Holocaust until my exposure to the relevant documents and witnesses at Nuremberg."[152]

This tendency to overlook the Holocaust was fought by American Jews and other Americans who empathized with the plight of the European Jews. Although such efforts had largely failed to rouse the White House during the killings, this pressure did make a noticeable impact in the planning of Nuremberg. The most important pressure came from the Treasury Department. Although Morgenthau did not want trials, he did want the Nazis to be punished for the Holocaust. In September 1944, the Treasury Department's Joseph O'Connell complained that in the State Department and the military there was "apparently a school of thought that believes we are substantially ham-strung in connection with such things as war crimes and what you do in Germany by international law, so called, and if it is acceptable to you [Morgenthau], we are working on a memorandum debunking that proposition, because it is the most completely phoney thing I have so far heard of." "Stimson takes that view," Morgenthau said. "It is a disgrace to the legal position to me," O'Connell replied, in a tidy critique of legalism, "because it is essentially an unlegalistic approach to the problem applying domestic constitutional principles to a world situation which has nothing in common with it."[153]

Stimson, in fact, saw trials as a way of restraining American Jewry from harsher vengeance. Briefing Truman on Germany, Stimson insisted that "the only way it could go right was to not allow the element of vengeance to come into the problem at all except, not through administration but through justice, the trial of war criminals. They should be punished and, they being punished, the rest of the country should be rehabilitated." Stimson then explicitly linked this kind of vengeance to the kind of "Semitism gone wild for vengeance" he had complained of before: "Then I told him of the problem of our Jewish people here and I recounted informally the episode of last summer at Quebec. I then told him the danger was not yet over and I told him of Barney Baruch's recent statement. He said they were all alike—they couldn't keep from meddling with it."[154]

Private American organizations had an impact, too. In August 1944, the American Jewish Conference appealed to Hull to make the extermination of the Jews a punishable crime.[155] Bernays noted the need to "satisfy the insistence of the minority groups that recognition should be given to the criminal character of the specific acts and policies of which they complain." Bernays wrote:

> To let these brutalities go unpunished will leave millions of persons frustrated and disillusioned. The fact that these acts are believed to be outside the jurisdiction of the United Nations War Crimes Commission as presently constituted has already aroused vigorous protest. Strong pressure is being brought upon the United States and British Governments by organized Jewish groups, representing their co-religionists and undoubtedly also expressing the views of many others who are not of their faith, to have these acts categorized and treated as war crimes. It must be anticipated that the pressure will grow stronger with time.[156]

Even the universalistic act of punishing the perpetrators of the Holocaust had some basis in particularistic domestic pressure.

In the end, the inclusion of the Holocaust in Nuremberg was guaranteed by the nightmarish reports from the liberation of Dachau and Belsen in April 1945 by American and British troops. Finally, the Allies were confronted with some of the reality of the Holocaust, shocking them into including it in their trial plans as they had not in their military plans. This flush of empathy came long after America had settled on a legalistic policy, in October 1944. The suffering of the Jews was far from the first concern of the American planners of Nuremberg.

America's Legalism

Morgenthau's rage, Stimson's legalism, the pressure of those who sympathized with European Jews, and the self-serving thrust of the American prosecution: these currents were what had sent Jackson to Nuremberg. American mass and elite outrage meant that America would surely choose some sort of punishment for Nazi war criminals. But power need not have paid reason the tribute of trials at Nuremberg. Stimson narrowly won the day with the argument that to choose anything other than trials was inconsistent with liberal domestic principles—that mass executions would be, in the last analysis, un-American. Nuremberg was the American thing to do.

BRITAIN

The British, not exactly swept away with a sense of the historical moment, opened their case at Nuremberg with a lie. Hartley Shawcross, the British attorney general serving in Nuremberg as Britain's chief prosecutor, told the court:

> There are those who would perhaps say that these wretched men should have been dealt with summarily without trial by "executive action"; that their personal power for evil broken, they should be swept aside into oblivion without this elaborate and careful investigation as to the part they played in plunging the world in war. Vae Victis. Let them pay the price of defeat. But that is not the view of the British Empire or the British Government.[157]

Actually, that had been largely the view of much of the British government. As Shawcross must have known, it was only late in the day that Britain had agreed to the trials, and only after America would not budge on the issue.

Like Morgenthau, the British government was intensely aware of the risks of legalism. But there was no British Stimson to insist on trials for the highest Nazi officials. Churchill's cabinet and the British public were bent on punishing Germany for the war it had waged against Britain—so much so that the thought of acquittals and other legal complications was intolerable. The British were still painfully aware of the Leipzig fiasco. So Britain mostly advocated summary executions for the top Nazi leaders.

This policy only went so far. Britain wanted trials for lower-level Germans accused of war crimes. When Stalin suggested shooting 100,000 German soldiers, Churchill was horrified. And the British idea of killing 50 to 100 top war criminals was more restrained than Morgenthau's possible 2,500. As a liberal state, Britain would extend its domestic standards of due process to almost all German war criminals—but not the hundred or so at the very top. This is the most significant evidence in this book against my argument: it shows that liberal states *tend* to be legalist, but are not *always*. Britain might have been as legalistic as America if Churchill and other British leaders had not been personally soured on legalism after World War I. This was a lapse in British legalism; the best that can be said of it is that it was only a partial lapse. In the end, when America insisted on trials, Britain went along.

Protecting Soldiers

Like America, Britain feared putting its soldiers at risk for the sake of war crimes prosecutions. Because an Allied decision had already been made to pursue unconditional surrender, there were for the most part no major additional risks from a strong war crimes policy. Churchill even sometimes argued that stigmatizing Hitler and his top aides as war criminals would help the war effort by discouraging the Germans: "Once however their names are published and they are isolated, the mass of the German people will infer rightly that there is a difference between these major criminals and themselves."[158] But in those cases where there was a trade-off between pursuing international justice and protecting British soldiers, Britain tended to choose the latter.

British officials feared German reprisals. When the Soviet Union started its 1944 Kharkov war crimes trials (see Soviet Union section below), Britain worried that this might prompt Germany to punish British and American prisoners.[159] The British paper that America agreed to at the Québec Conference recommended making no public announcements about war criminals, lest they "evoke reprisals against Allied individuals in German hands."[160]

After the Québec Conference, Churchill drafted a telegram to Stalin, on his and Roosevelt's behalf, suggesting summary execution of the Nazi leadership within six hours. (The first draft had that as one hour.) Churchill argued that "the question of their fate is a political and not a judicial one. It could not rest with judges however eminent or learned to decide finally a matter like this which is of the widest and most vital public policy."[161] But in October 1944, the War Cabinet reconsidered: "[I]n view of the danger of reprisals against British prisoners held by Germany it would be preferable not to take any action for the time being. On the whole it would be best to let events take their course," the Foreign Office noted.[162] The draft telegram was never sent to Stalin. As Churchill told the cabinet, "The danger of German retaliation against British prisoners in their hands could not be overlooked."[163]

In April 1945, Sir John Simon, the lord chancellor, noted to the War Cabinet that the Americans and "ourselves are in complete agreement that *nothing of these more detailed plans must be made public until the time is reached when British and American personnel who are now prisoners in German hands are safe.*" Simon continued: "I would repeat that neither the American Delegation nor we ourselves contemplate that anything should be made public about this detailed plan until British and American prisoners who are now prisoners in Germany are safe."[164] The War Cabinet echoed this.[165] Soon after, the Foreign Office modified a directive to British theater commanders on war criminals, adding the provision that "the individuals on the list should not be arrested at present *'as war criminals'* in view of possible reprisals, but as normal prisoners of war or on security grounds."[166] In the event, unconditional surrender meant that British forces would be occupying Germany no matter how Allied war criminals policy turned out.

Public Opinion

Britain's government was under tremendous public pressure to punish war criminals. Even leaving aside the cabinet's own rage, it is almost inconceivable that Parliament or public opinion would have let off the Nazis.[167]

Britons were hugely vengeful. After enduring the Battle of Britain and the Blitz, the British were more vindictive than the Americans. In a September 1944 Gallup poll, 97 percent of Britons thought that Hitler, Himmler, Göring, and other top Nazis should be punished—almost unanimity. Some 87 percent thought that members of the SS and Gestapo should be punished, even if there were no specific war crimes charges against the individuals.[168]

Churchill thought that Britain would not be able to go beyond shooting a few top Nazis.[169] Perhaps Britons would indeed have recoiled once the shooting started, but the polls show a far greater interest in punishment than in due process. Of the 97 percent who thought Hitler and other top Nazis should be punished, 53 percent preferred execution; 25 percent wanted exile and life imprisonment. Trials fell in a residual "other" category that included torture, Siberian exile, forced labor, turning them over to Poles or Jews, or "Nothing horrible enough for them." As for the Gestapo and SS, 21 percent wanted to shoot them with or without trial, 14 percent to imprison them, 9 percent to put them to forced labor, 6 percent to exile them, 5 percent to turn them over to Jews or Poles, and 8 percent to torture them (or "nothing horrible enough")—a total of 63 percent not specifically mentioning trials. Only 12 percent specified that the war criminals should be put on trial and punished—about as many as those pushing for forced labor. No British government could have ignored this bitter public outrage; but there was no great push here for legalism, just revenge.

Leipzig or Legalism?

This public fury had an unpleasantly familiar ring to British leaders who had personally gone through the Leipzig fiasco. In October 1941, Anthony Eden, the foreign secretary, made the first cut of British policy on war criminals, with Leipzig foremost in his mind:

> I am convinced that we should avoid commitments to "try the war criminals" and to "hang the Kaiser" (*alias* Hitler). I am fortified in this opinion by the experience of that ill-starred enterprise at the end of the last war. Long lists of war criminals were prepared by the Allies in accordance with . . . the Treaty of Versailles, but, when the carrying out of the provisions for trial by Allied courts was considered, the difficulties were seen to be insuperable and the scheme was abandoned.[170]

Wary, Eden would go no further than mooting an Allied declaration that German behavior was "contrary to the dictates of humanity; are a reversion to barbarism; and will meet with retribution, sure, sudden, and complete."[171] Soon after, when French hostages were shot in France, Churchill issued a statement on war crimes without giving any specifics about who would be punished or how:

> The butcheries in France are an example of what Hitler's Nazis are doing in many other countries under their yoke. The atrocities in Poland, in Yugoslavia, in Norway, in Holland, in Belgium, and above all behind the German fronts in Russia, surpass anything that has been known since the darkest and most bestial ages of mankind. . . . Retribution for these crimes must henceforward take its place among the major purposes of the war.[172]

This vagueness could not last. "Public opinion in this country," Eden noted, "is taking an increasing interest in this question." The exile Polish and Czechoslovak governments demanded redress. Private committees had started to lobby the Foreign Office, and the suffering of British soldiers was a direct spur to action: "[T]he extension of the war to the Far East and the conduct of the Japanese troops towards British troops and civilians have also given this country a new and direct interest in the question of war criminals." Eden, hoping "to avoid any parallel to the 'Hang the Kaiser' campaign," feared "that there is a serious danger of public opinion, both British and Allied, getting out of hand after the war unless some general decision of policy is reached during the war."[173]

So Eden drew up a broad outline of policy. The most important point in the first British plan was a distinction that would drive all of Britain's subsequent proposals: between major and minor war criminals. While British legalism still applied to the latter, the former were beyond the pale—and, echoing Arendt and Morgenthau, beyond law:

> [A] distinction should be drawn between outstanding enemy leaders, such as Hitler and Mussolini, and other enemy nationals. Judicial procedure would seem inappropriate for dealing with Hitler and Mussolini, and with a limited number of important enemy leaders such as Göring, Goebbels and Himmler. . . . The guilt of such individuals is so black that they fall outside and go beyond the scope of any judicial process. . . . Judicial procedure based upon the laws of war would be reserved for the crimes committed by enemy nationals other than outstanding leaders.[174]

Eden feared that prosecutions would founder, as at Leipzig, and insisted on avoiding "the delays and complications inseparable from setting up special tribunals." Wary of legal entanglements and wavering will, he preferred to follow "the precedent set in the case of Napoleon" for the major war criminals.[175] Better St. Helena than Leipzig.

Churchill himself had been burned by legalism during World War I, when he had disastrously tried to punish German U-boat crew members (see Leipzig chapter) and had become skeptical of the detention of accused Turkish war criminals (see Constantinople chapter). So Churchill was wary of too much legalism this time around. Under the Moscow Declaration, which Churchill had penned, lower-level war criminals would be punished by the Allied countries where the crimes had been committed. For the fifty to one hundred major war criminals left over, Churchill had a simple solution:

> As and when any of these persons fall into the hands of any of the troops or armed forces of the United Nations, the nearest officer of the rank or equivalent rank of Major-General will forthwith convene a Court of Inquiry, not for the purpose of determining the guilt or innocence of the accused but merely to establish the fact of identification. Once iden-

tified, the said officer will have the outlaw or outlaws shot to death within six hours and without reference to higher authority.[176]

To Churchill, this was a way of avoiding legalistic complications that might interfere with the punishment of the Nazis: "By this means we should avoid all the tangles of legal procedure."[177]

Still, Churchill was strongly legalistic in his approach to German war criminals not of the first rank. Churchill never advocated more than a hundred summary executions. At the Tehran Conference in 1943, when Stalin suggested shooting at least fifty thousand Germans, Churchill exploded. As American minutes recorded, Churchill

> took strong exception to what he termed the cold blooded execution of soldiers who had fought for their country. He said that war criminals must pay for their crimes and individuals who had committed barbarous acts, and in accordance with the Moscow Document, which he himself had written, they must stand trial at the places where the crimes were committed. He objected vigorously, however, to executions for political purposes.[178]

In his memoirs, Churchill wrote that he had furiously told Stalin:

> "The British Parliament and public will never tolerate mass executions. Even if in war passion they allowed them to begin they would turn violently against those responsible after the first butchery had taken place. The soviets must be under no delusion on this point."
>
> Stalin, however, perhaps only in mischief, pursued the subject. "Fifty thousand," he said, "must be shot." I was deeply angered. "I would rather," I said, "be taken out into the garden here and now and be shot myself than sully my own and my country's honour by such infamy."[179]

Denouncing "executions for political purposes," Churchill stormed out of the room when Stalin pressed the theme.[180]

The cabinet had its qualms, too. In November 1943, the War Cabinet was presented with Churchill's memorandum, in which he argued that "the process of preparing and publishing a relatively short list of the major war criminals would be calculated on the whole to shorten the War, since it would isolate these named war criminals from the other leading personages in enemy countries." But Churchill's proposal was blocked because it offended the legalist sensibilities of much of the cabinet:

The proposal that major war criminals on the suggested list should be shot as outlaws, without reference to higher authority, was felt by some Ministers to be open to grave objection. To shoot men without trial in this way would be to set a very dangerous precedent, however fully it might be justified in the cases of men who had undoubtedly committed what might be called a capital offence against civilization.[181]

Torn between legalism and Churchill's summary-execution plan, the cabinet could only decide to "record no formal decision" and to hold onto any major war criminals they might come across.[182] The cabinet was so divided that Eden, in June 1944, thought it would be "unwise to approach the United States or Soviet Governments on this difficult and delicate matter until His Majesty's Government have cleared their own minds."[183]

Britain's middle course was summary execution for Axis leaders and trials for the rest. Donald Somervell, then attorney general, worried: "[T]he issues being in the main political, if the Court was an Allied Court, it would be said that the result was a foregone conclusion, and the machinery of justice a façade and a farce." But Somervell was more assured about minor war criminals: "This cannot be said with regard to the trials of the subordinate war criminals."[184] He also believed that Germany's war crimes and the Holocaust were potential legal matters, and he thought seriously about command responsibility for these crimes.[185]

The British had nothing but contempt for show trials. Somervell disliked even the appearance of such impropriety. Judges, Simon wrote, "must, of course, act on their own judgment without any prompting from Executives—Our Anglo-American traditions make this the very cornerstone of criminal justice, and I would never consent to allow British judges to mount the Bench for the purpose of carrying out the order of any Government or combination of Governments."[186] Simon told McCloy that "there would be the strongest repugnance in this country" if the top war criminals got a Soviet-style trial.[187] Britain understood perfectly what legalism was; Britain simply did not want to apply it to Germany's leadership.

A consensus was emerging. When Churchill arrived at the Québec Conference, he brought a memorandum from Simon rejecting trials for Nazi leaders:

I am strongly of the opinion that the method by trial, conviction, and judicial sentence is quite inappropriate for notorious ringleaders such as Hitler, Himmler, Goering, Goebbels and Ribbentrop. Apart from the formidable difficulties of constituting the Court, formulating the charge, and assembling the evidence, the question of their fate *is a political, not a judicial, question.* It could not rest with judges, however eminent or learned, to decide finally a matter like this, which is of the widest and most vital public policy.[188]

As ever, Simon carefully noted that judicial procedure was to be denied only to a handful of top Axis leaders. For them, Simon found a rather English way of saying that they would be shot: "Upon any of these major criminals falling into Allied hands, the Allies will decide how they are to be disposed of, and the execution of this decision will be carried out immediately."[189] Roosevelt and Morgenthau accepted the paper, and agreed to send it on to Stalin and start drawing up a blacklist.[190]

There would be no repeat of Leipzig. The Allies, wrote British diplomat Alexander Cadogan, "did not mean to repeat the mistake which was made a quarter of a century ago when the demand for the surrender of 'wanted' criminals was postponed to the Treaty of peace. By that time many criminals had disappeared or successfully evaded capture."[191] Instead, as the Foreign Office put it, Britain had agreed on Churchill's "own original proposal that the major war criminals, once their names had been agreed, should be declared 'world outlaws' and that military Commanders in the Field should be empowered to execute them as soon as their identity has been established after capture."[192] For a brief moment, Anglo-American policy was to shoot the top Nazis.

This policy did not last long. Like Morgenthau, the British attracted the ire of Henry Stimson. In October 1944, Stimson clashed with Halifax, the British ambassador:

[I]ncidentally the question of the trial of the Nazi war criminals came up and I found that he was pretty well off the track and was thinking the best way would be to shoot them without trial. The result was a long lecture by me on the subject and bringing up points by me which he had apparently never heard before. We got keenly interested and we had a real debate on the subject which I think made a strong impression on him. At any rate I am to send to him my authorities and he is to send me some of the papers which show the British position on the subject.[193]

Stimson's great fight with Morgenthau over war crimes policy was also a fight with Britain.[194] Even after the demise of the Morgenthau Plan, Britain continued to resist Stimson's idea of trials for top Axis leaders. In April 1945, Roosevelt sent Rosenman to bring Britain into line on war criminals issues.[195]

Facing American displeasure, Britain tried to fudge. As a quasi-judicial compromise, Simon suggested setting up "an Inter-Allied judicial tribunal," then drawing up a "Document of Arraignment" laying out the general Allied accusations, and allowing "Hitler and Co. . . . an opportunity of coming before the tribunal and disproving the truth of its contents, if they could." Simon still saw "the gravest objections to putting upon a judicial tribunal the decision of what the punishment should be: that, at any rate, must be for the main Allied Governments to determine. It is a political decision of immense importance, for it may have a profound influence on the future history of the world." His arraignment plan "would justify the Allies in inflicting the severest punishment." While the plan would meet "the qualms of those who think that even Hitler should not be shot without trial, it avoids the interminable and endless dispute which would result from following ordinary procedure." And Hitler could not create a circus: "[T]he worst that could happen would be that he would make a long speech and possibly call some witnesses."[196]

Simon's plan got some support from Jan Smuts, South Africa's prime minister: "To shoot men without trial in this way would set a very dangerous precedent." Smuts hoped for "some middle course" short of a full trial.[197] The rest of the War Cabinet, led by Churchill, had no patience for Simon's quasi-judicial proposal. Indeed, British objections to legalism showed an unwillingness to compromise the integrity of their traditional judicial procedures—and a willingness to be blunt about it. The cabinet worried that

> the action taken against the Nazi leaders would be based neither on judicial trial nor on a political act of State, and we should get the worst of both worlds. Objections would be raised to the plan on the ground that it did not provide for a fair trial; and at the same time the Nazi leaders would be given an opportunity to deliver long speeches in justification of their actions. When the right to appear before a judicial tribunal was once conceded, the right to counsel could not be denied; and it was likely that delaying tactics would be adopted to spin out the proceedings to unseemly lengths. Moreover, as the result would be a foregone conclusion, these proceedings would tend to bring judicial proce-

dure into contempt. Finally, to put Hitler on trial in this way was bound to increase the prospect of his being regarded as a national martyr by subsequent generations of Germans.

For these reasons it was argued that it would be preferable that the Nazi leaders should be declared world outlaws and summarily put to death as soon as they fell into Allied hands.[198]

The cabinet that spoke freely of shooting Hitler nevertheless did not want to compromise its domestic legal standards with a rigged trial. Even at their harshest, the British had liberal scruples that would be quite alien to the Soviet Union.

For lesser offenders, the War Cabinet agreed to Bernays's scheme for trying the Gestapo and SS as whole organizations—that is, extending judicial procedure to the most notorious Nazi terror organs. But there remained, Simon wrote, "a fundamental difference of view between ourselves, who advocate summary execution on identification, and the Americans and Russians, who insist on some kind of judicial process for major criminals."[199] Stimson was unrelenting: "[T]he British have to my utmost astonishment popped out for what they call political action which is merely a euphemistic name for lynch law, and they propose to execute these men without a trial. Sir John Simon . . . while making a feeble attempt first to stand for a fair trial, has popped over to the views of the War Cabinet who wish to execute them at once when they are captured."[200] Stimson's shock suggests that he had expected that the British would prove as legalistic as the War Department.

On the brink of defeat, Simon drafted a final memorandum—eerily titled "The Argument for Summary Process against Hitler & Co."—for the British delegation at San Francisco to show to the Americans and Soviets. In his eloquent and disturbing case for "execution without trial," Simon assumed that Hitler, Mussolini, and other top Axis leaders must be killed. If Hitler was judged "in the manner that is necessary for reasons of justice in a criminal court," including standards of proof, the trial would be "exceedingly long and elaborate." Under British practice, Hitler would have to be given

> all the rights properly conceded to an accused person. He must be defended, if he wishes, by counsel, and he must be allowed to call any relevant evidence. According to British ideas, at any rate, his defence could not be forcibly shut down or limited because it involves a great expenditure of time. There is nothing upon which British opinion is

more sensitive in the realm of criminal procedure than the suspicion that an accused person on trial—whatever the depths of his crime—has been denied his full defence.[201]

On top of that, people might say "that the whole thing is a 'put-up job' designed by the Allies to justify a punishment they have already resolved on." As public opinion grew tired of a long trial, some would say, "The man should be shot out of hand." Hitler might also score some victories in the dock: "[I]f in the complicated and novel procedure which such a trial is bound to adopt—for Russian, American and British ideas must in some way be amalgamated—the defence secured some unexpected point, is there not a danger of the trial being denounced as a farce?" Finally, there was the problem of using international law to criminalize aggression.[202] The essence of the British objection to such a trial was that it would be a fair one, in keeping with British principles. It was precisely because the British knew what those domestic principles were that they did not want to apply them to the Nazi leadership.

This memorandum never got its chance. Finally yielding to its two major allies, Britain gave up. In May, the War Cabinet decided simply that any more opposition to trials would be "inexpedient." Britain would let the Allies draw up plans for a trial for the major war criminals.[203] Britain now aligned itself firmly with the American line, and started the preparations for Nuremberg, and Sir Hartley Shawcross's opening speech there.

What the British Were Putting on Trial: British Suffering, Not Jewish Suffering

Britain was concerned first and foremost with German war crimes against British citizens. In this self-centered outrage, at least, the British road to Nuremberg looked much like the British road to Leipzig.

From the start, Churchill had enshrined this kind of particularism by advocating local prosecutions. The occupied countries should be the ones to punish the Germans. Churchill did this out of a kind of modesty: Britain had not suffered anything like those under Nazi occupation on the Continent, and the victims deserved the right to punish. After getting the Moscow Declaration approved, Churchill wrote to the War Cabinet,

By this means an enormous amount of responsibility for administering retribution will pass from our hands to the many sovereign States who

191

have been outraged and subjugated and who have every right to be the judges of the treatment administered to those who have so horribly mistreated them. I consider this dividing up of the responsibility and retribution work to be one of the most wise and just steps which we in this country or in the United States could possibly take, for I am certain that the British nation at any rate would be incapable of carrying out mass executions for any length of time, especially as we have not suffered like subjugated countries.[204]

Other British officials were also respectful of the suffering of their allies on the Continent. Cadogan wrote:

I am acutely conscious of the fact that, while we in this country have had to pass through the Battle of Britain and have sustained grievous losses throughout the war in every field and element, we have succeeded in throwing back the invader from our own land and have, therefore, not experienced in our own towns and homes the frightful maltreatment which has been the fate of many of our European Allies during the period of German occupation.[205]

And Airey Neave, a British official at Nuremberg, remembered:

To the British soldier, who carried understatement to a ridiculous extreme, the German Army was "old Jerry." American troops, nearer the mark, invaded Europe calling upon the "Krauts" and "cock-suckers" to surrender. Those whose countries had been occupied were more bitter. The French cursed "the Boche" and there was nothing to compare with the fanatical hatred of the Soviet masses for the "Hitlerite murderers."[206]

But when it was Britons who were suffering, the British government was quick to anger. In July 1940, with France fallen and Britain under air assault, after Churchill's "finest hour" speech, Churchill said, "I never hated the Hun in the last war, but now I hate them like an earwig." Soon after the Battle of Britain in September 1940, Germany started dropping mines over London by parachute, so that they could not possibly be aimed at any military target. After a few nights of that, Churchill, an aide noted, was "becoming less and less benevolent towards the Germans, having been much moved by the examples of their frightfulness in Wandsworth, which he has been to see, and talks about castrating the lot!"[207]

This kind of outrage at crimes against Britons translated directly into war crimes policy. Eden thought that the Moscow Declaration entitled Britain to try the Germans who had abused British prisoners of war.[208]

While Britain and America sparred over trial plans, there was no contro-
versy about drafting a special "Royal Warrant" for putting Germans who
had abused British soldiers before a British military tribunal.[209] As in
World War I, Britain was particularly concerned with German submarine
warfare. The British delegation at San Francisco was instructed that the
British "hope to get Doenitz for the part he has played in the direction &
organisation of the barbarous methods of unrestricted U-boat warfare."[210] Britain remembered its own suffering.

The picture was also self-serving when it came to the Holocaust. During
the extermination, Britain had taken few serious steps to help the European Jews. Cadogan, for instance, refused to take in French Jewish children fleeing Vichy. Churchill backed bombing Auschwitz, but his preference was undermined by British officials who did not want to risk
"valuable" (that is, British) lives.[211]

To be sure, the British could be horrified at the extermination of the
Jews. The liberation of Buchenwald and Belsen, for instance, made a
clear impact on British planning, "so as to ensure that those responsible
for the crimes there committed are dealt with efficiently and speedily."[212]
And Churchill told Eden in July 1944 that the Holocaust was "probably
the greatest and most horrible single crime ever committed in the whole
history of the world."[213] But British policy was probably more accurately
represented by the attorney general, Somervell, who thought that "the
primary and main justification for punishing Hitler and his colleagues is
the policy which they have pursued in bringing about and conducting
the war." Nazi war crimes and the Holocaust were, to Somervell, a "very
important" but "secondary reason for punishment."[214]

British officials were of mixed mind about the status of the Holocaust
as a war crime. Simon thought that Hitler's persecution of the Jews "will
play a large part in the decision of the Allies as to his own fate," and that
the UNWCC's bungling of the question of punishing the perpetrators of
the Holocaust was a question that deserved the cabinet's attention. He
was sure that the massacre of Polish Jews was a war crime. But the killing
and persecution of German Jews seemed protected by German sovereignty: "It is, of course, perfectly clear that this does not come within the
category of a war crime, for a war crime essentially involves maltreatment
by the enemy of those who are not fellow-subjects of the enemy. . . . [T]o
seek to try by any sort of Allied or Inter-Allied court German officials for
acts done in Germany to German subjects (albeit Jews) . . . would raise
great legal difficulties."[215] These legal problems stayed on Simon's mind.

His quasi-judicial arraignment proposal included Nazi prewar antisemitic persecution, as well as "the charge that they had set out to maltreat and destroy the Jews."[216] Indeed, Simon argued that one advantage of sidestepping international law was that it would allow punishment for these cruelties.[217]

Others were more sanguine. Halifax wrote to Hull in August 1944 that Britain felt that the UNWCC

> should confine itself to collecting evidence of atrocities of this nature, e.g. those against Jews, only when perpetrated in occupied countries. It is felt that a clear distinction exists between offences in regard to which the United Nations have jurisdiction under International Law, i.e. war crimes, and those in regard to which they had not. Atrocities committed on racial, political or religious grounds in enemy territory fell within the latter category.[218]

The Foreign Office did not want—as Pell proposed—to expand "the scope of the UNWCC's work to include crimes committed by Germans against Germans." Instead, the British proposed to leave the matter to successor regimes in German-occupied countries, or German courts after an Allied victory.[219] Thus, Eden told the UNWCC that although Britain did not "wish to preclude the Commission from collecting any evidence which they feel would be of value in relation to the general extermination policy which has undoubtedly been carried out in occupied territory in circumstances which constitute war crimes," the "majority of these atrocities will have been committed against enemy nationals."[220] Ironically, this hedging was a step *back* for Britain, which had not hesitated in 1915 to condemn the Ottoman Empire for atrocities against Armenians who were Ottoman subjects.[221]

The British public was, if anything, more unsure how to proceed when the victims of Nazi atrocities were German Jews. In one poll, only 66 percent thought that the Allies should punish the Nazis in those cases, while 26 percent preferred, stunningly, to leave the matter up to the German people.[222] Unlike in America, where Bernays was aware of pressure from organized American Jewish groups to include the Holocaust in war crimes charges, the British records surveyed here say nothing about similar domestic pressures. And there was no British equivalent to Morgenthau—someone at the highest levels of government who was preoccupied with the Holocaust. Perhaps as a result, Britain tended to focus on aggressive war, rather than the Holocaust.

The Limits of Legalism

After Leipzig, British officials—many of whom, like Churchill, had been burned personally—were sharply skeptical about legalism for the top German leaders. This book does not argue that liberal states will always be legalist, but that they will overwhelmingly *tend* to be legalist. Even in its lapse for the fifty to one hundred top Axis leaders, Britain showed that it had distinct legalist tendencies: an unwillingness to consider show trials, a reticence about summary executions, and an insistence on legalism for lower-level war criminals. Accounting for British war crimes policy in 1944–45 takes a certain amount of special pleading—not enough to undermine this book's basic argument, perhaps, but still an uncomfortable exception.

THE SOVIET UNION

The defining Soviet statement on war criminals came early on, from Stalin himself, with brutal frankness. At the Tehran Conference in November 1943, Stalin and Molotov hosted a dinner at the Soviet embassy for Roosevelt and Churchill, as well as Eden, Hopkins, Averell Harriman, and other eminent Britons and Americans. In a toast, Stalin proclaimed that the Allies had to stiffen their resolve to keep Germany from launching a third world war. Thus, as the American minutes note, "At least 50,000 and perhaps 100,000 of the German Commanding Staff must be physically liquidated."[223]

In the stunned aftermath, only Roosevelt could react. "The President jokingly said that he would put the figure of the German Commanding Staff which should be executed at 49,000 or more," according to the American minutes. Roosevelt's second-rate joke did not defuse Churchill. In full cry, Churchill denounced "the cold blooded execution of soldiers who had fought for their country." (Stalin needled him for a "secret liking for the Germans.") Churchill insisted that war criminals would, under the Moscow Declaration, stand trial where they had committed their crimes. But he "objected vigorously" to political executions.[224]

It would hardly have been out of type for Stalin to kill 100,000 Germans, or more. Churchill's fit of high dudgeon—and a host of like-minded American and British complaints—made no obvious impact on the underlying Soviet attitude toward punishing war criminals, and ultimately to Nuremberg. The Soviet Union, having taken the brunt of Germany's military assault, was bitterly punitive—far more so than either America or Britain at their harshest. Stalin's grisly suggestion was part and parcel of this Carthaginianism. Soviet vengeance was utterly unhindered by liberal legalistic norms.

Stalin did confuse the issue somewhat by later insisting on trials. Churchill, not bothering to disguise his surprise, reported to Roosevelt in October 1944, after meeting with Stalin in Moscow, "On major war criminals U.J. [Uncle Joe] took an unexpectedly ultra-respectable line. There must be no executions without trial otherwise the world would say we were afraid to try them."[225] But there was an easy explanation for this shift: for the Soviets, these were to be show trials.

This was no particular secret to anyone, either in the American government or, later, in the delegations at Nuremberg. Stimson, the champion of bona fide war crimes trials, did not believe that Stalin had had a change of heart; in June 1944, Stimson reminded Roosevelt of "his conversation with Stalin concerning the liquidation of 50,000 German officers."[226] As early as September 1944, Marshall assumed that "in the case of joint tribunals the Russians would probably send military men as their representatives."[227] "The Soviets were used to political trials," says Bernard Meltzer, an American prosecutor at Nuremberg. Hull had even backed quick "drumhead" show trials as a way of currying favor with the Soviets.[228] Unfettered by any legalism, Stalin sought a dire retribution against the Nazis of the kind he had used against his domestic opponents.

Vishinsky and Vishinskyism, from Moscow to Nuremberg

Spectacular displays like Stalin's toast at Tehran aside, there were countless indications of a deeply punitive Soviet attitude toward Germany and its war criminals. Even leaving aside horrors like the battle of Stalingrad, Soviet civilians had suffered excrutiatingly in the German invasion. An American intelligence report in November 1944 noted that the Soviets would broadly purge as war criminals Nazi leaders, industrialists, landowners, and Germans who had used Russian labor.[229]

Britain saw the same pattern of heavy-handed and often arbitrary punishment. The British embassy in Moscow wrote that the Soviets had adopted

> something of the Old Testament adage of "An eye for an eye and a tooth for a tooth." This does not mean that the Russians, who, for all the Tartar strain in them, lack the coldly calculating Sadism of the *Herrenvolk*, will

indulge in wholesale butchery on the Maidanek model. But it does imply on present showing the mass deportations for forced labour in the Soviet Union of able-bodied Germans, including Germans belonging to minority groups in the satellite States, a tight squeeze of ex-enemy Governments in the matter of reparation deliveries and a ruthless attitude towards all elements in neighbouring countries suspected of collaborationism.[230]

As the Red Army moved west, the British Foreign Office worried that Soviet rage was getting out of control. In liberated parts of eastern Europe, the British saw "the completely cynical way in which the Russians dispose of, or allowed to be disposed of by their clients, persons who are objectionable or inconvenient as members of a class." The Foreign Office predicted a "heavy influx" of Germans fleeing from the Soviets, and noted:

> Certainly there will be genuine war criminals whom we ought to hand over to the Russians. But surely it would be madness to bind ourselves to handing over all and sundry on mere demand from the Russians? . . . We do not know how far the Russians will want to carry their retribution on the Germans, but according to what journalists told me in Moscow on first hand evidence, the Russian procedure is to take mere membership of an objectionable organisation or caste as sufficient reason for death.[231]

Compared to this Soviet fury, America and Britain often seemed almost docile. The Foreign Office, for example, wrote of Soviet perceptions of "the inadequacy and half-heartedness of our own arrangements for dealing with war criminals as compared with their own."[232] "We shall, I imagine, all have got rather tired of this war criminals business long before the Russians have dealt with more than a tiny fraction of the Germans who have committed the most abominable atrocities in the USSR," wrote a Foreign Office diplomat. "Russian and American views . . . will probably differ far more from the fact that the Russians will feel far more strongly about it than the Americans."[233] Churchill himself agreed. "After all," he wrote, "our ursine friends have a pretty strong view on the subject."[234]

So the Soviets moved faster on war crimes issues than the other Allies. By June 1942, while British and American policy was still gestating, the Soviet Union had already put out three notes on German war crimes. In January 1942, Molotov said, in typically fierce language,

The Soviet Government and its organs are conducting a detailed regis-
tration of all these evil crimes of the Hitlerite army. This is demanded
by the angered Soviet people, who call for vengeance. . . . The Soviet
people will never forget nor will they ever forgive these crimes. . . . The
Soviet Government . . . lays all the responsibility for these inhuman and
rapacious acts committed by the German troops on the criminal Hitlerite Government of Germany.[235]

In November 1942, the Soviets set up an Extraordinary State Commission
on German war crimes.[236] When the Majdanek death camp was liberated,
the Soviet Union swiftly set up another such commission specifically for
Majdanek.[237] In December 1943, *Izvestia* bragged that a military tribunal
in Kharkov was the first to punish German soldiers for war crimes.[238] The
trials, of three Germans and a Russian collaborator, served, as Harriman,
America's ambassador in Moscow, noted, to leave "no doubt of the intention of the Soviet authorities to hold the German Government and High
Command responsible for the crimes and atrocities committed in its
name and on its orders."[239] The accused were swiftly tried and hanged.[240]
In late November 1944, a special Polish court put six Nazis on trial for
atrocities at Majdanek.[241] Five of them were publicly executed in front
of what the Soviet press said was a crowd of twenty thousand jeering
spectators.[242]

   The Soviet Union was quick to use these proceedings as propaganda.
The Soviet press was full of grisly reports from this commission on war
crimes committed in regions now liberated by the Red Army.[243] Kennan,
then American chargé d'affaires in Moscow, wrote that the swift punishment of war criminals was a "principal" theme in the Soviet press, often
using "[t]he term purge (*chistka*)."[244] Almost half of *Pravda* and other
Soviet organs was devoted to the Kharkov trials.[245] It was not just the
Soviets who understood the propaganda purposes of war crimes trials—
the BBC broadcast Kharkov too[246]—but the Soviet approach stood out
in its vindictiveness. At Kharkov, one Soviet journalist concluded, "the
Hitlerite Germans are not a special race but a special breed of two-legged
animals brought up in special conditions of artificial savagery. This is a
dangerous breed. It should be annihilated and rendered harmless in the
interests of humanity and compassion."[247]

The Soviet Union revealed a radically different attitude toward the putative trials from their English-speaking Allies. British and American officials, particularly Harriman, worried that the Soviets took an essentially

political view of the punishment of war crimes. Even if the Soviets were taking their cues from their domestic procedures, these too were hugely politicized. As in Soviet domestic courts, where political expediency could determine guilt, so too Soviet international courts would punish Germans not only for violations of international law (as understood by the British and Americans) but also for broader offenses like being a German soldier or working for the Reich.[248]

The Soviets preferred rigged show trials, along the lines of the 1936–38 Moscow purge trials. American reporters covering Kharkov found "the self-abasing testimony of the accused . . . reminiscent of the famous purge trials but attributed this largely to the care exercised in selecting those who were placed on trial."[249] The Soviets did not relent as Allied planning progressed. "There were a lot of arguments between the Americans and the Russians about the [London] Charter," recalls Meltzer. Jackson, America's delegate to London, started his official report on those negotiations by noting politely that the "four nations whose delegates sat down in London to reconcile their conflicting views represented the maximum divergence in legal concepts and traditions likely to be found among occidental nations."[250]

Due process meant one thing to legalistic Americans and quite another to the Soviets. Jackson, in a minor miracle of understatement, wrote:

> Another fundamental opposition concerns the function of a judiciary. The Soviet views a court as "one of the organs of government power, a weapon in the hands of the ruling class for the purpose of safeguarding its interests". It is not strange that those trained in that view should find it difficult to accept or to understand the Anglo-American idea of a court as an independent agency responsible only before the law. It will not be difficult to trace in the deliberations of the Conference the influence of these antagonistic concepts. While the Soviet authorities accept the reality and binding force of international law in general, they do not submit themselves to the general mass of customary law deduced from the practice of western states.[251]

For the Soviets, indictments were statements of fact, and all that remained for the tribunal was to sentence the manifestly guilty Germans in the dock. "The facts were as in the indictments," Meltzer says, summarizing the Soviet point of view. "You look at the arguments over the sentencing," says Meltzer. "The Soviets wanted to hang everyone. Acquittals? They were indicted."

The Americans and Soviets had a long and heated series of arguments over their different conceptions of the tribunal. Jackson patiently tried to explain to the Soviets "what I would envisage in the light of our system."[252] In the London negotiations, Soviet delegate I. T. Nikitchenko said, "The policy which has been carried out by the Axis powers has been defined as an aggressive policy in the various documents of the Allied nations and of all the United Nations, and the Tribunal would really not need to go into that." Flabbergasted, Jackson replied, "If we are to proceed on that basis, why do we need a trial at all?" "The fact that the Nazi leaders are criminals has already been established," Nikitchenko said. "The task of the Tribunal is only to determine the measure of guilt of each particular person and mete out the necessary punishment—the sentences."[253]

Worse, the Soviet Union was guilty of many of the charges being leveled at Germany. On at least one occasion at the London Conference, the Americans threatened to walk out over this. Jackson, with more than a hint of exasperation, called this the "most serious disagreement": "The Soviet Delegation proposed and until the last meeting pressed a definition which, in our view, had the effect of declaring certain acts crimes only when committed by the Nazis. The United States contended that the criminal character of such acts could not depend on who committed them and that international crimes could only be defined in broad terms applicable to statesmen of any nation guilty of proscribed conduct."[254] This, of course, was the unsubtle Soviet solution to the problem that it was guilty of some of the same crimes as the Nazis. "Is it supposed . . . to condemn aggression or initiation of war in general or to condemn specifically aggressions started by the Nazis in this war?" asked Nikitchenko, at London. "If the attempt is to have a general definition, that would not be acceptable."[255] A. N. Trainin, in a book scrutinized for clues about Soviet motives and methods by his British and American peers at London, had written that aggression was "the most dangerous international crime," but quickly added: "It goes without saying that this does not refer to just wars, wars of liberation."[256]

Thus, Germans would be convicted, for instance, of a conspiracy to invade Poland, without any mention of the August 1939 Hitler-Stalin Pact to partition Poland. (The Nuremberg indictment did mention the Hitler-Stalin Pact: condemning Germany for violating it by invading the Soviet Union in 1941.)[257] Kennan was appalled at the hypocrisy: "The only implication this procedure could convey was, after all, that such crimes were justifiable and forgivable when committed by the leaders of one government, under one set of circumstances, but unjustifiable and unforgivable, and to be punished by death, when committed by another set of governmental leaders, under another set of circumstances."[258] Kennan meant this as withering criticism, but it described Nikitchenko's policy perfectly.

The Soviet team even brazenly charged the Germans with the massacres of Polish officers in Katyn forest—which were committed by the *Soviets*.[259] Cadogan skittishly insisted that it must be publicized that Katyn was a Soviet inclusion, and that the Soviets must lead the prosecution.[260] In the end, the Foreign Office considered these charges "undesirable," but did "not think that we can raise them with the Soviet Prosecutor. To do so will certainly create great difficulties, and I suggest that all we can do is to make it clear during the proceedings, and particularly if any question is raised, that this part of the case was prepared and put in by the Soviet Government, who naturally adopted their own wording and are responsible for the contents thereof."[261] When asked about Katyn in Parliament, the Foreign Office dodged: "The matter is a very delicate one . . . and the less that we can say about it the better."[262] The American team at Nuremberg was just as suspicious. Jackson tried to block the Katyn count outright, and, failing, decided to leave it to the Soviets.[263] "We had a lot of suspicions," says Meltzer. Polish officials had told Jackson that Katyn had been a Soviet massacre. In the end, the non-Soviet judges at Nuremberg made sure that their verdict did not mention Katyn.[264]

As with Kharkov, the Soviets used Nuremberg for propaganda on a variety of political causes.[265] For instance, Poland complained that the indictment made only a brief mention of crimes against Poles—a fact the British Foreign Office blamed on the Soviets.[266] Jackson and the British also took offense at the pointed Soviet references in the Nuremberg indictment to the Baltic "Soviet Socialist Republics,"[267] and the British cabinet officially notified the Soviet Union that such jargon was not a recognition of Soviet claims.[268] The Soviet press toed the line, too: for instance, *Red Star* argued against Anglo-Saxon legalism, as judgment had already been passed by the world.[269]

None of this suggests a sincere Soviet concern for fair trials. Jackson, a Morgenthau aide noted, "said they did not have any real discussions and all the Russians are saying is, 'Why didn't you try these men yesterday?' He [Jackson] isn't very optimistic about the Russians getting in the situation."[270] To the irritation of the other Allies, the Soviets insisted on wearing military uniforms at Nuremberg, strikingly distinguishing them from the others in civilian clothes.[271]

In a perfectly clear expression of this preference for Stalinist show trials, the Soviet Union called upon the abilities of no less than A. J. Vishinsky, the infamous prosecutor of the Moscow show trials.[272] In November 1945, as the trials were starting in Nuremberg, Vishinsky was sent to work with R. A. Rudenko, the Soviet chief prosecutor (who, even before Vishinsky arrived, would greet any request from the Americans by saying he had "to call Moscow").[273] The Americans were worried by Vishinsky's arrival, and he did nothing to calm their fears. "I propose a toast to the defendants," he said at a dinner in the Soviets' honor, hosted by Jackson. "May their paths lead straight from the courthouse to the grave!" Most of the guests drank before the toast was translated from Russian, and many of the Americans were appalled when they found out what they had just toasted.[274] As a British diplomat coolly recorded, at a second dinner party in Nuremberg with Jackson and the Western judges, the impresario of totalitarian show trials

> was very affable and made an amusing speech in which he made it quite clear that in his view the object of the trial was to ensure that the defendants were executed. This was not entirely to the liking of the American Judges and even Justice Jackson the American Prosecutor seemed rather alarmed. In private conversation Vyshinski harped on the theme that the defendants deserved death since the Soviet Union had suffered so much at their hands. He also seemed to think that there were too many documents being used and that the trial was proceeding too slowly.[275]

About a month later, back in Moscow, Vishinsky was well satisfied, and told the British ambassador that the Soviet delegation at Nuremberg looked forward to bringing "the trial to a successful conclusion." The ambassador got the point: "For Vyshinski and his compatriots a 'successful conclusion' means of course that most, if not all, of the accused will be hanged."[276] Rudenko's final words to the tribunal were: "I appeal to the Tribunal to sentence all the defendants without exception to the supreme penalty—death. Such a verdict will be greeted with satisfaction by all progressive mankind."[277]

Nikitchenko was the only judge to dissent from Nuremberg's final judgment. He objected to the acquittal of Hjalmar Schacht, Franz von Papen, and Hans Fritzsche (Nikitchenko had considered them guilty from the start); the sentencing of Rudolf Hess to life in prison instead of hanging; and the failure of the tribunal to designate the Reichscabinet, the General Staff, and the Army High Command as criminal organizations.[278]

In the end, Soviet policy on war criminals was harsher both in scale and in method than that of America and Britain. By 1963, trials in the American zone had sentenced 1,184 Germans, 450 of them to death. In the British zone, there were 1,085 sentences, of which 240 were death sentences. The Soviet Union sentenced some 10,000 Germans—about ten times the number sentenced by Britain or America.[279]

The Soviets remained true to their vision of Nuremberg to the end. Even at their most unrestrained, America and Britain never came close to the wild vengefulness of Stalin's Soviet Union. To Stalin and Vishinsky, the trials were to be propaganda exercises, not genuine exercises in due process that might risk the political objective of exacting vengeance. That was a risk that only liberal states would take.

Remembering Nuremberg

Somehow, the Nuremberg trials have evaded the attentions of the Federal Republic of Germany, which has memorialized so much of Germany's dark past. The hulking old *Justizgebäude* looms over Fürtherstrasse, west of the center of town, and still serves as a court. Room 600, where the great trial was held, has been preserved and given a plaque. From outside, one would have no idea what happened there.

But for those who believe in human rights, Nuremberg does not need a physical monument. Nuremberg remains legalism's greatest moment of glory. As such, it has been so exalted by advocates of war crimes trials that almost any noncongratulatory account of it will seem critical. Still, there is not much for legalists to like in Stimson's comments about Morgenthau's "Semitism gone wild for vengeance," Roosevelt's inattentiveness, Morgenthau's screeds, Churchill's proposal of summary executions for the top Nazis, the untamed democratic vengefulness of both American and British public opinion, and Stalin and Vishinsky's sordid efforts. It is only in retrospect that Nuremberg has become unimpeachable.

The single biggest defect, of course, was the concerted Soviet effort to make Nuremberg into a travesty. And the trials are incorrectly recalled as more selfless than they actually were. To the American and British governments, the trials were largely about aggression; to the Soviet regime, they were about propaganda.

But today, most people seem to think of Nuremberg as being primarily about its efforts to punish crimes against humanity, mostly meaning the Holocaust. In this sense, at least, Morgenthau—who was, all other anti-

Germany policies aside, the loudest voice in the White House speaking of Jewish suffering—made a significant contribution to the trials that he did not want. Nuremberg—and another Allied international military tribunal, this one for Japanese war crimes in the Far East—was followed by a series of international gestures aimed at outlawing crimes against humanity, including a UN General Assembly resolution in December 1946 affirming Nuremberg's charter and judgment, and the UN's 1948 adoption of the Genocide Convention.[280] "The recognition of crimes against humanity was the most important legacy of Nuremberg," says Richard Goldstone, the first chief prosecutor of the Hague and Arusha tribunals.[281] Political philosopher Judith Shklar, who did not forget what Nuremberg's planners had meant it to be, could only justify Nuremberg

> due to the revelations about crimes against humanity which it produced. For the American prosecution, however, this was not the main object of the Trial. Its real purpose was to try the Nazi leaders for having waged aggressive war. A conviction on these grounds, Justice Jackson felt, would make an enormous contribution to the future development of international law and order. It was, as such, directed at the remote future, at future generations of mankind. This in itself is a project of doubtful value. Moreover, in order to prove the charge of aggressive war, the distant past would also have to be explored, with all the difficulties inherent in attributing blame and praise for actions that have their beginnings in remote history. The result was that neither of the great ends of the Trial—its educative force among the spectators, and the rigorous attribution of guilt for specific acts—was well served. The future of international law was unaffected.[282]

Today, Shklar's justification of Nuremberg has won out over Stimson and Jackson's.

The Allies were interested parties, in both senses of the adjective. To many lawyers, this looks like a flaw; but it was also a great strength. Unlike today's tribunals in The Hague and Arusha, there was no lack of interest from the great powers at the end of World War II. So Nuremberg was not plagued with lack of resources, refusals to arrest suspects, and low-profile staff. Once the Nuremberg tribunal was up and running, critics could shake their heads at the show of victors' justice, but at least the victors took an interest in justice. The problem of The Hague and Arusha is that the world is not much interested in punishing war criminals; the problem of Nuremberg was that Morgenthau and Stalin, in their own ways, were *too* interested in punishing war criminals.

If Nuremberg was not created out of perfect goodwill, it was still far better than anything else that has been done at the end of a major war. The pressures on the Allies to choose summary execution were enormous, but they resisted in the name of domestic liberal decencies. Legalists are justified in seeing Nuremberg as a famous victory, even if they forget that the margin was razor-thin. In the end, America and Britain managed to produce something extraordinary. We have created nothing to compare with it since.

The Hague

H<small>E IS NOT A MAN</small> of great importance. He is neither a president nor a general, nor, by all accounts, a person with great political aspirations or indeed any particular ambition. Dusan Tadic is short, with small eyes, visibly nervous, and subdued. On May 7, 1996, Tadic had the dubious distinction of becoming the first accused war criminal in the gleaming new dock at the UN international criminal tribunal for the former Yugoslavia (ICTY), in The Hague. He is surrounded by four UN guards, in baby-blue uniforms; they do not look very tough, but neither does he. Still, if the charges against him are true, he is at least an unusually cruel person: he is accused of killing, mutilating, and beating Bosnian Muslim detainees in 1992 at the Bosnian Serb-run concentration camps of Omarska and Keraterm. There were rape charges, too, but they were dropped because a witness was afraid to testify.

Tadic doesn't take many notes, and is often visibly bored as the trial drags on. When an expert witness gives a history lecture that starts in the fourth century, Tadic's earphones are off by the 1910s. He has a vain way of brushing his hair back with thick fingers. But there are subtle signs of strain. On those rare moments when he glances at the gallery to see the press and international dignitaries and dissolute Dutch schoolchildren on a grim field trip, all these people here to watch him in the dock, he quickly averts his gaze. They stare at him through the bulletproof glass that encloses the courtroom; he stares away fixedly. Sometimes his eyelids flutter, in erratic twitchy blinks, and he rubs his eyes and puffs out his cheeks as if trying to compose himself.

The tribunal, sorely in need of good publicity, has flacked Tadic's trial as the opening of the first international war crimes trial since Nuremberg and Tokyo. The Nuremberg comparison is inevitable, but it is not a flattering one. Göring, Ribbentrop, and Jodl were the most powerful surviving men in Nazi Germany; Tadic is only a savage pawn in the Bosnian Serb forces. The Nazis stood their trial soon after the war ended; Tadic went on trial more than three years after the establishment of the tribunal in 1993. The leading Allied staff at Nuremberg were at the rank of attorney general or Supreme Court justice; the staff here, with perhaps two exceptions, are at best middle management. The Nazis were apprehended by victorious Allied armies at the end of the Allied crusade to liberate Europe; Tadic is in custody only because he had the bad luck to get arrested in 1994 by German police in Munich. As Tadic stood his trial, all of the more serious indicted figures—Radovan Karadzic, Ratko Mladic, and fifty-four more—were at large, as Western leaders refused to order the tens of thousands of NATO troops policing Bosnia's peace to arrest them.

Throughout the lands that had been Tito's Yugoslavia, indicted war criminals were in positions of power and comfort, intimidating their former victims with impunity. And never mind about Slobodan Milosevic or Franjo Tudjman, who had so far escaped indictment. (Milosevic was finally indicted in 1999; Tudjman was still publicly unindicted when he died in December 1999.) Historical comparisons only drove home how tokenistic the event was. As an official in the prosecutor's office had said, "The idea that because some thug who was a café owner has been indicted, that justice has been done—nothing could be further from the truth."

It was fitting that the tribunal's first trial was a token gesture. After all, the establishment of the Hague tribunal was an act of tokenism by the world community, which was largely unwilling to intervene in ex-Yugoslavia but did not mind creating an institution that would give the *appearance* of moral concern. The world would prosecute the crimes that it would not prevent. The tribunal was built to flounder.

At first, it did not disappoint. It staggered from one crisis to another: lack of funding; lack of intelligence cooperation from the great powers; lack of staff; threats of amnesties; inability to do investigations; inability to deter war criminals as the wars raged on in Bosnia; and, after the 1995 Dayton accords brought peace and sixty thousand NATO soldiers to Bosnia, a refusal by NATO to arrest the suspects indicted by the tribunal.

Above all, Western war crimes policy in ex-Yugoslavia has been driven by the desire to protect Western soldiers, not Bosnian civilians. Leaders like Bill Clinton and John Major, so solicitous of their own troops, showed an extraordinary ability to shrug off Bosnia's destruction. There were moments when Western public opinion seemed temporarily engaged, horrified by the images of concentration camps like Omarska in 1992, or by reports of mass rape, or by the televised carnage of both Sarajevo market massacres. Some influential constituencies did their best to push intervention, including some feminists (shocked by the use of rape as a weapon of ethnic war), many ethnic and religious leaders, and human rights activists. But for the most part, public opinion in the major democracies was not outraged enough at the slaughter in Bosnia to apply the kind of overwhelming pressure that pushed liberal governments after World War I and World War II to seek vengeance for crimes against their own citizens.

Without that kind of outrage, the tribunal could merely point out blame. International human rights groups and the press, often the tribunal's best advocates, nudged the process along—a crucial role, but no substitute for state power. The best hope was a handful of angry and legalistic senior Western officials, foremost among them Madeleine Albright, America's UN ambassador and later secretary of state, and Robin Cook, British foreign secretary under Tony Blair. Under their pressure, NATO in July 1997 started making a number of arrest raids, mostly of mid-level war crimes suspects. Protecting NATO soldiers remains the top priority—whether they were British and French UN peacekeepers, members of NATO's force in Bosnia after Dayton, or NATO pilots bombing Serb targets from a lofty altitude in the Kosovo war. Even NATO's arrests in Bosnia have been scrupulously designed to avoid Western casualties: in total, one British soldier has been wounded in such raids so far. With a new and forceful NATO mission in Kosovo, and with Milosevic finally indicted and Tudjman dead, the prospects seem brighter. Still, eight years after the discovery of concentration camps in Bosnia, and five years after genocide indictments, Karadzic and Mladic remain at large. Even if they are finally caught, the overall story of The Hague will be largely a dispiriting one.

Creating the Tribunal

Ustashas and Chetniks

In 1991, disintegrating Yugoslavia was a country that had failed to come to terms with its own brutal past. During World War II, the fascist Independent State of Croatia (NNDH) committed unspeakable atrocities against Serbs and Jews. This Nazi quisling state, led by Ante Pavelic, launched a locally unprecedented wave of ethnic slaughter in 1941.[1] Imitating their Nazi allies, the Ustashas—as the Croatian fascists were known—set up concentration camps for their campaign of ethnic killing, including the notorious Jasenovac camp.[2]

The Ustasha state was finally destroyed in May 1945, just after Nazi Germany surrendered. But the memories of the Ustasha slaughter locked Serbs and Croats in mutual suspicion. For Serbs, the terrors of Jasenovac were fresh. Some of the fiercest opposition to the Ustasha regime had come from the Serb monarchist Chetniks, led by Draza Mihailovic, which were increasingly chauvinist in their call for Serb rights. Many Croats feared that the Chetniks would take revenge for the Ustasha atrocities.[3] In Bosnia, while Muslims fought on all sides, some Muslims had backed the ruling Ustasha, and their atrocities prompted Chetnik reprisals in 1942 and 1943.[4]

Tito's communist regime swept all of this grim history under the rug.[5] His Partisans, unlike Mihailovic's Chetniks, had preferred to make multi-ethnic appeals to all Yugoslavs to resist fascism.[6] After the Ustasha state fell, Tito's victorious Partisans executed at least 20,000 and perhaps 40,000 people who had already surrendered, mostly Croats.[7] Tito (born Josip Broz) preferred to execute Ustasha war criminals on the spot, fearing that the spectacle of war crimes trials would only ignite anti-Croat rage among Serbs.[8] The Yugoslav communists presented all of Yugoslavia's nationalities as equal: no one nation was to be singled out for the wartime massacres or for collaborating with the Nazis, even though this flew in the face of facts.[9] Chetniks and Ustashas were put on the same moral plane.[10] In 1946, Tito turned on Mihailovic, staging a show trial for the Chetnik leader, whose forces had committed atrocities against Muslims in Sandzak and eastern Bosnia.[11]

The memories lingered. In the late 1980s and early 1990s, as Tito's Yugoslavia splintered, the history of the Ustasha era made easy ammunition for nationalists. Milosevic, rising to power in Serbia, whipped up ethnic hatred with speeches about the battle of Kosovo Polje in 1389, but he could more credibly scare Serbs by reminding them of the Ustashas. Franjo Tudjman, Croatia's nationalist president, was known for trying to downplay the number of deaths at Jasenovac, and revived the old fascist checkerboard *sahovnica* shield as the symbol of Croatia.[12] Nationalists in Serbia were quick to equate Tudjman's Croatia with Pavelic's.[13] Especially in the Krajina—a part of Croatia with a substantial Serb population, which would prove the flashpoint for the wars of Yugoslavia's disintegration—it was all too easy for Serb nationalists to argue that an independent Croatia would once again prove genocidal toward Serbs, that 1991 would be a replay of 1941.[14] It was not until 1999 that Dinko Sakic, Jasenovac's commandant, hiding out in Argentina, would be tried and convicted in Croatia.

From the Gulf to the Balkans

As Yugoslavia fell apart in 1991, the question of war criminals was fresh in Western minds, too, because of the Gulf War. President George Bush and Margaret Thatcher, the British prime minister, both called for a special UN tribunal for Iraqi war criminals.[15] In October 1990, Bush, with the image of Iraqi despot Saddam Hussein as Hitler in mind, had twice threatened Saddam with another Nuremberg.[16]

Bush's determination faded during the course of the crisis and war, but the idea lingered. As Milosevic stoked Serb nationalism, violence spread throughout the Balkans. First came Serbia's 1991 attacks on Slovenia and Croatia as they seceded from Yugoslavia—the latter war including the shelling of Dubrovnik and the sack of Vukovar, the first major crimes of these wars.[17] This was followed by the Serb onslaught in Bosnia, with devastating "ethnic cleansing" of Bosnia's Muslims and Croats. Serb paramilitary groups and the Bosnian Serb Army imprisoned and murdered local Bosnian leaders, and drove non-Serbs out of their villages, with widespread murder and rape. Western governments had a good sense of the brutal violence against civilians, and of the resulting flow of refugees: 1.1 million by the middle of July 1992. By the time the war ended in 1995, some 200,000 Bosnians had been killed.

Early in the war, Bush made it clear how low Bosnia ranked: "I don't think anybody suggests that if there is a hiccup here or there or a conflict here or there that the United States is going to send troops."[18] What movement there was would come from pressure from public opinion, led by the press and human rights activists. In July 1992, Human Rights Watch, a prominent group in an international human rights movement that had come of age since Nuremberg, called for an international tribunal to punish the perpetrators of war crimes and genocide.[19] On July 19, *Newsday*'s Roy Gutman published the first article about Bosnian Serb-run concentration camps, giving the first mention of names that would become notorious: Omarska, Keraterm, Trnopolje, and Manjaca. Bosnian Serb leader Radovan Karadzic denied that his forces were operating concentration camps. On August 6, Penny Marshall of ITN took Karadzic up on his rash offer to let journalists visit Omarska, and beamed chilling pictures around the world of emaciated Bosnian prisoners behind barbed wire.[20] "It looked like the Holocaust," says a senior Bush administration official. "Nobody pretended not to know."

It was only after such images that the UN Security Council took the first tentative step toward creating a tribunal. On October 6, while the killing continued apace in Bosnia, the Security Council unanimously voted to establish a "commission of experts" to gather evidence of war crimes in the former Yugoslavia.[21] Although France and Britain were not bold enough to vote against the resolution, they from the first saw the issue of war criminals as a potential impediment to making peace in ex-Yugoslavia, binding the hands of policymakers who might have to cut deals with criminal leaders. The UN bureaucracy in the office of legal affairs, and in particular Ralph Zacklin, a Briton, was also obstructionist, according to commission and tribunal staffers.

The commission was set up to go slow, stuffed with academic "old fogeys," as one commissioner put it. The chair, Frits Kalshoven, was an elderly retired law professor at Leiden, in Holland, who admitted he did not know why he had been picked. He was the only full-time member of the commission, which met infrequently and lacked the staff to carry out investigations. One commission member complained that the body was "a low-budget scapegoat." Kalshoven, as *Newsday*'s Gutman reported, was told by "authoritative persons" at the UN not to investigate Milosevic or Karadzic.[22]

Cherif Bassiouni, an Egyptian-American law professor at DePaul University who was on the commission, described Kalshoven as an "indoor scholar," and started pushing hard to make something of the commission. As time went on, Bassiouni—a human rights true believer—accumulated an impressive list of grudges against the UN bureaucracy, blaming France and Britain, with particular scorn for Zacklin as the instrument of obstructionism. Bassiouni raised $1.4 million from the MacArthur and Soros foundations (the latter led by a sympathetic Aryeh Neier), dwarfing the UN budget of $900,000. He stockpiled 65,000 pages of documentation, 300 hours of videotape, and a CD-ROM database. The commission had reports of 900 prison camps, about 90 paramilitary groups (mostly Serb, with ties alleged to the Yugoslav National Army and Serbia's Ministry of the Interior), 1,600 reports of rape, and 150 mass graves.

"It's never blatant," Bassiouni said of UN and European obstructionism, "unless you know how the system works." France, he says, turned over almost no evidence other than published reports to the Security Council. According to Bassiouni, when Holland offered $300,000 for travel expenses in May 1993, it took seven months for the UN to accept the money, after Bassiouni got senior Dutch officials to complain to UN officials.

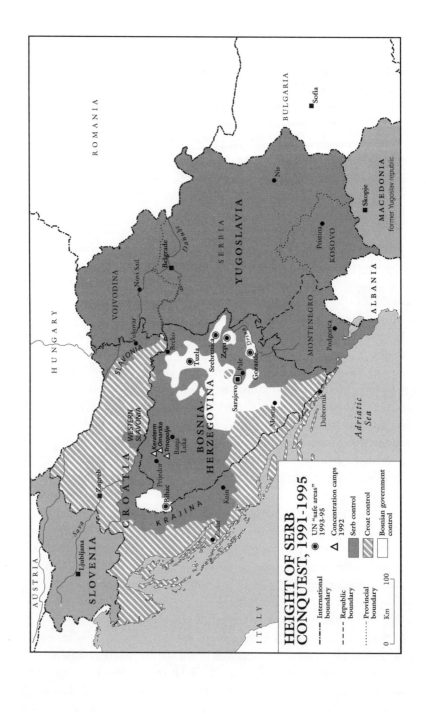

HEIGHT OF SERB
CONQUEST, 1991-1995

◉ UN "safe areas"
   1993-95
△ Concentration camps
   1992
   Serb control
   Croat control
   Bosnian government
   control

─··─ International
     boundary
─ ─ ─ Republic
     boundary
········· Provincial
     boundary

0   100
Km

In August 1993, Kalshoven resigned, leaving the commission officially in Bassiouni's hands. By then, even Kalshoven was publicly complaining about British and French foot-dragging. Britain had not given either money or manpower, he said. When Kalshoven asked Britain to provide combat engineers for a mass grave excavation at Ovcara, outside Vukovar, Britain never bothered to respond. "Britain hasn't done anything for us—nothing at all," Kalshoven complained. "At a practical level we haven't received any help in particular from France and the U.K.," he said in December 1993. "If they didn't want us to participate actively, they shouldn't have voted for us."[23] In April 1994, Bassiouni says, the UN bureaucracy shut down the commission, over Bassiouni's loud complaints that only the Security Council should be able to do that.[24] "Things did not start as a conspiracy," Bassiouni says. "But it wound up with all the characteristics of a conspiracy."

Absent at the Creation

"If there's no international will to stop the killing," said a frustrated UN Security Council ambassador in July 1993, "I don't see how there can be will to have a tribunal." By the end of 1992, Serb forces had conquered 70 percent of Bosnia, and the great powers were still refusing to stop them. "The administration's initial impulse was to cover it up," says Warren Zimmermann, Bush's ambassador to Yugoslavia, of the atrocities. Muhamed Sacirbey, Bosnia's UN ambassador, recalls that proposals for a tribunal were "all intended to defuse the call for military action then," postponing intervention now by promising justice later.

America's position at first was to talk big and carry no stick. "I know of no instance where the violence was targeted by the Bush administration as war crimes," says David Gompert, then the National Security Council staffer on Eurasia. "That would be awkward for our policy." After months of studied disinterest from the Bush administration about the Balkan "hiccup," on December 16, 1992, Lawrence Eagleburger, Bush's secretary of state and a former ambassador to Yugoslavia, gave a dramatic speech at the Geneva peace talks. Eagleburger invoked "a moral and historical obligation not to stand back a second time in this century while a people faces obliteration." He specifically called for charges against Milosevic, Karadzic, and Bosnian Serb Army chief Ratko Mladic for "crimes against humanity," as well as lower-level figures like the notorious Serb paramilitary leaders Vojislav Seselj and Zeljko Raznatovic (Arkan), and a Serb soldier named Borislav Herak who had confessed killing scores of Bosnians to a Bosnian court.[25] There was "dead silence" in the room, Eagleburger recalled, and David Owen, the European Union's mediator, "made it clear he considered my remarks unhelpful."[26]

This sounded impressive, and, relative to other Western reaction to date, it was. But the speech came a month after Bush had lost the presidential election to Bill Clinton, so no one expected the lame-duck Eagleburger to deliver much of anything.[27] On top of that, Eagleburger billed his speech as a spontaneous outburst prompted by a conversation with Elie Wiesel.[28] "I don't have the sense that there was any intention of following up," says Zimmermann. "It was a kind of one-shot expression of irritation and opposition to Milosevic."

Clinton had blasted Bush during the 1992 campaign for coddling tyrants in Beijing and Belgrade, calling for war crimes charges. "If the horrors of the Holocaust taught us anything," Clinton said on August 5, "it is the high cost of remaining silent and paralyzed in the face of genocide. We must discover who is responsible for these actions and take steps to bring them to justice for these crimes against humanity."

But when Clinton was in Bush's shoes, Clinton shifted to the awkward position that he was against crimes against humanity but not prepared to send troops to stop them. After the Vance-Owen plan, which divided Bosnia into ethnic cantons, was proposed, Clinton read a book called *Balkan Ghosts*, which reportedly convinced him that the region was chronically violent and persuaded him to distance himself from Vance-Owen and from air strikes against Bosnian Serb forces.[29] In May 1993, Warren Christopher, Clinton's secretary of state, toured European capitals to sound out America's allies on a policy of lifting the arms embargo on Bosnia and launching air strikes against the Bosnian Serbs (known as "lift-and-strike"); when the Europeans refused to endanger their UN peacekeeping troops on the ground, the administration essentially shrugged and abandoned both lift-and-strike and Clinton's campaign oratory. On May 18, at a congressional hearing, Christopher proclaimed Bosnia "a problem from hell," born of ancient and therefore presumably unmanageable ethnic hatreds.[30] He turned Holocaust analogies against the Bosnians, not the Serbs: "It's been easy to analogize this to the Holocaust, but I never heard of any genocide by the Jews against the German people."[31] On May 21, Clinton stuck by his refusal to send American ground troops to Bosnia: "We don't want our people in there, basically in a shooting gallery."

What did that leave for America to do? Set up a war crimes tribunal, but one without teeth. The Clinton administration's policy had the form of legalism, insofar as it preferred law over other forms of political action, but without the outrage that would be necessary to use law effectively. Law became a euphemism for inaction.

The images from Omarska and elsewhere made some kind of gesture necessary, as Klaus Kinkel, Germany's foreign minister, admitted. In August 1992, he had suggested a tribunal[32]—a legalist proposal from a country that was constitutionally incapable of military intervention. According to American diplomats, France and Britain seemed to oppose a tribunal, but did not want to be seen blocking one. The cynicism of the Security Council was not complete: Madeleine Albright, America's UN ambassador, herself a former Czech refugee from both Nazism and Communism, fought hard for a strong tribunal. It was against this background—nightmare images from Bosnia, coupled with a fundamental Western unwillingness to stop the Serb rampage—that on February 22, 1993, the Security Council unanimously passed a resolution deciding "that an international tribunal shall be established for the prosecution of persons responsible for serious violations of international humanitarian law committed in the territory of the former Yugoslavia since 1991."[33] True to UN form, the court was born with precisely that as its mouthful of an official name, stuck on its letterhead and fax cover sheets: The International Tribunal for the Prosecution of Persons Responsible for Serious Violations of International Humanitarian Law Committed in the Territory of the Former Yugoslavia since 1991.

Picking Goldstone

The West's stance toward Bosnia was perfectly summed up by Clinton on April 20: "The U.S. should always seek an opportunity to stand up against—at least speak out against—inhumanity."[34] So the most heated politicking was not over whether or not to have a tribunal; that could be a token gesture. The pitched debate was over the real question: what *kind* of tribunal?

The tribunal was evidently intended by many countries to be just another kind of reprimand, not an actual court with defendants in the dock. Even Albright did not seem confident that anyone would ever be arrested: "The Tribunal will issue indictments whether or not suspects can be taken into custody. They will become international pariahs."[35]

There were two main kinds of opposition. First, more simply, those states that routinely abused human rights at home or abroad were afraid of setting a precedent that might eventually bring them into the dock.

"They fear the UN might do this to them," said a senior American official. Russia thought of its record in Chechnya, as well as its traditional ties to Serbia. Li Zhaoxing, China's UN ambassador, said that a court should rest on treaties, not Security Council fiat, and that the special ex-Yugoslavia case "shall not constitute any precedent."[36] After Tiananmen Square and Tibet, everyone knew what that meant.

Second, France and Britain were leading the UN Protection Force (UNPROFOR) in Bosnia, which saw its mandate as not to take sides but only to protect the delivery of humanitarian aid. Britain had 2,700 soldiers on the ground, and France 4,000.[37] UNPROFOR's rules of engagement did not allow it to fire on forces attacking civilians, only to return fire if UNPROFOR itself came under fire—rules that earned it the derisive Bosnian nickname of Un-Protection Force. Hoping to get their soldiers out of harm's way, Britain and France were inclined toward a quick settlement in Bosnia. A serious war crimes tribunal might indict men like Milosevic and Karadzic, who would presumably be needed for such a deal. A tribunal, which could not help but indict more Serbs than Bosnians, might expose British and French peacekeepers to Serb reprisals. Many French and British diplomats and military officials tended to see all sides in ex-Yugoslavia as equally guilty, and dismissed Albright's pro-Bosnian rhetoric as cheap: America did not have troops on the ground.

It seemed easy enough to cripple the tribunal without attracting the kind of embarrassing headlines that would come from open opposition to it. The evidence depended largely on victim testimonials, which would be harder to gather as time went on, or if perpetrators could threaten potential witnesses. "Valuable evidence, forensic and testimonial, is disappearing by the day," said Jeri Laber, executive director of Helsinki Watch. The UN bureaucracy was slow-moving, and the usual UN budgetary debates would further hamper things. Then there were the legal complexities of drafting a statute for the tribunal, which took three months.[38]

The selection of eleven judges was the first hurdle. America put up Gabrielle Kirk McDonald, a talented former Texas district judge—not much of a gesture, except of Albright's wish to put a woman on the court. There were groans at the complete list, which included nominations by oppressive regimes like Zaire, Iran, and Peru, plus the breakaway ex-Yugoslav states of Croatia and Slovenia. Egypt—not America—nominated Bassiouni. Bosnia nominated Catharine MacKinnon, a feminist American law professor who would later be criticized by human rights activists for exaggerating rape statistics.[39] "The breakdown on judges resembles the breakdown on [Bosnia] policy," said a senior Western diplomat. "Those who want to do the most have the least power in the Security Council, and those who want to do the least have veto power."

But when the UN General Assembly made its choices, the list wound up hack-free, with at least three high-profile judges: two prominent Egyptian and Canadian jurists, and, above all, Antonio Cassese, a compassionate and well-respected Italian international law professor and human rights advocate, who was named as the tribunal's president, or chief judge.[40] Bosnia's Sacirbey complained that there were no Muslims on the bench, showing "maybe outright bias towards Muslims."

In November, the eleven judges took office in The Hague.[41] It was a sobering experience. Cassese would later reckon that the Security Council had "thought we'd never become operational. We had no budget, we had nothing. Zero." The judges were being paid on an ad hoc basis until the end of 1993. They were not even sure that the tribunal would stay in The Hague.[42] There were a few computers, and two weeks of rent paid for a few rooms in the Peace Palace, the seat of the International Court of Justice (the other hamstrung UN tribunal in town). "Some of us were saying, 'Let's go slow,' " said McDonald.[43] But not Cassese, who set about finding the tribunal a headquarters in a slightly run-down building shared with a Dutch insurance firm, and starting work on a single courtroom and on a twenty-four-cell jail. The tribunal drew up rules of procedure, wrestling in particular with how to try crimes of sexual assault.[44] Worst of all, the tribunal had no indictments and no cases, for a simple reason: there was no prosecutor to bring them.

The selection of a prosecutor was a protracted, politicized fiasco.[45] It was clear that a weak prosecutor would doom the tribunal to obscurity. But because the prosecutor did not answer to anyone in making indictments, a bold prosecutor could indict Milosevic, Karadzic, or Tudjman. "That's the key," said Sacirbey. "If the office of the prosecutor is undermined for political expediency, the entire process is in jeopardy of making a mockery of the international legal system."

Bassiouni, still fuming over his fights with France and Britain, was actively lobbying to get the tribunal's top job, with backing from Boutros Boutros-Ghali, an old friend from Egypt who was now UN secretary-general. But Christopher had decided the prosecutor should not be an American, and Bassiouni quickly ran into resistance from predictable quarters. "There are certainly some members of the Security Council that are not too enthusiastic about having an aggressive prosecutor who is likely to disrupt political processes," Bassiouni said—with Britain obviously in mind. "They prefer a tame or manageable prosecutor to suit their political agenda. I'm obviously not one of those persons."

Although British officials would only call Bassiouni "controversial," Britain pointedly put forward its alternative: a Scottish prosecutor named John Duncan Lowe. Bosnia and its supporters saw this as an attempt to neutralize the tribunal. "We cannot have a European, and especially not an Englishman," said a pro-Bosnian Security Council representative. "Britain cannot negotiate and give absolution at the same time." A senior Western diplomat was more blunt: "If you're a Bosnian, do you want a *Brit* as your prosecutor? If you're France or Britain or Russia, do you want an outspoken Muslim?" Compromise candidates from Canada, Argentina, and Kenya were met with derision, says a Security Council ambassador. Later, Sacirbey went further: "Bassiouni was, behind the scenes, negated as a prosecutor because he was Muslim."

Predictably, this all blew up. Albright preferred Bassiouni over Lowe, but neither was likely to get a majority of the fifteen votes in the Security Council, and she wanted a unanimous vote to show world consensus.[46] (British officials would later also profess not to have wanted a split in the Security Council, which rang a little false since they had nominated the candidate that split the council in the first place.) Boutros-Ghali forced the issue in August 1993 by nominating Bassiouni, who was shot down by Britain. Boutros-Ghali then nominated India's attorney general, who was blocked by Pakistan.[47]

Next, Diego Arria, Venezuela's UN ambassador, a sympathizer with Bosnia who had pushed hard for Bassiouni, suggested one of his own: Ramon Escovar Salom, the attorney general of Venezuela, a figure almost totally unknown to most of the Security Council. Bosnia trusted Arria, and Boutros-Ghali nominated Escovar. No one objected, and in October, the Security Council named Escovar as prosecutor.

No one, that is, except Escovar. He accepted on the condition that he could stay in Venezuela until February 1994 to continue a corruption probe against a former president there. In mid-January, he interviewed an Australian war crimes prosecutor, Graham Blewitt, to be deputy prosecutor. "The same day he brought me before the tribunal," Blewitt recalls, "before the judges in plenary, and said, 'We've found a good deputy prosecutor, and now I'm not going to take up the position of prosecutor, and I'm out of here.'" Escovar resigned and became Venezuela's interior minister.[48] These were not exactly the actions of a man burning to do righteous deeds in Bosnia.[49] Back to square one, America suggested a former U.S. attorney. This time it was Russia's turn to object, recalling a deal not to name anyone from a NATO country for major international Bosnia jobs, which also blocked a Canadian candidate.[50] Tempers were running short.

It was at this point that Nelson Mandela saved the day. By now, Cassese was considering asking his fellow judges to resign en masse in protest. At the same time, quietly taking matters into his own hands, Cassese approached his ideal choice: Richard Goldstone, a high-profile South African judge. Goldstone was interested, but wanted to safeguard the seat he was sure to get on South Africa's new Constitutional Court. Mandela, democratic South Africa's first president, encouraged by a phone call from Christopher, agreed to hold Goldstone's place open while Goldstone served as prosecutor. "He certainly encouraged me," Goldstone says, of Mandela. "He thought it was important to take what was the first offer of a major international position after South Africa ceased to be a pariah." Mandela's intervention was a pure fluke, but the Security Council dared not play games with the heroic Mandela's pick. Cassese, ecstatic, faxed his fellow judges a Latin note with the traditional Vatican message heralding a new pope: "Habemus papum!"[51] On July 8, the Security Council unanimously approved Goldstone. He took office the next month.

The tribunal had spent eighteen months without a prosecutor.

Pope Goldstone

Richard Goldstone, the man who was supposed to breathe life into the tribunal, does not act dynamic. He is short, stern, and almost owlish. His most striking physical characteristic is the faint beginning of jowls, which gives the incorrect impression that he is almost constantly frowning. He has a pedantic and precise way of speaking, choosing every word with care. (He and Cassese made an odd pair: the top judge with the temper of a prosecutor, and the top prosecutor with the temper of a judge.) Goldstone seems, in a word, lawyerly.

But Goldstone's reputation at The Hague was, almost from the start, quite the opposite: as a politico. A student anti-apartheid activist at the University of the Witwatersrand in Johannesburg, he had worked his way up to the Transvaal Supreme Court and then the appellate division of South Africa's Supreme Court. Although some democratic activists criticized him for taking a judicial appointment from the apartheid state, he had managed to preserve a liberal reputation, and had found in apartheid's patina of legality a direct challenge to his faith in law as an instrument of substantive justice.

For Goldstone, politics often lurked behind law. In 1992, Goldstone pointed out that most South African judges "applied such [apartheid] laws without commenting upon their moral turpitude. A significant number, however, did not remain silent"—a group in which Goldstone included himself, and which he thought helped the courts' credibility. With his typical precision, Goldstone said: "Frequently it is difficult to decide where moral precepts and standards end and where strictly political doctrine begins. In that area, in my view, if a judge is to err, it should be on the side of defending morality."[52]

Goldstone's belief in the interplay of politics and law was further shaped by the job that made his name (and bore it): chairing a government commission of inquiry into political violence from 1991 to 1994, better known as the Goldstone commission. The commission mostly criticized apartheid South Africa's police, as well as the Zulu-based Inkatha Freedom Party and Mandela's African National Congress. Goldstone later said he was shocked at how high up apartheid's brutality went. In many ways, Goldstone's task at the commission paralleled his responsibilities at The Hague. He was independent in his choice of cases; there were more cases than he could possibly investigate, so he had to choose instructive ones; his court had strictly limited powers; and he was executing a legal mandate in a highly politicized environment.

It is never clear exactly to what extent Goldstone—no naïf—saw himself as truly apolitical. On the one hand, in public he declared himself to be simply executing a mandate. "I've got no function other than to expose the causes of violence," he told *The Los Angeles Times.* "And whatever the political consequences of what we find, so be it."[53] On the other hand, in 1992 he had implied that the line between morality and law was not always bright, and that moral considerations should guide judges. However he resolved these tensions, it was with this background that Goldstone left South Africa for The Hague.

He arrived to find a shambles. Goldstone was appalled at the slow-moving UN bureaucracy, which he had to "beg and cajole" to do its work. "A bureaucracy made up of civil servants from 186 countries is more than 186 times worse," Goldstone would later complain. Some members of the prosecutor's staff were still figuring out the situation in ex-Yugoslavia, and the tribunal admitted it was having problems finding enough qualified investigators.[54] In December 1994, Goldstone reckoned he needed twice the number of staff he had, including lawyers and investigators.[55]

Blewitt had started work on fourteen investigations, often of low-level figures.[56] It was a daunting task. The tribunal had to excavate mass graves, find witnesses to crimes that had happened two years ago, create a witness protection unit, counsel rape victims, and cull eyewitness fact from recycled rumor. The early work relied on the commission of experts' best work, a report on Prijedor, which prosecutors would nevertheless later criticize. Some documents from the commission of experts might be forgeries by Croatian intelligence, says a former commission member. It would be enormously difficult to meet legal standards of proof.

Then there was the huge problem of money. In 1993–94, the UN at first proposed the shockingly small sum of $562,300 for investigations—including witness travel, interviews with refugees, forensic experts, translators, and protection, according to former Bassiouni aide Tom Warrick. In December 1993, the UN General Assembly gave the tribunal $5.6 million for the first half of 1994, so the court could only make contracts for those six months. That meant it could not sign a lease, hire long-term staff, or buy equipment for investigations. This scared away many potential staffers.[57] As the tribunal put it in an official report, the court "was operating with one hand tied behind its back."[58]

In April 1994, the General Assembly gave over another $5.4 million to cover expenses until the end of December 1994. The tribunal could now sign a lease for its Churchillplein headquarters in The Hague, but the sum was still hopelessly inadequate. (By way of comparison, the tribunal's 1999 budget was over $94 million.) The tribunal only had one courtroom for three chambers; the prosecutor's office was desperately trying to recruit serious staff; and the judges were still drawing their salary on an ad hoc basis.[59] In July, twenty prosecutors and investigators were sharing a single telephone to call outside of Holland.[60] It was only in July 1994 that the prosecutor's office felt capable of starting field investigations.[61] The UN's two budget committees tried to cut the budget by 20 percent for 1994.[62] Goldstone had to fly to UN headquarters in New York, cap in hand.[63]

Small wonder that the UN, and particularly its office of legal affairs, continued to frustrate the tribunal. "You know, I used to think that on the list of people who wanted to get Ralph Zacklin, Cherif [Bassiouni] was number one," said an official after watching Goldstone fume in a meeting. "Now he's number two." When Zacklin was mentioned, one senior tribunal official snapped, "Arrogant little shit." Asked about

Zacklin (who has since been promoted to UN assistant secretary-general for legal affairs), Goldstone chuckled: "That is below the belt."

Governments were slow to stuff Goldstone's pockets. America was the most generous, giving $3 million for computers and, crucially, seconding twenty-two investigators and prosecutors. This was a huge shot in the arm (the total number of prosecution staffers was only sixty-seven),[64] although it would later cause grumbling about the dominance of the "American mafia" and UN disapproval of more American hires, plus the usual complaints about America's delinquency in paying UN dues. Major's Britain gave $30,500 and one staffer. France gave nothing. Sweden, Denmark, Malaysia, and Pakistan were all more generous than Britain and France.

To the frustration of American officials, this European foot-dragging reflected a general European sense of the Balkans as an endless quagmire for European soldiers. France and Britain, said a senior American diplomat, were "further along the line toward reconciliation without justice." "When faced with a formal decision in the Security Council, they're helpful," said an American official, of the British. "When they have to do something voluntarily, they aren't." British Foreign Office diplomats were evasive when asked if they would use sanctions for states that rebuffed the tribunal. The problem, said a British official, was "indicting people [when] you may be negotiating with them."

America was more enthusiastic, but still underwhelming. In February, after a Bosnian Serb shell exploded in Sarajevo's Markale market, Clinton snapped, "Until these folks get tired of killing each other . . . bad things will continue to happen." Steve Walker, a Croatia desk officer and Balkans specialist at the State Department, who resigned in protest of Clinton's inaction in 1993, says that the State Department was "barely going through the motions," doing just enough to outperform America's more reluctant allies. "Saying we supported the war crimes tribunal was easy," he said. Albright was more serious, but it was clear she had no great backing in Washington. Even John Shattuck, the assistant secretary of state for human rights, kept expectations low. "Justice doesn't have to ultimately mean putting people behind bars," Shattuck said. "I would not measure [the] tribunal in terms of how many people go to jail, or top-level people, because the number is going to be very low. Success is a commitment to establish principles of accountability, getting out the truth."

In the face of all this, Goldstone's immediate task was to show that the tribunal was viable and relevant. He insisted that no one on the political and military ladder was immune, and that he preferred to aim at the top. But his first indictments were far lower down. On November 4, 1994, the tribunal confirmed Goldstone's first indictment: of the commander of the Susica camp in Bosnia, accused of crimes against humanity in the summer of 1992.[65] There were no illusions that Bosnian Serbs would turn him over. On November 8, Goldstone asked Germany to defer to The Hague's jurisdiction the prosecution of Tadic, a Bosnian Serb in German custody, already indicted by Germany for crimes at Omarska.[66] Tadic would be the first person in the tribunal's custody.

Goldstone knew he needed to raise the tribunal's visibility, and even the judges were urging him to issue more indictments.[67] Although some of the early indictments are unlikely to hold up in court, they seemed necessary at the time. Not everyone agreed. "We waste our time going after these small fish," said a Goldstone staffer. Cassese was against "trying small fry." In 1997, a senior tribunal official would describe the list of indictees as "this fucking list of idiots." Some of these cases rested on a small number of witnesses; if two or three could be intimidated out of testifying, said nervous prosecutors, then the case would collapse. (In February 1998, Robert Gelbard, an American envoy, would publicly say that America thought many indictments "will not stand up in court."[68] Louise Arbour, Goldstone's successor, has dropped indictments against seventeen suspects.)

By far the worst problem was the unfolding bloodbath in ex-Yugoslavia. Goldstone came into office while Serb forces continued to besiege Sarajevo and other Bosnian towns, and in the aftermath of the brutal 1993–94 war between Bosnian Croat forces and the Bosnian government. Except for the Bosnian government, authorities in ex-Yugoslavia viewed The Hague with contempt. Serbia, blocking international investigations, complained that the tribunal was biased against Serbs. Against this, the tribunal could only threaten to report noncompliance with its orders and arrest warrants to the Security Council.[69]

To no avail. Cassese formally protested five times, and each time got roughly the same reply from the Security Council.[70] "We deplore their attitude, we condemn their attitude. Either deplore or condemn," Cassese said. "Maybe next time they'll find a third word." Relying on a reluctant UN and NATO to enforce its edicts, the tribunal could only inconvenience and stigmatize its suspects. Goldstone often pointed out that it was hard to be a world leader if one could not travel. Under the tribunal's Rule 61, Goldstone could hold a public hearing on the evidence against suspects being shielded by recalcitrant Balkan authorities.[71] But Goldstone had no troops.

Protecting Soldiers

NATO had the troops. In all of The Hague's early difficulties, the fundamental hurdle was the West's refusal to take military action against war criminals in ex-Yugoslavia.

A dread of Serb reprisals against UNPROFOR lay at the root of French and British fears of being seen as less than impartial.[72] UNPROFOR's guidelines made it perfectly clear that humanitarianism yielded pride of place to self-protection: "The execution of the mandate is secondary to the security of UN personnel."[73] David Owen later wrote, "I believe Mladic knew that UN troops were his ultimate safeguard against NATO air power."[74]

To the frustration of its NATO allies, America refused to send troops into Bosnia. Colin Powell, chairman of the Joint Chiefs of Staff under Bush and then Clinton, later wrote: "No American President could defend to the American people the heavy sacrifice of lives it would cost to resolve this baffling conflict."[75] In 1993, Clinton's choice of a lift-and-strike policy had the advantage of not embroiling American soldiers in ground combat. But it risked UNPROFOR troops, so the Europeans scotched the idea.[76] America's reluctance to risk troops overseas was only strengthened in October 1993, when eighteen American soldiers were killed in Somalia while trying to catch faction leader Muhammad Farah Aideed.

Such American reticence complicated the tribunal's work, as for instance in the excavation of a mass grave in a field at Ovcara, near Vukovar, where some 260 Croats from Vukovar hospital had allegedly been executed by Milosevic's Yugoslav National Army in 1991. The forensic investigators at Ovcara were led by Physicians for Human Rights, a Boston-based organization. But when the group asked for military engineers, in June 1993, the State Department and the Pentagon—to Albright's chagrin—refused, fearing Serb attacks.[77] (Britain, according to Kalshoven, never even replied to a similar request.)[78] "If you want us to deploy soldiers," said James Rubin, Albright's spokesman and confidant, "you need more soldiers to protect them, a whole 'nother level of commitment which the United States government has not reached."

224

The investigators had to settle for about 150 Dutch army volunteers. According to Eric Stover of the UN team, they had to beg permission from the local Serb authorities, who demanded the exhumation of a mass grave with dead Serbs. In October 1993, the UN team set out, and eerily found itself being housed in barracks that backed onto a training ground for Arkan's Tigers, a savage Serb paramilitary group. The UN team was only able to clear away the overgrowth at Ovcara before the local Serb general, Milan Milovanovic, sitting beneath a picture of Milosevic, ordered them out.[79]

As the war dragged on, both Britain and France lost all stomach for the UNPROFOR mission. Most of Major's cabinet wanted Britain's 5,500 troops out of Bosnia before the winter of 1995–96, and France warned that it would bring its 5,000 UNPROFOR soldiers home if America did not make a military commitment in Bosnia.[80]

America was no more enthusiastic. Clinton resented the media's focus on war crimes in Bosnia. "They keep trying to force me to get America into a war," Clinton once said.[81] "The president was being asked here to go out on a limb with an issue that had no constituency," says Dick Morris, Clinton's former pollster and strategist (who has since turned against Clinton). In May 1995, Clinton tentatively said that America "should be prepared to assist NATO" if NATO asked. The White House panicked as Clinton's approval ratings dropped and Morris warned of public perceptions of another Vietnam. Clinton backtracked, vowing to send troops to help British and French soldiers only if there was no fighting going on.[82]

There was a vivid example of the West's emphasis on its own soldiers in May 1995. On May 25, NATO planes finally struck at Bosnian Serb forces that had defied a NATO ban on shelling Sarajevo, a UN–designated "safe area." The Serb forces retaliated by shelling all six "safe areas" in Bosnia, including a shell that killed seventy-one people in Tuzla. This did not faze NATO. But then the Serbs took more than 350 UNPROFOR soldiers hostage, chaining one Canadian soldier to a Bosnian Serb Army ammunition dump. Holbrooke, a lone hawk, argued to Christopher that NATO should demand the release of hostages and continue bombing if the Serbs refused. Instead, the American government decided to quietly put off air strikes, fearing Serb retaliation against the hostages. Britain, France, and Canada caved in, stopping the air strikes and starting quiet talks to get their hostages back. Bernard Janvier, the UN force commander in Bosnia, requested and got a meeting with Mladic. Janvier told Yasushi Akashi, the UN special representative on Bosnia, "We are no longer able to use air power because of the obvious reason that our soldiers are on the ground." Akashi announced that UNPROFOR would stick to "strict" peacekeeping.[83] And on September 10, Janvier met with Mladic, at the request of President Jacques Chirac of France, to ask for the release of two downed French pilots.[84]

The nadir came with the Srebrenica massacre in July 1995. As he conquered Srebrenica, Mladic took 450 Dutch UNPROFOR troops hostage as a hedge against NATO air strikes. "Srebrenica taught us that our lives were less valuable than the lives of the UN soldiers," one survivor said later. "That, for us, was the final truth."[85] A Bosnian officer said that, for the West, thirty Dutch hostages in Serb hands were worth more than 30,000 Muslims. On July 10, Joris Voorhoeve, the Dutch defense minister, did decide to risk thirty Dutch lives if there were NATO bombings; but the NATO raids never came. The Clinton administration's first reaction to Srebrenica was to avoid having to risk its own troops—not by rescuing the Bosnians, but the Dutch UN troops. Akashi met with Mladic to try to free the UNPROFOR hostages and to let the International Committee of the Red Cross check on thousands of Muslim prisoners.[86] In an impetuous flash of Western courage, Chirac suggested to Clinton sending French and American troops to liberate Srebrenica. Clinton, incredulous, refused, as did Britain and Holland. America also dismissed Chirac's proposal that American helicopters fly French troops into the threatened enclave of Gorazde, a mission seen as too risky for the American pilots; instead, NATO threatened air strikes.

But when a single American life was on the line, America could make spectacular efforts. As American soldiers were dying in Somalia in 1993, Clinton had exploded: "We're not inflicting pain on these fuckers. . . . When people kill us, they should be killed in greater numbers. . . . I believe in killing people who try to hurt you, and I can't believe we're being pushed around by these two-bit pricks."[87] In Bosnia, he got his chance. Just over a month before Srebrenica's fall, a Bosnian Serb Army missile shot down an American F-16, leaving its pilot, Scott O'Grady, trapped behind Serb lines. O'Grady was rescued six days later by Marine commandos.[88] Clinton himself was notified in the White House residence by a midnight phone call. "He was just gleeful," remembers Dick Morris, "like he was at a basketball game." O'Grady—an American war hero, without an American war—returned home to national acclaim and a White House reception with Clinton, Vice President Al Gore, William Perry, the secretary of defense, and John Shalikashvili, chairman of the Joint Chiefs of Staff. When NATO finally started bombing Bosnian Serb forces soon after, Clinton remembered the area where O'Grady had been downed, and wanted to strike there on principle. "Did he value American lives more than Bosnian lives?" says Morris, of Clinton. "Damn right he did. He's president of the United States."

"An Academic Exercise"

Even with Goldstone at the helm, the tribunal staggered through much of 1995. Its 1995 budget of $25 million was insufficient for witness protection and investigations, and prosecutors worried they were not getting crucial intelligence from Western governments.[89] Goldstone, who took media relations seriously, could use his high profile to appeal directly to Western public opinion. In retrospect, Goldstone is not sure if he made enough noise or not: "[P]ossibly if one had been less gracious and less diplomatic at that point, it may have been worse. . . . We were a very new institution. We had to establish our own credibility." Goldstone could also put pressure on the West simply by issuing more indictments. On February 13, he indicted twenty-one Bosnian Serbs for running the Omarska concentration camp in 1992. Camp commander Zeljko Meakic was slapped with the first indictment ever for genocide.[90] But of the twenty-one, only the low-level Tadic was available for trial. "Not a terribly intelligent person," sniffed a Goldstone staffer.

The idea was to build upward from such cases. Hopes quickly faded for a "smoking gun" document that would directly implicate Milosevic in "ethnic cleansing" in Bosnia.[91] Instead, the prosecutors could only hope to build slowly on divisions among the nationalist Serb and Croatian leadership. During Serbia's 1993 parliamentary elections, for instance, the regime's men had accused Seselj's paramilitaries of war crimes; Seselj fired back that he would go to The Hague, but "I don't see how I could go without Slobodan Milosevic."[92] Seselj would later claim to have "incontestable proof" that Milosevic, not Karadzic or Mladic, was commanding the war in Bosnia.[93] Relations between Milosevic's regime in Belgrade and the Bosnian Serb leaders in Pale were always fractious and often poisonous. If a mid-level leader could be put on trial, he might give information on higher-ups to save himself. The cases against senior figures, if Goldstone dared, would rest on command responsibility: showing that leaders must have either ordered, or known of and not prevented, war crimes.

This was no small task. Because the Serbs were utterly uncooperative, it was easier to gather evidence from Bosnians and, to a lesser extent, Croats—ironically, the Serb accusation of bias made it more likely that

The Hague would indict Serbs. Many of the early indictments aimed low, at figures too uninvolved in the chain of command to incriminate the major leaders. It was difficult to trace the chains of command in Serbia and the Bosnian Serb power structure, and the links with paramilitary groups were particularly murky. These were some of the possible reasons why Goldstone did not publicly indict prominent thugs like Arkan and Seselj. Asked about Arkan and Seselj, Goldstone said, "The only thing I can say to anybody who thinks people should be indicted who haven't been indicted: give us the evidence. And by evidence I don't mean allegations. I mean witnesses or documents with which we can go to court." Holbrooke writes that he repeatedly pressed Goldstone to indict Arkan, but got no answer.[94] (In June 1997, Arkan would claim that he was exonerated because he had not been indicted.[95] It was not until September 1997 that Arkan was finally secretly indicted—more than five years after his war crimes made him notorious.)

How high could the tribunal dare to aim? The most obvious—and delicate—target was Milosevic, who had driven Yugoslavia into collapse and war. In the event, Milosevic would not be indicted until 1999, for atrocities in Kosovo. But as early as 1991, his JNA had committed war crimes in its war with Croatia, and Western intelligence had no doubts that Serbia was helping the Bosnian Serb Army and Serb paramilitaries. Roy Gutman, a respected journalist, argues that under Serbia's own chain of command, Milosevic bore command responsibility for Serb paramilitary groups.[96] But indicting Milosevic might set off a political earthquake. Goldstone insisted that he did not care. "If we get evidence, we'll give priority to higher-ups," said Goldstone in November 1995, when asked about indicting Milosevic. "I don't exclude anybody. If we haven't indicted someone by now, it's because we don't have evidence." He firmly denies that there was ever any pressure to spare Milosevic.

Other tribunal staffers admitted to more nervousness. Because the standards of proof for an indictment are lower than those required for a conviction, some staffers in the prosecutor's office figured they could indict Milosevic, but they were not sure they could get a conclusive conviction in court. People in the prosecutor's office liked to quote a proverb (although no one was sure where it was from): "If you're going to strike at the king, make sure you kill him." It would be irresponsible and mortally embarrassing to lodge a weak indictment against a major figure.

Then there were the political problems: disrupting Balkan diplomacy, and testing the limited tolerance of the Security Council. Milosevic was cultivating an image of himself as a useful interlocutor for the West. It is impossible to believe that Goldstone was not aware of these considerations, although he would vociferously deny that politics played any role in his decision. "I think there'll be hesitation from the prosecutor," said one Goldstone staffer. "Politically, you don't want to dislocate someone from the political process." Hague staffers might not have needed to worry; a senior Clinton administration official says that an indictment would not have prevented America from negotiating with Milosevic.

Tudjman, the other major nationalist seen as useful by the West, also seemed to be off the hook. Prosecutors, while aiming at Bosnian Croat atrocities in the Lasva Valley, said they were having difficulties definitively linking him to those operations. "I just don't think it's going to happen," said a Goldstone staffer. "Making a Greater Croatia is not a war crime." Moreover, says a Bosnian diplomat, Bosnia was somewhat circumspect in its accusations against Croatia, realizing that Croatian support was needed to balance against the Serb forces.

That left Karadzic and Mladic. The Bosnian Serb leaders had a vile reputation in the West, and Karadzic was increasingly in ill odor in Belgrade.[97] Marginalizing Karadzic and Mladic might help peacemaking efforts. "You have two options," said a Goldstone staffer. "A, you can indict Milosevic and be shut down. B, or you can do low-level [indictments] and do a few trials, like Mladic and Karadzic." Though not as bold as indicting Milosevic, it was still a heady prospect. Goldstone thought that the Security Council probably had never thought that creating the tribunal would lead to the indictment of Karadzic and Mladic.

"Goldstone really pushed on Karadzic and Mladic, to the point of rebellion," remembers a member of Goldstone's staff. "He wanted it sooner rather than later." The Bosnian government was also investigating Karadzic and Mladic, which helped force Goldstone's hand. On April 21, 1995, Goldstone asked Bosnia to suspend its investigation and defer to The Hague instead.[98] Finally, after issuing another round of lower-level indictments,[99] Goldstone threw his thunderbolt: on July 25, he indicted Karadzic and Mladic for genocide and crimes against humanity.[100]

The indictment, bringing together investigative work from several teams, was a kind of accounting for much of the Serb war in Bosnia. The charges were a grotesque litany of the cruelty Karadzic and Mladic had presided over: shelling and sniping at civilians in Sarajevo and other towns; camps like Omarska, Keraterm, Trnopolje, Luka, and Manjaca[101];

the sacking of mosques and Catholic churches; murder, rape, and torture. There was also one count for taking UNPROFOR troops hostage
two months earlier.[102]

European countries, used to negotiating with Karadzic and Mladic,
were startled to have them named as pariahs.[103] "I never thought that that
was insurmountable," recalls Warren Christopher, "or that the tribunal
shouldn't do what it needed to do because of the negotiating process."
Other diplomats, including some at the State Department, were more
alarmed. After all, America had often reached out to Karadzic. In December 1994, America had broken the Contact Group ban on meeting Karadzic by sending envoy Charles Redman to Pale,[104] and Jimmy Carter had
met with Karadzic and Mladic at around the same time. (A British,
French, and American delegation had personally met with Mladic in Belgrade two days before he was indicted, albeit to threaten him with air
strikes.) One tribunal official said he feared that Goldstone's move would
be an invitation for the Europeans to "turn the heat up on Goldstone.
They'll find he's made of asbestos." Goldstone says he did not worry
much about incurring the Security Council's wrath: "You know, obviously
it would be naïve not to take into account all realities. But it was really
done as, if you like, as an academic exercise. Because our duty was clear.
We weren't going to be dissuaded from doing it by any prognostica-
tions—good or bad—as to what effect it would have." Serbia had talked
of allowing the tribunal to open a one-person office in Belgrade (which
Goldstone called "a slight chink in the opening of a door if one had
extremely good eyesight"); that, and whatever other tiny gestures Serbia
might have made, were now put on hold. Predictably, the Pale leadership
denounced the tribunal as anti-Serb.

The indictment of Karadzic and Mladic was, like so much of the tribunal's work, simultaneously revolutionary and hopelessly insufficient. Before Goldstone could issue the actual indictment on July 25, Karadzic
and Mladic had made it clear exactly how seriously they took the West's
muted warnings about war crimes, and Goldstone's moves toward indicting them. On July 11, Mladic led his Bosnian Serb Army into Srebrenica, one of six Bosnian towns ostensibly under UN protection. "In the
end," Mladic bragged, "the fate of Srebrenica's Muslims lies in my
hands."[105] Bosnian Serb forces then proceeded to slaughter at least seven
thousand Muslims at Srebrenica—the single worst crime against humanity in Europe since World War II. The very day that The Hague indicted

Karadzic and Mladic, Mladic's forces took Zepa, another UN "safe area."[106]

NATO Strikes

It was only after Srebrenica that the White House began to rethink its Bosnia policies, with Clinton increasingly convinced that the Bosnian Serb leadership only reacted to military force.[107] On August 10, Albright gave a withering denunciation of the Bosnian Serbs at a closed session of the UN Security Council, unveiling classified U-2 spy plane photographs of mass graves near Srebrenica. Holbrooke started a new diplomatic shuttle. Holbrooke was chosen for his toughness, which Christopher thought would let him deal with all the parties—including the Serb war criminals.[108]

Clinton and Holbrooke were horrified when three senior American diplomats were killed when their armored personnel carrier skidded off the treacherous Mount Igman road into Sarajevo, which they had to take because the Serb authorities would not them use Sarajevo's airport. These American deaths drove home the horrors in Bosnia to the administration in a way that untold thousands of Bosnian deaths had not. In his memoirs, which begin with a harrowing account of the fatal trip over Igman, Holbrooke wrote: "Within the Administration, the loss of three friends on Mount Igman carried a special weight; the war had, in effect, come home."[109]

The balance of forces on the ground was swinging against the Serbs. In early August, Croatia reconquered the Krajina. The last straw came when, on August 28, Bosnian Serb shelling killed thirty-eight people in Sarajevo's downtown marketplace. Unlike thousands of shells before, this one got a reaction. After the fall of Srebrenica and Zepa, with NATO careful to get UN troops out of Gorazde, with UN personnel out of Serb territory, and with Bihac secure, for the first time since 1992 there were no UNPROFOR forces vulnerable to Serb hostage-taking.[110] (NATO's motivations were not altogether humanitarian; since late 1994, under a secret plan called Op-Plan 40104, NATO was committed to sending 60,000 troops—including 20,000 Americans—to extricate UNPROFOR, a mission that might be just as risky as enforcing a peace and much more ignominious.) On August 29, NATO planes unleashed a massive bombing campaign against Bosnian Serb positions. In September, a Croatian and Bosnian offensive was driving Serb forces out of northwestern Bosnia. And as the bombs fell, Holbrooke shuttled around the Balkans trying to translate the unprecedented strikes into a peace initiative.

The Milosevic Strategy

Would America deal with Karadzic and Mladic? "I don't think any of us were very enthusiastic about dealing with people who were indicted," Christopher says. "I think we were all queasy about that." Holbrooke makes a point of distancing himself from Karadzic and Mladic in his memoirs, and he publicly excoriated them for Srebrenica, calling the massacre a crime against humanity reminiscent of Himmler and Stalin.[111] Anthony Lake, then Clinton's national security advisor, is more sanguine: "There's always a balance between achieving justice and understanding the importance of setting precedent for the future, so that other future war criminals will reflect, and sacrificing future lives on the altar of justice for the past. And I think that to arrive at an absolutist answer on either side of that argument is wrong." In private, some American leaders were more circumspect. "I had no problem with that," says a senior American official, of Holbrooke meeting Karadzic and Mladic.

But the real point was not the indictments, but that the White House increasingly saw Karadzic and Mladic as useless interlocutors, unlike Milosevic. In the spring of 1995—before Goldstone's indictments—Robert Frasure, Holbrooke's deputy, had got the American government to follow what American officials called "the Milosevic strategy": dealing with Milosevic and pressuring him to deliver the Bosnian Serbs. If "the Balkan political hit man" did his bit, America would relax the sanctions that were crippling Serbia's economy. This strategy would force Serbia and the Bosnian Serbs together—ending what Frasure, who had held many talks with Milosevic, had once called "the good Serb–bad Serb game."

Holbrooke decided to back Frasure (who would die in the Igman crash) to the hilt. Half a year before NATO started bombing, Holbrooke writes in his memoirs, he had decided to negotiate only with Milosevic.[112]

The Bosnian government accepted the substance of the Milosevic strategy. In late August, Alija Izetbegovic, Bosnia's president, and Sacirbey had agreed that the Americans could only meet with Karadzic or Mladic if the two Bosnian Serb leaders were in a delegation led by Milosevic in Belgrade.

If the Milosevic strategy did not work out, then America would have to think about setting up a second channel to the Bosnian Serb leaders. America kept a number of back channels open to the Bosnian Serb leadership: through EU envoy Carl Bildt, Janvier, and Russian deputy foreign minister Igor Ivanov (although Andrei Kozyrev, Russia's foreign minister, had urged Lake to try the Milosevic strategy). Bildt frequently checked in with the Bosnian Serb leaders, and Janvier had a number of negotiations with Mladic during NATO's bombing campaign. Clinton himself would be kept apprised of the Janvier-Mladic talks by a phone call from Willy Claes, NATO's secretary-general, on September 2.

Karadzic also tried to reach out to America through Jimmy Carter, most notably in a letter on August 28, hinting at accepting America's peace efforts. Carter had the letter faxed to Holbrooke the same day, although American officials seem not to have taken it particularly seriously. For now, the Milosevic strategy was the order of the day. In his memoirs, Holbrooke writes that he would meet with Karadzic so long as Karadzic was in a delegation led by Milosevic's regime.[113]

Still, these channels to the Bosnian Serbs, according to American officials, seemed to make Milosevic nervous. If he could not deliver the Bosnian Serbs, then sanctions on Serbia would remain in place. Holbrooke's team arrived in Belgrade on August 30, as NATO's air war was just getting under way. Milosevic greeted them with a letter—known as the Patriarch letter, because it was witnessed by the patriarch of the Serbian Orthodox Church—in which Karadzic, Mladic, and the other Bosnian Serb leaders agreed to subordinate themselves to Milosevic in a joint Serb delegation. In his memoirs, Holbrooke writes that he gave Milosevic a stern lecture that Karadzic and Mladic could not be part of any peace conference. When Milosevic said that the indicted men were necessary to make peace, Holbrooke offered to help arrest them personally if they dared set foot in America. "You have just shown us a piece of paper giving you the power to negotiate for them," Holbrooke told Milosevic. "It's your problem."[114]

Milosevic was not willing to completely sell out the Bosnian Serb leaders. Although Milosevic often insulted Karadzic to the Americans (once calling him a "crazy, dumb maniac"), Milosevic also tried to shield Karadzic from being frozen out of diplomacy because of war crimes accusations. On September 1, in Belgrade, Milosevic asked Roberts Owen, the legal adviser on Holbrooke's team, to postpone the issue of whether indicted war crimes suspects might be disqualified from high office in Bosnia. The Americans thought that Milosevic was worried that this would prove too much for the Bosnian Serbs. "In the house of a man just hanged," Milosevic told Owen, "don't talk about rope."

American diplomats also worried that the Bosnian Serbs were too splintered and disparate for Milosevic to deliver.[115] The most dramatic example came when NATO tried a pause in its bombing, in hopes that the Bosnian Serbs, under pressure from Milosevic, might be ready to capitulate and pull back their heavy weapons besieging Sarajevo. Not Mladic. Instead, the Bosnian Serb general sent Janvier a ranting letter calling NATO worse than Hitler, which made some American diplomats question Mladic's sanity. So NATO started bombing again, with some diplomats left skeptical of the Milosevic strategy. James Pardew, the Pentagon man on the shuttle team, wrote that the bombing pause had shown that Milosevic could not deliver Mladic after all. Mladic was the crucial Bosnian Serb leader, Pardew thought, and worried that the Milosevic strategy might lead to a dead end: that Mladic would not accept a deal cut with Milosevic, and that this deal would only pave the way for concessions to Mladic.

The Milosevic strategy did not mean that the Americans could avoid the prospect of dealing directly with Karadzic and Mladic. Flying into Belgrade overnight on September 12–13, Holbrooke writes, he weighed the moral implications of meeting with war criminals.[116] Holbrooke writes that he was "deeply influenced" by the examples of Raoul Wallenberg and Folke Bernadotte, who "had decided to deal with a mass murderer in order to save lives."[117] The comparison is unenlightening. Wallenberg was a young attaché in the Swedish legation in German-occupied Budapest in 1944, desperately trying to give protective Swedish passports to Hungarian Jews as the Nazis were deporting them to be murdered; Holbrooke was the assistant secretary of state of the United States, the planet's only superpower and the leader of the planet's most powerful military alliance, which was massively bombing the Serb leadership into submission.

The Americans had previously sounded out Goldstone about meeting Karadzic and Mladic. Goldstone had told the Americans that he would not mind if there was a meeting with Karadzic and Mladic in Belgrade, although some State Department officials had thought it would be more seemly to meet the two men inside Bosnia. Goldstone claims not to remember this green light, but does not dispute it. He says that indicted suspects were innocent until proven guilty, and that if the Americans chose to deal with Karadzic and Mladic, "that was their affair."

In his memoirs, Holbrooke writes that it was "acceptable to meet with Karadzic and Mladic if it would help the negotiations." The Americans, Holbrooke writes, would "not ask to meet the two men, but would see them, if Milosevic suggested it. . . . We would not meet with any Bosnian Serbs—indicted or unindicted—if they presented themselves as a separate delegation or tried to negotiate on their own."[118] In other words, the issue for Holbrooke was upholding Milosevic's primacy, not Goldstone's indictments.

Milosevic almost immediately forced the issue. On September 13, at his villa outside Belgrade, Milosevic told Holbrooke that Karadzic and Mladic were in another villa nearby. Holbrooke writes: "I simply hated the two men for what they had done—including, indirectly, causing the deaths of our three colleagues." But so long as Milosevic led the delegation, and kept Karadzic and Mladic from "historical bullshit," the Americans would deal with them. Holbrooke, by his own account, only asked Milosevic if Karadzic and Mladic could be helpful.[119] Holbrooke does not mention that their presence on Serbia's soil was a direct violation of international law; all states are obliged to comply with the Security Council and arrest tribunal indictees.

Holbrooke, disgusted, refused to shake hands with the indicted men, although other Americans did. Karadzic tried to subvert the Milosevic strategy by bringing up his ties to Carter, implying that Karadzic had another channel to the Americans. Holbrooke slapped Karadzic down for this, and Milosevic later specifically told Holbrooke that Holbrooke had done well to disabuse Karadzic of any such illusions. Holbrooke called Christopher to describe the scene; the secretary of state knew full well that his assistant secretary was talking with international fugitives. After two o'clock in the morning on September 14, the Pale contingent—including Karadzic and Mladic—signed an American paper pledging to end the siege of Sarajevo.[120]

Unbeknownst to the public, the Americans held one more meeting with Karadzic. On September 23, an American delegation—made up of State Department Balkans director Christopher Hill, Roberts Owen, Pardew, Belgrade chargé d'affaires Rudolph Perina, and State Department Serbia desk officer John Burley—held secret talks with Karadzic himself in Belgrade. Milosevic told the team that Karadzic would be negotiating. This, Hill said, was fine, with the standard caveat that Karadzic could not be the head of the Serb delegation. These talks went no more smoothly than the last ones with Karadzic. He insisted on Republika Srpska—the self-styled Bosnian Serb state—being an independent state, not merely the Serb part of a central Bosnian state. He called the proposed joint presidency "one-half of hell." Once again, the Americans turned to Milosevic to whip the Bosnian Serbs into line. And once again, Milosevic did.

Not everyone was comfortable with the Milosevic strategy. Sacirbey, as Bosnia's foreign minister, complained that the Americans were spending too much time in Belgrade. Christopher worried about such reliance on Milosevic, and many American diplomats seemed to think that the Bosnian Serbs could not be entirely frozen out. And, of course, there was always the embarrassment of Milosevic's dirty hands—Serbia's war crimes in Croatia and its links to the Bosnian Serb Army and to Serb paramilitaries.

In particular, the Americans were horrified by Serbia's ties to Arkan. Holbrooke personally raised this issue with Milosevic twice. First, on September 30, Holbrooke met with Shattuck in Zagreb, where Shattuck was investigating human rights abuses around the region. Holbrooke and Shattuck both wanted to look unbiased, and they thus decided that Shattuck should try to find evidence of Croatian abuses against Serbs in the Krajina. But Shattuck was appalled at reports that Arkan was once again engaged in his trademark brand of savage "ethnic cleansing," this time targeting Muslims near Banja Luka. When Holbrooke, traveling on to Belgrade later that day, complained about Arkan to Milosevic, Serbia's president shrugged it off as a "peanut issue" that would be taken care of.

It wasn't. By late October, Shattuck was still gravely worried about the situation in Banja Luka. Holbrooke had bluntly told Milosevic that Arkan's atrocities smacked of another Srebrenica, and demanded that Arkan be stopped. When Holbrooke brought Arkan up again over dinner in Belgrade on October 19, Milosevic lashed back with a diatribe, refusing to see Serb war crimes as a legitimate issue and instead telling of the suffering inflicted on Serbs by sanctions and war crimes by Croats and Muslims. Besides that, Milosevic claimed that he had no control over Arkan.

Holbrooke had had the CIA prepare a declassified memorandum to shoot down this implausible claim. As prearranged, Pardew now pounced, producing the CIA memorandum and putting it on the table next to Milosevic. In his memoirs, Holbrooke calls this paper "powerful and incriminating."[121] The CIA noted that Arkan all but certainly had the approval of Serbia's state security services, and might even be acting on its orders. Arkan, the report said, had long had ties to Serbia's Ministry of the Interior. Nor did the CIA believe that these Serbian government agencies could be doing such things without approval from Milosevic himself.

Milosevic recoiled. He refused to touch the memorandum or even look at it, and leaned away from it. Pardew left the paper for him. A Milosevic aide told Pardew that he had forgotten something. He hadn't, Pardew said. Milosevic could have it.

Hard-pressed both by NATO's bombing and by Bosnian and Croatian forces, the Bosnian Serbs capitulated. Holbrooke brokered a cease-fire, which was signed by Milosevic—and Karadzic, under Milosevic's watchful eye. On October 5, Izetbegovic refused to sign it because of the presence of the despised Bosnian Serbs' signatures. He signed a photocopy with those signatures taken off.[122] By then, American diplomats thought that Milosevic was sure that he had Karadzic and Mladic in his pocket.

DAYTON AND THE HAGUE

The next step was a November peace conference, to be held at Wright-Patterson Air Force Base in Dayton, Ohio. There were three key issues for The Hague, each of which will be discussed in turn below. First, what role would Karadzic and Mladic play at the talks? Second, what would the Dayton accords say about the arrest and marginalization of war criminals? And third, what could the tribunal do to make sure it would not be bargained away during the talks?

Who Speaks for Pale?

The Milosevic strategy meant that Karadzic and Mladic were not needed at Dayton. Still, there were some indications—most dramatically, Holbrooke's and then Hill's meetings with Karadzic—that the Americans were prepared to do a limited amount of business with indicted war criminals if that would serve the interests of a peace settlement. On September 8, Christopher said he had not ruled out dealing with Karadzic and Mladic, despite their indictments. "There are some practical logistical problems that might arise in that situation," Christopher publicly admitted. "But we recognize we need to deal—with respect to finding a peace settlement—with the leaders of the Bosnian Serbs as well as the leaders of Serbia. And so, we have not ruled out dealing with them."[123] (A State Department lawyer working on ex-Yugoslavia went one better: "Conceivably, legally, you can negotiate with these guys if they're in jail.")

Right before Dayton, Holbrooke reminded journalists that World War II humanitarians negotiated with Himmler.[124] According to one senior American diplomat who worked on Dayton and the talks preceding it, Holbrooke briefly considered giving Karadzic and Mladic some role—presumably from overseas—if that would help the talks. If that is true, Holbrooke must have quickly ruled out the idea. What would happen if Karadzic came to America? "We'd throw him in jail," said a senior American official. Would Karadzic play any role? If he did, this official said, he would have to play it "over the telephone."[125]

But Milosevic was vital, and could not be kept at arm's length, let alone branded as a war criminal. Holbrooke was worried about Milosevic's dark record, and particularly that damning evidence would surface *during* Dayton. That would make it harder to continue to rely on Milosevic. Early in Dayton, the State Department's intelligence wing (INR) filed a report which concluded that American intelligence had no hard evidence implicating Milosevic. Two 1993 reports by INR had drawn the same conclusions.

The Americans had another headache. When the site for the talks was being chosen, Albright had not liked the prospect of letting war crimes suspects like Milosevic and the Bosnian Serb delegates onto American soil. Karadzic, visiting New York in 1993, had been slapped with a lawsuit for wartime atrocities by Bosnian plaintiffs under an American statute, and the State Department's legal staff worried that the same thing might happen to Milosevic and some of the Bosnian Serb delegates. According to State Department memorandums, Milosevic, who craved a whiff of Manhattan air, would run less risk of getting sued if he hid out at Wright-Patterson Air Force Base.

Unaware that the CIA seemed not to have the goods on him, Milosevic was particularly sensitive about press reports on Serb war crimes. Here, the Americans showed signs of distinct ambivalence about covering for him. Shattuck continued to highlight the war crimes issue by traveling around Bosnia, heading off to Banja Luka again on November 9. Before Dayton, Holbrooke had publicly announced that the State Department was helping reporters trying to reconstruct the events at Srebrenica. On the eve of Dayton, both *The New York Times* and *The Washington Post* had printed "take-outs" on Srebrenica, huge and damning pieces detailing the slaughter. Stung, at Dayton, Milosevic rumbled about a press conspiracy. On November 3, *The New York Times* again drew Milosevic's fire for a piece about Goldstone's insistence that any peace accords include provisions for turning over war crimes suspects. This time, when Milosevic complained to the Americans, Holbrooke told Milosevic that the American government had not leaked the offending story.

But the bottom line was the Milosevic strategy. American officials privately pointed out that Milosevic was the elected leader of Serbia. The tribunal, a State Department official said, had "accidentally served a political purpose: it isolated Karadzic and left us with Slobo." A senior British official says, "Milosevic was not just prepared to speak for the Bosnian Serbs, he was determined to do so." Although Milosevic's lies angered Holbrooke, the Milosevic strategy stuck. When the Bosnian Serb delegation resisted compromise on the proposed map, Holbrooke had his team freeze out the Bosnian Serbs. (In an eerie note of solicitude for his Bosnian Serb rivals, Milosevic asked for Mladic's hometown to be included in Republika Srpska, the Serb entity in Bosnia.) In the end, the Bosnian Serb delegates were stunned when they saw the deal Milosevic had cut for them. The Americans briefly panicked when they noticed there was no Bosnian Serb signature on the Dayton accords. Milosevic laughed this off as "bullshit" and promptly got the signatures—including Karadzic's.[126] Karadzic did not come to Dayton; he was not needed.

Not Hunting War Criminals

Most of the crucial decisions about what American soldiers would do to arrest Bosnia's war criminals were made *before* the delegations arrived in Dayton. The White House and the Pentagon were reluctant to make arrests, animated by a sense of how unpopular a vigorous Bosnia mission would be among most Americans. In 1995, on the eve of Dayton, Dick Morris says he did a poll for Clinton that asked Americans their opinion on seven or eight tasks that American soldiers might be called upon to do in Bosnia, like disarming the Bosnian Serbs and repatriating refugees. "The arrest of war criminals was the one that they most opposed using American troops for," says Morris, "I think probably because of the heritage of Somalia, hunting for the bad guy [Aideed]." Morris wanted Clinton to assure the American public that "we're not going to be rummaging around in the mountains looking for war criminals." Clinton, told of the poll results, said that America would not do that. "He was quite adamant," says Morris.

Morris thinks that Bosnia's war criminals were never "well enough known for them to be hated." This is in stark contrast to bitter public awareness after World Wars I and II. Morris, sounding a bit like the topic was the New Hampshire primary, reckons Karadzic only had 20 percent name recognition, as against a presumed 100 percent for Saddam Hussein. "I don't think that the public ever really *got* that Karadzic was a son of a bitch," Morris says. "Because he wasn't a head of state, just a general, I think most people didn't know the name." (As if to underscore his point, Morris is confusing Karadzic with Mladic, who was the general.[127])

The Republican-led Congress, which Clinton had once called "the most isolationist Congress since the 1930s," dreaded American casualties. This prompted Perry and Shalikashvili to announce that their soldiers would wrap up their Bosnia mission in a year. Holbrooke notes that 70 percent of Americans did not want American troops in Bosnia at all.[128]

The military did not want this mission, and wanted to keep its responsibilities to a minimum.[129] Christopher says, "So this was basically State pushing for more responsibility than the Pentagon was prepared to take, and lower echelons of the Pentagon were very unenthusiastic." A week before Dayton, according to Holbrooke's memoirs, the military did not even want NATO's Implementation Force (IFOR) to be deployed in Bosnian Serb territory or on Bosnia's international borders, and they only wanted to "encourage" the parties to withdraw their heavy weapons. Nor did the military want IFOR to have the authority to investigate war crimes, react to "over the horizon" reported attacks on international workers, or respond to major human rights violations. Even the International Police Task Force (IPTF) was to be denied arrest powers. Finally, Holbrooke writes, "the Pentagon opposed any mandate or obligation to arrest indicted war criminals. Needless to say, I disagreed."[130]

On October 25, Holbrooke writes, at a White House meeting, the Pentagon and a reluctant State Department agreed that IFOR would not be responsible for arresting war criminals.[131] Shalikashvili retreated slightly from this stand in a second White House meeting on October 27: "[W]e do not wish to be obligated to arrest war criminals, but we will accept the authority to arrest them if we get the chance."[132] This was evidently not much more than a fig leaf over the Pentagon's basic unwillingness to arrest war criminals.

On October 31, the American delegation had its final White House meeting with Clinton and Gore before departing for Dayton. Clinton, in Holbrooke's account, was focused on American soldiers, sobered by both Somalia and the impending decision to send troops into Bosnia. Holbrooke made a last-ditch plea on Karadzic and Mladic:

> I said that there was one critical issue I had to raise, even though it was difficult. "If we are going to create a real peace rather than an uneasy

cease-fire," I said, "Karadzic and Mladic will have to be captured. This is not simply a question of justice but also of peace. If they are not captured, no peace agreement we create in Dayton can succeed." There was silence at the Cabinet table.[133]

That silence was, presumably, a final endorsement for a weak arrests policy.

The Bosnian delegation at Dayton did not realize that American policy on war criminals was in its essence already set. The American and European delegations came together to pressure the Bosnians, a process Sacirbey, then Bosnia's foreign minister, describes as "kind of like pissing on each other's hands and saying we're cleaning our hands."

According to members of Bosnia's delegation, Bosnia proposed putting eight points about war criminals in the peace accords and the Bosnian constitution: explicit provisions that the parties would have to arrest and extradite war criminals; automatic sanctions for noncompliance; and mechanisms to purge war crimes suspects from the police, the military, and officeholders. Holbrooke supported the idea but was overruled by Washington, which saw this as mission creep.[134] Although the Americans, with Holbrooke's support, accepted some of Bosnia's other suggestions, IFOR's mandate was not on the table. Sacirbey, who handled the war crimes portfolio for Bosnia at Dayton, says that Holbrooke simply told him that Bosnia's proposal was "impossible." "The U.S. figured, we've got to convince the Serbs across the parking lot to sign onto it," says Paul Williams, a former State Department official serving as legal advisor to the Bosnian delegation. The issue of war criminals, the Bosnians were told, was "a deal-breaker."

Instead, the Americans put forward the Pentagon's preferred language: IFOR would not have to arrest war criminals, but it would have the authority to do so. This was a huge step back from what the Bosnians had proposed. Unlike the Bosnians, the Americans did not want to put the war criminals issue in the annex on IFOR.

The American delegation had a tough tactic to lean on the reluctant (and squabbling) Bosnians. According to Sacirbey and Bosnian officials at Dayton, an American diplomat told the Bosnians that Goldstone had approved this language. "That took the wind out of the Bosnians' sails," says Williams. The Bosnians unhappily agreed to the American proposal. Told of this incident later, Goldstone was appalled. "Absolutely not," he said. "120 percent false. I was not asked and I would not consent." "We never signed off on anything," says Blewitt. "That's a lie."

As ever, America emphasized protecting American lives. Christopher said that NATO would not send in peacekeepers if Karadzic and Mladic were still in power, posing a risk to American troops—a baffling position that the American negotiators quickly backed away from. Holbrooke insisted to Milosevic that Bosnian Serb forces free David Rohde, a *Christian Science Monitor* reporter captured while discovering evidence of the Srebrenica massacres,[135] and even got Christopher to write Milosevic a stern letter demanding Rohde's release.

The Europeans were even less enthusiastic. According to Williams, Bildt told the Bosnians not to mention war criminals, figuring that Milosevic would never accept it. Britain and France did not want sanctions over war criminals, Williams says. Russia tried to edit the annex that covered IFOR to water down the force's mandate. According to Goldstone, Russia "vigorously opposed" an American suggestion at Dayton that IFOR be obliged to arrest the war criminals.[136]

Worst of all was Milosevic's modest proposal for Karadzic. Milosevic merely wanted to trounce him in elections, by pressing the many Bosnian Serb refugees in Belgrade to vote against Karadzic. On November 3, Milosevic told Holbrooke that excluding Karadzic from Bosnian elections would only make him a martyr. Holbrooke shot Milosevic's idea down.

A few days before Dayton was initialed, Goldstone had no illusions that IFOR would track down war criminals. How could Mladic end up in jail? "The only two possibilities are, one, is he voluntarily gives himself up," Goldstone said. "The other scenario is it's going to become in the political interests of whoever's running the part of the former Yugoslavia he's in to have him turned over. Or I suppose, third, he can be a pariah in a self-imposed prison." Goldstone did not mention IFOR at all.

The View from The Hague

As Dayton started, Goldstone and Blewitt seemed exhausted and worn down. Watching Dayton from the cheap seats in The Hague, the tribunal's staff worried that the tribunal might be bargained away as a sweetener to a peace deal.

Amnesties had long been a cause of concern in The Hague. In November 1993, Albright said that America was against amnesties. But when Carter brokered a cease-fire with Karadzic and Mladic in December 1994, tribunal officials worried that Carter might throw amnesties into the deal. Going into Dayton, Holbrooke said, "We are not going to compromise the war tribunal's proceedings."[137] Did Cassese worry about amnesties? "Yes. Of course. Before Dayton I was worried and Goldstone and I decided to take some steps and to approach some of the leading powers to impress upon them the idea that amnesty would be unacceptable. And they said, 'Yes, we fully agree.' " A senior American official said, "The war crimes tribunal isn't going to mess with our peace talks; we're not going to mess with the war crimes tribunal." As Yehuda Mirsky, Shattuck's spokesman, put it during Dayton, "In this building there is a consensus that the tribunal won't be bargained away in a vulgar way."

That of course left open the possibility of undermining the tribunal in nonvulgar ways. Goldstone insisted that the tribunal be a part of any settlement. First, at his most lawyerly, Goldstone said, "We're a creature of the Security Council. It's an apolitical mandate. We have to do our job. I protect the professional interests of the tribunal." Second, more practically, he argued, "I don't think any 'peace'—and I say it in quotation marks—that's established at the expense of justice will lead to a long-term resolution."

At the start of Dayton, Goldstone wrote to Albright, his best ally, asking that America make the surrender of war criminals a part of any peace accord.[138] Goldstone said he had received American assurances that there would be no amnesties. On November 7, Cassese pointedly gave a speech to the UN General Assembly, complaining that forty-one of forty-three indicted suspects were believed to be in Serbia or Bosnian Serb territory. "Our tribunal is like a giant who has no arms and legs," Cassese said. "To walk and work, he needs artificial limbs. These artificial limbs are the state authorities."[139]

When rumors reached The Hague from Belgrade that Karadzic and Mladic might be amnestied, Goldstone uncharacteristically exploded in public: "What politicians have the moral, legal or political right to forgive people charged with genocide and crimes against humanity—for the deaths of tens of thousands of people—without consulting the victims? I just find it abhorrent." If the world community backed a deal that let Milosevic's regime shelter Karadzic and Mladic, Goldstone warned, "then all of us at the tribunal would question whether it was worthwhile pursuing the work."[140]

The tribunal issued three major indictments during the Dayton conference, aiming at senior figures. This was what Holbrooke had feared, although the indictments did not derail the Milosevic strategy. Sacirbey says he had been tipped off—he refuses to say by whom—that these indictments were coming, and was anticipating them as a way of raising the profile of the war criminals issue. First, on November 7, the tribunal indicted three senior JNA officers—Mile Mrksic, Miroslav Radic, and Ve-selin Sljivancanin—for command responsibility in the 1991 Vukovar hos-pital massacre that had allegedly left the victims in the Ovcara mass grave.[141] The first indictment aiming at Serbia proper, this was a shot directly across Milosevic's bow.

Next, on November 10, The Hague indicted a group of Bosnian Croats—including Bosnian Croat leader Dario Kordic and his military chief Tihomir Blaskic—for atrocities against Muslims in 1993 in central Bosnia's Lasva Valley.[142] The tribunal tried to get these indictments out before Dayton, Blewitt says, to defuse accusations of anti-Serb bias. "Tudj-man in particular was pissed off," recalls Sacirbey. Peter Galbraith, then the American ambassador to Croatia, says, "The immediate impact of the Lasva Valley ones was that Tudjman transferred, removed Blaskic from being head of the HVO [the Bosnian Croat militia] and made him in-spector of the army." This was reported in the press as a promotion,[143] but Galbraith differs: "Since when is being commander of your own army a less important job than *inspector* of an army?" Galbraith says. "It was clearly President Tudjman's idea of getting him out of the way." Still, on Galbraith's account, at best, Tudjman's idea of compliance with the tribunal was to kick his indicted officer upstairs.[144]

Finally, on November 16, the tribunal issued a new indictment against Karadzic and Mladic for genocide, crimes against humanity, and war crimes at Srebrenica.[145] Goldstone staffers say they hurried to have the second Karadzic-Mladic indictment ready for Dayton. Was this Gold-stone's way of reminding Dayton's negotiators of The Hague? "Not at all," Goldstone said. Purely coincidental? "[I]t was really happenstance," he said. "We've issued indictments when they've been ready." But Blewitt, Goldstone's deputy prosecutor, has said that the Dayton indictments were timed to remind negotiators of the war criminals and to make it harder to dispose of the tribunal.[146] It was coincidental that the indict-ments were largely ready then, says Blewitt, but "we wanted to make sure that we were going to be part of the Dayton solution, whatever came out of it, that we were going to be part of the deal."

To get America's attention, on November 15 and 16, Goldstone made the rounds in Washington, meeting with Lake, Perry, and Shattuck, as well as CIA director John Deutch, and Strobe Talbott, deputy secretary of state. With Perry, Lake, and Deutch, Goldstone focused on intelligence cooperation, a crucial issue. Someone had leaked a letter from Gold-stone complaining about the "disappointing" quality of the American intelligence he got. Goldstone wanted information about alleged conversations between Mladic and JNA chief of staff Momcilo Perisic during the Srebrenica massacres, which could implicate Milosevic in Srebrenica.[147] Still, after his meetings in Washington, Goldstone said he got "[e]verything and more than I could have expected."

Goldstone says he also talked to Shattuck and Talbott about Dayton. After the Washington meetings, Goldstone said he was "not privy to the negotiations nor would I wish to be." Might there be amnesties? "You can rule that out absolutely." The Americans, Goldstone said, agreed that "the parties should be required to cooperate," including turning over suspects. But Holbrooke was "acting very much in the political domain," and Goldstone knew that "the interests of justice may be relegated to a secondary status in the talks."

The Americans did sound a number of reminders at Dayton that The Hague was of some importance. Principles aside, Holbrooke understood the practical usefulness of The Hague, as a way of cementing the Milosevic strategy. And the war crimes issue, Shattuck has noted, was a nonnegotiable demand for Christopher. In his opening speech on November 1, Christopher made human rights and the punishment of war crimes one of four basic principles for a settlement. Earlier the same day, Christopher had personally raised the issue of human rights with Milosevic— reminding Milosevic that his good reputation was by no means assured. And on November 10, Christopher again asked Milosevic to cooperate with The Hague. This time, Christopher reiterated his public comment that America might not send IFOR troops so long as Karadzic and Mladic were in power. Milosevic seemed hesitant to promise that they would be deposed. Christopher urged Milosevic to find ways to go around the two indicted leaders, as done in the Patriarch letter.

In the end, Dayton's text was either opaque or minimalist. "The references to war criminals in Dayton are glancing," says Major General William Nash, the American commander of multinational IFOR forces. "At best." The parties were to "cooperate fully" with the tribunal,[148] including with evidence-gathering and arrests.[149] Indicted persons were to be barred from public office in Bosnia,[150] despite Milosevic's efforts. And IFOR, as America had wanted, was given the right "to monitor and help ensure compliance" with Dayton, but was under no obligation to arrest indicted war criminals.[151]

Finally, just before the gala signing ceremony in Paris, on December 14, Clinton himself issued a top-level but rather vague private warning to Milosevic, Tudjman, and Izetbegovic of the importance of letting the tribunal do its work. Clinton also made a point of reassuring Izetbegovic—who desperately wanted to get rid of Karadzic and Mladic—that elections would be a way of getting war crimes suspects out of Bosnia's political life.

In Paris, Milosevic also got a final payoff for his part in the Milosevic strategy. Clinton briefly met with each of the three presidents, and Milosevic evidently reveled in his few moments of face-time. (The White House did not, trying to divert press attention from the one-on-one meeting between the two men.) Clinton told Milosevic that Milosevic would have to continue to lean on the Bosnian Serbs to make Dayton work, and that Dayton would not have been possible without him. Very possibly, but it would not have been necessary either.

Peace and the Search for Justice

Pax Americana

"This NATO force in Bosnia will be the biggest, toughest, and the meanest dog in town," promised Perry. Starting on December 16, some 60,000 IFOR troops moved into Bosnia, bringing a sudden peace. The American troops, black and white and Latino, were a walking advertisement for multiethnicity.

At Dayton, Izetbegovic had once told Perry that the Bosnian Serbs, like the defeated Nazis, should have terms imposed upon them; Perry reminded Izetbegovic that Bosnia had not defeated the Serb forces. But NATO, of course, had, even though the victors politely called themselves a peacekeeping force. Before the arrival of IFOR, it had been easy to say that The Hague could never approximate Nuremberg: no victor, no victor's justice. But now all that had changed, with even the Bosnian Serbs cowed.[152] By common consensus, the implementation of the military side of the Dayton accords went off with remarkable efficiency. It was the civilian side that lagged. And one critical component of the civilian side was the question of war criminals.

If there was ever a moment for arresting the indicted war criminals, the arrival of IFOR was it. But IFOR's policy on apprehending war criminals had been set by a White House that was scrupulous about avoiding casualties (and was aware of the upcoming presidential election).[153] This had not been America's war, and thus the retributive desires of Arthur Balfour or Henry Morgenthau Jr. were quite alien to Clinton's White

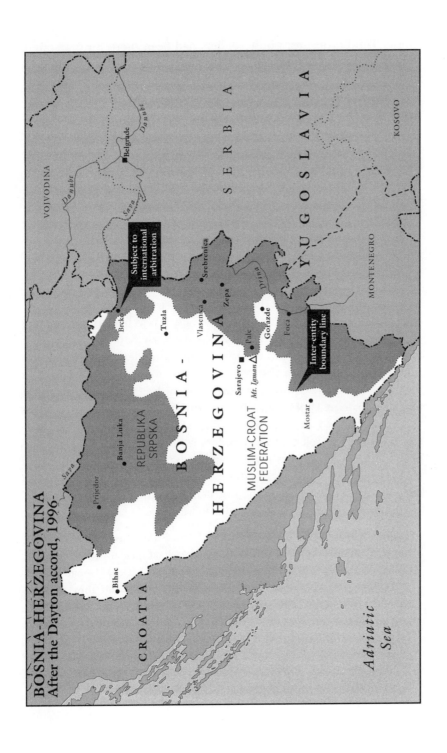

BOSNIA-HERZEGOVINA
After the Dayton accord, 1996-

VOJVODINA

Danube

Belgrade

Danube

Sava

S E R B I A

Y U G O S L A V I A

KOSOVO

MONTENEGRO

Subject to international arbitration

Srebrenica

Žepa

Drina

Inter-entity boundary line

Brcko

Tuzla

Vlasenica

Goražde

Foca

Pale

B O S N I A -

Sarajevo

Mt. Igman

REPUBLIKA SRPSKA

Banja Luka

H E R Z E G O V I N A

Prijedor

MUSLIM-CROAT FEDERATION

Mostar

C R O A T I A

Bihac

Adriatic Sea

House. The Europeans, whose soldiers had been there for years, were already sick of ex-Yugoslavia and dreaded angry mobs and guerrilla attacks.

Until July 1997, despite fierce criticism from the press and human rights activists, IFOR stuck with its policy: it would arrest war criminals if its soldiers stumbled upon them in the course of their regular peacekeeping duties, but IFOR would not seek out the men on The Hague's list. Even Christopher says that "the execution left many of us disappointed. We thought there were opportunities that were simply not seized." Goldstone was harsher. "We'll arrest people when they come into our laps," he said in 1996. "Anybody who made that policy either was stupid or not serious. I'm not sure which it was. Because it couldn't have really been considered that arrests would take place with that policy. Not a single arrest has taken place, and not one, in my view, is going to take place."

By the time Goldstone left the tribunal in October 1996, IFOR had indeed not made a single arrest. Nash recalls, "[W]e had so much going on at the time that our energy level in the early days was focused on those military tasks *specified* in Dayton that were clear and articulated. And we concentrated on that. We were trying to get the armies back in the barracks, get the equipment stored." According to a senior Pentagon official, the Joint Chiefs were briefed on Dayton's military provisions (known as Annex 1-A), but not on going after war criminals. NATO military commanders felt that their orders from their political bosses had been perfectly clear. Nash says that he had clear instructions from NATO's member states, with "political guidance that was very specific in its non-pursuit provisions, of the instructions to the military command."

This suited the military. As a senior Pentagon official put it,

> There's a resistance to mission creep. There's a resistance to policing. . . . You don't want to have another Somalia, especially when public opinion is dicey anyway on the whole Bosnia mission. DoD [Department of Defense] doesn't want to send soldiers on a mission they're not trained for. If you're Clinton, do you start taking ten casualties a day and go full-bore after Karadzic and Mladic? And then have Congress say we weren't so sold on this in the first place?

Another senior American military official later recalled, "If you did [arrests of Karadzic and Mladic] in January 1996, then you've taken on belligerent status. Then you've got a guerrilla war. There'd be sniping and bombs." To Holbrooke's chagrin, Admiral Leighton Smith, the American IFOR commander, went on Pale Television to deny that he had the authority to make arrests.[154]

The Europeans also made no secret of their reluctance. A senior British Ministry of Defence official said that Mladic and Karadzic "were surrounded by large numbers of heavily-armed well-trained bodyguards, who were not stupid, who appeared from time to time to our embarrassment in front of the cameras and the media, but always surrounded and in the middle of large numbers of civilians. A major firefight would have resulted in large numbers of casualties of innocent civilians as well as the military personnel." Nobody had the stomach for that. As this British official added, "[B]oth Mladic and Karadzic in terms of Serb public opinion were very important political players, and if IFOR and NATO had been perceived as acting partially particularly against those two individuals, we were genuinely worried about the impact on the broader peace process, the process of reunification and nation-building would be even more difficult." British military officials continued to worry that arresting Karadzic or Mladic would spark reprisals or splinter the Bosnian Serb leadership.[155]

Russia, still in the throes of its uncertain transition to liberal democracy, was overtly obstructionist. Russian nationalist politicians professed traditional affinities for the Serbs, as fellow Orthodox Slavs.[156] The Hague was seen as being as much of an American show as Dayton and was therefore resented. On December 11, 1995, Andrei Kozyrev, Russia's foreign minister, had said that Karadzic and Mladic's indictments should be frozen.[157] As Cassese recalls, "[T]he Russian ambassador came to see me on a Sunday [December 11] with instructions from Kozyrev asking whether it was technically and legally possible to freeze those arrest warrants, and I said, no, it is impossible." The two called Goldstone to confirm that stance. Goldstone says he got "a telephone call from the Russian ambassador. It was a request and it was very very promptly refused."

Karadzic, though stigmatized by his indictment and barred under Dayton from holding office, proved quite capable of fulminating against IFOR and Muslims, even without shuttling around Geneva and New York. Returning from Dayton in triumph on November 22, 1995, Holbrooke met with Clinton and Gore at the White House and warned that the capture of Karadzic and Mladic was "the most critical issue that was not resolved at Dayton." Holbrooke writes: "I repeated my view that if the two men, particularly Karadzic, the founder and leader of a still unrepentant separatist movement, remained at large, full implementation of the agreement would be impossible. The President concurred, saying, 'It is best to remove both men.' Without giving a direct instruction, he asked the military to consider the issue."[158]

Soon after, Holbrooke wrote to Milosevic to demand that Milosevic rein in the Pale Serbs. Holbrooke later wrote: "[O]n the future of Kara-dzic and Mladic, Milosevic remained adamant; he could not, and would not, deliver the two men to an international tribunal."[159] This was an overt Serbian violation of the Dayton accords, even before it had been formally signed in Paris.

A Wrong Turn

With so many former antagonists in close proximity, it was almost inevitable that perpetrators and victims would meet, and not amicably. On January 30, 1996, Djordje Djukic, a general in the Bosnian Serb Army and a Mladic crony, and Aleksa Krsmanovic, a Bosnian Serb Army colonel, took a wrong turn and stumbled into the hands of Bosnian police in Sarajevo. Djukic had been the head of logistics for the Bosnian Serb Army, and Krsmanovic had done the same for the Sarajevo area—logistics that facilitated war crimes like the Sarajevo sniping campaign. As such, even though they had not been indicted by The Hague, the Bosnian government named them as suspected major war criminals and started preparations for a trial in a Bosnian courtroom. Djukic "really was the conscious presence of Serbia in Bosnia," Sacirbey later recalled. "He knew how logistics were being directed and where they came from."

Starved for suspects in custody, and presumably leery of a trial in Bosnia's courts, Goldstone quickly issued an arrest warrant for Djukic and Krsmanovic. The West did not appreciate The Hague's interference. "Justice Goldstone complicated matters considerably," Holbrooke writes in his memoirs.[160] IFOR was scandalized. "[M]y first personal reaction was that it was going to be very hard to conduct business," says Nash. "I thought Judge Goldstone made a very serious mistake in having a nonindicted individual brought to The Hague."

Milosevic insisted that Djukic and Krsmanovic be freed. Mladic publicly ordered the Bosnian Serb Army to end cooperation with IFOR. At the time, this looked like a moment of great danger, but this was more show than anything else. "We never stopped talking," Nash later admitted. "At my level, I did not hold any meetings, because with me came the press and that type of stuff, and they wouldn't meet with me. My colonels, both at the brigade and battalion levels, met with VRS [Bosnian Serb Army] counterparts near daily throughout that two- or three-week period that they broke off relations with IFOR. We kept up day-to-day at the low level and we kept doing our business." Holbrooke flew to Belgrade, where Milosevic told him that Djukic was slowly dying of cancer, and that both captives were "simple soldiers" who should be freed at once.[161]

To NATO, the Djukic arrest was an unwelcome sneak preview of what might happen if IFOR moved against the war criminals. The Pentagon worried that Mladic would kidnap American soldiers. Was it worth going after Djukic even if that meant an IFOR soldier from Nebraska got killed? "Absolutely," Goldstone said. "Because not arresting them can have the same effect. Who's going to decide? It's a question of choosing whose crystal ball you're going to look into." As it turned out, it was not Americans who bore the brunt of Serb anger, but passengers on a bus in the Sarajevo suburb of Ilidza, who were shot at in reprisal sniping.

Everyone knew that keeping Djukic and Krsmanovic in a Bosnian jail was dangerous. So French IFOR troops whisked Djukic and Krsmanovic out of their Sarajevo jail and into American helicopters bound for The Hague. As Holbrooke writes, not without irritation,

> they were held for months by Goldstone before the charges against Colonel Krsmanovic were dropped and General Djukic, now close to death from cancer, was released.
>
> Christopher and I were greatly disturbed by this incident. The seizure of the two men, neither of whom were ever indicted, had disrupted the implementation process and set a bad precedent for the future. We determined to try to prevent any repetition of such an incident before it became a pattern.[162]

Actually, although Krsmanovic was never charged, The Hague hastily indicted Djukic.[163] He would die of cancer in May.

On February 18, the Dayton signatories established "Rules of the Road" that said that suspects could only be apprehended if The Hague had previously reviewed a warrant. But Bosnians interpreted the Djukic affair differently: if IFOR's foot-dragging continued, the Bosnian government might take matters into its own hands.

IFOR versus ICTY

NATO's unwillingness to arrest war criminals was a constant sore point with The Hague and the Bosnian government. An IFOR commander points out that his troops went into Bosnia without its officers having lists of who the indicted war criminals were, or their pictures, or instructions for the troops; those steps were not taken until well into January 1996. IFOR, blaming The Hague for providing shoddy information, complained that it had photographs of only 15 of the 52 suspects, many of them indistinct or blurry. IFOR's "Wanted" poster had pictures of only 17 of the 52 suspects, many of them hopelessly indistinct.

As IFOR and the Bosnian Serb Army (VRS) sized each other up, there were real risks of confrontation. A senior American military officer says, "[W]e should have put a tank battalion in Pale, day one." IFOR and human rights officials say there was at least one major face-off at Vlasenica around April—which, according to these sources, may well have been because the Serbs thought IFOR was there to arrest Mladic. At a road checkpoint, a Serb officer belligerently told an American lieutenant to move his platoon. The American refused and moved in more forces, checking in with both his company and battalion commanders. Nash recalls, "[W]e just said, 'You want to fight? Today's a good time, this is a good place.' " The Serb forces backed down. In the background of this— possibly explaining the VRS's strong reaction—were rumors that Mladic's black Mercedes had been moving along that road in recent weeks. During the confrontation, IFOR had scouts out looking for a black Mercedes.[164]

Human Rights Watch wrote, "[I]t is increasingly evident that IFOR soldiers are making every effort not to 'encounter' the two most notorious of indicted persons," Karadzic and Mladic.[165] More obliquely, a senior American official says, "On the one hand, I agreed that our military were not a police force, but on the other hand, under the rules of engagement, they damn well ought to be picking up anybody they came in contact with. There were a number of times on which I recall pressing them to implement those rules of engagement as vigorously as possible." American IFOR troops were accused of keeping away from Han Pijesak, Mladic's mountain headquarters, in the American zone,[166] although IFOR officials say they had close to a full tank battalion there and kept the area under surveillance.

When enterprising journalists went looking, they managed to find many of the indicted men.[167] The foreign press corps in Sarajevo kept up a drumbeat on the issue, aggressively asking IFOR briefers why the war crimes suspects were still at large. Perversely enough, these kinds of embarrassing stories in the press may have sometimes been welcomed in the White House. "I frankly regarded that as positive negative publicity," says Morris. "People saw that we weren't doing too much, and that helped views of the mission."

IFOR was also reluctant to be dragged into war crimes investigations, most notably the excavation of mass graves. These digs were a grisly mix of sophisticated medical detective work and cruder steps. The rough location of the sites was found by satellite photography and survivor accounts; but to find the precise spot, investigators would sometimes simply drive a long metal probe into the ground, pull it back up, and smell the tip for the methane stench of rotting corpses. Rows of investigators had to comb the fields for every scrap of evidence. This kind of inch-by-inch searching was not exactly the first thing one wanted to do in a countryside that might have land mines. The Serb authorities took an obvious interest in the digs. When tribunal investigators went to the Nova Kasaba field, near Srebrenica, where some of the mass executions took place, a crowd of Serb military men showed up, too. IFOR preferred not to expose its soldiers to fields that might be hiding mines, nor to antagonize the Bosnian Serbs by digging up evidence of their worst atrocities.[168]

The mass graves became a flashpoint between Goldstone, Albright, and Shattuck on the one hand, and IFOR on the other. "Initially we did not have enough forces in January and February to provide guarding of sites," says Nash. On January 21, Shattuck tried to force the issue by visiting mass grave sites around Srebrenica. Smith immediately publicly rebuffed Shattuck: "NATO is not, I repeat, NATO is not going to provide specific security, or in other words guarantee security, for teams investigating these grave sites." Nash says that when public officials "are making public statements that we should do certain things, and trying to put extraordinary pressure on the military to take independent actions in line with their quoted views, I don't think that's helpful."

Albright kept pushing. Joining tribunal investigators at Pilica, near Srebrenica, in March, she threw down a gauntlet: "Mladic and Karadzic need to know that their days of roaming around are numbered."[169] By then, a senior IFOR official says, IFOR had drawn up lists of sites to check several times daily, personally and through remote technology. The investigators proved, from the military's point of view, simply a pain to work with. As one IFOR commander complains:

> There was also a lack of clarity on which sites the tribunal was interested in. And they had a lack of specificity as to *this* site, *this* piece of ground

right here, this road junction intersection or this soccer field are the fields and we want them watched. And they could not produce a list, and a location. . . . [T]hey were very difficult to work with, because they were not well coordinated in their efforts. They didn't know exactly where they wanted to go, they wanted to kind of explore. They would hear a rumor and suddenly decide they wanted to go check out an area. We'd explain to them, we don't operate on an ad hoc basis, that if they want to go look at an area, we needed about 24 hours to brief our soldiers and make a reconnaissance, organize the security, and . . . coordinate with the local police authorities.

In April, when tribunal investigators arrived at Srebrenica, American IFOR commanders refused to clear the sites of land mines, so the tribunal had to turn to a private humanitarian minesweeping organization. On July 7, at Cerska, near Srebrenica, where IFOR feared to tread, mine-sniffing dogs from the Norwegian Peoples Aid rushed in.[170]

IFOR ultimately agreed only to provide "area security" for the forensic excavators during the day, but when The Hague's investigators left, IFOR did, too. There was overnight monitoring, but not protection, says a senior IFOR official. In at least one instance, a site was disturbed, although a senior IFOR official says it was only an inch or two of topsoil. Not only were investigators nervous about snipers, but they feared that leaving open mass graves unguarded in Bosnian Serb territory was an invitation to tampering or booby traps. So two American investigators, Bill Haglund and John Gerns, would sleep by the grave, without IFOR protection.[171] In August, the UN administration in Eastern Slavonia mineswept the area around the Ovcara mass grave, but with a twenty-ton demining vehicle that trashed the grave site itself.[172]

With the arrival of IFOR, the focus of politicking over the tribunal had shifted away from budgetary issues. But the tribunal still felt underfunded. The budget had grown—about $11 million in 1994, $28 million in 1995, and almost $41 million in 1996—but did not keep pace with the increasingly large caseload. In 1995, France and Britain gave nothing in voluntary contributions, while America gave $700,000 and eighteen staffers. Even major countries did little for the tribunal if they had soldiers on the ground: Britain sent three staffers, but its voluntary contribution of $31,700 for video and computer equipment was less than the $105,000 given by Soros's Open Society Institute or the $500,000 from the Rockefeller Foundation.[173] The tribunal remained near the bottom of the list of Western priorities in Bosnia.

Noncompliance

Serb intransigence became an excuse for Croat intransigence, and vice versa. Of the fifty-three men indicted by February, seven were Croats, but Croatia and Bosnian Croat authorities complained that they were being pressured to extradite suspects while Milosevic shielded his three indicted JNA officers. In Vitez, Croats were enraged by the tribunal's indictments of Kordic and other Bosnian Croats. Ivica Rajic, the first Croat indicted by the tribunal, was arrested by Bosnian Croats for separate murders of Croats. He was soon freed, to the anger of American, Bosnian, and tribunal officials, who said this was a violation of Dayton. Kordic, the most prominent Croat suspect, was living in a Zagreb apartment.[174]

Karadzic and Mladic were far from intimidated. Mladic brazenly went skiing near Sarajevo in March, telling the television reporters who filmed him that he had no worries of being arrested. Karadzic went to a session of the Bosnian Serb parliament in Pale, with no evident fear of Italian IFOR troops who patrolled Pale.

More than even Mladic, it was Karadzic who attracted the attention of American officials, by undermining Dayton. After lying low when IFOR first arrived, Karadzic soon resurfaced to intimidate Serbs sympathetic to Dayton. "They can't arrest me," Karadzic bragged to reporters. "I am going to travel whenever I feel I need to travel." Holbrooke writes:

> Of all the things necessary to achieve our goals in Bosnia, the most important was still the arrest of Radovan Karadzic. . . . As we had told the President and his senior advisers even before Dayton, Karadzic at large was certain to mean Dayton deferred or defeated. Nothing had changed six months later, except that Karadzic was rebuilding his position. While the human-rights community and some members of the State Department, especially John Shattuck and Madeleine Albright, called for action, the military warned of casualties and Serb retaliation if an operation to arrest him took place. They said they would carry it out only if ordered to do so directly by the President; thus if anything went wrong the blame would fall on the civilians who had insisted on the operation, including the President himself. This was a heavy burden to lay on any president, particularly during an election year, and it was hardly surprising that no action was taken to mount, or even plan, an operation against Karadzic in 1996 or 1997.[175]

That is, for the first two years of the NATO mission in Bosnia, there was no *planning* of a raid on Karadzic.

By July, the White House had decided to try to get Karadzic out of the political spotlight, but not to actually arrest him. A senior American official says, "My recollection is that NATO was not prepared to mount the force or take the risk to do the things necessary to arrest him, so the next best choice was to get him out of the government." Holbrooke writes, "The Administration's goal was to remove Karadzic from power or significantly weaken him through diplomatic pressure, thus defusing the pressure for a military operation."[176] And a senior IFOR officer was also receptive to the idea of using "all the other means necessary to screw him up," like breaking Karadzic's fabled cigarette and gasoline monopolies. (More cryptically, another senior American diplomat says, "[W]e were looking into a number of alternatives to our troops making arrests." The official adds, "[W]e were looking at getting other folks to do it." The official refused to elaborate.)

Nonmilitary pressure could sometimes have an impact on Serbia and Croatia. Trying to sideline Blaskic by moving the indicted Bosnian Croat military leader into Croatia's army, Tudjman miscalculated. "A lot of diplomatic pressure was brought to bear on the Blaskic case," says Galbraith. "He also was in the Croatian army, he was the inspector of the army, and he was on Croatian soil. So it was easy for the Croatian authorities to make sure that he went." Tripped up by his own machinations, Tudjman tentatively agreed to turn in Blaskic by the end of March.[177] Blaskic resisted, demanding he be put under house arrest, not in the tribunal's jail. On March 30, Perry visited Zagreb, threatening to slash Croatia's international financial and military aid. Finally cowed, Tudjman implausibly announced that Blaskic had volunteered to surrender himself. Because Blaskic was ostensibly going voluntarily, Croatia set no extradition precedent.

Milosevic would not turn over any of the forty-five Serbs still at large,[178] and made it clear that the three suspects in Milosevic's own army could sleep easy. In a surreal scene, one of them—as well as Mladic himself—confidently attended the Belgrade funeral of their fellow indicted suspect, Djukic, who had died of cancer.[179] But Milosevic did agree to turn over two unindicted men to The Hague for questioning: Drazen Erdemovic and Radoslav Kremenovic. Because they were not indicted, Milosevic, like Tudjman, could claim he was not setting a precedent of extradition. Erdemovic—who opportunistically served in Bosnian, Croat (he was a Croat by ethnicity), and Serb forces in Bosnia—claimed to be an unwilling participant in the Srebrenica massacre, forced to kill Muslims or be shot himself.[180] Fearing his former Serb comrades, Erdemovic was looking to turn himself in to The Hague, and was arrested by Serbian secret police after giving interviews to *Le Figaro* and ABC News.[181] Milosevic was on the spot, and this time he reluctantly yielded to American pressure: after a month, Erdemovic was delivered to The Hague.[182]

Bosnia, the government that had the least to account for, gave "fulsome" cooperation, Goldstone said. On March 21, The Hague made its first indictments against suspects under the Bosnian government's control, with Bosnian Serbs as the victims.[183] In May, Bosnia became the first ex-Yugoslav government to carry out a Hague arrest warrant, arresting two Bosnian Muslims accused of murdering and torturing Serbs at the Celebici camp in 1992. Bosnia had its misgivings about this, and it is possible that if the suspects were more important figures, Bosnia would have been more reluctant. (Two other Celebici suspects, a Bosnian Croat and a Bosnian Muslim, had already been arrested in Vienna and Munich before they were indicted by The Hague.)[184] Ironically, the refusal of Serbia and Republika Srpska (the Serb entity in Bosnia) to cooperate with the tribunal hampered the Celebici indictments: Goldstone had to get Serb witnesses to travel to another country to give evidence. A tribunal that was regularly excoriated in the Serb nationalist press as being anti-Serb found itself with mostly Croats and Muslims in custody.[185]

While America explored options other than arresting Karadzic, The Hague did what it could to turn up the heat. On May 7, The Hague opened its first trial, of Dusan Tadic.[186] The Tadic trial's opening was supposed to be a gala media event (so many reporters showed up that they had to work out of two big red tents pitched on the tribunal's front lawn), but things kept going wrong. The tribunal had hoped to make history with rape charges, but they were dropped on the morning the trial started because a witness was afraid to testify in The Hague. The prosecution's opening statement—not even given by Goldstone—was tepid and easily outshone by the defense's Michail Wladimiroff, a prominent Dutch criminal lawyer who elegantly quoted Grotius. One judge mispronounced Balkan terms such as "Ustasha" and "Herzegovina." The first witness, James Gow, a respected academic at King's College, London, put the press to sleep and scared off live television coverage; years later, the mere mention of his erudite performance would make prosecutors groan. (Tadic, during his trial, would paint a gory watercolor titled "Dr Gow + Serbs.") And it was impossible to forget that Tadic, a pawn in the Bosnian Serb hierarchy, was nobody's idea of a major suspect.

Goldstone kept lobbying NATO, and America in particular.[187] On May 20, he met with Christopher, Perry, and Shalikashvili, urging them to arrest Karadzic, Mladic, and the other fugitives. Goldstone says that Christopher and Shalikashvili "made it quite clear that the policy wasn't going to be changed." Christopher's recollections are more placid: "The meetings I had with him were relatively brief, they were not detailed, they basically were a laying-on of hands, expressing appreciation for what he was doing." When Goldstone returned to The Hague, he for the first time publicly vented his frustration at IFOR. "Unless some of those indicted people become suicidal," Goldstone told *The New York Times*, "it's not going to happen."[188] Cassese also spoke out, suggesting reimposition of full sanctions against the Bosnian Serbs and Serbia.

In June, The Hague indicted eight Bosnian Serb paramilitary officers for the rape and enslavement of Bosnian Muslim women at the Foca prison camp in 1992[189]—the first international rape charges since Tokyo and the first time that crimes of sexual assault were listed as war crimes in their own right. There is no sign that this got NATO's attention.

Finally, aiming higher than the lowly Tadic, in June and July the tribunal convened a special session about Karadzic and Mladic under its Rule 61, which allows a public hearing to air evidence and issue a new arrest warrant. Some of the urgency to dig up the Srebrenica mass grave sites was due to the deadline of the Rule 61 hearing. For over a week, the court heard details of Mladic's direct role in Srebrenica's fall, and was riveted by testimony by Erdemovic and by an anonymous survivor of the massacre.

None of this changed any minds in Washington. The White House hoped Bosnian elections, scheduled for September 14, would marginalize Karadzic's loyalists. Bosnia complained that there could be no fair elections while the war criminals were at large to intimidate voters.

With the White House worried that Milosevic would not sideline Karadzic and Mladic after all, Holbrooke flew to Bosnia and Serbia on another shuttle. On July 6, Smith had said publicly that IFOR was patrolling in Pale, but "[t]hat's as far down that path as I want to go. I do not have orders to go out and hunt down Dr. Karadzic." On July 18, in Belgrade, Holbrooke demanded that Karadzic leave Bosnia and that the Serbs cooperate with the tribunal.[190] Momcilo Krajisnik, a Bosnian Serb leader, refused to send Karadzic out of Bosnia. "If we won't do it with 60,000 troops in the country," Holbrooke told *The New York Times* afterward, "why would Milosevic do it and launch a Serb civil war?"[191] They settled on having Karadzic resign as president of Republika Srpska and of his Serb nationalist political party, and on keeping Karadzic's image off television screens and campaign posters. All that was needed was Karadzic's signature, and to get it, Milosevic had no difficulty finding the man that IFOR kept missing. Holbrooke got what the American government wanted: the pressure to arrest Karadzic was off for the rest of year.[192]

The Bosnians fumed. Before Holbrooke's shuttle, Ejup Ganic, Bosnia's vice president, had threatened to pull out of the elections if Karadzic and Mladic were not arrested. The International Crisis Group, a well-respected organization monitoring the implementation of Dayton, recommended that the elections be put off because of difficulties in implementing the civilian provisions of Dayton. One of the key failures, in addition to crucial issues like the repatriation of refugees, was the continuing influence of war criminals at large. Karadzic posters were plastered all over Republika Srpska, and Serb nationalist leaders spoke frequently and warmly of him.[193] When the Organization for Security and Cooperation in Europe (OSCE) stood behind its decision to give a green light to the elections, Bosnians joked that OSCE stood for "Organization to Secure Clinton's Election."

Privately, one senior White House official admitted that leaving Karadzic in Republika Srpska was akin to leaving Göring and Göbbels in Germany after World War II. But when asked publicly about Karadzic and Mladic, White House officials were relentlessly "on message": focus on the September elections in Bosnia, and downplay the fact that Karadzic was at large. On a presidential campaign trip in California, Leon Panetta, the White House chief of staff, was asked under what conditions America would move against Mladic or Karadzic. "We really have to keep the primary mission of our forces there in mind," said Panetta, "which is that they're there to provide security and support for the other IFOR forces, and their mission is not to go out and arrest Karadzic. Now if they confront Karadzic, then they are supposed to take him into custody, so that pretty much remains the mission of our forces." Similarly, Clinton aide George Stephanopoulos said, "We haven't yet succeeded at holding everyone accountable for the war crimes, you're right, but we also can't do anything that would jeopardize the elections right now."

NATO and OSCE officials had argued that arresting Karadzic might create a nationalist backlash right before the elections. But no backlash was needed. In the September 14 voting, nationalists of all three ethnicities triumphed over multiethnicists. Biljana Plavsic, handpicked by a hopeful West to succeed Karadzic, was voted president of Republika

Srpska. Plavsic was a fierce nationalist, and seemed incapable of condemning even the worst Serb atrocities. She had visited Arkan during the height of his Tigers' "ethnic cleansing" and kissed him on the cheek. "I always kiss the heroes," she had explained.[194] In 1994, she had said that Serb-Muslim mixed marriages "lead to an exchange of genes between ethnic groups, and thus to a degeneration of Serb nationhood." Milosevic, no stranger to nationalist excess, had once said that Plavsic should be put in a mental institution.[195] Plavsic was not Karadzic, but she had no strong incentive not to keep up Karadzic's politics.

Arbour Takes Over

By the beginning of 1996, a frustrated Goldstone was saying he wanted to be back in South Africa by the summer. In October, he left to take up a seat on South Africa's Constitutional Court, as promised by Mandela. Before going, he handpicked a successor: Louise Arbour, a judge on the Ontario Court of Appeal and a former criminal law professor. Because of the tribunal's rape cases, Goldstone wanted a woman to succeed him. On February 22, Boutros-Ghali had named Arbour as Goldstone's replacement. (With Goldstone's reputation behind Arbour, it was far too late in the day for the Security Council for a rerun of its 1993–94 shenanigans.)

Arbour is a charming, petite person with a Québécois accent. Her good cheer makes her far more approachable than Goldstone; on a whim on a recent vacation, she got a tattoo on one foot and ankle.[196] Arbour made her name with a report criticizing a riot squad in an Ontario jail. Arbour had been a member of a three-judge Ontario Court of Appeal panel that upheld the acquittal of a man accused of helping deport Jews in German-occupied Hungary during World War II—a ruling that made her a startling choice to some Canadian human rights activists. A fine jurist and a thoroughly decent person, Arbour was not yet in Goldstone's league when it came to international politicking.[197] "When you've been a judge for a decade, you're used to speaking in orders that get obeyed," she said, after her first year in The Hague. "So this is a new environment in which to operate. There's lots of frustrations about things that are not happening the way they should. And by 'should,' I mean should morally, logically, by just about any measure—except wrong-headed politics, I suppose."

By the time Goldstone left, many staffers had complaints about the "political animal." "He wants to be the big man, and he leaves us with all this," said one, despairing at Goldstone's earlier indictments. The worst thing that could happen, tribunal staffers said, was that Milosevic would flood them with low-level suspects, overwhelming the tribunal by compliance. When there were rumors that Goldstone might get the Nobel Peace Prize, some members of his own staff grumbled. "You are dealing with not enough money, not enough staff, bureaucrats, big egos, and small minds," said an official in the prosecutor's office. "At least The Hague is quiet when you go home at night." There was appreciation for all Goldstone had done, but the honeymoon was over.

The tribunal had a knack for self-inflicted wounds. NATO countries worried that The Hague would accidentally leak classified information turned over as evidence. There was only one reliable encrypted telephone, in the chief prosecutor's office, which tribunal officials said was maintained by the CIA. A witness in the Tadic trial announced that the Bosnian government had ordered him to perjure himself. In a worrying lapse of security, a Croatian refugee, for some reason carrying a red rose, managed to get past two security points and into the main tribunal itself.[198] Mevludin Oric, one of the tribunal's best witnesses of the Srebrenica massacre, said that he might not testify because the tribunal was not protecting his family from Serb reprisals.[199]

Arbour started with next to no knowledge of ex-Yugoslavia or Rwanda. At first, she proved more cautious and conservative than Goldstone, frowning on show-boating "CNN justice." Arbour was less willing than Goldstone to play to the media, which some of her staff (and all of the journalists) thought was a mistake. Goldstone would later privately express considerable irritation with her for not playing to the press and, in the fall of 1998, for not trying hard enough to get into Kosovo.

Unbeknownst to outsiders, Arbour had something big up her sleeve. Soon after taking office, she decided to start making sealed—that is, secret—indictments. These would allow the military the advantage of surprise, although at the expense of the tribunal's usual public denunciation of a suspect. The decision to use sealed indictments impressed NATO. It suggested seriousness.

Arbour had plenty of targets. In Prijedor, as Elizabeth Neuffer of *The Boston Globe* found, the police were still dominated by Hague suspects, charged with atrocities at Omarska, including accused concentration camp commander Zeljko Meakic. Simo Drljaca, who had run much of Prijedor's 1992 "ethnic cleansing" as the police chief then, was now running much of Prijedor.[200] Drljaca would be one of the first to be slapped with a sealed indictment.

Still, many American officials, and not just in the Pentagon, were not displeased with the status quo. One senior American diplomat said, "I'm not disappointed at where things are now." It would have been better to have Mladic and Karadzic in the dock, this official said, "[b]ut when this was set up, one knew that that wasn't going to happen, immediately, and the idea was first to have a system of accountability. Whether you got the defendants or not, you have the system of accountability." The tribunal could stigmatize its suspects, and "they will always have to worry that at *some* point *somebody's* going to grab 'em." There might be a new regime in Republika Srpska, the official speculated, or an Israeli-style commando squad. "They can't travel. What does it profit a man to have accumulated all the wealth that Karadzic has if he has to spend it in Pale? He will never see the sea again in his entire life." But he might not ever see The Hague either—unless something dramatically changed.

ALBRIGHT AND COOK'S MOMENT

"The Mother of All the Tribunals"

The 1996 American elections had almost nothing to do with Bosnia, let alone a tougher war crimes policy. If anything, the imminent election made Clinton doubly eager to avoid losing soldiers. But after Clinton's reelection, he made history by naming the first woman secretary of state: Madeleine Albright, suddenly elevated from UN ambassador.

Goldstone, the State Department liked to recall, had called Albright "the mother of all the tribunals." To Albright, herself twice a refugee from Nazi and Soviet totalitarianism in Czechoslovakia, the wars in Bosnia were horribly reminiscent of Nazism. She was not afraid of using force, nor of browbeating the Pentagon when it was reluctant to do battle. While most American officials had grown up in the shadow of Vietnam, she said, her views of the world had been formed by another searing experience. "My mindset is Munich," she liked to say.[201]

She saw no shortage of Chamberlains in the West's sluggish reaction to war crimes in Bosnia. "The war, itself, is the result of premeditated armed aggression," she said in a harsh speech at the U.S. Holocaust Memorial Museum in April 1994. "Bosnian Serb leaders have sought a 'final solution' of extermination or expulsion to the problem of non-Serb populations under their control." Albright supported military intervention, in the form of lift-and-strike. Since 1993, she had been the loudest American advocate for the tribunal. "We oppose amnesty for the architects of ethnic cleansing," she said in that 1994 speech. "We believe that establishing the truth about what happened in Bosnia is *essential* to—not an *obstacle* to—national reconciliation. And we know the Tribunal is no substitute for other actions to discourage further aggression and encourage peace." The tribunal, Albright said, would deter war criminals now and in the future, help bring reconciliation, and strengthen international law. But she knew the difficulties too. "This is not Nuremberg," she said. "The accused will not be the surrendered leaders of a broken power."[202] She emphasized money, investigations, staff, and political will.

Albright, in short, was a true believer, in a tradition going back at least to Lloyd George. But she could not plausibly claim any mandate to rethink America's war crimes policy, neither from the 1996 election nor from any discernible shift in Clinton's thinking on Bosnia. She was acting as equal parts Morgenthau and Stimson—both pressing for punishment per se and for legalism—against the Pentagon and the White House. Unlike Morgenthau, though, her calls for punishment found little public echo. Whatever risks she would take in a firmer policy on war criminals, she would be held personally responsible.

Albright versus Cohen

The stage was set for a confrontation between the Pentagon and the State Department. The Pentagon started by offering what seemed like a compromise. In December 1996, at a NATO summit, Perry, the outgoing American defense secretary, called for the creation of a special police force to arrest war criminals. France and Italy were cool to the plan. The idea, according to Shalikashvili, was to distance NATO forces—which were to shift from being called IFOR to SFOR, for Stabilization Force—from any arrests and thus diminish the chance of retaliation. This police force might not even be under NATO command.[203] The NATO ministers agreed, Perry said, "that bringing these indicted war criminals to justice is an important mission—but is not an SFOR mission."[204]

Perry's successor was less conciliatory. William Cohen, a Republican, said that American troops would be out of Bosnia in eighteen months and would not hunt down war criminals while there. In March 1997, Cohen warned, "If they choose not to pursue peace, that is going to be their choice." Was peace "something they wish to pursue or do they want to go back to slaughtering each other?"[205] Cohen's hands-off approach to

Bosnia would inevitably conflict with Albright's activism, with war crimes issues as a crucial test.

Albright ratcheted up the volume, taking public stands that would make it harder for America to retreat from her pledges without embarrassment. On January 31, 1997, Arbour visited Albright in Washington. Their conversation covered administrative issues, Arbour says, and only in another session in The Hague in May did they focus on the question of arrests. After America threatened to block international loans, Croatia handed over Zlatko Aleksovski, a Croat prison camp leader, but this did not satisfy Albright. He was "not a significant figure," said a tribunal official. On May 15, Albright met with Mate Granic, Croatia's foreign minister, and specifically asked for the surrender of a list of indicted war criminals to The Hague.[206]

As Albright and Cohen sparred, Clinton remained a cipher. Asked about the proposed special police force, on January 29, he gave a cautious, rambling answer (in which he kept confusing SFOR with UNPROFOR). It would be, Clinton said, "very difficult for them to do the mission." But since Dayton, everyone had known "that they couldn't walk away from this evidence of war crimes and that there needed to be some way of proceeding, but that there was no way that you could effectively do the job of UNPROFOR [sic], which was the most important thing to try to stabilize the country and the borders, and, in effect, make that the primary mission."[207] On the other hand, Clinton was also quite capable of giving the impression that he was closer to Albright's view. After a meeting with Clinton at the White House on March 26, Izetbegovic declared, "We received clear assurances that the war criminals will be brought to justice." Izetbegovic also said: "I can say only my impression—that would be the special units."[208]

Clinton ordered Samuel (Sandy) Berger, his national security advisor, to mediate between the two sides. In April and May, Berger conducted a full-blown policy review on Dayton.[209] At a White House meeting on May 16, Albright and Cohen reviewed Bosnia policy issue by issue, with Berger trying to find compromises. While Cohen still wanted American troops out of Bosnia by July 1998, he agreed to have the international forces there be more active in the interim—including arresting some war criminals.[210]

Emboldened, Albright started putting her plans for war criminals into practice. The State Department created a new post of ambassador-at-large for war crimes issues, and gave it to David Scheffer, a long-time Albright advisor. Robert Gelbard, the American special envoy to the Balkans, tried unsuccessfully to press Milosevic into surrendering indicted war criminals under Serbia's control.[211]

Albright kept ratcheting up the stakes, next with a high-profile tour of Europe. On May 28, she pointedly visited the tribunal, delivering a stem-winder of a speech calling justice "the heart of American policy toward Bosnia."[212] She went to a Portugal summit of NATO foreign ministers, which issued a call for bolder steps on the issue of war criminals.[213] Then she proceeded on a tough, whirlwind tour of ex-Yugoslavia. On May 31, in Zagreb, Albright bluntly asked Tudjman about Dario Kordic's where-abouts and threatened personally to block loans to Croatia from the International Monetary Fund. Winging on to Belgrade later the same day, Albright told Milosevic to turn over Serbia's three indicted JNA officers or risk international isolation. "Words are cheap," she told Milosevic. "Deeds are coin of the realm." Finally, proceeding to Bosnia the next day, she went to Banja Luka, in Republika Srpska, to hector Plavsic about Bosnian Serb intransigence.[214]

Albright's victory was not total. Almost nothing was more controversial than putting soldiers at risk in arresting war criminals. On May 22—several days after Cohen and Albright had ostensibly reached an under-standing—Cohen distanced the Pentagon from her more muscular ap-proach to Dayton. Arresting war criminals, Cohen said, "puts them [NATO troops] at great risk. . . . They are not police officers, they are not people who are trained to arrest. Their function is quite different."[215] A meeting of NATO defense ministers echoed Cohen, freezing an Ameri-can proposal to arrest some war criminals.[216]

But Albright had the good luck to acquire an unexpected important ally. In May, Tony Blair's Labour Party thrashed Major's Tories in British elections. After years of diffidence or quiet obstructionism from Britain, the tribunal now found itself getting warm support from Robin Cook, Blair's moralistic foreign secretary. "We're just leaving these guys around?" said a baffled Foreign Office diplomat, of the fugitives. At a G-7 summit in Colorado, France and Italy agreed to more planning on how to arrest some war criminals.[217] Confronting Karadzic's loyalists, Plavsic (the West's rather dubious alternative Bosnian Serb leader) emerged triumphant from a June power struggle in Republika Srpska. Soon after, stories began to appear in the press about American plans to arrest Kara-dzic, reportedly drawn up by the CIA and the Pentagon's Special Forces but not yet approved by Clinton.[218]

Meanwhile, Arbour was secretly trying to force NATO's hand. "We were working virtually nonstop on the arrest issue," she recalls. Arbour called the bluff the Pentagon had written into Dayton. Under its own rules of engagement, SFOR was supposed to arrest suspects it routinely encountered. In a country as small as Bosnia, this had to have been happening in many places. The tribunal knew that SFOR troops in Prijedor would encounter Drljaca, the Serb head of Prijedor's police, who had played a key role running the Keraterm and Omarska concentration camps.[219] Instead of driving Drljaca underground by publicly indicting him, Arbour in March got a sealed indictment. "We gave it to SFOR," says Blewitt, the deputy prosecutor, "and said, well, we know you were encountering this guy, and you can set up the encounter in a way that's not going to cause any loss of life. You're in the driving seat. The guy doesn't know he's indicted." This, Blewitt recalls, caused "an almighty ruckus in NATO and elsewhere. There was a lot of resistance and pressure, trying to get us to back off. Because they were saying that it was just unfair that these people were not given the opportunity to flee—in effect, that was what they were saying. So we didn't back off at all. We just said that we'll go public and expose you for the fraud you are. And a lot of heated words."

Arbour had another card to play. Jacques Klein, the American head of the UN authority in Eastern Slavonia (UNTAES), was a bold and forceful military man. When Arbour told him that Slavko Dokmanovic, the former mayor of Vukovar, was secretly indicted and in Klein's territory, Klein had him arrested without incident and sent him to The Hague on June 27. "And there were no adverse consequences," Arbour says, "and I think it certainly did set a more favorable climate for SFOR to be more proactive." The Hague had finally offered NATO a safer way of making arrests.

Operation Tango

"What we did was not the same as Auschwitz and Dachau, but it was a mistake," said Milan Kovacevic, who had helped run Omarska, in a stunning 1996 interview. "It was planned to have a camp for people, but not a concentration camp. Omarska was planned as a reception centre. . . . But then it turned into something else. I cannot explain the loss of control. I don't think even the historians will find an explanation in the next 50 years. You could call it collective madness."[220] Kovacevic, the director of Prijedor hospital, would not have much longer as a free man to boozily contemplate his sins.

Kovacevic was in his office at the hospital when NATO finally struck. Early in the morning of July 10, British SFOR troops launched two well-organized arrest raids in Prijedor. Arbour had secretly indicted the two targets, Kovacevic and Drljaca, for complicity in genocide in running Omarska, on March 13. Only SFOR and The Hague knew. The two men were important figures, not like the lowly Tadic.[221]

Kovacevic, unarmed, surrendered and was whisked to The Hague. Drljaca was fishing in a lake not far from Omarska when SFOR helicopters came after him. Living up to his violent reputation, Drljaca pulled a pistol and fired on the British commandos who had left their helicopters, hitting one of them in the leg. Drljaca was immediately mowed down.[222] This was not altogether unwelcome to NATO. A State Department official coolly pointed out that Drljaca's death proved that SFOR would kill, a fact that would scare other fugitives.

In a sign of Cook's activism, it was British troops who led the raid. America provided logistical support; Clinton had been notified a week before that the raid—called Operation Tango in SFOR parlance—was coming, and had decided it did not pose an undue risk to NATO troops.[223] Berger explained that SFOR troops had regularly come into contact with Kovacevic and Drljaca in their routine duties, and thus this arrest fell under SFOR's rules of engagement.[224] This was, in its own way, an official confirmation of what human rights activists had long suspected: that SFOR often bumped into indicted war criminals.

The reaction in Republika Srpska was angry. Krajisnik, now the Serb representative on Bosnia's joint presidency, asked Serbs "not to take revenge on the young SFOR soldiers"[225]—a statement that sounded more threatening than soothing. Pro-Karadzic radio broadcasts claimed that Drljaca had been murdered, and Plavsic condemned the killing.[226] A State Department official shrugged off the nationalist rhetoric at Drljaca's funeral as "organized top-down backlash."

In the days after the raid, there were three apparently anti-Western bombings. One American soldier was lightly wounded by a man with a sickle;[227] another suffered minor injuries from a bomb.[228] NATO officials, including Clinton, grimly let it be known that reprisals would bring dire consequences.[229]

Not every country had changed its stripes like Britain. The Russian Foreign Ministry denounced "cowboy raids,"[230] and Yevgeny Primakov, the Russian foreign minister, warned Cook not to launch any more.[231] And as American officials let *The New York Times* know, France had been involved in planning a second raid in the French zone but, fearing casualties, had backed out early in July.[232] This French reticence was particularly discouraging because Karadzic was presumed to be in and around Pale, in the French zone.

The plan, said a State Department official, was to go after the people SFOR could easily grab: the most undefended and unpopular war crimes suspects. "Low-hanging fruit first," says a British diplomat. Drljaca, famed for his venality and known locally as "Mr. 10%" for skimming his percentage off of all dealing in Prijedor, was a good example. "Everyone just heaved a sigh of relief," says a British official, when this "gangster" was killed.

It was still not clear whether Karadzic and Mladic would be arrested.[233] Before the raid, there had been a debate among human rights activists and government officials about whether to go after Karadzic first, or to arrest lesser figures before him. "If you're going to kill a snake, why not cut at the head?" asked a senior State Department official, before the raid. "There are people under Karadzic and Mladic who would like to see them fall anyway, like Biljana Plavsic. If you grab some, you might scare them into something desperate, the ones who are sitting in cafés."

Mladic ostentatiously surfaced in plain view: he went to his son's wedding in Belgrade and spent a week enjoying the Montenegrin seaside.[234] Mladic tended to attract less Western attention than Karadzic because he was not meddling in Republika Srpska's politics as vigorously as Karadzic, and because he was presumed to be better guarded. But the net was tightening around Karadzic. On August 9, Holbrooke told Milosevic that Karadzic might be arrested if he did not stay out of Republika Srpska's politics as he had pledged to do.[235] Wesley Clark, the new NATO supreme commander, made the threatening gesture of a visit to Pale.[236] Karadzic was stripped of police protection, and increasingly marginalized as the West threw its influence behind Plavsic.[237] NATO officials kept leaking that Karadzic would soon be in The Hague, one way or another.[238]

The raid never came. In a stunning story in *The Washington Post*, France was said to have wrecked a potential raid when one of its officers tipped off Karadzic, who is presumed to be in the French zone. The raid would have involved hundreds of well-armed NATO troops, to overwhelm Karadzic's bodyguards.[239] In *The New York Times*, officials denied that there had been a specific plan to catch Karadzic.[240] As of July 1998, plans to arrest Karadzic and Mladic were reportedly scuttled, thanks to fears of NATO casualties and Serb backlash.[241]

Since Operation Tango, the tribunal has been strengthened both by further arrest raids and by continuing support from Cook and Albright.

Karadzic has been marginalized, although moderates—like Milorad Dodik, who served as prime minister—remain in short supply in Republika Srpska. France remains particularly cautious, possibly because of memories of French hostages taken in 1995. American officials complained that France only accepted the surrender of a fugitive when there was no way to avoid it.[242] British and American officials blame France for the fact that Karadzic remains at large.

Under firm pressure from Albright and Cook, Tudjman finally made a gesture of compliance with The Hague, in the hopes, say American diplomats in Zagreb, of winning back Croatian control of Eastern Slavonia. After America (to Arbour's chagrin) promised a trial within three to five months for suspects who turned themselves in voluntarily, The Hague found itself swamped by an unprecedented load of ten suspects. On October 6, Dario Kordic and nine other Bosnian Croats went to The Hague of their own accord, or at least of Tudjman's.

There have been several more SFOR arrest raids—all carefully planned to avoid any NATO casualties. "If you're going to do it," says a senior British official, "why take casualties?" France remains the most reluctant. Alain Richard, France's defense minister, has accused The Hague of "show justice" and has said that suspects must be arrested without any bloodshed; Arbour retorted that the French zone was "absolutely safe" for fugitives. On December 18, Dutch SFOR troops arrested two Bosnian Croats for atrocities at Ahmici in 1993. On January 22, 1998, American SFOR soldiers launched the first raid in which they directly participated, briskly arresting Goran Jelisic, who had bragged that he was "the Serb Adolf" in Brcko in 1992. British troops arrested three Omarska suspects in April and May. By March, four Bosnian Serbs had turned themselves in, evidently frightened by SFOR's raids.

As SFOR took The Hague more seriously, it also got frustrated with the tribunal's occasional blunders. SFOR hated the thought of arresting fugitives charged in the unreliable early indictments; there was no point risking NATO soldiers arresting low-level people who might not be convicted. In May, Arbour withdrew fourteen of these indictments, preferring to focus her limited resources on bigger fish. Then there were two deaths in custody, both of which fed Serb nationalist images of The Hague as an anti-Serb kangaroo court. Dokmanovic, soon before his verdict was to be handed down, hanged himself on June 29; Kovacevic died of an aortic aneurysm on August 1. And French SFOR forces killed a Serb suspect in an arrest raid in Foca.

Some fugitives are presumed to have fled Bosnia for Serbia, which still shields war crimes suspects. "Bosnia is no longer so cozy," Arbour says, with thirty people in custody. "So the natural place to go is Serbia." Mladic reportedly has lived in Belgrade for years.

SFOR's raids have continued, and have even begun to aim higher. On December 2, 1998, American SFOR troops arrested General Radislav Krstic, a senior Bosnian Serb officer accused of a major role in the Srebrenica massacre. This prompted loud Russian and Serb protests. Within Bosnia, arrests still continue, even after the Kosovo war. An accused Keraterm shift commander was nabbed on June 7, 1999, and Radoslav Brdjanin, a senior wartime Karadzic crony, was arrested by British SFOR soldiers at a roadblock on July 6. In August, Momir Talic, the Bosnian Serb military chief of staff, made the mistake of attending a conference in Vienna, unaware that he was under a sealed indictment. He was arrested by plainclothes Austrian police and sent to The Hague—the highest-ranked military suspect in custody. On October 25, SFOR arrested Damir Dosen, accused of atrocities while a shift commander at the Keraterm camp. In a dramatic raid on December 20, British SFOR troops apprehended General Stanislav Galic, who had commanded the Sarajevo-Romanija Corps of the Bosnian Serb Army as it mercilessly shelled Sarajevo's people from 1992 to 1995. It has presumably concentrated Mladic's mind to see so many of his top subordinates—Krstic, Talic, and Galic—all wind up in The Hague. Later the same week, in Foca, SFOR also arrested another war crimes suspect, Zoran Vukovic.

France may have had a change of heart. On January 25, 2000, French SFOR forces made their first successful arrest, of Mitar Vasiljevic, charged with murdering Bosnian civilians while Vasiljevic served in Seselj's paramilitary White Eagles. French troops struck again on April 3 in Pale, blasting open a door to arrest Momcilo Krajisnik, a prominent Karadzic aide who had been speaker of the Bosnian Serb assembly and, later, the Serb representative on Bosnia's three-person presidency after Dayton. Krajisnik, whose histrionics at Dayton and subsequent reluctance to implement the deal struck there had infuriated Western diplomats from Holbrooke on down, became the most important political figure in custody at The Hague. "Force protection is our number one priority," said a senior Clinton administration official the day of the arrest. But White House officials say they have learned that SFOR can do arrest raids that do not threaten NATO's troops in Bosnia.

The tribunal's bitter relationship with Croatia may have taken a sharp turn for the better with the death of Tudjman from cancer in December 1999 and the election of Stipe Mesic as president in February 2000. As Tudjman's medical condition worsened, Croatia had questioned the tribunal's jurisdiction over two Croatian military offensives, known as Operation Flash and Operation Storm. It took furious sparring and American pressure to convince Croatia to turn over indicted war crimes suspect Vinko (Stela) Martinovic, and even more arm-twisting over the fate of Mladen (Tuta) Naletilic, an indicted Bosnian Croat paramilitary leader whom Croatia claimed was too ill to go to The Hague. McDonald, the tribunal's president after Cassese, formally complained in August 1999 to the Security Council about Croatian noncompliance. Blewitt, undiplomatically stating what was perfectly obvious, said that perhaps Tudjman's imminent death might herald better relations between Zagreb and The Hague; for this, Croatia's justice minister demanded his resignation, and luridly called Blewitt's comment "aggressive, morbid and necrophilic."[243]

Mesic, who has already testified at The Hague, promises to cooperate with the tribunal, allow Serb refugees to return, and stop Croatia's support for the Bosnian Croats. He has said that there can be no progress in the Balkans without Milosevic in The Hague, and even offered to return to The Hague to testify against him.

The Hague, once so desperate for a defendant in custody that it ballyhooed Tadic's trial, now pushes SFOR to arrest fugitives in the groups in which they were indicted, so that all the Lasva Valley or Foca suspects can be tried together conveniently. The tribunal has so many suspects in custody that its officials have begun to complain that they cannot try them fast enough—a welcome predicament, if seen in the light of the early days in The Hague. But even though Bosnia's future stability is far from assured, the focus of The Hague has shifted to Kosovo.

THE WAR FOR KOSOVO

Indicting Milosevic

In the fall of 1998, Milosevic's repression of ethnic Albanians in Kosovo—the issue that had, in 1987, sparked the wars that destroyed Tito's Yugoslavia[244]—once again took center stage. Under three specific Security Council resolutions, the Hague tribunal had jurisdiction over Kosovo—a province of Serbia and therefore under the tribunal's mandate to pursue war crimes committed in ex-Yugoslavia since 1991. The Hague was nowhere near ready to do any serious investigations, as senior tribunal officials privately admitted.

In October 1998, Milosevic's justice minister and foreign minister publicly denied the tribunal's jurisdiction. Arbour wrote a letter to Milosevic requesting access to Kosovo for on-site investigations. But much of Arbour's team was denied visas, and Arbour herself only got a seven-day single-entry visa and a warning that she had no right to go to Kosovo, although she could go to Belgrade, where Milosevic's regime had filled her calendar with meetings with Yugoslav officials. "I'm not going to negotiate about jurisdiction," she fumed. "I'm entitled by law."

In November, Holbrooke brokered a last-minute deal to avert air strikes. The deal did not mention The Hague. "The absence of language suggested we had no jurisdiction," Arbour said. But the deal, which even American officials in Belgrade said could not last, did not stick. A massacre of forty Kosovars, in the town of Racak, brought American accusations of "crimes against humanity." Fearful of losing face, NATO convened peace talks in Rambouillet, France. Milosevic refused to attend, evidently afraid that he might be under secret indictment by The Hague. In the talks, the Yugoslav delegation tried to build in amnesty for atrocities in Kosovo.

Arbour kept pressing. In January 1999, she showed up at the Macedonian border demanding entry to Yugoslavia in order to gather evidence in Racak. True to form, Milosevic's regime turned her away.

After the failure of Rambouillet, NATO unleashed its second massive bombing campaign in the Balkans, on March 24. Clinton ruled out ground troops. NATO kept the safety of its pilots ahead of the Kosovars, despite prescient warnings that Serb forces might start a wave of massive "ethnic cleansing." Milosevic's fourth war—after Slovenia, Croatia, and Bosnia—was, as usual, vicious, with paramilitaries leading the atrocities. In total, according to Western estimates, over a million Kosovar Albanians were displaced, and perhaps 10,000 killed, with massacres in places like Velika Krusa and Djakovica.

The Hague came under criticism for moving too slowly. After Britain said that Mladic was involved in this round of savagery, Mladic appeared in Belgrade to deny it. With Britain also accusing Arkan's Tigers of taking a role in the Kosovo atrocities, Arbour announced that Arkan had been under sealed indictment for a year and a half. "She's a bitch," Arkan said.

This time around, Western minds—led by Cook and Albright—had changed about Milosevic.[245] Turning against the Milosevic strategy, American and European leaders now began to argue that Milosevic should have been indicted and that it would have been better to have gotten Karadzic on trial so that he could rat out Milosevic.[246] As refugees streamed out of Kosovo, NATO officials accused Yugoslavia of genocide and compared

Milosevic not just to Hitler, but also Stalin and Pol Pot. George Robertson, Britain's defense secretary, called Milosevic a "serial ethnic cleanser" and accused him of "genocidal violence." The State Department warned nine Yugoslav military commanders that they might be charged with war crimes. And Clinton pointedly asked, "Think the Germans would have perpetrated the Holocaust on their own without Hitler?"

In stark contrast to Western secretiveness during the Bosnia war, NATO governments now began to share serious intelligence with The Hague, including data from spy satellites over Kosovo. The classified information was packaged and analyzed so that The Hague could use it relatively easily. Cook even appointed a special Kosovo war crimes coordinator, in charge of channeling British intelligence to The Hague.

Arbour warned Milosevic and other top Serb officials that they could face prosecution; the "ethnic cleansing" continued unabated. Temporarily shelving some of its Bosnia investigations, the tribunal sent investigators to Macedonia and Albania to interview Kosovar refugees and issue swift indictments. The OSCE began using a uniform questionnaire for interviews with Kosovar refugees to build a database for The Hague. Arbour flew to France, Britain, Germany, and America to appeal for help, so The Hague could do investigations in "real time." On April 30, Arbour visited Albright in Washington and lobbied for the arrest of war crimes suspects in Bosnia as a way of deterring Yugoslav atrocities in Kosovo.

The impact of this was flattened when Arbour told American officials that she was planning to resign soon. This was no particular surprise; it was an open secret that Arbour had had enough of The Hague and was a likely choice for the next seat on Canada's Supreme Court. But NATO cringed at the thought of opening the tribunal's top job to Russian and Chinese pressures in the Security Council at a time when both countries were fuming at NATO.[247] Igor Ivanov, Russia's foreign minister, had even suggested that NATO personnel might be hauled before the tribunal.

Arbour, swarmed by reporters, cut a defiant figure when she made her move on May 27, as the war raged on. Eight years after Dubrovnik and Vukovar, she finally indicted Slobodan Milosevic for crimes against humanity in Kosovo. Mirroring Western priorities, there were no accusations over atrocities in Bosnia or Croatia, although Arbour said that she might make more charges. Arbour also charged Serbia's president Milan Milutinovic, Yugoslav army chief of staff Dragoljub Ojdanic, Yugoslav minister of internal affairs Vlajko Stojilkovic, and Yugoslavia's deputy prime minister. The indictment, based on accounts of several massacres, ends with a chilling list of the names of those presumed killed. Boldly, Arbour said, "[T]he evidence upon which this indictment was confirmed raises serious questions about their suitability to be the guarantors of any deal, let alone a peace agreement." (This was the opposite position from Goldstone's secret green light to the Americans about meeting Karadzic and Mladic back in 1995.)

But Arbour then undermined the tribunal by jumping ship. Two weeks after indicting Milosevic, Arbour announced her resignation, leaving the repercussions of her single biggest decision to her successor.

America and Britain publicly cheered the indictments, while American officials privately fretted that they would derail cease-fire negotiations. Viktor Chernomyrdin, Russia's envoy on Kosovo, complained that a new obstacle had been put up. How could the great powers negotiate with indicted war criminals? In the event, with a minimum of nose-holding. On June 2, Chernomyrdin and EU envoy Martti Ahtisaari flew to Belgrade to talk directly to Milosevic and Ojdanic. (Talbott worked with Chernomyrdin and Ahtisaari but stayed away from Belgrade.) This was, if anything, a less impromptu decision to do business with indicted war criminals than Holbrooke's meeting with Karadzic and Mladic just before Dayton, although that was invoked as a precedent. "I had no problem with dealing with Milosevic over Kosovo," says a senior American official. Ojdanic and Stojilkovic were excluded from cease-fire talks with NATO. Milosevic defiantly promoted Ojdanic.

When the NATO–led Kosovo Force (KFOR) entered, unopposed, into Kosovo in June, the soldiers were closely followed by a dozen teams of investigators working for The Hague, totaling some three hundred people. The task was overwhelming. But this time, at least, they worked on relatively fresh graves and recent memories among Kosovars, and there was substantial backup from the FBI and other Western government agencies. Even though the tribunal had only indicted five Yugoslav leaders over Kosovo, NATO forces apprehended over a dozen war crimes suspects, not yet indicted by The Hague. The rage of many Kosovar Albanians against the Serbs is one of the biggest obstacles to a peaceful Kosovo. Russia, demanding a peacekeeping role, stipulated that its troops would not arrest any war criminals. Presumably, many war crimes suspects will head for the haven of Serbia.

NATO would not touch Milosevic. "If he remains in Serbia inside the confines of Serbia," Clinton said, "presumably he's beyond the reach of the extradition powers of the other governments. But sometimes these things take a good while to bear fruit." He added: "I think it's [Milosevic's indictment] a very important thing. But I do not believe that the NATO allies can invade Belgrade to try to deliver the indictment, if you will."[248]

That leaves the prospect of Milosevic's overthrow from within. Belgrade has been swept with gangland-style executions, with Arkan himself mysteriously gunned down in the lobby of the Hotel Intercontinental on January 15, 2000. But it is not clear if these killing reveal a crumbling regime, or if they are the work of the regime or at least have the regime's blessing. Yugoslavia is unlikely to get foreign aid so long as Milosevic rules. Milo Djukanovic, the democratic president of Montenegro, has promised to comply with The Hague, including arresting Milosevic if he sets foot in Montenegro, Yugoslavia's smaller republic—an extraordinary limitation on Yugoslavia's president. The indictment of Ojdanic makes an army coup unlikely, and Vuk Draskovic, Serbia's main opposition leader, encouraged Milosevic's resignation by saying that he would not turn Milosevic over to The Hague. Still, Arbour says, "the world is a much smaller place for them."

The world is smaller still for Dusan Tadic, who was convicted in May 1997 and sentenced to twenty years in jail. The tribunal in The Hague has grown to be far stronger than its reluctant creators would have imagined back in 1993. With greater NATO support in Bosnia and Kosovo, it could get stronger still. Arbour's successor, Carla Del Ponte, Switzerland's federal prosecutor, has inherited an institution far more robust than what Goldstone had. But with atrocities of such a nightmarish scale, and with a Western commitment that waxes and wanes, the outlook is still uncertain. The tribunal has come a long way from the Tadic trial, but it is still a far cry from the kind of broad accountability that was provided at Nuremberg.

Still, the UN has made two other stabs at creating institutions to punish war criminals. There is The Hague's sister tribunal in Arusha, Tanzania, investigating the genocide in Rwanda in 1994 and subsequent crimes there; and the putative permanent ICC, approved at a UN meeting in Rome in July 1998. After the travails of the war crimes tribunal in The Hague, the ability of the world to create token institutions is not in doubt; but the ability of the world to use such institutions to bring reconciliation to shattered societies is still an open question. "With war criminals walking free—they must pay," says Dragica Levi, in a smoky office in Sarajevo. Levi is a committed Bosnian multiethnicist, herself Jewish but insistent in her tolerance, who stayed in Sarajevo throughout the war to help run La Benevolencija, a philanthropy run by Sarajevo's Jewish community. "If you lost your husband and the killer is walking free, you must have hate in your heart. If you did something you have to pay for it. It is normal."

Conclusion

IN JULY 1915, at the height of the Ottoman slaughter of the Armenians in Turkey, someone made a humanitarian typographical error. A prominent American missionary leader in New York state, James Barton, sent a desperate telegram to Robert Lansing, Woodrow Wilson's secretary of state, begging for America to save the Armenians. But Barton somehow garbled his point: "Advices from different parts of Turkey report inhuman treatment of Americans by Turks. Cannot something be done to alleviate the horrors?"[1]

This got the American government's attention. "The Department has received no reports of any inhuman treatment of Americans by the Turks, and would be pleased to receive details from you if you have received information to this effect," Lansing replied, with more than a hint of smugness. "The Department believes, however, that the 'Americans' in your telegram should have read 'Armenians.' "[2]

It was precisely this kind of distinction that the Young Turks were counting on to let them commit their deportations uninterrupted. When Henry Morgenthau Sr., the American ambassador in Constantinople, appealed for mercy to Talaat, the Ottoman interior minister, Talaat snapped: "Are *they* Americans?"[3] That was not the right answer to give to Morgenthau, but it was about right for someone like Lansing. Lansing, no doubt, did not approve of what Talaat was doing; but what mattered above all to the secretary of state was that the victims were not—however poorly a missionary might type—Americans.

This is a small but revealing episode. This book has tried to explain under what circumstances states will support international war crimes tribunals. Lansing gave the simple answer: mostly, when liberal states have been the victims of war crimes. The single best guarantee of a stung and moralistic reaction from a liberal state has been its own victimization. But there are also reasons to think that the answer may be broader and more complicated than that, and that liberal states could, over time, be made to be less selfish and more concerned with the suffering of innocents who do not happen to be their own citizens. The story of the politics of war crimes tribunals is really the story of the constant tension between liberal ideals and cruder self-interest.

The Power of Selfishness

For the most part, the selfish impulses have won out. This much, at least, makes sense through a realist prism: there is a powerful emphasis on protecting one's own citizens and one's own soldiers.

The single biggest challenge for international war crimes tribunals has been the unwillingness of even liberal states to endanger their own soldiers either by arresting war criminals or in subsequent reprisals. Holbrooke, among others, has explained the Pentagon's reluctance to pursue Bosnian war criminals as a product of what he calls Washington's "Vietmalia syndrome,"[4] referring to the casualties of Vietnam and Somalia. But the extreme unwillingness of Western leaders to put their soldiers at risk for the sake of international justice in Bosnia—what I have called the O'Grady phenomenon, after the American pilot rescued from Bosnia—is not simply a post-Vietnam or post-Somalia artifact. The roots go far deeper than that.

States have been amazingly consistent in their refusal to pay for international justice in the lives of their own soldiers. As early as 1815, the British squadron that finally captured Napoleon was instructed that the king valued the life a single British sailor as much as Napoleon's. The trend runs throughout this century: from Churchill's fiasco with the U-boat crews, to France's secret 1916 agreement on prisoners with Germany, to the British deal with Atatürk to swap accused Turkish war criminals for British prisoners, and to the American decision not to prosecute Hirohito lest the Japanese fight on. One of the most important—and crude—reasons for the triumph of Nuremberg was that it did not require any additional risks for Allied soldiers, since the Allies had demanded an unconditional Axis surrender before settling on a war crimes policy.

This is the real backdrop for the fear of Serb reprisals that has dominated Western military deployments in ex-Yugoslavia, whether in UNPROFOR, IFOR, SFOR, or KFOR. It was only after the civilian side of the Dayton accords had come to the brink of collapse, with Karadzic prominently flouting NATO's authority, and after the fortuitous elevation of Albright and Cook, that NATO made its first arrest raids. Even so, one outstanding feature of these raids has been their trepidation about taking risks. Unpopular and marginal war crimes suspects may get nabbed, but not a well-defended and popular figure like Mladic. Even in the Kosovo war, NATO insisted on humanitarianism on the cheap, refusing to send ground troops even as Milosevic's "ethnic cleansing" killed thousands of Kosovars and put a million of them out of their homes.

Some victims count more than others. Even liberal states have mostly pursued international justice when their citizens had been the victims of war crimes. In World War I, offenses against the British—the deaths of Fryatt and Cavell, U-boat warfare, Zeppelin raids—became national rallying points in Britain. France and Belgium, the two countries that had suffered under German occupation, all but howled for prosecutions. When Americans died at the hands of German U-boat crews, the Wilson administration found its voice on war crimes. As British plans for trials for Ottoman war criminals unraveled, British officials tried to hold onto Turks accused of crimes against Britons to the end, showing more solicitude for Britons than for Armenians.

This explains in large part why aggression was seen as the primary international crime after both world wars. Nuremberg was meant to put the Nazi leaders on trial for the crime that most directly harmed the Allies: starting the war. Many Israelis and West Germans saw the subsequent Eichmann and Auschwitz trials as a necessary way of focusing attention on the Holocaust in a way Nuremberg had not. The Tokyo tribunal went to equal lengths to put Japanese leaders in the dock for aggression, even though Japan had not committed a genocide. The most notorious Japanese atrocity against the Chinese, the Rape of Nanking, was not the focus of Allied prosecutions.

In this light, the relative lack of Western interest in war crimes in ex-Yugoslavia and Rwanda makes a crude kind of geopolitical—if not moral—sense. The slaughters of Armenians and Jews were carried out by wartime enemies of the most powerful liberal states; the slaughters of Bosnians and Tutsi were a project by groups against whom the West bore no particular grudge. If America had for some other reason been in a war against the Bosnian Serbs or the Rwandan Hutu, Bush and Clinton might have been quicker to take steps to stop their criminality—witness Bush's sudden discovery of the criminal nature of Saddam Hussein's regime after the Iraqi invasion of Kuwait. It was the great misfortune of Rwandans and Bosnians to be able to make appeals to the West only in moral terms.

The Power of Idealism

The picture is not all bleak. There are genuine principled impulses in the behavior of liberal states, pushing back against more selfish impulses.

Although citizens tend to come before foreigners, liberal states also have a universalistic strand built in: a domestic ideology that sees rights as universal and inviolable, which can thus force liberal states to worry about the plight of foreigners. This struggle between the self-serving and humanitarian impulses in states comes up over and over again. There were powerful diplomats and ordinary citizens in the West horrified by the sack of Belgium, the Armenian genocide, the Holocaust, the genocide in Rwanda, and the ravaging of Bosnia and Kosovo. NATO is currently showing considerable seriousness about helping the Hague tribunal prosecute war crimes in Kosovo. In full cry, this humanitarianism can be a potent force in the making of a liberal state's foreign policy. This does not leave much space for humanitarianism, but it does leave some. Lansing was more typical than Barton, and more powerful than Barton, but there are people like Barton all the same.

Of course, the decision about whether to seek punishment is not always entirely in the hands of elite decision makers. Public opinion weighs in powerfully. Even Castlereagh could not afford to shrug off popular outcry for the punishment of Bonapartists in 1815; even Prussian and Soviet leaders had to take into account punitive pressures from below. And such public sentiments are particularly hard to muzzle in liberal states.

By 1918, the force of public opinion made it all but inevitable that the Allies would decide to punish German war criminals.[5] Lloyd George and Clemenceau were both acutely aware of popular outrage, with Lloyd George even running a hugely successful anti-German campaign in elections immediately after the end of the Great War. Even more skeptical politicians like Churchill felt compelled to campaign on trying the kaiser. And polls in Britain and America during World War II show overwhelming public approval for punishing the Nazis.

Often the leaders are just as enthusiastic: one thinks of Liverpool, Blücher, Lloyd George, Balfour, Calthorpe, Clemenceau, Poincaré, Churchill, both Morgenthaus, Roosevelt, Stimson, Albright, and Cook. There was usually a good fit between elite and public sentiment. The obvious exception is that American public opinion was more enthusiastic about punishing the kaiser than the Wilson administration was.[6] This, of course, was not the biggest misjudgment Wilson made about the extent to which the American public stood behind him.

Sometimes elites will push for war crimes trials even when public opinion is disengaged. Here, the only examples are Albright, Holbrooke, and Cook, forcing through the first NATO arrests of Bosnian war crimes suspects despite the forecasting of Dick Morris. They are being even more vigorous in Kosovo. (There is nothing to stop a decision maker from getting out in front of public opinion; but Albright, Holbrooke, and

279

Cook are taking a huge risk if anything goes wrong. It would only take a few dead SFOR or KFOR soldiers to tarnish their forthright stance.)

Nonstate actors can also pitch in. They do not feature in most of this book, for the simple reason that they mostly did not exist until after World War II, and took time to gather strength. Amnesty International, the biggest global human rights group, was not founded until 1961. Because of the lack of examples, this book does not try to account definitively for the precise impact of various tactics by human rights groups.[7] But it is clear that a complete account of The Hague and Arusha must include the role of groups like Human Rights Watch, Médecins sans Frontières, and the Open Society Institute, as well as the role of the press. The expertise and cash of nongovernmental organizations helped keep The Hague viable, and the pressure of continuing reports of massive violations of human rights made the feeble reaction of Western governments that much more embarrassing.[8] All told, a liberal government can find itself being lobbied for an idealistic policy from all corners: from public opinion, principled decision makers, opposition parties, and nongovernmental organizations.

And finally, there is legalism. The actions of liberal states in this book cannot be explained convincingly without an account of their principled ideas. Liberal states have taken a legalistic approach to the punishment of war criminals, even when so doing has greatly complicated international diplomacy. If the historical episodes in this book are typical, then legalism seems to arise exclusively in liberal states, ones where civil rights are respected at home.

Legalism was not born at Nuremberg; it just came of age there. The exportation of liberal domestic norms of due process has been an important fact of international relations since at least World War I. The legalistic efforts at the end of World War I rival the more famous projects after World War II. Indeed, in some ways, legalism actually was *more* expansive in earlier days, when the notion of outlawing war was seen as a critical part of the legalist project, instead of as a dead end.

Even liberal states can be sorely tempted to dispense with such niceties as trials (as Prussia and the Soviet Union would have) and simply execute war criminals. These temptations were epitomized by Morgenthau Jr. and by Churchill, once he turned against legalism after disastrously pushing it in 1915. In World War II polls, democratic electorates, too, were decidedly nonlegalistic. Legalism seems to be an elite phenomenon—a product of liberalism, not of democracy per se.

But no matter how bloodthirsty democratic citizenries were, there was a countervailing tendency in American and British politics that demanded legalism. Even the British government, soured on trials by Leipzig, would only hear of executing fifty to one hundred top Axis leaders at the end of World War II. Churchill insisted on trials for lower-level war crimes suspects, and was furious at Stalin's suggestion of mass executions of Germans. Stimson doggedly fought his bureaucratic rivals for a legalistic approach, invoking the Bill of Rights and the Supreme Court. There was nothing overdetermined about Stimson's victory; the most that one can credibly argue is that liberal states will have their legalists, and that they will *tend* to win. Certainly, Stimson's kind of arguments would have been unthinkable in an illiberal state, and incomprehensible to Blücher or Stalin in a way they were not to Roosevelt. In the event, this legalism meant that, at the end of the greatest conflagration in human history, the victors extended the protection of due process to their defeated enemies in Nuremberg and Tokyo.

When war and massacre tore apart Yugoslavia and Rwanda, the reaction of the great liberal powers was legalist. One of the most potent arguments for intervention was that war crimes were being committed, especially when images of Serb concentration camps conjured up (not quite correctly) memories of the Holocaust. If Serb forces were committing crimes against humanity in Croatia and Bosnia (and later Kosovo), and if Hutu forces were committing crimes against humanity in Rwanda, then the appropriate reaction was to create a war crimes tribunal like that at Nuremberg.

Of course, there was a distinct tokenism to this legalism. Unlike in World War II, this time legalism came easily to America and other NATO countries. The outrage of the public, or of decision makers in the mold of Morgenthau Jr., was largely absent. To be sure, the West insisted on giving the benefit of due process to ex-Yugoslav and Rwandan war criminals. For those few Western leaders who were genuinely enraged at "ethnic cleansing," it was impressive that they would tame their anger with legalism. But for the rest, it was no great feat to impose the form of legalism on policies that were never meant to be serious.

All told, this legalism may sometimes seem eccentric, absurdly pious, or an impediment to substantive justice; but it is certainly *principled*. Legalists can be sincerely horrified at violations of the norms of war and serious in their intention to punish the offenders. There is at least some idealistic clay to work with here.

POWER AND JUSTICE

Nuremberg and Tokyo—and Leipzig and Constantinople before them—were roundly criticized as conquerors' courts.[9] This was their great flaw, and their great advantage. True, the Allies sat in judgment because of the morally arbitrary fact of having won a war. "Chance is the supreme judge in war and not Right," Lloyd George wrote.[10] But with the anger and bitterness of wartime came a resolute desire to punish the war criminals, to translate chance into right.

In contrast, the Hague tribunal was widely applauded as the first truly international war crimes court. "This is a truly international institution," said tribunal president Cassese. "It is an expression of the entire world community, not the long arm of four powerful victors."[11] But this was both a moral strength and a practical weakness. The punishment of Axis war criminals was a matter of the first order for the Allies; the punishment of ex-Yugoslav war criminals was not Bill Clinton's problem. Clinton, after all, is president of the United States, and that office has weighty responsibilities: health care, tax breaks, Kenneth Starr, and other matters that furrow brows at the White House in a way that Bosnia and Rwanda did not.

If there is to be, despite American objections, a serious permanent war crimes tribunal—the ICC—then liberal governments will have to make a far stronger commitment to international justice than they have in the 1990s.[12] What made Nuremberg suspect made it strong; what made The Hague unimpeachable made it weak. For Clinton—and for the American public—legalist words have often been a substitute for real political actions in Bosnia and Rwanda. As Judith Shklar once wrote, "The idea that all international problems will dissolve with the establishment of an international court with compulsory jurisdiction is an invitation to political indolence. It allows one to make no alterations in domestic political action and thought, to change no attitudes, to try no new approaches and yet appear to be working for peace."[13]

There is, after all, a self-serving case for a more legalist world. Liberal states would be better off in a world where aggression and violent bigotry are punished. Multiethnic societies like America, India, and Nigeria have a particular interest in seeing law tame ethnic conflict (Clinton has nervously compared America's multiethnicity with Bosnia's).[14] Or perhaps better-informed liberal publics could push their governments to greater humanitarianism. And Western militaries—who have recently tried to obstruct legalistic projects—have a particular interest in the enforcement of the laws of war. Soldiers are some of the only Americans who, as part of their occupation, are by definition at risk of becoming the victims of war crimes—witness Malmédy, or the UNPROFOR hostages in Bosnia. Any military commander would shudder at the thought of operating in a region where the enemy routinely abused prisoners of war.

Even if states are often self-serving in their pursuit of international justice, a more universalistic brand of justice can hitch a ride on a particular state. The high-water mark of international justice, Nuremberg, was an example of just that. Today almost nobody remembers the quixotic American crusade to outlaw war itself, but the category of crimes against humanity is well-established. But this drift to universalism can only happen if there is a robust tribunal in existence.

In the last analysis, the two international war crimes tribunals in The Hague and Arusha stand largely as testaments to the failure of America and the West.[15] Had the West managed to summon the political will to stop the slaughters in Rwanda and Bosnia, there would have been no need for these two fragile experiments in international justice. No war crimes, no war crimes tribunals. But having abdicated the responsibility of stopping war crimes, the West has now put its faith in weak international institutions to restore the world community's good name. No matter how successful the two tribunals may come to be in the fullness of time—including, of course, the unhappy possibility that they will be forgotten as completely as Leipzig and Constantinople—they will not be able to fulfill that task. Legalism will never make up for the lives lost; but legalism is all we have now.

Epilogue: Do War Crimes Tribunals Work?

*You want to execute them for the right reasons, if you want to
do anything for the future peace of the world.*
—*Justice Robert Jackson*

L IBERALS have never been prone to make modest claims about the importance of international war crimes tribunals. Madeleine Albright, visiting the Hague tribunal in 1997, said:

Justice is essential to strengthen the rule of law, soften the bitterness of victims' families, and remove an obstacle to cooperation among the parties. It will help ensure that our forces can depart Bosnia without the fear that renewed violence threatening U.S. interests might one day return. It will establish a model for resolving ethnic differences by the force of law rather than the law of force.[1]

In Pristina in July 1999, after the Kosovo war, Albright said, "[W]e believe that justice is a parent to peace." Throughout this book, legalists have set a dizzying array of lofty objectives for international war crimes tribunals. They are to bring justice, establish peace, outlaw war altogether, erase bitterness, or establish new international norms that will help lift us out of anarchy.[2] The Hague tribunal, in an annual report, modestly argued that it was essential to peace in ex-Yugoslavia: "[I]t would be wrong to assume that the Tribunal is based on the old maxim *fiat justitia et pereat mundus* (let justice be done, even if the world were to perish). The Tribunal is, rather, based on the maxim propounded by Hegel in 1821: *fiat justitia ne pereat mundus* (let justice be done lest the world should perish)."[3]

These kinds of sweeping claims have become accepted as a kind of orthodoxy among many human rights activists, often backed up only with the example of Nuremberg's success. For at least a century, legalists have made arguments similar to Albright's about the need to prosecute war criminals. But although most people have a sense that prosecuting war criminals is a morally good thing to do, there is no reliable proof that so doing will always have good *results*. Without a systematic study of failures like Leipzig as well as successes like Nuremberg, we are left with our scruples and our hunches, but no sturdy consensus built on empirical study.

There are many reasons to be skeptical of the notion that war crimes trials are always appropriate. Due process may interfere with substantive justice, through technical acquittals and delays in punishing people who richly deserve it. The spectacle of foreign-imposed trials may cause a nationalist backlash. Or a moralistic insistence on punishing war crimes may make it impossible to do business with bloodstained leaders who, however repulsive, might end a war. When politics is linked to law, crucial flexibility is lost—potentially with catastrophic results.

In this epilogue, I will take a first cut at analyzing the liberal case for war crimes tribunals, outlining realist critiques and then looking in depth at each of the five main arguments commonly made by liberals. Then I will try to bolster these traditional arguments with a rather less idealistic argument: international tribunals are better than the usual alternative, which is simple vengeance by the aggrieved parties. It is not that these complicated and often muddled trials are too noble to question; it is that the other options would be worse.

The Realist Argument: The Dangers of Backlash

Realists, from E.H. Carr to Kenneth Waltz, have long been skeptical of the ability of law to play a productive role in international relations. The two most powerful realist criticisms of war crimes trials are that such efforts will perpetuate a war, or destabilize postwar efforts to build a secure peace.

Raymond Aron argued that threats of war crimes trials would only make war more brutal:

> Would statesmen yield before having exhausted every means of resistance, if they knew that in the enemy's eyes they are criminals and will be treated as such in case of defeat? It is perhaps immoral, but it is most often wise, to spare the leaders of the enemy state, for otherwise these men will sacrifice the lives and wealth and possessions of their fellow citizens or their subjects in the vain hope of saving themselves. If war as such is criminal, it will be inexpiable.[4]

It is hard to say whether Aron's specific argument stands up, for the trade-off between justice and peace is rarely so stark. In World War II, the Allied decision to demand unconditional surrender was taken well before anyone had conceived of Nuremberg or Tokyo. If anything, The

285

Hague's indictment of Karadzic helped Holbrooke, by giving a nonpolitical reason to shunt Karadzic aside in the pursuit of America's "Milosevic strategy." In the Kosovo war, Milosevic's indictment did not stop NATO from negotiating a cease-fire with his regime. Still, the general concern is not so easily dismissed.

As for the second realist critique, it is easier to see the impact of nationalist backlash. This kind of backlash comes up over and over again in this book. Talleyrand, having had his ear bent a few times too many by the British about punishing Bonapartists, would later complain that Louis XVIII's blacklist was "a clumsy and mad act, which could only create difficulties and risks for the royal government."[5] Soberingly, in Weimar Germany, Allied calls for war crimes trials stirred up nationalist resentment across much of the political spectrum. And in the Ottoman Empire, anti-British backlash helped undermine the sultanate when it cooperated with British legalism.

The risk of backlash is present in Bosnia today, too. Moderates in Republika Srpska (such as they are), like Milorad Dodik, face a similar problem to that of Louis XVIII, Matthias Erzberger, and Damad Ferid. If Dodik lets Karadzic and his cronies meddle in politics, they may undermine Dodik; if Dodik helps SFOR deliver Karadzic to The Hague, anti-Western resentment may undermine Dodik. Small wonder that Dodik has tested the waters cautiously, letting SFOR carry out a few arrests of war criminals and then watching to see how threatening the backlash is.

NO JUSTICE, NO PEACE

Liberals are well aware of the risks of backlash, too; and yet they still argue that the benefits of war crimes tribunals outweigh them. Realists see justice as dangerous to a durable peace; liberals argue that there is no durable peace without justice.

The liberal case, as made in the aftermath of wars this century—and echoed in current debates about the ICC—can be broken down into a series of five major arguments. Liberals argue that international war crimes tribunals build up a sturdy peace by, first, purging threatening enemy leaders; second, deterring war criminals; third, rehabilitating former enemy countries; fourth, placing the blame for atrocities on individuals rather than on whole ethnic groups; and, fifth, establishing the truth about wartime atrocities. Each of these will be discussed in turn below.

Upon closer examination, only one of these arguments—that tribunals establish a definitive record—seems to be unambiguously worthy. All of the others are much muddier. Purging threatening leaders can be an important part of reforming a conquered country, but it may require a serious military commitment to ride out the nationalist backlash set off by foreign-imposed justice. Although some less ideological regimes may be deterred by the threat of war crimes prosecutions, those bent on mass slaughter—the Ottoman Empire, Nazi Germany, Republika Srpska—have shrugged off such warnings. Trials may help the rehabilitation of a defeated country, but only as one element in a broader program of national reconstruction. And no international tribunal has ever dreamed of prosecuting more than a fraction of the guilty individuals, so trials tend not to put the blame where it fairly belongs. In sum, the traditional liberal arguments make a fair case, but not one overwhelming enough to silence all critics.

Purging Threatening Leaders

The direct liberal reply to realist warnings about backlash is that a country can never be stable while dangerous leaders are still at large. Karadzic and other war crimes suspects can undermine Dayton; Milosevic can undermine the whole region's stability.

In December 1918, Allied leaders weighing Wilhelm II's trial had precisely the same debate, with Sonnino, Italy's foreign secretary, taking the realist line against Lloyd George's liberal line:

> *Baron Sonnino* . . . questioned the desirability of making a scape-goat. Was not St. Helena useful to the Bonapartists? The answer was "Yes"; and the *régime* of Napoleon III had been the result.
> *Mr. Lloyd George* replied that St. Helena was not so useful to the Bonapartists as the ex-Kaiser in Holland with £30,000,000 at his disposal would be to his party in Germany.[6]

It was that kind of logic that made Castlereagh write in 1815 that the "Principal Dangers" to European peace were the fact that Napoleon and many Bonapartists were still at large.[7] In 1919, the British high commissioner in Constantinople justified keeping Said Halim and other important Young Turks in custody in much the same terms:

> [I]f the accused were to escape, they would immediately form the nucleus of all the inveterate supporters of the C.U.P., from which disorders,

even in the Capital, of the most serious kind might be apprehended, to the grave disadvantage not only of the present Government but also of the Allies, both in their moral and their material interests.[8]

It is not enough, legalists argue, just to get rid of these leaders. For public attitudes to shift, criminal leaders must be tried—their aura of mystery shattered by showing their weaknesses and stupidities, and their prestige deflated by the humiliation of standing in the dock.

The best examples of the success of this approach are the two great Allied international military tribunals at Nuremberg and Tokyo. As one historian notes, "[T]he massive, bitter opposition to the IMT that some of Germany's critics had predicted did not materialize."[9] But while the success of Nuremberg is well known, one must remember Leipzig and Constantinople, too. Why the different outcomes after World War I and World War II?

This is a huge question, but the critical factors seem to be the strength of the opposition to the victorious countries' trying to impose trials, the extent of other punitive measures, the perception of hypocrisy, and the depth of the victors' military commitment. The Constantinople process fell apart as the Young Turks and Atatürk resisted the sultanate, and Britain was in no position to resist militarily as Turkey descended into civil war. Similarly, the Leipzig process floundered as German rightists wore down the legitimacy of Weimar, without a clear Allied commitment to stop that. German backlash was further encouraged by the many other punitive provisions of Versailles. Conversely, after World War II, the Allies, while not brooking any Nazi revivalism, tried to restore Germany rather than humiliate it. As Germans heard more about Nazi aggression and atrocities, they came to renounce Nazism.

Tentative as this analysis is, it is only partially encouraging when one considers NATO's current mission in Bosnia. Among Bosnian Serbs, at least, there has been considerable potential for anti-Western backlash. Many Serbs resent Dayton for reasons unrelated to its war criminals provisions: returning Serb-conquered territory to the Bosnian government, the possibility of refugees returning to their prewar homes, and so on. Karadzic and Mladic still have significant support. By January 1997, almost two-thirds of Bosnian Serbs had a very favorable opinion of Mladic, and about one-fifth had a somewhat favorable impression of him.[10] Karadzic is less popular, but in January 1997 still had a very favorable image among over half of Bosnian Serbs; about one-third had a somewhat favorable opinion. While IFOR refused to pursue Karadzic in the first year after Dayton, his popularity actually went up.[11] His popularity has dwindled since NATO started arresting war crimes suspects, but as late as October 1999, 73 percent of Bosnian Serbs in Republika Srpska had a favorable opinion of him[12]—numbers that any Western politician would envy. (Dodik polled less well, but not as poorly as many had feared. Against Karadzic's 36 percent very-favorable mark, Dodik got 18 percent. And 53 percent of Bosnian Serbs in Republika Srpska had a very or somewhat favorable view of Dodik. The frightening point is that 19 percent had a very unfavorable opinion of Dodik, against only 4 percent for Karadzic.)[13]

So far, SFOR's sporadic arrest raids have not provoked significant Serb reprisals. But after the first SFOR raid, 84 percent of Bosnian Serbs thought SFOR should not hunt war crimes suspects.[14] Even Dodik worried, in February 1998, that the prospect of Karadzic and Mladic's arrests "is a nightmare for the Serb Republic. We are aware of our obligations from Dayton. We have had the media creating heroic myths among the people. We cannot change such attitudes in just one month."[15] The hope is that as time goes by, Bosnian Serbs are getting used to Dayton and to the arrest of war criminals. It is enormously heartening that Krajisnik's arrest—a possible preview of a Karadzic arrest—did not cause any appreciable disruptions or violence.

In Kosovo, if there is Serb backlash, it cannot be as threatening because the prewar population was nine-tenths Kosovar Albanian. As for the rest of Yugoslavia, and the question of whether The Hague's indictment of Milosevic will hasten his ouster, it is simply too soon to tell. In Tudjman's Croatia, the regime loudly scorned The Hague, with the justice minister even flying to Split to welcome home a convicted Croat war criminal who had been released in May 1999 for time served. But Tudjman's death has allowed the election of a new government that says it will cooperate with The Hague.

The most alarming possibility is that it might not take too much backlash to make SFOR, or KFOR, cut and run. Even while waging the Kosovo war, NATO showed no stomach for more than a handful of casualties. High-profile reprisals—say, a Beirut-style bombing in Sarajevo's Old Town, a guerrilla attack on American SFOR troops in Tuzla, or the seizure of Western hostages—could quickly erode Western support for an extended stay in Bosnia. The governments of Lloyd George, Wilson, and Churchill all worried hugely about their own soldiers; one should not expect anything less self-centered from Clinton and Blair.

Deterring War Criminals

The champions of war crimes tribunals have argued for about a century that the existence of such a court will deter potential criminals. In May 1915, after the Allies threatened the Young Turk leaders with personal responsibility, the Armenian Patriotic Association wrote gratefully to the British Foreign Office: "The victims of Ottoman fraud and cruelty cannot be brought back to life, but the fear of personal responsibility and threatened condign punishment for their wilful misdeeds may deter the criminal minded officials and their rascally myrmidons from committing other crimes."[16] In the speech that convinced the Imperial War Cabinet to demand Wilhelm II's trial, Frederick Smith argued, "[L]et the ruler who decides upon war know that he is gambling, amongst other hazards, with his own personal safety." As for preventing U-boat warfare, Smith said: " 'If I do it and fail,' the Tirpitz of the next war must say, 'I, too, shall pay for it in my own person.' "[17] In 1944, the War Refugee Board's John Pehle wrote, "The failure to punish the criminals of World War I may well have removed a deterrent to the commission of brutalities against civilian populations in this war, including the mass murder of the Jews."[18] Fifty years later, at the U.S. Holocaust Memorial Museum, Albright said:

> *Even the threat of punishment for war crimes can save lives.*
>
> The prospect of war crimes trials in the latter stages of World War II caused some Nazi leaders to modify their treatment of Jews and other prisoners. In former Yugoslavia, each time the prospect of punishing war criminals has been publicized, the treatment of detainees has improved and atrocities have diminished. Today, there are signs that some of the worst violators of human rights are being deprived of their authority by one-time protectors who now fear justice under the law.
>
> In short, the more serious we are about the Tribunal, the greater the potential deterrent the Tribunal will be. If this means that one village that would otherwise be attacked is spared; that one woman who would otherwise be violated is respected; that one prisoner who would otherwise be executed is allowed to live—the existence of the Tribunal would be validated on these grounds alone.[19]

Albright also argued for a long-term global deterrent: "If the architects of war and ethnic cleansing in Bosnia go unpunished, the lesson for would-be Milosevic's around the world will endanger us all."[20] "There's only one deterrent," says Richard Goldstone, "and that's detection and punishment."[21]

Despite these claims, it is far from clear that war crimes tribunals have much of a deterrent effect, either in the near- or long-term.[22] The short-term difficulties are daunting. Even the best-established domestic legal systems are incapable of deterring all murderers, or even all shoplifters. International war crimes tribunals face a far greater challenge. These tribunals, after all, are meant to deal with the most bloody of crimes; men willing to commit mass murder are terribly difficult to dissuade. In many of the cases when war crimes tribunals have been mooted, a regime has devoted itself to expelling or exterminating an ethnic group: Armenians, Jews, Bosnian Muslims, Rwandan Tutsi. Such a regime may be undeterrable by anything short of massive military force, and maybe not even that. When legalistic threats do come, these mass killings are already well underway, so the accused are already criminally liable and thus may think they have nothing to gain by stopping now. Although some collaborators and lower-level agents may be cowed, especially if there are military threats behind the legalistic ones, such genocidal regimes are unlikely to be swayed by threats of prosecution.

That was the Allied experience when dealing with the Ottoman Empire during World War I. Henry Morgenthau Sr., the American ambassador in Constantinople, who delivered the direct Allied threat of prosecution in 1915, reported:

> I have repeatedly spoken to the Grand Vizier and pleaded earnestly with Minister of the Interior and Minister of War to stop this persecution. My arguments were unavailing except as to Constantinople. . . . *They state that it is the Union and Progress committee's nationalistic policy which they refused to modify even when Russia, France, and Great Britain threatened Ottoman Cabinet Ministers with personal responsibility.* Turkish authorities desire to avail themselves of present conditions when three of the great powers are at war with them, Italy in strained relations, and the two others are their allies and therefore will not interfere when they are successfully defending the formidable attack at the Dardanelles.[23]

By their own account, even to a pro-Armenian interlocutor like Morgenthau, the Ottoman leaders had not lessened their persecution of the Armenians.

Nazi Germany dedicated itself single-mindedly to the extermination of the Jews.[24] Even during Stalingrad—when one would have expected that all available resources would be thrown into fending off the Soviet

Union—Germany relentlessly continued the Holocaust. In December 1942, the Allies issued a stern declaration warning that the Germans responsible for exterminating the European Jews would be brought to justice,[25] but the death camps continued their systematic murders until they were liberated by the Allies.[26] In July 1944, Eden, reinforced in his complacency, said: "[T]here are unfortunately no signs that the repeated declarations made by His Majesty's Government in association with the other United Nations of their intention to punish the instigators and perpetrators of these frightful crimes have moved the German Government and their Hungarian accomplices either to allow the departure of even a small proportion of their victims or to abate the fury of their persecution."[27] Even orders from the top need not stop extermination campaigns. With the war clearly lost and Dachau in American hands, Himmler in May 1945 explicitly ordered an end to the death marches of Jews, fearing that continued murders would embarrass him in talks with America.[28] Stimson noted that "Himmler himself was sending refugees to Switzerland apparently in the hope that he would thus get some credit and appeasement with the American Jews to soften the punishment which he is expecting as a war criminal."[29] But even a direct order from the highest levels did not stop the Germans from further murders. Himmler was not deterred until just short of the bitter end, and even that did not stop his underlings.[30]

Allied threats did seem to have some success when not directly confronting Germany over the Holocaust. There is some evidence that Germany could be deterred from committing war crimes against Americans. Stimson noted a case where two American prisoners of war were spared from execution when another prisoner threatened "the names and their commandants would be given to the Americans for punishment after the war by court martial."[31] And the Allies scored some successes when dealing with Axis satellites. After hearing of an Allied threat to bomb Hungarian and German institutions in Budapest (including a list of names of Hungarians and Germans deporting Jews to Auschwitz), Hungary belatedly ordered an end to the deportations.[32] Allied threats against Axis satellites might well have saved many Jews from deportation from Rumania, Bulgaria, Hungary, and Italian-occupied parts of France, Greece, and Yugoslavia.[33] And it is possible that the Allied threats about war crimes would have had more impact on Germany and its satrapies if the Allies had emphasized the Holocaust more in their declarations. As historian David Wyman suggests,

Roosevelt, Churchill, and the Pope might have made clear to the Nazis their full awareness of the mass-murder program and their severe condemnation of it. If, in addition, Roosevelt and Churchill had threatened punishment for these crimes and offered asylum to the Jews, the Nazis at least would have ceased to believe that the West did not care what they were doing to the Jews. That might possibly have slowed the killing. And it might have hastened the decision of the SS, ultimately taken in late 1944, to end the extermination. Even if top Nazis brushed the threats aside, their subordinates might have been given pause.[34]

Only twice, both in 1942, did the Allies warn the Nazis specifically about the persecution of the Jews. Seven of the Allies' public threats, including the Moscow Declaration, did not mention the Jews at all.[35]

The Hague tribunal—and Western nonmilitary pressure in general—has done little to dissuade war crimes in ex-Yugoslavia. In the summer of 1992, for instance, the UN warned Bosnian Serb leaders that expelling Muslims and Croats was a war crime, to no avail.[36] The creation of the Hague tribunal—remote and hamstrung as it has been—did not seem to change the picture radically. The most dramatic failure in Bosnia was the fall of Srebrenica in July 1995, with Mladic overseeing the massacre of seven thousand Bosnian Muslims[37]—two years after the creation of the tribunal, and shortly after it became clear that the tribunal was about to indict Karadzic and Mladic. Cassese considers Srebrenica one of his court's biggest failures. Goldstone was more circumspect. "Well, firstly, indictments on their own aren't enough. There have to be arrests, trials and convictions," he says. But he also argues that "no criminal justice system is going to stop crime. It can only curb it. And what crimes might have been committed that weren't committed obviously it's impossible to say." And in Kosovo in 1999, specific threats from The Hague did not stop Milosevic's forces from mass killings and expulsions.

The picture is not entirely bleak. After the sinking of the *Lusitania*, Wilson threatened to hold Germany accountable for the loss of American lives; so Bethmann, despite Tirpitz's vociferous objections, managed to stop attacks on large passenger ships.[38] (This lasted until January 1917, when the Reichstag, Wilhelm II, and Hindenburg overruled Bethmann.[39]) In 1916, a muted American protest over German deportations of French citizens from Lille and Roubaix convinced Germany to desist.[40]

In August 1992, when Western journalists revealed the existence of the Serb-run Omarska concentration camp, with horrific television images of Bosnian Muslim prisoners evocative of the Holocaust, Karadzic agreed to evacuate the camp.[41] (Karadzic's forces continued their attacks on civilian targets throughout the rest of the war.) David Scheffer, America's ambassador-at-large for war crimes issues, claims that local authorities in Bosnia would sometimes ameliorate prison conditions to avoid punishment.[42] Peter Galbraith, as American ambassador to Croatia, raised the issue of war crimes in a Croat-run prison camp in a meeting with Mate Boban, a Bosnian Croat leader. "I listened to him spew off crap for about an hour and a half, and then I really let him have it," Galbraith remembers. Slamming down a fist, Galbraith continued:

> I said, "I have people who were just in the camp on, I forget, three days before, and here's what they found!" And I warned him, that these were war crimes. I said, frankly, holding prisoners in inhumane conditions: that's a war crime. And using food as a weapon, which he admitted to me that he was doing: I said, that's a war crime. And I said shelling purely civilian targets like east Mostar is a war crime. . . . And he said, "Oh, you don't understand, blah blah blah." And the next day he called up and announced that they were releasing prisoners en masse, and in fact I think that day they released 700 prisoners. . . . And then later I went public on the BBC, which was then replayed in the Croatian media, suggesting that Boban might be responsible for war crimes. In fact, raising this issue led to very significant improvements in the camps, they changed some leadership, and then they released the people by December, all of them. . . . And again, it was the sense of accountability, and of course made it clear to the Croatians that to the extent that they supported these guys they too could be held accountable. But I thought the whole war crimes issue was a very effective tool to stopping war crimes.

Galbraith also believes that the Hague tribunal's indictment of Milan Martic, the president of the self-styled Serb statelet in the Krajina, for a rocket attack on Zagreb "had a significant deterrent effect in terms of blocking further missile attacks at the time of Operation Storm," the August 1995 Croatian offensive that retook the Krajina. Goldstone has also claimed that Croatian soldiers in the Krajina, fearing indictment, were more restrained than they might have been.[43]

From these accounts, it seems that deterrence is at best a limited success—dissuading some war crimes, but not general programs of extermination. It is no great surprise that weak tribunals, like The Hague, do little to deter potential offenders. But even more credible efforts, like the Allied threats against the Ottoman Empire or Nazi Germany, met with little success when trying to dissuade genocide. Even military threats do not always work in such situations. This is not to say that such threats are ill-advised; to the contrary, they are moral necessities. And it is possible that more strongly worded and strongly backed threats might have more of an impact. But one should also keep one's expectations in check: war criminals are war criminals.

Some advocates of tribunals have a longer-term view of deterrence: that in the long run, the establishment of international norms or law can deter potential war criminals globally. The notion of global deterrence is not in itself implausible. Even states in total war may shy from breaking some norms, as when Nazi Germany and the Soviet Union held back from using chemical weapons in World War II.[44] But the picture is, once again, a mixed one: Hitler did not restrain himself from U-boat warfare against British merchant ships, and Britain did not hold back from massive bombing of Germany despite Britain's fear of a German response in kind.[45]

At a minimum, long-run deterrence of war crimes would require a relatively credible threat of prosecution: that is, a series of successful war crimes tribunals that became so much an expected part of international affairs that no potential mass murderer could confidently say that he would avoid punishment. The world would have to set up tribunals significantly more intimidating than the UN's two current courts for ex-Yugoslavia and Rwanda. The proposed ICC would likely help, but only if it somehow receives political support from the same great powers who have largely neglected the ex-Yugoslavia and Rwanda tribunals for so long. The combined impact of the Nuremberg and Tokyo trials did not have an obvious deterrent effect after the 1940s. Given the disappointing record so far of specifically targeted efforts at deterrence, it is hard to be overly optimistic.

Rehabilitating Renegade States

Nuremberg's glory is partially a reflected glory. The rehabilitation of Germany after World War II is one of the great political successes of the century, turning a fascist enemy into a democratic ally; Nuremberg gains prestige as part of that terrific success. Stimson saw trials as a first step toward rehabilitation.[46]

But Nuremberg was only the most spectacular element in a broader Allied program of denazification. According to sophisticated polling by the American occupation authorities, about two-thirds of Germans in the American zone supported Nuremberg, and half thought that all the defendants were guilty.[47] But many Germans were distracted by the ruin of their country and the shock of defeat. As time went on, German distaste for war crimes trials grew. Four years after Nuremberg, only 38 percent of German respondents in the American zone thought well of subsequent trials.[48] By 1949, many Germans disapproved of Allied trials of industrialists and senior military men.[49] In 1950, even Konrad Adenauer, the West German chancellor, asked the Allies to end all war crimes trials and to be more lenient in punishing convicted war criminals.[50] West Germany's own trials for Auschwitz and Majdanek, held in 1963–65 and 1975–81 respectively, as well as Israel's trial of Eichmann, helped drive home German guilt, but only after a new postwar West German generation had come to the fore.[51]

The picture in Japan is less encouraging. The 1946–48 Tokyo tribunal and other postwar trials had much less of an impact.[52] There are many possible reasons: the shock of Hiroshima and Nagasaki; a sense of being singled out for aggressions that were not unprecedented; an American emphasis on a natural law tradition and Anglo-American trial proceedings that found little local echo in Japan; the long, technical, and sometimes dubious proceedings; the absence of a Japanese equivalent to the Nazi Holocaust, despite such horrors as the Nanking slaughters; and an American occupation policy that was losing interest in democratization.[53] A British intelligence report noted that "the Japanese people do not understand the nature of the imputed guilt and are inclined to think that the principal crime of the accused is that they lost the war. . . . It seems possible that, with the usual tricks of memory assisted by nationalist propaganda, in a relatively short time most of the accused will be regarded as martyrs."[54] Tokyo, Shklar wrote, was "a complete dud."[55] Compared to West Germany, Japan's progress looks unimpressive; still, if Serbia could move as far from militarism as Japan has, the south Balkans would be a much calmer place.

If one takes Germany as a best-case scenario, one must be modest about one's hopes for a quick rehabilitation. It is not that tribunals have no positive effect, but that the effect is far from decisive, and certainly not quick. The popular image of Nuremberg as a lightning catharsis, transforming Germany at a stroke from a thoroughly Nazi country to a penitent democratic one, is much overstated. Rather, the Nuremberg experience suggests war crimes tribunals are not a quick fix, but part of a much more ambitious and time-consuming project of social engineering.

Putting the Blame on Individuals, Not Ethnic Groups

The basic argument here—a common one—is that, in Albright's words, "responsibility for these crimes does not rest with the Serbs or Croats or Muslims as *peoples*; it rests with the *people* who ordered and committed the crimes. *The wounds opened by this war will heal much faster if collective guilt for atrocities is expunged and individual responsibility is assigned.*"[56] Richard Goldstone has made the same case,[57] as has a prominent analyst of the Rwandan genocide.[58] Once again, this is not a new idea.[59] In June 1815, the commander of the Austrian army proclaimed: "Frenchmen! it is for you to decide for peace or war. Europe wishes to be at peace with France, but she will make war against the usurper of the French throne."[60] Stimson, disdaining the "indiscriminate condemnation of the German people as a hopelessly evil race,"[61] wanted to pin blame specifically on the Nazi leadership.[62] And Churchill hoped that "the mass of the German people will infer rightly that there is a difference between these major criminals and themselves."[63]

Appealing as it may sound, this ideal has proved terribly difficult to translate into practice. How broadly or narrowly does one draw the circle of guilt? As Aron wrote,

> If it is a question of punishing not the state or the nation but the persons by whose agency the state has committed the "crime against the peace," a single formula would be quite satisfactory, the one that occurs in several speeches of Sir Winston Churchill: *One man, one man alone.* If one man alone has taken the decisions that have committed a people, if one man alone possessed absolute power and acted in solitude, then this man incarnated the criminal state and deserves to be punished for the nation's crime. But such a hypothesis is never completely fulfilled, the leader's companions have shared in his decision, have conspired with him against peace and for conquest. How far is the search for the guilty to be carried? To what degree are the duties of obedience or national solidarity to be considered as absolving excuses?[64]

Some leaders have spread the blame widely. Austen Chamberlain found it

> impossible to distinguish the guilt of the ex-Kaiser from the guilt of the people who welcomed and applauded and supported him throughout. If you are going to treat the ex-Kaiser as the sole root of evil, you are going to acquit the German people. I think it is too early to do that

before you are satisfied that their change of mind and heart is complete and permanent. I think there is a great danger for our own people in teaching them that the ex-Kaiser alone was to blame and that the German people were as innocent as lambs.[65]

Australia's W. M. Hughes largely agreed: "I think that 85 per cent. of the German people are as bad as the ex-Kaiser ever was, and are as deserving of death; but I am not in favour of this 85 per cent. getting off free and sheltering under the blood of this man."[66] Similarly, during World War II, Roosevelt himself complained,

> Too many people here and in England hold to the view that the German people as a whole are not responsible for what has taken place—that only a few Nazi leaders are responsible. That unfortunately is not based on fact. The German people as a whole must have it driven home to them that the whole nation has been engaged in a lawless conspiracy against the decencies of modern civilization.[67]

Telford Taylor remembered being attacked as "soft on Germany" for suggesting in 1945 that not all SS members deserved death.[68]

Even the broadest application of legalistic principles will only allow the conviction of actual perpetrators—those who really committed crimes. But there will always be a wider circle of bystanders and collaborators, who may not bear actual criminal culpability but can reasonably be said to bear a moral taint. In 1915, some Germans cheered the sinking of the *Lusitania*.[69] Karl Jaspers, weighing German responsibility for Nazism, distinguished between criminal, political, moral, and metaphysical guilt.[70] Many Germans who did not actually take part in the Holocaust still have some moral—if not legal—culpability for venerating Hitler while knowing full well about *Mein Kampf* and the Nuremberg Laws. There are many Bosnian Serbs who did not actually commit war crimes but supported Karadzic; and Milosevic has plenty of enthusiasts. Will even trials of actual war criminals make it impossible for Bosnians and Kosovars to see a wider moral taint among many Serb nationalists?

As it turns out, those agonizing decisions about the extent of complicity tend never to be faced, for simple logistical reasons. After a war or mass slaughter, the massive number of perpetrators overwhelms the capacity of any legal institutions. But if one does not want to put on hundreds of thousands of trials, nor to declare whole organizations criminal (as was done at Nuremberg), then a legalistic approach will of necessity let off huge numbers of war criminals.

The sheer scale of these atrocities defies any normal notion of accountability. At best, a war crimes tribunal will punish the *most* guilty. No state has ever contemplated catching every war criminal, however much each criminal might deserve it. Lloyd George, reviewing an early list of German war criminals in 1919, "was rather taken aback at the idea of more than 1,500 separate trials."[71] Millerand icily told Germany that the Allied lists "did not include all the authors of the innumerable crimes committed during the war by German nationals," only the ones with the gravest responsibility.[72] Calthorpe, Britain's high commissioner in Constantinople, thought that "to arrest all those who deserve it would be too immense a task."[73] De Robeck, a subsequent high commissioner, wrote: "I have never thought it would be either practicable or politic to attempt to bring to justice all persons who took a part in the deportations or massacres. Justice and policy alike require, however, that an endeavour should be made to bring to justice a certain number of those who played the most active rôles, whether as originators, organisers or executants."[74] And many Class A Japanese war crimes suspects were released when the Allies dismissed the charges.[75]

Even the planners of Nuremberg realized that their efforts would never come close to doing justice to all war criminals. In September 1944, McCloy told Morgenthau Jr., "there may be arguments as to how far down you should go but we can't undertake to eliminate immediately every member of the Nazi Party." "Why not?" asked Morgenthau. "Because there are too many of them," said McCloy. "I think there are 13 million."[76] The British cabinet feared that an "intolerable burden might be placed on the military courts" if they had to try all alleged Gestapo members.[77] Jackson worried that the trial of all Gestapo members "would involve literally hundreds of thousands of trials if we reached all members, would it not?"[78]

Faced with this problem, even Stimson did not always manage to keep from spreading blame more broadly. Bernays wrote, "It will never be possible to catch and convict every Axis war criminal, or even any great number of them, under the old concepts and procedures."[79] The War Department's proposal of trying whole Nazi organizations cast a broader net, but at the cost of blurring distinctions among individuals. Jackson admitted:

> The difficulty in our case is that we have in the neighborhood of perhaps 200,000 prisoners. We don't want to have 200,000 trials. Some of them

perhaps ought to be tried individually on charges of individual criminal actions; but also they should be tried for their part in the planning of extermination of minorities, the aggressive warfare, the atrocities against occupied nationals, and offenses of that character. We think this should be done in a single effort so far as the collective guilt is concerned.[80]

Clearly, there is a difference between declaring all SS men criminals and declaring all Germans criminals, or between saying that all of Arkan's Tigers are criminals and that all Serbs are criminals. But the conspiracy scheme would likely have been met by a chilly reception from Goldstone or Arbour.

Daniel Jonah Goldhagen calculates that there were at least 100,000 perpetrators of the Holocaust, perhaps as many as 500,000.[81] But by 1948, by Taylor's reckoning, only 3,500 Germans had been tried (not just for murdering Jews but for other war crimes, too).[82] The only purge that would have come close to the mark was that proposed at Tehran by Stalin, although the 100,000 on Stalin's list would have been very different from the 100,000 Goldhagen has in mind. Even the most prodigious effort ever to purge war criminals did not even come close to placing individual guilt where it belonged.

The same problems are around today. Gérard Prunier estimates there were between 80,000 and 100,000 murderers in the Rwandan genocide: "Since it would be mad to add a second genocide to the first, it is out of the question to kill all the killers. But the desire for vengeance can be assuaged if the real organisers, the 'big people', go to the gallows."[83] The Arusha tribunal has indicted only thirty-five Rwandans. Although the Rwandan government has tens of thousands of accused *génocidaires* in its jails, even the RPF leadership admits that there cannot be trials for every killer. "It's materially impossible to judge all those who participated in the massacres, and politically it's no good, even though it's just," said one RPF leader.[84] The Bosnian Serb soldiers who fired shells indiscriminately into Tuzla or Zepa are war criminals; the snipers in the hills around Sarajevo are war criminals. But they are not going to be tried. The Hague has publicly indicted only eighty-one men.

Tribunal justice is inevitably symbolic: a few war criminals stand for a much larger group of guilty individuals. Thus, what is billed as individual justice actually becomes a de facto way of exonerating many of the guilty.

The good news is that this kind of whitewash could be politically useful. A narrow and well-focused purge may be less likely to spark a nationalist backlash. Surprisingly enough, the Nuremberg trial of the major war criminals was *more* popular among Germans than subsequent trials for lower-level war criminals. As Allied prosecutions turned from the top Nazi leaders to German military figures and professionals, the German public grew more restive. While it was not so hard for Germans to understand why a Göring or a Streicher was a special case, when the Allied prosecutions reached lower levels, the question was begged why Soviets were not on trial, too.[85] In Japan, there was great sympathy for the lower-level (Class B and Class C) war criminals.[86]

There is a certain logic to this reaction. The average German might find it easy to see that Ribbentrop bore unusual guilt and could be punished as a way of expiating Allied anger without posing any threat to less prominent Germans; but when Allied prosecutors aimed lower, ordinary Germans would be personally threatened. Similarly, trials conducted by the Muslim-Croat Federation in Bosnia could well be more threatening to the average Bosnian Serb than a trial of Karadzic in The Hague, because the Federation trials aim at minor war criminals. "Some are VRS Serbs who blew up a building, no one got hurt, you get fifteen years," says Hansjörg Strohmeyer, who monitors the trials for the Office of the High Representative (OHR) in Sarajevo. "For this Serb, he saw his mates doing much worse things."

In this light, many of the early trials in The Hague of low-level war criminals have been exactly the wrong approach. Quick, high-profile trials of high-ranked suspects would be better. The trial of Dusan Tadic, the low-level Bosnian Serb who was the first to stand in the dock in The Hague, was precisely the opposite of what one wants out of an international war crimes tribunal: a long and rather inconclusive trial of a minor figure. Serbs can plausibly argue that there were countless Tadics in the Bosnian Croat militia and, less plausibly, in the Bosnian Army. Trying a Karadzic or a Mladic may offend Serbs, but it does not concentrate the mind with a sense of personal peril.

So the idea that war crimes tribunals will individualize guilt turns out to be fraught with ambiguity. In practice, the logistical and political obstacles to a complete accounting tend to spare many perpetrators, collaborators, and bystanders. This may be useful, insofar as it lessens the danger of nationalist backlash; but it is hardly anything for legalists to cheer about.

Establishing the Truth

Of the five main liberal arguments for war crimes tribunals, this is the least controversial. Liberals argue that the denial of atrocity is in fact part and parcel of committing atrocity.[87] For instance, when a Bosnian Serb shell killed scores of civilians in Sarajevo's Markale market in 1994, Karadzic claimed that the Bosnians had faked the incident with corpses from the morgue.[88]

Small wonder that a thorough debunking has long been seen as one of the most important functions of a war crimes tribunal. Goldstone said, "[F]undamental to all forms of justice is official acknowledgment of what happened, whether by criminal process or truth commission."[89] Ernest Pollock, Britain's solicitor general after World War I, said the Allies' lists of war criminals "would remain for all time a record of German brutality."[90] After World War II, even British officials who did not want to risk a trial of the Nazi leadership admitted that a definitive historical record would be useful.[91] Jackson demanded as much evidence as possible, to make "a record of this thing so that the man to write the story of this twenty years from now can bank on it."[92] Stimson noted with satisfaction that no less than John Maynard Keynes "went out of his way to say that it is vitally important to make such a record of the great evil." And Stimson himself noted that one advantage of a conspiracy approach was that "the flexibility of evidence which is allowed would permit us to make a full and public record of the whole evil system of Nazism."[93]

This was a clear success of Nuremberg: an extraordinary trove of testimony and documentation. The SS's files alone filled six freight cars. Jackson later told Truman that the documentary record he had assembled came out to over five million pages.[94] (The Tokyo tribunal amassed thirty thousand pages of evidence.[95]) Afterward, Nuremberg published eleven volumes of documents and twenty-two volumes of the proceedings, at around five hundred pages per volume.[96] Alan Bullock, a historian, recalled reading all those volumes: "And I became intensely excited about them because—you can argue whichever way you want about whether it's justice or not—but from the point of view of the historian the Nuremberg trials were an absolutely unqualified wonder. I mean, the greatest coup in history for historians. The capture of the records of the most powerful state in the world immediately after the event!"[97] After the Eichmann trial, Arendt wrote, "Even today, eighteen years after the war, our knowledge of the immense archival material of the Nazi regime rests to a large extent on the selection made for prosecution."[98]

The Allies went to great lengths to make clear to Germans what the defendants at Nuremberg were accused of by broadcasting on German radio, showing documentaries, and distributing pamphlets.[99] American military police marched a thousand Weimar residents to Buchenwald, just liberated, to drive home to the Germans the horrors of Nazism: the piles of bodies and the emaciated survivors.[100] The Allied information campaign made more Germans face up to the reality of the Holocaust and Germany's responsibility for aggression.[101] These efforts have helped build a powerful German culture of remembering and atoning.[102]

The failed trials for the Young Turks show the opposite outcome. Like Jackson, some British officials had seen the need to set the historical record straight in Turkey.[103] But the failure of the Constantinople trials scotched that hope. As the Constantinople prosecutions were collapsing, the British Foreign Office worried that the evidence in the court's files was disappearing.[104] To this day, the Turkish government—a successor of Atatürk's government, not of the Ottoman Empire at all—goes to considerable lengths to deny the persecution of the Armenians.[105] One cannot imagine Germany doing anything remotely like this, and Nuremberg is part of the reason.

Even in the best of circumstances, it is hard to prevent war criminals from destroying the evidence. After the war was lost, Japanese militarists set off bonfires, destroying records of the secret police and military, transcripts of imperial conferences, cabinet deliberations, and records on prisoners of war and on campaigns in China. Some Japanese officers killed witnesses of war crimes, and by the end of August 1945, over a thousand Japanese officers had committed suicide.[106]

Of course, tribunals have no monopoly on truth-telling. Many tribunals have been preceded by a weak evidence-gathering commission of some kind: the Mazhar Inquiry Commission before Constantinople, the UNWCC before Nuremberg, and the Kalshoven commission of experts before The Hague. It was human rights groups and reporters—Roy Gutman of *Newsday*, Penny Marshall of ITN, John Burns of *The New York Times*, Christiane Amanpour of CNN, and many courageous others—that focused Western attention on Bosnia. But what Jackson had in mind was something more spectacularly public, with access to new documents and with high-level men in the dock giving testimony.[107] (South Africa's Truth and Reconciliation Commission partly fits the bill, although it is a domestic body.) In 1998 in The Hague, Stipe Mesic, the last president of communist Yugoslavia (and later Croatia's president after Tudjman's death), testified that Borisav Jovic, Serbia's representative on Yugoslavia's multiperson presidency, had said that Serbia had designs on two-thirds of Bosnia. Mesic also testified that Tudjman had told him about a 1991 meeting with Milosevic, who said that Bosnia was "untenable" and that Tudjman could have the parts that Serbia did not want. Paddy Ashdown, leader of Britain's Liberal Democrat Party, testified about a boozy 1995 dinner with Tudjman, where Tudjman, writing on a napkin, carved up Bosnia between Serbia and Croatia.

The absence of a well-established historical record facilitates denial that atrocities ever happened. For instance, Karadzic denies that there were executions at Srebrenica in July 1995.[108] There is already a fringe in Europe that wildly claims that the horrific ITN television footage of emaciated Bosnian prisoners at the Bosnian Serb-run Trnopolje concentration camp, in August 1992, was faked.[109] As time goes on, that fringe may grow. The Hague can fight that.

JUSTICE OR VENGEANCE

The five standard liberal arguments in favor of war crimes tribunals are far from weak, but they are not totally convincing either. But what alternative is there to legalism? Realists argue that the alternative to international tribunals, with their attendant risks of backlash, is a painless kind of forgetting. Not so. In fact, the more likely alternative to international tribunals is vengeance—often in an untamed form that would be more destabilizing than international trials. The victims of war crimes are unlikely to be as willing to turn the other cheek as outsiders are. Americans and Europeans may be glad to forget Serb and Croat enormities, but Bosnians and Kosovars will not. Once large-scale war crimes have been committed, there will almost inevitably be efforts to punish the perpetrators. If so, better an impartial international tribunal than national prosecutions or vigilantism.

The Least Awful Alternative

As in domestic society, a great advantage of international legalism is that it institutionalizes and moderates desires for revenge. As Shklar wrote, Nuremberg "replaced private, uncontrolled vengeance with a measured process of fixing guilt in each case, and taking the power to punish out of the hands of those directly injured."[110] The end of a war or series of atrocities is a time with great potential for further violence, even if the perpetrators have been conquered. International tribunals can regularize and tame what might otherwise turn into a bloodbath.

This is a very real danger. There is no telling what might have happened if the Morgenthau Plan had in fact gone into effect, with Allied execution squads fired up with the passions of victory and acting with insufficient oversight from above—and that is not even considering what Stalin might have done. As Herbert Wechsler wrote,

> [W]ho can doubt that indiscriminate violence, a blood bath beyond power of control, would have followed an announcement by the responsible governments that they were unwilling to proceed? If nothing else was to be accomplished, it was essential that some institutional mechanism be provided that would reserve the application of violence to the public force, to cases in which punishment might serve a constructive purpose and in which reason would conclude that it was deserved.[111]

And surely the backlash engendered by a huge series of summary executions by foreign enemies would be worse than anything caused by international trials.

If the international community does not punish war criminals, then in many cases the victims will be tempted to take justice into their own hands. In 1918, a group of American soldiers impetuously crashed into Holland to try to capture Wilhelm II, getting as far as the estate where he was then hiding out[112]; but the problem is usually far less farcical. Wherever victims and perpetrators meet, there is the risk of vigilantism of one kind or another. Having escaped British and Ottoman justice, Young Turk leaders like Talaat and Said Halim were hunted down and killed by Armenian assassins.

After World War II, there were retribution killings throughout Europe, from France and Holland to Hungary and Yugoslavia.[113] Abba Kovner, a former leader of the Vilna ghetto uprising, set up a group called Nakam ("Revenge" in Hebrew) to poison the drinking water in West Germany, to kill six million Germans. When the Labor Zionist establishment angrily rejected this plan, Nakam in 1946 settled on a lesser revenge: poisoning German prisoners at the Stalag 13 prisoner-of-war camp (two thousand were poisoned, although none died).[114]

Nakam's poison plans were rebuffed by Ben-Gurion and the Haganah, but not so for assassinations of individual Nazis. "Because we were weak," said a vigilante who eventually became Israeli army chief of staff, "and did not have our own country, and did not have power, we avenged. It was not a nice act." A number of Germans were killed, but Ben-Gurion fought back further calls for revenge, fearing that vigilantism would undermine support for a Jewish state.[115] Israel extended the rule of law even to Eichmann, and later John Demjanjuk. During the Eichmann trial, as Arendt pointed out—with Tehlirian, Talaat's assassin, in mind—some Israelis argued that Eichmann should simply have been gunned down in Buenos Aires.[116] What is most striking, though, is the extent to which Israelis and Jews were willing to let law take the place of vigilantism.

Some of the same dangers are present today in Bosnia and Kosovo.[117] The Hague tribunal, said Sacirbey, was "essential to discourage individuals from taking justice into their own hands, in acts of revenge." Told of the assassinations of Young Turks, Sacirbey, reflecting the frustration of many Bosnians at the sluggish pace of justice in The Hague, said he expected that Bosnians might follow the Dashnak example if The Hague gave no satisfaction, and that he would "condone it." After the second Markale market massacre in Sarajevo, in 1995, Izetbegovic said, "And regarding the criminals, I want to let them know that we will pay back in kind, and very soon. That day is not far away."[118] Naser Oric, the Bosnian Army officer who was supposed to defend Srebrenica in July 1995, sent a chilling message after the massacre to General Milenko Zivanovic, the leader of the Bosnian Serb Army's Drina Corps: "[T]he score is one, nothing."[119] As reporter David Rohde wrote, "A young Ratko Mladic may have been born during the fall of Srebrenica."[120] Some Bosnian Muslims in Gorazde spoke of killing Milan Lukic, a Bosnian Serb thought to be responsible for killings there in 1992.[121] In 1995 and 1997 polls, about half of the Bosnian Muslims did not want to forget the injustices of the past and concentrate on the future; about a third felt that strongly.[122] There is no poll data on Kosovo yet, but there is no doubting Kosovar Albanian rage against Serbs. In July 1999, fourteen Kosovar Serbs were massacred, presumably as indiscriminate revenge. Kosovar Albanian desires for retribution against the Serbs remain a primary obstacle to the multiethnic Kosovo that the UN wants.

Accused Hutu *génocidaires* who are released from overcrowded Rwandan jails are sometimes killed by Tutsi vigilantes.[123] When Placide Koloni, a deputy governor during the genocide, was freed in 1995 from jail in Gitamara, he was almost immediately killed, along with his wife, two daughters, and a servant. One prisoner in Gitamara jail later said, "When we see how Koloni was killed, we'd rather be in here than out there." And more broadly, Rwanda's continuing struggle against Hutu extremists based in Congo has sparked a huge war, involving many of the other countries in the region.[124]

Of course, no legal institution will make assassins and vigilantes instantly wink out of existence. But a visible international effort to bring justice will undermine the argument that the victims have no recourse but assassination, and will give incentives for responsible leaders, whether Ben-Gurion or Izetbegovic, to rein in their extremists. And many Bosnians say that they would be satisfied by seeing justice done in a court in The Hague. Hurem Suljic, a Bosnian Muslim survivor of Srebrenica, has said that he has no desire for revenge against the Serbs, but only asks that Ratko Mladic be tried.[125]

Even if there is no vigilantism, leaving rough justice totally up to the victims can be dangerous. The victorious RPF regime in Rwanda holds as many as 130,000 suspected *génocidaires* in Rwandan jails, in appalling conditions and with scant prospect of ever standing trial.[126] The new regime is hardly bound by legalism. For over two and a half years, the courts were simply shut down. Even with the best will in the world, a court system short on pencils and police inspectors, and subject to intimidation from outside the courtroom, would have found the conditions in Rwanda next to impossible.[127] "In the climate of bitterness and suspicion which prevails after the genocide," wrote Amnesty International in a scathing report, "many defendants accused of genocide are considered guilty unless proved innocent." Defendants would get only eight days to prepare for trial, often without writing materials or aid for the illiterate; judges had only six months of training; prosecutors faced political pressure. In April 1997, there were only sixteen defense lawyers in Rwanda for 100,000 defendants.[128]

In April 1998, the Rwandan regime held public mass executions for twenty-two accused *génocidaires*, shot to death in front of jeering crowds after having been given trials that struck many human rights groups as unfair.[129] Soon after, some two thousand prisoners pled guilty in the hopes of avoiding the same fate.[130] Much of the blame for this must go to the glacial pace of justice at the UN's Arusha tribunal, hampered by ineptitude and corruption. (The Rwandan government had voted against the creation of the UN tribunal because it would get the top suspects but not impose the death penalty.) By the time of the April 1998 executions, Rwandan courts had tried 346 people, convicting a third of them to death and a third to life imprisonment, and only acquitting twenty-six.[131] In the same time period, the Arusha court had not finished trying a single person (Jean Kambanda, prime minister during the genocide, had pled guilty). The tribunal had also been blasted for incompetence and corruption by an internal UN investigation.[132] Rwanda's government was furious when the Arusha tribunal in November 1999 ordered that a Hutu leader, Jean-Bosco Barayagwiza, be freed because he had been detained for too long before standing trial. No one should have expected the Rwandans to be as unconcerned about the punishment of the genocide as the UN was.[133]

Bosnia, too, has long had its own war crimes prosecutions, which are noticeably more legalist than Rwanda's and do better at coexisting alongside international efforts. When Goldstone decided to indict Karadzic and Mladic, he had the Bosnian government yield its cases against them to The Hague's jurisdiction. The weakness of the Hague tribunal encourages Bosnians to run their own trials. There are two official Bosnian government institutions collecting evidence: a state commission for war crimes and the Ministry of the Interior's state security service. By November 1994, the former had gathered evidence for 7,100 cases and incriminated 17,000 individual suspects, according to Mirsad Tokaca, the commission's secretary.[134] In practice, since Dayton, Bosnia's Muslim-Croat Federation has been far more restrained. In November 1997, OHR was tracking seven ongoing trials and ten ongoing appeals cases in the Federation; twelve Federation trials had been closed.[135]

Some of these trials are basically fair, according to OHR, but many are not. The cases sometimes rest on the 1977 Yugoslav criminal code, and many judges and prosecutors are steeped in the old ways of Communist jurisprudence. As OHR human rights monitor Hansjörg Strohmeyer, in Sarajevo, says,

> There are trials where judges make an effort, the procedure is acceptable. But the verdict raises concerns: the sentence is too high. Or you have a politicized case like [Ibrahim] Djedovic [a member of parliament who supports Izetbegovic's rival Fikret Abdic], where it's flawed from the beginning. Where you limit space for an effective defense. Or you get cases where due process can't be reached because there's no interentity judicial cooperation.

OHR officials worry that the Bosnian government will be too harsh in its sentencing of Bosnian Serb soldiers who were drafted. Many accused Serbs would prefer to be tried in The Hague. "A lot of people say, take us to The Hague," says Strohmeyer. "Tomorrow. They have no confidence in the system here."

There is a constant danger of politicization. Bosnia has put on one high-profile trial that was a clear travesty. In a spectacular 1993 genocide trial, Sretko Damjanovic, a Bosnian Serb soldier, was sentenced to death for killing Kasim and Asim Blekic and four other Bosnian Muslims. But in 1997, the Blekic brothers turned up alive in a Sarajevo suburb. According to OHR, unless they are Abdic supporters like Djedovic, the Federation government has yet to prosecute any Muslims. (Sacirbey denies this, pointing to courts-martial for Bosnian Army soldiers.) The Federation trials are almost all against low-level Bosnian Serbs who fought against Bosnian government forces or civilians.

Obviously, these are potential flashpoints. What would have happened if there had not been an international tribunal when the Bosnian government apprehended Djordje Djukic, a Bosnian Serb Army general and Mladic crony, in 1996? Much as the Bosnian Serbs scorn the Hague tribunal, they presumably would have been even angrier to see Djukic facing war crimes charges in a Bosnian government court. After the Djukic crisis, The Hague and NATO set up "Rules of the Road" that let the Hague tribunal review the war crimes cases of local authorities. This helps cut down on local abuses; but so would a more aggressive international effort to preempt Bosnian efforts. In February 1998, Bosnian intelligence agents in Sarajevo captured Goran Vasic, a Bosnian Serb soldier accused of shooting to death Hakija Turajlic, the Bosnian vice president, inside a French UNPROFOR armored personnel carrier in 1993. In a tense standoff, Serbs took Muslim hostages in reprisal. The Bosnians were, unsurprisingly, unrepentant.[136] Once again, it would have been easier to have The Hague deal with this case. If Karadzic and Mladic had not been indicted by The Hague, they would have surely been indicted by the Bosnian government.

Croatian courts have been busy with war crimes cases against Serbs, often extremely dubious ones. Tudjman's regime issued a 1990–96 general amnesty for the Serbs who rebelled against Croatian control in the Krajina, but, according to Western diplomats and human rights workers in Zagreb, Croatia keeps its Serbs off-guard by not letting them know who is safe and who is still suspected of war crimes that go beyond the amnesty. As of October 1997, the court in Zadar said it still had to look at approximately 10,000 cases against Serb rebels. Some of these trials prove provocative. In April 1997, a local Croatian court in Zadar tried Momcilo Perisic, then chief of staff of the Yugoslav army, and eighteen other Yugoslav officers in absentia, sentencing Perisic to twenty years in jail for ordering artillery attacks on Zadar in 1991. (Croatia has refused to allow The Hague to evaluate the credibility of this case.) This, predictably, infuriated Serbia.

Serbia, in turn, is far from pure. In July 1992, for instance, a Belgrade military court sentenced seven Croats from Vukovar to death or lengthy jail terms, based on confessions that, according to Helsinki Watch, were extracted through torture. This prompted an American diplomat in Belgrade to endorse international trials: "Removing prosecution of offenders from domestic judicial systems—civilian and military—seems to us the only viable way to avoid compounding the bitterness caused by the war with new injustices, which would further delay reconciliation within the former Yugoslavia."[137] After the Kosovo war, local courts in Serbian towns like Nis and Leskovac charged NATO leaders—including Clinton, Blair, Chirac, Albright, and Cook—with war crimes.[138]

If the international community will not step in, then vengeance will be left in the hands of the victims. They may not be legalistic; they may have highly politicized trials (as in Croatia) or show trials (as in Republika Srpska and Serbia); they may find that the pressure of trying war criminals overwhelms their judicial system (as in Rwanda); or they may prefer revenge to legalism. It is simply not an alternative to pretend that war crimes did not happen. Justice, of a sort, will be done; the only question is whether it will be finely tuned or crude.

Do war crimes tribunals work? The only serious answer is: compared to what? No, war crimes trials do not work particularly well. But they have clear *potential* to work, and to work much better than anything else diplomats have come up with at the end of a war. A well-run legalistic process is superior, both practically and morally, to apathy or vengeance. True, the track record of war crimes tribunals so far has not been particularly impressive, except—and this is a big exception—for Nuremberg. But the track records of other approaches to defeated foes leave even more to be desired. The task is to do a tribunal, and to do it properly. If at first you don't succeed, try again.

* *Afterword to the Paperback Edition* *

THE JAILERS took away Slobodan Milosevic's belt and shoelaces. Milosevic's family has a storied history of suicides: his favorite uncle, Milislav Koljensic, shot himself in the head when Milosevic was a boy; some years later, in 1962, while Milosevic was in law school, his father, Svetozar Milosevic, also shot himself; and ten years later, in 1972, his mother, Stanislava Milosevic, hanged herself. Before Slobodan Milosevic's arrest in Belgrade, he had vowed that he would not be taken alive. According to Milosevic's own defense lawyer, the deposed and newly imprisoned leader—stuck in a dismal Belgrade jail facing the bleak prospect of trial for corruption there and likely also a war crimes trial in The Hague—was on tranquillizers and sunk deep in depression.[1] So nobody was taking any chances. The Yugoslav authorities did not want to have to explain a successful Milosevic suicide to the country and the world.

Even after the Kosovo war, Bill Clinton had publicly announced that NATO was not going to get Milosevic out of Belgrade and into The Hague. Once again, the West was hardly about to risk its troops for the sake of international justice. So it was left to the Serbs to face down their own leadership, or to endure it. This might have smacked of cynicism; but in October 2000, the Serbs surprised the world with a sudden revolution that ousted Milosevic.

International justice got a huge boost from national Yugoslav politics. Skepticism about the tribunal has been replaced, for the moment, with heady optimism. Once Milosevic was out of power, with his political base having seemingly vanished all but overnight, and with increasing American and international pressure for a war crimes trial, there was precious little keeping Serb authorities from surrendering him to The Hague in June 2001—for a trial that represents a high watermark for international justice.

REVOLUTION

Indicting Milosevic

It had been just about the worst possible time for a computer to crash. On Friday, May 21, 1999, in The Hague, Louise Arbour and her staff worked late into the night preparing their indictment of Slobodan Milosevic. She had been painfully criticized for moving slowly on the Kosovo violence in the winter and spring of 1998. (This was, she says, partly due to an opinion from her staff that, because the prosecutor's office did not know if the KLA counted as an organized military force answerable to the Geneva Conventions, the tribunal might not have jurisdiction.) Now, with NATO at war over Kosovo, her indictment was finally almost finished. The work was cut short when a computer failed. Technical glitches aside, the indictment was ready for Arbour's signature on Saturday. She then turned it over to a judge to review the indictment.

Arbour also had to worry about protecting UN personnel. On Monday, May 24, when she appeared before Judge David Hunt, he issued a nondisclosure order that would expire on May 27 at noon. Under this order, the prosecutor could reveal the existence of the indictment to other parties for security reasons. This was an important concern—once again, a reflection of the West's overriding interest in its own citizens. As Arbour stood before the judge, the UN had a secret team of fact finders at work in Kosovo. (When Arbour had first heard of the UN mission, she had been upset, and had gone to Kofi Annan, the UN secretary-general, to complain that by sending a separate mission, the UN was freezing out the tribunal—itself a UN body. Annan had agreed, but feared that insisting on the inclusion of a Hague investigator would make Yugoslavia refuse to let in the UN mission at all, just as Arbour had been barred from visiting Kosovo after the Racak massacre.[2] It had been no small struggle to get Yugoslav approval for this mission. So finally, a compromise had been reached: one tribunal investigator would go with the UN team, but, in deference to Yugoslavia, would not be officially identified as such.) So now Arbour, knowing that the UN staffers were vulnerable on the ground, wanted to be sure that news of the indictment would not reach Belgrade until the team was safely out of Yugoslavia by Thursday, their scheduled departure date.

Arbour knew that the UN was probably not the only body that was up to tricks in Kosovo. So she wanted to give some advance warning to others. For three days, Milosevic's indictment was a secret—although one that, Arbour knew, would soon leak out. (By May 25, senior NATO officials had heard rumors that Milosevic was about to be indicted.)[3] There was no point in keeping the indictment secret permanently; Milosevic was not going to be snatched by a surprise commando raid like the ones NATO carried out in Bosnia. But Arbour wanted to let some governments know what she had done before Milosevic did. She did not want to jeopardize the security of anyone, if it could be helped.

Arbour personally broke the news to Annan that she had an indictment. She had difficulty establishing a secure communication line with the secretary-general, so finally wound up jumping on a plane to Stockholm to tell him face-to-face, and then returning to The Hague a few hours later. Annan was glad to have advance notice so that he could look after the UN team. His main concern, say tribunal officials, was the negotiations being carried on between Milosevic and EU envoy Martti Ahtisaari and Russian negotiator Viktor Chernomyrdin, which could be wrongfooted by an indictment of Milosevic and his senior staff.

Rather than going one by one to a range of governments to break the news, Arbour used one-stop diplomacy: she told the Dutch foreign minister, and told him he could spread the news to whomever needed to know. The news spread with astonishing speed. By Wednesday evening, it had reached high levels in the American government, as well as NATO commander Wesley Clark.[4] The Americans were upset. Arbour had never been clear in her own mind if the Americans wanted an indictment or not, but in any case she thought they would have liked to participate in choosing the timing of the indictment. But by passing the chore of breaking the news to the Dutch foreign minister, she also avoided hearing the brunt of NATO's response. Finally, on May 27, Arbour went public with the indictment.

But in the end, NATO's bombs spoke louder than anything else. Milosevic might have been enraged by his indictment, but he finally chose to get a ceasefire. However much the indictment rankled, he was still esconced as president of Yugoslavia—what must have seemed a position of perfect immunity.

"He's Finished"

It was a familiar kind of gamble. Confident of its grip on the people, with the opposition in its habitual disarray, a dictatorship would allow a quick election—and discreetly rig the results if they didn't go the right way.

It is also a gamble that almost always blows up in the dictator's face, from Brazil to Pakistan.[5] When he decided to call an early election, to take place in September 2000, Milosevic surely must not have predicted how badly things would go. He could have waited until the following June, but he saw the main chance now. Ironically enough, he may have been pushed by a brief surge of popularity from the NATO bombing, which he might have wanted to capitalize on to shore up his regime's legitimacy. Whatever Milosevic might have had in mind, on September 24, Yugoslavs went to the polls to pick a president.

It is no wonder that Milosevic's democratic opponents did not exactly make him tremble. The opposition had managed momentarily to unify itself into something called the Democratic Opposition of Serbia (DOS), a fractious assortment of eighteen opposition groups, fronted by Vojislav Kostunica. Kostunica was an unlikely moderate. He frowned on violence and had never served in any of Milosevic's tainted administrations, but his Serb nationalist credentials were impeccable. A former Belgrade University law professor and opposition parliamentarian, he had struggled against Tito's federalism and turned to Serb nationalism. During the war in Bosnia, Kostunica's sympathies lay with Radovan Karadzic. So Kostunica campaigned against both Milosevic and NATO, bitterly railing against the alliance's bombing campaign. He was no softer on The Hague, denouncing it as a tool of American power and refusing to hear of turning over Milosevic. Kostunica, quiet and reserved, presented himself as high-minded and incorruptible—a welcome respite after the institutionalized gangsterism of the Milosevic era.[6]

The election was, in the end, no contest. Kostunica bested Milosevic by, staggeringly, almost half a million votes. Milosevic's regime, stunned and desperate, worked hard to paper up the extent of the defeat, but the margin was so colossal as to defy electoral fraud. The best Milosevic's loyal election commission could suggest was that Kostunica had done better than Milosevic, but had not cleared the majority threshold, and that there would have to be a second round of balloting. The Constitutional Court, stacked with Milosevic's people, declared the election results canceled and called for a new election sometime before Milosevic's term expired.

This was not the first time Milosevic's back had been against this particular wall. In 1996, he had tried to sweep away the opposition Zajedno coalition's victory in local elections. When Zajedno (Serbo-Croatian for "Together") took to the streets in protest, Milosevic rode it out for three months, letting the opposition factions jockey and bicker among themselves, and finally conceding. But this time, Milosevic's vote fraud set the stage for nothing short of revolution. As opposition crowds began to gather and strikes spread, Serbia seemed on the road either to another Tiananmen Square or another Ceauçescu. The DOS demanded that Milosevic concede to Kostunica.

Protests spread daily. It wasn't just the urban elites who turned on Milosevic. Many of the protestors were from rural areas. Importantly, coal miners in Kolubara, south of Belgrade, went on strike in protest of Milosevic's attempts to hijack the election. They withstood an appeal by Yugoslav army chief of staff Nebojsa Pavkovic (himself a miner's son, and one of the few top Yugoslav officers in Kosovo not indicted by The Hague), which showed that the army might well leave Milosevic to his fate rather than turn against the demonstrators. Scenting change, even the state media, including Serbian state television and the daily newspaper *Politika*, began to move toward a more independent line in their news coverage—something they had not felt necessary during the years of Milosevic's propaganda barrages against Albanians and Croats and Bosnians.

By October 5, the crowds in Belgrade were enormous, numbering in the hundreds of thousands, cheering and waving flags. Some of the demonstrators went beyond mere protests, storming the grand old Parliament building and facing down riot police. The police fired tear gas outside the Parliament, but then fell back. At their gentlest, student demonstrators chanted, "He's finished!" Others were rougher: "Slobodan, Slobodan, save Serbia and kill yourself!" Fire swept through the Parliament and the state television building. Whatever legitimacy Milosevic might have claimed was gone, and if he was to save his regime, the only way was to shoot at the crowds. But this option never materialized. Many policemen preferred not to do Milosevic's dirty work for him, and the army evidently seemed reluctant. In the event, the Tanjug state news service (which went over to the opposition) reported two deaths and sixty-five injuries. Kicking away Milosevic's last hope of foreign rescue, Igor Ivanov, Russia's foreign minister, flew to Belgrade to meet Milosevic on October 6 and tell him that Russia recognized Kostunica's victory.[7]

As his regime crumbled around him, Milosevic was nowhere to be seen. Finally the speculation about Milosevic's whereabouts ended when, standing in front of a Yugoslav flag, he stiffly made a televised concession to Kostunica on October 6, complete with a lame boilerplate line that could have come from the most ordinary defeated pol: "I myself, relieved by the end of the enormous responsibility that I have borne for a whole decade, plan to rest a little, to spend more time with my family."[8]

Kostunica Balks

With Milosevic turfed out of power, the world quickly shifted its policy toward Yugoslavia—a country that Kostunica proudly declared "liberated." The question, both in Washington and in European capitals, jerked from what kind of sanctions to impose to what kind of aid to offer. The EU drew up an emergency aid package; the oil embargo vanished; the World Bank opened a Belgrade office and hinted that Yugoslavia could become a member state. But a crucial sticking point was the arrest and trial of Milosevic and other war crimes suspects.

Kostunica dug in his heels. His opposition sprang from two sources. First, he seemed more interested in Serb reconciliation than in revenge against the Milosevic regime. Kostunica, with his ambitions to unite the Serbs, knew that many Serbs had voted for Milosevic and that some of Yugoslavia's most prominent politicians were implicated in Milosevic's deeds, and he might also have worried that the security forces had some residual loyalties to Milosevic.[9] "An instant trial in The Hague would endanger the very fragile democratic process here," Kostunica warned. During the October revolution, he had called for nonviolence, and taken care to calm hotheads who wanted to march to Dedinje, the posh Belgrade suburb where Milosevic lived.

Second, Kostunica affected a principled skepticism about The Hague. Emphasizing his background as a thoughtful constitutional lawyer who had translated *The Federalist Papers* into Serbo-Croatian, he scorned The Hague. In his first state television interview, on October 5, he did not mince words: "[T]his is a political institution and not a legal institution; actually it is not a court at all. The Hague court is not an international court, it is an American court and it is absolutely controlled by the American government. It is a means of pressure that the American government uses for realizing its influence here. . . . Many people ask about Slobodan Milosevic and my answer was clearly *no*."[10] While not shy about accusing NATO of war crimes in its bombing of Yugoslavia, the furthest Kostunica seemed prepared to go on Serb war crimes was a formula that would hardly satisfy Bosnians or Kosovars: before the September 24 election, Kostunica had told *The New York Times* that he backed a state truth commission that would look at all the crimes of ex-Yugoslavia's wars.[11] He also suggested looking at crimes "a few years ago and maybe a few decades ago," evidently implying a look at World War II and the Ustasha period.[12]

While the revolution was still unsteady, and with Kostunica facing possible secessionist challenges in Montenegro and Kosovo, Western capitals toned down discussions of Milosevic's fate. Even Madeleine Albright, usually the most vociferous voice against Milosevic, was prepared to bide her time: "We believe in the importance of accountability for what Milosevic has done," she said, but emphasized that "the important thing is to get him out of any position of any kind of power." Strobe Talbott, America's deputy secretary of state, said America would not immediately insist on Kostunica turning over Milosevic. And Robin Cook, Britain's foreign secretary, also usually a strong advocate for The Hague, floated the idea of Milosevic first going on trial for corruption in Yugoslavia and then later for war crimes at the UN tribunal.

The Hague also sent somewhat mixed signals. Carla Del Ponte, the chief prosecutor, asked for a meeting with Kostunica after the December parliamentary elections in Serbia, and moved quickly to reopen an office in Belgrade, which had been closed during the Kosovo war. Graham Blewitt, her deputy prosecutor, said that Kostunica should have some time to confront the question of Milosevic's trial, and did not slam the door on a discussion of Yugoslavia launching its own investigations of Milosevic, although he insisted on The Hague's primacy.

Kostunica's own signals were less muddy. Pocketing an aid package at an EU summit in Biarritz on October 14, Kostunica said of The Hague, "The question of cooperation is a fact, but it cannot be one of our priorities." Kostunica found it easier to concentrate on Milosevic's crimes against Serbs, like rampant corruption and electoral fraud, which, for all the horrors of his regime, did not hold a candle to what had happened in Kosovo, let alone Bosnia. One of Kostunica's first moves as president was attending the reburial of a Serb poet in Trebinje, in Republika Srpska—a symbolic gesture of pan-Serb solidarity that terrified Bosnians, although the OHR pressured Kostunica into a quick trip to the Sarajevo airport afterward to meet Bosnian officials. And Kostunica continued to blast The Hague as not really being interested in justice, while praising South Africa's Truth and Reconciliation Commission.[13]

But as it became clear that Kostunica was consolidating his hold on power day by day, the West grew more impatient. On January 4, 2001, Goran Svilanovic, a human rights activist serving as Yugoslavia's new foreign minister, met Albright at the State Department, where she pushed for turning over Milosevic to The Hague. Svilanovic took a softer line than Kostunica, saying that there could be a UN war crimes prosecution of Milosevic but it would have to be held in Yugoslavia. Momcilo Grubac, Yugoslavia's justice minister, urged indicted Yugoslavs to follow Biljana Plavsic, the former Bosnian Serb leader who had turned herself over to The Hague, although Zoran Djindjic, about to become Serbia's prime minister, was horrified that she had been indicted.

Kostunica, zigging as Svilanovic zagged, stunned the West and much of his own DOS by meeting with Milosevic himself on January 13 to discuss

Montenegro and Kosovo. At the same time, Kostunica also unleashed his legal reasoning: admitting that Yugoslavia had signed Dayton and the Geneva Conventions, but still insisting that Yugoslavia's constitution did not allow for extradition of Yugoslav citizens. Kostunica, who had met Milosevic, refused to meet with Del Ponte if she came to Belgrade, but then changed his mind, saying that he wanted to discuss NATO's use of depleted uranium munitions and question whether there was really evidence of a Serb massacre at Racak.

Their meeting went just about as badly as could be expected. Del Ponte, not known for her mildness, brought a list of some of The Hague's secret indictments to ask Kostunica to arrest at least four Serb suspects in Yugoslavia (Kostunica had said that he would publish any such indictments that Del Ponte gave him). In the meeting, Kostunica accused the tribunal of anti-Serb bias, even though Del Ponte had started an investigation into atrocities by Kosovar Albanians against Serbs. After an hour, Del Ponte stormed out of the meeting and refused to talk to reporters.[14] "I absolutely did not like him," she told La Stampa. "He just fired off a volley of unjustified accusations."[15]

The crucial piece of pressure, in the end, came from the U.S. Congress. Russia's Ivanov said that the tribunal ought to be closed down; the EU did not condition aid tightly on cooperation with The Hague; and George W. Bush, America's new president, had shown scant interest in the Balkans on the campaign trail, and frowned on Clinton's peacekeeping and nation-building efforts. But Congress concentrated the Bush team's minds with a firm deadline of March 31, when the Bush administration would have to certify that Yugoslavia had cooperated sufficiently with The Hague to qualify for a $100 million financial aid package, as well as for American support for Kostunica's efforts to get World Bank and International Monetary Fund assistance. This was a crucial issue as Kostunica's government, strapped for cash after years of economic sanctions, struggled to restructure its World Bank debt and get low-interest loans.

The cumulative pressure from Washington and The Hague began to take a toll. Kostunica continued to accuse NATO of war crimes and to float the idea of a Belgrade trial for Milosevic, but much of the DOS wanted to turn Milosevic over. The interior minister admitted that Milosevic had been put under police surveillance, and the justice minister said that war crimes suspects would have to go to The Hague eventually. After meeting with Colin Powell, Bush's secretary of state, on February

2, Djindjic announced that Yugoslavia would start criminal proceedings against Milosevic.

Del Ponte suggested on February 20 that Kostunica could demonstrate his seriousness by turning over Bosnian Serb suspects, perhaps starting at Mladic's suburban Belgrade home. NATO and CIA officials thought Karadzic was also sometimes hiding out in Yugoslavia, and even the Yugoslav interior minister admitted that about fifteen indictees were at large in the country. This was no secret. Among them were Milan Milutinovic, Serbia's powerful president during Milosevic's federal Yugoslav presidency; Dragoljub Ojdanic, Milosevic's defense minister; and the so-called "Vukovar three," Yugoslav army officers accused of a 1991 massacre of Croats. But Kostunica made no moves, even keeping the defiant Milutinovic as Serbian president for the time being. In short order, Serbia's interior minister announced that Mladic had vanished.

The possibility of a double standard raised hackles in Croatia. Stipe Mesic, Croatia's president, had come under withering domestic criticism for cooperating fully with The Hague, turning over Bosnian Croat suspects, and starting to hold war crimes trials for Croats accused of atrocities against Serbs. Both for consistency and for Serbia's own democratic progress, Mesic argued, the international community must hold all countries—Yugoslavia included—to the same standards.[16]

The noose around Milosevic's neck appreciably tightened when Rade Markovic, the former chief of Milosevic's notorious state security service, was arrested on charges of ordering an assassination attempt on Vuk Draskovic, a Serb opposition leader. The Serbian interior minister announced that Milosevic was being investigated on corruption charges—a huge step, although small beer compared to The Hague's charges of crimes against humanity. In what might have been a conciliatory gesture, Graham Blewitt, the deputy prosecutor, suggested holding some of Milosevic's UN war crimes trial in Belgrade.

Yugoslavia's credibility had been undermined by the inconsistency of the statements coming from Belgrade. But the White House, which would make the crucial choice about whether to certify Yugoslavia as sufficiently cooperative with The Hague, was unsure what to do. Even as the March 31 deadline approached, there were a number of disagreements within the new Bush administration about how to proceed. American officials did not offer Yugoslavia a definitive list of necessary steps, but did say that they wanted Milosevic arrested, if not sent to The Hague, and at least one other war crimes suspect transferred to The Hague. The latter seemed easier to accomplish. On March 12, Blagoje Simic, formerly the Serb mayor of the Bosnian town of Samac, became the first Yugoslav citizen to surrender himself to The Hague. A few days later, on March 23, plainsclothes Belgrade police arrested Milomir Stakic, a Bosnian Serb accused of running the Omarska and Keraterm concentration camps, and sent him to The Hague—the first such arrest by Serbian authorities, and presumably a last-ditch attempt to show enough Serb cooperation to win White House certification. (Confusingly, Kostunica criticized Stakic's arrest and extradition as illegal.)

According to American officials, James Dobbins, the assistant secretary of state for European affairs, simply wanted to certify Yugoslavia and move on. There were even some divisions within Dobbins's staff. Other American officials, including Pierre-Richard Prosper, named as ambassador-at-large for war crimes issues, argued that the Yugoslavs would have to carry through an arrest of Milosevic. Prosper, although not yet confirmed by the Senate, dug in his heels. Powell was not given a clear unanimous recommendation by the State Department, say American officials. Powell conferred with Bush, but, according to American officials, the decision finally came down to Powell himself over the coming weekend.

The Battle of Uzicka Street

The U.S. Congress had set a March 31 deadline—and at around 2:30 A.M. on March 31, masked Yugoslav special police finally came for Milosevic. The former strongman was inside the villa at 11 Uzicka Street in Dedinje, with his wife, Mirjana Markovic, and their daughter Marija Milosevic, as a gun battle raged outside. Milosevic said that he would not be taken alive. But two arrest attempts failed, with the police forced back by Milosevic's bodyguards. A small crowd chanted their loyalty to Milosevic, facing off against police. Throughout a bewildering night, rumors raced around Belgrade, while the police kept the villa surrounded.[17]

Equally baffled in Washington, American officials were not sure that Milosevic would survive the raids. He might be killed while resisting arrest; he might commit suicide rather than go to jail; or he might be intentionally killed by Serbs who wanted to get rid of him once and for all, or who feared what he might tell prosecutors either in Belgrade or The Hague.

The Serbian interior ministry said that Milosevic was under house arrest on charges of corruption and abuse of power, but that Milosevic had refused to accept an arrest order. Djindjic said he had no idea what was going on, and had been watching the movie *Gladiator* (about political treachery and violence in ancient Rome) on television. Kostunica huddled with his top aides and announced that no one was above the law.

The police appeared ready to try again when, after a protracted siege and lengthy negotiations, Milosevic finally surrendered around 4 A.M. on April 1. He was whisked away in a convoy of five cars, heading for Belgrade's Central Prison. Milosevic had reportedly waved a gun and threatened to kill himself and his wife and daughter; his daughter had also fired a few shots, reportedly at a Djindjic envoy.[18] It could have been much bloodier. The police say they found a staggering arsenal in the compound: two armored personnel carriers, some thirty automatic weapons, two cases of hand grenades, and more.[19] According to the Serbian interior minister, Milosevic had been told that he would not face war crimes charges, which helped convince him to go peacefully. If the government did make those promises, Milosevic was more than a little unwise to rely on them.

Milosevic in The Hague

Milosevic's obsession with The Hague seems only to have grown, as he waited to go there. In an interview with *La Stampa* before his arrest in Belgrade, he wildly called The Hague "an illegal and immoral institution, invented as reprisal for disobedient representatives of a disobedient people—as once there were concentration camps for superfluous peoples and people." He also said, "It's the same form of intimidation that the Nazis used first against the Jews and then against all the Slav people."[20] From his Belgrade jail, he issued a statement: "the criminal proceedings against me are a political fix ordered by the new authorities, with the aim of besmirching and belittling my work over many years, and especially the fact that I stood up against the world's power-brokers in the interests of the state and the people."[21] When he was served with his Hague indictment in his Belgrade cell, Milosevic refused to take it, leaving it at the door.[22]

But this was all too late. Even after arresting Milosevic, the Yugoslav government remained under pressure to send him to The Hague. Del Ponte was demanding the "immediate transfer of the accused Milosevic." Bosnia and Croatia, as well as Kosovar Albanian politicians, called for a Hague trial. Bush urged Yugoslavia to send him to face trial for crimes against humanity. Most importantly, Powell had given his certification, but now threatened to skip a June 29 international donors' conference in Brussels if Yugoslavia did not continue its cooperation with The

Hague—an American move that might have scared away other major donors like Japan and the World Bank, scotching any Yugoslav hopes of raising the billion dollars that the country desperately needed.

Once again, Kostunica initially hung tough. "It should never happen," he said, of Milosevic's extradition, while allowing that there ought to be a war crimes trial in Yugoslav courts.[23] The inevitable demonstrations for Milosevic's release were small and mostly made up of middle-aged or old protestors, although public opinion seemed unenthusiastic about a Hague trial.[24] Kostunica decided to go through with his mooted truth commission, although two members resigned soon after being named to it.[25] When the UN tribunal's registrar came to Belgrade with a warrant for Milosevic, the Serbian justice minister initially refused to take it, instead asking for indictments against Bosnians, Croats, and Kosovars.

But Kostunica's line was eroding fast. As the donors' conference approached, Yugoslav authorities began to discover evidence that Milosevic's security forces tried to dispose of the corpses of Kosovar Albanians, allegedly on personal orders from Milosevic. These revelations, the first time Yugoslav authorities have begun to make a case that Milosevic and his cronies were involved in war crimes, were a way of softening up Serb public opinion before sending Milosevic to the UN tribunal—and making sure Milosevic did not become a martyr. Yugoslavia has also charged almost 200 of its own officers with war crimes in Kosovo, which could also help persuade Serbs of the Milosevic regime's enormities.

In the end, Milosevic's surrender came only after a fiery, high-stakes showdown between Kostunica and Djindjic. When the government could not get a nationalist coalition party to go along with an extradition law in parliament, Djindjic and the rest of the DOS persuaded a reluctant Kostunica to go along with a special decree instead, which would allow the extradition of Milosevic and the other war crimes suspects in Yugoslavia. With timing that could hardly be coincidental, on June 23, just before the donors' conference, the Yugoslav cabinet adopted the decree. This was enough to get America to go to the donors' conference.

In a last-ditch effort, Milosevic's lawyers complained that the decree was illegal. Djindjic and his supporters were startled when they learned that Yugoslavia's Constitutional Court was about to strike down their decree. They called a meeting, but Kostunica failed to show up. This, say Western officials, so angered the rest of the DOS that they decided to put Milosevic on an airplane at once. Scorning the Constitutional Court as a tool of Milosevic, Serbian government authorities pressed ahead with Milosevic's transfer even without a firm legal foundation.

Shipping off this supremely paranoid man seemed to bring out the paranoia in all those involved. At every stage, Serb and Western officials held their breath waiting for something to go wrong. There was no shortage of people who would rather have Milosevic dead than testifying. Djindjic's people, afraid that the army might stop them, used two decoy cars, so three cars went to three different airports without anyone being sure which had Milosevic. They also had an airplane from Montenegro as another distraction.[26] But nothing untoward happened. Exactly twelve years after a notorious Kosovo speech that unleashed Serb nationalism, on June 28, 2001, Milosevic was put on a Serbian helicopter to Tuzla.

His first stop—with perfect symbolism—was an American military base in Bosnia, the country that had suffered the most from Milosevic's rule. American officials were considerably relieved when he touched down. Milosevic was then loaded onto a British airplane to The Hague, before a helicopter ride for the final trip to the UN detention unit. Head bowed, he was marched to the compound.

If Milosevic had fancied there would be mass outrage in Serbia, he was largely mistaken. Kostunica, letting Djindjic take the heat, still said that the extradition "could not be considered legal or constitutional." Yugoslavia's prime minister resigned in protest of the extradition, and Russia mildly condemned the move. But the demonstrators in Belgrade, no more than 3,000 strong, were nothing compared to the masses of October. Djindjic may well take heart from the faint public reaction, although Serbs might be angrier to see some of their other leaders follow Milosevic to The Hague. There will still be opportunities for backlash to set in, when Yugoslavia makes good on its pledge to send fifteen more of its indicted citizens to the tribunal, including such prominent figures as Milutinovic, Ojdanic, and Milan Martic.

They are not the only ones sleeping poorly. Mesic's Croatia has stepped up its cooperation with The Hague. NATO has not stopped its arrest raids in Bosnia, even with the younger Bush in the White House. On April 15, just two weeks after Milosevic's arrest, SFOR apprehended Dragan Obrenovic, a lieutenant general in the Bosnian Serb Army, charged with genocide for his role at Srebrenica. Radovan Karadzic, for all his lunatic defiance (he told a Bosnian newspaper that he expected to be nominated for the Nobel prize), may find himself trapped either in a tightening net in Bosnia, or at the mercy of the new authorities in Yugoslavia.[27] The same goes for Ratko Mladic, who had cut an ostentatiously high profile around Belgrade before the revolution. As I write this afterword in July 2001, Karadzic and Mladic are still at large—but their days seem numbered, and in small digits. American officials, saying that the White House is resolved to act, even speak of winding down the hunts for other war crimes suspects if the high-priority ones can be seized. From its feeble beginnings, the tribunal has reached a barely imaginable milestone.

AFTER MILOSEVIC

The fall of Milosevic is not the only story. The cause of international justice has been lurching forward on all fronts. The successes, however limited, of the two UN ad hoc tribunals for ex-Yugoslavia and Rwanda have led to movement toward more tribunals for Cambodia and Sierra Leone. The ICC is gaining some momentum, and will most likely come into being in the near future. And as most dramatically demonstrated in part by the seizure of Augusto Pinochet in London, national courts have taken up the cause of war crimes trials.

Of course, all of these efforts must be judged by what they actually accomplish for the victims. Tokenism is not enough. Milosevic's trial is a landmark, but there have been similar landmarks before—like the Constantinople trials—that came and went. The trial's success, assuming that Milosevic can be convicted, can only be measured in its ability to bring some satisfaction to the victims and rehabilitate the Serb polity.

Nor should the successes of accountability become a palliative, an excuse to push forward with the punishment of war crimes while slackening on the prevention of war crimes. The time to stop Milosevic was 1986, when he put Serbia on the road to war, not 2001. The putative tribunals for Cambodia and Sierra Leone make the point clear: as with Bosnia and Rwanda, these are two places where the international community has little to brag about. But human rights and accountability have become almost an expected part of the Western agenda, which in itself is a considerable accomplishment. There are enough signs of progress that, after so many reversals and failures in modern history, one might be forgiven for temporarily dropping the habitual gloom.

"A Victim of Circumstances"

Politics still lurks behind the advance of human rights. Thus, progress has been the slowest against the strongest states. Against a major power, like Russia or China or America, the bite of unwelcome international norms is much weaker. The imposition of legalistic norms, not surprisingly, is vastly easier when it is a matter of strong states pushing a human rights agenda on weaker states. The diplomacy of human rights is still power politics, but power politics in the name of justice.

Many of the successes of the Rwanda war crimes tribunal at Arusha have been due to the weakness of many African states, which have not been willing or able to withstand international pressure for extraditions of the scattered genocidal Hutu leadership. As a partial result, the Rwanda tribunal, for all its administrative chaos and friction with the Rwandan government, has been able to prosecute an impressive roster of the major figures in the 1994 genocide. Jean Kambanda, the former Rwandan prime minister, was arrested in Kenya, as was Eliezer Niyitegeka, who had been the minister of information; Jérôme Bicamumpaka, formerly Rwanda's foreign minister, and Théoneste Bagosora, who had been the director of cabinet at the defense ministry, were nabbed in Cameroon; Edouard Karemera, former interior minister, in Togo; Joseph Nzirorera, president of the National Assembly, in Benin; Jean-Paul Akayesu, the mayor of Taba, in Zambia; and Mathieu Ngirumpatse, director-general of the foreign ministry, in Mali. In 1998, the Arusha court convicted Kambanda for genocide and crimes against humanity—an achievement comparable to a Milosevic conviction.

But the picture looks very different when it is a powerful state being bullied, no matter how much the powerful might deserve to wind up in the dock. Russia has come in for withering criticism from human rights groups for its contemptible conduct of the wars in Chechnya. Official Western criticism has been disapproving, although more muted. But Vladimir Putin, waging the second round of the war, has also found that his Chechen campaign—unlike Boris Yeltsin's—can be hugely popular among Russians.[28] Putin fiercely defends his war in Chechnya,[29] and refused to meet with Mary Robinson, the UN high commissioner for human rights. Although Russia has opened more than eighty cases against its own soldiers, senior Russian officials have made sympathetic comments about Russian soldiers accused of war crimes. Sergei Ivanov, Russia's defense minister, has described Yuri Budanov, a colonel in a tank regiment who confessed to strangling an eighteen-year-old Chechen girl, as "a victim of circumstances."[30]

China, too, is not so easily bullied on human rights issues, despite its cruel treatment of political dissidents and harsh rule in Tibet.[31] Soon after taking office, Clinton signed an executive order giving China a year to take serious steps on a variety of human rights issues, including releasing political prisoners and allowing dissidents to leave the country. If China did not, then America would slap it with tough trade penalties—revoking China's most-favored-nation (MFN) trade privileges. Chinese leaders resented the linkage of trade with human rights, and, when John Shattuck, then assistant secretary of state for democracy and human rights, quietly met in Beijing with Wei Jingsheng, a prominent Chinese dissident, the Beijing regime responded by arresting Wei and other dissidents in Beijing and Shanghai. When Warren Christopher, then secretary of state, went to Beijing, Li Peng, China's hardline premier, literally pounded his chair as he railed against American arrogance about human rights. Even though the White House knew that China had not met even the administration's vague conditions for progress on human rights, the Clinton administration publicly backed away from its MFN threat.[32] And since the NATO bombing of the Chinese embassy in Belgrade, China is even more resistant to Western humanitarianism.

Still, if one is going to try to push China around on human rights, there is something to be said for trying to enmesh it in the relevant international institutions. Alastair Iain Johnston, a China specialist, has argued that China takes a keen interest in participation in international institutions.[33] Certainly, China has not minded contributing a judge to The Hague, and joined the rest of the Security Council in creating the tribunal and appointing its prosecutors, which tends implicitly to legitimize the idea of international prosecutions of war crimes and human rights violations.

America, in particular, has been slow to allow itself to be judged by the ideals that it trumpets for the rest of the world. Clinton had David Scheffer sign the ICC treaty on America's behalf at the last possible minute, on December 31, 2000; the administration of George W. Bush seems only too happy to let the Senate trash the ICC treaty, for fear that America's global security commitments might expose its soldiers to politicized prosecutions. This is not a hypothetical concern: Milosevic's Yugoslavia launched sham prosecutions of NATO officials for the Kosovo bombing campaign, although Kostunica quickly sidelined them.

The dilemma for human rights groups is that America is more than just another country that ought to be under the ICC's jurisdiction. A powerful liberal state like America is also a crucial engine for tangible progress on human rights.[34] American officials point to Milosevic's extradition as proof of how crucial American support would be for the success of the ICC. And NATO is unlikely to be the subject of a serious bona fide war crimes investigation; after all, it took considerable care in the Kosovo war to choose legitimate military targets, and to hit them accurately. For all that, Americans are not exactly enthusiastic about considering past American war crimes. The My Lai investigation was botched. Robert McNamara has somehow managed to return to polite society, and even to lecture Americans once again about how to conduct foreign policy.[35] When John Kerrey, a former U.S. senator and Vietnam veteran who is now president of New School University, was accused of killing Vietnamese civilians in 1969 during a confusing wartime raid, American public debate rarely considered actually investigating Kerrey, let alone his superiors.[36] This is hardly the right example, especially for a country whose military deserves praise for teaching its soldiers the laws of war. Somehow, when it comes to our own crimes, suddenly everything is in shades of grey.

Universal Jurisdiction

Rather than set up new international courts to prosecute war criminals, some human rights activists have pushed to use existing national courts to do the job. The easiest way to do this, politically and legally, is when one's own citizens have been the victims—allowing a country's own courts to prosecute the foreigners who victimized its citizens. For example, George H. W. Bush arrested Panamanian strongman Manuel Noriega for drug charges during the 1989 invasion of Panama, and approved an operation to abduct Pablo Escobar Gaviria, the Colombian drug lord running the notorious Medellin cartel.[37] More expansively, under the principle of universal jurisdiction, any state can bring to book those responsible for crimes against humanity and war crimes. In some countries, treaties like the Torture Convention or the Geneva Conventions automatically become part of the domestic law; in others, treaty obligations must be specifically ratified or supplemented with domestic implementing legislation. Germany and Belgium have taken the lead in prosecuting, respectively, Serbs and Rwandans.

The politics of universal jurisdiction are inevitably messy. Skeptics—led by Henry Kissinger, who evidently likes to travel hassle-free—worry that sovereignty is being sacrificed, and that some countries will launch politicized prosecutions against enemy officials.[38] After all, if every country's courts can reach far and wide, then surely some of them will launch frivolous or malicious prosecutions. As with international trials, only liberal countries will go to pains to have fair procedures, and even then the prosecutions may get tangled up in the politics of democratization or peacemaking.

But at least so far, the political costs of universal jurisdiction have kept it from spreading too far. Presidents and prime ministers will have much the same hesitations about using legalism for a national war crimes trial as about using legalism for an international war crimes prosecution. Even liberal governments do not relish too much involvement in human rights crusades—which are all too often expensive, legally difficult, and diplomatically painful. It is more common for a war criminal to slip away incognito to another country than it is for that country to catch and prosecute him. Eichmann and Pinochet may yet prove to be the exception, not the rule.[39]

After all, Idi Amin is resting easy in Saudi Arabia; Milton Obote, another Ugandan, in Zambia; Paraguay's Alfredo Stroessner, in Brazil; and Emmanuel "Toto" Constant, the founder of a notorious Haitian death squad, in Queens, New York.[40] In 1976, France allowed one of the terrorists allegedly involved in the Munich Olympics massacre to go free, despite Israeli and West German attempts to extradite him. In 1999, Izzat Ibrahim al-Duri, a senior Iraqi official, sought medical help in Austria; despite calls for a trial for Duri's role in the slaughter of Iraq's Kurds, Austria let him go. Later that same year, Mengistu Haile Mariam, the former Ethiopian dictator in exile in Zimbabwe, went to South Africa, also for medical treatment; South Africa snubbed Ethiopian calls for extradition, and let him slip back to Zimbabwe. And in 2000, Senegal indicted Hissène Habré, the brutal former dictator of Chad, for crimes against humanity, but Abdoulaye Wade, Senegal's president, later let it drop.[41] Kissinger need not panic just yet.

More legitimately, many liberals worry that the exercise of universal jurisdiction may interfere with democratization. After all, in a negotiated transition to democracy, the outgoing dictatorship usually secures for itself some kind of amnesty.[42] If these amnesties are then scotched by foreign judges, then future dictators may cling to power until the bitter end. This is, in a way, the domestic-level equivalent of the dilemma faced by Holbrooke when he decided to negotiate with Milosevic and Karadzic. Some of the most prominent human rights activists believe either that weakened dictators are not in much of a position to insist on amnesty, or that such amnesties are illegitimate and should be overcome.[43]

At a minimum, universal jurisdiction should be seen as a likely reaction to continued impunity. In other words, the less that one likes universal jurisdiction, the more one ought to like the idea of a well-institutionalized international forum where such cases can be heard. (This is a point missed by Kissinger, who has equal reservations about the ICC and universal jurisdiction.)[44] If one condemns both universal jurisdiction and international war crimes courts, then that leaves the victims with precious few options.

"False Tribunal"

In his first court appearance at The Hague, on July 3, 2001, Milosevic resorted to an old argument. At his arraignment, instead of entering a plea, he coolly denounced the tribunal, in his imperfect English, as a NATO tool: "I consider this tribunal false tribunal and indictments false indictments." He thus joined the long tradition of accused war criminals who consider their own trial nothing more than victors' justice, from Wilhelm II to Göring to Tojo.

Milosevic's variation on the argument is no particular improvement on it. It has been echoed in part by some Serb and Western analysts, from rightists with a dislike for international law to leftists with a dislike for American power.[45] And it has an echo in the region. Kostunica, playing to the kind of nationalist backlash that undermined Leipzig and Constantinople, did not watch the televised arraignment as it would have been "too painful," but once again blasted The Hague: "There is no impartiality, but only the expression of selective justice."

Of course, Milosevic, of all people, can't complain too much about power politics. It was Western power that got him into the court, but it was Milosevic's own power that had kept him—and his cronies and subordinates—out of it. Nor does Milosevic deserve much sympathy as the object of victors' justice. In a limited way, what goes on in The Hague is victors' justice of a kind, but only inasmuch as all justice relies on a certain measure of force. It is victory that makes justice *possible*, but the fairness of the process is what makes it justice. Compared to what the Allies planned for Wilhelm II and Talaat, let alone what Morgenthau or Stalin planned for the Nazi leadership, The Hague's kind of victors' justice is pretty mild stuff.

Milosevic, and his half-hearted defenders in Serbia and elsewhere, have pointed to the Hague court as the embodiment of a Western double standard. To be sure, it would be nice to have a tribunal that could pass—and enforce—judgment against all countries, weak or strong. But in a world where impunity is the rule, waiting for perfectly comprehensive justice could mean waiting forever—which is why violent nationalists bother calling for comprehensiveness in the first place.

Comprehensiveness, after all, is no friend to Milosevic. If comprehensiveness means a thorough exploration of war crimes committed by Croats, as well as by Bosnians and Kosovar Albanians, then comprehensiveness is firmly on The Hague's agenda. But it must also mean a thorough accounting for Milosevic's legacy. After all, Milosevic's trial will hardly constitute real justice unless the indictment is changed to include crimes in Bosnia, not just Kosovo. A Bosnia command-responsibility indictment will be far more complicated to make, since the Serb chain of command is murkier than it was Kosovo. Goldstone and Arbour's work on the various chains of command—to Milosevic, as well as to Tudjman and even to Izetbegovic—was relatively rudimentary. But The Hague must finish the job now.[46] On top of The Hague's work, Milosevic's image is also under attack back in Yugoslavia. There are a number of scenarios being explored that might combine Yugoslav and UN investigations. Milosevic could be returned to Belgrade to face Yugoslav corruption charges during the UN tribunal's lengthy pretrial phase, which could take as long as a year. Selectivity, in short, is Milosevic's best hope.

In a bizarre way, Milosevic is one of the lucky ones. He does not face a Vishinsky or a firing squad. He does not even face a court made up entirely of judges from enemy countries. There were television cameras to cover live his outburst at his arraignment, and he will have plenty of chances to get his message out to the world press.

He is, in short, a beneficiary of legalism, that odd trait of the liberal countries that he scorns. In this curious hybrid court of law, he is free—probably for the last time, if he is convicted—to speak his mind. The irony is not a small one: legalism allows him the opportunity to denounce legalism. But his fate is no longer a matter for diplomats, but for trial lawyers. His words are just words, not commands; and he can be answered in kind by words from the prosecutors and the judges and, above all, some of his victims. Slobodan Milosevic will have to sit in The Hague and listen to witnesses tell how their families were killed.

* Acknowledgments *

IT TAKES a lot of local good faith to chronicle so much international bad faith.

This book is in memory of my grandfathers, Nate Basserabie and Chona (Joe) Bobrow. Wise and good men, they are both missed beyond what words can say. My love, too, to my wonderful grandmothers, Gert Basserabie and Bess Bobrow, and to my terrific family, Arthur, Karen, and Warren Bass.

I owe a great debt to my Harvard dissertation committee. Without Stanley Hoffmann's unique blend of humane wisdom, formidable learning, and friendship, this book would not have been possible. Stephen Peter Rosen's good-humored skepticism was bracing and invaluable. And Anne-Marie Slaughter pushed me toward understanding the intersection of law and international relations. For help at Harvard, thanks to Eva Bellin, Peter Berkowitz, Grzegorz Ekiert, Chris Gelpi, Danny Goldhagen, Iain Johnston, Bob Keohane, Rod MacFarquhar, Harvey Mansfield, Andy Moravcsik, Susan Pharr, Louise Richardson, Michael Sandel, and Celeste Wallander. Judith Shklar's influence is still enormous, not least in this book. At Princeton, Sheri Berman, Kent Eaton, Jim Doig, Michael Doyle, Aaron Friedberg, Joanne Gowa, Fred Greenstein, Jeff Herbst, George Kateb, Atul Kohli, Kate McNamara, Anne Sartori, Ken Schultz, and Dick Ullman offered useful insights and encouragement.

Mike Grunwald cheerfully endured me and this project for over five years. I can think of nothing more flattering than for someone to find— either from our discussions, his insightful editing, or osmosis—Grunwald-style reporting and writing in these pages. Samantha Power shared her passion for Bosnia and her deep knowledge of human rights issues. Jennifer Pitts unsparingly kept the arguments sharp. Peter Canellos, the best editor in Boston, carefully edited huge portions, improving every passage he touched.

At *The Economist*, I am forever grateful to Daniel Franklin for the tremendous fun of working in his Washington bureau. Ann Wroe, the American editor, is a dream of a boss, including indulgently allowing me to write for her from Boston while I was in graduate school. Thanks, too, to Brian Beedham, Bill Emmott, Charles Grant, John Heilemann, Sebastian Mallaby, Zanny Minton-Beddoes, Yvonne Ryan, Xan Smiley and Brooke Unger. At *The New Republic*, a consistent voice against brutality in Bosnia, particular thanks to Marty Peretz, and to Nurith Aizenman, Peter Beinart, Jonathan Cohn, Chuck Lane, Andrew Sullivan, and Leon Wieseltier. Thanks, too, to Barry Gewen and Sara Mosle of *The New York Times* and Richard Leiby and Jodie Allen, then at *The Washington Post.*

Chris Bennett of the International Crisis Group and *The Economist* put a roof over my head in Sarajevo. Other reporters shared insights and beers in Bosnia, Serbia, and The Hague: David Rohde of *The New York Times*, Charlie Trueheart of *The Washington Post*, Stacy Sullivan, Elizabeth Neuffer of *The Boston Globe*, and Donatella Lorch of NBC. Natasa Kandic and Bogdan Ivanisevic of the Humanitarian Law Center in Belgrade, a brave Serbian human rights group, helped me travel to Serbia as the crisis in Kosovo worsened.

Thanks to fellow graduate students who pitched in: Ben Berger, Bill Burck, Kanchan Chandra, Page Fortna, Wendy Franz, Jason Furman, Anna Grzymala-Busse, Michael Hiscox, Mala Htun, Sharon Krause, Rory MacFarquhar, Patchen Markell, Rob Mickey, Kathleen O'Neill, Jeff Ritter, Andy Sabl, Curt Signorino, Liz Stanley, and Al Tillery. Richard Primus set me straight on legalism; Dan Libenson and Mark Wiedman added lawyerly insights.

At Princeton University Press, thanks to Fred Appel, Walter Lippincott, Malcolm Litchfield, Ian Malcolm, Chuck Myers, and a strikingly thoughtful anonymous reviewer. Graham Douglas drew up excellent maps. Madeleine Adams and Jennifer Backer efficiently handled production and editing.

Anna Sweeney of the State Department provided Bosnia polling data. Will Ferroggiaro of the National Security Archive helped me with the Freedom of Information Act. Thanks to the staff of the Public Records Office in Kew, London; the Archives diplomatiques at the Quai d'Orsay, Paris; the National Archives II in College Park, Maryland; Widener Library at Harvard; and Firestone Library at Princeton. The research bill was generously footed by Harvard's Center for European Studies and Center for International Affairs, the Krupp Foundation, and the MacArthur Foundation. Thanks, one and all.

G.J.B.
Princeton
February 2000

* *Notes* *

Note on Sources

This book is based on archival records and memoirs and, for the ex-Yugoslavia sections, on an extensive series of interviews with knowledgeable sources, including government officials at the highest levels short of head of state. I interviewed figures including Richard Goldstone, Louise Arbour, Antonio Cassese, Anthony Lake, Warren Christopher, John Shattuck, Dick Morris, Graham Blewitt, Peter Galbraith, Warren Zimmermann, Muhamed Sacirbey, and over three hundred others over the course of five years. I relied on sources in the American, British, French, Bosnian, Croatian, and Serbian governments, in the UN (including the Hague tribunal), NATO, the OHR in Bosnia, human rights groups, and elsewhere. Many sources were interviewed several times, including Goldstone and Arbour. I went to Bosnia, Serbia, and Croatia for research, as well as The Hague and Western capitals; some of the most thought-provoking interviews were conversations with ordinary Bosnians, Croatians, Serbians, and Kosovars, and with Western soldiers and aid workers in ex-Yugoslavia. The people listed above spoke on the record at least some of the time. But many of the interviews, including those with top-ranking officials, were conducted "on background"—I use the information, but protect the identity of the source. There are many useful facts I was told off the record and are therefore not printed here.

Some of the reporting was originally done for *The Economist*, as well as *The Washington Post* and *The New Republic*. I have been greatly helped by other reporters, whose coverage (often under dangerous conditions) and goodwill were invaluable. When I'm relying on another reporter, I footnote. All other quotations without footnotes are from my own reporting, except for readily available public statements by major leaders.

Documents are cited as follows: from the British Public Records Office, in Kew, London, as FO (Foreign Office papers) or CAB (Cabinet papers); from America's National Archives II, in College Park, Maryland, by R.G. (record group); from France's Archives diplomatiques, in the Quai d'Orsay, Paris, by série and sous-série. Unless otherwise noted, Quai d'Orsay records are from série Europe 1918–1940. *FRUS* refers to the official *Foreign Relations of the United States* volumes. Henry Stimson's diaries, unpublished, are at Yale University. Translations from French sources are my own unless otherwise noted.

A small number of contemporary State Department documents declassified under the Freedom of Information Act are available on-line at http://foia.state.gov/. Until vastly more records are declassified, no account of policy toward ex-Yugoslavia—including this book—can be seen as definitive.

Chapter One
Introduction

1. See Marcus Tanner, *Croatia: A Nation Forged in War* (New Haven: Yale University Press, 1997), pp. 289–90, and the Hague tribunal's second amended indictment: *Prosecutor of the Tribunal* against *Tihomir Blaskic*, IT-95-14-T, 25 April 1997. See also the

original indictment: *Prosecutor of the Tribunal* against *Kordic et al.*, IT-95–14-T, in *International Criminal Tribunal for the former Yugoslavia Yearbook 1995* (New York: UN, 1995), pp. 229–39.

2. ICTY *Bulletin*, nos. 5–6, 24 April 1996. A second courtroom was built years later, and then a third.

3. Unbeknownst to most reporters covering the tribunal—myself most definitely included—the prosecutor's office had been issuing secret indictments.

4. One academic mistakenly writes, "History's first international criminal court was the Nuremberg Tribunal," and in his book's subtitle forgets the Tokyo trials (Michael Scharf, *Balkan Justice: The Story behind the First International War Crimes Trial since Nuremberg* [Durham, N.C.: Carolina Academic Press, 1997], p. 3).

5. In two of these cases, the Napoleonic Wars and the Gulf War, in the end the victors chose not to hold trials; these cases are included as counter-examples.

6. Telford Taylor, *Nuremberg and Vietnam: An American Tragedy* (Chicago: Quadrangle, 1970), p. 24.

7. Ibid., p. 18.

8. For examples of Indian legalism, see B. N. Mehrish, *War Crimes and Genocide: The Trial of Pakistani War Criminals* (Delhi: Oriental Publishers, 1972), and S. C. Chaturvedi, "The Proposed Trial of Pakistani War Criminals," *Indian Journal of International Law*, vol. 11, no. 4 (October 1971), pp. 645–54. For an English-language sketch of the politics, see, variously, "Bangla Govt. Decides on a Genocide Probe," *Hindustan Times*, 2 January 1972, p. 1; "War Crimes Panel Demand" and "JS for Handing over War Criminals to Bangla," *Hindustan Times*, 3 January 1972, p. 6; L. M. Singhvi, "Trial at the Bar of Humanity," *Hindustan Times Sunday World*, 9 January 1972, pp. 11–12; "Mujib Rejects Links with Pak: Genocide Trial Demanded under UN Aegis," *Hindustan Times*, 11 January 1972, p. 1; "No Immunity to War Criminals, India Tells UN," *Hindustan Times*, 18 January 1972, pp. 1, 10; "POWs' Trial Will Do Harm, Says Bhutto," *Hindustan Times*, 5 May 1972, p. 1; "Dacca Defers Trials Till after Talks," *Hindustan Times*, 27 May 1972, p. 1.

9. Telford Taylor, *Anatomy of the Nuremberg Trials: A Personal Memoir* (New York: Knopf, 1992), p. 641.

10. Paul Lewis, "Top 5 on U.N. Council Back Call for Inquiry on Iraqi War Crimes," *New York Times*, 21 October 1990, p. A12; Marc Fisher, "Germany, Passive in Gulf War, Takes Initiative on Refugees," *Washington Post*, 17 April 1991, p. A23; and Adam Roberts, "The Laws of War in the 1990–91 Gulf Conflict," *International Security*, vol. 18, no. 3 (winter 1993–94), pp. 174–75.

11. See Martin Indyk speech, Washington Institute for Near East Policy, 18 May 1993, pp. 14–15. On Anfal, see Human Rights Watch-Middle East, *Iraq's Crime of Genocide: The Anfal Campaign against the Kurds* (New Haven: Yale University Press, 1995); Jonathan C. Randal, *After Such Knowledge, What Forgiveness?* (New York: Farrar Straus Giroux, 1997); and Middle East Watch and Physicians for Human Rights, *The Anfal Campaign in Iraqi Kurdistan: The Destruction of Koreme* (New York: Human Rights Watch, 1993).

12. This book owes its greatest debt to a work of political theory, not international relations, which emphasizes moral questions over empirical ones: Judith N. Shklar's magnificent *Legalism: Law, Morals, and Political Trials* (Cambridge, Mass.: Harvard University Press, 1986).

13. Closely related is the question of why states continue to support a war crimes tribunal after its establishment. The dynamics do not seem to change much, although once a tribunal is up and running, some states find it embarrassing to abolish it.

14. It is important for political theory, too. Shklar wrote "of the great puzzles raised by the trials of war criminals. How should one assign responsibility for acts committed by public agents, not on their own initiative, but as members of governmental organizations? Who can try such people? These are not minor issues in contemporary political theory" ("Hannah Arendt as Pariah," in *Political Thought and Political Thinkers* [Chicago: University of Chicago Press, 1998], Stanley Hoffmann, ed., p. 372).

15. In Henry Morgenthau Jr., *Morgenthau Diary—Germany* (Washington, D.C.: U.S. Government Printing Office [GPO], 1967), vol. 2, 18 May 1945, p. 1508.

16. See Sheldon Glueck, *The Nuremberg Trial and Aggressive War* (New York: Knopf, 1946), p. 10.

17. Martin Gilbert, *Churchill: A Life* (London: Minerva, 1992), p. 677; Robert Dallek, *Franklin D. Roosevelt and American Foreign Policy, 1932–1945* (New York: Oxford University Press, 1995), p. 472.

18. War crimes trials were included in the Treaty of Versailles, the preeminent example of a harsh peace. But the American advocates of war crimes trials at the end of World War II were also against the many punitive measures of the Morgenthau Plan, which included summary executions of war criminals.

19. In Richard H. Minear, *Victors' Justice: The Tokyo War Crimes Trial* (Princeton: Princeton University Press, 1971), p. 3. In September 1945, Tojo had made much the same point more emphatically. "I should like not to be judged by a conqueror's court," he said, and then shot himself. He survived (Arnold C. Brackman, *The Other Nuremberg: The Untold Story of the Tokyo War Crimes Trials* [New York: William Morrow, 1987], p. 44).

20. G. M. Gilbert, *Nuremberg Diary* (New York: Farrar Straus, 1947), p. 4. Göring later said, "As far as the trial is concerned, it's just a cut-and-dried political affair, and I'm prepared for the consequences. I have no doubt that the press will play a bigger part in the decision than the judges. —And I'm sure that the Russian and French judges, at least, already have their instructions. I can answer for anything I've done, and can't answer for anything I haven't done. But the victors are the judges . . . I know what's in store for me" (pp. 12–13).

21. Série Europe 1918–1929, sous-série Allemagne, vol. 28, Wilhelm II to Hindenburg, 5 April 1921. For a similar complaint by Turks, see FO 371/6505/E13968, Turkish prisoners (Ali Ihsan, Tevfik, Sabit, Djemal, Ibrahim Hakki, Hilmi, etc.) to Curzon, 1 September 1921.

22. "The World Tries Again: Making Rules for War," *The Economist*, 11 March 1995, p. 23.

23. Richard Rhodes, "The General and World War III," *New Yorker*, 19 June 1995, p. 48.

24. See Kenneth Anderson, "Nuremberg Sensibility: Telford Taylor's Memoir of the Nuremberg Trials," *Harvard Human Rights Journal*, vol. 7 (spring 1994), pp. 281–93.

25. Immanuel Kant, "To Perpetual Peace: A Philosophical Sketch," in *Perpetual Peace and Other Essays* (Indianapolis: Hackett, 1983), Ted Humphrey, trans., p. 110. See also Hedley Bull, *The Anarchical Society: A Study of Order in World Politics* (New York: Columbia University Press, 1977), p. 89.

26. Plato, *Republic* (New York: Basic Books, 1968), Alan Bloom, trans., book 1, 339a, p. 16. Thrasymachus is talking about justice internal to a regime, so his skepticism is even more radical than that of most realists.

27. On realists and liberals, see Michael W. Doyle, *Ways of War and Peace: Realism, Liberalism, and Socialism* (New York: W. W. Norton, 1997).

28. Raymond Aron, *De Gaulle, Israel and the Jews* (London: André Deutsch, 1969), John Sturrock, trans., p. 27.

29. Thucydides, *Peloponnesian War*, p. 221.

30. As Robert Keohane, a thoughtful critic of realism's limitations, wrote, "From a Realist perspective, it is remarkable how moralistic governments often are in discussing their obligations and those of others" (*After Hegemony: Cooperation and Discord in the World Political Economy* [Princeton: Princeton University Press, 1984], p. 126).

31. E. H. Carr, *The Twenty Years' Crisis, 1919–1939* (1939; reprint, New York: Harper and Row, 1964), pp. 64, 148.

32. Henry Kissinger, *Diplomacy* (New York: Simon and Schuster, 1994). Unsurprisingly, Kissinger has no stomach for pursuing war criminals in Bosnia ("Limits to What the U.S. Can Do in Bosnia," *Washington Post*, 22 September 1997, p. A19).

33. A.J.P. Taylor, *The Struggle for Mastery in Europe, 1848–1918* (Oxford: Oxford University Press, 1971), p. 574.

34. A.J.P. Taylor, *The Origins of the Second World War* (New York: Atheneum, 1961), p. xxviii.

35. Ibid., p. xiii.

36. A.J.P. Taylor, *Bismarck: The Man and Statesman* (New York: Knopf, 1955), p. 79.

37. George F. Kennan, *American Diplomacy* (Chicago: University of Chicago Press, 1984), p. 95. See also Richard Ullman, "The U.S. and the World: An Interview with George Kennan," *New York Review of Books*, 12 August 1999, pp. 4, 6.

38. Morgenthau—no relation to Henry Morgenthau Sr. or Jr.—was not totally allergic to legalism. He considered it "inevitable that certain rules of law should govern these [inter-state] relations" (Hans J. Morgenthau, *Politics among Nations: The Struggle for Power and Peace* [New York: Knopf, 1964], 3rd ed., p. 276), offered moral judgments about wartime justice (pp. 233–59), and even specifically considered international courts (pp. 290–93).

39. In Robert Jackson, introduction to Whitney R. Harris, *Tyranny on Trial: The Evidence at Nuremberg* (Dallas: Southern Methodist University Press, 1954), p. xxxiii. See also Morgenthau, *Politics among Nations*, p. 237.

40. Henry A. Kissinger, *A World Restored: Metternich, Castlereagh, and the Problems of Peace 1812–1822* (Boston: Houghton Mifflin, 1973), p. 138.

41. Ibid., p. 140.

42. Kenneth N. Waltz, *Theory of International Politics* (Lexington, Mass.: Addison-Wesley, 1979), p. 111.

43. Ibid., p. 93ff.

44. Ibid., pp. 112–13.

45. John Mearsheimer, "The False Promise of International Institutions," *International Security*, vol. 19, no. 3 (winter 1994–95), p. 7.

46. George F. Kennan, *Memoirs, 1925–1950* (New York: Pantheon, 1983), p. 261.

47. The international structure is often indeterminate; structural explanations, like Waltz's, cannot account for the variation in outcomes (and cannot dismiss that variation as unimportant unless realists are prepared to argue that events like the Hundred Days and Nuremberg are unimportant). True, Waltz aims at a theory of international relations, not of specific foreign policies. But this often does not stop neorealists from trying to explain foreign policy decisions, as Stephen Walt does with great skill in *The Origins of Alliances* (Ithaca, N.Y.: Cornell University Press, 1987).

48. Functional explanations therefore do not suffice.

49. Gérard Prunier, *The Rwanda Crisis: History of a Genocide* (New York: Columbia University Press, 1997), p. 355. He ultimately favors trials, but scorns the fact that the UN tribunal will not use the death penalty.

50. See Shklar, *Legalism*, p. 167, and "A Life of Learning," in Bernard Yack, ed., *Liberalism without Illusions: Essays on Political Theory and the Political Vision of Judith N. Shklar* (Chicago: University of Chicago Press, 1996), p. 274.

51. Robert Penn Warren, *All the King's Men* (New York: Harvest, 1996), p. 136.

52. Arendt to Karl Jaspers, 17 August 1946, in their *Correspondence, 1926–1969* (New York: Harcourt Brace, 1992), Lotte Kohler and Hans Saner, eds., p. 54. See also Martha Minow, *Between Vengeance and Forgiveness: Facing History after Genocide and Mass Violence* (Boston: Beacon, 1998), pp. 121–22.

53. CAB 66/25, Eden war criminals memorandum, W.P. (42) 264, 22 June 1942.

54. FO 371/4173/68097, Calthorpe to Balfour, 20 April 1919.

55. CAB 66/25, Eden war criminals memorandum, W.P. (42) 264, 22 June 1942.

56. *Trial of the Major War Criminals before the International Military Tribunal* (Nuremberg: Secretariat of the Tribunal, 1947), vol. 1 (hereafter *IMT*), pp. 139–40, 146; Taylor, *Anatomy*, pp. 91–94. Jackson said that public opinion would not tolerate letting off Krupp, "the very symbol of aggressive warfare"; but he had no choice (FO 371/50999/U9574, Nuremberg chief prosecutors meeting, 10:30 A.M., 9 November 1945).

57. Philip R. Piccigallo, *The Japanese on Trial: Allied War Crimes Operations in the East, 1945–1951* (Austin: University of Texas Press, 1979), p. 95.

58. "Tadic Case: The Verdict," ICTY press release, CC/PIO/190-E, 7 May 1997. For an analysis, see Roy Gutman, "Confusion in War Crimes Cases," *Newsday*, 13 May 1997, p. A16. The ruling was overturned on appeal in July 1999, with a finding that the war had been international.

59. Why doesn't the United States assassinate foreign leaders? Why do Nazi war crimes prosecutions continue to this day, when Germany is thoroughly rehabilitated?

60. See P. J. Marshall, ed., *The Writings and Speeches of Edmund Burke: India: The Launching of the Hastings Impeachment* (Oxford: Clarendon Press, 1991), vol. 6.

61. Howard M. Sachar, *A History of Israel: From the Rise of Zionism to Our Time* (New York: Knopf, 1989), vol. 1, pp. 536, 595.

62. *United States v. William L. Calley, Jr.*, 22 U.S.C.M.A. 534 (1973). In 1962, Neil Sheehan, a war reporter in Vietnam, wondered if America's leaders should be "placed in the dock and made to stand trial for their lives" for Vietnam (William Prochnau, *Once Upon a Distant War* [New York: Vintage, 1996], p. 282). It was Sheehan's concern about war crimes that led to the publication of the Pentagon Papers in *The New York Times*. Sheehan had written a huge review of books alleging war crimes in Vietnam ("Should We Have War Crime Trials?" *New York Times Book Review*, 28 March 1971). Daniel Ellsberg, a young Pentagon official who had turned against the war, had also

become obsessed with war crimes. He had tried to leak the Pentagon Papers to Senator William Fulbright of Arkansas, but Fulbright refused to have them. When Ellsberg saw Sheehan's article on war crimes, he decided to leak the Pentagon Papers to Sheehan (David Halberstam, *The Powers That Be* [New York: Dell, 1979], pp. 789–92).

63. Ze'ev Schiff and Ehud Ya'ari, *Israel's Lebanon War* (New York: Simon and Schuster, 1984), Ina Friedman, trans., pp. 281–85. A liberal might point out that these are both instances of democracies engaged in unpopular wars; that may say something about how and when countries will come to hold genuine convictions about norms, but such second-image arguments are beyond the scope of neorealism.

64. Raymond Aron, *Peace and War: A Theory of International Relations* (New York: Praeger, 1967), Richard Howard and Annette Baker Fox, trans., p. 114.

65. Ingo Müller, *Hitler's Justice: The Courts of the Third Reich* (Cambridge, Mass.: Harvard University Press, 1994), Deborah Lucas Schneider, trans., p. 52.

66. See Robert C. Tucker and Stephen F. Cohen, eds., *The Great Purge Trial* (New York: Grosset and Dunlap, 1965), especially p. ix.

67. FO 371/39010/C17547/14/62, Somervell memorandum to Churchill, "Germany: Trial of Hitler and His Colleagues," 15 December 1944.

68. Max Weber, *Economy and Society* (Berkeley: University of California Press, 1978), Guenther Roth and Claus Wittich, eds., vol. 2, p. 647. Italics added.

69. Adam B. Ulam, *Stalin: The Man and His Era* (Boston: Beacon Press, 1989), p. 619n.5.

70. Waltz, *Theory of International Politics*, pp. 76–78, 93–101, 102–23, 127–28.

71. Plato, *Republic*, 556e-567b, pp. 245–46.

72. See Stanley Hoffmann, "Rousseau on War and Peace," in his *Janus and Minerva: Essays in the Theory and Practice of International Politics* (Boulder, Colo.: Westview Press, 1987).

73. Vladimir I. Lenin, *Imperialism: The Highest Stage of Capitalism* (New York: International Publishers, 1939); J. A. Hobson, *Imperialism: A Study* (London: George Allen and Unwin, 1902); Joseph A. Schumpeter, *Imperialism and Social Classes* (New York: Kelly, 1951), Heinz Norden, trans.

74. Kant, *Perpetual Peace*.

75. Samuel Huntington, *American Politics: The Promise of Disharmony* (Cambridge, Mass.: Harvard University Press, 1981), p. 237. Huntington argues that American foreign-policy institutions "have existed in uneasy and fundamentally incompatible coexistence with the values of the prevailing ideology" (p. 238). See also Louis Henkin, *How Nations Behave: Law and Foreign Policy* (New York: Columbia University Press, 1979), p. 62, and Mark Danner, *The Massacre at El Mozote* (New York: Vintage, 1994), pp. 9–10.

76. Samuel P. Huntington, *The Soldier and the State: The Theory and Politics of Civil-Military Relations* (Cambridge, Mass.: Belknap Press of Harvard University Press, 1985), p. 457; see also pp. 143–57.

77. Aaron L. Friedberg, *In the Shadow of the Garrison State: America's Anti-Statism and Its Cold War Grand Strategy* (Princeton: Princeton University Press, 2000).

78. David Lumsdaine, *Moral Vision in International Politics: The Foreign Aid Regime, 1949–1989* (Princeton: Princeton University Press, 1993), p. 22.

79. Ibid., pp. 23–24.

80. Andrew Moravcsik, "A Liberal Theory of International Politics," *International Organization*, vol. 51, no. 4 (fall 1997), p. 518.

81. Huntington, *Soldier and the State*, p. 150. See also, for instance, Helen Milner, "International Theories of Cooperation among Nations: Strengths and Weaknesses," *World Politics*, vol. 44, no. 3 (April 1992), pp. 466–96; Robert O. Keohane, "International Institutions: Two Approaches," in his *International Institutions and State Power: Essays in International Relations Theory* (Boulder, Colo.: Westview, 1989); and Peter B. Evans et al., eds., *Double-Edged Diplomacy: International Bargaining and Domestic Politics* (Berkeley: University of California Press, 1993).

82. The literature is large, and growing. See Kant, *Perpetual Peace*; Michael W. Doyle, "Liberalism in World Politics," *American Political Science Review*, vol. 80, no. 4 (December 1986), pp. 1151–69; Doyle, "Kant, Liberal Legacies, and Foreign Affairs, part 1," *Philosophy and Public Affairs*, vol. 12, no. 3 (summer 1983), pp. 205–35; Doyle, "Kant, Liberal Legacies, and Foreign Affairs, part 2," *Philosophy and Public Affairs*, vol. 12, no. 4 (fall 1983), pp. 325–53; Bruce Russett, *Grasping the Democratic Peace: Principles for a Post–Cold War World* (Princeton: Princeton University Press, 1993); John M. Owen IV, *Liberal Peace, Liberal War: American Politics and International Security* (Ithaca, N.Y.: Cornell University Press, 1997), and "How Liberalism Produces Democratic Peace," *International Security*, vol. 19, no. 2 (fall 1994), pp. 87–125; Bruce Russett and Zeev Maoz, "Normative and Structural Causes of Democratic Peace, 1946–1986," *American Political Science Review*, vol. 87, no. 3 (September 1993), pp. 624–38.

83. Like Owen, I argue that it is liberalism, not democracy, that is the causal factor. (Owen, *Liberal Peace, Liberal War*, pp. 15–17.)

84. It is for this reason that the history of international war crimes tribunals is bound up in the history of the two preeminent liberal states, Britain in the nineteenth century and America in the twentieth century.

85. Shklar, *Legalism*, p. 144.

86. *The Paquete Habana*, Supreme Court of the United States, 1900, 175 U.S. 677, 20 S.Ct. 290.

87. 28 U.S.C. §1350. For more on the Alien Tort Statute, see the critical decisions in *Filartiga* v. *Pena-Irala*, United States Court of Appeals, Second Circuit, 1980, 630 F.2d 876; *Tel-Oren* v. *Libyan Arab Republic*, 726 F.2d 774 (D.C. Cir. 1984); and *Forti* v. *Suarez-Mason*, United States District Court, Northern District California, 1987, 672 F. Supp. 1531. See also Anne-Marie Burley, "The Alien Tort Statute and the Judiciary Act of 1789: A Badge of Honor," *American Journal of International Law*, vol. 83, no. 3 (July 1989), pp. 461–93.

88. "Thugs Brought to Book: The Law," *The Economist*, 22 March 1997, pp. 31–32.

89. Michael Walzer, *Just and Unjust Wars: A Moral Argument with Historical Illustrations* (New York: Basic Books, 1992), pp. 319–21.

90. CAB 23/43, Imperial War Cabinet 39, 28 November 1918, 11:45 A.M., p. 4. Italics added.

91. *Public Papers of Woodrow Wilson: War and Peace: Presidential Messages, Addresses, and Public Papers 1917–1924* (New York: Harper, 1925), Ray Stannard Baker and William E. Dodd, eds., vol. 5, p. 11.

92. Jackson to Truman, 6 June 1945, in *Report of Robert H. Jackson, United States Representative to the International Conference on Military Trials: London, 1945* (Washington, D.C.: U.S. Department of State, 1947), pp. 48–50. Italics added.

93. Kennan, *American Diplomacy*, p. 95. See also Kissinger, *World Restored*, pp. 328–29.

94. For a standard data set, see J. David Singer and Melvin Small, *Correlates of War Project: International and Civil War Data, 1816–1992* (Ann Arbor, Mich.: Inter-University Consortium for Political and Social Research, April 1994), ICPSR 9905.

95. Eugene Davidson, *The Trial of the Germans: An Account of the Twenty-Two Defendants before the International Military Tribunal at Nuremberg* (1966, reprint, Columbia: University of Missouri Press, 1997), p. 11.

96. Brackman, *The Other Nuremberg*, p. 52.

97. Soviet dissent, *IMT*, pp. 342–64.

98. The cynicism was not complete. Nikitchenko did not object to lighter sentences than death for Walter Funk, Karl Dönitz, Erich Räder, Baldur von Schirach, Albert Speer, and Constantin von Neurath.

99. Shklar, *Legalism*, p. 1.

100. For classic statements, see Max Weber, "The Social Psychology of the World Religions," in *From Max Weber: Essays in Sociology* (New York: Oxford University Press, 1958), H. H. Gerth and C. Wright Mills, eds. and trans., p. 280; John Maynard Keynes, *The General Theory of Employment, Interest and Money* (London: Macmillan, 1936), p. 383; and Isaiah Berlin, "Two Concepts of Liberty," in his *Four Essays on Liberty* (Oxford: Oxford University Press, 1969), pp. 118–19. More recently, see Judith Goldstein, *Ideas, Interests, and American Trade Policy* (Ithaca, N.Y.: Cornell University Press, 1993); Doyle, *Ways of War and Peace*, p. 21; Jack Snyder, *Myths of Empire: Domestic Politics and International Ambition* (Ithaca, N.Y.: Cornell University Press, 1991), pp. 1–10, 31–60; Peter A. Hall, ed., *The Political Power of Economic Ideas: Keynesianism across Nations* (Princeton: Princeton University Press, 1989), p. 361; Judith Goldstein and Robert O. Keohane, "Ideas and Foreign Policy: An Analytical Framework," in Goldstein and Keohane, eds., *Ideas and Foreign Policy: Beliefs, Institutions, and Political Change* (Ithaca, N.Y.: Cornell University Press, 1993), pp. 29–30; Kathryn Sikkink, *Ideas and Institutions: Developmentalism in Brazil and Argentina* (Ithaca, N.Y.: Cornell University Press, 1991); Kathleen R. McNamara, *The Currency of Ideas: Monetary Politics in the European Union* (Ithaca, N.Y.: Cornell University Press, 1998); Sheri Berman, *The Social Democratic Moment: Ideas and Politics in the Making of Interwar Europe* (Cambridge, Mass.: Harvard University Press, 1998); Thomas Risse-Kappen, "Ideas Do Not Float Freely: Transnational Coalitions, Domestic Structures, and the End of the Cold War," *International Organization*, vol. 48 (spring 1994), pp. 185–214; Owen, *Liberal Peace, Liberal War*; and Daniel Jonah Goldhagen, *Hitler's Willing Executioners: Ordinary Germans and the Holocaust* (New York: Knopf, 1996), pp. 9, 21. For a social constructivist perspective, emphasizing the power of culture, see Peter J. Katzenstein, ed., *The Culture of National Security: Norms and Identity in World Politics* (New York: Columbia University Press, 1996); Elizabeth Kier, *Imagining War: French and British Military Doctrine between the Wars* (Princeton: Princeton University Press, 1997); Alastair Iain Johnston, *Cultural Realism: Strategic Culture and Grand Strategy in Chinese History* (Princeton: Princeton University Press, 1995); and Alexander Wendt, "Anarchy Is What States Make of It: The Social Construction of Power Politics," *International Organization*, vol. 46, no. 2 (spring 1992), pp. 391–425, as well as his "The Agent-Structure Problem in International Relations Theory," *International Organization*, vol. 41, no. 3 (summer 1987), pp. 335–70, and "Constructing International Politics," *International Security*, vol. 20, no. 1 (summer 1995), p. 73. On

the power of human rights ideals, see Margaret E. Keck and Kathryn Sikkink, *Activists beyond Borders: Advocacy Networks in International Politics* (Ithaca, N.Y.: Cornell University Press, 1998), p. 119, and Martha Finnemore, *National Interests in International Society* (Ithaca, N.Y.: Cornell University Press, 1996), p. 87.

101. For a typical expression of frustration, from a political scientist who believes that ideas are important explanatory variables, see Robert A. Dahl, *Polyarchy: Participation and Opposition* (New Haven: Yale University Press, 1971), pp. 181–88.

102. For a critique of the norm-based argument for the democratic peace on these grounds, see Joanne Gowa, "Democratic States and International Disputes," *International Organization*, vol. 49, no. 3 (summer 1995), pp. 514–16; and Henry S. Farber and Joanne Gowa, "Polities and Peace," *International Security*, vol. 20, no. 2 (fall 1995), pp. 125–26. More generally, see Kenneth Shepsle, "Comment," in Roger Noll, ed., *Regulatory Policy and the Social Sciences* (Berkeley: University of California Press, 1985), pp. 234–36.

103. See Stanley Hoffmann, *Duties beyond Borders: On the Limits and Possibilities of Ethical International Relations* (Syracuse, N.Y.: Syracuse University Press, 1981). Deliberately, I am examining liberal and illiberal states, not democracies and nondemocracies. Democratic public opinion might well tolerate summary executions, as will be shown in the chapters on Leipzig and Nuremberg. But liberalism tends to preclude that option. For a similar distinction, see Owen, *Liberal Peace, Liberal War*, pp. 15–17.

104. R. J. Rummel, *Power Kills: Democracy as a Method of Nonviolence* (New Brunswick, N.J.: Transaction, 1997), pp. 91–98. This is faint praise, and intentionally so. Racial discrimination is of course perfectly possible in liberal societies, but it is often accompanied by a sense of shame: a realization, slowly rising to the surface, that such bigotry is a betrayal of the liberal legacy.

105. Russett, *Grasping the Democratic Peace*, p. 31.

106. The argument that such domestic norms can make a decisive impact on foreign policy is a familiar one from the democratic peace literature. Zeev Maoz, for instance, finds that domestic executions correlate directly with the likelihood of a country's involvement in foreign conflict. Maoz finds that democratic norms reduce the likelihood of conflict abroad (ibid., pp. 86–92).

107. Anglo-French conference, London, 13 December 1919, 11 A.M., in E. L. Woodward and Rohan Butler, eds., *Documents on British Foreign Policy 1919–1939: Volume II: 1919* (London: His Majesty's Stationery Office, 1948), 1st ser., pp. 756–57.

108. There is of course substantial hypocrisy here. While liberal states do not carry out atrocities at home, they do in *guerre à outrance*: Hiroshima, Dresden, My Lai, No Gun Ri. And liberal states have also carried out brutal colonial projects, and capped that in wars of decolonization, as France did in Algeria. For those who take their liberal principles seriously, this is a source of considerable anguish. Sometimes liberals plead good motives (e.g., Truman had never aspired to destroy Hiroshima, but did so in order to end the war; see Lucy S. Dawidowicz, *The Holocaust and the Historians* [Cambridge, Mass.: Harvard University Press, 1981], pp. 17–19). Sometimes domestic norms will belatedly try to reassert themselves over wartime practices, as after My Lai and after Sabra and Shatila. For more on these moral dilemmas, see Walzer, *Just and Unjust Wars*, p. 325; Shklar, *Legalism*, p. 164; Taylor, *Nuremberg and Vietnam*; and Seymour M. Hersh, *My Lai 4* (New York: Random House, 1970). The most I will claim is

NOTES TO CHAPTER ONE

that liberal states are often aware that they are not being true to their domestic traditions, whereas illiberal states usually feel no such dilemma. Liberal states pushing for war crimes tribunals are frequently hypocritical—but not always, and not completely. In contrast, as Shklar put it: "Crimes against humanity were not something that the Nazis engaged in merely because they were an occupying power in hostile territory. They engaged in them because they were Nazis" (*Legalism*, p. 164).

Still, the important analytical point for this book is that liberal politics at home can lead to liberal politics abroad. The example of European colonialism cuts both ways, for the end of Europe's imperialism was driven by, among other things, the spread of liberal ideas (J. Daniel Philpott, Jr., "Revolutions in Sovereignty: On Ideas, Power, and Change in International Relations," Ph.D. diss., Harvard University, 1995, pp. 188ff). Burke wanted "to enlarge the circle of national justice to the necessities of the empire we have obtained" (opening speech, "Impeachment of Warren Hastings," in Burke, *Works* [London: John C. Nimmo, 1887], vol. 9, p. 343). Less frequent violations of *jus in bello* will also presumably follow the growth of liberalism. Explaining the precise lags and hypocrisies is a matter for future work; it would only confound this book if I claimed that liberal ideas invariably and promptly spill over into foreign policy. But much of this book is dedicated to explaining when liberal states will betray their own principles by letting war criminals go free. The spread of liberal ideas is slow and tortuous, whether these ideals are confronting racism, colonialism, or the punishment of war criminals.

It should also be pointed out that those who deplore the war crimes committed by liberal states may find them all the more reason to support war crimes tribunals, which create additional pressures for all sides to obey standards of *jus in bello*. Judge Radhabinod Pal's blistering dissent at Tokyo rested on a *tu quoque* argument, and Jackson was wary of charging Nazis for indiscriminate bombing: "[W]e left out of our draft the destruction of villages and towns, because I have seen the villages and towns of Germany. I think that you will have great difficulty distinguishing between the military necessity for that kind of destruction as distinguished from some done by the Germans, assuming the war to be legitimate. It seems to me that those subjects invite recriminations that would not be useful in the trial" (Jackson, *Report*, 25 July 1945, p. 380). Such arguments are more likely to resonate in liberal states than in illiberal ones.

109. CAB 66/42, Churchill war criminals note, War Cabinet, W.P. (43) 496, 9 November 1943.

110. See Robert L. Holmes, *On War and Morality* (Princeton: Princeton University Press, 1989), pp. 152–59. On the enduring power of the natural law tradition in just war theory, see James Turner Johnson, *Just War Tradition and the Restraint of War: A Moral and Historical Inquiry* (Princeton: Princeton University Press, 1981), pp. 85–118.

111. Marshall, *Writings and Speeches of Edmund Burke*, p. 346.

112. Louis Henkin, *Constitutionalism, Democracy, and Foreign Affairs* (New York: Columbia University Press, 1990), p. 100. See also Black's plurality opinion in *Reid* v. *Covert*, 354 U.S. 1, 17 (1957). It would be theoretically possible to have a liberal state that rests on a social contract only among its citizens, but Henkin rejects that reading of the Constitution. This opens the door for America to do things like harangue China about human rights violations within China.

113. Louis Henkin, *Foreign Affairs and the Constitution* (New York: W. W. Norton, 1972), p. 254.

114. Russett, *Grasping the Democratic Peace*, p. 32.

115. Israel is not a clear-cut case, because it is both liberal and Zionist. Many Israelis, and not just those on the left, would agree with novelist Amos Oz: "[T]here always have been those who contend that we are forbidden to adopt the murderous methods of the enemy, that we are forbidden, unconditionally and without 'it depends,' to be war criminals, even when war criminals seek to destroy us. And if there have been some war criminals among us—and there have been—we must isolate and denounce them and not turn their 'precedents' into the norm. It is forbidden to commit war crimes—and not because 'crime doesn't pay.' . . . No. It is forbidden simply because it is forbidden. Period. This is an axiom" (*The Slopes of Lebanon* [New York: Harcourt Brace Jovanovich, 1989], Maurie Goldberg-Bartura, trans., p. 188).

116. Holmes, *War and Morality*, pp. 153–54.

117. William Ewart Gladstone, *Bulgarian Horrors and the Question of the East: The Turco-Servian War* (New York: Lovell, Adam, Wesson, 1876); Vahakn N. Dadrian, "Genocide as a Problem of National and International Law: The World War I Armenian Case and Its Contemporary Legal Ramifications," *Yale Journal of International Law*, vol. 14, no. 2 (summer 1989), pp. 233–38.

118. CAB 23/43, Imperial War Cabinet 37, 20 November 1918, noon, London, p. 8.

119. Henry Morgenthau Sr., *Ambassador Morgenthau's Story* (Garden City, N.Y.: Doubleday, Page, 1918), pp. 333–34. Morgenthau later even turned Talaat's gibe around, wearing his transcendence of ethnicity as a badge of honor: "I can think of no greater honour than to be recalled because I, a Jew, have been exerting all my powers to save the lives of hundreds of thousands of Christians" (p. 379).

120. Shklar, *Legalism*, p. 128. For a superb critical account of the Tokyo trials, see John W. Dower, *Embracing Defeat: Japan in the Wake of World War II* (New York: Free Press, 1999), pp. 443–84. See also Minear, *Victors' Justice*, and Radhabinod Pal, *International Military Tribunal for the Far East: Dissentient Judgment* (Calcutta: Sanyal and Co., 1953).

121. Henkin, *Foreign Affairs and the Constitution*, p. 254.

122. Jackson, *Report*, p. xi.

123. Piccigallo, *Japanese on Trial*, p. 91.

124. Anderson, "Nuremberg Sensibility," p. 290.

125. See Roy Gutman and David Rieff, eds., *Crimes of War: What the Public Should Know* (New York: Norton, 1999), pp. 155, 177–78, 282–85, 342–43.

126. Genocide was not codified as an international crime until after World War II, but the Allies condemned the extermination of the Armenians as criminal in 1915. There were rape charges against Japanese defendants after World War II, and the Hague and Arusha tribunals are breaking new legal ground in prosecuting rape as a war crime. But for much of this book, the basic definition of a war crime is largely unchanged. The one big exception is aggression, seen as a crime after both world wars, but not today.

127. The most dubious case is the Tokyo tribunal. For criticisms, see Ian Buruma, *The Wages of Guilt: Memories of War in Germany and Japan* (New York: Meridian, 1994);

Minear, *Victors' Justice*, and Dower, *Embracing Defeat*. Piccigallo argues that the vast majority of the Allied trials were fair, often remarkably so (*Japanese on Trial*, pp. 213–15).

128. See, for instance, Frederic Herbert Maugham, *U.N.O. and War Crimes* (London: J. Murray, 1951), including an anti-Nuremberg postscript by Lord Hankey that manages to never mention the Holocaust.

129. John F. Kennedy, *Profiles in Courage* (New York: Harper and Row, 1964), pp. 231–44.

130. Quoted in Alpheus Thomas Mason, *Harlan Fiske Stone: Pillar of the Law* (New York: Viking, 1956), p. 716.

131. For more sustained rebuttals, see Richard A. Posner, *The Problems of Jurisprudence* (Cambridge, Mass.: Harvard University Press, 1990), pp. 228–39, and Carlos Santiago Nino, *Radical Evil on Trial* (New Haven: Yale University Press, 1996), pp. 149–58.

132. Hannah Arendt, *Eichmann in Jerusalem: A Report on the Banality of Evil* (London: Penguin, 1994), p. 5. See also Tom Segev, *The Seventh Million: The Israelis and the Holocaust* (New York: Hill and Wang, 1994), Haim Watzman, trans., pp. 323–66, and Pnina Lahav, *Judgment in Jerusalem: Simon Agranat and the Zionist Century* (Berkeley: University of California Press, 1997).

133. See Richard J. Goldstone, *Do Judges Speak Out?* (Johannesburg: South African Institute of Race Relations, 1993).

134. Alexis de Tocqueville, *The Old Regime and the French Revolution* (1856; reprint, New York: Doubleday, 1983), Stuart Gilbert, trans., pp. 191–92.

135. Shklar, *Legalism*, p. 148.

136. Charles S. Maier, *The Unmasterable Past: History, Holocaust, and German National Identity* (Cambridge, Mass.: Harvard University Press, 1988), p. 74.

137. In Müller, *Hitler's Justice*, p. 140.

138. Ibid., p. 79.

139. Ibid., pp. 81–119.

140. Quoted in William L. Shirer, *The Rise and Fall of the Third Reich: A History of Nazi Germany* (New York: Simon and Schuster, 1990), p. 1070. See also Müller, *Hitler's Justice*, p. 148, and Karl Dietrich Bracher, *The German Dictatorship* (New York: Holt, Rinehart and Winston, 1970), Jean Steinberg, trans., p. 459. Hitler was not speaking of Stauffenberg, who, along with three other officers, had been shot already, but of thousands of friends and relatives of alleged conspirators.

141. In Shirer, *Rise and Fall of the Third Reich*, p. 1070.

142. Tucker and Cohen, *Great Purge Trial*, p. xxiii.

143. Ulam, *Stalin*, p. 413.

144. Václav Havel, "The Trial," in his *Open Letters: Selected Writings 1965–1990* (New York: Knopf, 1991), pp. 104–5.

145. That is, realism underpredicts and liberalism overpredicts the incidence of war crimes tribunals.

146. These arguments are, for political scientists, a series of brittle hypotheses, derived from international relations theory. In the dissertation that this book is based on, they are explicitly treated as such. The subsequent case study chapters are attempts to falsify these hypotheses by testing them against empirical evidence (see Karl R. Popper, *The Logic of Scientific Discovery* [New York: Harper and Row, 1968]). The

dependent variable—support for a tribunal—is a *preference*, not necessarily any particular political outcome. My null hypothesis, drawing on neorealism, is: (1) either liberal or illiberal states only set up war crimes tribunals as a way of punishing a defeated enemy; and (2) the tribunals thus set up are indistinguishable from each other; it makes no difference which state is pushing for the tribunal. The *n* in this study is not just five, but actually twenty: various countries reacting in five extensive cases and three lesser case studies. (For a more detailed explanation of my methodology, see my "Judging War: The Politics of International War Crimes Tribunals," Ph.D. diss., Harvard University, 1998, pp. 75–99.) On case study methods, see Gary King, Robert O. Keohane, and Sidney Verba, *Designing Social Inquiry: Scientific Inference in Qualitative Research* (Princeton: Princeton University Press, 1994), p. 45. See also Stephen Van Evera, *Guide to Methods for Students of Political Science* (Ithaca, N.Y.: Cornell University Press, 1997), pp. 49–88. I have selected some of my cases precisely in order to have variation on the explanatory variables (liberal and illiberal states, outraged and indifferent public opinion, etc.). I have not selected on the dependent variable (King, Keohane and Verba, *Designing Social Inquiry,* pp. 129–38. Van Evera is less strict about selecting on the dependent variable [*Guide to Methods*, p. 47]). See also David Collier, "The Comparative Method: Two Decades of Change," in Dankwart A. Rustow and Kenneth Paul, eds., *Comparative Political Dynamics: Global Research Perspectives* (New York: Harper Collins, 1991), pp. 7–31; Harry Eckstein, "Case Study and Theory in Political Science," in Fred I. Greenstein and Nelson W. Polsby, eds., *Handbook of Political Science*, vol. 7, *Strategies of Inquiry* (Reading, Mass.: Addison-Wesley, 1975), pp. 79–137; Alexander L. George and Timothy J. McKeown, "Case Studies and Theories of Organizational Decision Making," in *Advances in Information Processing in Organizations* (Greenwich, Conn.: JAI Press, 1985), vol. 2, pp. 21–58; and Arend Lijphart, "Comparative Politics and Comparative Method," *American Political Science Review,* vol. 65, no. 3 (September 1971), pp. 682–98. For more specific discussions of how to do good case study work, see Theda Skocpol, *States and Social Revolutions: A Comparative Analysis of France, Russia and China* (Cambridge: Cambridge University Press, 1979), p. 36; Walt, *Origins of Alliances*, pp. 11–121; Jeffrey W. Legro, *Cooperation under Fire: Anglo-German Restraint during World War II* (Ithaca, N.Y.: Cornell University Press, 1993), pp. 46–51; and Alon Peled, *A Question of Loyalty: Military Manpower in Multiethnic States* (Ithaca, N.Y.: Cornell University Press, 1998), pp. 10–15.

147. I will not dwell much on the distinction made above between liberal and illiberal states, mostly because the countries in question in my case studies fit easily. There are finer distinctions to be made (Stalin's Soviet Union was noticeably more illiberal than Wilhelmine Germany; Churchill's Britain was a parliamentary democracy unlike Roosevelt's presidential democracy), but I cannot imagine anyone suggesting, say, lumping Britons and Soviets together.

148. Hans Morgenthau, "Human Rights and Foreign Policy," in Kenneth W. Thompson, ed., *Moral Dimensions of American Foreign Policy* (New Brunswick, N.J.: Transaction, 1984), p. 344. See also Walzer, *Just and Unjust Wars*, pp. 101–2.

149. It has the further advantage of being easy to identify empirically, and is not time-dependent: the protection of soldiers is much the same thing from 1815 to 2000.

150. George Stephanopoulos, *All Too Human: A Political Education* (New York: Little, Brown, 1999), p. 214.

151. Huntington, *Soldier and the State*, p. 69. He quotes an American captain (p. 68) who in 1946 wrote that the military professional "must be the 'no' man for idealism and wishful thinking."

152. Eugène Ionesco, *Rhinoceros* (New York: Grove Press, n.d.), Derek Prouse, trans., pp. 78–79.

153. Taken together with my second proposition, this is, oddly, slightly paradoxical advice for war criminals. A war criminal who takes a liberal state's soldier hostage can pressure the liberal state to give up on justice. But if the war criminal kills that soldier, the war criminal incurs the liberal state's wrath and increases the risk of facing a war crimes trial.

154. Kennan, *American Diplomacy*, p. 93.

155. William Ewart Gladstone, "Germany, France, and England," in his *Gleanings of Past Years, 1843–77* (London: John Murray, 1879), p. 256.

156. See Keck and Sikkink, *Activists beyond Borders*.

157. Andrew Moravcsik argues that international pressure "works when it can work through free and influential public opinion and an independent judiciary" ("Explaining International Human Rights Regimes: Liberal Theory and Western Europe," *European Journal of International Relations*, vol. 1, no. 2 [1995], p. 158).

158. Samuel P. Huntington, *The Third Wave: Democratization in the Late Twentieth Century* (Norman: University of Oklahoma Press, 1991), pp. 211–31. See also Guillermo O'Donnell and Philippe C. Schmitter, *Transitions from Authoritarian Rule: Tentative Conclusions about Uncertain Democracies* (Baltimore: Johns Hopkins University Press, 1986), pp. 28–32; Nino, *Radical Evil on Trial*; Neil J. Kritz, ed., *Transitional Justice: How Emerging Democracies Reckon with Former Regimes* (Washington, D.C.: United States Institute of Peace, 1995), 3 vols.; Aryeh Neier, *War Crimes: Brutality, Genocide, Terror, and the Struggle for Justice* (New York: Times Books, 1998), pp. 56–74, 96–107; Tina Rosenberg's extraordinary *The Haunted Land: Facing Europe's Ghosts after Communism* (New York: Vintage, 1996); and Kader Asmal, Louise Asmal, and Ronald Suresh Roberts, *Reconciliation through Truth: A Reckoning of Apartheid's Criminal Governance* (New York: St. Martin's Press, 1997).

159. Sikkink, *Ideas and Institutions*, p. 2. See also Stephen D. Krasner, "Structural Causes and Regime Consequences: Regimes as Intervening Variables," in Krasner, ed., *International Regimes* (Ithaca, N.Y.: Cornell University Press, 1983), pp. 1–21; Robert O. Keohane and Joseph S. Nye, *Power and Interdependence* (Boston: Little, Brown, 1977).

160. Keohane's book is mostly written from an egoist perspective, but he does admit that reducing moral obligations to a strategy of reciprocity is "probably too cynical" (*After Hegemony*, pp. 126–27), because of principled officials, like Woodrow Wilson and Jimmy Carter, and electorates. On this account, Keohane at least implies that moralism comes into foreign policy from domestic principles, presumably democratic ones. Keohane himself is concerned about the ethical value of cooperation (pp. 10–11, 247–57).

161. "For Realists, in other words, the early postwar regimes rested on the *political hegemony* of the United States," Keohane wrote. "Thus Realists and Institutionalists could both regard early postwar developments as supporting their theories" (*After Hegemony*, p. 9).

162. One could also argue that the legacy of Nuremberg is itself a kind of institution, a banner carried by human rights groups if not by other institutions. Nuremberg,

after all, was a product of American hegemony, and could have effects that outlasted that hegemony, shaping the beliefs and expectations of actors half a century later. A neoliberal institutionalist could argue that the emergence of the Hague and Arusha tribunals only show how far-reaching the legacy of Nuremberg was. Merely by claiming the mantle of Nuremberg, the Hague tribunal made it impossible for the UN Security Council to abolish it outright even when the member states might have secretly wanted to do so.

Chapter Two
St. Helena

1. CAB 24/85, G.T. 7806, Second Interim Report of the Commission of Enquiry into Breaches of the Laws of War, 3 June 1919, appendix: H. Hale Bellot, "Memorandum on the Detention of Napoleon Buonaparte."

2. CAB 23/43, Imperial War Cabinet 37, 20 November 1918, noon; CAB 28/5, Allied Conference, London, 2 December 1918, I.C.-98; and série Europe 1918–1940, sous-série Allemagne, vol. 25, Allizé to Pichon, 23 November 1918. Napoleon's fate came up in the planning for Nuremberg, too. (See, for instance, Memorandum for the President, 18 January 1945, in Bradley F. Smith, ed., *The American Road to Nuremberg: The Documentary Record, 1944–1945* [Stanford, Calif.: Hoover Institution Press, 1982], p. 109.) A French general once reminded Ratko Mladic that Napoleon had ended up at St. Helena. Mladic laughed (Roger Cohen, *Hearts Grown Brutal: Sagas of Sarajevo* [New York: Random House, 1998], p. 234).

3. Kissinger, *World Restored*, p. 140.

4. Ibid., p. 139.

5. Rory Muir, *Britain and the Defeat of Napoleon, 1807–1815* (New Haven: Yale University Press, 1996), p. 325.

6. Castlereagh, 3rd ser., iii, pp. 498–99, in CAB 24/85, Bellot appendix to Commission of Enquiry report, p. 381.

7. Russett, *Grasping the Democratic Peace*, p. 15.

8. Tocqueville, *Old Regime*, p. 206.

9. Muir, *Britain and Defeat of Napoleon*, p. 377.

10. Quoted in Kissinger, *World Restored*, p. 134.

11. Muir, *Britain and Defeat of Napoleon*, pp. 369–70.

12. Henry Houssaye, *1815: La première restauration, le retour de l'île d'Elbe, les Cent Jours* (Paris: Perrin, 1911), vol. 1, p. 459. *The Morning Post, The Observer,* and other papers were similar.

13. Ibid., pp. 459–63.

14. Wellington to Beresford, 7 August 1815, in Arthur Wellesley, Duke of Wellington, *Despatches, Correspondence, and Memoranda of Field Marshall Arthur, Duke of Wellington, K.G.* (London: J. Murray, 1867–80), vol. 8, p. 231.

15. Castlereagh to Liverpool, 3 August 1815, in Robert Stewart, Viscount Castlereagh, *Correspondence, Despatches, and Other Papers of Viscount Castlereagh, Second Marquess of Londonderry* (London: John Murray, 1853), Charles William Vane, ed., 3rd ser., military and diplomatic, vol. 2, p. 451.

16. As Kissinger puts it, not without admiration, "[I]t is symptomatic of his conception of statesmanship that Castlereagh, even at this moment when he stood practically alone, disdained concessions to popular opinion" (*World Restored*, p. 183).

17. FO 92/21, Castlereagh to Liverpool, 7 July 1815.

18. The definitive account is still Henry Houssaye, *1815: Waterloo* (Paris: Perrin, 1910), vol. 2, 67th ed.

19. Liverpool to Castlereagh, 30 June 1815, in Arthur Wellesley, Duke of Wellington, *Supplementary Despatches and Memoranda of Field Marshal Arthur, Duke of Wellington, K.G.* (London: John Murray, 1863), vol. 10, p. 631. This letter can also be found in Castlereagh, *Correspondence*, vol. 2, pp. 504–6, and in C. K. Webster, ed., *British Diplomacy, 1813–1815: Select Documents Dealing with the Reconstruction of Europe* (London: G. Bell, 1921), p. 340.

20. Even some first-rate authors have been tempted to read backward. For instance, Edward Vose Gulick, writing in the shadow of Nuremberg, says: "With regard to making examples of war criminals, he [Castlereagh] merely went through the motions" (Gulick, *Europe's Classical Balance of Power* [1955; reprint, New York: W. W. Norton, 1967], p. 273).

21. CAB 24/72, Committee of Enquiry into Breaches of the Laws of War, Interim Report, 13 January 1919, p. 29.

22. Paul Schroeder, a diplomatic historian, accuses Napoleon of waging a criminal foreign policy, but he too mostly focuses on Napoleon's destruction of the international order, not on specific atrocities (except the execution of the Duc d'Enghien) ("Napoleon's Foreign Policy: A Criminal Enterprise," *Journal of Military History*, vol. 54, no. 2 [April 1990], pp. 147–62). French forces were accused of massacring prisoners in Jaffa in 1799, but this incident does not come up in the 1815 debate over Napoleon's fate.

23. Liverpool to Castlereagh, 30 June 1815, in Wellington, *Supplementary Despatches*, vol. 10, p. 631.

24. FO 92/24, Castlereagh to Liverpool, 17 August 1815, 35e séance, annexe no. 1. Italics in original.

25. Wellington to Castlereagh, 11 August 1815, in Arthur Wellesley, Duke of Wellington, *The Dispatches of Field Marshal the Duke of Wellington, During His Various Campaigns in India, Denmark, Portugal, Spain, the Low Countries, and France, from 1799 to 1815* (London: John Murray, 1838), John Gurwood, ed., vol. 12, p. 599. See also Wellington to Castlereagh, 19 Sept 1815, in Wellington, *Dispatches*, vol. 12, pp. 638–39.

26. Convention of Paris, 3 July 1815, in Wellington, *Dispatches*, vol. 12, p. 542.

27. Liverpool to Castlereagh, 7 July 1815, in Castlereagh, *Correspondence*, vol. 2, p. 416.

28. See also Liverpool to Castlereagh, 11 August 1815, in ibid., p. 479; and Liverpool to Castlereagh, 28 July 1815, in ibid., pp. 446–47.

29. Liverpool to Castlereagh, 7 July 1815, in ibid., p. 416.

30. Ibid.

31. FO 92/21, Castlereagh to Liverpool, 10 July 1815.

32. C. K. Webster, *The Foreign Policy of Castlereagh, 1812–1815: Britain and the Reconstruction of Europe* (London: G. Bell, 1931), p. 464. See also "E.B." to Wellington, 8 July 1815, in Wellington, *Supplementary Despatches*, vol. 10, p. 676.

33. Castlereagh to Liverpool, 7 July 1815, in ibid., p. 676.

34. Castlereagh to Liverpool, 8 July 1815, in Castlereagh, *Correspondence*, vol. 2, p. 418.

35. Castlereagh to Liverpool, 3 August 1815, in ibid., p. 451.

36. FO 92/21, Castlereagh to Liverpool, 10 July 1815; FO 92/21, Castlereagh to Liverpool, 12 July 1815.

37. Metternich to Mary (daughter), 13 July 1815, in *Memoirs of Prince Metternich, 1773–1815* (New York: Charles Scribner's Sons, 1880), Mrs. Alexander Napier, trans., vol. 2, p. 610.

38. "E.B." to Wellington, 7 July 1815, in Wellington, *Supplementary Despatches*, vol. 10, p. 674. Castlereagh might have exaggerated Louis XVIII's popularity (FO 92/21, Castlereagh to Liverpool, 8 July 1815), but Metternich was more skeptical: "There were loud cries of 'Vive le Roi!' If the devil had appeared suddenly he would have been equally well received. Provided that a Frenchman can shout, he is content" (Metternich to Mary, 26 July 1815, in Metternich, *Memoirs*, p. 614).

39. Liverpool to Castlereagh, 15 July 1815, in Castlereagh, *Correspondence*, vol. 2, p. 431.

40. Ibid., p. 432.

41. FO 92/21, Castlereagh memorandum, 15 July 1815.

42. FO 92/21, Castlereagh to Liverpool, 17 July 1815, no. 13.

43. FO 92/21, Castlereagh to Liverpool, 17 July 1815, no. 14.

44. Joseph Fouché, *Memoirs of Joseph Fouché, Duke of Otranto, Minister of the General Police of France* (London: William W. Gibbings, 1892), p. 461.

45. FO 92/21, Castlereagh to Liverpool, 17 July 1815, no. 13.

46. FO 92/22, Castlereagh to Liverpool, 24 July 1815, no. 18.

47. Charles Maurice, Duc de Talleyrand-Périgord, *Mémoires 1754–1815* (Paris: Plon, 1982), p. 761.

48. Fouché, *Memoirs*, p. 467.

49. FO 92/22, Louis XVIII ordinance, 24 July 1815, enclosure to Castlereagh to Liverpool, 24 July 1815, no. 18.

50. Houssaye, *1815*, vol. 1, p. 313.

51. Talleyrand, *Mémoires*, p. 761.

52. A. Hilliard Atteridge, *The Bravest of the Brave* (London: Methuen, 1912), pp. 334–36.

53. Muir, *Britain and Defeat of Napoleon*, p. 367.

54. Liverpool to Canning, 4 August 1815, in Arthur Wellesley, Duke of Wellington, *Supplementary Despatches, Correspondence, and Memoranda of Field Marshal Arthur, Duke of Wellington, K.G.* (London: John Murray, 1864), vol. 11, p. 95.

55. Castlereagh to Liverpool, 3 August 1815, in Castlereagh, *Correspondence*, vol. 2, p. 451; Muir, *Britain and Defeat of Napoleon*, p. 367. A British Whig, Sir Robert Wilson, helped Lavalette escape, reflecting Whig shock at the death sentences.

56. See Atteridge, *Bravest of the Brave*; René Floriot, *Le procès du Maréchal Ney* (Paris: Hachette, 1955); and John Foster, *Napoleon's Marshal: The Life of Michel Ney* (New York: William Morrow, 1968).

57. Atteridge, *Bravest of the Brave*, pp. 342–48.

58. Harold Kurtz, *The Trial of Marshal Ney: His Last Years and Death* (New York: Knopf, 1957), pp. 312–13.

59. Atteridge, *Bravest of the Brave*, p. 369.

60. Castlereagh to Liverpool, 24 July 1815, in Castlereagh, *Correspondence*, vol. 2, p. 436. Their crime was treason against the French crown, not war crimes.

61. Castlereagh to Liverpool, 24 July 1815, in ibid., p. 436; Melville to Keith, 28 July 1815, in ibid., p. 444. Savary appears on the royal blacklist as Rovigo, his lordly title.

62. Savary to Romilly, 1 August 1815, in *Memoirs of the Life of Sir Samuel Romilly, Written by Himself; With a Selection from His Correspondence* (London: John Murray, 1841), vol. 2, pp. 379–83.

63. Maitland to Melville, 31 July 1815, in Romilly, *Memoirs*, p. 383.

64. Romilly, *Memoirs*, p. 386; CAB 24/85, Bellot appendix to Commission of Enquiry report.

65. J. G. Lockhart, *The Peacemakers 1814–1815* (London: Duckworth, 1932), p. 148.

66. Leo Tolstoy, *War and Peace* (Oxford: Oxford University Press, 1991), Louise Maude and Aylmer Maude, trans., p. 1.

67. Romilly, *Memoirs*, p. 379.

68. Liverpool to Castlereagh, 7 July 1815, in Wellington, *Supplementary Despatches*, vol. 10, p. 678.

69. Metternich to Mary, 13 July 1815, in Metternich, *Memoirs*, pp. 610–11.

70. See, for instance, Cathcart to Castlereagh, 21 June 1815, in Castlereagh, *Correspondence*, vol. 2, p. 382.

71. Baron von Müffling, *Passages from My Life; Together with Memoirs of the Campaign of 1813 and 1814* (London: Richard Bentley, 1853), Philip Yorke, ed., p. 269.

72. Gneisenau to Müffling, 29 June 1815, in ibid., p. 274. In 1804, much of Europe had been scandalized by the kidnapping and killing of the Duc d'Enghien, a Bourbon.

73. Gneisenau to Müffling, 27 June 1815, in ibid., pp. 272–73. On the March 1815 declaration outlawing Napoleon, see Enno E. Kraehe, *Metternich's German Policy: Volume II: The Congress of Vienna, 1814–1815* (Princeton: Princeton University Press, 1983), p. 330.

74. Kraehe, *Metternich's German Policy*, vol. 2, p. 330.

75. Müffling, *Passages*, p. 252.

76. Ibid., pp. 252–23.

77. Wellington to Stuart, 28 June 1815, in Wellington, *Dispatches*, vol. 12, p. 516. Blücher's name is omitted in this version, but is in Castlereagh, *Correspondence*, vol. 2, pp. 386–87. That version wrongly uses "Parisians" instead of "Prussians."

78. Gneisenau to Müffling, 29 June 1815, in Müffling, *Passages*, p. 275. Italics added.

79. Anecdotes and Conversations from Mr. Croker's Note Books, 26 October [1825], Croker Papers, i, pp. 327–28, in CAB 24/85, G.T. 7806, Bellot appendix, p. 369.

80. Kraehe, *Metternich's German Policy*, vol. 2, p. 330.

81. Liverpool to Castlereagh, 7 July 1815, in Castlereagh, *Correspondence*, vol. 2, pp. 416–17. "No chance of escape" might mean literally that: no chance of escaping from French jails, or of escaping another exile as he did Elba. Or it might mean no chance of acquittal.

82. FO 92/21, Castlereagh memorandum, 15 July 1815.

83. FO 92/21, Castlereagh to Liverpool, 17 July 1815, no. 13.

84. FO 92/21, Castlereagh to Liverpool, 12 July 1815.

85. FO 92/21, Castlereagh to Liverpool, 17 July 1815, no. 14.

86. Ibid.

87. Liverpool to Castlereagh, 21 July 1815, in Castlereagh, *Correspondence*, vol. 2, p. 434.

88. Liverpool to Castlereagh, 3 August 1815, in ibid., p. 453.

89. Romilly, *Memoirs*, p. 379.

90. Muir, *Britain and Defeat of Napoleon*, p. 368. In *Jane Doe* v. *Karadzic* and *Kadic* v. *Karadzic*, Karadzic was ordered to appear in a New York court or risk a massive default settlement in a civil case; he refused to come (Karadzic letter, author's files, 28 February 1997).

91. FO 92/22, 22e séance, annexe no. 56, 1 August 1815.

92. FO 92/24, Castlereagh to Liverpool, 24 August 1815, no. 38.

93. FO 92/24, Castlereagh to Liverpool, 17 August 1815, 35e séance, annexe no. 1. Italics in original.

94. FO 92/24, Castlereagh to Liverpool, 24 August 1815, no. 40.

95. Muir, *Britain and Defeat of Napoleon*, p. 371.

96. Hajo Holborn, *A History of Modern Germany 1648–1840* (New York: Knopf, 1964), pp. 387–88.

97. Ibid., pp. 393–98; James J. Sheehan, *German History 1770–1866* (Oxford: Clarendon Press, 1989), pp. 252–53, 310.

98. Sheehan, *German History*, pp. 291, 312; Holborn, *Modern Germany*, p. 395.

99. Kissinger, *World Restored*, p. 139.

100. Gneisenau to Müffling, 27 June 1815, in Müffling, *Passages*, p. 273.

101. Atteridge, *Bravest of the Brave*, p. 329.

102. Houssaye, *1815*, vol. 1, pp. 458–59.

103. Liverpool to Castlereagh, 28 July 1815, in Castlereagh, *Correspondence*, vol. 2, p. 445.

104. Müffling, *Passages*, pp. 267–68.

105. FO 92/21, Castlereagh to Liverpool, 8 July 1815.

106. FO 92/21, Müffling to Wellington, 14 July 1815.

107. Wellington to Castlereagh, 14 July 1815, in Wellington, *Dispatches*, vol. 12, p. 558.

108. FO 92/21, Castlereagh memorandum, 15 July 1815.

109. In A.J.P. Taylor, *Bismarck: The Man and Statesman* (New York: Knopf, 1955), pp. 86–87, 124. See Moritz Busch, *Our Chancellor* (New York: Scribner's Sons, 1884), vol. 1, William Beatty-Kingston, trans., p. 99.

110. During World War II, Churchill publicly professed not to see Napoleon's case as even relevant. Asked about it in Parliament in September 1944, he replied: "I do not see that it occurs at all. Napoleon gave himself up, and threw himself upon the mercy of Britain, and he was kept for the rest of his life as a prisoner of State." (FO 371/39003/C13199.) For his part, Chief Justice Stone in 1945 wrote, of Nuremberg, "The best that can be said for it is that it is a political act of the victorious States which may be morally right, as was the sequestration of Napoleon about 1815. But the allies in that day did not feel it necessary to justify it by an appeal to nonexistent legal principles" (Mason, *Harlan Fiske Stone*, p. 715).

111. CAB 23/43, Imperial War Cabinet 37, 20 November 1918, noon, p. 11. Lloyd George also used the case of Napoleon as a way of insulting Wilhelm II: "There is no

legend you can create about a creature of this kind. Napoleon fought; he was actually under fire; and he showed great talent and power which won the admiration of the world, but the ex-Kaiser is a poor wretched thing who never showed any strength of character or any brilliancy of mind, and I do not believe anything could create a legend for him or for that poor miserable creature of a son." (Ibid., p. 9.)

CHAPTER THREE
LEIPZIG

1. My thinking, and the shape of this chapter, has been much influenced by a superb history: James F. Willis, *Prologue to Nuremberg: The Politics and Diplomacy of Punishing War Criminals of the First World War* (Westport, Conn.: Greenwood, 1982). This narrative follows his version, which should stand as the standard account. Still, I have done my own research in British, French, and American records—not because of any quibbles with Willis's version, but because documents that serve as proof for me may not have been part of Willis's own research agenda.

2. CAB 66/19, Eden memorandum, 5 October 1941, W.P. (41) 233. See also CAB 66/25, Eden memorandum, 22 June 1942, W.P. (42) 264.

3. Henry Morgenthau Jr., *Morgenthau Diary—Germany* (Washington, D.C.: GPO, 1967), vol. 1, p. 487.

4. Morgenthau to Truman, 29 May 1945, in *Morgenthau Diary*, vol. 2, pp. 1543–44.

5. Marc Ferro, *The Great War 1914–1918* (London: Routledge and Kegan Paul, 1973), Nicole Stone, trans., p. 227. Ferro puts France's war dead at 1.35 million; Lloyd George and Eugen Weber put it at 1.4 million (Weber, *The Hollow Years: France in the 1830s* [New York: Norton, 1994], p. 11). John Keegan has two million (*The First World War* [New York: Knopf, 1999], pp. 5–6).

6. In this book, I use "legalism" to mean the belief that war criminals should be put on trial; but here, referring to Wilson, it means a broader sense that laws ought to govern actions. The meaning should be clear from context.

7. It would make my argument neater if Wilson had joined Lloyd George and Clemenceau wholeheartedly. But whatever one thinks of the wisdom or jurisprudence of Allied and American efforts after the Great War, they still stand as a testament to the enduring power of legalist ideas.

8. CAB 66/25, law officers' annex to Eden memorandum, 22 June 1942, W.P. (42) 264.

9. "Winning This War," 6 May 1916 speech, in Lloyd George, *The Great Crusade: Extracts from Speeches Delivered during the War* (New York: George H. Doran, 1918), p. 23.

10. Willis, *Prologue*, p. 12; Herbert Henry Asquith, *Memories and Reflections 1852–1927* (Boston: Little, Brown, 1928), vol. 2, p. 48.

11. Ferro, *Great War*, p. 227.

12. Asquith, *Memories and Reflections*, vol. 2, p. 67.

13. Willis, *Prologue*, pp. 16–17.

14. In David Lloyd George, *War Memoirs of David Lloyd George: 1918* (Boston: Little, Brown, 1937), vol. 6, p. 229.

15. Asquith, *Memories and Reflections*, vol. 2, p. 64.

16. FO 383/32/38804, Greene to Foreign Office, 29 March 1915.

17. FO 383/32/45699, Jagow to Grey, 16 April 1915 (via U.S. embassy).

18. FO 383/61/65321, Gerard to Page, 17 May 1915.

19. Willis, *Prologue*, p. 20.

20. FO 383/32/45699, filed 17 April 1915.

21. Blanche E. C. Dugdale, *Arthur James Balfour 1906–1930* (New York: G. P. Putnam's Sons, 1937), pp. 96–100. See also Asquith, *Memories and Reflections*, vol. 2, pp. 123–24.

22. See Gordon A. Craig, *Germany 1866–1945* (New York: Oxford University Press, 1980), pp. 369–70. For Britain's indignant reaction to the *Lusitania* sinking, see Page to Bryan, 8 May 1915, *FRUS: 1915 Supplement: The World War* (Washington, D.C.: GPO, 1928), p. 385.

23. FO 383/61/74605, 8 June 1915.

24. In Harold Nicolson, *King George the Fifth: His Life and Reign* (London: Constable, 1952), p. 273.

25. FO 383/61/76338, Grey to Page, 12 June 1915.

26. FO 383/61/77744, 14 June 1915.

27. In FO 383/61/76883, 9 June 1915.

28. Charles Hobhouse, *Inside Asquith's Cabinet: From the Diaries of Charles Hobhouse* (London: John Murray, 1977), Edward David, ed., p. 238.

29. Frances Stevenson, *Lloyd George: A Diary* (London: Hutchinson, 1971), A.J.P. Taylor, ed., p. 46.

30. Willis, *Prologue*, pp. 27–28.

31. Doris Kearns Goodwin, *No Ordinary Time* (New York: Simon and Schuster, 1994), p. 73.

32. FO 383/195/140584, admiralty to Foreign Office, 18 July 1916; FO 383/195/147519, Maxse to Foreign Office, 28 July 1916.

33. FO 383/195/149202, Grey to Laughlin, 7 August 1916.

34. FO 383/195/154624, 2 August 1918, or FO 383/195/156104, 7 August 1916, for instance.

35. See, for instance, FO 383/195/149910, FO 383/195/150468, FO 383/195/150572, FO 383/195/153003, and FO 383/195/162678.

36. "The Kaiser's Murder List," *Weekly Dispatch*, 30 July 1916; in FO 383/195/150473.

37. House of Commons, 31 July 1916, pp. 2069–70; in FO 383/195/150417, 31 July 1916.

38. FO 383/195/151547, Grey to Bertie and Buchanan, 2 August 1916.

39. FO 383/195/156595, Buchanan to Grey, 7 August 1916; FO 383/195/157823, Granville to Grey, 9 August 1916.

40. Willis, *Prologue*, p. 33.

41. FO 383/195/165378, 18 August 1916.

42. Willis, *Prologue*, p. 35.

43. In Lloyd George, *War Memoirs*, vol. 6, p. 229.

44. G.T. 5928, Prisoners of War, in FO 383/474/115077, 10 October 1918. See also CAB 23/8, War Cabinet 484 and Imperial War Cabinet 35, 11 October 1918, 4 P.M.; FO 383/474/115112, 9 October 1918 meeting; and FO 383/474/115781, 17 October 1918 meeting.

45. In Lloyd George, *War Memoirs*, vol. 6, p. 261.

46. Ibid., pp. 258–59.

47. CAB 23/8, War Cabinet 484 and Imperial War Cabinet 35, 11 October 1918, 4 P.M.

48. Ibid. See also FO 383/474/115726.

49. Lloyd George, *War Memoirs*, vol. 6, pp. 384–85. The armistice is on pp. 381–95.

50. CAB 23/8, War Cabinet 488, 17 October 1918, 11:30 A.M.

51. CAB 23/14, War Cabinet 494A, 31 October 1918, noon, p. 10.

52. FO 371/3227/207705, Balfour to Townley, 14 December 1918. On Wilhelm II's border crossing, see Virginia Cowles, *The Kaiser* (New York: Harper and Row, 1963), p. 405.

53. Sous-série Allemagne, vol. 25, Allizé to Foreign Ministry, 12 November 1918.

54. David Lloyd George, *Memoirs of the Peace Conference* (New Haven: Yale University Press, 1939), vol. 1, pp. 54–55.

55. Ibid., p. 55. For public outcry, see FO 371/3227/213745, 31 December 1918.

56. CAB 23/43, Imperial War Cabinet 37, 20 November 1918, noon, p. 6. Italics added.

57. Ibid.

58. Asquith, *Memories and Reflections*, vol. 2, p. 84.

59. CAB 23/43, Imperial War Cabinet 37, 20 November 1918, noon, p. 7. Italics added.

60. Ibid.

61. CAB 23/43, Imperial War Cabinet 37, 20 November 1918, noon, pp. 7–8.

62. Ibid., p. 8. Where the legal status of the crime was less dubious, Hughes was stoutly legalist.

63. Ibid.

64. Ibid.

65. CAB 23/43, Imperial War Cabinet 37, 20 November 1918, noon, p. 9.

66. Ibid.

67. CAB 23/43, Imperial War Cabinet 37, 20 November 1918, noon, p. 10.

68. Ibid.

69. CAB 23/43, Imperial War Cabinet 37, 20 November 1918, noon, pp. 10–11.

70. Ibid., pp. 10–12.

71. Lloyd George, *Memoirs of the Peace Conference*, vol. 1, p. 65.

72. CAB 23/43, Imperial War Cabinet 37, 20 November 1918, noon, p. 12. The committee had looked at "framing charges against the ex-Emperor of Germany . . . [f]or the crime against humanity of having caused the war" and for wartime violations of international law.

73. See CAB 24/72, Committee of Enquiry into Breaches of the Laws of War, *Interim Report*, 13 January 1919. The committee pointed out that Napoleon III had been held as a prisoner of war in 1870; that German military manuals allowed for the possibility that a sovereign might be a prisoner of war; and that any prisoner of war could be tried for war crimes. One of the precedents referred to was the trials, in Transvaal and Orange Free State courts, of Boers accused of war crimes against British soldiers in the course of the Boer War. Foreshadowing Leipzig, they were acquitted.

74. CAB 23/43, Imperial War Cabinet 39, 28 November 1918, 11:45 A.M., pp. 2–3.

75. Smith was not just taking a page out of Burke, but also out of Kant: "[U]nder a nonrepublican constitution, where subjects are not citizens, the easiest thing in the world to do is to declare war. Here the ruler is not a fellow citizen, but the nation's owner, and war does not affect his table, his hunt, his places of pleasure, his court festivals, and so on. Thus, he can decide to go to war for the most meaningless of reasons, as if it were a kind of pleasure party" (*Perpetual Peace*, p. 113).

76. CAB 23/43, Imperial War Cabinet 39, 28 November 1918, 11:45 a.m., pp. 3–4. Italics added.

77. Ibid., pp. 4–5.

78. Ibid., p. 5.

79. Cowles, *Kaiser*, p. 409.

80. Lloyd George, *War Memoirs*, vol. 6, p. 214. See also K. G. Robbins, "Public Opinion, the Press and Pressure Groups," in F. H. Hinsley, ed., *British Foreign Policy under Sir Edward Grey* (Cambridge: Cambridge University Press, 1977), pp. 70–88, and Ebba Dahlin, *French and German Public Opinion on Declared War Aims, 1914–1918* (Stanford: Stanford University Press, 1933), pp. 9–12.

81. CAB 23/43, Imperial War Cabinet 39, 28 November 1918, 11:45 A.M., p. 6.

82. Lloyd George, *Memoirs of the Peace Conference*, vol. 1, p. 109. Lloyd George denied ever using the slogan, "Hang the kaiser," which became notorious.

83. Willis, *Prologue*, p. 59.

84. Ibid., p. 61.

85. CAB 28/5, I.C.-98, Allied conversation, London, 2 December 1918, 11 A.M., p. 6.

86. Ibid., p. 5.

87. Ibid., p. 7.

88. Ibid.

89. CAB 28/5, I.C.-99, Allied conversation, London, 2 December 1918, 4 P.M., pp. 3–4.

90. Willis, *Prologue*, p. 68.

91. FO 371/4271/9019, 13 January 1919.

92. FO 371/4271/62362, Commission on the Responsibility of the Authors of the War and on the Enforcement of Penalties (hereafter CRAWEP), report to preliminary peace conference, 29 March 1919. For the French version, see série Paix 1914–20, vol. 64, "Rapport présenté à la Conférence des Préliminaires de Paix par la Commission des Responsabilitiés des Auteurs de la Guerre et Sanctions," 29 March 1919.

93. CRAWEP third meeting, 12 March 1919, 11 A.M., in R.G. 256, M-820, roll 141, vol. 115, 181.1201/3.

94. FO 371/4271/62362, CRAWEP report, 29 March 1919, pp. 11–14, 19. Big countries, like America and Italy, got three judges; small ones, like Belgium and Czechoslovakia, got one.

95. Brockdorff-Rantzau to Clemenceau, 29 May 1919, *FRUS: 1919: The Paris Peace Conference* (Washington, D.C.: GPO, 1946), vol. 6, p. 875; Clemenceau to Brockdorff-Rantzau, 16 June 1919, in ibid., p. 926.

96. For a famous critique, see John Maynard Keynes, *The Economic Consequences of the Peace* (London: Macmillan, 1920).

97. A first draft had arraigned Wilhelm II "not for an offence against criminal law, but for a supreme offence against international morality and the sanctity of treaties."

Lloyd George had complained that this made it sound as if Wilhelm II had not broken any criminal law, and thus, with Wilson's approval, changed it to the wording used in the treaty (Wilson, Lloyd George, and Clemenceau meeting, 1 May 1919, *FRUS: 1919: The Paris Peace Conference* [Washington, D.C.: GPO, 1946], vol. 5, p. 389).

98. Text in Willis, *Prologue*, pp. 177–78.

99. Ibid, p. 85; Craig, *Germany*, pp. 425–26.

100. In Willis, *Prologue*, p. 99.

101. FO 371/4271/97114, Robertson to Foreign Office, 2 July 1919.

102. FO 371/4271/92228, Curzon to Townley, 19 June 1919; FO 371/4292/98689, Curzon to Derby, 4 July 1919.

103. FO 371/4292/98689, Curzon to Derby, 4 July 1919.

104. Bethmann Hollweg to Clemenceau, 25 June 1919, in FO 371/4271/97972 and in *FRUS: 1919: Peace Conference*, vol. 6, pp. 756–57; Allied meeting, 28 June 1919, in ibid., pp. 751–52.

105. FO 371/4271/96763, 30 June 1919.

106. See FO 371/4274/201293, 3 June 1920. Lloyd George had proposed trying Wilhelm II in England in June 1919, to no noticeable enthusiasm whatsoever from Clemenceau (Allied meeting, 26 June 1919, *FRUS: 1919: Peace Conference*, vol. 6, p. 701).

107. CAB 23/11, War Cabinet 598, 23 July 1919, noon, p. 4. On interning Wilhelm II in Dover Castle, see Anglo-French conference, London, 13 December 1919, 3:30 P.M., *Documents on British Foreign Policy: 1919*, p. 774.

108. FO 371/4272/172018; Clemenceau to Dutch queen, 15 January 1920, *FRUS: 1919: The Paris Peace Conference* (Washington, D.C.: GPO, 1946), vol. 9, pp. 887–88.

109. FO 371/4272/172018, Graham to Foreign Office, 19 January 1920.

110. FO 371/4272/173085, Graham to Foreign Office, 23 January 1920.

111. FO 371/4272/175168, Hardinge to Graham, 28 January 1920.

112. FO 371/4272/175736, Graham to Curzon, 3 February 1920.

113. See FO 371/8755/C19278/347/18, memorandum on Dutch negotiations over ex-kaiser, 12 November 1923.

114. FO 371/4272/173512, Foreign Office (for Lloyd George) to Derby, 30 January 1920.

115. FO 371/4272/175501, Foreign Office to Graham, 31 January 1920.

116. FO 371/4272/176756, Graham to Foreign Office, 6 February 1920; FO 371/4273/184757, Graham to Curzon, 9 March 1920.

117. FO 371/4273/182006, Graham to Curzon, 27 February 1920.

118. FO 371/4273/183163, Graham to Foreign Office, 4 March 1920.

119. FO 371/4274/198732, Graham to Curzon, 16 May 1920.

120. FO 371/4271/114096, Malcolm to Balfour, 5 August 1919.

121. FO 371/4271/21235, 1 August 1919.

122. FO 371/4271/114350, 9 August 1919.

123. FO 371/4274/200596, Villiers to Curzon, 26 May 1920.

124. British, French, and Italian meeting, Paris, 15 January 1920, *Documents on British Foreign Policy: 1919*, p. 886.

125. Anglo-French conference, London, 13 December 1919, 11 A.M., in ibid., pp. 756–57.

126. Allies and America meeting, Paris, 20 January 1920, 10:30 A.M., in ibid., p. 928. For another set of minutes for the same meeting, see *FRUS: 1919: Peace Conference*, vol. 9, pp. 905–6.

127. Willis, *Prologue*, p. 128.

128. FO 371/4273/185867.

129. Five Great Powers meeting, 15 September 1919, *FRUS: 1919: The Paris Peace Conference* (Washington, D.C.: GPO, 1946), vol. 8, p. 214.

130. Anglo-French conference, London, 13 December 1919, 11 A.M., *Documents on British Foreign Policy: 1919*, pp. 756–57.

131. British, French, and Italian delegations meeting, Paris, 15 January 1920, ibid., p. 886.

132. FO 371/4271/11529, Balfour to Lloyd George, 11 August 1919. British intelligence thought that Erzberger's government could endure it (FO 371/4271/116306, Malcolm to director of military intelligence, 14 August 1919).

133. FO 371/4271/11529, Balfour to Lloyd George, 11 August 1919.

134. FO 371/4271/11529, Lloyd George to Balfour, 13 August 1919.

135. FO 371/4272/173894, Kilmarnock to Foreign Office, 26 January 1920. Kilmarnock's enthusiasm for the entire war crimes project may be judged by his habit of putting the words "war criminals" in quotations.

136. FO 371/4272/173512, Derby to Curzon, 26 January 1920.

137. FO 371/4272/174733, Lersner to Millerand, 25 January 1920.

138. FO 371/4272/176123, Derby to Foreign Office, 4 February 1920. The note had to be delivered by the French chargé d'affaires in Berlin. See also CAB 23/20, Cabinet 9 (2C), 5 February 1920, noon.

139. FO 371/4272/176446, British embassy in Berlin to War Office, 5 February 1920.

140. FO 371/4272/176737, Kilmarnock to Foreign Office, 5 February 1920. The time had come, Kilmarnock wrote, for a decision with "stupendous consequences": Would the British government now flatten Germany, or try to let it rebuild itself even if that meant backing off on war criminals? (FO 371/4272/178427, Kilmarnock to Curzon, 10 February 1920.)

141. CAB 23/20, Conference of Ministers, 25 February 1920.

142. FO 371/4272/174733, Lersner to Millerand, 25 January 1920; sous-série Allemagne, vol. 571, Lersner to Millerand, 25 January 1920. See also sous-série Allemagne, vol. 571, note attached to Lersner to Millerand, 25 January 1920.

143. Sous-série Allemagne, vol. 571, Réponse du Conseil Supreme des Alliés aux Observations des Allemands, 14 February 1920. See FO 371/7529/C16860, Negotiations respecting Trial of War Criminals under Articles 228 to 230 of Treaty of Versailles.

144. FO 371/4272/178427, Lloyd George, "Sanctions: Reply to the German Note of January 25th 1920," 13 February 1920.

145. Sous-série Allemagne, vol. 571, Millerand to Lersner, 7 May 1920; first Allied list for Leipzig, filed as an annex to sous-série Allemagne, vol. 571, Note sur la question des coupables a livrer par l'Allemagne, Secrétariat Général, Conference de la Paix, n.d.

146. FO 371/4273/182435, 3 March 1920.

147. FO 371/5861/C-9216, German War Criminals, 4 May 1921. See also FO 371/4731/C9103, Curzon to Derby, 20 October 1920.

148. FO 371/4731/C4965/13/18, Rolin-Jaequemyns to Foreign Office, 9 July 1920.

149. FO 371/5860/C1186, 19 January 1921.

150. FO 371/5862/C11245, Woods note, 26 May 1921.

151. Sous-série Allemagne, vol. 575, Neton to Foreign Ministry, 26 July 1921.

152. FO 371/5864/C22014, 19 November 1921.

153. FO 371/5863/C15779, Leipzig report, 28 July 1921.

154. Ibid.

155. FO 371/7529/C17096, Allied-German negotiations on war criminals, 7 January 1922.

156. FO 371/7529/C17096, 9 December 1922.

157. CAB 24/125, C.P.-3006, Pollock memorandum on Leipzig trials, 2 June 1921.

158. FO 371/5862/C11430, 2 June 1921.

159. Willis, *Prologue*, pp. 134–35.

160. FO 371/5863/C14050, 9 July 1921.

161. FO 371/5864/C20103, 19 October 1921.

162. FO 371/5864/C20103, 20 October 1921.

163. FO 371/7529/C4338, 23 March 1922.

164. FO 371/7529/C7164/555/18, Curzon to Hardinge, 19 May 1922.

165. Série Europe 1918–1929, sous-série Allemagne, vol. 577, St.-Aulaire to Poincaré, 31 March 1922.

166. FO 371/7529/C17096, 9 December 1922.

167. W. M. Jordan, *Great Britain, France, and the German Problem 1918–1939: A Study of Anglo-French Relations in the Making and Maintenance of the Versailles Settlement* (Oxford: Oxford University Press, 1943), pp. 5–6.

168. French archival records on this period are less comprehensive and candid than those in Britain, particularly about internal debates. This section is thus of necessity somewhat more tentative than the preceding one. My analysis is also supported—and supplemented—by Willis, *Prologue.*

169. Pierre Miquel, *La paix de Versailles et l'opinion publique française* (Paris: Flammarion, 1972), p. 239.

170. Willis, *Prologue*, p. 14.

171. Ibid., pp. 14–15.

172. FO 383/195/177588, Cambon to Grey, 6 September 1916.

173. Willis, *Prologue*, p. 33.

174. Série Paix 1914–1920, vol. 64, Foreign Ministry minute, 4 August 1916.

175. Série Paix 1914–1920, vol. 64, Project de convention entre la France et la Grande-Bretagne, 5 August 1916. For a later draft, see série Paix 1914–1920, vol. 64, Projet de convention pour assurer le châtiment des crimes ennemis, 2 May 1917.

176. Lloyd George, *War Memoirs*, vol. 6, p. 258.

177. Série Paix 1914–1920, vol. 64, Foch to Clemenceau, 6 September 1918.

178. Lloyd George, *Memoirs of the Peace Conference*, vol. 1, p. 54. See also Earl of Ronaldshay, *The Life of Lord Curzon* (London: Ernest Benn, 1928), vol. 3, pp. 226–27.

179. CAB 23/7, War Cabinet 475, 20 September 1918, p. 5. See also série Paix 1914–1920, vol. 64, Bertie to Foreign Ministry, 18 November 1918.

180. CAB 23/43, Imperial War Cabinet 37, 20 November 1918, noon, p. 10.

181. Miquel, *L'opinion publique française*, pp. 238–39.

182. Lloyd George, *Memoirs of the Peace Conference*, vol. 1, p. 55.

183. CAB 23/43, Imperial War Cabinet 37, 20 November 1918, noon, p. 6.

184. CAB 28/5, I.C.-98, Allied conversation, London, 2 December 1918, 11 A.M., p. 5.

185. Bonar Law said there was "no doubt that public sentiment was with M. Clemenceau" (ibid).

186. CAB 28/5, I.C.-98, Allied conversation, London, 2 December 1918, 11 A.M., p. 7.

187. CAB 28/5, I.C.-99, Allied conversation, London, 2 December 1918, 4 P.M., p. 3.

188. Ibid.

189. CRAWEP third meeting, 12 March 1919, 11 A.M., in R.G. 256, M-820, roll 141, vol. 115, 181.1201/3. See also CRAWEP meeting, 25 February 1919, 11 A.M., in R.G. 256, M-820, roll 144, vol. 118, 181.12301/4.

190. Allied meeting, 25 June 1919, *FRUS: 1919: Peace Conference*, vol. 6, p. 670.

191. Ibid., p. 677.

192. Sous-série Allemagne, vol. 26, Allied declaration (signed Clemenceau), 27 June 1918.

193. Sous-série Allemagne, vol. 26, Réponse à la Holland (Extradition de l'ex-Empereur), 14 February 1920. See also série Paix 1914–1920, vol. 66, Réponse à la Holland, 2 February 1920.

194. Série Paix 1914–1920, vol. 66 (microfilm), Benoist to Foreign Ministry, 1 February 1920.

195. Ibid.

196. Série Paix 1914–1920, vol. 66, Laroche to embassies, 20 February 1920.

197. CAB 23/43, Imperial War Cabinet 37, 20 November 1918, noon, p. 6.

198. Série Paix 1914–1920, vol. 66, Millerand note, 9 March 1920.

199. See Jordan, *German Problem*, pp. 66–69; and Édouard Bonnefous, *Histoire politique de la Troisième République: L'Après-guerre, 1919–1924* (Paris: Presses Universitaires de France, 1968).

200. Sous-série Allemagne, vol. 571, Lefèvre to Millerand, 13 January 1921.

201. Anglo-French conference, London, 13 December 1919, 11 A.M., *Documents on British Foreign Policy: 1919*, pp. 756–57.

202. Ibid.

203. British, French, and Italian delegations meeting, Paris, 15 January 1920, in Anglo-French conference, London, 13 December 1919, 11 A.M., *Documents on British Foreign Policy: 1919*, p. 887. See also Five Great Powers meeting, 16 January 1920, *FRUS: 1919: Peace Conference*, vol. 9, p. 863.

204. CAB 23/20, Cabinet 9 (2C), 5 February 1920, noon; série Paix 1914–1920, vol. 64, L'Extradition, 30 January 1920.

205. In FO 371/4272/177849, Grahame to Foreign Office, 9 February 1920.

206. For a draft, see série Paix 1914–1920, vol. 66, projet, 2 February 1920.

207. Sous-série Allemagne, vol. 571, Millerand to Lersner, 3 February 1920.

208. Jordan, *German Problem*, p. 72.

209. Sous-série Allemagne, vol. 571, Lefèvre to Millerand, 13 January 1921.

210. Sous-série Allemagne, vol. 574, ligue Soutien Sarthois to Foreign Ministry, 24 June 1921.

211. Sous-série Allemagne, vol. 575, Allied conference, Paris, 12 August 1921, pp. 12–14.

212. Sous-série Allemagne, vol. 574, Matter note, 6 July 1921.

213. Ibid.

214. Sous-série Allemagne, vol. 574, Samalens to Foreign Ministry, 5 July 1921. "In a court of any other country than Germany STENGER couldn't have escaped conviction," editorialized *The New York Times*. "Thus the German mentality is shown to be unaltered: and the proposed punishment of war criminals is a farce" ("Convicting Itself," *New York Times*, 9 July 1921; in sous-série Allemagne, vol. 575).

215. Sous-série Allemagne, vol. 574, Samalens to Foreign Ministry, 6 July 1921.

216. Sous-série Allemagne, vol. 574, Samalens to Foreign Ministry, 7 July 1921.

217. Sous-série Allemagne, vol. 574, Briand to Laurent, 7 July 1921.

218. Sous-série Allemagne, vol. 574, Samalens to Foreign Ministry, 9 July 1921. See sous-série Allemagne, vol. 575, Matter to Briand, 12 July 1921.

219. Sous-série Allemagne, vol. 575, Matter, Leroux, and Manneville to Briand, 12 July 1921.

220. Sous-série Allemagne, vol. 574, Briand to French ambassadors in London and Brussels, 7 July 1921.

221. Sous-série Allemagne, vol. 574, Montille to Foreign Ministry, 10 July 1921.

222. Sous-série Allemagne, vol. 575, Laurent to Foreign Ministry, 11 July 1921.

223. Sous-série Allemagne, vol. 575, Samalens to Foreign Ministry, 11 July 1921.

224. FO 371/5863/C14493, Cheetham to Curzon, 15 July 1921.

225. Sous-série Allemagne, vol. 575, Laurent to Foreign Ministry, 13 July 1921. See also FO 371/5863/C14316, D'Abernon to Foreign Office, 13 July 1921.

226. Sous-série Allemagne, vol. 575, Allied conference, Paris, 12 August 1921, pp. 16–17. See also sous-série Allemagne, vol. 575, Quai d'Orsay meeting, 13 August 1921, 10:30 A.M.

227. Série Paix 1914–1920, vol. 64, Project de convention entre la France et la Grande-Bretagne, 5 August 1916.

228. Sous-série Allemagne, vol. 576, Instructions à donner au délégués français à la Commission des coupables, 15 December 1921.

229. Sous-série Allemagne, vol. 576, Souvenez-vous to Briand, 9 December 1921.

230. Sous-série Allemagne, vol. 575, Allied conference, Paris, 12 August 1921, pp. 16–17.

231. See, for instance, ibid., p. 17; sous-série Allemagne, vol. 576, Instructions à donner au délégués français à la Commission des coupables, 15 December 1921.

232. Sous-série Allemagne, vol. 571, 3 June 1920, Göppert to Millerand; judgment copied in sous-série Allemagne, vol. 571, Bonnevay to Foreign Ministry, 24 February 1921.

233. See sous-série Allemagne, vol. 571, 12 March 1921.

234. Sous-série Allemagne, vol. 576, Note: Jugement des coupables de guerre, 20 October 1921.

235. Sous-série Allemagne, vol. 576, Briand statement, 21 October 1921.

236. Sous-série Allemagne, vol. 576, verdicts throughout; FO 371/7529/C11741, Pollock to Foreign Office, 15 August 1922.

237. Sous-série Allemagne, vol. 577, Bonnevay to Briand, 9 January 1922.

238. Sous-série Allemagne, vol. 577, Laurent to Foreign Ministry, 15 January 1922.

239. Sous-série Allemagne, vol. 578, Poincaré to Margerie, 3 June 1922.

240. Sous-série Allemagne, vol. 580, Poincaré to Maginot, 14 October 1922.

241. Sous-série Allemagne, vol. 577, Laurent to Foreign Ministry, 10 February 1922.

242. Sous-série Allemagne, vol. 578, Poincaré to Margerie, 3 June 1922.

243. Jordan, *German Problem*, pp. 70–71. The French troops withdrew on May 17, 1920, once German forces had pulled out.

244. Ibid., p. 77.

245. Sous-série Allemagne, vol. 577, instructions to Laurent, 7 February 1922; sous-série Allemagne, vol. 577, Poincaré to St.-Aulaire, 24 March 1922.

246. FO 371/7529/C7164/555/18, Curzon to Hardinge, 19 May 1922.

247. Série Europe 1918–1929, sous-série Allemagne, vol. 577, St.-Aulaire to Poincaré, 31 March 1922.

248. Sous-série Allemagne, vol. 28, Poincaré to London, Rome and Brussels, 13 November 1923. At the same time, Poincaré asked Foch and the ministers of war and the navy to explore France's military options, including viable ones if France had to act alone (sous-série Allemagne, vol. 28, Poincaré note, 13 November 1923).

249. Sous-série Allemagne, vol. 28, Crewe statement, 19 November 1923; sous-série Allemagne, vol. 580, Crewe memorandum, 18 November 1923; sous-série Allemagne, vol. 580, Poincaré to Maginot, 15 November 1923.

250. Willis, *Prologue*, p. 141.

251. Ferro, *Great War*, p. 227.

252. Ernest R. May, *The World War and American Isolation 1914–1917* (Cambridge, Mass.: Harvard University Press, 1959), pp. 40–41. See also Arthur S. Link, *Wilson* (Princeton: Princeton University Press, 1960, 1961, 1965), vols. 3–5.

253. Lansing to Wilson, 21 November 1916, *FRUS: The Lansing Papers 1914–1920* (Washington, D.C.: U.S. GPO, 1939), vol. 1, p. 43.

254. May, *American Isolation*, p. 147.

255. Lansing to Bryan, 28 August 1914, *FRUS: Lansing Papers*, vol. 1, p. 29.

256. Wilson to Bryan, 4 September 1914, ibid., p. 33.

257. Wilson to Lansing, 17 June 1915, ibid., p. 38.

258. Lansing to Wilson, 21 September 1916, ibid., p. 569.

259. See Jan van der Hoeven Leonhard, *Les Déportations belges: À la lumière des documents allemands* (Harlem: Tjeenk Willink, 1931).

260. Lansing to Grew, 29 November 1916, *FRUS: 1916 Supplement: The World War* (Washington, D.C.: GPO, 1929), p. 71.

261. Lansing to Wilson, 21 November 1916, *FRUS: Lansing Papers*, vol. 1, pp. 43–44. Lansing thought the French deportations might be justified by "military expediency."

262. May, *American Isolation*, pp. 179–84.

263. In Lansing to Gerard, 19 October 1914, *FRUS: Lansing Papers*, vol. 1, p. 35.

264. Lansing to Wilson, 23 November 1914, ibid., pp. 35–37; Wilson to Lansing, 26 November 1914, ibid., p. 37. When condemning war crimes was not at odds with neutrality and he could speak for his own conscience, Lansing had less hesitation. He urged protests to Germany, Britain, and France for the "reprehensible and utterly indefensible" use of mines on the high seas (Lansing to Bryan, 18 February 1915, ibid., pp. 37–38). America did lodge one complaint against the Allies: in October

1915, America denounced the British blockade as a violation of international law (May, *American Isolation*, pp. 325–27).

265. Wilson to Lansing, 27 November 1916, *FRUS: Lansing Papers*, vol. 1, p. 44.

266. May, *American Isolation*, p. 171; Thomas J. Knock, *To End All Wars: Woodrow Wilson and the Quest for a New World Order* (Princeton: Princeton University Press, 1992), p. 61.

267. Lansing to Wilson, 21 September 1916, *FRUS: Lansing Papers*, vol. 1, pp. 569–70; Wilson to Lansing, 29 September 1916, ibid., pp. 570–71; Lansing to Wilson, 2 October 1916, ibid., pp. 571–72; Knock, *To End All Wars*, pp. 60–61.

268. Ibid.; May, *American Isolation*, pp. 179–80.

269. See Gerard to Lansing, 3 May 1916, *FRUS: 1916 Supplement*, p. 253.

270. Lansing on Bernstorff conversation, 20 April 1916, *FRUS: Lansing Papers*, vol. 1, p. 556.

271. Knock, *To End All Wars*, pp. 152–53. On public opinion, see ibid., pp. 170–75, and Daniel M. Smith, *Robert Lansing and American Neutrality 1914–1917* (Berkeley: University of California Press, 1958), pp. 83–131.

272. May, *American Isolation*, pp. 179–80; Knock, *To End All Wars*, pp. 60–61.

273. May, *American Isolation*, p. 181.

274. Morgenthau Sr., *Ambassador Morgenthau's Story*, p. 398.

275. See May, *American Isolation*, pp. 153–55.

276. Bryan to Gerard, 13 May 1915, *FRUS: 1915 Supplement*, pp. 393–96. For the unrepentant German reply, blaming the steamer company for taking the risk, see Jagow to Gerard, 28 May 1915, ibid., pp. 419–21. For further American-German disputes over liability for the *Lusitania* sinking, see, for instance, Lansing to Wilson, 24 January 1916, *FRUS: Lansing Papers*, vol. 1, pp. 520–22; Wilson to Lansing, 24 January 1916, ibid., p. 522; Lansing memorandum, 25 January 1916, ibid., pp. 523–24.

277. May, *American Isolation*, pp. 134–38, 149–59.

278. Ibid., p. 146.

279. Lansing to Wilson, 2 February 1917, *FRUS: Lansing Papers*, vol. 1, p. 591.

280. Draft Lansing note to Bernstorff if talks fail, 26 January 1916, ibid., p. 527.

281. Page to Bryan, 18 December 1915, *FRUS: 1915 Supplement*, p. 646.

282. Lansing to Penfield, 6 December 1915, ibid., pp. 623–25.

283. Lansing memorandum, 21 December 1915, *FRUS: Lansing Papers*, vol. 1, p. 503.

284. Lansing to Gerard, 18 April 1916, *FRUS: 1916 Supplement*, pp. 232–37. For Jagow's unapologetic response, see Gerard to Lansing, 11 April 1916, ibid., pp. 227–29. See also Knock, *To End All Wars*, pp. 73–74.

285. Lansing suggested insertion, 10 April 1916, *FRUS: Lansing Papers*, vol. 1, p. 543. Bethmann hinted that he might try the U-boat commander who sank the *Sussex* (Gerard to Lansing, 24 April 1916, ibid., p. 560).

286. In Willis, *Prologue*, p. 39.

287. Lansing to Wilson, 27 March 1916, *FRUS: Lansing Papers*, vol. 1, pp. 537–39. See May, *American Isolation*, pp. 191–94. See also the stinging American draft note, *FRUS: Lansing Papers*, vol. 1, pp. 540–42.

288. In Willis, *Prologue*, p. 39.

289. In May, *American Isolation*, p. 359.

290. Ibid., pp. 151, 356. See also Wilson to Lansing, 17 May 1916, *FRUS: Lansing Papers*, vol. 1, pp. 568–69.

291. Craig, *Germany*, pp. 380–81.

292. May, *American Isolation*, p. 167.

293. Lansing to Wilson, 19 November 1915, *FRUS: Lansing Papers*, vol. 1, pp. 491–93; Lansing memorandum, 25 January 1916, ibid., pp. 523–25.

294. Lansing to Wilson, 10 May 1916, ibid., p. 568.

295. Wilson address to Congress, 3 February 1917, *FRUS: 1917 Supplement 1: The World War* (Washington, D.C.: GPO, 1931), pp. 109–12.

296. Wilson address to Congress, 2 April 1917, ibid., pp. 195–99.

297. Ibid., p. 199.

298. See May, *American Isolation*, pp. 404–15, 416–24, 427.

299. Lloyd George, *Memoirs of the Peace Conference*, vol. 1, p. 139.

300. Ferro, *Great War*, p. 227.

301. Lloyd George, *Memoirs of the Peace Conference*, vol. 1, p. 120.

302. Ibid., p. 114.

303. Ibid., pp. 139–40.

304. CAB 23/43, Imperial War Cabinet 39, 28 November 1918, 11:45 A.M., p. 6.

305. Lansing to Wilson, 21 November 1916, *FRUS: Lansing Papers*, vol. 1, pp. 43–44.

306. Lansing to Wilson, 31 January 1917, ibid., p. 583.

307. In Lloyd George, *War Memoirs*, vol. 6, pp. 259–60.

308. Lansing to Wilson, 27 September 1918, *FRUS: The Lansing Papers 1914–1920* (Washington, D.C.: GPO, 1940), vol. 2, p. 156.

309. Lansing to Wilson, 4 October 1918, ibid., pp. 159–60.

310. Willis, *Prologue*, pp. 42–45.

311. Lloyd George, *War Memoirs*, vol. 6, p. 260.

312. In Willis, *Prologue*, p. 47.

313. Here I use "legalist" in Shklar's broader sense, not necessarily referring to war crimes.

314. In Lloyd George, *Memoirs of the Peace Conference*, vol. 1, pp. 141–42.

315. In Lloyd George, *War Memoirs*, vol. 6, p. 231.

316. CRAWEP meeting, 4 March 1919, 11 A.M., in R.G. 256, M-820, roll 144, vol. 118, 181.12301/5.

317. Willis, *Prologue*, p. 47. See Robert Lansing, *The Peace Negotiations: A Personal Narrative* (New York: Houghton Mifflin, 1921), p. 33.

318. Lansing wrote, "I considered a judicial tribunal the most practical agency for removing causes of war" (*Peace Negotiations*, p. 68).

319. Lloyd George, *Memoirs of the Peace Conference*, vol. 1, p. 87; Knock, *To End All Wars*, pp. 108, 198–99.

320. Curzon's words, not Clemenceau's. CAB 23/43, Imperial War Cabinet 37, 20 November 1918, noon, p. 7.

321. CAB 28/5, I.C.-99, Allied conversation, 2 December 1918, 4 P.M., pp. 2–4. See also FO 371/3227/198754, Foreign Office to Barclay and Bayley, 2 December 1918; Miller to House, 3 December 1918, pp. 335–36, *FRUS: 1919: The Paris Peace Conference* (Washington, D.C.: GPO, 1942), vol. 1; and Miller to House, 6 December 1918, ibid., p. 341.

322. FO 371/3227/199367, Grahame to Foreign Office, 3 December 1918.

323. Lloyd George, *Memoirs of the Peace Conference*, vol. 1, p. 86.

324. Wilson, Lloyd George and Clemenceau meeting, 5 May 1919, *FRUS: 1919: Peace Conference*, vol. 5, pp. 470–71.

325. In Willis, *Prologue*, p. 47.

326. Five Powers meeting, 25 June 1919, *FRUS: 1919: Peace Conference*, vol. 6, p. 677.

327. Allied meeting, 26 June 1919, ibid., p. 700. See also Lansing to Wilson, 26 June 1919, ibid., pp. 704–6.

328. Willis, *Prologue*, pp. 67–77.

329. CRAWEP meeting, 27 March 1919, 10:30 A.M., in R.G. 256, M-820, roll 141, vol. 115, 181.1201/10.

330. CRAWEP third meeting, 12 March 1919, 11 A.M., in R.G. 256, M-820, roll 141, vol. 115, 181.1201/3.

331. Ibid.

332. CRAWEP meeting, 4 March 1919, 11 A.M., in R.G. 256, M-820, roll 144, vol. 118, 181.12301/5.

333. Ibid.

334. Ibid.

335. In Willis, *Prologue*, p. 75. Lansing says nothing about the report in his *Peace Negotiations*.

336. See James Brown Scott, "The Trial of the Kaiser," in Edward Mandell House and Charles Seymour, eds., *What Really Happened at Paris: The Story of the Peace Conference, 1918–1919* (New York: Charles Scribner's Sons, 1921), pp. 231–58.

337. FO 371/4271/62362, CRAWEP report, 29 March 1919, Annex II, American Reservations, p. 51.

338. Ibid., p. 52.

339. Ibid., p. 55.

340. Ibid., pp. 54–56.

341. Ibid., p. 61.

342. Ibid., p. 62.

343. In Jackson, *Report*, p. 299.

344. Willis, *Prologue*, pp. 77–80.

345. Ibid., p. 78.

CHAPTER FOUR
CONSTANTINOPLE

1. See Richard G. Hovannisian, *Armenia on the Road to Independence* (Berkeley: University of California Press, 1967), p. 49. In this chapter, in order to minimize confusion by following usages in British documents, I often refer to the genocide as the Armenian massacres or deportations, as well as using rather archaic spellings of Turkish names (Djemal, not Cemal, and Talaat, not Talât).

2. Djemal Pasha, *Memories of a Turkish Statesman—1913–1919* (New York: George H. Doran Co., 1922), p. 132. The captives were Said Halim Pasha, Hairi Effendi, Halil Bey, Ibrahim Bey, and Shukri Bey; the escapees were the troika of Enver, Talaat, and Djemal.

3. See, for instance, Rouben Paul Adalian, *Remembering and Understanding the Armenian Genocide* (Yerevan: National Commission of the Republic of Armenia on the 80th Commemoration of the Armenian Genocide, 1995), p. 29.

4. There are only a handful of accounts other than this chapter, most of them fragmentary and some polemical. For an excellent version that emphasizes legal issues over political ones, see Dadrian, "Genocide as a Problem of National and International Law." Dadrian draws on this article in *The History of the Armenian Genocide* (Oxford: Bergahn Books, 1995), pp. 303–43. He also thoughtfully sifts through the evidence from the tribunal in "The Documentation of the World War I Armenian Massacres in the Proceedings of the Turkish Military Tribunal," *International Journal of Middle East Studies*, vol. 23, no. 4 (November 1991), pp. 549–76. Unlike Dadrian, I am primarily interested here in British politics. On the Malta period, see Willis, *Prologue*, pp. 153–63. Akaby Nassibian discusses the May 1915 declaration in *Britain and the Armenian Question 1915–1923* (London: Croom Helm, 1984), pp. 70–75. See also Haigazn K. Kazarian, "Turkey Tries Its Chief Criminals: Indictment and Sentence Passed down by Military Court of 1919," *The Armenian Review*, vol. 24 (winter 1971), p. 3; Arthur Beylerian, ed., *Les Grandes Puissances, l'Empire ottoman et les Arméniens dans les archives françaises 1914–1918* (Paris: Sorbonne, 1983), pp. lxi–lxii; G. S. Graber, *Caravans to Oblivion: The Armenian Genocide, 1915* (London: Wiley, 1996), pp. 157–68; Nino, *Radical Evil on Trial*, p. 5; and Annette Höss, "The Trial of Perpetrators by the Turkish Military Tribunals: The Case of Yozgat," in Richard G. Hovannisian, ed., *The Armenian Genocide: History, Politics, Ethics* (London: Macmillan, 1992), pp. 208–21. For English transcripts of the Ottoman courts-martial, which were published at the time in issues of the official Ottoman gazette, *Takvim-i Vekayi*, see Vartkes Yeghiayan, ed., *The Armenian Genocide and the Trials of the Young Turks* (La Verne, Calif.: American Armenian International College Press, 1990). A caveat: I have only been able to check their accuracy against a few translations in Constantinople newspapers. For an apologetic anti-Armenian account, see Kamuran Gürün, *The Armenian File: The Myth of Innocence Exposed* (Istanbul: K. Rustem, 1985), pp. 233–39.

5. Lloyd George, *War Memoirs*, vol. 6, p. 276.

6. Ibid., p. 280.

7. CAB 28/5, I.C.-99, Inter-Allied Conference, London, 2 December 1918, 4 P.M.

8. See, for instance, FO 371/4172/24783, Webb to Foreign Office, 13 February 1919.

9. I did not find anything of value on the punishment of Turkish war criminals in the archives of the Ministère des Affaires étrangères at the Quai d'Orsay in Paris, and am thus loath to say much more. There are a few documents on the May 1915 declaration in Beylerian, ed., *Grandes Puissances*, pp. 15, 17–18, 21–29.

10. See R.G. 59, microfilm M-353, roll 6, 867.00/798–2, Morgenthau to Lansing, 18 November 1915. Lansing passed this report on to Wilson (R.G. 59, M-353, roll 6, 867.00/798–2, Lansing to Wilson, 13 January 1916). The story of American outrage at mass ethnic slaughter in the twentieth century turns out to be also largely the story of a father and a son, both Henry Morgenthaus. Morgenthau *père* served under Woodrow Wilson as the American ambassador to the Ottoman Empire from 1913 to 1916; Morgenthau *fils* was the secretary of the treasury for Franklin Roosevelt at the

end of World War II, and was bitterly outraged at the Holocaust. Both men were lonely voices in their respective administrations—calling for end to the killing, and going largely unheeded. See Morgenthau Sr., *Ambassador Morgenthau's Story.*

11. In July 1915, Morgenthau wrote: "Persecution of Armenians assuming unprecedented proportions. Reports from widely scattered districts indicate systematic attempt to uproot peaceful Armenian populations and through arbitrary arrests, terrible tortures, whole-sale expulsions and deportations from one end of the Empire to the other accompanied by frequent instances of rape, pillage, and murder, turning into massacre, to bring destruction and destitution on them" (Morgenthau to Lansing, 10 July 1915, *FRUS: 1915 Supplement,* p. 982). A month later, he literally begged: "I earnestly beg the Department to give this matter urgent and exhaustive consideration with a view to reaching a conclusion which may possibly have the effect of checking this Government [Turkey] and certainly provide opportunity for efficient relief which now is not permitted. It is difficult for me to restrain myself from doing something to stop this attempt to exterminate a race, but I realize that I am here as Ambassador and must abide by the principles of non-interference with the internal affairs of another country" (Morgenthau to Lansing, 11 August 1915, ibid., p. 986). Ignored in Washington, Morgenthau Sr. did manage to attract the attention of the Young Turks; Djemal wrote bitterly about the "imbecile confederates of the Morgenthau stamp" (Djemal, *Memories of a Turkish Statesman,* p. 299). In 1916, Lansing did ask Germany to try to restrain Turkey from its intent "to annihilate a Christian race" (Lansing to Grew, 1 November 1916, *FRUS: 1916 Supplement,* p. 858).

12. Hovannisian, *Armenia,* p. 55. The chargé d'affaires in Turkey suggested breaking off relations to protest "barbarous methods," but there was no follow-up (Philip to Lansing, 1 October 1916, *FRUS: 1916 Supplement,* p. 856).

13. Lansing to Philip, 12 February 1916, *FRUS: 1916 Supplement,* p. 847. Lansing's outrage was far from complete: "In the case of the Armenians I could see that their well-known disloyalty to the Ottoman Government and the fact that the territory which they inhabited was within the zone of military operations constituted grounds more or less justifiable for compelling them to depart from their homes. It was not to my mind the deportation which was objectionable but the horrible brutality which attended its execution." Lansing called this brutality "one of the blackest pages of this war" (Lansing to Wilson, 21 November 1916, *FRUS: Lansing Papers,* vol. 1, p. 42).

14. May, *American Isolation,* p. 338. See also R.G. 59, M-365, roll 2, 711.67.

15. May, *American Isolation,* p. 419.

16. Hovannisian, *Armenia,* p. 55.

17. Lloyd George, *Memoirs of the Peace Conference,* vol. 1, p. 117.

18. William Linn Westermann, "The Armenian Problem and the Disruption of Turkey," in House and Seymour, eds., *What Really Happened at Paris,* p. 179.

19. FO 371/4271/62362, CRAWEP report, 29 March 1919, Annex II, American Reservations, p. 61.

20. Without more evidence, this is all that can be safely said. I found nothing on America's attitude toward the Constantinople trials in *FRUS,* the National Archives, or various memoirs, and only a few references to America in the British files (for instance, FO 371/4173/69050 and FO 371/6504/E6311).

21. See W. E. Gladstone, *Political Speeches in Scotland, November and December 1879* (London: W. Ridgway, 1879).

22. See Roy Jenkins, *Gladstone* (London: Macmillan, 1995), pp. 399–414, and R. T. Shannon, *Gladstone and the Bulgarian Agitation 1876* (London: Harvester Press, 1975).

23. Gladstone, *Bulgarian Horrors*, pp. 9–10.

24. Marc Trachtenberg, "Intervention in Historical Perspective," in Laura W. Reed and Carl Kaysen, eds., *Emerging Norms of Justified Intervention* (Cambridge, Mass.: American Academy of Arts and Sciences, 1993), p. 25; Nassibian, *Britain and the Armenian Question*, p. 33.

25. Jenkins, *Gladstone*, p. 627.

26. FO 371/2484/22083, 25 February 1915; FO 371/2484/25073, 4 March 1915; FO 371/2484/25167; FO 371/2484/28172; FO 371/2485/41444; FO 371/2485/101144, 26 July 1915. "The difficulty is that the Turks would immediately take reprisals on the Armenians actually in their power, and massacres would immediately follow," worried a Foreign Office diplomat (FO 371/2485/106769, 4 August 1915). Even Sir Mark Sykes was denied permission to foment Armenian unrest (FO 371/2485/115866, 3 August 1915, Sykes to Maxwell). See also FO 371/2485/126836, 7 September 1915; FO 371/2485/136059, 22 September 1915; FO 371/2485/196024, 21 December 1915; and Arnold J. Toynbee, *Armenian Atrocities: The Murder of a Nation* (London: Hodder and Stoughton, 1915), p. 70.

27. FO 371/2488/171151, 29 October 1915.

28. FO 371/2490/148384, 12 October 1915.

29. Paul W. Schroeder, *Austria, Great Britain, and the Crimean War: The Destruction of the European Concert* (Ithaca, N.Y.: Cornell University Press, 1972), p. 41.

30. Hovannisian, *Armenia*, pp. 44, 47.

31. FO 371/2484/22083, 25 February 1915.

32. FO 371/2485/138029, 24 September 1915. Britain disapproved.

33. FO 371/2485/40247, 6 April 1915; FO 371/2485/46558, 20 April 1915.

34. Lloyd George, *Memoirs of the Peace Conference* (New Haven: Yale University Press, 1939), vol. 2, pp. 811–12.

35. Lloyd George wrote, "Abdul Hamid and the Young Turks had deliberately set themselves to the simplication of the Armenian difficulty by exterminating and deporting the whole race, whom they regarded as infidels and traitors. In this savage task they had largely succeeded" (ibid., p. 650). "[T]he Turk is a blight and a curse wherever he pitches his tent, and . . . he ought in the interests of humanity to be treated as such. When a race which has no title to its lands other than conquest, so mis-manages the territories it holds by violence . . ., the nations have a right—nay, a duty—to intervene in order to restore these devastated areas to civilisation" (p. 876).

36. CAB 23/44 (part 2), 19 May 1918, 3 P.M. meeting.

37. FO 371/2488/134706, 20 September 1915. He had Enver in mind.

38. On the considerable—though hardly unlimited—power of public opinion in World War I Britain, see K. G. Robbins, "Public Opinion, the Press and Pressure Groups," in Hinsley, ed., *British Foreign Policy under Sir Edward Grey*.

39. See H.A.L. Fisher, *James Bryce* (New York: Macmillan, 1927). Unlike most British pro-Armenians, Bryce had actually visited the Ottoman Empire; see his *Transcaucasia and Ararat, Being Notes of a Vacation Tour in the Autumn of 1876* (London: Macmillan,

1896). After the war, Bryce preferred rough justice: "Enver and Talaat, the two chief villains, ought to be hanged if they can be caught" (Willis, *Prologue,* pp. 61–62).

40. FO 371/2488/108070, 29 July 1915.

41. In Toynbee, *Armenian Atrocities,* p. 14.

42. FO 371/2488/148483, 6 October 1915.

43. FO 371/2488/172811, 17 November 1915, Lord A. Williams.

44. FO 371/2488/148483, 6 October 1915.

45. Nassibian, *Britain and the Armenian Question,* pp. 44–50. On the role of pressure groups, see Robbins, "Public Opinion," pp. 82–86.

46. Nassibian, *Britain and the Armenian Question,* pp. 48–49.

47. Toynbee, *Armenian Atrocities,* p. 27.

48. On the press, see Robbins, "Public Opinion," pp. 76–82.

49. FO 371/2488/143477, 2 October 1915.

50. FO 371/2488/148680, 11 October 1915.

51. See, for instance, FO 371/2488/125295, 4 September 1915; FO 371/2488/140259, 10 September 1915; FO 371/2488/143153, 16 September 1915, on Trebizond; FO 371/2488/153862, 20 October 1915; FO 371/2488/198351, 9 December 1915, on Van; FO 371/2488/200063, 28 December 1915; and FO 371/2489/82061, 22 June 1915; FO 371/2490/130287, 13 September 1915.

52. For instance, FO 371/2488/140654, British Armenian Committee to Grey, 27 September 1915.

53. FO 371/2488/152040, 16 October 1915.

54. See, for instance, Lord Newton's comments in FO 371/6505/E1377, Lords, 10 November 1921.

55. FO 371/4172/12905, 7 January 1919.

56. FO 371/4172/41634, Webb to Foreign Office, 9 March 1919.

57. On general political conditions in Turkey in 1915, and the domination of Ittihadists, see R.G. 59, M-353, roll 6, 867.00/797, Morgenthau to Lansing, 4 November 1915. "They have annihilated or displaced at least two thirds of the Armenian population and thereby deprived themselves of a very intelligent and useful race," Morgenthau Sr. wrote. See also R.G. 59, M-353, roll 6, 867.00/798–2, Morgenthau to Lansing, 18 November 1915.

58. FO 371/2488/51009, 27 April 1915.

59. Russian Embassy to French Foreign Ministry, 26 April 1915, in Beylerian, ed., *Grandes Puissances,* pp. 14–15; FO 371/2488/51010, Buchanan to Foreign Office, 29 April 1915. At around the same time, Russia noted threateningly that "there are many Mussulmans in Russian territory and that these enjoy immunity from religious persecution" (Bryan to Morgenthau, 27 April 1915, *FRUS: 1915 Supplement,* p. 980).

60. FO 371/2488/59097, Foreign Office to Bertie, 18 May 1915; with slightly different wording, British Embassy to French Foreign Ministry, 19 May 1915, in Beylerian, ed., *Grandes Puissances,* p. 25.

61. Delcassé to Cambon, 27 April 1915, in Beylerian, ed., *Grandes Puissances,* p. 15.

62. Grey noted, "[I]t would appear that the massacres were not all on one side, and that the Armenians for a time held Van and disposed of a good many Turks" (FO 371/2488/58350, 10 May 1915). See FO 371/2488/58350, 11 May 1915. On May 13, 1915, the Foreign Office wrote: "We might tell Sir H. [Henry] McMahon what little we know: that there has been a rising in Van (?), suppressed by the Turks, who are

apparently encouraging massacres throughout Armenia." "No more is known at present," the same official added a day later (FO 371/2488/59096, 13 May 1915). Britain was forced to rely on America's judgment that Armenian Catholic reports were credible (FO 371/2488/51010, 27 April 1915). This was not just a British problem: Morgenthau Sr. wrote, "Reliable information can be secured only by investigation in the localities, which the Ottoman Government will not allow now" (Morgenthau to Bryan, 2 May 1915, *FRUS: 1915 Supplement*, p. 981). It was only by July that Morgenthau Sr. was confident he knew what was really happening (Morgenthau to Lansing, 10 July 1915, ibid., p. 982).

63. FO 371/2488/58350, 10 May 1915.

64. FO 371/2488/58350, Grey to Bertie, 11 May 1915. This argument is eerily similar to one of John McCloy's explanations for why the Pentagon would not bomb Auschwitz: "[S]uch an effort, even if practicable, might provoke even more vindictive action by the Germans" (in David S. Wyman, *The Abandonment of the Jews: America and the Holocaust 1941–1945* [New York: Pantheon, 1984], p. 296).

65. FO 371/2488/59097, Bertie to Foreign Office, 12 May 1915.

66. FO 371/2488/58387, Buchanan to Grey, 11 May 1915. See also FO 371/2488/59205, 12 May 1915; Russian Embassy to French Foreign Ministry, 11 May 1915, in Beylerian, ed., *Grandes Puissances*, p. 23.

67. FO 371/2488/58387, 12 May 1915.

68. From the receiving end, this kind of pan-Christian outrage looked like bigotry. Some of the Turks accused of war crimes would complain bitterly to Curzon that "only Mohammedans and Turks have been singled out as victims of oppression, and the British officials in Constantinople have made themselves blind tools of a mediaeval sort of crusading spirit and religious fanaticism" (FO 371/6505/E13968, Ali Ihsan, Tevfik, Sabit, Djemal, Ibrahim Hakki, Hilmi, etc., to Curzon, 1 September 1921).

69. See, for instance, FO 371/4172/41634, Webb to Foreign Office, 9 March 1919.

70. FO 371/2488/63095, Bertie to Foreign Office, 19 May 1915.

71. FO 371/2488/63903, Bertie to Foreign Office, 21 May 1915. France did not want to appear pro-Christian lest it alienate Muslims living under French colonial rule (French Foreign Ministry to British Embassy in Paris, 20 May 1915, in Beylerian, ed., *Grandes Puissances*, p. 26).

72. FO 371/2488/65759, 24 May 1915. See also Russian Embassy to French Foreign Ministry, 24 May 1915, in Beylerian, ed., *Grandes Puissances*, p. 29.

73. The term gained a certain currency even in the 1910s. In 1918, Robert Borden, Canada's prime minister, said that Wilhelm II had committed "a crime against humanity" by starting World War I (CAB 23/43, Imperial War Cabinet 37, 20 November 1918, noon, p. 7), and Lloyd George recalled then "a growing feeling that war itself was a crime against humanity" (Lloyd George, *Memoirs of the Peace Conference*, vol. 1, p. 55). Lloyd George accused Wilhelm II of "offences against international law and against humanity" (CAB 23/43, Imperial War Cabinet 39, 28 November 1918, 11:45 A.M., p. 6). It was sometimes used broadly to mean moral offenses—namely, starting World War I—that might or might not strictly qualify as crimes under international law (CAB 23/43, Imperial War Cabinet 37, 20 November 1918, noon, p. 12).

74. FO 371/2488/59097, Foreign Office to Bertie, 18 May 1915.

75. In Sharp to Bryan, 28 May 1915, *FRUS: 1915 Supplement*, p. 981.

76. They were Enver, Talaat, Djemal, Nazim (the former secretary-general of Itti-had ve Terraki), Bahaeddin Shakir (a top Ittihadist), Azmi Bey (a former chief of public security and governor general of Beirut), Bedri Bey (another former chief of public security), Ismail Hakki Pasha (a former senior official in the Ministry of War), and Djemal Azmi (who had been *vali* of Trebizond). Enver made the list twice, for ordering a march of British prisoners of war across the desert from Kut-al-Amara (FO 371/4273/185867).

77. FO 371/4271/62362, CRAWEP report, 29 March 1919, pp. 3, 19.

78. CAB 23/43, Imperial War Cabinet 37, 20 November 1918, 12 noon.

79. CAB 28/5, I.C.-99, Allied Conference, London, 2 December 1918, 4 P.M.

80. Ahmed Tevfik served from November 1918 to March 1919; then Damad Ferid Pasha ruled from March to October 1919, and again (after brief stints by Ali Riza Pasha and Salih Hulusi Pasha) from April to October 1920; then Ahmed Tevfik again, from October 1920 to November 1922 (Stanford J. Shaw and Ezel Kural Shaw, *History of the Ottoman Empire and Modern Turkey: Reform, Revolution and Republic: The Rise of Modern Turkey, 1808–1975* [Cambridge: Cambridge University Press, 1977], vol. 2, pp. 439–40).

81. See ibid., pp. 332–33.

82. During the debate over the May 1915 Allied declaration, the British Foreign Office had suggested a historical analogy with the Damascus massacre of 1860. (See Albert Hourani, *A History of the Arab Peoples* [Cambridge, Mass.: Belknap Press of Harvard University Press, 1991], p. 277.) Then, after a massacre of Christians by the Druze, Napoleon III had sent six thousand troops to Lebanon, "only to find that Fuad Pasha had already exacted punishment for the Damascus massacre, and that they could not get hold of the Druse ringleaders. The final result was the establishment of the autonomy of the Lebanon under a Christian Governor-General, and we must provide the parallel to that by defeating the Turks, not by writing to them." The key lesson that Grey drew from this was that it was European pressure that had made the Ottomans punish the Druze: "Fuad Pa. was forced to inflict punishment" (FO 371/2488/51010, 28 April 1915).

83. In Lloyd George, *Memoirs of the Peace Conference*, vol. 2, p. 651.

84. FO 371/4174/98910, Damad Ferid to Clemenceau, 30 June 1919, War Cabinet WCP 11 02.

85. FO 371/4172/20440, Text of Conditions of [Mudros] Armistice with Turkey, filed 6 February 1919. The armistice showed continuing concern for the Armenians, including demanding the immediate surrender of interned Armenians to the Allies (clause 4) and a stipulation that "[i]n case of disorder in the six Armenian vilayets the Allies reserve to themselves the right to occupy any part of them" (clause 24).

86. David Fromkin, *A Peace to End All Peace: The Fall of the Ottoman Empire and the Creation of the Modern Middle East* (New York: Avon, 1989), pp. 404–5.

87. CAB 23/14, War Cabinet 491B, 26 October 1918, p. 23; FO 371/4172/10991, 14 January 1919.

88. FO 371/4173/44216, Deedes report, War Office, 20 March 1919. Lower-level British officials were equally arrogant. On May 11, 1921, British military police arrested Tevfik Pasha, the grand vizier, for not having the proper numbers on his car. The furious dignitary was taken to a nearby police station, identified, and released (R.G. 59, M-353, roll 10, 867.00/1416, Bristol to Hughes, 18 May 1921).

89. Lloyd George, *Memoirs of the Peace Conference,* vol. 2, p. 834.

90. Höss, "Trial of Perpetrators," pp. 210–11.

91. FO 371/4172/2391, 2 January 1919.

92. Ibid.

93. FO 371/4172/12905, 7 January 1919.

94. FO 371/4172/14375, Calthorpe to Foreign Office, 22 January 1919.

95. FO 371/4172/13592, 10 January 1919. Britain reassured the sultan that "His Majesty's Government would unquestionably insist on punishment of guilty, that they would certainly prevent public disorder" (FO 371/4172/14375, Calthorpe to Foreign Office, 22 January 1919).

96. FO 371/4172/12905, 7 January 1919.

97. FO 371/4172/13694, 24 January 1919.

98. CAB 23/9, War Cabinet 516, 15 January 1919, noon. Lloyd George was absent.

99. FO 371/4172/14375, Calthorpe to Foreign Office, 22 January 1919.

100. FO 371/4172/16321, Calthorpe to Foreign Office, 28 January 1919. The suspect was Reshid Bey, the former *vali* of Diarbekir.

101. FO 371/4172/16321, Calthorpe to Foreign Office, 28 January 1919.

102. FO 371/4172/16731, Calthorpe to Foreign Office, 30 January 1919.

103. FO 371/4172/7682, Calthorpe to Foreign Office, 30 January 1919. The men included Midhat Shukri, the secretary-general of Ittihad ve Terraki, and Rahmi, presumably the ex-*vali* of Smyrna. Others like Said Halim, the grand vizier in 1915, were being kept under surveillance.

104. FO 371/4172/18989, Calthorpe to Foreign Office, 1 February 1919.

105. FO 371/4174/118377, Constantinople high commission Greek-Armenian section to Foreign Office, 1 August 1919.

106. FO 371/4172/23004, 9 February 1919. There was even a particularly satisfying bonus: "Reshid Bey was recaptured on February 6th and thereupon killed himself."

107. Foreign Office to Law Officers, 10 July 1919, after FO 371/4174/98243.

108. FO 371/4173/44516, 19 March 1919. Balfour had it in for Djavid Bey. See also FO 371/4172/31131, 21 February 1919.

109. FO 371/4172/31131, 21 February 1919. The minister was Ismail Djambolat; the intellectual was Zia Goukalp. (On the latter, see Ahmed Emin, *Turkey in the World War* [New Haven: Yale University Press, 1930], pp. 189–93. See also Shaw and Shaw, *History,* vol. 2, pp. 301–4.) Also arrested were Hussein Djahid, Midhat Shukri, and Rahmi, ex-*vali* of Smyrna. There may have been some overlap in these various lists. At around the same time, Nuri Pasha was also arrested and taken to face a British military court at Batum (FO 371/4172/30796, 22 February 1919).

110. R.G. 59, M-353, roll 7, 867.00/861, enclosure in Heck to Lansing, 11 March 1919.

111. FO 371/4173/46680, 23 March 1919. This was explicitly meant to encourage British goodwill; Moustapha Rechid, the foreign minister who had got the full force of Calthorpe's ire, promised to pursue "all the authors of the ravages committed during the war on the occasion of the deportation of the Armenians" (FO 371/4173/47293, 26 March 1919). Calthorpe was duly impressed: "The Government appear sincerely to intend to bring specific charges against all the arrested persons, and to

accomplish as expeditiously as possible their trial by a new Court Martial more effi-cient than that set up the Tewfik Pasha's Government" (FO 371/4173/55120, Cal-thorpe to Balfour, 22 March 1919).

112. FO 371/4172/41632, 11 March 1919. "New Govt. making rapid progress," the Foreign Office noted, by now almost blasé about the arrest of the high and mighty. "Said Halim is but a poor catch, but Javid would be a very big one indeed." On these arrests, see also R.G. 59, M-353, roll 7, 867.00/861, Heck to Lansing, 11 March 1919; and R.G. 59, M-353, roll 7, 867.00/853, Sharp to Lansing, 10 March 1919. On Said Halim's regime, see Hasan Kayali, *Arabs and Young Turks: Ottomanism, Arabism, and Islamism in the Ottoman Empire, 1908–1918* (Berkeley: University of California Press, 1997).

113. FO 371/4173/55120, Calthorpe to Balfour, 22 March 1919. In order: Ibrahim Halil Bey, Rifat Bey, Ali Munif Bey, Fethi Bey, Shukri Bey, Ibrahim Bey Pirizade, and Ahmed Nessimi Bey.

114. FO 371/4173/55120, Calthorpe to Balfour, 22 March 1919. In order: Mussa Kiazim Effendi, Reshad Bey, and Sabandjali Hakki Bey.

115. Hairi Effendi: FO 371/4173/55120, Calthorpe to Balfour, 22 March 1919.

116. FO 371/4173/55120, Calthorpe to Balfour, 22 March 1919.

117. FO 371/4174/136069, de Robeck to Curzon, 21 September 1919. In that group fell Said Halim, Ahmed Nessimi, Ali Munif, Ferid, Fethi, Hadji Adil, Halil, Hairi, Ibrahim, Ismail Djambolat, Midhat Shukri, Rahmi, and others.

118. FO 371/4173/46680, 23 March 1919.

119. Seifeddin Bey Bin Riza: FO 371/4174 /105794, 6 July 1919.

120. In order: Hadji Adil Bey, Kiazim Bey, and the *valis*, Rahmi Bey, Mehmed Kemal Ben Arif, Sabit Bey Bin Moustafa Vehbi, Mehmed Memdouh Bin Tayar, Ali Osman Bin Ali Osman, and Ibrahim Bedreddin Bey. For a complete listing, see FO 371/4173/62442, after Webb to Curzon, 7 April 1919.

121. Ibid.

122. Damad Ferid told Lewis Heck, the American commissioner in Constantino-ple, that the wartime Ittihadist regime had been "a horrible group [of] bandits," and that he was "determined to punish guilty and to divulge [*sic*] honor of Turkey before the world." But he worried about the "many unionists [Ittihadists] among the army officers" (R.G. 59, M-353, roll 7, 867.00/858, Heck to Sharp, 24 March 1919).

123. For a skeptical view from Ahmed Riza Bey, a liberal Ottoman parliamentarian who wanted to punish those guilty of Armenian massacres, see R.G. 59, M-353, roll 7, 867.00/867, Heck to Lansing, 2 April 1919, and R.G. 59, M-353, roll 7, 867.00/868, Heck to Lansing, 4 April 1919.

124. FO 371/4173/55120, Calthorpe to Balfour, 22 March 1919.

125. FO 371/4172/7682, 30 January 1919, Calthorpe to Foreign Office.

126. Heck warned, "The Ferid Pasha cabinet has become so active in its arrests of the members of the Committee of Union and Progress, that political elements which do not belong to that party are beginning to fear that if they show too much activity the Government may also turn against them. . . . The arrests of members of the former government and its partisans continue both in Constantinople and in the prov-inces. . . . Persons who are not directly in sympathy with the present cabinet, express the opinion that if these arrests continue on a large scale, there may be trouble, since it is popularly believed that many of them are made from motives of personal

vengeance or at the instigation of the Entente authorities, especially the British" (R.G. 59, M-353, roll 7, 867.00/868, Heck to Lansing, 4 April 1919).

127. FO 371/4173/44216, Deedes report, War Office, 20 March 1919.

128. Reuter, 31 May and 2 June 1919, in FO 371/4173/84678, 6 June 1919 filed. See also FO 371/4173/57319, British delegation in Paris to Curzon, 11 April 1919.

129. This appearance of impropriety was left, of course, to the French to point out: "French Government feel that it would be still more impossible to transport guilty persons out of Turkish territory to be tried by a Court which is normally not competent to judge such cases and by reason of its situation not in a position to collect evidence and to examine all the indispensable witnesses. Such a step would in their opinion, far from having that appearance of justice which is so necessary for the two Allies in their dealings with population formerly under Turkish yoke, risk giving impression of a kind of vengeance and might result in increasing popularity which certain of the guilty Turkish officials are far from having lost through their own acts" (FO 371/4172/28138, Derby to Foreign Office, 19 February 1919).

130. FO 371/4172/41634, Webb to Foreign Office, 11 March 1919. The garbling is in the cypher.

131. FO 371/4172/41634, Webb to Foreign Office, 9 March 1919. Damad Ferid took office on March 4.

132. Höss, "Trial of Perpetrators," p. 210. For transcripts in French of the Yozgat, Trebizond, and Kharput trials, see Jean-Marie Carzou, *Un génocide exemplaire: Arménie 1915* (Paris: Flammarion, 1975), pp. 233–46.

133. Haigazn K. Kazarian, "A Turkish Military Court Tries the Principal Genocidists of the District of Yozgat," *The Armenian Review*, vol. 25 (summer 1972), p. 36. I have not been able to confirm independently the veracity of all details of this record. But substantially similar versions—precise phrases have not survived translation from Turkish into English or French, sometimes by way of Armenian—are in Carzou, *Génocide exemplaire*, pp. 233–36, and Yeghiayan's collection of transcripts, *Armenian Genocide and the Trials of the Young Turks*, pp. 155–58.

134. For a transcript from *Takvim-i Vekayi*, see Kazarian, "Turkish Military Court," pp. 35–39, and Carzou, *Génocide exemplaire*, pp. 233–36.

135. FO 371/4173/61185, 17 April 1919.

136. FO 371/4173/72536, Hoyland paper, filed 13 May 1919.

137. FO 371/4173/72743, Hoyland report M.63, 26 April 1919.

138. FO 371/4173/72536, 21 April 1919.

139. FO 371/4173/61185, 17 April 1919.

140. FO 371/4173/61185, 22 April 1919.

141. The men in the dock were Said Halim Pasha, Shukri Bey, Ali Munif Bey, Ahmed Nessimi Bey, Ibrahim Bey, Zia Goukalp, Atif Bey, Midhat Shukri Bey, and Djavid Bey; the others in absentia were Djemal, Nazim Atif Bey, and Bahaeddin Shakir ("Le Procès de l'Union et Progres: Les anciens ministres au banc des accusés," *Le Spectateur d'Orient* [Constantinople], 29 April 1919, in FO 371/4173 folio p. 370). Kazarian's version adds Riza, Khalil, and Kemal, and omits Ali Munif ("Turkey Tries Its Chief Criminals," pp. 5–6).

142. In Kazarian, "Turkey Tries Its Chief Criminals," p. 10.

143. Fromkin, *Peace to End All Peace*, p. 404.

144. R.G. 59, M-353, roll 7, 867.00/881, Ravndal to Wallace, 29 May 1919.

145. FO 371/4173/69050, 17 April 1919.

146. FO 371/4173/80105, 16 May 1919.

147. FO 371/4173/84188, 4 June 1919.

148. "Deportation of Turkish Suspects: Eventual Trial by Allies," Reuter, 31 May 1919, in FO 371/4173/84678, 6 June 1919.

149. Foreign Office to Law Officers, 10 July 1919, after FO 371/4174/98243; also in FO 371/5091. See also FO 371/5091/E15109, Malta Internees, 8 November 1920.

150. FO 371/4173/84435, 18 May 1919.

151. FO 371/4173/83001, 21 May 1919. See *Spectateur d'Orient*, 21 May 1919.

152. FO 371/4174/88761, Calthorpe to Curzon, 30 May 1919.

153. FO 371/5090/E15109, Malta Internees, 8 November 1920.

154. R.G. 59, M-353, roll 7, 867.00/881, Ravndal to Wallace, 29 May 1919; FO 371/5091/E15109, Malta Internees, 8 November 1920. Ravndal explained Britain's move as a result of "the excitement prevailing among the Turks and the dilatoriness of the judicial authorities in dealing with the trial of the Unionist leaders." The dozen Turks in Mudros were transferred in September 1920 to Malta.

155. Among them: Ali Munif Bey, Fethi Bey, Halil Bey, Shukri Bey, Ibrahim Bedreddin Bey, Hairi Effendi, and Sabit Bey. Also in Malta were Hilmi Bey, governor of Kirk-Killissée, being held for the massacre of Armenians in Trebizond; Hamduh, governor general of Mosul; Abbase Pasha, former minister of public works; Mahmoud Kaimil Pasha, former commander of the Fifth Army, suspected of deportations; Ferid Bey, the secretary of Ittihad ve Terakki at Constantinople, for massacres; Colonel Djevid Bey, former military commander of Constantinople (not to be confused with Djavid Bey, the finance minister who escaped to Germany; see FO 371/4173/83002, 21 May 1919); Kemal Bey, former supply minister; Hadji Adil Bey, president of the Chamber of Deputies; Djevdet Bey, former governor of Ankara; Zekeria Zihni Bey, former governor general of Adrinople; and Hadji Ahmed Pasha, a former minister of war—and Enver's father (FO 371/4174 /96951, 17 June 1919; FO 371/4174/88768, Calthorpe to Curzon, 31 May 1919). For a detailed list of fifty-three, see FO 371/4174/88768, Calthorpe to Curzon, 31 May 1919. Typically confusing, it includes no less than three Chukri Beys, two of them (Midhat Chukri Bey and Chukri Bey) listed as former ministers of public instruction.

156. FO 371/4173/81368, 29 May 1919. About half of the forty-one were accused of Armenian massacres, with the rest "deported as a war precautionary measure" (FO 371/4174/118377, Constantinople high commission Greek-Armenian section to Foreign Office, 1 August 1919). In his Malta internees memorandum (FO 371/5091/E15109, 8 November 1920), W. S. Edmonds puts the total at sixty-eight, not sixty-seven.

157. FO 371/4174/88761, Calthorpe to Curzon, 30 May 1919. An American diplomat called the court-martial "characteristically dilatory . . . showing little disposition to be severe or rapid in judgement" (in R.G. 59, M-353, roll 7, 867.00/841, Sharp to Lansing, 8 February 1919).

158. On the trial of Talaat, Enver, and others, see "Le Procès des Unionistes," *Entente*, 26 June 1919.

159. "Les Poursuite contre les unionistes," *Spectateur d'Orient*, 13 June 1919.

160. FO 371/4174/113166, 21 July 1919; "Unionistes libérés," *Spectateur d'Orient*, 14 June 1919.

161. FO 371/4174/105794, 6 July 1919.

162. "Le Procès de l'Union et Progrès: Evasion d'un ancien ministre," *Spectateur d'Orient*, 3 June 1919.

163. FO 371/4174/123322, 22 August 1919; FO 371/4174/119573, 20 August 1919.

164. FO 371/4174/113166, 21 July 1919; "Unionistes libérés," *Spectateur d'Orient*, 14 June 1919.

165. FO 371/4174/156721, 29 November 1919.

166. FO 371/4174/98243, Corcoran to Foreign Office, 4 July 1919.

167. The other two sentenced to die were Djemal and Nazim; the three facing fifteen years were Djavid, Mustafa Sheref, and Moussa Kiazim; and Rifaat and Hashim were acquitted.

168. FO 371/4174/118392, Webb to Foreign Office, 7 July 1919. The attached French version of the verdict is consistent with the English verdict in Kazarian, "Turkey Tries Its Chief Criminals," pp. 19–25. Insignificant differences in phrasing aside, the only substantive difference is that Kazarian includes a special dissent by one of the judges further implicating the convicted—a final paragraph perhaps overlooked by the British high commission.

169. FO 371/4174/118392, filed 20 August 1919.

170. "Les unionistes," *Spectateur d'Orient*, 14 July 1919.

171. FO 371/4174/136069, de Robeck to Curzon, 21 September 1919.

172. FO 371/4174/158721, de Robeck to Curzon, 17 November 1919.

173. High Commissioner telegram 677, 3 April 1919, cited in FO 371/4174/118377, Constantinople high commission Greek-Armenian section to Foreign Office, 1 August 1919.

174. Dadrian, "Genocide as a Problem of National and International Law," p. 283.

175. Willis, *Prologue*, p. 154.

176. Otto Liman von Sanders, *Five Years in Turkey* (Annapolis, Md.: Naval Institute Press, 1927), pp. 324–25; FO 371/4173/57782, 12 April 1919.

177. FO 371/4173/68097, Calthorpe to Balfour, 20 April 1919.

178. CAB 28/5, I.C.-99, Inter-Allied Conference, London, 2 December 1918, 4 P.M.

179. FO 371/4174/118377, Constantinople high commission Greek-Armenian section to Foreign Office, 1 August 1919.

180. FO 371/4173/52689, 7 January 1919.

181. FO 371/4174/118377, Constantinople high commission Greek-Armenian section to Foreign Office, 1 August 1919.

182. FO 371/4172/2391, 2 January 1919.

183. FO 371/4172/14375, Calthorpe to Foreign Office, 22 January 1919.

184. FO 371/4172/41634, Webb to Foreign Office, 11 March 1919. For efforts to set such standards, see FO 371/4173/47590, Thwaites paper, 25 March 1919; FO 371/4172/7176, 13 January 1919; FO 371/4172/21128, Foreign Office to Calthorpe, 5 February 1919; and FO 371/4173/47590, CIGS to GOCs Egypt and Constantinople, 8 February 1919.

185. Foreign Office to law officers, 10 July 1919, after FO 371/4174/98243; FO 371/4174/113957, "Turkey—Armistice With," filed 9 August 1919.

186. FO 371/4174/136069, de Robeck to Curzon, 21 September 1919.

187. FO 371/4174/118377, Constantinople high commission Greek-Armenian section to Foreign Office, 1 August 1919. Their sources were usually the Bureau d'information Armenienne, or the testimony of Armenian survivors.

188. Ibid.

189. FO 371/5089/E879, 19 February 1920: regarding Thwaites proposal for Ali Ihsan Pasha.

190. FO 371/4173/66315, List of Undesirable Persons, filed 30 April 1919.

191. FO 371/4174/136069, de Robeck to Curzon, 21 September 1919.

192. FO 371/4173/83002, 21 May 1919.

193. FO 371/4174/163689, de Robeck to Curzon, 6 December 1919.

194. FO 371/5090/E12676, 14 October 1920.

195. FO 371/4175/170564, 2 January 1920. These prisoners were Prince Halm Mohamed Abbas, Shukri Bey, and Ahmed Pacha Hadji.

196. FO 371/5090/9934, 16 August 1920; FO 371/4174/118377, Constantinople high commission Greek-Armenian section to Foreign Office, 1 August 1919.

197. I have done my best, but I have occasionally been as stumped as the British.

198. FO 371/4173/68109, 20 April 1919.

199. FO 371/4174 /156721, 29 November 1919.

200. FO 371/4174/136069, de Robeck to Curzon, 21 September 1919.

201. FO 371/4174/118377, Constantinople high commission Greek-Armenian section to Foreign Office, 1 August 1919; Foreign Office to law officers, 10 July 1919, after FO 371/4174/98243.

202. FO 371/4174/136069, de Robeck to Curzon, 21 September 1919.

203. FO 371/5090/E12804, 5 October 1920.

204. FO 371/4174/136069, de Robeck to Curzon, 21 September 1919. De Robeck did not want to free even those against whom he knew he could not build a legal case.

205. FO 371/5091/E14130, 26 October 1920.

206. FO 371/5089/E569, 23 February 1920.

207. FO 371/4174/158721, de Robeck to Curzon, 17 November 1919.

208. Shaw and Shaw, *History*, vol. 2, p. 346. The new grand vizier was Ali Riza Pasha.

209. FO 371/5089/E1347, 12 February 1920.

210. FO 371/4174/136069, de Robeck to Curzon, 21 September 1919.

211. On partition plans for the Ottoman Empire, see Paul C. Helmreich, *From Paris to Sèvres: The Partition of the Ottoman Empire at the Peace Conference of 1919–1920* (Columbus: Ohio State University Press, 1974); and Shaw and Shaw, *History*, vol. 2, pp. 330–32.

212. The treaty is in Willis, *Prologue*, pp. 180–81; see also FO 371/5091/E15109, Malta Internees, 8 November 1920.

213. Shaw and Shaw, *History*, vol. 2, p. 356.

214. Ibid., p. 348. It was Ali Riza who resigned. Salih Hulusi Pasha served briefly as grand vizier in between Ali Riza and Damad Ferid.

215. FO 371/4174/136069, de Robeck to Curzon, 21 September 1919.

216. FO 371/4174/158721, de Robeck to Curzon, 17 November 1919.

217. FO 371/5089/E1346, 12 February 1920.

218. FO 371/5089/E3395, 15 April 1920.

219. FO 371/5089/E2293, 20 January 1920.

220. FO 371/5089/E1075, 5 March 1920.

221. FO 371/5089/E2293, 11 March 1920. That included Ali Ihsan Pasha, Mehmet Tewfik Bey, Fethi Bey, Rahmi Bey, Ferid Bey, Ali Munif Bey, Ahmed Agayeff, Halli Bey, Zia Goukalp, Shukri Bey, Ahmed Nessimi Bey, and others.

222. For sixteen such suspects, FO 371/4175/163689, de Robeck to Curzon, 6 December 1919; for sixty, Malta Internees, FO 371/5091/E15109, 8 November 1920.

223. Fromkin, *Peace to End All Peace*, p. 428.

224. Martin Gilbert, *Winston S. Churchill: Vol. III: 1914–1916: The Challenge of War* (Boston: Houghton Mifflin, 1971), pp. 188–89.

225. CAB 23/44 (part 2), 10 December 1919, 5 p.m. meeting, p. 9.

226. Gilbert, *Churchill*, vol. 3, p. 556.

227. Fromkin, *Peace to End All Peace*, p. 432–33.

228. Churchill had in mind Rahmi Bey, the governor general of Smyrna from 1916 to 1918. The Foreign Office accused Rahmi—despite his opening to the Entente—of being a stalwart Ittihadist and of deporting between 200,000 and 250,000 Greeks from the Asia Minor coast in May and June 1914, with "not inconsiderable massacres" in the process (FO 371/5090/E5815, 29 May 1920).

229. FO 371/5090/E6825, Sinclair to Campbell, 17 June 1920.

230. FO 371/5090/E10303, 19 July 1920.

231. There is no record of exactly what Curzon said to Churchill in the cabinet meeting; the best approximation comes from the memorandum Curzon had his staff prepare (FO 371/5090/E10303, Tilley to Curzon, 22 July 1920).

232. FO 371/5090/E10303, Fitzmaurice memorandum for Curzon for cabinet meeting, 21 July 1920.

233. FO 371/5090/E10431, 25 August 1920.

234. CAB 23/22, 4 August 1920 meeting.

235. FO 371/6503/E6274, 1 June and 24 May 1921.

236. FO 371/6502/E5845, 20 May 1921. Italics in original.

237. FO 371/6504/E8745, Edmonds memorandum, 3 August 1921.

238. FO 371/6503/E6728 22 June 1921.

239. Ibid., 13 June 1921.

240. FO 371/6505/E10023, Smith to Constantinople, 24 August 1921.

241. In one accounting, the Foreign Office reckoned it had demanded 141 men for crimes against British soldiers, and only seventeen for crimes against Armenians (FO 371/5091/E15109, Malta Internees, 8 November 1920). The sixty Turks who wound up at Malta for Armenian massacres, as it says in this memorandum, must have been arrested by the Ottomans and then taken from the jails of the Ottoman courts-martial to Malta.

242. FO 371/4173/66315, 9 April 1919.

243. FO 371/6502/E5845, 20 May 1921.

244. FO 371/5091/E15109, Malta Internees, 8 November 1920.

245. FO 371/4174/158721, de Robeck to Curzon, 17 November 1919.

246. FO 371/4174 /158721, Edmonds to de Robeck, 5 December 1919.

247. FO 371/5090/E11651, 9 September 1920.

248. FO 371/5090/E12773, 15 October 1920.

249. FO 371/5090/E12831, Rawlinson to Edmonds, 12 October 1920. On other hostages, see FO 371/5090/E12831, 18 October 1920.

250. FO 371/6504, C.P. 3269, Laming Worthington-Evans memorandum on prisoner release talks, 29 August 1921. "Colonel Rawlinson's captivity has been made the subject of no little political discussion in Great Britain," noted Rear-Admiral Mark Bristol, the American high commissioner in Constantinople (R.G. 59, M-353, roll 10, 867.00/1460, Bristol to Hughes, 23 November 1921).

251. FO 371/6503/E7597, 4 July 1921.

252. FO 371/5090/E11697, Lord Rawlinson to Curzon, 16 August 1920.

253. FO 371/5091/E15116, 24 November 1920.

254. FO 371/5090/E11697, Fitzmaurice memorandum for Curzon, 19 August 1920.

255. FO 371/5090/E12256, 22 September 1920.

256. FO 371/5091/E15109, Malta Internees, 8 November 1920. In total, by November 1920, about 150 men had been deported from Turkey to Malta. Twenty were freed relatively quickly, and another twenty-six were recommended for release by the Constantinople high commissioner as soon as the peace treaty was ratified. Of the rest, twelve were held for abusing British prisoners of war; about sixty for atrocities against Armenians; about six for violating the armistice; and about twenty-five as political prisoners. This almost adds up.

257. FO 371/6504/E7597, 3 July 1921.

258. FO 371/6504, C.P. 3269, Worthington-Evans memorandum on prisoner release talks, 29 August 1921; FO 371/6502/E3707, 29 March 1921. The swap was no secret; America knew all about it (R.G. 59, M-353, roll 10, 867.00/1409, Bristol to Hughes, 24 May 1921; R.G. 59, M-353, roll 10, 867.00/1421, Bristol to Hughes, 25 May 1921) and the press was notified ("Britain Releases Malta Deportees," *Orient News*, 21 May 1921, in R.G. 59, M-353, roll 10, 867.00/1421).

259. FO 371/6503/E6274, 1 June and 24 May 1921.

260. FO 371/6504, C.P. 3269, Worthington-Evans memorandum on prisoner release talks, 29 August 1921. They were Tewfik Hadi, Ismail Djambolat Bey, Mumtaz Bey, Atif Bey, Ferid Bey, Kadri Bey Buessin, Zecheria Bey Zihmi, Djimdoz Bey Saleh, Ahmed Pacha Hadji, Riza Hamid, Zulfi Bey Mohammed, Prince Halm Mohammed Abbas, Prince Halm Mohammed Said, Midhat Chukri Bey, Badji Adil Bey, Zia Goukalp, Tewfik, Halil Mehmed Saleh, Ali Munif Bey, Ahmed Shukri Bey, Ahmed Aghayeff, Toussoun Hussein Bey, Mohammed Arif Bey, Murcel Hakky Pasha, Mehmed Essad Pasha, Hussein Raouf Bey, Ahmed Chevket Bey, Mustafa Wassif Bey, Mehmed Sheref Bey, Ahmed Faik Bey, Nouman, Ali Said Pasha, Hazif Suleiman, Djelal Noury, Abdul Salam Pasha, and Ali Djenani Bey.

261. On an earlier listing, the charges against Prince Halm Mohamed Abbas, Halil Mehmed Saleh, Shukri Bey, and Ahmed Pacha Hadji seemed politicized (FO 371/4175/170564, 2 January 1920).

262. FO 371/6505/E8745, 10 August 1921.

263. FO 371/6504/E8745, 3 August 1921.

264. FO 371/6505/E9724, 26 August 1921.

265. FO 371/6504/E8745, Wood (for Hewart) to Foreign Office, 29 July 1921. Italics added.

266. Ibid.

267. FO 371/6504/E10239, 9 September 1921; FO 371/6504/E10023, Rumbold to Curzon, 30 August 1921.

268. FO 371/6504/E10023, Rumbold to Curzon, 30 August 1921. Italics added.

269. FO 371/6504/E10023, Harington to Rumbold, August 1921.

270. FO 371/6504/E10411, Army Council, War Office, to Foreign Office, 16 September 1921.

271. FO 371/6504/E10411, 16 September 1921.

272. Ibid.

273. Ibid.

274. FO 371/6504/E10411, 19 September 1921.

275. FO 371/6504/E10662, 27 September 1921.

276. FO 371/6505/E11192, Rumbold to Curzon, 4 October 1921. See also FO 371/6505/E11614, 20 October 1921.

277. FO 371/6505/E10963, Rumbold to Curzon, 27 September 1921.

278. FO 371/6505/E11012, de Robeck to Admiralty, 4 October 1921.

279. FO 371/6505/E11012, 5 October 1921.

280. *Times*, 6 October 1921. Also see *Times*, 11 October 1921.

281. FO 371/6505/E12091, 2 November 1921. See also R.G. 59, M-353, roll 10, 867.00/1460, Bristol to Hughes, 23 November 1921.

282. FO 371/6505/E12880, 25 November 1921.

283. FO 371/6505/E13323, 28 November 1921.

284. Alfred Rawlinson, *Adventures in the Near East 1918–1922* (New York: Dodd, Mead, 1924), p. 353.

285. Ibid. O'Grady's memoir, with ghostwriter Jeff Coplon, is *Return with Honor* (New York: Doubleday, 1995).

286. FO 371/6505/E12511, 29 October 1921.

287. For sixteen such suspects, FO 371/4175/163689, de Robeck to Curzon, 6 December 1919; for sixty, FO 371/5091/E15109, Malta Internees, 8 November 1920.

288. FO 371/6505/E8745, 10 August 1921.

289. See Shaw and Shaw, *History*, vol. 2, pp. 365–69.

290. Lloyd George, *Memoirs of the Peace Conference*, vol. 2, p. 872.

291. See Clive Foss, "The Turkish View of Armenian History: A Vanishing Nation," in Hovannisian, ed., *Armenian Genocide*, pp. 269–77.

292. Shaw and Shaw, *History*, vol. 2, pp. 315–17. This goes further than Djemal Pasha, who as much as admits the deportation of 1,500,000 Armenians and the death of 600,000 (*Memories of a Turkish Statesman*, p. 280). As Beylerian writes, "Les auteurs d'un ouvrage récent sur l'Empire ottoman, Stanford Shaw et Ezel Kural-Shaw, indiquent à peine 200.000 personnes disparues; mais où est passé alors le reste du peuple arménien?" (*Grandes Puissances*, p. lxiii).

293. FO 371/4174/136069, de Robeck to Foreign Office, 21 September 1919.

294. FO 371/6505/E12761, 3 November 1921.

295. Kazarian, "Turkey Tries Its Chief Criminals," p. 7.

296. For British complaints about Talaat and Enver's anti-British efforts, see Kilmarnock to Curzon, 4 March 1920, *Documents on British Foreign Policy 1919–1939* (London: Her Majesty's Stationery Office, 1960), 1st ser., vol. 9, p. 119; Curzon to Kilmarnock, 6 March 1920, in ibid., p. 122; Curzon to Derby, 8 March 1920, in ibid., p. 125; Derby to Curzon, 9 March 1920, in ibid., pp. 125–26; and Curzon to Kilmarnock, 1 May 1920, in ibid., p. 456.

297. In his otherwise unrepentant memoirs, Djemal wrote (for an English-speaking audience): "Public opinion will recognise that I had nothing to do with the deportations and Armenian massacres. . . . I am equally innocent of ordering any massacres; I have even prevented them and cause all possible help to be given to all emigrants at the time of the deportations" (*Memories of a Turkish Statesman*, p. 279).

298. Jacques Derogy, *Resistance and Revenge: The Armenian Assassination of the Turkish Leaders Responsible for the 1915 Massacres and Deportations* (New Brunswick, N.J.: Transaction, 1990), A. M. Berrett, trans., p. xxvii.

299. Ibid. There are popular Armenian rumors that the killers were actually Armenians.

300. Kazarian, "Turkey Tries Its Chief Criminals," p. 7.

301. Edward Alexander, *A Crime of Vengeance: An Armenian Struggle for Justice* (New York: Free Press, 1991); Derogy, *Resistance and Revenge*, pp. xix–xxi. On whether Israeli agents should have followed Tehlirian's example and shot Eichmann in Buenos Aires, see Arendt, *Eichmann in Jerusalem*, p. 265.

CHAPTER FIVE

NUREMBERG

1. Jackson, *Case against the Nazi War Criminals*, p. 3.

2. In the most recent popular book on Nuremberg, in 447 pages, Joseph E. Persico devotes only two paragraphs to the Morgenthau Plan's notion that the German war criminals did not deserve trials (*Nuremberg: Infamy on Trial* [New York: Viking, 1994], p. 15). For an excellent overview, see Bradley F. Smith, *The Road to Nuremberg* (New York: Basic Books, 1981).

3. For a typical error of this kind, see Scharf, *Balkan Justice*, p. xiii.

4. For a historically accurate view, see Richard A. Primus, *The American Language of Rights* (Cambridge: Cambridge University Press, 1999), pp. 213–15.

5. CAB 66/25, Eden memorandum, W.P. (42) 264, 22 June 1942, Annex No. 2 to law officers' memorandum.

6. FO 371/39005/C15057, 26 October 1944.

7. CAB 66/25, Eden memorandum, W.P. (42) 264, 22 June 1942. In June 1942, the Czechoslovak exile government drew up a list of German war criminals, including Hitler, who would be tried and executed immediately upon liberation.

8. FO 371/39010/C12588/14/62, UNWCC report, 19 September 1944. The Soviet Union boycotted, complaining that the UNWCC was dominated by former British colonies. For a typically disparaging assessment, see FO 371/39010/C17673/14/62, 11 December 1944.

9. Halifax to Hull, in Smith, ed., *American Road to Nuremberg*, p. 16; Bernays memorandum, 15 September 1944, in ibid., p. 34.

10. For a typically gloomy evaluation, see 22 January 1945 memorandum to Truman, in *Morgenthau Diary*, vol. 2, pp. 1524–25.

11. Churchill to Stalin and Roosevelt, 12 October 1943, *FRUS: 1943* (Washington, D.C.: GPO, 1964), vol. 1, pp. 556–57.

12. Simon memorandum, 4 September 1944, in Smith, ed., *American Road to Nuremberg*, p. 32.

13. Moscow Declaration, in ibid., pp. 13–14.

14. Ibid.

15. Herbert Wechsler, *Principles, Politics, and Fundamental Law: Selected Essays* (Cambridge, Mass.: Harvard University Press, 1961), p. 140; Smith, *Road to Nuremberg*, p. 4. Bradley F. Smith has no connection with a Holocaust-denier of the same name with a different middle initial (Deborah E. Lipstadt, *Denying the Holocaust: The Growing Assault on Truth and Memory* [New York: Free Press, 1993], pp. 183–208).

16. Gilbert, *Nuremberg Diary*, p. 7.

17. *Henry L. Stimson Diaries*, vol. 50, 29 March 1945, p. 208.

18. For a slightly less trustworthy version, see Stimson and McGeorge Bundy, *On Active Service in War and Peace* (New York: Harper and Row, 1948), pp. 565–91.

19. Thus, Jackson could *start* his report on the London Charter by asserting that the "United States, at the close of World War II, found itself in possession of high-ranking prisoners" (Jackson, *Report*, p. v).

20. *Stimson Diaries*, vol. 52, 10 August 1945, p. 72.

21. Brackman, *The Other Nuremberg*, p. 47; Piccigallo, *Japanese on Trial*, pp. 16–17.

22. FO 371/39004/C14080, Obligations of Theatre Commanders in Relation to War Crimes, C.C.S. 705, 2 October 1944.

23. State Department to Harriman, in *FRUS: Diplomatic Papers 1944*, vol. 4, Europe (Washington, D.C.: GPO, 1966), p. 1198.

24. *Stimson Diaries*, vol. 49, 15 December 1944, p. 96. See also *Stimson Diaries*, vol. 50, 25 January 1945, p. 74.

25. See, for instance, Richard Breitman, *Official Secrets: What the Nazis Planned, What the British and Americans Knew* (New York: Hill and Wang, 1998), pp. 192–211, and Wyman, *Abandonment of the Jews*, p. 203.

26. *Morgenthau Diary*, vol. 1, p. 448.

27. Ibid., 4 September 1944, p. 490. This speech does not hold up well against Morgenthau Sr.'s own impressions. First, Morgenthau Sr. put the number of deported Greeks at 100,000, a factor of ten less than what his son reckoned. Second, Morgenthau Sr. saw these deportations as a precedent for more brutal ones: "It was probably for the reason that the civilized world did not protest against these deportations that the Turks afterward decided to apply the same methods on a larger scale not only to the Greeks but to the Armenians, Syrians, Nestorians, and others of its subject peoples" (Morgenthau Sr., *Ambassador Morgenthau's Story*, p. 323).

28. John Morton Blum, *Roosevelt and Morgenthau* (Boston: Houghton Mifflin, 1970), p. xvi.

29. *Morgenthau Diary*, vol. 1, 4 September 1944 meeting, p. 490.

30. Ibid., p. 664.

31. Ibid., p. 490. The specific issue at hand was the Ruhr, but Morgenthau's concern is wider. See also ibid., pp. 426–28.

32. Brief for a Conference with the President, *Stimson Diaries*, vol. 48, 25 August 1944, p. 24.

33. Taylor, *Anatomy*, pp. 108, 110.

34. *Morgenthau Diary*, vol. 1, 4 September 1944 meeting, p. 491.

35. Memorandum of Conversation with the President, *Stimson Diaries*, vol. 48, 25 August 1944, p. 29.

36. FDR to Stimson, 26 August 1944, *Morgenthau Diary*, vol. 1, pp. 443, 445.

37. For a sympathetic biography, see Godfrey Hodgson, *The Colonel: The Life and Wars of Henry Stimson 1867–1950* (New York: Knopf, 1990).

38. Wyman, *Abandonment of the Jews*, p. 314.

39. Frederick R. Whitridge et al. to Wilson, 25 November 1916, *FRUS: Lansing Papers*, vol. 1, p. 44.

40. *Morgenthau Diary*, vol. 1, 28 August 1944, p. 447.

41. Ibid., p. 427.

42. As the Soviet Union ran amok in the territories it captured, Stimson continued to worry about Soviet cruelty. He complained of "awkward demands" being made by the Soviets, that America turn over to them German prisoners with Russian citizenship, whom Stimson feared would be executed. "I pointed out that this was contrary to the traditions of sanctuary that the English peoples always had . . . and besides it violated the rules of the Geneva protocol towards prisoners of war. We were responsible for these prisoners and this ought not to be done. Unfortunately the step had already been taken. Nevertheless in spite of that I refused to sign the letter which McCloy had drawn for me consenting to it. . . . Let them take their own Germans that they capture but not ours. Otherwise we will be running into trouble with the treaties and with our own public opinion when the Russians wreak their will on such Germans" (*Stimson Diaries*, vol. 50, 16 January 1945, p. 48).

43. FDR-Stimson conversation on Germany occupation, 8 June 1944, *Stimson Diaries*, vol. 48, p. 93. In his preparatory notes for a meeting with Roosevelt, Stimson wrote: "Keeps us away from Russia during occupational period. Let her do the dirty work but don't father it" (*Stimson Diaries*, vol. 48, 25 August 1944, p. 24).

44. *Stimson Diaries*, vol. 48, 23 October 1944, p. 176.

45. *Stimson Diaries*, vol. 48, 26 August–3 September 1944, p. 30.

46. McCloy-Stimson conversation, 28 August 1944, in Smith, ed., *American Road to Nuremberg*, p. 23.

47. *Stimson Diaries*, vol. 48, 4 September 1944, p. 33. This was a favorite theme of Stimson's. On September 5, 1944, in a stormy meeting with Morgenthau, Stimson "pointed out to my colleagues . . . that it was very singular that I, the man who had charge of the Department which did the killing in the war, should be the only one who seemed to have any mercy for the other side; and Marshall and I [later] laughed over this circumstance together" (*Stimson Diaries*, vol. 48, 5 September 1944, p. 37).

48. Post-Surrender Germany program, 4 September 1944, *Morgenthau Diary*, vol. 1, pp. 508–9; Morgenthau Plan, 5 September 1944, in Smith, ed., *American Road to Nuremberg*, pp. 27–29. Italics added.

49. Smith, ed., *American Road to Nuremberg*, pp. 27–29. See also the draft plan, *Morgenthau Diary*, vol. I, pp. 463–75.

50. Allen Weinstein and Alexander Vassiliev, *The Haunted Wood: Soviet Espionage in America, the Stalin Era* (New York: Random House, 1999). White did not drive policy on war criminals; Morgenthau did.

51. *Morgenthau Diary*, vol. 1, p. 486.

52. Group Meeting, 7 September 1944, ibid., p. 559.

53. Between October 1946—when the trial of major war criminals at Nuremberg ended—and April 1949, American tribunals issued 185 indictments of high-level Germans accused of war crimes. The United States army also tried 1,700 Germans. Of the Germans before American tribunals, excluding the army's, about a hundred were

convicted (Thomas Alan Schwartz, *America's Germany: John J. McCloy and the Federal Republic of Germany* [Cambridge, Mass.: Harvard University Press, 1991], p. 157). Over 500 American military tribunals indicted 1,941 Germans, among them concentration camp guards and soldiers accused of killing American combatants. Of these, 1,517 were convicted; 324 were sentenced to death and 247 to life in jail (Richard L. Merritt, *Democracy Imposed: U.S. Occupation Policy and the German Public, 1945–1949* [New Haven: Yale University Press, 1995], p. 149n.5.)

54. Taylor, *Nuremberg and Vietnam,* pp. 27–28.

55. *Morgenthau Diary,* vol. 1, pp. 486–87.

56. Ibid.

57. Ibid.

58. George H. Gallup, ed., *The Gallup Poll: Public Opinion 1935–1971* (New York: Random House, 1972), vol. 1: 1935–48, p. 339 (hereafter cited as Gallup).

59. Ibid., p. 507.

60. Ibid., p. 501.

61. Ibid., pp. 477–78.

62. Smith, *Road to Nuremberg,* p. 229.

63. *Stimson Diaries,* vol. 48, 4 September 1944, p. 34.

64. *Morgenthau Diary,* vol. 1, p. 503.

65. *Stimson Diaries,* vol. 48, 5 September 1944, p. 35.

66. *Morgenthau Diary,* vol. 1, p. 494. That was at the Moscow Conference on October 22, 1943, where Hull phrased it slightly more delicately: "at sunrise on the following day there would occur a historic incident" (*FRUS: 1943,* vol. 3 [Washington, D.C.: GPO, 1963], p. 612). See also *Morgenthau Diary,* vol. 1, p. 447.

67. *Morgenthau Diary,* vol. 1, p. 526.

68. *Morgenthau Diary,* vol. 1, 5 September 1944, pp. 521–24. Morgenthau and Hopkins mulled about having Stimson vent his views in front of Roosevelt, in the hopes of turning the president against the War Department for good. "And let him know where Stimson stands," Morgenthau added cannily. Even better: "[L]ook, Harry, I think it's terribly important to let Stimson blow off like that in front of the President." Hopkins, giddy after the meeting, hoped that in that case, Roosevelt "might blow right up in Stimson's face. That would settle it, you know. Stimson would see there was no more use talking" (ibid).

69. *Stimson Diaries,* vol. 48, 5 September 1944, p. 36.

70. *Morgenthau Diary,* vol. 1, p. 532.

71. *Stimson Diaries,* vol. 48, pp. 36, 44; War Department memorandum, *Morgenthau Diary,* vol. 1, p. 532.

72. Stimson-Cramer conversation, 5 September 1944, in Smith, ed., *American Road to Nuremberg,* pp. 25–27.

73. *Stimson Diaries,* vol. 48, 7 September 1944, p. 49. Stimson did not mention Eisenhower.

74. *Stimson Diaries,* vol. 48, 7 September 1944, pp. 51–52.

75. *Stimson Diaries,* vol. 48, 9 September 1944, p. 57.

76. Stimson to FDR, 9 September 1944, in *Stimson Diaries,* vol. 48, pp. 60–61, and *Morgenthau Diary,* vol. 1, p. 613. Italics added.

77. *Stimson Diaries,* vol. 48, 11 September 1944, p. 67.

78. *Stimson Diaries,* vol. 48, 14 September 1944, p. 74.

79. *Stimson Diaries*, vol. 48, 13 September 1944, p. 71.

80. Québec Directive, 15 September 1944, *Morgenthau Diary*, vol. 1, p. 621.

81. Treasury meeting, 19 September 1944, ibid., pp. 625. As Stimson put it, "[T]he President had sent a decision flatly against us in regard to the treatment of Germany. Apparently he has gone over completely to the Morgenthau proposition and has gotten Churchill . . . with them" (*Stimson Diaries*, vol. 48, 16–17 September 1944, p. 81).

82. *FRUS: Quebec Conference* (Washington, D.C.: GPO, 1972), p. 467.

83. *Stimson Diaries*, vol. 48, 20 September 1944, p. 92.

84. Treasury meeting, 19 September 1944, *Morgenthau Diary*, vol. 1, pp. 624–25.

85. *Stimson Diaries*, vol. 48, 16–17 September 1944, p. 82.

86. Stimson to FDR, 15 September 1944, *Stimson Diaries*, vol. 48, pp. 83–84.

87. Morgenthau to FDR, in *Morgenthau Diary*, vol. 1, pp. 631–32. The paper evidently came out between September 20 and 25, 1944.

88. *Stimson Diaries*, vol. 48, 20 September 1944, pp. 92–93.

89. "Morgenthau Plan on Germany Splits Cabinet Committee," *New York Times*, 24 September 1944, pp. 1, 8. See also Lansing Warren, "Own Aides Shaping Peace, Hull Hints," *New York Times*, 26 September 1944, p. 11.

90. In a November 1944 Gallup poll, 34 percent of Americans wanted to destroy Germany as a political entity (Morgenthau's position), 32 percent wanted to supervise and control Germany, and 12 percent wanted to rehabilitate Germany (Stimson's position) (Gallup, p. 470; see also p. 426.)

91. Gallup, p. 499. Among college-educated Americans, 71 percent preferred close supervision of German industry, and only 6 percent wanted pastoralization.

92. Dallek, *Roosevelt and American Foreign Policy*, p. 477.

93. *Stimson Diaries*, vol. 48, 25 September 1944, p. 105. Stimson had carefully noted the Sunday front-page "reports of the alleged 'split in the Cabinet' " in the press. *Alleged* split? (*Stimson Diaries*, vol. 48, 23–24 September 1944, p. 104).

94. *Morgenthau Diary*, vol. 1, p. 633.

95. Ibid., p. 670.

96. *Stimson Diaries*, vol. 48, 27 September–1 October 1944, p. 109.

97. *Stimson Diaries*, vol. 48, 3 October 1944, p. 117.

98. *Stimson Diaries*, vol. 49, 4 November 1944, p. 5.

99. Bernays memorandum, "Trial of European War Criminals," 15 September 1944, in Smith, ed., *American Road to Nuremberg*, p. 36.

100. Ibid.

101. *Stimson Diaries*, vol. 48, 24 October 1944, pp. 179–80.

102. Bernays memorandum, 15 September 1944, in Smith, ed., *American Road to Nuremberg*, p. 36.

103. To Keynes (*Stimson Diaries*, vol. 49, 19 November 1944, p. 35) and Roosevelt (*Stimson Diaries*, vol. 49, 21 November 1944), among others.

104. Smith, *The Road to Nuremberg*, p. 75.

105. *Stimson Diaries*, vol. 48, 24 October 1944, p. 180.

106. *Stimson Diaries*, vol. 48, 27 October 1944, p. 188. This is a reference, extremely rare in Stimson's diaries, to the Holocaust.

107. *Morgenthau Diary*, vol. 2, 18 May 1945, p. 1504.

108. Among those who found this bizarre was Morgenthau. "I don't know, I'm not a lawyer," Morgenthau said to Jackson. "I might—can anyone give me an example in the history of the world where you have found an organization guilty? Has any court

ever convicted an organization?" "You have quite a number of antitrust cases where you have convicted trade organizations," Jackson replied. "Individuals," said Morgenthau. "But I agree with you that there is much to be unconventional about this," Jackson conceded. "If there isn't, there is no sense doing it" (ibid., p. 1505).

109. Dower, *Embracing Defeat*, p. 463.

110. *Stimson Diaries*, vol. 50, 21 January 1945, p. 62. Italics added.

111. FDR memorandum, 3 January 1945, in Smith, ed., *American Road to Nuremberg*, p. 92.

112. Morgenthau to Truman, 29 May 1945, *Morgenthau Diary*, vol. 2, pp. 1544–45.

113. Ibid.

114. Quoted in ibid., 18 May 1945, p. 1508.

115. Smith, *Road to Nuremberg*, pp. 201–4.

116. Arendt, *Eichmann in Jerusalem*, p. 6. See Segev, *Seventh Million*, and Lahav, *Judgment in Jerusalem*.

117. Jackson, *Case against the Nazi War Criminals*, p. 3.

118. FO 371/50988/U7378, Shawcross to Bevin, 10 September 1945.

119. FDR to Stettinius, 3 January 1945, in Smith, ed., *American Road to Nuremberg*, p. 92.

120. In *Department of State Bulletin*, 27 October 1946, p. 776.

121. In 1931, Stimson stopped a grant to Columbia University because, as he put it, "of the tremendous Jewish influence" there. (Hodgson, *Colonel*, p. 373.) McCloy recalled Morgenthau as "a deeply passionate member of the Jewish race. He felt his racial position was affronted by the activities of the Hitler regime" (in an interview with, of all people, Henry Morgenthau III, *Mostly Morgenthaus: A Family History* [New York: Ticknor and Fields, 1991], p. 372).

122. Hodgson, *Colonel*, p. 259.

123. *Stimson Diaries*, vol. 48, 3 October 1944, p. 118. For Stimson's own misrepresenting, see *Stimson Diaries*, vol. 48, 16–17 September 1944, p. 82, and 14 September 1944, p. 74.

124. Hodgson, *Colonel*, p. 373.

125. *Stimson Diaries*, vol. 48, 4 September 1944, p. 34.

126. For Stimson's rather muted reaction to a meeting with a congressional delegation that had visited Buchenwald, Dachau, and Nordhausen, see *Stimson Diaries*, vol. 51, 9 May 1945, pp. 109–10.

127. Martin Gilbert, *Auschwitz and the Allies* (London: Holt, Rinehart and Winston, 1981), pp. 299–322; Wyman, *Abandonment of the Jews*, pp. 288–307.

128. Stimson to FDR, 9 September 1944, *Stimson Diaries*, vol. 48, p. 61; *Morgenthau Diary*, vol. 1, p. 614. Italics added.

129. For the Nuremberg tribunal's rebuttal, see its judgment in Henry J. Steiner and Philip Alston, eds., *International Human Rights in Context: Law, Politics, Morals* (Oxford: Clarendon, 1996), pp. 103–9.

130. *Stimson Diaries*, vol. 50, 19 January 1945, pp. 57–58.

131. Wechsler, *Principles, Politics, and Fundamental Law*, p. 145.

132. Taylor, *Nuremberg and Vietnam*, p. 84.

133. *Stimson Diaries*, vol. 50, 18 January 1945, p. 54. See also Stimson, "The Nuremberg Trial: Landmark in Law," *Foreign Affairs*, vol. 25, no. 2 (January 1947), pp. 179–89.

134. Taylor, *Anatomy*, p. 44.

135. Jackson, *Report*, 25 July 1945, pp. 381–84.

136. Ibid., 19 July 1945, p. 299. Italics added.

137. Ibid., pp. ix, xii.

138. Jackson, *Report*, 23 July 1945, p. 331.

139. Ibid., 30 April 1945, p. 36.

140. *Stimson Diaries*, vol. 50, 8 January 1945, p. 24.

141. *Stimson Diaries*, vol. 50, 25 January 1945, p. 74.

142. Gordon Dean, preface, to Jackson, *Case against the Nazi War Criminals*, p. v.

143. Yuki Tanaka, *Hidden Horrors: Japanese War Crimes in World War II* (Boulder, Colo.: Westview, 1996), pp. 2–3; Gallup, pp. 388, 508–9. On popular stereotypes, see Paul Fussell, *Wartime: Understanding and Behavior in the Second World War* (Oxford: Oxford University Press, 1989), pp. 115–29.

144. James J. Weingartner, *Crossroads of Death: The Story of the Malmedy Massacre and Trial* (Berkeley: University of California Press, 1973); Gerhard L. Weinberg, *A World at Arms: A Global History of World War II* (Cambridge: Cambridge University Press, 1994), pp. 766–67.

145. Smith, *Road to Nuremberg*, pp. 114–18.

146. *Stimson Diaries*, vol. 49, 26 December 1944, p. 120.

147. Wyman, *Abandonment of the Jews*; Breitman, *Official Secrets*. See also Lucy Dawidowicz, "Could America Have Rescued Europe's Jews?" in her *What Is the Use of Jewish History?* (New York: Schocken, 1992), and the essays in Verne W. Newton, ed., *FDR and the Holocaust* (New York: St. Martin's, 1996), especially Michael R. Marrus, "Bystanders to the Holocaust," pp. 151–58, and, for a defense of Roosevelt, Arthur M. Schlesinger Jr., "Did FDR Betray the Jews? Or Did He Do More Than Anyone Else to Save Them?" pp. 159–61.

148. See American Jewish Conference to Hull, 25 August 1944, in Smith, ed., *American Road to Nuremberg*, p. 18.

149. Wyman, *Abandonment of the Jews*, pp. 189–90.

150. Taylor, *Anatomy*, p. 28.

151. Pehle to Stettinius, 28 August 1944, in Smith, ed., *American Road to Nuremberg*, p. 22.

152. Taylor, *Anatomy*, p. 26.

153. Treasury meeting, 19 September 1944, *Morgenthau Diary*, vol. 1, p. 626.

154. *Stimson Diaries*, vol. 52, 3 July 1945, pp. 12–13.

155. American Jewish Conference to Hull, 25 August 1944, in Smith, ed., *American Road to Nuremberg*, p. 19.

156. Bernays memorandum, 15 September 1944, in ibid., p. 34.

157. FO 371/50998/U9561, Shawcross address, 4 December 1945.

158. FO 371/39004/C13753, FDR and Churchill to Stalin (draft), 2 October 1944.

159. Winant to Hull, 28 January 1944, *FRUS: 1944*, vol. 4, pp. 1204–5.

160. Simon memorandum, 4 September 1944, in Smith, ed., *American Road to Nuremberg*, p. 32; FO 371/39004/C13753, 3 October 1944.

161. FO 371/39004/C13753, FDR and Churchill to Stalin (draft), 2 October 1944. Churchill signed the draft on September 17, 1944 and gave it to the cabinet on October 3. See also W.P. (44) 555, Eden war criminals memorandum, 3 October 1944, in FO 371/39003/C13529.

162. FO 371/39005/C14328/G, 30 October 1944.

163. War Cabinet minutes 131 (44), 4 October 1944, in FO 371/39003/C13561/G.

164. CAB 66/64, Simon memorandum, W.P. (45) 225, 9 April 1945, pp. 110 (Simon's italics), 112.

165. CAB 65/50, W.M. (45) 43, War Cabinet meeting, 12 April 1945, 3:30 P.M., p. 24.

166. FO 371/51019/U, Obligation of Theatre Commanders in relation to War Criminals, 27 April 1945. Underline in original.

167. CAB 66/64, Simon memorandum, W.P. (45) 225, 9 April 1945, p. 110; FO 371/50972/U2371, Ward memorandum, 8 April 1945.

168. FO 371/39202/13673; FO 371/39202/16398. The poll was by the British Institute of Public Opinion; its findings are also in Gallup, pp. 463–64.

169. CAB 66/42, Churchill war criminals memorandum, W.P. (43) 496, 9 November 1943, p. 266.

170. CAB 66/19, Eden memorandum, 5 October 1941, W.P. (41) 233. The British were not the only ones scared off of legalism by Leipzig. In a passionate memorandum that he ultimately decided not to send to Truman, Morgenthau wrote: "I am fearful that unless we drastically change our attitude toward the punishment of war criminals we will have an even worse fiasco than we had after the last World War." After the last war, he argued, international lawyers, including the Americans on the commission, threw up a host of technicalities, and the German court at Leipzig was inadequate. So "the criminals were free to plan new and unheard of atrocities for the next war" (Morgenthau to Truman, 29 May 1945, in *Morgenthau Diary*, vol. 2, pp. 1543–44).

171. CAB 66/19, Eden memorandum, 5 October 1941, W.P. (41) 233.

172. CAB 66/25, Annex No. 1 to law officers' memorandum, annex to Eden memorandum, W.P. (42) 264, 22 June 1942.

173. CAB 66/25, Eden memorandum, W.P. (42) 264, 22 June 1942.

174. Ibid.

175. Ibid. For more on legalism's limits, see ibid., annex by the law officers.

176. CAB 66/42, Churchill war criminals memorandum, W.P. (43) 496, 9 November 1943, pp. 265–66.

177. Ibid.

178. Bohlen minutes, Soviet embassy dinner, 29 November 1943, *FRUS: The Conferences at Cairo and Tehran 1943* (Washington, D.C.: GPO, 1961), p. 554. See also Martin Gilbert, *Winston S. Churchill: Vol. VII: Road to Victory 1941–1945* (Boston: Houghton Mifflin, 1986), pp. 580–81.

179. Churchill, *The Second World War* (London: Cassell, 1952), vol. 5, p. 330. Churchill was never convinced that Stalin was just joking.

180. In the fall of 1944, Churchill told Stalin of "the difficulties in international law" in trying major war criminals, but Stalin insisted on trials—show trials, as it turned out—if there were to be executions (FO 371/39005/C14765, Churchill to Roosevelt, 22 October 1944).

181. CAB 65/36, War Cabinet 152 (43), 10 November 1943, 6 P.M., p. 154.

182. Ibid.

183. CAB 66/51, Eden memorandum, 16 June 1944, W.P. (44) 330. The most Eden could do was draw up a list of major German and Italian war criminals, which he

hoped to keep under fifty (CAB 66/51, Attlee memorandum, 26 June 1944, W.P. [44] 345).

184. FO 371/39010/C17547/14/62, Somervell memorandum, 15 December 1944.

185. Like Stimson and Bernays, Somervell thought the Holocaust and other German atrocities were "secondary" to the "primary and main justification for punishing Hitler and his colleagues," which was "the policy which they have pursued in bringing about and conducting the war." Unlike Stimson and Bernays, however, Somervell insisted that waging aggressive war was "not a 'war crime' as recognised by International Law" (ibid). There is an obvious irony here, with Britain renouncing a principle it had itself established in the Versailles treaty.

186. Simon to Rosenman, 6 April 1945, in Smith, ed., *American Road to Nuremberg*, p. 150.

187. FO 371/51019/U3294, 16 April 1945.

188. Simon memorandum, 4 September 1944, in Smith, ed., *American Road to Nuremberg*, p. 32 (Simon's italics).

189. Ibid., p. 33.

190. *FRUS: Quebec*, p. 467.

191. FO 371/39005/C14854, Cadogan to Hurst, 28 October 1944.

192. FO 371/39004/C13753, 3 October 1944. See FO 371/39005/C14328/99/G, 9 November 1944.

193. *Stimson Diaries*, vol. 48, 9 October 1944, pp. 131–32.

194. *Stimson Diaries*, vol. 50, 19 January 1945, p. 58.

195. CAB 66/64, Simon memorandum, W.P. (45) 225, 9 April 1945.

196. Ibid. See Simon to Rosenman, 6 April 1945, in Smith, ed., *American Road to Nuremberg*, p. 150.

197. CAB 65/50, W.M. (45) 43, War Cabinet meeting, 12 April 1945, 3:30 P.M.

198. Ibid.

199. CAB 66/65, Simon memorandum, W.P. (45) 281, 3 May 1945, especially Annex B: The Argument for Summary Process against Hitler & Co.

200. *Stimson Diaries*, vol. 51, 27–29 April 1945, p. 79.

201. CAB 66/65, Simon memorandum, W.P. (45) 281, annex B, 3 May 1945 (drafted 16 April 1945).

202. Ibid.

203. CAB 65/50, War Cabinet 57, W.M. (45) 57, 3 May 1945, 6 P.M., pp. 331–32.

204. CAB 66/42, Churchill war criminals memorandum, 9 November 1943, W.P. (43) 496.

205. FO 371/39005/C14854/14/62, Cadogan to Hurst, 28 October 1944.

206. Airey Neave, *Nuremberg* (London: Hodder and Stoughton, 1978), p. 63.

207. Gilbert, *Churchill: A Life*, pp. 668, 677.

208. FO 371/39003/C13210/14/62, Eden to Churchill, 3 October 1944.

209. CAB 66/64, Simon memorandum, W.P. (45) 225, 9 April 1945.

210. FO 371/51019/U3450/29/G, Foreign Office to San Francisco, 5 May 1945.

211. Gilbert, *Auschwitz and the Allies*, pp. 77, 341; see also pp. 299–322, and Breitman, *Official Secrets*.

212. FO 371/51019/U3450/29/G, Foreign Office to San Francisco, 5 May 1945.

213. Gilbert, *Auschwitz and the Allies*, p. 341.

214. FO 371/39010/C17547/14/62, Somervell memorandum, 15 December 1944.

215. CAB 66/50, Simon UNWCC memorandum, 2 June 1944, W.P. (44) 294, p. 3.

216. CAB 66/64, Simon memorandum, 9 April 1945, W.P. (45) 225.

217. CAB 66/65, Simon memorandum, 3 May 1945, W.P. (45) 281, annex D.

218. Halifax to Hull, 19 August 1944, Smith, ed., *American Road to Nuremberg*, p. 16.

219. FO 371/39005/C14744, 30 October 1944. .

220. FO 371/39005/C14744, Eden to Hurst, 9 November 1944.

221. It is not clear from my research exactly what role was played here by British antisemitism. In the documents I read, I found only the occasional expression of genteel antisemitism. For instance, a British diplomat at Nuremberg reported to Ernest Bevin: "It is not an impressive crowd: indeed one's first impression of the Grand Hotel is that one has suddenly been transported to Jaffa or Tel Aviv. It is perhaps natural that the Jews should congregate at the trial of those who did their best to wipe out their race from the face of Europe. But it is a regrettable fact that the Jews who throng the corridors of the Grand Hotel neither inspire confidence nor command respect, least of all from the German staff" (FO 371/51003/U9934, Pink to Bevin, 29 November 1945).

222. FO 371/39202/13673; FO 371/39202/16398.

223. Bohlen minutes, Soviet embassy dinner, 29 November 1943, in *FRUS: Cairo and Tehran*, p. 554.

224. Ibid.

225. FO 371/39005/C14765, Churchill to Roosevelt, 22 October 1944.

226. *Stimson Diaries*, vol. 47, 8 June 1944, p. 93.

227. *Stimson Diaries*, vol. 48, 4 September 1944, pp. 33–34.

228. *Morgenthau Diary*, vol. 1, p. 494.

229. OSS study no. 2337, 28 November 1944, in ibid., p. 770.

230. CAB 66/63, Balfour memorandum, 12 March 1945, W.P. (45) 156. Eden was impressed and circulated the paper.

231. FO 371/50972/U2371, Ward memorandum, 8 April 1945.

232. FO 371/39004/C14255, 6 October 1944.

233. FO 371/39005/C104872/G, 23 October 1944.

234. FO 371/39004/C14255, Churchill to Eden, P.M.'s personal minute M.1003/4, 5 October 1944.

235. In CAB 66/25, Eden memorandum, 22 June 1942, W.P. (42) 264.

236. *FRUS: 1942*, vol. 3, p. 473.

237. Harriman to Hull, 19 August 1944, *FRUS: 1944*, vol. 4, p. 1208.

238. Harriman to Hull, 16 December 1943, *FRUS: 1943*, vol. 3, p. 847.

239. Harriman to Hull, 23 December 1943, ibid., p. 851.

240. Harriman to Hull, 24 December 1943, ibid., p. 851.

241. Kennan to Hull, 29 November 1944, *FRUS: 1944*, vol. 4, p. 1209.

242. Harriman to Hull, 6 December 1944, ibid., p. 1211.

243. Ibid., p. 1207.

244. Kennan to Hull, 19 October 1944, *FRUS; 1944*, p. 1209.

245. Harriman to Hull, 20 December 1943, *FRUS: 1943*, vol. 3, p. 849.

246. Winant to Hull, 23 December 1943, ibid., p. 849. For an evaluation of the Soviets' propaganda purposes—for "whipping up and keeping alive a spirit of vengeance" among Soviet citizens, reminding the world of Soviet suffering, frightening the SS and German soldiers, and putting ultimate responsibility on the German leadership—see Harriman to Hull, 23 December 1943, ibid., pp. 850–51. Harriman wanted to follow the Soviets' lead and use Kharkov as a way of intimidating German troops (Harriman to Hull, 27 December 1943, ibid., p. 853).

247. Harriman to Hull, 16 December 1943, ibid., p. 848.

248. FO 371/39005/C104872/G, 23 October 1944.

249. Harriman to Hull, 23 December 1943, *FRUS: 1943*, vol. 3, p. 851. The Americans did not doubt that the Germans were guilty and did not otherwise fault the Soviet procedures.

250. Jackson, *Report*, p. v.

251. Ibid, p. vi.

252. Ibid., 26 June 1945, p. 76.

253. Ibid., 19 July 1945, p. 303.

254. Jackson, *Report*, pp. vii–viii.

255. Ibid., 25 July 1945, p. 387.

256. A. N. Trainin, *Hitlerite Responsibility under Criminal Law* (London: Hutchinson, 1945), A. J. Vishinsky, ed., Andrew Rothstein, trans., p. 37.

257. Nuremberg indictment number 1, in U.S. Department of State, *Trial of War Criminals* (Washington, D.C.: GPO, 1945), p. 89.

258. Kennan, *Memoirs*, p. 261.

259. See Taylor, *Anatomy*, p. 639. That Katyn was committed by the Germans was a standard Soviet canard; see *Soviet Government Statements on Nazi Atrocities* (London: Hutchinson, 1946? [n.d.]), pp. 107–36; and Ulam, *Stalin*, p. 583.

260. FO 371/50988/U7358, Cadogan note, 27 September 1945. When news of the Katyn massacre reached London, Cadogan on June 18, 1943, noted a British report "making the case against the Russians for the Katyn murders, and drawing the inference that it was terrible to be on friendly terms with a Government that can do such things. I pointed out that, years before Katyn, the Soviet Government made a habit of butchering their own citizens by the 10,000's, and that if we could fling ourselves into their arms in 1941, I don't know that Katyn makes our position more delicate. The blood of Russians cries as loud to Heaven as that of Poles. But it's very nasty. How can Poles *ever* live amicably alongside Russians, and how can *we* discuss with Russians execution of German 'war criminals', when we have condoned this?" (*The Diaries of Sir Alexander Cadogan, O.M., 1938–1945* [New York: G.P. Putnam's Sons, 1972], David Dilks, ed., p. 537). Taylor lets the British off the hook by garbling the quote: "How can *we* discuss with Russians execution of German 'war criminals', when they have done this?" (Taylor, *Anatomy*, p. 467).

261. FO 371/50988/U7358, draft Nuremberg indictment, 22 September 1945.

262. FO 371/50990/U8261, 13 October 1945.

263. Harris, *Tyranny on Trial*, p. 252.

264. Davidson, *Trial of the Germans*, pp. 71–74. For more on Soviet chicanery, see Taylor, *Anatomy*, pp. 466–72, and Neave foreword in Louis FitzGibbon, *The Katyn Cover-Up* (London: Tom Stacey, 1972).

265. The Soviet Union also took pains to make sure that Nuremberg would not give the Germans the opportunity to score a few final propaganda points. In a draft of the London Charter, the Soviets wrote: "All attempts to use trial for Nazi propaganda and for attacks on the Allied countries should be decisively ruled out." There was no American equivalent to this (Jackson, *Report*, pp. 84, 178). See also Natalya Lebedeva, "Stalin and the Nuremberg Trial," *Moscow News*, no. 11, 24–30 March 1995, p. 12.

266. FO 371/51002/U9824, 10 December 1945.

267. Jackson reservations, 6 October 1945, *IMT*, vol. 1, p. 95; FO 371/50988/U7358, draft Nuremberg indictment, 22 September 1945.

268. FO 371/50988/U8048G, Cabinet 38 (45), 9 October 1945.

269. FO 371/50990/U8402, 12 October 1945.

270. *Morgenthau Diary*, vol. 2, p. 1561.

271. Taylor, *Anatomy*, p. 122.

272. Judith Shklar pointed out that anyone who advocates using trials as a part of a political process runs the risk of being accused of Vishinskyism (*Legalism*, pp. 143–44). This was not a risk that bothered the Soviet Union much.

273. Taylor, *Anatomy*, p. 209.

274. Ibid., p. 211.

275. FO 371/50998/U9445, Dean to Foreign Office, 28 November 1945.

276. FO 371/51004/U10023, Kerr to Foreign Office, 14 December 1945.

277. Taylor, *Anatomy*, p. 500.

278. Nikitchenko dissent, *IMT*, vol. 1, pp. 342–64.

279. Davidson, *Trial of the Germans*, p. 30.

280. True to form, when the Genocide Convention was passed, the Soviet Union would exclude political groups from the possible victims of genocide (Lawrence J. LeBlanc, *The United States and the Genocide Convention* [Durham, N.C.: Duke University Press, 1991]).

281. Richard Goldstone, *Prosecuting War Criminals* (London: David Davies Memorial Institute of International Studies, August 1996), occasional paper no. 10, p. 2.

282. Shklar, *Legalism*, pp. 170–71.

Chapter Six
The Hague

1. Tanner, *Croatia*, pp. 141–67. On the lack of historical antecedents in Bosnia to the Ustasha atrocities, see Noel Malcolm, *Bosnia: A Short History* (New York: New York Univeristy Press, 1996), and Robert J. Donia and John V. A. Fine Jr., *Bosnia & Hercegovina: A Tradition Betrayed* (New York: Columbia University Press, 1994).

2. The precise death toll in the camps remains unclear: the official Communist figure was 600,000, and Tudjman stunned Serbs in the 1970s by claiming that only one-tenth that number had been killed (Tanner, *Croatia*, p. 152).

3. Aleksa Djilas, *The Contested Country: Yugoslav Unity and Communist Revolution 1919–1953* (Cambridge, Mass.: Harvard University Press, 1991), pp. 144–46.

4. Malcolm, *Bosnia*, pp. 184–92. See Ivo Banac, *The National Question in Yugoslavia: Origins, History, Politics* (Ithaca, N.Y.: Cornell University Press, 1984), pp. 359–78.

5. Roy Gutman, *A Witness to Genocide* (New York: Macmillan, 1993), pp. xxi–xxii; Aryeh Neier, *War Crimes: Brutality, Genocide, Terror, and the Struggle for Justice* (New York: Times Books, 1998), pp. 114–16.

6. Tim Judah, *The Serbs: History, Myth and the Destruction of Yugoslavia* (New Haven: Yale University Press, 1997), p. 120.

7. Ibid., p. 130.

8. Richard West, *Tito and the Rise and Fall of Yugoslavia* (New York: Carroll and Graf, 1996), p. 210.

9. Djilas, *Contested Country*, pp. 162–63; Laura Silber and Allan Little, *Yugoslavia: Death of a Nation* (New York: TV Books, 1995), pp. 28–29.

10. Judah, *Serbs*, p. 132.

11. Ibid., pp. 120–21; West, *Tito*, pp. 208–9.

12. Silber and Little, *Yugoslavia*, pp. 84–85, 98; Cohen, *Hearts Grown Brutal*, pp. 306–13, 501.

13. Judah, *Serbs*, pp. 132–33.

14. Silber and Little, *Yugoslavia*, p. 93.

15. Cassese introduction in ICTY, *The Path to The Hague: Selected Documents on the Origins of the ICTY* (The Hague: United Nations, 1996), p. 9.

16. U.S. Department of State, *Dispatch*, 12 November 1990, p. 260, in ibid.

17. Warren Zimmermann, *Origins of a Catastrophe: Yugoslavia and Its Destroyers—America's Last Ambassador Tells What Happened and Why* (New York: Times Books, 1996), p. 158.

18. Gutman, *Witness to Genocide*, p. xvii.

19. Helsinki Watch, *War Crimes in Bosnia-Hercegovina* (New York: Human Rights Watch, 1992), pp. 1–7, 18, 156–57, 193–94. See Neier, *War Crimes*, pp. 123–25.

20. Silber and Little, *Yugoslavia*, pp. 248–52. See also Ed Vulliamy, *Seasons in Hell: Understanding Bosnia's War* (New York: Simon and Schuster, 1994).

21. UN Security Council Resolution 780 (1992), S/25274. The echo of the UNWCC was evidently intentional—ironically, given how feeble a step toward Nuremberg the UNWCC was in its day.

22. In Gutman, *Witness to Genocide*, pp. 150–56.

23. Patrick Bishop and Barbara Smit, "Britain 'Snubbed War Crimes Team,' " *Daily Telegraph*, 4 December 1993, p. 16. See also Robert Block and Stephen Castle, "MPs Unite in Condemning Britain's Record on War Crime Prosecutions," *Independent*, 8 August 1993, p. 14.

24. See also Philippe Naughton, "Yugoslav War Crimes Investigator Assails U.N.," Reuters, 18 March 1994. For a summary of the commission's findings, see the excerpt, "Interim Report of the Commission of Experts," UN S/25274, 2 January 1993, in W. Michael Reisman and Chris T. Antoniou, eds., *The Laws of War: A Comprehensive Collection of Primary Documents on International Laws Governing Armed Conflict* (New York: Vintage, 1994), pp. 387–92. In 1994, the commission's files were in the hands of the Hague tribunal (*ICTY Yearbook 1994* [New York: UN, 1994], p. 119).

25. In *Path to The Hague*, pp. 55–57.

26. Carla Anne Robbins, "Balkan Judgments," *Wall Street Journal*, 13 July 1993, p. A1.

27. See Owen, *Balkan Odyssey* (New York: Harcourt Brace, 1995), p. 86.

28. Robbins, "Balkan Judgments." Eagleburger would later say that he would probably give the war criminals amnesty in exchange for a peace agreement ("An Exercise in Hypocrisy," *60 Minutes*, CBS News, 4 October 1994).

29. Silber and Little, *Yugoslavia*, p. 287. See Robert D. Kaplan's controversial *Balkan Ghosts: A Journey through History* (New York: St. Martin's Press, 1993).

30. Silber and Little, *Yugoslavia*, p. 288. See also Elizabeth Drew, *On the Edge: The Clinton Presidency* (New York: Simon and Schuster, 1994), pp. 138–63.

31. Gutman, *Witness to Genocide*, p. xxxviii.

32. In *Path to The Hague*, p. 67.

33. UN Security Council resolution 808 (1993), in *ICTY Basic Documents 1995* (New York: UN, 1995), pp. 143–45.

34. In Drew, *On the Edge*, p. 153.

35. UN Security Council, 25 May 1993, 9 p.m., S/PV. 3217.

36. Ibid.

37. AP, 14 December 1992.

38. UN Security Council resolution 827 (1993), passed on 25 May 1993, in *ICTY Basic Documents 1995*, pp. 1–27.

39. List provided by Security Council ambassador, 13 August 1993. On MacKinnon, see Neier, *War Crimes*, pp. 179–91.

40. See Cassese's *International Law in a Divided World* (Oxford: Oxford University Press, 1986), and *Violence and Law in the Modern Age* (Princeton: Princeton University Press, 1988).

41. The other judges were: Georges Abi-Saab of Egypt; Jules Deschênes of Canada; Elizabeth Odio Benito, of Costa Rica, the vice president; Adolphus Karibi-Whyte of Nigeria; Claude Jorda of France; Haopei Li of China; McDonald; Rustam Sidhwa of Pakistan; Ninian Stephen of Australia; and Lal Chand Vohrah of Malaysia (UN secretary-general's office, 5 December 1994).

42. ICTY 1994 Report (A/49/342; S/1994/1007), in *ICTY Yearbook 1994*, p. 90.

43. William W. Horne, "The Real Trial of the Century," *American Lawyer*, September 1995, pp. 5ff.

44. *ICTY Yearbook 1994*, p. 102; *ICTY Basic Documents 1995*.

45. This draws on my "Courting Disaster: The U.N. Goes Soft on Bosnia. Again," *New Republic*, 6 September 1993, pp. 12–14.

46. In a straw poll by Albright, Bassiouni got the support of America, Japan, and five nonaligned governments; Lowe was backed by Britain, France, Russia, China, Spain, and two others. Brazil voted for Amos Wako, the former attorney general of Kenya (Stanley Meisler, "Bosnia War Crimes Dispute Divides Security Council," *Los Angeles Times*, 11 September 1993, p. A3).

47. In Stanley Meisler, "Jury Still Out on Bosnian War Crimes Tribunal Created by U.N.," *Los Angeles Times*, 25 December 1993, p. A5.

48. Stanley Meisler, "U.N. Names South African Judge as Balkans War Crimes Prosecutor," *Los Angeles Times*, 25 December 1993, p. A5.

49. HRW-Helsinki, "The War Crimes Tribunal: One Year Later," February 1994.

50. Stephen Engelberg, "Balkan War-Crimes Prosecution Bogs Down," *New York Times*, 7 July 1994, p. A5.

51. Latin for "We have a pope!" (Horne, "Real Trial of the Century").

52. Richard J. Goldstone, *Do Judges Speak Out?* (Johannesburg: South African Institute of Race Relations, 1993), pp. 21–24.

53. Scott Kraft's interview, *Los Angeles Times*, 21 March 1993, p. M3.

54. *ICTY Yearbook 1994*, p. 117.

55. Marlise Simons, "Bosnian Rapes Go Untried by the U.N.," *New York Times*, 7 December 1994, p. A12.

56. *ICTY Yearbook 1994*, p. 4.

57. Ibid., p. 117.

58. Ibid., pp. 90–91.

59. Ibid.

60. Thomas S. Warrick, "War Crimes: Don't Let Them Get Away with It," *Washington Post*, 20 December 1994, p. A21.

61. *ICTY Yearbook 1995* (New York: UN, 1995), p. 259.

62. Warrick, "War Crimes." The committees are the Fifth Committee and the Advisory Committee on Administrative and Budgetary Questions (ACABQ).

63. In December 1994, I asked Boutros-Ghali why Goldstone was in New York asking for more UN funding. "Your information is not precise," Boutros-Ghali said. "He is in Rwanda." This was less than responsive.

64. *ICTY Yearbook 1994*, p. 117.

65. *Prosecutor of the Tribunal* against *Dragan Nikolic*, IT-94–2-1.

66. In the matter of Dusko Tadic, *ICTY Yearbook 1994*, pp. 39–66.

67. ICTY press release CC/PIO/003-E, 1 February 1995.

68. AP, 25 February 1998. Arbour publicly dismissed Gelbard's comments as "without foundation and purely speculative."

69. *ICTY Yearbook 1994*, p. 103.

70. See, for instance, the tribunal's formal Rule 61 protest against Serbia for sheltering three indicted JNA officers (Cassese to Somavia, 24 April 1996, author's files).

71. *ICTY Yearbook 1994*, p. 20.

72. Owen to EU foreign ministers, 22 July 1994, in Owen, *Balkan Odyssey*, p. 309.

73. In David Rohde, *Endgame: The Betrayal and Fall of Srebrenica* (New York: Farrar Straus Giroux, 1997), p. 28.

74. Owen, *Balkan Odyssey*, p. 314.

75. Colin Powell with Joseph E. Persico, *My American Journey* (New York: Random House, 1995), pp. 577–78.

76. Drew, *On the Edge*, pp. 155–56.

77. Elaine Sciolino, "U.S. Won't Send Troops to Seek Croats' Bodies," *New York Times*, 24 June 1993, p. A12.

78. Bishop and Smit, "Britain 'Snubbed War Crimes Team.' "

79. "The World Tries Again: Making Rules for War," *The Economist*, 11 March 1995, pp. 21–23; Eric Stover and Gilles Peress, *The Graves: Srebrenica and Vukovar* (Berlin: Scalo, 1998), pp. 110–12. See also Carol J. Williams, "Serbian Authorities Thwart U.N. War Crimes Investigation in Balkans," *Los Angeles Times*, 21 November 1993, p. A8.

80. Mark Danner, "Bosnia: The Great Betrayal," *New York Review of Books*, 26 March 1996. Canada and other countries participated in UNPROFOR, of course, but this account emphasizes the bigger powers.

81. Dick Morris, *Behind the Oval Office: Winning the Presidency in the Nineties* (New York: Random House, 1997), p. 245.

82. Ibid., p. 253. See also Stephanopoulos, *All Too Human*, pp. 355, 381.

83. See Danner, "Great Betrayal," and Rohde, *Endgame*, pp. 27, 361. See also Owen, *Balkan Odyssey*, pp. 348–52.

84. Richard Holbrooke, *To End a War* (New York: Random House, 1998), p. 146.

85. Goldstone, foreword to Stover and Peress, *Graves*, p. 13.

86. Rohde, *Endgame*, pp. 188, 309, 68–69, 122–23, 177, 309–10.

87. Stephanopoulos, *All Too Human*, p. 214.

88. See ibid., pp. 355–57; Morris, *Behind the Oval Office*, p. 254; Mary Pat Kelly's breathless *"Good to Go": The Rescue of Capt. Scott O'Grady, USAF, from Bosnia* (Annapolis, Md.: Naval Institute Press, 1996); and O'Grady's own *Return with Honor.* On Milosevic's role in the rescue, see Owen, *Balkan Odyssey*, p. 351.

89. "Justice Collides with Peace: Bosnia," *The Economist*, 18 November 1995, p. 58.

90. *Prosecutor of the Tribunal* against *Meakic and others*, 13 February 1995; tribunal press release, CC/PIO/004-E, 13 February 1995; and Roger Cohen's front-page "Tribunal Charges Genocide by Serb," *New York Times*, 14 February 1995, p. A1.

91. See Roger Cohen, "Serb Defector Offers Evidence on War Crimes," *New York Times*, 13 April 1995, pp. A1, A12. The tribunal was skeptical of these documents, but Cohen, a superb reporter, seems more impressed with the basic gist. (Cohen, *Hearts Grown Brutal*, pp. 409–11.)

92. "Peace and Justice, Warring Angels: War Crimes," *The Economist*, 29 April 1995, pp. 62–63.

93. AP, 23 January 1996.

94. Holbrooke, *To End a War*, p. 190.

95. Reuters, 4 June 1997.

96. Roy Gutman, "Peacemaker?" *Newsday*, 3 October 1995, p. A5. See also Gutman, "Federal Army Tied to Bosnia Crimes," *Newsday*, 1 November 1995, p. A4.

97. Zimmermann, *Origins of a Catastrophe*, p. 175.

98. See *ICTY Yearbook 1995*, p. 254. Also on the list was Mico Stanisic, the self-styled minister of internal affairs in Pale.

99. On July 21, 1995, Goldstone indicted Dusko Sikirica and twelve others at the Keraterm camp; Slobodan Miljkovic and six others for the 1992 "ethnic cleansing" of Bosanski Samac in Bosnia's Posavina corridor; and Goran Jelisic (who called himself the "Serb Adolf") and Ranko Cesic for 1992 atrocities at the Luka camp near Brcko. Jelisic was charged with genocide.

100. Goldstone also indicted Milan Martic, president of the self-styled Republic of Serb Krajina (RSK) for a May 1995 rocket attack on Zagreb.

101. The commanders of Omarska, Susica, and Keraterm—Zeljko Meakic, Dragan Nikolic, and Dusko Sikirica—had already been separately indicted.

102. *Prosecutor of the Tribunal* against *Radovan Karadzic and Ratko Mladic*, IT-95-5-I, 25 July 1995.

103. See, for instance, Owen, *Balkan Odyssey*, pp. 390, 325, 332.

104. Ibid., p. 332. Owen thinks that Holbrooke sent Redman.

105. Rohde, *Endgame*, p. 179.

106. Ibid., p. 329.

107. Stephanopoulos, *All Too Human*, p. 383; Bob Woodward, *The Choice* (New York: Simon and Schuster, 1996), pp. 253–69.

108. Ibid., p. 268. Woodward does not specifically name Karadzic and Mladic, but they are the only people who fit that description.

109. Holbrooke, *To End a War*, p. 373. See also ibid., p. 81, and Cohen, *Hearts Grown Brutal*, pp. 451–52.

110. Owen, *Balkan Odyssey*, p. 357.

111. Holbrooke, *To End a War*, p. 90.

112. Ibid., p. 98.

113. Ibid., p. 99.

114. Ibid., pp. 107–8.

115. When Srebrenica fell, Milosevic had responded to an American démarche by dodging the blame.

116. Ibid., p. 147.

117. Ibid.

118. Ibid. See Holbrooke, "The Road to Sarajevo," *New Yorker*, 21 and 28 October 1996, p. 100.

119. Holbrooke, *To End a War*, p. 148.

120. Ibid., p. 152.

121. For Holbrooke's account of the second meeting, see *To End a War*, pp. 211–12. Hill was also underwhelmed by the CIA memorandum that Pardew gave to Milosevic.

122. Ibid., p. 197.

123. Reuters, 8 September 1995. Christopher added, "that does not mean that we are in any way compromising the efforts of the War Crimes Tribunal."

124. Gary J. Bass, "Settling with the Enemy: The Dicey Politics of Negotiating Peace in the Balkans with Accused War Criminals," *Washington Post*, 29 October 1995, p. C2.

125. Senior U.S. official, interview, 10 October 1995. I am grateful to Daniel Franklin, Washington bureau chief of *The Economist*, who asked these questions for me.

126. Holbrooke, *To End a War*, p. 310.

127. In *Behind the Oval Office*, Morris writes of "Ratko Mladac" (p. 252), not Mladic, and says that Karadzic "was wanted by the International Court of Justice" (p. 261), not the war crimes tribunal.

128. Holbrooke, *To End a War*, p. 219.

129. Ibid., p. 217.

130. Ibid., pp. 220–21.

131. Holbrooke, *To End a War*, advance proofs, p. 230. This passage was excised from the published version.

132. Holbrooke, *To End a War*, p. 222.

133. Ibid., p. 226.

134. See ibid., p. 271.

135. See ibid., pp. 251, 254–56, 263.

136. Goldstone, *Prosecuting War Criminals* (London: David Davies Memorial Institute of International Studies, August 1996), occasional paper no. 10, p. 21. It is not clear when, if ever, the Americans—presumably the people from the State Department—made such a suggestion.

137. Bass, "Settling with the Enemy."

138. Stephen Engelberg, "Panel Seeks U.S. Pledge on Bosnia War Criminals," *New York Times*, 3 November 1995, pp. A1, A12. Sacirbey would later formally ask the Americans and the Contact Group to make cooperation with The Hague a precondition for relaxing sanctions.

139. *ICTY Yearbook 1995*, pp. 311–16.

140. Reuters, 14 November 1995.

141. *Prosecutor of the Tribunal* against *Mile Mrksic, Miroslav Radic, and Veselin Sljivancanin*, IT-95–13–1, 7 November 1995.

142. *Prosecutor of the Tribunal* against *Dario Kordic, Tihomir Blaskic, Mario Cerkez, Ivica Santic, Pero Skopljak, Zlatko Aleksovski*, IT-95–14-T, 10 November 1995. This was the second indictment of Croats. On August 29, Bosnian Croat commander Ivica Rajic was indicted for leading a 1993 attack on Stupni Do, Bosnia (ICTY press release CC/PIO/017-E, 6 September 1995).

143. Myself included ("Justice Collides with Peace: Bosnia," p. 58). "Well," Galbraith said, "that was just snide journalism."

144. Goldstone was not the only person hassling Tudjman. The Americans, hoping to bolster the shaky Muslim-Croat Federation in Bosnia, brought up Croat atrocities. Holbrooke had Shattuck meet with Tudjman and Izetbegovic, demanding that he be able to continue his investigations and hoping that refugees would be able to return home. It took a dose of Holbrooke's trademark temper to get Tudjman and Izetbegovic to agree even to this.

145. *Prosecutor of the Tribunal* against *Radovan Karadzic and Ratko Mladic*, IT-95–18-I, 16 November 1995.

146. *ABA Journal*, April 1996.

147. Michael Dobbs, "War Crimes Prosecutor Says U.S. Information Insufficient," *Washington Post*, 7 November 1995, p. A19. Goldstone has said that the administration had leaked the letter. On the Perisic-Mladic intercepts, see Cabell Bruce, "Belgrade Blamed," *Newsday*, 12 August 1995.

148. Dayton Peace Agreement (DPA), Annex 1-A: Agreement on Military Aspects of the Peace Settlement, Article X.

149. DPA, Annex 4: Constitution, Article II: Human Rights and Fundamental Freedoms, paragraph 8.

150. DPA, Annex 4: Constitution, Article IX: General Provisions, paragraph 1.

151. DPA, Annex 1-A: Agreement on the Military Aspects of the Peace Settlement, Article VI, 2(a).

152. Silber and Little, *Yugoslavia*, p. 360.

153. Holbrooke, *To End a War*, p. 335.

154. Ibid., p. 341.

155. Some of these worries were outlined in a Ministry of Defence memorandum to John Major. I am indebted to Charles Grant, then defense editor of *The Economist*, for relaying this information to me.

156. James Gow, *Triumph of the Lack of Will: International Diplomacy and the Yugoslav War* (New York: Columbia University Press, 1997), pp. 184–95; David MacKenzie, *Serbs and Russians* (New York: Columbia University Press, 1996).

157. Jane Perlez, "Serbs Say Captive French Pilots Are to Be Released Today," *New York Times*, 12 December 1995, p. A10.

158. Holbrooke, *To End a War*, pp. 327–28.

159. Ibid., p. 332.

160. Ibid., p. 345.

161. Ibid.

162. Holbrooke, *To End a War*, p. 346.

163. *Prosecutor of the Tribunal* against *Djordje Djukic*, IT-96–20-I, 29 February 1996.

164. This paragraph is based on an interview with Nash and background interviews with IFOR and human rights officials.

165. HRW-Helsinki, "A Failure in the Making: Human Rights and the Dayton Agreement," vol. 8, no. 8 (D), June 1996, p. 29.

166. Philip Shenon, "G.I.'s in Bosnia Shun Hunt for War-Crime Suspects," *New York Times*, 2 March 1996, p. A4.

167. Johanna McGeary and Alexandra Stiglmayer, "Face to Face with Evil," *Time International*, 13 May 1996, pp. 18–23. *Newsweek*'s Stacy Sullivan started a "War Criminals Watch," taking an IFOR "Wanted" poster and checking off each suspect she found.

168. See Stover and Peress, *Graves*, pp. 138–48.

169. Ibid., pp. 166–67.

170. Rohde, *Endgame*, pp. 346–47; Stover and Peress, *Graves*, p. 148. This was hardly ideal: dogs might miss up to 20 percent of the land mines.

171. Ibid., pp. 148–50.

172. Ibid., pp. 151–52.

173. *Bulletin*, no. 2, 22 January 1996.

174. John Pomfret, "Wanted for War Crimes, Yet Free to Be in Zagreb," *Washington Post*, 8 June 1996, p. A22.

175. Holbrooke, *To End a War*, p. 338.

176. Ibid., p. 353.

177. Steven Erlanger, "Balkan Leaders Again Promise to Carry Out Accord on Bosnia," *New York Times*, 19 March 1996, pp. A1, A6.

178. Cassese to Somavia, 24 April 1996, author's files.

179. HRW-Helsinki, "Failure in the Making," p. 29.

180. Stover and Peress, *Graves*, pp. 168–70.

181. Renaud Girard, "Confession d'un Criminel de Guerre," *Le Figaro*, 8 March 1996; Garrick Utley, "Srebrenica: The Confession," ABC News, 7 March 1996.

182. Rohde, *Endgame*, p. 345.

183. *Prosecutor of the Tribunal* against *Zejnil Delalic, Zdravko Mucic, Hazim Delic and Esad Landzo*, IT-96–21-T, 21 March 1996.

184. In a case of mistaken identity, Germany also arrested Goran Lajic, a Bosnian Serb thought to be one of thirteen Keraterm indictees, near Nuremberg. Lajic was freed in June 1996 (Order, 17 June 1996, IT-95–8-T).

185. By this point, The Hague had indicted forty-six Serbs (three of them from Serbia proper), seven Croats, and three Muslims. It had six suspects in custody: Tadic, a Serb, Blaskic, a Croat, plus three Muslims and one Croat on Celebici charges.

186. "On Trial: War Crimes," *The Economist*, 11 May 1996, pp. 50–51.

187. See NATO Press Release (96)74, 9 May 1996.

188. Jane Perlez, "War Crimes Prosecutor Vents Frustration," *New York Times*, 22 May 1996, p. A8.

189. *Prosecutor of the Tribunal* against *Dragan Gagovic, Gojko Jankovic, Janko Janjic, Radomir Kovac, Zoran Vukovic, Dragan Zelenovic, Dragoljub Kunarac, Radovan Stankovic* ("Foca"), IT 96–23-I, June 26, 1996.

190. Holbrooke, *To End a War,* p. 355.

191. Jane Perlez, "Top Bosnian Serb Agrees to Resign," *New York Times,* 20 July 1996, p. A1.

192. Holbrooke, *To End a War,* pp. 356–57.

193. International Crisis Group, Sarajevo, "Elections in Bosnia and Herzegovina," 13 August 1996, pp. 4–5.

194. Samantha Power, "Pale Imitation: Meet Republika Srpska's New Democrats," *New Republic,* 14 October 1996, p. 18.

195. Gutman, "NATO's Aid May Hand Real Power to Plavsic," p. A6.

196. Carol Off, "The Prosecutor," *Elm Street,* summer 1999, p. 32.

197. For a glowing profile, see ibid., pp. 29–38.

198. This happened during the Blaskic trial, on June 24, 1997. There were reporters, myself included, sitting mystified in the press cubicles on the first floor of the tribunal as the UN police hustled the man out.

199. Mike O'Connor, "War Crimes Witness May Refuse to Testify," *New York Times,* 30 May 1996, p. A6. For Mevludin Oric's experiences, see Rohde, *Endgame.*

200. Elizabeth Neuffer, "Bosnia's War Criminals Enjoy Peacetime Power," *Boston Globe,* 29 October 1996, pp. A1, A20.

201. See "Madeleine s'en va-t-en guerre," *The Economist,* 16 August 1997, pp. 21–22.

202. Albright, "Bosnia in Light of the Holocaust: War Crimes Trials," speech at U.S. Holocaust Memorial Museum, 12 April 1994.

203. William Drozdiak, "U.S. Urges Formation of Special Police Unit for War Crimes Duty," *Washington Post,* Wednesday, 18 December 1996, p. A25. See also Steven Erlanger, "U.S. Ponders Special Force to Arrest War Suspects," *New York Times,* 19 December 1996, p. A11; briefing by Kenneth Bacon, assistant secretary of defense for public affairs, 28 January 1997, 1:30 P.M.

204. Reuters, 18 December 1996.

205. Reuters, 4 March 1997.

206. U.S. Department of State, briefing #75 by Nick Burns, 15 May 1997, 1:26 P.M.

207. White House, Office of the Press Secretary, "Remarks by the President at C-in-C's Meeting," 29 January 1997, Army Conference Room, the Pentagon, 10:25 A.M.

208. Slobodan Lekic, AP, 26 March 1997. See also White House, Office of the Press Secretary, 26 March 1997, Mike McCurry briefing, 1:36 P.M.

209. Holbrooke, *To End a War,* pp. 359–61.

210. This information is from a remarkable story by Steven Erlanger, then chief diplomatic correspondent of *The New York Times:* "On Bosnia, Clinton Supports Albright against Cohen View," *New York Times,* 12 June 1997, pp. A1, A12.

211. Reuters, 26 May 1997.

212. Albright-Arbour press availability, The Hague, 28 May 1997.

213. Reuters, 30 May 1997.

214. See "Trials, Tribulations and Tribunals," *The Economist,* 28 June 1997, pp. 50–51; Tyler Marshall, "Albright Blisters Balkan Leaders," *Los Angeles Times,* 1 June 1997,

p. A1; and Roy Gutman, "Albright: Chastise Serbs for Crimes," *Newsday*, 2 June 1997, p. A1.

215. UPI, 22 May 1997.

216. William Drozdiak, "NATO Chiefs Block Call for Pursuit of War Criminals," *Washington Post*, 13 June 1997, p. A36.

217. Tyler Marshall, "France, Italy Support Clinton's Bosnia Stance," *Los Angeles Times*, 21 June 1997, p. A1.

218. James Risen, "U.S. Formed Plan to Nab Serb Suspect," *Los Angeles Times*, 6 July 1997, p. A1. For a story sourced from OHR, see Jonathan C. Randal, "West Reportedly May Arrest Indicted Serb Karadzic as War Criminal," *Washington Post*, 6 July 1997, p. A20.

219. Judah, *Serbs*, pp. 229–30, 232–33.

220. Ed Vulliamy, "Horror Hidden beneath Ice and Lies," *Guardian*, 19 February 1996, p. 9.

221. On Kovacevic, see Judah, *Serbs*, p. 236, and Tina Rosenberg, "Defending the Indefensible," *New York Times Magazine*, 19 April 1998, pp. 46–56, 69; on Drljaca, see Neuffer, "Bosnia's War Criminals Enjoy Peacetime Power," pp. A1, A20.

222. Details from Rod Nordland, "War Criminals, Beware," *Newsweek*, 21 July 1997, p. 12.

223. Barry Schweid, AP, 10 July 1997.

224. Berger briefing, Warsaw, 10 July 1997, 3:44 P.M. Warsaw time.

225. Michael Evans and Tom Walker, "Former Police Chief Stood No Chance Once He Had Made the Fatal Mistake of Shooting at the Advancing Soldiers," *Times* (London), 11 July 1997.

226. Anna Husarska, "Tell the Serbs Who the Bad Guys Are," *Los Angeles Times*, 11 July 1997, p. 9.

227. AP, 15 July 1997; Mike O'Connor, "Serbs Threaten Retaliation for War-Crime Arrests, U.N. Says," *New York Times*, 17 July 1997, p. A6; Edward Cody, "U.S. Soldier in Bosnia Wounded in Sickle Attack," *Washington Post*, 17 July 1997, p. A24.

228. Reuters, 19 July 1997.

229. AP, 15 July 1997.

230. Reuters, 11 July 1997.

231. Reuters, 14 July 1997. See also Sergei Baibakov, "Russia to Keep Clear of Hunting War Crime Suspects," *TASS*, 5 November 1997.

232. Steven Erlanger, "France Balked at 2d NATO Raid in Bosnia," *New York Times*, 16 July 1997, p. A1.

233. Bradley Graham and Rick Atkinson, "NATO Remains Uncertain about Future Pursuit of Suspected War Criminals," *Washington Post*, 19 July 1997, p. A16; Richard Boudreaux, "In Bosnia, It Isn't Exactly Open Season on Karadzic," *Los Angeles Times*, 12 July 1997, p. 4; and UPI, 10 July 1997.

234. Jane Perlez, "A Vacation Fit for a King of Fugitives," *New York Times*, 3 August 1997, p. A8.

235. Edward Cody, "Serb May Be Seized, U.S. Envoys Warn," *Washington Post*, 10 August 1997, p. A1.

236. AFP, 13 August 1997.

237. Tracy Wilkinson, "West Turns Up Heat on Serb Strongman," *Los Angeles Times*, 17 August 1997, p. 4; Roy Gutman, "NATO's Aid May Hand Real Power to Plavsic," *Newsday*, 30 August 1997, p. A6.

238. See, for instance, Lee Hockstader, "The Rumor Heard 'Round the World," *Washington Post*, 27 September 1997, p. A14; Roy Gutman, "The Noose Tightens on Karadzic," *Newsday*, 15 September 1997, p. A17. See also Lee Hockstader, "Troops Seize Bosnian Serb TV Towers," *Washington Post*, 2 October 1997, p. A1.

239. R. Jeffrey Smith, "Secret Meetings Foiled Karadzic Capture Plan," *Washington Post*, 23 April 1998, p. A1.

240. Steven Erlanger, "French Said to Hurt Plan to Capture Karadzic," *New York Times*, 23 April 1998, p. A11.

241. Tim Weiner, "U.S. Cancels Plans for Raid on Bosnia to Capture 2 Serbs," *New York Times*, 26 July 1998, p. A1. On a special American arrest squad whose mission was evidently cancelled, according to that *Times* story, see Richard J. Newman, "Hunting War Criminals: The First Account of Secret U.S. Missions in Bosnia," *U.S. News & World Report*, 6 July 1998, p. 45.

242. Smith, "Secret Meetings Foiled Karadzic Capture Plan," p. A1.

243. AFP, 2 December 1999.

244. See Noel Malcolm, *Kosovo: A Short History* (New York: New York University Press, 1998).

245. See Ed Vulliamy and Patrick Wintour, "Hawks Smell a Tyrant's Blood," *Observer*, 30 May 1999, p. 15.

246. Jane Perlez, "Step by Step: How the U.S. Decided to Attack, and Why the Move Came So Fast," *New York Times*, 26 March 1999, p. A9; Raymond Bonner, "Tactics Were Barrier to Top Serb's Indictment," *New York Times*, 29 March 1999, p. A9.

247. Raymond Bonner, "Tribunal Chief Plans to Quit, Causing U.S. to Fear for Fate of Milosevic Case," *New York Times*, 30 April 1999, p. A12.

248. Clinton statement, Élysée, Paris, 17 June 1999.

CHAPTER SEVEN
CONCLUSION

1. Barton to Lansing, received 14 July 1915, *FRUS: 1915 Supplement*, p. 984.

2. Lansing to Barton, 19 July 1915, ibid.

3. Morgenthau Sr., *Ambassador Morgenthau's Story*, p. 330.

4. Holbrooke, *To End a War*, p. 217.

5. Willis, *Prologue*, p. 50.

6. Ibid., pp. 37–48. See, for instance, James M. Beck, *The Evidence in the Case: A Discussion of the Moral Responsibility for the War of 1914* (New York: G. P. Putnam's Sons, 1915).

7. See Peter Haas, "Introduction: Epistemic Communites and International Policy Coordination," *International Organization*, vol. 46, no. 1 (winter 1992), pp. 1–36; and Margaret E. Keck and Kathryn Sikkink, *Activists beyond Borders: Advocacy Networks in International Politics* (Ithaca, N.Y.: Cornell University Press, 1998).

8. Still, nonstate actors were mostly influential insofar as they could bring pressure on liberal states. There is only so much that a human rights activist or a reporter can

do. Governments have vastly more money than foundations, and the prosecutorial and investigative talents of the FBI and Justice Department personnel seconded to The Hague by the American government were crucial. Above all, only states can impose sanctions, operate spy satellites (at least for now), arrest war criminals, and go to war. Real changes in Bosnia policy came when Albright and Cook were elevated to the rank of foreign minister—when people basically of one mind with the people in these nonstate actors suddenly became state actors themselves.

9. See, for instance, Montgomery Belgion, *Epitaph on Nuremberg: A Letter Intended to Have Been Sent to a Friend Temporarily Abroad* (London: Falcon Press, 1946); Wilbourn E. Benton and Georg Grimm, eds., *Nuremberg: German Views of the War Crimes Trials* (Dallas: Southern Methodist University Press, 1955); and Minear, *Victors' Justice.*

10. Lloyd George, *War Memoirs*, vol. 6, p. xi.

11. Cassese speech at UN, 14 November 1994, in *ICTY Yearbook 1994*, pp. 136–37.

12. For a pro–ICC argument, see Neier, *War Crimes*, pp. 252–60; for a pessimistic assessment, see David Rieff, "Court of Dreams," *New Republic*, 7 September 1998, pp. 16–17.

13. Shklar, *Legalism*, p. 134.

14. Peter Baker, "Clinton Has Bosnia on His Mind," *Washington Post*, 10 August 1997, p. A1.

15. See Philip Gourevitch, *We Wish to Inform You That Tomorrow We Will Be Killed with Our Families: Stories from Rwanda* (New York: Farras Straus Giroux, 1998), pp. 248–52.

CHAPTER EIGHT
EPILOGUE

1. Albright statement at ICTY, 28 May 1997.

2. See, for instance, Bernays memorandum, 15 September 1944, in Smith, ed., *American Road to Nuremberg*, p. 36.

3. ICTY 1994 Report to UN, *ICTY Yearbook 1994*, p. 87.

4. Aron, *Peace and War*, p. 115.

5. Talleyrand, *Mémoires*, pp. 761–62.

6. CAB 28/5, I.C.-98, Allied conversation, London, 2 December 1918, 11 A.M., p. 5.

7. FO 92/21, Castlereagh memorandum, 15 July 1815. Kissinger disagrees: "The fate of Napoleon was of no immediate consequence in the European balance, but it served as a touchstone of the mind of the Allies" (*World Restored*, p. 140).

8. FO 371/4174/88761, Calthorpe to Curzon, 30 May 1919.

9. Merritt, *Democracy Imposed*, p. 161.

10. U.S. Information Agency, *Public Opinion in Bosnia Hercegovina: Volume IV: One Year of Peace* (Washington, D.C.: USIA, February 1997), p. 115.

11. Ibid., p. 114.

12. State Department polling, October 1999.

13. Ibid.

14. USIA opinion analysis, 4 August 1997.

15. BBC broadcast summary, 21 February 1998; from Radio Bosnia-Hercegovina, Sarajevo, 19 February 1998, 2 P.M. GMT.

16. FO 371/2485/66687, 26 May 1915.

17. CAB 23/43, Imperial War Cabinet 39, 28 November 1918, 11:45 A.M., pp. 2–5.

18. Pehle to Stettinius, 28 August 1944, in Smith, ed., *American Road to Nuremberg*, p. 22.

19. Albright, "Bosnia in Light of the Holocaust: War Crimes Trials," 12 April 1994. Her italics.

20. Ibid.

21. Some human rights activists are more skeptical, like Aryeh Neier of the Open Society Institute. See his "What Should Be Done about the Guilty?," *New York Review of Books*, 1 February 1990, pp. 32–35.)

22. As many authors have pointed out, it is always hard to trace the functioning of deterrence, because it is hard to spot the empirical evidence of something that did not happen. I will look only at cases of specific threats and the reaction to them. For a more detailed discussion of how to tell when deterrence is going on, see Paul K. Huth, "Extended Deterrence and the Outbreak of War," *American Political Science Review*, vol. 82, no. 2 (June 1988), pp. 439–41; Christopher H. Achen and Duncan Snidal, "Rational Deterrence Theory and Comparative Case Studies," *World Politics*, vol. 41, no. 2 (January 1989), pp. 160–63; Richard Ned Lebow and Janice Gross Stein, "Rational Deterrence Theory: I Think, Therefore I Deter," *World Politics*, vol. 41, no. 2 (January 1989), pp. 218–23; and Paul Huth and Bruce Russett, "Deterrence Failure and Crisis Escalation," *International Studies Quarterly*, vol. 32 (1988), pp. 37–44.

23. Morgenthau to Lansing, 10 July 1915, *FRUS: 1915 Supplement*, p. 983. Italics added.

24. On the status of the Holocaust as a critical Nazi foreign policy objective, see, for instance, Lucy S. Dawidowicz, *The War against the Jews 1933–1945* (New York: Bantam, 1986), pp. 88–149; and Eberhard Jäckel, *Hitler's World View: A Blueprint for Power* (Cambridge, Mass.: Harvard University Press, 1981), Herbert Arnold, trans., p. 53.

25. Wyman, *Abandonment of the Jews*, p. 75. Similar threats were issued by Roosevelt and Hull in 1944 (ibid., p. 237), although the credibility of these statements may have been undermined by the omission of any specific mention of the extermination of the Jews in the 1943 Moscow Declaration and the Québec Conference proclamation (ibid., p. 256).

26. Raul Hilberg, *The Destruction of the European Jews* (New York: Holmes & Meier, 1985), pp. 251–58.

27. Gilbert, *Auschwitz and the Allies*, p. 265.

28. Goldhagen, *Hitler's Willing Executioners*, p. 356.

29. *Stimson Diaries*, vol. 50, 2 March 1945, p. 153.

30. Goldhagen, *Hitler's Willing Executioners*, p. 357. These killers were not for the most part SS men, Nazi stalwarts, or otherwise unusually motivated ideologues.

31. *Stimson Diaries*, vol. 50, 8 January 1945, p. 24.

32. Gilbert, *Auschwitz and the Allies*, p. 266.

33. Wyman, *Abandonment of the Jews*, pp. 331–32.

34. Ibid., pp. 334–35.

35. Ibid., p. 397.

36. Silber and Little, *Yugoslavia*, p. 248.

37. See Rohde, *Endgame*; Chuck Sudetic, *Blood and Vengeance: One Family's Story of the War in Bosnia* (New York: W.W. Norton, 1998); and Jan Willem Honig and Norbert Both, *Srebrenica: Record of a War Crime* (London: Penguin, 1996).

38. Craig, *Germany*, pp. 370–71.

39. Ibid., pp. 380–81.

40. Lansing to Wilson, 15 November 1916, *FRUS: Lansing Papers*, vol. 1, p. 42. For the American warning, see Lansing to Gerard, 21 June 1916, *FRUS: 1916 Supplement*, p. 858.

41. Silber and Little, *Yugoslavia*, pp. 250–52. On the discovery of the camps by ITN's Penny Marshall, *The Guardian*'s Ed Vulliamy, and *Newsday*'s Roy Gutman, see Gutman, *Witness to Genocide*, and Vulliamy, *Seasons in Hell*.

42. David Scheffer, "International Judicial Intervention," *Foreign Policy*, vol. 102 (spring 1996).

43. Deutsche Presse-Agentur, 26 January 1996.

44. Jeffrey W. Legro, *Cooperation under Fire: Anglo-German Restraint during World War II* (Ithaca, N.Y.: Cornell University Press, 1995), pp. 1–34. See also Richard M. Price, *The Chemical Weapons Taboo* (Ithaca, N.Y.: Cornell University Press, 1997).

45. Legro, *Cooperation under Fire*, pp. 31–32.

46. *Morgenthau Diary*, vol. 1, p. 532.

47. Merritt, *Democracy Imposed*, pp. 160–61, 157. Such polls must be taken with a grain of salt. American analysts assumed a 10 percent bias in any questions about Nazism. Pro-Nuremberg responses can also be seen as self-serving: blaming the Nazi leadership in order to exculpate themselves or to mollify the vengeful Allies.

48. Ibid., p. 163.

49. Schwartz, *America's Germany*, p. 159.

50. Ibid., p. 165.

51. Buruma, *Wages of Guilt*, p. 148.

52. Ibid., p. 162.

53. Dower, *Embracing Defeat*, pp. 443–84.

54. FO 371/54728/U6329, intelligence report on indictments of major war criminals, 17 May 1946.

55. Shklar, *Legalism*, p. 181.

56. Albright, "Bosnia in Light of the Holocaust: War Crimes Trials," 12 April 1994. Her italics.

57. Stover and Peress, *Graves*, p. 138.

58. Prunier, *Rwanda Crisis*, p. 342.

59. I made it, somewhat thoughtlessly, in "Settling with the Enemy," *Washington Post*, 29 October 1995, p. C2.

60. Marshal de Schwarzenberg proclamation, 23 June 1815, in Metternich, *Memoirs*, vol. 2, p. 607.

61. *Stimson Diaries*, vol. 48, 23 October 1944, p. 176.

62. McCloy-Stimson conversation, 28 August 1944, in Smith, ed., *American Road to Nuremberg*, p. 23.

63. FO 37/39004/C13753, draft of suggested Churchill-Roosevelt telegram to Stalin, 2 October 1944.

64. Aron, *Peace and War*, pp. 114–15. Italics in original.

65. CAB 23/43, Imperial War Cabinet 37, 20 November 1918, noon, p. 9.

66. Ibid., p. 10.

67. FDR to Stimson, 26 August 1944, in *Morgenthau Diary*, vol. 1, pp. 443–45.

68. Taylor, *Anatomy*, p. 42.

69. Craig, *Germany*, pp. 369–70.

70. Karl Jaspers, *The Question of German Guilt* (New York: Dial Press, 1948).

71. Anglo-French conference, London, 13 December 1919, 11 A.M., *Documents on British Foreign Policy: 1919*, p. 757.

72. Sous-série Allemagne, vol. 571, Millerand to Lersner, 3 February 1920.

73. FO 371/4172/2391, 2 January 1919.

74. FO 371/4174/136069, de Robeck to Foreign Office, 21 September 1919.

75. Dower, *Embracing Defeat*, p. 454.

76. *Morgenthau Diary*, vol. 1, 7 September 1944, p. 559.

77. CAB 65/50, War Cabinet 57, W.M. (45) 57, 3 May 1945, 6 P.M., p. 331.

78. Jackson, *Report*, 29 June 1945, p. 112.

79. Bernays memorandum, 15 September 1944, in Smith, ed., *American Road to Nuremberg*, p. 35.

80. Jackson, *Report*, 2 July 1945, pp. 129–30.

81. Goldhagen, *Hitler's Willing Executioners*, p. 167.

82. Taylor, *Nuremberg and Vietnam*, p. 28.

83. Prunier, *Rwanda Crisis*, p. 342.

84. In Gourevitch, *Tomorrow We Will Be Killed*, p. 246.

85. Merritt, *Democracy Imposed*, pp. 170–71.

86. Buruma, *Wages of Guilt*, p. 169.

87. Prunier, *Rwanda Crisis*, p. 241; Mark Thompson, *Forging War: The Media in Serbia, Croatia and Bosnia-Hercegovina* (Luton, Bedfordshire: University of Luton Press, 1999).

88. Mark Danner, "Bosnia: The Turning Point," *New York Review of Books*, 5 February 1998, p. 35.

89. In Kader Asmal, Louise Asmal, and Robert Suresh Roberts, *Reconciliation through Truth: A Reckoning of Apartheid's Criminal Governance* (New York: St. Martin's Press, 1997), p. 13.

90. Anglo-French conference, London, 13 December 1919, 11 A.M., in *Documents on British Foreign Policy: 1919*, p. 758.

91. CAB 66/64, Simon war criminals memorandum, W.P. (45) 225, 9 April 1945, folio p. 111.

92. *Morgenthau Diary*, vol. 2, 18 May 1945, pp. 1507–9.

93. *Stimson Diaries*, vol. 49, 19 November 1944, p. 35.

94. Davidson, *Trial of the Germans*, pp. 33–34.

95. Dower, *Embracing Defeat*, p. 450.

96. See also R.G. 238: World War II war crimes records (Nuremberg).

97. In Ron Rosenbaum, *Explaining Hitler: The Search for the Origins of His Evil* (New York: Random House, 1998), p. 81.

98. Arendt, *Eichmann in Jerusalem*, p. 231.

99. Merritt, *Democracy Imposed*, p. 151.

100. "Forced Tour of Buchenwald: Weimar Citizens Shown Round," *Times*, 18 April 1945; in FO 371/50972/U2654.

101. Merritt, *Democracy Imposed*, p. 209.

102. See Maier, *Unmasterable Past.* On the weaker sense of atonement in East Germany, see Jeffrey Herf, *Divided Memory: The Nazi Past in the Two Germanys* (Cambridge, Mass.: Harvard University Press, 1997).

103. FO 371/4173/44216, Deedes report, 20 March 1919.

104. FO 371/6504/E8745, Edmonds memorandum, 3 August 1921.

105. Alexander, *Crime of Vengeance*, pp. 4–5, 195.

106. Brackman, *The Other Nuremberg*, pp. 40, 44.

107. This is not to say that the inherently dramatic spectacle of a war crimes trial should be put before the narrow legalistic function of a court: hearing evidence and determining guilt or innocence. For an argument for "liberal show trials," see Mark Osiel, *Mass Atrocity, Collective Memory and the Law* (New Brunswick, N.J.: Transaction, 1998); for a critique, see Samantha Power, "The Stages of Justice," *New Republic*, 2 March 1998, p. 38ff.

108. Interview in Pazit Ravina, "Atrocities, What Atrocities?" *Times* (London), 11 February 1996.

109. Luke Harding, "A Shot That's Still Ringing," *Guardian*, 12 March 1997, p. T2.

110. Shklar, *Legalism*, p. 158.

111. Wechsler, *Principles, Politics and Fundamental Law*, pp. 143–44.

112. T. H. Alexander, "They Tried to Kidnap the Kaiser—and Brought Back an Ash Tray," *The Saturday Evening Post*, 23 October 1937, pp. 5–7, 84–89.

113. See István Deák, "Resistance, Collaboration, and Retribution during World War II and Its Aftermath," *Hungarian Quarterly*, vol. 35 (summer 1994), pp. 62–74; Benjamin Frommer, "Retribution against Nazi Collaborators in Postwar Czechoslovakia," Ph.D. diss., Harvard University, 1999; and Peter Novick, *The Resistance versus Vichy: The Purge of Collaborators in Liberated France* (New York: Columbia University Press, 1968).

114. Segev, *Seventh Million*, pp. 140–46.

115. Ibid., pp. 146–52.

116. Arendt, *Eichmann in Jerusalem*, p. 265.

117. John Pomfret, "Atrocities Leave Thirst for Vengeance in Balkans," *Washington Post*, 18 December 1995, p. A1.

118. Silber and Little, *Yugoslavia*, p. 361.

119. Zivanovic interview with Stacy Sullivan of *Newsweek*. I am grateful to her for providing me with this interview. See Rohde, *Endgame*, p. 381.

120. Rohde, *Endgame*, p. 375.

121. Jonathan C. Randal, "In Gorazde, Thirst Rises for Revenge: Hague Trial's Verdict Too Little, Too Late," *Washington Post*, 8 May 1997, p. A20.

122. USIA, *Public Opinion in Bosnia Hercegovina*, p. 127.

123. Power, "Stages of Justice," p. 38.

124. Gourevitch, *Tomorrow We Will Be Killed*, pp. 242–43.

125. Rohde, *Endgame*, p. 385.

126. For an excellent overview, see Human Rights Watch and Fédération Internationale des Ligues des Droits de l'Homme, *Leave None to Tell the Story: Genocide in Rwanda* (New York: HRW-FIDH, 1999), pp. 747–65.

127. Gourevitch, *Tomorrow We Will Be Killed*, pp. 239–52.

128. Reuters, 8 April 1997.

129. James C. McKinley Jr., "Firing Squads Execute 22 Convicted of Genocide in Rwanda," *New York Times*, 25 April 1998, p. A1.

130. AFP, May 15, 1998.

131. McKinley, "Firing Squads Execute 22," p. A1.

132. UN report A/51/789, 6 February 1997.

133. This is not to say that Rwanda should not be allowed to run its own prosecutions. But the UN must find a modus vivendi between Arusha's and Kigali's brands of justice, recognizing legitimate Rwandan grievances but trying to maintain legal standards, too. See José Alvarez, "Crimes of State/Crimes of Hate: Lessons from Rwanda," *Yale Journal of International Law*, vol. 24, no. 2 (1999), pp. 355–483.

134. Jasminka Sabic, "War Criminals Must Be Brought to Justice," *Vecernje Novine* (Sarajevo), 29 October 1994, pp. 4–5; English version in BBC broadcasts summary, 7 November 1994. See also Robert Fisk, "Bosnia Opens War Crime Files," *Independent*, 18 July 1993, p. 1.

135. Office of the High Representative, *Trial Status Report* (Sarajevo: OHR, November 1997).

136. R. Jeffrey Smith, "Suspect Seized in '93 Bosnia Death," *Washington Post*, 7 February 1998, p. A20; Sacirbey interview, 27 May 1998.

137. State Department 08249/101627Z, Rackmales to Christopher, July 1992.

138. Institute for War and Peace Reporting, *Balkan Crisis Report*, no. 91, 9 November 1999.

Afterword to the Paperback Edition

1. Reuters, 2 April 2001. See Dusko Doder and Louise Branson, *Milosevic: Portrait of a Tyrant* (New York: Free Press, 1999), pp. 14–26, and Laura Silber, "Milosevic Family Values," *New Republic*, 30 August 1999, p. 23.

2. See Wesley K. Clark, *Waging Modern War: Bosnia, Kosovo, and the Future of Combat* (New York: PublicAffairs, 2001), pp. 159–60.

3. Ibid., p. 325. See also *Prosecutor* v. *Milosevic et al.*, IT-99-37, Judge David Hunt, Decision on Review of Indictment and Application for Consequential Orders, 24 May 1999.

4. Clark, *Waging Modern War*, p. 325.

5. Samuel P. Huntington, *The Third Wave: Democratization in the Late Twentieth Century* (Norman, Okla.: University of Oklahoma Press, 1991), pp. 174–92; Timothy Garton Ash, *The Magic Lantern: The Revolution of '89 Witnessed in Warsaw, Budapest, Berlin, and Prague* (New York: Random House, 1990), pp. 14–15, 25.

6. See Steven Erlanger, "Serbia's Reluctant Revolutionary Calmly Looks Beyond the Chaos," *New York Times*, 6 October 2000, p. A1.

7. For excellent accounts, see variously, Steven Erlanger and Roger Cohen, "How Yugoslavia Won Its Fight for Freedom," *New York Times*, 15 October 2000, p. A1; Fredrik Dahl, Reuters, 6 October 2000; Katarina Kratovac, "Milosevic Concedes Election Defeat," AP, 6 October 2000; Eric Witte, International Crisis Group Yugoslavia Situation Report no. 3, 6 October 2000; Steven Erlanger, "Yugoslavs Claim Belgrade for a New Leader," *New York Times*, 6 October 2000, p. A1; Jeffrey Smith, "Yugoslav Masses Seize Belgrade," *Washington Post*, 6 October 2000, p. A1; Paul Watson and Zoran Cirjakovic, "Protesters Seize Yugoslav Parliament," *Los Angeles Times*, 6 October 2000, p. A1.

8. This translation is from Reuters, "Milosevic Concedes Election Defeat," 6 October 2000.

9. When a transition happens suddenly and decisively, as in Yugoslavia, one would expect much greater opportunities for prosecuting the ancien régime. The two most serious recent attempts to prosecute at the domestic level came in Argentina and Greece, where the military governments quickly collapsed after the humiliation of losing a war—a pattern that must have sounded familiar in Belgrade. Kostunica may have had more room for maneuver than, say, Nelson Mandela and Václav Havel did.

10. CNN, 5 October 2000.

11. Steven Erlanger, "The Serbs Ask a Chance to Judge Their Own Guilt," *New York Times*, 15 October 2000, Week in Review, p. 5.

12. Carlotta Gall, "Yugoslav Leader Treads Softly at Poet's Rite in Bosnia," *New York Times*, 23 October 2000, p. A3.

13. Renaud Girard, "Vojislav Kostunica: 'Milosevic a signé son arrêt de mort politique,'" *Le Figaro*, 19 December 2000, p. 4.

14. R. Jeffrey Smith, "Kostunica Faces Test Over Extradition of Serbs for War Crimes," *Washington Post*, 21 January 2001, p. A33; Radio B92, 23 January 2001.

15. AFP, 5 Februrary 2001.

16. See Stjepan Mesic, "The Serbs' Choice," *New York Times*, 29 March 2001, p. A27.

17. See wire reports from AP, UPI, and Reuters, as well as Jeremy Scahill, "How Milosevic's loyalist thugs fought Serbian police to a bloody stand-off," *Telegraph*, 1 April 2001, p. 2.

18. R. Jeffrey Smith, "Yugoslav Ex-Leader Ends Standoff," *Washington Post*, 1 April 2001, p. A1, and Steven Erlanger, "Serb Authorities Arrest Milosevic to End Standoff," *New York Times*, 1 April 2001, p. A1.

19. AP, 2 April 2001.

20. AP, 3 February 2001. See also Milosevic's interview with Dragan Bisenic, "'I Am an Ordinary Man'/'I Was a Dictator,'" *Ha'aretz*, 23 March 2001.

21. BBC, 3 April 2001.

22. BBC, 3 May 2001.

23. Steven Erlanger, "Yugoslav Chief Says Milosevic Shouldn't Be Sent to Hague," *New York Times*, 3 April 2001, p. A3.

24. Only 11 percent wanted to see Milosevic in The Hague, 59 percent preferred a Belgrade trial, and 20 percent said he should be freed. As for what his worst crimes were, 40 percent said abuse of power, 18 percent said loss of Serb territory in Croatia and Kosovo, and 18 percent said he was simply innocent. (Reuters, 13 April 2001.)

25. For a thoughtful partial defense of Kostunica's approach, see Alex Boraine, "Reconciliation in the Balkans?" *New York Times*, 22 April 2001, p. A17.

26. Carlotta Gall, "Serbian Tells of Spiriting Milosevic Away," *New York Times*, 1 July 2001, p. A8.

27. See Scott Peterson, "The Karadzic Capture That Almost Was," *Christian Science Monitor*, 27 April 2001, p. 8.

28. See Henry Hale, "Is Russian Nationalism on the Rise?" Program on New Approaches to Russian Security, Harvard University, policy memorandum no. 110; Susan B. Glasser, "Putin's War Persists as Sentiment Shifts," *Washington Post*, 28 July 2001, p. A1; Anatol Lieven, *Chechnya: Tombstone of Russian Power* (New Haven, Conn.: Yale

University Press, 1999), pp. 217-18; David Remnick, *Resurrection: The Struggle for a New Russia* (New York: Random House, 1997), pp. 260-91.

29. See Vladimir Putin, with Nataliya Gevorkyan, Natalya Timakova, and Andrei Kolesnikov, *First Person*, trans. Catherine A. Fitzpatrick (New York: PublicAffairs, 2000), pp. 139–44.

30. Marcus Warren, "Moscow Minister Backs Colonel who Strangled Girl, 18," *Telegraph*, 17 May 2001, p. 20.

31. See James D. Seymour, "Human Rights in Chinese Foreign Relations," in Samuel S. Kim, ed., *China and the World: Chinese Foreign Relations in the Post–Cold War Era* (Boulder, Colo.: Westview, 1994), pp. 202–25.

32. Patrick Tyler, *A Great Wall: Six Presidents and China* (New York: PublicAffairs, 1999), pp. 393–94, 406–10.

33. See Alastair Iain Johnston and Paul Evans, "China and Multilateral Security Institutions," in Alastair Iain Johnston and Robert S. Ross, eds., *Engaging China: The Management of an Emerging Power* (London: Routledge, 1999), pp. 235–72.

34. As G. John Ikenberry argues, channeling American power through international institutions may make it seem less threatening to other countries (*After Victory: Institutions, Strategic Restraint, and the Rebuilding of Order after Major Wars* [Princeton: Princeton University Press, 2001]).

35. For a stinging critique of cheap forgiveness, see "Mr. McNamara's War," *New York Times*, 12 April 1995, p. A24.

36. Gregory L. Vistica, "What Happened in Thanh Phong," *New York Times Magazine*, 29 April 2001, pp. 51–57, 66–68, 133. For typical commentary, see Richard Cohen, "The War-Is-War Excuse," *Washington Post*, 10 May 2001, p. A31, and Gabriel Schoenfeld, "Bob Kerrey, War Criminal?" *Commentary*, July–August 2001, pp. 38–44. For an exception, see Daniel Jonah Goldhagen and Samantha Power, "Kerrey Should Be Investigated," *Boston Globe*, 3 May 2001, p. A15.

37. Bob Woodward, *The Commanders* (New York: Simon & Schuster, 1991), pp. 87, 113, 159, 170. The Escobar raid was supported by Dick Cheney, then defense secretary and now vice president. For other examples of American assertiveness, see William Glaberson, "U.S. Courts Become Arbiters of Global Rights and Wrongs," *New York Times*, 21 June 2001, p. A1.

38. Henry A. Kissinger, "The Pitfalls of Universal Jurisdiction," *Foreign Affairs*, July–August 2001, pp. 86–96. Overlooking Leipzig and Constantinople, he wrongly sees the idea of judging leaders as "outlaws" as "quite new" (p. 87). Kissinger, invoking democratic control, prefers Chilean jurisdiction for Pinochet, or perhaps an ad hoc international tribunal. But if democracy is the point, what is so democratic about an ad hoc tribunal? Nor does Kissinger's emphasis on democracy stop him from offering a qualified defense of Pinochet's overthrow of Salvador Allende's democratically elected government, as well as a defense of Pinochet as "a fashionably reviled man of the right" (pp. 88–92), as if the families of the three thousand people "disappeared" by Pinochet's regime were simply being trendy. (See *Informe de la Comisión Nacional de Verdad y Reconciliación*, 3 vols. [Santiago: CNVR, 1991], and Eugenio Ahumada et al., *Chile: La Memoria Prohibida*, 3 vols. [Santiago: Pehuén, 1989].)

39. America wouldn't necessarily need to use universal jurisdiction to go after Pinochet. In 1976, a Pinochet agent set off a car bomb outside the Chilean embassy in Washington, D.C., killing former Allende cabinet minister Orlando Leterlier as well

as an American, Ronni Moffitt. (Simon Collier and William F. Sater, *A History of Chile, 1808–1994* [Cambridge: Cambridge University Press, 1996], pp. 361–63; Hugh O'Shaugnessy, *Pinochet: The Politics of Torture* [New York: New York University Press, 2000], pp. 97–98; Mary Helen Spooner, *Soldiers in a Narrow Land: The Pinochet Regime in Chile* [Berkeley: University of California Press, 1994], pp. 125–26, 133–35, 224–26, 250.)

40. On Constant, see David Grann, "Giving 'The Devil' His Due," *Atlantic*, June 2001, pp. 55–75.

41. See Human Rights Watch, *The Pinochet Precedent: How Victims Can Pursue Human Rights Criminals Abroad* (New York: Human Rights Watch, September 2000).

42. Huntington, *Third Wave*, pp. 215–17.

43. See Kenneth Roth's introduction, in Geoffrey Robertson, *Crimes Against Humanity: The Struggle for Global Justice* (New York: Free Press, 2000), p. xxx; and Aryeh Neier, *War Crimes: Brutality, Genocide, Terror, and the Struggle for Justice* (New York: Times Books, 1998), pp. 100–107.

44. If Kissinger really likes ad hoc international tribunals, then it is not such a huge conceptual leap to consider a permanent one. His conditions for setting up an ad hoc tribunal—an unrepresentative local regime, or a national regime that will not prosecute properly ("Pitfalls of Universal Jurisdiction," p. 95)—would seem to apply equally to the ICC.

45. Aleksa Djilas, "Viewpoint: The Politicised Tribunal," in Institute for War and Peace Reporting, *Tribunal Update*, no. 230, 16–21 July 2001; Michael Mandel, "Milosevic Has a Point,"*Globe and Mail*, 6 July 2001, p. A15; Shlomo Avineri, "Yes, Milosevic Is Bad, but So Is Selective International Justice," *International Herald Tribune*, 3 July 2001, p. 8; Charles Krauthammer, "Milosevic in the Dock: At What Price?" *Time*, 9 July 2001, p. 32.

46. Del Ponte has said that she plans to indict Milosevic for crimes committed by Serb forces in Bosnia, but two of her self-imposed deadlines, the end of December 2000 and then May 2001, have come and gone without any public charges. (See Roy Gutman, "Milosevic Faces New Indictment," *Newsday*, 27 September 2000, p. A33; Mirko Klarin, "Analysis: Milosevic's Other Indictments," in Institute for War and Peace Reporting, *Tribunal Update*, no. 219, 30 April 2001.) Ironically, while in jail in Belgrade, Milosevic himself has clarified his own links to the Serb campaigns in Bosnia, by trying to evade embezzlement charges by explaining that state funds had secretly been going to the Bosnian Serbs.

* *Index* *